Studies in Irish Legal History

Studies in Irish Legal History

W.N. Osborough

FOUR COURTS PRESS

Set in 10 on 12 point Bembo for
FOUR COURTS PRESS LTD
Fumbally Lane, Dublin 8, Ireland
e-mail: info@four-courts-press.ie
and in North America
FOUR COURTS PRESS
c/o ISBS, 5804 N.E. Hassalo Street, Portland, OR 97213.

A catalogue record for this title
is available from the British Library.

ISBN 1-85182-447-2

Printed in Great Britain
by MPG Books Ltd, Bodmin, Cornwall

Contents

Preface

There is no single-volume account of the history of law in Ireland. Those who would aspire to obtain an understanding of the subject, unfortunately for them, must perforce turn to a succession of different books, even to master the rudiments – to such classic texts as Fergus Kelly's *A guide to early Irish law*, G.J. Hand's *English law in Ireland, 1290-1324* and F.E. Ball's *The judges of Ireland, 1221-1921*. Should they be prompted to take their studies further, comfort is at hand in the realization that a wealth of additional information remains available, waiting only to be extracted, secreted as it so often is in the pages of learned journals or in the growing number of pertinent monographs (some of which, I am happy to say, have been produced under the aegis of the recently established Irish Legal History Society). There is, in truth, no shortage of primary as well as of secondary source-material for the dedicated researcher to latch onto. If this material, contrary to expectation, cannot itself furnish all the answers, it at least usually possesses the merit of pointing in the right direction, and likewise, where answers are not now available and never will be (a distressingly frequent occurrence), of explaining in coherent language why to have ever set out to solicit them was to have embarked on a fool's errand.

The present selection of legal historical essays covers a broad chronological spectrum, but it cannot, and does not, claim to fill the gap that, to the discredit of Irish legal and historical scholarship, self-evidently persists. The invitation to bring this selection before a wider audience (an invitation for which I am most grateful to Four Courts Press) has been accepted, however, largely out of the conviction that, despite irrefutable proof of recent progress, the discipline of Irish legal history continues to suffer from a measure of neglect on the part of lawyers and historians alike, and that the publication of the selection at this juncture may go some small part of the way to remedy a disturbing state of affairs. At the same time, I should be less than honest if I did not frankly admit that no less compelling an inducement has been the belief, fostered by several years' teaching of the subject, that the story of the law on the island of Ireland is a story worth relating for its own sake – even in the form of the bits and pieces of that story which are alone assembled here.

What indeed constitutes an extraordinary saga evinces far more of a unity than has customarily been supposed, or as scholars with their different predilections have sometimes been prepared to recognize. The point is appreciated by generations of students who have struggled to make sense of the 'several fishery' lawsuits litigated through the courts of the Irish Free State in the 1920s and 1930s – such reported lawsuits as *Moore* v. *A.G.* [1934] IR 44 and *Little* v. *Cooper* [1937] IR 1. The Table of Contents for the present volume furnishes confirmation too. There the reader will find that, over the course of three hundred and more pages, the author is making it his business to try to say something – something he trusts is comprehensible as well as germane – about each of the legal traditions that at one time or another have helped to chart the fortunes of law in Ireland – from the brehon law to canon law and from Roman law to the common law. (European law is too recent a novelty to attract more than a passing reference.) The reader will thus encounter on the route such very different personages as Giolla na Naomh mac Duinnshléibhe Mhic Aodhagáin (Irish jurist), Panormitanus (canonist), Gaius (Roman jurist), and Sir Thomas Molony (last lord chief justice of Ireland).

That said, the majority of the essays featured here do, as it happens, investigate topics that fall peculiarly within Ireland's common law heritage. For good or for ill, membership of the family of the common law was the hand dealt by History from the pack, and from the time of the common law's second reception in the country at the start of the seventeenth century such membership has been constant and has endured. The reader will discover that these topics embrace such key issues as Irish law reporting and pre-Act of Union statute law as well as facets of the history of the organization of the legal profession's lower branch – the attorneys and solicitors. Changes to the common law-grounded legal system between 1796 and 1926 are described in two separate studies which are roughly complementary. Other matters explored include the penal laws directed against Catholics in the eighteenth century, and one species of property loss (stolen vehicles) sustained during the conduct of the Anglo-Irish war in the earlier twentieth century. In both instances there will be found tentative discussion of the nature of the challenge that these different episodes presented to the Irish judicial bench of the respective epochs.

The thirteen pieces that make up *Studies in Irish Legal History* are reprinted versions of essays written by me over the last thirty years and which appeared originally in the journals and books that are listed in the accompanying Acknowledgments. I am grateful for permission to reprint them in this collection. In bringing together the essays for publication, it seemed best not to attempt to standardize modes of citation. A modest amount of revision, however, has been undertaken. In the main, this consists of additional material I thought it appropriate to incorporate. Some mistakes, too, have been corrected. Since I have tried to deal with law over so many centuries, it is only right that I should accept that some errors very probably remain. None of these, let me hasten to add, should of course be laid at the door of the very many people who, in so many different ways, assisted me when the essays were first written, and to whose assistance heartfelt thanks are paid seriatim. I should like to take this opportunity also to pay tribute to the various librarians and archivists in Ireland and elsewhere who down the years have been of such immeasurable aid to me as I have sought to unravel at least a few of the mysteries in which the story of law in Ireland has been enshrouded. I should also like to thank Helen Litton for preparing the Index. For grants in aid of publication I am most grateful to both the Faculty of Law and the Academic Publications Fund of University College Dublin.

'In Search of Irish Legal History: A Map for Explorers' opens the collection. Preoccupied with the question of sources, this piece does not underestimate the difficulties that face the would-be researcher into Ireland's legal past. Far from it. Paradoxically though, the tone of this introductory essay is decidedly exuberant The choice has been deliberate. I make no attempt to hide that the challenge of penetrating and demystifying the legal history of Ireland promises considerable frustration and very likely an equal amount of disillusionment. But there is a brighter side too. Taking up the challenge also holds out the prospect of experiencing excitement – the thrill of discovering something not previously known, something, too, perhaps, not even suspected.

Acknowledgments

1 'In search of Irish legal history: a map for explorers', *Long Room*, 35 (1990) 28-38.

2 'Roman law in Ireland', in W.N. Osborough (ed.), *Essays in honour of John M. Kelly* (Dublin, 1994) (= *Irish Jurist*, xxv-vii), pp 212-68.

3 'The Irish custom of tracts', *Irish Jurist*, xxxii (1997) 439-58.

4 'The legislation of the pre-Union Irish Parliament', introduction to the 1995 reprint of *The Irish Statutes revised edition: 3 Edward II to the Union, AD 1310-1800* (1885) (Dublin, 1995), pp A-U.

5 'Letters to Ireland: professional enlightenment from the English bench', in Finbarr McAuley and David O'Keeffe (eds), *Essays in honour of Geoffrey J. Hand* (Dublin, 1996) (= *Irish Jurist*, xxxi), pp 226-54.

6 'Ecclesiastical law and the reformation in Ireland' in R.H. Helmholz (ed.), *Canon law in Protestant lands* (= *Comparative Studies in Continental and Anglo-American Legal History*, xi) (Berlin, 1992), pp 223-52.

7 'The regulation of the admission of attorneys and solicitors in Ireland, 1600-1866' in D. Hogan and W.N. Osborough (eds), *Brehons, serjeants and attorneys: studies in the history of the Irish legal profession* (Dublin, 1990), pp 101-51.

8 'Puzzles from Irish law reporting history' in Peter Birks (ed.), *The life of the law: proceedings of the Tenth British Legal History Conference*, Oxford 1991 (London and Rio Grande, 1993), pp 89-111.

9 'Catholics, land and the popery acts of Anne', in T.P. Power and Kevin Whelan (eds), *Endurance and emergence: Catholics in Ireland in the eighteenth century* (Dublin, 1990), pp 21-56.

10 The Irish legal system, 1796–1877' in Caroline Costello (ed.), *The Four Courts: 200 years* (Dublin 1996), pp 33-79.

11 'Law in Ireland, 1916–1926', *Northern Ireland Legal Quarterly*, xxiii (1972) 48-81.

12 'Forcibly commandeered transport and owners' insurance: the deciding of two test cases in the 1920s', *Irish Jurist*, xi (1976) 105-25.

13 'The title of the last lord chief justice of Ireland' *Irish Jurist*, ix (1974) 87-98.

In Search of Irish Legal History: A Map for Explorers

There is a second 'massacre of St Bartholomew' – the product of the fertile genius of Victor Hugo. In *Quatrevingt-treize*, a novel that traces the course of the royalist revolt in the Vendée in 1793, Hugo introduces the reader to the child hostages, René-Jean, Gros-Alain and Georgette. Detained in the library in the royalist stronghold of the Tourgue, the three set out to destroy one of the library's most prized possessions: a magnificent folio volume, known for its religious content as 'St Bartholomew'. The children first tear out the picture pages. The volume falls to the floor where it is used for soccer practice. Worse is to come:

> Tout prestige disparut; René-Jean se précipita, Gros-Alain se rua, et joyeux, éperdus, triomphants, impitoyables, déchirant les estampes, balafrant les feuillets, arrachant les signets, égratignant la reliure, décollant le cuir doré, déclouant les clous des coins d'argent, cassant le parchemin, déchiquetant le texte auguste, travaillant des pieds, des mains, des ongles, des dents, riants, roses, féroces, les trois anges de proie s'abattirent sur l'évangéliste sans défense.[1]

The episode in the library of the Tourgue will serve to fix the first feature on the map. Those who would seek to fathom the mysteries of Irish legal history must adjust to the disconcerting discovery that their task has been made immeasurably more difficult from the widespread destruction of indigenous legal records. No category of record has escaped: from Gaelic Ireland a number of law tracts, it is known, have not survived (Bretha Luchtaine, for instance);[2] from the Ireland of the common law various series of chancery rolls, statute rolls and plea rolls; from ecclesiastical sources episcopal registers and collections of wills – again, no one can be quite certain how many, so great is the loss.

As with Hugo's delinquent nursery some share of this destruction can legitimately be ascribed to children. Gorges Edmund Howard, that most prolific of Ireland's eighteenth-century legal authors, recounts, in the preface to his treatise on the Irish exchequer, how he himself, whilst a boy, may have assisted in the destruction of manuscript material of which only very much later he came to recognise the true worth. The family had inherited four volumes of legal notes kept by Dudley Loftus, also celebrated as an antiquarian and orientalist. These notes were looked

1 Victor Hugo, *Oeuvres romanesques complètes* (Paris, 1962), p. 1373. 2 Fergus Kelly, *A guide to early Irish law* (Dublin, 1988), p. 269.

upon as junk and had been employed for miscellaneous household purposes. Out of the four, a single volume, Howard would have us believe, alone was to survive unscathed.[3]

The devastation wrought by adults has naturally been more widespread. Here veritable horror stories abound, some of very recent date indeed. The Rev. Philip Dwyer's fine nineteenth-century history of the diocese of Killaloe is notable for the number of original documents he managed to track down, transcribe and print. Dwyer wished he had been able to locate even more, but an attitude of mind still too prevalent amongst senior churchmen had scarcely conduced to the survival of any. He tells a grim tale to illustrate the point:

> On the death of a dignitary holding a high place in one of the united dioceses, his widow performed suttee, not of herself, but with a large pile of most valuable ancient books and papers belonging to the diocese.[4]

The ravages wrought by accidental, as opposed to deliberate, destruction probably constitute the greater proportion. The losses that occurred at the Public Record Office in the Dublin Four Courts complex in 1922 as a result of explosion and fire are documented and their significance generally appreciated.[5] Less well-known is the sequence of earlier fires. In 1304 one such fire at St Mary's Abbey in Dublin destroyed a collection of chancery rolls and documents covering the administration of the previous decade.[6] In 1711, in a fire at the then Custom House in Dublin, there perished many of the records of the Irish privy council.[7] By the 1750s most of the court records still extant had been transferred to the Bermingham Tower in Dublin Castle where they were housed in ten deal presses. Around 1758, however, five of these presses were consumed by fire, and virtually all the plea rolls from the reigns of James I and Charles I literally went up in smoke.[8]

Sheer neglect exacted its toll as well. In 1674 Michael Tisdall, writing from Dublin to William Petyt, keeper of records at the Tower of London, paints a depressing picture. Many records then stored in the Bermingham Tower were, he writes,

> made altogether useless by water falling in there being not so much care taken to keep the places dry, and of those that remained there is no abstract or directory extant, and the place does not yield an encouragement to labour.[9]

John Lodge's account, dated 1758, of the conditions in which parliament rolls and chancery records were being kept at that time in the Rolls office at the old King's

3 G.E. Howard, *A treatise of the exchequer and revenue of Ireland*, 2 vols. (Dublin, 1776), i, preface, p. iii n. 4 Philip Dwyer, *The diocese of Killaloe from the reformation to the close of the eighteenth century* (Dublin, 1878), p. 156. 5 Herbert Wood, 'The public records of Ireland before and after 1922', *Transactions of the Royal Historical Society*, 5th series, 13 (1930), 17; Margaret Griffith, 'A short guide to the Public Record Office of Ireland', *Irish Historical Studies*, 8 (1952–3), 45. 6 Herbert Wood, *A guide to the records deposited in the Public Record Office of Ireland* (Dublin, 1919), introduction, p. x. 7 Ibid., p. ix. 8 Ibid., pp ix–x. 9 J.C. Davies, *Catalogue of manuscripts in the library of the honourable society of the Inner Temple*, 2 vols. (London, 1972), ii, p. 177. I am grateful for this reference to Dr Colum Kenny.

Inns – the site of the present Four Courts – demonstrates very clearly that official policy had not altered. Matters indeed may have regressed. The building, Lodge wrote,

> is in a very ruinous state, being supported by props from top to bottom. The weight of the pleadings is so great that there is reason to fear the sinking of the floors, which should fall in, should the props give way. The roof is shored up from end to end, and in danger of falling in by every high wind. The slates are stripped by every storm, and the window cannot be kept in repair, so that the records daily suffer by dust and moisture. The whole building is so shook by tempests, that the clerks have quitted their desks in fear, and locked up the office.[10]

The transfer of King's Inns records to the Inns' new premises in Henrietta Street took place in 1804. The tradition is that the records were removed in an open cart, and many records were simply lost in transit.[11]

The rebellion of 1641 occasioned a considerable degree of administrative dislocation. It too has been blamed for the disappearance of a substantial quantity of records. Writing to Clarendon in 1663, the earl of Orrery blamed the rebellion for the loss of the records of the Presidency Court of Munster.[12] In a law-suit in 1858, involving the rights of the dean and chapter of Kildare, where accurate historical data was at a premium, it was pointed out that no early records existed for St Bridget's cathedral; this gap too was attributed to the rebellion of 1641.[13]

Tisdall, in his letter to Petyt in 1674, advanced one further explanation for the extent of the losses he had detected even then: the practice of theft and embezzlement.[14] An official report, drawn up a century and half before, in 1537, indicates that this was nothing new. The report showed that keepers of records had been known to embezzle 'suche mynymentes as shulde made agaynst them, or ther fryndes.' Self-interest represented a permanent temptation; for remedy, the report canvassed the establishment of a central repository with proper attendant security.[15]

Ironically, the Victorians' sense of order and attachment to historical scholarship inspired the concentration of Irish legal and other public records in the last great central repository to be opened to receive them, the new Public Record Office of 1867. Ironically, for it was this concentration which alone made possible the greatest loss of all that was to occur when the Four Courts were devastated in 1922 in an action that signalled the commencement of the Irish Civil War.

10 Wood, *Guide*, p. xi. **11** *King's Inns admission papers 1607-1867*, eds. Edward Keane, P.B. Phair and T.U. Sadleir (Dublin, 1982), p. viii. **12** Wood, *Guide*, p. 267. **13** *Ecclesiastical commissioners* v. *Dean and chapter of Kildare* (1858) 7 Irish Chancery Reports 144. **14** Davies, *Catalogue*, ii, p. 177. **15** Wood, *Guide*, pp viii, xiv-xvi.

II

On their journey together to Northanger Abbey, Henry Tilney teases Catherine Morland over the surprises he assures her lie in wait at their destination. There would be strange discoveries to be made in the ante-chamber of her bedroom, for instance:

> In repassing through the small vaulted room … your eyes will be attracted towards a large old-fashioned cabinet of ebony and gold … Impelled by an irresistible presentiment, you will eagerly advance to it, unlock its folding doors, and search into every drawer; – but for some time without discovering any thing of importance … At last, however, by touching a secret spring, an inner compartment will open – a roll of paper appears: – you seize it – it contains many sheets of manuscript – you hasten with the precious treasure into your own chamber, but scarcely have you been able to decipher 'Oh! thou – whomsoever thou mayst be, into whose hands these memoirs of the wretched Matilda may fall' – when your lamp suddenly expires in the socket, and leaves you in total darkness.

Late next day, settled in her apartment at Northanger and anxious to explore it, Catherine espies a large antique black cabinet similar to the one evoked by Henry during the journey. The cabinet is locked but, eventually, the key turns and a series of drawers of different sizes stands revealed. Nothing remarkable transpires until Catherine tries the small central drawer:

> At length it did open; and not vain, as hitherto, was her search; her quick eyes directly fell on a roll of paper pushed back into the further part of the cavity, apparently for concealment. Her heart fluttered, her knees trembled, and her cheeks grew pale.

Maddeningly, at this precise juncture, Catherine's candle goes out – exactly, it would appear, again as Henry had envisaged. Resolution of the mystery had accordingly to be deferred to the following morning. How were Catherine's expectations to be dashed, however! The roll of paper she fancied might perhaps have contained the memoirs of some sequestered nun is identified as nothing more exciting than an inventory of linen.[16]

This passage from *Northanger Abbey* is a light-hearted spoof directed by Jane Austen at writers of the Gothic novel. But it will in addition serve to fix the second feature on the map. The serious explorer at work in the field of Irish legal history must be prepared not only to adjust to the quantum of records destroyed but also to face the additional psychological challenge of frequent disappointment. The source-material may have survived but it may prove difficult to locate it. And even where the material is traced, it may not yield the answers the explorer craves, or yield these easily.

16 Jane Austen, *Northanger Abbey*, chs. 5, 6, 7.

Take Irish grand jury records to which, as yet, sadly, no general index exists. These records are scattered in libraries and other repositories throughout the country. A dramatic account of the finding of a collection of such records for Co. Meath straddling the period 1760 to 1830 was published some years ago by Rev. John Brady: the ingredients were an ancient safe, a mislaid key and a determined priest.[17] In his article, Brady draws attention to evidence furnished by records of this class for the payment of interpreters in eighteenth and nineteenth-century Irish criminal prosecutions. It might also have been expected that grand jury presentment records would shed much-needed light on the history of road construction in the several Irish counties. Alas, this does not seem to be the case, at least in the professional assessment of J.H. Andrews:

> Attempts to unravel the sequence of road construction from the presentment records of [Donegal] and other counties have proved unrewarding: the presentment descriptions are often too indefinite for roads to be identified and it is not always possible to distinguish the making of new roads from the repairing of old ones.[18]

There is another formidable hazard: the decipherment of surviving manuscript material. The combination of law French or Latin and court hand can cause even the most dedicated explorer to falter. And it is only slight comfort to learn that the associated difficulties constitute a complaint of long standing. 'I have severall things out of ye Old Rolls', wrote Archbishop King at the end the seventeenth century,

> and there are no clerks in yt or any other offices that I can find can understand old french, this makes ye matter very troublesome … Not one clerke in the Rolls knew where any thing was or could read or understand it when found.[19]

Mary Hickson's narrative, published in 1884, of how she came to locate records of the proceedings of the Cromwellian high court of justice that sat in Dublin between 1652 and 1654, teaches another salutary lesson. The records survive in a small square octavo volume, part of the collection of manuscripts bequeathed to Trinity College in 1745 by Dr John Stearne, bishop of Clogher. Miss Hickson's discovery was the product of patient detective work. The reward was not as great as might have been hoped, however, for, as Miss Hickson explains, the records in their state of preservation were loath to disgorge their secrets:

> The writing … is most difficult to decipher and I had to procure the able assistance of Mr Edward Impey, a Record Agent, long trained in such work in the London Public Record Office, to make the selections hereafter given. Some of the notes are quite impossible to decipher, the writing is so crabbed, and the abbreviations so numerous …[20]

17 John Brady, 'Irish interpreters at Meath assizes', *Ríocht na Mídhe*, 2 (1959), 62. **18** J.H. Andrews, 'Road planning in Ireland before the railway age', *Irish geography*, 5 (1964–8), 17 n. 34. **19** Quoted, Wood, *Guide*, p. xiv. **20** Mary Hickson, *Ireland in the seventeenth century*, 2 vols. (London, 1884), ii, p. 160.

So far as I am aware, forgery has not been isolated as presenting any particular snare in this field of historical research. Other potential sources of frustration and disillusionment persist however, none more so than references to earlier or contemporary records that are not now traceable or are definitely lost. Early entries in the 'Black Book' of King's Inns (1607–1730) allude to the existence of other records of the society: in 1628 there is mention of a 'great gilt rowle', in 1636 of 'a bundle of wrytings which belong to ye house', and in 1637 to pension rolls and to a book of admissions obtained from the Herald of Arms.[21] None of these have apparently survived. In John Alcock's pamphlet of 1838 on the controversy occasioned by Baron Richards's refusal to be guided by majority decisions on judicial interpretations of the franchise law, reference will be found to a journal maintained by the most junior judge in which a record was entered of legal questions arising on assize on which the returning judges would seek the views of their colleagues.[22] No such journal is traceable today either. James Ferguson, one of the band of intrepid explorers of the Victorian era, made a considerable personal sacrifice in order to acquire medieval Irish court records that mysteriously surfaced in the Germany of his day. Following purchase, the collection was brought carefully back to Ireland, eventually finding its way into the new Public Record Office.[23] Like so much else, what Ferguson strove so hard to acquire on behalf of his adopted country went up in flames in 1922.

III

Alexander Pushkin's story 'Dubrovsky' shows how a trivial disagreement can provoke an act of gross injustice that leads in turn to a sanguinary trail of vengeance. Andrei Gavrilovich Dubrovsky (Dubrovsky *père*) and Kiril Petrovich Troyekurov were landowners, neighbours and friends, though Troyekurov was markedly richer. One day Dubrovsky *père* visits his friend's property and is shown the kennels where over five hundred hounds lived in warmth and comfort. He lets fall the observation that he suspects Troyekurov's dogs are housed better than his servants. One of the latter resents the remark whereupon Dubrovsky demands that Troyekurov should make him apologise. Troyekurov refuses. In consequence, the two friends drift apart. Subsequently, first by way of jest but then in deadly earnest, Troyekurov resolves to teach his neighbour a lesson. He will go to law and challenge the title of Dubrovsky *père* to his estate. As a wealthy landowner, Troyekurov has easy access to the best available talent, talent, which in the shape of the lawyer Shabashkin, does not flinch from resorting to underhand tactics. The court sits, declares the estate is Troyekurov's and orders the eviction of Dubrovsky *père*. The perpetration of this grotesque act of injustice is more than matched by the cruelties later practised by Dubrovsky *fils* in avenging the treatment meted out to his father.

21 T. Power, 'The "Black Book" of King's Inns: an introduction with an abstract of contents', *Irish Jurist*, 20 (1985), 135 at 137. **22** John Alcock, *Observations concerning the nature and origin of the meetings of the twelve judges for the consideration of cases reserved from the circuits* (Dublin and London, 1838), p. 12. **23** Charles Haliday, *The Scandinavian kingdom of Dublin*, ed. J.P. Prendergast, 2nd ed. (Dublin, 1884), preface, pp xxviii–xxix.

It is essential to Pushkin's literary purpose that the text of the decree pronounced by the relevant court should be reproduced. The longwindedness of legal documents in general, and the specious logic in which authorisation for the forcible dispossession of someone like Dubrovsky *père* might be cloaked: both required an exemplar. Fortunately, as Pushkin became aware, one was to hand in the records of the Kozlov District Court in the province of Tambov. There a law-suit had dragged on from 1826 to 1832, as a consequence of which, by another act of comparable injustice, a poor landowner was actually deprived of his lands in favour of a rich one. Once Pushkin had secured a copy of this decree, all he had to do was to change the names of the principals to Dubrovsky and Troyekurov and also – so as to avoid the attentions of the tsarist censor – to alter the dates.[24] Not every English edition of Pushkin's story includes the text of this decree, as amended. The omission is easy to understand: the text itself occupies over five pages in the Penguin Classics edition of 1962.

This brief excursus into Russian literary history will serve to fix the third and final feature on our map. In the quest for Irish legal history, the handicaps are undoubtedly severe: there has been much destruction of records and many other sorts of disappointment crowd the route. But the detail on the composition of Pushkin's story has a message too: in Irish legal history the opportunity is frequently extended to make discoveries that are germane, possibly even of great interest. Any discovery will help to enhance the understanding of Ireland's legal past; a few may enable the researcher to take matters a critical stage further, where, for example, they happen to shed light on how legal doctrines and procedures peculiar to Ireland may have come to evolve.

In rare instances celebrated legal discoveries have been the outcome of archaeological excavation. In 1902, in the Mesopotamian desert, a team of French archaeologists unearthed the gigantic block of diorite, now in the Louvre, upon which there was found inscribed the laws of Hammurabi.[25] More recently, in 1981, near Seville in Spain, the use of metal detectors led accidentally to the recovery of six bronze tablets recording the proceedings of the senate at Irni in the first century AD; these illuminated various facets of administrative and judicial practice in Rome's Spanish province.[26] Discoveries of a similar order – though by no means as dramatic – could conceivably still occur in Ireland. Last century significant finds of ancient manuscripts were made at Cashel (BL Add. Ms. 11809) and at Lismore (the *Book of Lismore*), for instance, when buildings were being repaired and restored.[27] Naturally, though, the chance of such finds being repeated in the future must, as the years pass, become increasingly remote.

The sort of discovery that is there to be made and that I have principally in mind is likely to be, rather, the product of painstaking work among manuscripts and print-

24 Alexander Pushkin, *The queen of spades and other stories*, trans. Rosemary Edmonds (London, 1962), pp 69–74. Mr John Murray of the Department of Russian, Trinity College Dublin, has, in addition, kindly directed my attention to N.V. Izmailov, 'Two documents in Pushkin's work', which appears in *Pushkin, issledovaniya i materialy* (Pushkin, research and materials) (Leningrad, 1982), x, p. 305. **25** See C.H.W. Woods, *The oldest code of laws in the world* (Edinburgh, 1903). **26** P.B. Birks, 'New light on the Roman legal system: the appointment of judges and conduct of trial', *Cambridge Law Journal*, 47 (1988), 36. **27** Lord Killanin and M.V. Duignan, *Shell guide to Ireland* (London, 1962), see entries for 'Cashel' and 'Lismore'.

ed books. Already, happily an amount of progress can be reported. In the 1940s a researcher at work in Marsh's Library in Dublin identified among the library's manuscript collection transcripts of a number of the acts passed by James II's Irish parliament of 1689, not apparently extant in any form – in print or in manuscript – elsewhere.[28] Concealed in one of the published volumes of Blake family papers is a real curiosity, in no way connected either with the Blake family or with Co. Galway: a record of an arbitral decree of 1482 handed down in the Desmond palatinate of Kerry, probably at Dingle, in a dispute that had arisen over shipping dues and rights of admiralty at Ventry.[29] Again, a paragraph in the minutes of evidence published alongside the report of a mid-nineteenth century parliamentary inquiry comes as close as it may ever prove possible to do to furnish an explanation for the origins of Ireland's judicially invented suspended sentence: an initiative born of frustration when politicians and churchmen became embroiled in controversy over allegations of proselytism in Irish penal institutions, and penal reform was delayed.[30] Of equal interest must be any evidence that touches on the origins of the Irish civil bill: such evidence is to hand in the marginal notes to the narrative of a mid-eighteenth century law-suit contained in one of the volumes of Robinson manuscripts preserved in the Pearse Street Public Library in Dublin[31] and also, somewhat more conveniently, if less interestingly, in the Irish law reports for 1897.[32]

Law reports constitute a distinct genre of historical source-material. Though somewhat intimidating on first acquaintance, their general importance in the present connection should not be underestimated. The sort of information that lies buried in them is exemplified by the accounts they furnish of two very different law-suits, one of 1865 date, the other of 1835. In the case from 1865[33] the then lord lieutenant had been sued, and the court, to assist itself in the task of deciding how to proceed, referred back to the last known occasion in Ireland when similar litigation had been initiated. This was in 1792 when Napper Tandy had commenced proceedings against the earl of Westmoreland. The report of the 1865 case prints the text of all the orders made in the course of the earlier litigation by the court of exchequer, orders that were made between 26 June and 28 November 1792. In the case from 1835 the entire Irish judicial bench was summoned by the lord chancellor to proffer an opinion on the major contentious professional question of the hour: whether, following the assimilation of the Irish and British currencies in the preceding decade, fees on retainers due Irish solicitors and attornies were to be calculated in terms of the old-style Irish currency or the new-style British.[34] Though the outcome possesses obvious interest, more immediately instructive is the fact that the reporters, Lloyd and Goold, obligingly reproduce

28 Marsh's Library, Dublin, Ms.Z 2.1.7. **29** *Blake family records 1300 to 1600*, ed. M.J. Blake (London, 1902), p. 42. **30** *Report from the select committee on criminal and destitute children: together with the minutes of evidence ...*, House of Commons Sessional Paper 1852–53 (674), xxiii, p. 342 (366). **31** Gilbert Collection, Pearse St Public Library, Ms. 40, p. 138. **32** *R.* v. *Justices of Tipperary* [1897] 2 Irish Reports 486 at 490–1 (judgment of Johnson J in footnotes). See now D.S. Greer, 'The development of civil bill procedure in Ireland' in J.F. McEldowney and Paul O'Higgins, eds., *The common law tradition: essays in Irish legal history* (Dublin, 1990), p. 27. **33** *Luby* v. *Woodhouse* (1865) 17 Irish Common Law Reports 618. **34** *Case of the Solicitors and Attornies* (1835) Lloyd & Goold's Reports 349.

the full text of the Irish government proclamation of 1637 which had sought to establish a comparable uniformity between the two currencies, the Irish and the English, at that time.

Reports of nineteenth-century Irish cases in fact commonly reproduce an abundance of other historical evidence. In a dispute from the 1820s and '30s between Trinitarians and Unitarians over possession of the Presbyterian meeting-house at Clough, Co. Down, entries from the eighteenth-century records of the Synod of Ulster are carefully sifted for any indication of early Unitarian tendencies.[35] In the dispute of 1833 over the advowson of Rathweir, Killucan, the parties included among their proofs: the regal visitation book of 1615, the entry book of First Fruits of the exchequer, a visitation book of 1633, an inquiry conducted under the Commonwealth in 1653, and replies to questions asked later in the same century by Bishop Dopping of Meath.[36] An equally rich documentary vein is tapped in the series of Irish several fishery cases, most spectacularly perhaps in the first of the series – *Malcomson* v. *O'Dea*[37] – that focussed on fishing rights in a stretch of the Shannon close to Limerick. Other law-suits of the same general vintage quote, discuss or refer to records in a host of miscellaneous residual categories: decrees of the courts (the prerogative, chancery, equity exchequer), municipal records, the books of survey and distribution drawn up under the Restoration land settlement, besides many others.[38]

In relation to searches through the earlier Irish law reports (a period extending roughly from the 1780s to the 1860s), one is regularly made to sense that genuine discoveries lie just around the corner. C.R. Milward, in the preface to his collection of ecclesiastical law reports (1847), alludes to the precarious state of the records of the Irish prerogative court before Dr Radcliff was appointed judge in 1816, and sets out to explain how such a situation had arisen.[39] Nor are the law reports the exclusive fount of such unexpected enlightenment. A parliamentary paper, published in 1867, supplies comprehensive details on one group of Irish ecclesiastical appeals which, prior to 1782, could be heard by an English court of delegates and which, apparently, frequently were: cases arising within the sphere of clerical disciplines.[40] Staying with matters ecclesiastical, there is the huge challenge represented by any attempt to frame a detailed reconstruction of the extraordinary affair of the Rev. Lemuel Mathews, archdeacon of Down.[41] Between 1694 and 1711, and possibly even beyond, Matthews fought a sustained and tortuous legal and political battle to reverse the sentence of deprivation against him imposed by special royal commissioners appointed to investigate malad-

35 *Dill* v. *Watson* (1836) 2 Jones's Reports 48. **36** *Bishop of Meath* v. *Marquis of Winchester* (1833) Alcock & Napier's Reports 508. **37** (1863) 10 House of Lords Cases 593; 11 English Reports 1155. **38** For example, *McDonnell* v. *Alcorn* [1894] 1 Irish Reports 274 (the prerogative and equity exchequer); *Neill* v. *Duke of Devonshire* (1882–3) 8 Appeal Cases 135 (chancery); *A.G.* v. *Corporation of Cashel* (1842) 3 Drury & Warren's Reports 294 (municipal records); *Knox* v. *Earl of Mayo* (1858) 7 Irish Chancery Reports 563 (books of survey and distribution). **39** C.R. Milward, *Reports of cases argued in the court of prerogative in Ireland and in the consistory court of Dublin during the time of the late rt.hon. John Radcliff LL.D* (Dublin, 1847), preface, p. vii. **40** *Appeals in causes of doctrine or discipline made to the high court of delegates, from its erection by the 25 Henry VIII c.19 A.D. 1533 until its abolition by the 2 & 3 Will. IV c. 92 A.D. 1832*, House of Commons Sessional Papers 1867–8 (199), lvii, 75. **41** For an account of the affair see G.T. Stokes, *Some worthies of the Irish church* (London, 1900), pp 234–40.

ministration in the northern dioceses of Down and Connor in the established church. The case is best regarded as a vast jig-saw puzzle with an unhealthy preponderance of missing pieces. Happily, one central piece of the puzzle has recently been located by the Irish Manuscripts Commission and can now be set confidently in place. A volume of documents published in 1983 prints a letter from one of the commissioners, Bishop King, to Sir Robert Southwell in London, warning him against Chief Justice Pine of the Irish king's bench: in legal proceedings in Ireland in 1696, Pine had, according to King, taken up cudgels on Matthews's behalf and was pressing to have the case reopened; he was, therefore, 'dangerous' and was not to be encouraged.[42]

The King letter solves one problem. A letter from the Irish privy council to its English counterpart and forwarded in the autumn of 1641 solves several. It will suffice to mention two: the origins and scope of conciliar jurisdiction in Ireland and the approach of government in accelerating the process of assimilation between Gaelic law and the common law in the immediate aftermath of the Nine Years' War. The letter is long and detailed and its composition was interrupted by the outbreak of the Irish rebellion in October. It was included in the collection of manuscripts belonging to the marquis of Drogheda, transcribed for the Historical Manuscripts Commission.[43] Particularly for the light the letter casts on the mechanics of what may be termed 'the second reception of the common law in Ireland', omission of any allusion to it from existing historical surveys of the period borders on the inexcusable.

IV

In *Pilgrim's Progress* the progress of Christian and his wife Christiana is interrupted by a succession of traveller's nightmares. There is the Slough of Despond to cross and the Valley of Humiliation to pass through; earlier there had been the encounter with Doubting Castle and its inhabitants, Giant Despair and his wife Diffidence. The journey of the Irish legal history explorer is punctuated likewise by the appearance on the horizon of landmarks equally calculated to cause dismay, disillusionment and – certainly where the deliberate destruction of source-material can be vouched for – even dread. But these obstacles, I would contend, though formidable, can be surmounted, for, if the analogy with John Bunyan's masterpiece is permissible – and plainly it should not be stretched too far – there is a Promised Land and it beckons all the time: 'After this, I beheld until they were come unto the Land of Beulah, where the sun shineth night and day.'

42 *The bishopric of Derry and the Irish Society of London*, eds. T.W. Moody and J.G. Simms, 2 vols. (Dublin, 1983), ii (1670–1705), p. 170. **43** *Historical Manuscripts Commission*, 9th report (1883), pt. 2, appendix, pp 310–15.

Roman Law in Ireland

> I wish some worthy lawyer would read the law diligently, and show the several heads from which these laws of ours are taken. They beyond the seas are not only diligent, but very curious in this kind; but we are all for profit and *lucrando pane*, taking what we find at market, without enquiring whence it comes.
>
> Sir Henry Spelman

Roman arms never invaded Ireland, or so it is generally believed. The system of Roman law was universally installed in the wake of conquest elsewhere. An early opportunity for this system to leave its impress on the history of law in Ireland too thus never presented itself.

It could easily have been otherwise. No permanent settlement ensued from Julius Caesar's incursion into Britain in 54 BC, but it did in the aftermath of the emperor Claudius's expedition of 43 AD. This settlement endured until the early years of the fifth century, when the last of the Roman legions were withdrawn. Not long after the Claudian conquest, Agricola, who served as governor of Roman Britain between 78 and 84, did actually contemplate the seizure of Ireland. In the year 82 Agricola was campaigning in south-west Scotland – today's Dumfries and Galloway – and possibly reached a point from where one should be able to make out, at least in decent weather, far to the west the coastlines of the modern Irish counties of Down and Antrim – an enticing prospect indeed. Tacitus, Agricola's son-in-law, to whom we are indebted for the details, stresses the strategical considerations that lay uppermost in Agricola's calculations.[1] Accepting (erroneously, as any atlas will confirm) that Ireland was geographically positioned between Britain and Spain, Agricola reckoned that, by investing it and securing it, a valuable link would be forged between the other two existing Roman provinces. Preliminary plans were laid. Navigational data was assembled. Political intelligence, too, began to be collected, principally, it may be conjectured, from an Irish chieftain banished to Britain as a result of some local quarrel and whose friendship Agricola was assiduously engaged in cultivating.[2] In Tacitus's brief account, no reference is made to special allurements that Ireland might have been thought to hold out. There is no mention, for instance, of the mineral wealth and the pearls (possibly derived from the fresh water pearl mussel *margaritifera margaritifera*),

1 Tacitus, *Agricola*, xxiv. **2** Ibid.

natural resources which furnished both Julius Caesar and Claudius with an extra justification for invading Britain and that doubtless served equally well as a bribe to forestall the opposition of Britannosceptics on the Senate.[3] In the case of Ireland, hard information for the Romans in fact seems to have been in short supply, though stories abounded concerning all the remoter regions of the western seas – stories of severe weather, unknown birds, fabulous sea-monsters and the like.[4] Agricola was later to tell Tacitus that, in his estimation, Ireland might have been conquered and held by but a single legion with an accompanying auxiliary force.[5] A recent editor of the *Agricola*, cognisant perhaps with the problems of military deployment faced by the commanders of crown forces in Ireland in the present century, unhesitatingly labelled this logistical assumption as 'optimistic', which 'might well make a thoughtful reader gasp'.[6] Whatever the cause, Agricola's proposal to invade Ireland was soon abandoned. It does not appear that such a proposal was ever seriously entertained again thereafter; or if it was, the proof is not to hand.[7]

3 Suetonius, *De vita Caesarum*, i, 47; Tacitus, *Agricola*, xii. **4** Tacitus, *Annales*, ii, 24. **5** Tacitus, *Agricola*, xxiv. **6** H. Mattingly in his introduction to the Penguin Classics ed. of the *Agricola* and the *Germania* (London, 1948), p. 14. **7** There is an ambiguous reference to a possible conquest of Ireland in, of all places, Juvenal's notoriously anti-homosexual second satire (lines 159-61): 'arma quidem ultra/ litora Iuvernae provimus et modo captas/ Orcadas ac minima contentos nocte Britannos.' The sense is that, despite the debauchery in Rome, the Roman legions abroad had continued to notch up successes: 'Our arms indeed we have pushed beyond the shores of Ireland to the newly-conquered Orkneys and the Britons who enjoy short nights.' If the passage carries the connotation that there was indeed a later expedition, one theory goes that this expedition must have met with a reverse. • The whole question of contact between Ireland and Rome during this period (as well as later and earlier) was the theme of a colloquium held at the Royal Irish Academy in November 1975. The resultant published papers contain a detailed examination of all the evidence that bears on Hiberno-Roman relations: the literary, that derived from finds of coins, that from archaeological field-work generally. Of particular value in the present context are J.F. Killeen, 'Ireland in the Greek and Roman writers' (1977) 76 *Proc. R.I.A.*, section c, p. 207; J.J. Tierney, 'The Greek geographic tradition and Ptolemy's evidence for Irish geography', ibid., p. 257; J.D. Bateson, 'Further finds of Roman material from Ireland', ibid., p. 171; Michael Dolley, 'Roman coins from Ireland and the date of Patrick', ibid., p. 181; Etienne Rynne, 'The La Tène and Roman finds from Lambay, County Dublin: a reassessment', ibid., p. 231; Charles Thomas, 'Imported late-Roman Mediterranean pottery in Ireland and western Britain: chronologies and implications', ibid., p. 245; R.B. Warner, 'Some observations on the context and importation of exotic material in Ireland, from the first century BC to the second century AD', ibid., p. 267. • Killeen and Warner both discuss the views of those who consider there may have been an invasion of Ireland after 82. It is a theme to which Warner has returned in a more recent general survey of Hiberno-Roman contact ('The earliest history of Ireland' in Michael Ryan (ed.), *The illustrated archaeology of Ireland* (Dublin, 1991), pp 112-16). The nature of the archaeological artefacts brought to light in recent years in the south-east of Ireland and the concentration of them there has led Warner to pose two rhetorical questions for the Irish history of the second and third centuries AD (at p. 116): 'Can we really escape the conclusion that at least the aristocracy of the south-east were Romanised Britons and Gauls, and is there even reason to suspect a military campaign in the area?' • The circumstances in which in earlier times attention was drawn to Ireland's having avoided invasion by Rome are themselves not without interest. A prologue, specially commissioned for a performance in Dublin shortly after the restoration of Charles II in 1660 of an English version of Corneille's *Pompée*, for example, contained the following lines apropos the career of Julius Caesar: 'When he the Thames, the Danube, and the Nile,/ Had stain'd with blood, Peace flourished in this isle …' (J.T. Gilbert, *History of the city of Dublin*, 3 vols. (Dublin, 1854-9), ii, 66-7). • Archbishop Ussher, in his formidable tract on the divine right of kings, *The power communicated by God to the prince, and the obedience required of the subject; briefly laid down and confirmed out of the holy scriptures, the testimony of the primitive church, the dictates of right reason, and the opinion of the wisest among the heathen writers* (C.R. Elrington (ed.), *The whole works of the most rev. James Ussher, D.D.*, 17 vols. (Dublin, 1864), xi, 235), first published in England a few

If Agricola had pressed ahead with an invasion in 82 and been successful, the likelihood must be that the Roman legal system would have been transplanted into Hibernian soil. The permanence of the transplant would by no means have been assured however if the experience that Britain underwent following the removal of its Roman garrison may serve as a guide. During the earlier centuries of the occupation of Britain, Roman cultural influence had been extensive. Latin was spoken, Roman dress was adopted, Roman building styles and religious practices became firmly established. Legal difficulties arising in Britain and referred to the emperor for final adjudication might even bring forth a decision that would enter the corpus of Roman law itself: a constitution of the emperor Constantine that settled a tax dispute, probably originating in conflict between Roman and Celtic notions of land ownership in Roman Britain, was thus to find its way into the Theodosian Code promulgated in 438.[8] Before the legions were withdrawn in the fifth century, however, a cycle of Anglo-Saxon incursions had started and these incursions predictably gathered momentum after the final departure of the Romans. A conspicuous casualty was the legal regime that the Romans had introduced and that they had over the centuries refined. In 1885, the future Lord Justice Scrutton, in his remarkable Yorke essay on the impact of Roman law on English law, writing of the situation in England at this period, bleakly concluded that 'the vestiges of Roman influence can hardly have endured with any permanence in face of the anarchy of invasion which swept over them'.[9] More recently, J.F. Winkler has indicated his concurrence with that verdict:[10]

> Where the Anglo-Saxons settled, Roman law seems to have disappeared entirely. During the fifth century through the mid-seventh centuries, the early English occupied most of Roman Britain and displaced, assimilated, or enslaved the Roman-British. As they did so, they appear to have retained such legal customs as they had received from their continental ancestors. There is no significant evidence that these pagan warriors, farmers and herdsmen, whose

months after the restoration of Charles and some five years after Ussher's own death, again refers to Ireland's same lucky escape. The allusion surfaces in the course of an intriguing passage where Ussher warns of the dangers of civil war, and of how, in particular, the latter was prone to precipitate the intervention of some foreigner in a country's own affairs, 'which', Ussher asserts (Elrington (ed.), *Ussher's works*, xi, at 364), 'how ready a way it is to subvert the state of any such distracted kingdom, and to bring it under the subjection of foreigners, we need not seek further for proof than from our own Ireland. For when one of the petit kings of this nation was by domestical dissension driven out of his country, Julius Agricola received him indeed under the colour of courtesy and friendship, but retained him only till occasion should serve, that he might use this as a means to subdue the whole island unto the Roman government. And howsoever that project then failed, by the recalling of Agricola unto Rome from his lieutenantship in Brittany [sic]: yet afterward, when, upon like occasion, Dermot, King of Leinster, was forced by his rebellious subjects to crave the aid of King Henry II for the restoring of him to his kingdom, this association produced that effect which now we see, that the Irish lost their dominion, and became subject to the crown of England even until this day.'

8 C.E.Stevens, 'A possible conflict of laws in Roman Britain', (1947) 37 *Journal of Roman Studies* 132. **9** T.E. Scrutton, *The influence of the Roman law on the law of England* (Cambridge, 1885), p. 4. For an equally instructive guide to the rather different developments in Scotland, see Peter Stein, 'The influence of Roman law on the law of Scotland', (1963) 8 *Juridical Review* 205. **10** J.F. Winkler, 'Roman law in Anglo-Saxon England', (1992) 13 *Journal of Legal History* 101 at 102.

political and social organisation was rudimentary, were influenced by the legal concepts and rules of late antique Roman Britain.

II

The history of law in Ireland effectively commences with the reduction to writing of its laws in the early law tracts.[11] The relationship between the indigenous legal tradition as reflected in this material and other legal traditions, including Roman law, now merits consideration. In 1865 the Brehon law commissioners published the first volume in the Ancient Irish Law series. Responsibility for writing the preface to this introductory volume was given to W.N. Hancock, one of the editors of the series and a polymath who did not shrink to put pen to paper on an intimidating range of topics.[12] In his preface – a fascinating pot pourri that nonetheless still deserves to be read – Hancock advanced the claim that Roman law codification might have both inspired and served as a model for the writing down of the early Irish law texts. 'The preparation and publication of the Theodosian Code', Hancock declared,[13]

> are events of such importance that the knowledge of them would be rapidly diffused through the provinces of the Roman empire. The success of the Christian bishops in securing the requisite modification of pagan laws, by the imperial authority of Theodosius at Constantinople and Valentinian at Rome, would spread with equal rapidity to the Christian missionaries throughout the world. St Patrick, a Roman citizen, a native of a Roman province, and an eminent Christian missionary, would be certain to obtain early intelligence of the great reform of the law of the empire, and of the great triumph of the Christian church. He would naturally be influenced in the work in which he was engaged by so remarkable a precedent, and would facilitate the conversion of the Irish and strengthen the church he was founding, by recognising all that was good in the pagan laws of Ireland, and only insisting on such modifications and adaptations as Christian morality and Christian doctrine rendered indispensable; and such is precisely the course which St Patrick is described in the introduction to the Senchus Mor as having pursued.

The episode to which Hancock is here alluding tells how the murder of St Patrick's charioteer prompted the establishment of a committee that then oversaw the writing down of the laws of Ireland in such a manner as to ensure their compliance with Christian belief and doctrine. St Patrick's mission to Ireland occurred in the first half of the fifth century and was thus contemporaneous with the promulgation of Theodosius's code. Hancock's thesis, therefore, was by no means far-fetched. There are serious snags with it even so. First, it is now settled that the Irish law tracts only

11 Fergus Kelly, *A guide to early Irish law* (Dublin, 1988), passim. **12** J.F. McEldowney, 'William Nielson Hancock (1820-88)', (1985) 20 *Irish Jurist* 378; R.S. Harrison, *Irish insurance: historical perspectives 1650-1939* (Cork, 1992), pp 37-9, 41-3. **13** *Ancient laws and institutes of Ireland*, i (Dublin, 1865), pp xii-xiii.

began to be set down in writing from the seventh century – very much later than the time of Patrick's mission.[14] But secondly – and this condemns the thesis out of hand – as the late D.A. Binchy has shown,[15] the narrative in the prologue to the Senchus Már as to how the laws came to be written down has to be dismissed as a fabrication, not least because the language in which it is cast identifies the entire passage as a later addition, albeit, some would have it, composed of elements of a respectable enough pedigree. Whether these are to be dated to before or after the Viking invasions is the bone of contention.[16]

Hancock's foray into historical scholarship – not perhaps his strongest suit – plainly bristled with a number of misunderstandings. Nevertheless, the instincts that propelled him – to offer an explanation where one had never before been attempted and to admit the possibility of cross-cultural influence – were fundamentally sound. In recent years, the question of the exact provenance of the substance of all early Irish legal material (including the rules of law as such) has again begun to command an amount of attention. The influence of the bible, particularly that of the Old Testament; the influence of the writings of the early church fathers: these have already been assessed.[17] The quest for links of this sort had earlier been anticipated by Kathleen Hughes who, in her important book on sources for the history of early Christian Ireland, drew attention to the close connections existing then between the secular laws and ecclesiastical legislation.[18]

A possible role for Roman law is much more difficult to chart. The flavour of a great deal of the content in the tracts themselves derives, as A.P. Smyth has phrased it, from 'a native Irish rather than a Christian Roman tradition'.[19] Eoin MacNeill and D.A. Binchy, representatives of an older school in Celtic scholarship, have likewise stressed the unique characteristics of the early Irish legal material. Some influence attributable to Roman law, exerted though the instrumentality of early canon law, they were alone prepared to concede.[20] The problem with this somewhat loose-ended discussion, however, has been the failure to keep clearly in mind the precise question to which attention is being directed. If by the term 'Roman law' something is to be understood other than the classical law of the Justinianic compilations of the sixth century which only finally began to penetrate western Europe from the eleventh century onwards, it is unsafe to seek to stand over the verdict of MacNeill and Binchy in the absence of more substantial evidence than they themselves were apparently able or prepared to adduce.

The entire question is worth subsuming within a broader examination of the migration of Roman law into the legal systems of western Europe in general,[21] and of

14 Fergus Kelly writes (*Guide to early Irish law*, p. 225): 'The manuscripts in which the law-texts are found date mainly from the 14th-16th centuries AD, but the linguistic evidence shows that many of these texts were originally written in the 7th-8th centuries.' **15** D.A. Binchy, 'The pseudo-historical Prologue to the Senchas már', (1975-6) 10-11 *Studia Celtica* 15. **16** Nerys Patterson, 'Gaelic law and the Tudor conquest of Ireland: the social background of the sixteenth century recensions of the pseudo-historical Prologue to the Senchas már', (1991) 27 *Irish Historical Studies* 197. **17** Donnchadh Ó Corráin, Liam Breatnach and Aidan Breen, 'The laws of the Irish', (1984) 3 *Peritia* 382. **18** Kathleen Hughes, *Early Christian Ireland: introduction to the sources* (Cambridge, 1972), chs. 2 and 3. **19** In his review of Kathleen Hughes's book (above): (1973) 13 *Studia Hibernica* 170. **20** D.A. Binchy, 'De fontibus juris Romani', (1983) 15 *Celtica* 13. **21** See general-

its possible migration into the legal systems of early Christianised Britain and Ireland in particular. In relation to Britain and Ireland, this is not a topic upon which it is possible to pronounce with any degree of confidence: the evidence is exiguous and what there is is difficult to interpret. Winkler, in his study of the possible impact of Roman law on Anglo-Saxon England, has drawn attention to the familiarity with certain concepts of late Roman law displayed in the educational work of Theodore of Tarsus at Canterbury in the seventh century. Such modest amounts of knowledge, he went on to point out, may very well not have survived the Venerable Bede's notorious onslaught on the teaching of secular law that came soon after. Winkler stressed the absence throughout the Anglo-Saxon period of any evidence whatsoever for the circulation of the Justinianic compilations of the sixth century.[22] Much of what he has to say is obviously of interest in an Irish context.

Set beside this dismal inventory, an awareness nevertheless seems to be growing that in both Anglo-Saxon England and Celtic Ireland native marriage law may have been infiltrated by Roman ideas to a larger extent than has hitherto been supposed or thought possible. In this connection, Winkler has singled out recognition of the dowry for England,[23] and Donnchadh Ó Corráin has done likewise for Ireland. Indeed, as regards much of native early Irish marriage law, Ó Corráin has gone so far as to assert that the imprint of late Roman law is unmistakable – on the shape of *lánamnas comthinchuir*, or marriage of common convenience; on the marriage of soldiers; and, most significant of all, on provision for divorce.[24] Ó Corráin has offered the following tentative conclusions:[25]

> It seems highly likely that much of the Roman legal framework in matters relating to marriage was brought into Ireland by missionaries ... they may also have brought with them the prudent tolerance in regard to divorce and marriage which one observes in the decisions of the synods of the fifth century.

A partial, if minor, rehabilitation of Hancock would thus seem to be under way.

Ó Corráin's argument supporting the notion of a transplant must remain in the realm of speculation, but, in its own terms, it does not lack persuasiveness. At the same time, it merits emphasis that the doctrines on which he concentrates appear to have been a concoction of classical and late imperial law with a soupçon of early native law. If in Ireland borrowing occurred, which seems likely, such borrowing, it bears repeating, was being effectuated by members of a learned class as familiar with secular as they were with ecclesiastical law. Any 'reception' that may have taken place has to be accepted therefore as by no means an orderly channelling of law flowing in a natural and unadulterated stream.

ly O.F. Robinson, T.D. Fergus and W.M. Gordon, *An introduction to European legal history* (Abingdon, 1985), ch. 1. **22** Winkler,'Roman law in Anglo-Saxon England', (1992) 13 *Journal of Legal History* 101 at 107. **23** Ibid., at 110, n. 151. **24** Donnchadh Ó Corráin, 'Marriage in early Ireland', in Art Cosgrove (ed.), *Marriage in Ireland* (Dublin, 1985), p. 5 at pp 13, 18, 19-20. **25** Ibid., at p. 20.

III

From the arrival of the Anglo-Normans in the late twelfth century to the end of the Nine Years War at the start of the seventeenth two distinct legal systems cohabited within Ireland: the brehon law in Gaelic and gaelicised areas and the common law in areas of Anglo-Norman, or English, settlement. Over the years the differences between these two systems became blurred in certain respects: each was to influence the other.[26] For purposes of the present exercise, it seems wisest nevertheless to sketch the continuing fortunes of Roman law in Ireland over this period of four centuries and more, assuming a background of, basically, two separate cultural milieux.

It is not easy to form an accurate picture of the administration of law in Gaelic and gaelicised parts of the country – the Ireland of the brehon law – for the period stretching from the twelfth century to the seventeenth.[27] The law texts of the early Christian era continued to be copied; indeed the manuscript tradition itself, in nearly all instances, goes back no further than the fourteenth to sixteenth centuries.[28] Evidently, a knowledge of some kind of the doctrinal tradition embodied in these texts managed to be preserved. Yet, a crucial question admits of no simple answer: what actually happened when a dispute broke out and the services of some brehon were engaged to resolve it? An issue of paramount concern to us – identification of the sources of enlightenment to which the brehon might have had recourse as he set about formulating his award – cannot easily be resolved largely on account of the paucity of the evidence that might bear on it.[29] Isolating the factors likely to have played some part is probably all that can or should be attempted. Classical Irish law of the early Christian period, if only in an attenuated form, may still have exerted a great deal of influence. This is the view of Nerys Patterson who has presented her argument attractively and with some force.[30] No less influential may have been the canon law of the medieval church, with its roots in Roman law: here the fact that in some regions of the country the same person might be discovered discharging the dual roles of brehon and of diocesan official, or ecclesiastical court judge,[31] is clearly of great interest. Important likewise, though from an altogether different perspective, are the indications of frequent resort to arbitration for the settlement of disputes: a product of the diverse legal regimes existing within Ireland and of the retention of the idea that law itself was primarily personal rather than territorial but, above all, of the imperative need to secure an acceptable modus vivendi when conflict threatened an unwanted breakdown of law and order.[32]

26 Gearóid MacNiocaill, 'The interaction of laws', in James Lydon (ed.), *The English in medieval Ireland* (Dublin, 1984), p. 105. **27** A stimulating discussion of this entire question is Nerys Patterson, 'Brehon law in late medieval Ireland: "antiquarian and obsolete" or "traditional and functional"?', (1989) 17 *Cambridge Medieval Celtic Studies* 43. **28** See n. 14 above. **29** The oral context of much Gaelic legal practice entails, in Patterson's view, that the lack of evidence should occasion no surprise: 'Brehon law in late medieval Ireland', at 48–9. **30** 'I cannot see any compelling reasons for doubting that the Irish jural tradition was continuous and functional, and that its persistence as a system, with identifiable institutions, depended upon the availability of the law tracts as an anchor for legal learning': Patterson, 'Brehon law in late medieval Ireland', at 63. **31** Katharine Simms, 'The brehons of later medieval Ireland', in Daire Hogan and W.N. Osborough (eds.), *Brehons, serjeants and attorneys: studies in the history of the Irish legal profession* (Dublin, 1990), p. 51 at pp 71–2. **32** Some useful material is assembled in Richard Sharpe, 'Dispute settlement in medieval

Might Roman law too have had direct influence, that is, exerted an influence other than that which was being transmitted indirectly through the medium of canon law?

That within Gaelic and gaelicised Ireland a certain awareness of Roman law and an interest in it prevailed is suggested by a curious text embedded in a recension of one of the law tracts.[33] This is an account, written in modern Irish, probably no earlier than the fifteenth century, of the supposed origins of Roman law itself. The text is at page 59 of TCD MS. 1337,[34] where it occupies the space surrounding a quadrilateral centre-piece given over to an obscure dictum of one Cormac ua Cuind. The text stands in total isolation and thus is in marked contrast to other literary disquisitions on legal origins to be found in ancient source-material. In his *Annals*, Tacitus, for example, similarly includes a digression on the origins of law, but this is a natural progression from the immediately preceding discussion by him of the *Lex Papia Poppaea*.[35]

The passage in TCD MS. 1337 has been edited by Binchy and translated by him as follows:[36]

> Here is how the imperial law had its beginning: there were two cities in Greece named Athens and Sparta. And the manner in which the people of that city [called] Sparta had their law was through memory and learning by heart. The people of the other city, Athens, were accustomed to have their law in writing. And equally [for both] the law consisted of their customs and ordinances according to their own natural reasoning. And it was from these two cities that the Romans took their model and instruction when Romulus was their chief. He ordered the Romans to have ten wise men who would preserve in memory the customs and usages they had taken from the above-mentioned Greek cities. And full powers for a year were given to them to do that. The result was that they had their law [engraved] on ten tables within that year. And whatever difficulties arose [afterwards] were put into two other tables in addition, with the result that it was named the law of the Twelve Tables. And [subsequently] when many doubts about that law of the Twelve Tables arose, the name *ius civile* was given to it, i.e. civil law. And after that there arose law-suits and matters for decision, and a certain number of these were established so that there should not be a superfluity of them, and they were given the name of *legis actiones*. And it is Gaius Flaius [Gnaeus Flavius] who devised the *legis actiones*. And the names of the Decemvirate are [given] elsewhere: Ploc, Plut, Plocar?, Rucon, etc.

Binchy laboured to make sense of this extraordinary farrago of truth, half-truth and blatant falsehood. As to the source from which the copyist might have obtained his information, a possible candidate would have been the *Etymologiae* of Isidore of Seville,

Ireland: a preliminary enquiry', in Wendy Davies and Paul Fouracre (eds.), *The settlement of disputes in early medieval Europe* (Cambridge, 1986), p. 169. See, too, for Wales, Llinos Beverley Smith, 'Disputes and settlements in medieval Wales: the role of arbitration', (1991) 106 *English Historical Review* 835. **33** D.A. Binchy, 'De fontibus juris Romani', (1983) 15 *Celtica* 13. **34** Formerly H.3.18. The Irish text will be found in the *Corpus iuris hibernici*: C.I.H. 602.34-603.15. **35** Tacitus, *Annales*, iii, 75. **36** 15 *Celtica* 14-15.

a text certainly in circulation in Ireland as early as the seventh and eighth centuries. While the *Etymologiae* furnished a version of the origins of Roman law, the excerpt from MS. 1337 included detail not to be discovered there, nor, in Binchy's judgment, anywhere else either. Binchy's own hesitant solution to the riddle was that the version could have been based on some epitome, no other copies of which survive, that circulated at the time; or, perhaps, on the faulty recollection of a conversation held with a student from Ireland who had been studying civil law abroad, possibly in Oxford.[37]

This bizarre synopsis can legitimately be regarded as nothing other than a gratuitous display of inaccurate antiquarian learning. It would be dangerous to treat it as irrefutable proof of a general familiarity, on the part of brehons as a class, with Roman law, still less of any disposition by them to make use of the rules of Roman law in the settlement of disputes brought before them. Tangible proof demonstrating that Roman law was actually employed in just such a fashion is obviously what is needed. Proof of this kind for the later medieval period is not wholly lacking; sadly, though, it is more often inferential than absolutely clear-cut. What relates to legal business in Galway for the fifteenth and sixteenth centuries – not, however, business transacted before brehons – will be examined shortly. Two other scraps of evidence may be mentioned here. In 1562, the lord deputy, the earl of Sussex, wrote a letter to Queen Elizabeth in which he described the brehon law as essentially 'a corrupt kind of civil law'.[38] The phrase is derogatory doubtless, but the analogy is eloquent. The well-known contemporaneous description of the native Irish set down in *Holinshed's Irish chronicle* contains a glimpse of the 'common schools of leachcraft and law' which the student entered as a child and where he stayed for 16 to 20 years. This is our second scrap of evidence. The account tells of the students 'connyng by rote the Aphorismes of Hypocrates, and the civil institutes, with a few other paringes of those faculties'.[39] One cannot be absolutely sure, but this looks very like a reference to Justinian's *Institutes*.

IV

At the end of the sixteenth century and at the start of the seventeenth the Gaelic order was superseded, and the way accordingly lay clear for a second 'reception' of the common law in the island. Paradoxically, elements within Gaelic society had not been opposed to development along these lines,[40] but, naturally, the manner of the final accomplishment of that reception – in the wake of resort by the crown to force of arms – left ample fuel for future resentment.[41] From the standpoint of the English government in Ireland, once victory in the Nine Years War had been assured, the

37 Ibid., 15-17. **38** *Cal. Carew MSS., 1515-74*, p. 331. **39** *Holinshed's Irish chronicle the histoire of Irelande from the first inhabitation thereof, unto the yeare 1509, collected by Raphaell Holinshed, and continued till the yeare 1547 by Richard Stanyhurst*, eds. Liam Miller and Eileen Power (Dublin, 1979), p. 14. **40** Patterson, 'Gaelic law and the Tudor conquest of Ireland', (1991) 27 *Irish Historical Studies* 197. **41** Note the widescale emigration from Munster to France, and to Paris in particular, which led to forced repatriation by boat in 1606: David Buisseret, *Henry IV* (London, 1984), pp 14-45; idem, 'The Irish at Paris in 1605', (1964-5) 14 *Irish Historical Studies* 58; *Cal. S. P. Ire., 1603-06*, pp 496-8.

immediate priority was consolidation of its authority by the adoption of a novel legal programme.[42] A system of assizes encompassing for the first time ever the whole island was promptly set in place.[43] A cheap and expeditious method of commencing civil law-suits was soon made available as well, in the shape of the so-called civil bill.[44] Brehons vanished; the brehon law, too, was earmarked for extinction. Whatever the fate of Roman law hitherto in Gaelic and gaelicised regions had been, its fortunes from this moment on in the history of Ireland were inextricably linked with the stance evinced towards it by the common law – by the judges of its courts and by the members of its legal professions.

From the late twelfth century onwards, in areas of Ireland subject to Anglo-Norman or English influence, the impact of Roman law can safely be presumed to have been identical with the impact of Roman law in England. There, two features may be remarked upon, both of which show that, contrary to popular belief, England by no means set out deliberately to shun the mainstream legal tradition of Europe.

First, it has been established that direct citation of Roman law in the common law courts was by no means unprecedented, the practice only apparently falling into disuse in the course of the fourteenth century.[45] Secondly, there is the magisterial thirteenth-century figure of Bracton who was to play a key role in introducing into the common law in its formative years doctrines borrowed from Roman law. Bracton incorporated within his celebrated treatise, *De legibus et consuetudinibus Angliae* (*On the laws and customs of England*),[46] either directly or via Azo, William of Drogheda and others, many passages taken straight from the Justinianic compilations of the sixth century, which, from the eleventh century, as has already been noted, had begun to enjoy a general currency in western Europe. Estimates of the amount of unreconstructed Roman law in Bracton's treatise have varied enormously. In 1885 Scrutton calculated the number of express citations at twelve from the *Digest*, ten from the *Code* and one from the *Institutes*.[47] By 1968 such estimates had been shown to be woefully inadequate, S.E. Thorne then writing that, in the first third of *De legibus* alone, there were to be found quotations from almost 200 different sections of the *Digest*.[48] Accompanying this scholarly volte-face was the belated acknowledgment of the fact that Bracton had been a more than competent civilian. F.W. Maitland's contradictory impression was revealed as quite misleading.[49] Bracton's influence indeed lives on. Such vestiges of Roman law that remain secreted within common law doctrine today owe their place there in a great number of instances to the legacy of Bracton. Two modern Irish cases, to be

42 H.S. Pawlisch, *Sir John Davies and the conquest of Ireland: a study in legal imperialism* (Cambridge, 1985). **43** John McCavitt, ' "Good planets in their several spheares" – the establishment of the assize circuits in early seventeenth century Ireland', (1989) 24 *Ir. Jurist* 248. **44** D.S. Greer, 'The development of civil bill procedure in Ireland', in J.F. McEldowney and Paul O'Higgins (eds.), *The common law tradition in Ireland: essays in Irish legal history* (Dublin, 1990), p. 27. **45** Scrutton, *Influence of Roman law on the law of England*, pp 71-2. And now see D.J. Seipp, 'The reception of canon law and civil law in English common law courts before 1600', (1993) 13 *Oxford Journal of Legal Studies* 388. **46** Bracton, *On the laws and customs of England*, ed. G.E. Woodbine, transl. with revisions and notes by S.E. Thorne, 4 vols. (Cambridge, Mass., 1968-77). **47** Scrutton, *Influence of Roman law on the law of England*, p. 80. **48** Bracton, *On the laws and customs of England*, i, p. xxxvi (translator's intro. by S.E. Thorne). **49** Bracton, *On the laws and customs of England*, i, pp xxxii-xl (Thorne's important review of Bractonian scholarship).

examined below, in which Roman doctrine associated with donations *mortis causa* and with the law of alluvion was to undergo exhaustive analysis, substantiate the leading part played by Bracton in such reception of Roman law as took place within the common law tradition of England and Ireland. Recognition of this is even clearer from the more frequent and more extensive discussion of Bracton's legacy in England.[50]

The common law tradition of England revolves as much around institutions as it does around doctrine and procedure. It was this composite tradition that gradually became distinctive, and, by the end of the middle ages, it can be regarded as a fait accompli. From the arrival of the Anglo-Normans in Ireland, areas of English settlement in the country had professed a fidelity to the common law of England that was extensive and deep-rooted. Interestingly, however, it is at this later juncture that such fidelity began to show undeniable signs of faltering.

For the western sea-port of Galway data has survived which indicates that resort to Roman law in the handling of law-suits was had there in the fifteenth and early sixteenth centuries. The principal piece of evidence concerns a commercial suit brought originally before a court in Galway and which is referred to in the records of the Irish parliament for 1476-7, in the reign of Edward IV.[51] This parliamentary record conveys the clearest of impressions that Roman law, variously described as 'the civil law' or 'the law of the emperor', was then being commonly utilised in the resolution of litigation. The town of Galway, soon to be elevated in status by Richard III's charter of 1484, may be seen at the time as an isolated settlement which, though surrounded by Gaelic or gaelicised territory, was not entirely impervious to English governance. A major element in the evidence for the use made of Roman law in late medieval-early modern Ireland is properly viewed then as an incident in the history of a 'common law' area. That the individual, alleged, quite irregularly, to have applied Roman law in settling the litigation, was no less a personage than the sovereign or portreeve of Galway himself, one William Fitzsaundre Lynch, is of additional significance. The further circumstance that the Irish parliament, having heard the complaint brought before it by the dissatisfied party, ordered the entire affair to be retried before the Irish court of King's Bench[52] supports the classification as well.

The principal protagonists in the dispute were Germyn Lynch, a Galway merchant described as a goldsmith, and Walter White and Gerot Lewes, two merchants from Limerick. Lynch was engaged in trade between Ireland and the Iberian peninsula, owning a ship, the *Mary Leybourne*. Lynch's commercial dealings with White and Lewes, which precipitate the later legal proceedings, started when the *Mary Leybourne* put into Kinsale on the south coast at the end of a stormy passage back from Portugal. Lynch found himself short of money to pay for essential repairs – the mast had been broken and other damage sustained – and availed of the services of a third Limerick merchant, an Esmond Torger, to arrange the necessary loans: £10 from White and £13 6*s*. 8*d*. from Lewes. Lynch got the money to pay for the repairs, and the *Mary*

50 Not everything was to be plain sailing, as is made clear by D.E.C. Yale in his '"Of no mean authority": some later uses of Bracton', in M.S. Arnold et al. (eds.), *On the laws and customs of England: essays in honor of S.E. Thorne* (Chapel Hill, N.C., 1981), p. 383. **51** *Stat. rolls, Ire., 12 & 13-21 & 22 Edw. IV*, pp 570-7. **52** Ibid., pp 572-3.

Leybourne set sail. The bonds evidencing the nature and extent of Lynch's indebtedness to White and Lewes were duly handed over to the latter.

According to Lynch's complaint, it was agreed that the loans would be repaid either in Bruges in Flanders or in London through Torger, the agent who had arranged the loan. Also according to Lynch, the sums in question were in fact later paid back in London, having been given to a Lombardy banker there, a Carle Camby. Despite what Lynch regarded as clear proof that the loans had been repaid, White and Lewes, who had retained their bonds – evidence of the original loans – maintained that they had not. In his complaint, Lynch went on to name the persons who, in his view, had instigated White and Lewes to open proceedings against him in the court of Galway's sovereign. William Fitzsaundre Lynch, the holder of the office of sovereign in the relevant year, was also alleged to have conducted the resultant suit 'according to the law of the emperor called civil law and not according to the law of England' (solonq la ley del Empoure appelle la ley du Civile & nient solonq la ley le Roy dengletre).[53] The outcome, a decree against Germyn Lynch, included the award to White and Lewes, in satisfaction of the imagined debt, of property in Galway belonging to Lynch, which had earlier involved the latter in outgoings of 200 marks. What had happened, Lynch protested, was 'contrary to all law, faith and justice' (contarie a toute ley foialte & conscience).[54]

The eventual outcome of Lynch's petition is not known. The statute rolls reveal that the Irish parliament granted the petition, and ordered White, Lewes, Torger and William Fitzsaundre Lynch and others to explain themselves to the Irish King's Bench by a specified date. In addition, the parliament instructed William Fitzsaundre Lynch to bring with him to the court a record of the tainted proceedings. A particular concern of the parliament's was also to ensure that, in the event of the Galway court's decree being reversed, Germyn Lynch would be reinstated in his property in Galway.[55]

The long entry summarising Lynch's complaint and recording the parliament's reaction to it dates from 1476/7. Additional evidence for the use of Roman law in the courts in Galway is furnished by the terms of a municipal ordinance for 1519.[56] This stipulated:

> That no Irish judge nor lawire shall plede in no man's cause or matter within this towne or courte for it agreeth not with the King's law, nay yet the Emprors, in many placis.

Making sense of the ordinance is not easy, though it is plain enough that a determined effort was being made to outlaw resort to brehon law. The phrase 'nay yet the Emprors' presents the challenge. A possible reading is that the common law had been recently reintroduced into Galway, but had not yet entirely displaced Roman law. This is Kenneth Nicholls's interpretation,[57] which is certainly a legitimate one.

The interpretation gathers indirect support from other details in the parliamentary record for 1476/7 of Germyn Lynch's petition. Lynch went to some trouble to indicate the possible reasons why resort had been had to Roman law to deal with the claim

53 Ibid., p. 572. **54** Id. **55** Ibid., pp 574–7. **56** HMC, *10th report, app. V* (1885), p. 395. **57** Kenneth Nicholls, *Gaelic and gaelicised Ireland in the middle ages* (Dublin, 1972), pp 48–9.

against him. There was a scarcely veiled insinuation of corrupt practice but, besides that, Lynch dwelt on two other interconnected matters: ignorance in the west of Ireland of the common law and, possibly more crucial, the lack of personnel designated by the common law dispensation to oversee the due execution of writs and decrees:[58]

> et coment nulx viscounts sount en lez Countees delymyk et Connaght ne nulx homes lerez p[er] lez qux la ley du Roy poet estre execute.

The absence of effective law enforcement machinery was to vex the Irish parliament as well. The order they drew up to deal with the eventuality that the Galway court's decree might be overturned directed the issuance of the appropriate writs to such individuals as could be relied upon to restore Germyn Lynch to his property in Galway. This testifies to an institutional hiatus which it is most unlikely could have been speedily rectified.

Galway's important trading links with Spain and Portugal may have rendered it particularly susceptible to civil law influence. The date of Lynch's petition falls squarely within a period that witnessed a resurgence of Roman law on the continent. It is vital to recall, too, the vacuum that Roman law may then have filled, and the reasons for its emergence. Galway was geographically remote, but it had experienced an intellectual isolation as well, both as regards knowledge of common law doctrine and acquaintance with common law enforcement machinery. In 1972 Kenneth Nicholls first called attention to the legal position in Galway. 'It seems certain', he then wrote,[59] 'that Irish law in the later medieval period was strongly influenced by Roman law'. Whilst much has subsequently been made of this bold assertion,[60] the true state of affairs must remain debatable. The paucity of the surviving documentary evidence is one reason for caution; Nerys Patterson's stout defence of the integrity of the jural tradition associated with brehon law[61] is another.

V

The completion of the conquest of Ireland coincided with the emergence in England of a more radical approach towards an array of legal issues. Criticism of the amount of medieval obfuscation that continued to disfigure the law was becoming vocal. Partly in response, but motivated by an independent professionalism too, the courts were set to evolve impressive innovations in basic legal doctrine. Symptomatic yet again, in a series of constitutional test cases, a proportion touching on the relationship with other

58 *Stat. rolls, Ire., 12 & 13 – 21 & 22 Edw. IV*, p. 572. **59** Nicholls, *Gaelic and gaelicised Ireland*, p. 44. **60** Maurice Craig, the architectural historian, for instance, has drawn from it the inference that the isolation to which these legal records appear to lend credence may have helped to give St Nicholas's collegiate church in Galway (which is fourteenth century) 'the very individual character it retains': *The architecture of Ireland from the earliest times to 1880* (London and Dublin, 1982), p. 80. **61** Patterson, 'Brehon law in late medieval Ireland', (1989) 17 *Cambridge Medieval Celtic Studies* 43.

tribunals recognised by the legal system of the day, the common law courts were to find themselves moving to the centre of the political stage, whether they especially desired this or not.

The new chapter that was opening in the history of law in Ireland at the commencement of the seventeenth century thus opened in the midst of a debate in England concerning all manner of things connected with the law – with judicial institutions, with legal doctrines, with constitutional objectives – a debate which, at times, was to assume a frankly propagandist tone. If the discussion on the various issues that had arisen was of immediate interest in England, and indeed was largely carried on there, it was not a discussion thought to be irrelevant in Ireland, nor one from which certain benefits for Ireland might not ultimately be hoped to accrue.

It was confidently expected that the completion of the conquest would speed the infiltration of English doctrine and procedure into Ireland. Among the values that at the same time it was sought to inculcate, in order, as it were, to smooth the transition, was recognition of one particular jurisprudential bonus conferred by the tie with England – the distinctiveness of the common law and its innate excellence too. But there is a second Irish interest to the debate. A focus of attention was the comparison to be drawn between the common law tradition and the civilian tradition grounded on Roman law (a tradition with which the sons of Irish recusant gentry families sent to the continent for their education[62] would naturally be becoming increasingly acquainted). Here, as it chanced, a significant intervention was to be registered in a law book published in Dublin in 1615.

Of the self-appointed spokesmen for the common law who regarded the latter both as a proud expression of nationalism and an essential safeguard of liberty, Sir Edward Coke (1552-1634) was undoubtedly the most celebrated. The second part of his *Institutes* was published, posthumously, in 1642. It consists of a jumble of commentaries on Magna Carta and on other important English statutes of the medieval and early modern periods. In the final paragraph of the proem Coke contrasted the technique he had adopted throughout with that of the typical glossator or commentator on the continent. The superiority of a legal tradition founded exclusively on judge-made law, to which Coke here lay claim, could not perhaps have been better expressed:[63]

> Upon the Text of the Civill Law, there be so many glosses and interpretations, and again upon those so many Commentaries, and all these written by Doctors of equall degree and authority, and therein so many diversities of opinions, as they do rather increase than resolve doubts, and incertainties, and the professors of that noble Science say, That it is like a Sea full of waves. The difference then between those glosses and Commentaries, and this which we publish, is, that their glosses and commentaries are written by Doctors, which be Advocates, and so in a manner private interpretations: And our Expositions or Comment-

62 Helga Hammerstein, 'Aspects of the continental education of Irish students in the reign of Queen Elizabeth I', in *Historical Studies: VIII*, ed. T.D. Williams (Dublin, 1971), p. 137. **63** Edward Coke, *The second part of the institutes of the lawes of England* (London, 1642), proem.

aries upon Magna Charta, and other Statutes, are the resolutions of Iudges in Courts of Iustice in Judiciall courses of proceeding, either related and reported in our Books, or extant in judiciall Records, or in both, and therefore being collected together shall (as we conceive) produce certainty, the Mother and Nurse of repose and quietnesse, and are not like to the waves of the Sea, but *Statio bene fida peritis*: for *Iudicia sunt tanquam Iuris dicta.*

Coke's assault on the civilians in the proem to the second part of his Institutes was relatively short. An earlier assault, mounted by another self-appointed spokesman, Sir John Davies (1569-1626), successively James I's solicitor general and attorney general in Ireland, was longer, ranged more widely and essayed to probe more deeply. In 1615 Davies published in Dublin the first collection of Irish law reports. The preface, which touches on various preoccupations of English and, possibly, to some degree, also of Irish lawyers of the period, devotes considerable space to an examination of the respective merits of the common law, on the one hand, and of the civil law and of Roman law, on the other.

At the outset Davies highlighted the same vice to which Coke was later to return, even employing the same metaphor attributed to the civilians which Coke was also to borrow. 'The civilians themselves confesse', Davies wrote,[64] 'that their lawe is a seafull of waves'. The text of it, Davies continued,[65]

being digested into so many volumes, & so many Doctors interpreting the Text, & twice as many more Commenting uppon their interpretations, & so glosse uppon glosse, & booke upon booke, & every Doctors opinion being a good authority fitt to be cited & vouched among them, must needes breed distraction of opinions and uncertainty in that lawe.

The common law, he averred, was in all respects superior:[66]

Our native Common lawe is farre more apt & agreeable, then the Civile or canon lawe, or any other written lawe in the worlde besides.

The explanation lay in the fact that the common law had been built on robust common sense and the practical acumen of an independent, island race:[67]

This lawe therefore doth demonstrate the strength of witt and reason, and selfe sufficiencie which hath beene alwayes in the people of this land, which have made their owne lawes out of their wisdome & experience (like a silke-worme that formeth all her webb out of her selfe onely) not begging or borrowing a forme of a common-weale, either from Rome, or from Greece, as all other nations of Europe have done, but having sufficient provision of lawe & Iustice

64 Sir John Davies, *Le primer report des cases & matters en ley resolues & adiudges en les courts del roy en Ireland* (Dublin, 1615), f. 4v. **65** Id. **66** Ibid., f. 2v. **67** Ibid., ff 2v-3.

> within the land, have no neede *Iustitiam & iudicium ab alienigenis emendicare*, as King Iohn wrote most nobly to Pope Innocent the third.

Davies's excoriation of civil law (and of its parent, Roman law) embraced a number of further arguments, which, whatever about those already rehearsed, were hardly persuasive. Who, Davies interjected,[68] had ever seen the need to supply a gloss or commentary on any classic text of the common law?

> But of the professors of our lawe, who ever yet hath made any glosse or interpretation uppon our Master Litleton? though into that little booke of his, he hath reduced the principall groundes of the common lawe, with exceeding great Iudgement & authority, & with singular Method & order? and yet if hee had beene an author in the Civill or Canon lawe, I dare say, there had beene, by this time, so many Comments and glosses made uppon him, as the bookes written uppon this booke onely, would have beene more in number, then all the volume of our lawe at this day.

The riposte to this tirade that straightaway suggests itself is that Coke, following his own dismissal from office in 1616, i.e. one year after Davies published his reports, was to set about to do just that. Coke's commentary on Littleton, the first part of his *Institutes*, was published in 1628.[69]

A hostage of a very different species was committed to fortune when, in a long excursus, Davies upbraided Roman law for its temerity in admitting a right to counsel in serious criminal cases:[70]

> as our Iudges do discountenance bad Counsellors, so doth our Lawe abhore the defence & maintenance of bad causes, more then any other lawe in the world besides. … And this is one cause, among others why our lawe doth not allowe counsell unto such as are indicted of Treason, Murder, Rape, or other capitel crimes: So as never any Professor of the lawe of England hath beene knowne to defend (for the matter of fact) any Traytour, Murderer, Ravisher or Thief, being indicted & prosecuted at the suite of the King. *Turpe reos empta miseros defendere lingua*, saieth the Poet, & therefore it is an honor unto our lawe, that it doth not suffer the Professors thereof to dishonor themselves (as the Advocats & Orators in other countries do) by defending such offenders. For example whereof wee have extant divers Orations of Cicero, one *pro C. Rabirio perduellionis reo*, another *pro Roscio Amerino* who was accused of Parricide, & another *pro Milone* who was accused of Murder.

The corollary was that a good lawyer could not honestly undertake the defence of a foul and desperate cause, a proposition, Davies was glad to note,[71] that was roundly supported by Aquinas.

68 Ibid., ff 4v–5. **69** Edward Coke, *The first part of the institutes of the lawes of England, or a commentarie upon Littleton, not the name of a lawyer onely, but of the law itself* (London, 1628). **70** Davies, *Le primer report*, f. 7. **71** Ibid., f. 7v.

In nailing his colours to the mast in so unequivocal a fashion, Davies neglected to mention that contemporary practice within the civilian tradition (despite his assertion to the contrary) could also be at odds with what had happened under Roman law. In the year of his own death, there occurred in France the notable refusal to allow the comte de Chalais to be defended by counsel at his trial for treason in Nantes.[72] The main point that deserves emphasis, however, is that the attitude of Davies on this practical question and that of others who thought like him was very soon to be vigorously disowned. By 1695 the English parliament had swung round to the view that, in regard to prosecutions for treason at least, a right to counsel should be accorded.[73] The preamble to the enabling act thus enshrined an approach that was diametrically opposed to that of Davies:[74]

> Whereas nothing is more just and reasonable than that persons prosecuted for high treason and misprision of treason whereby the liberties lives honour estates blood and posterity of the subject may bee lost and destroyed should bee justly and equally tried and that persons accused as offenders therein should not bee debarred of all just and equal means for defence of their innocencies in such cases …

Interestingly, it was to take seventy more years before the Irish parliament, in 1765, enacted a measure conceding an entitlement to the exercise of the identical privilege in Ireland.[75] And it was to be seventy more years after that before, in 1836, the right to defend oneself by counsel was finally granted in felony cases in both England and Ireland.[76]

Despite the bluster, as Hans Pawlisch has convincingly demonstrated, Davies was far from being uniformly hostile to the civil law tradition of his day. There was on the continent a great deal of contemporary learning, based in part on interpretations of Roman law, devoted to questions such as sovereignty and the prerogative;[77] and this learning was deployed so frequently by Davies that the resultant picture must, as Pawlisch has written,[78] 'cast doubt upon the conventional notions of an insular common law tradition'. There were extensive allusions, too, to the history of Rome in the arguments Davies set down both in his law reports and in his earlier historical

72 Victor-L. Tapié, *France in the age of Louis XIII and Richelieu*, transl. and ed. D. Mc N. Lockie (London, 1974), p. 161. On the other hand, as is also well known, in 1408 the duke of Burgundy, John the Fearless, was permitted the services of John Parvus to present the defence at his trial in Paris for instigating the murder of the duke of Orleans, the brother of King Charles VI, the preceding year. See Roland Mousnier, *The assassination of Henry IV* (London, 1973), pp 83–6. **73** For the background see Holdsworth, *H.E.L.*, vi, 233–4. **74** 7 & 8 Will. III, c. 3: An act for regulating of trials in cases of treason and misprision of treason. **75** 5 Geo. III, c. 21 (Ir.): An act for the better regulating of trials in cases of high treason under the statute of the twenty-fifth of Edward the third. The preamble to the Irish Act of 1765 is a good deal shorter: 'Whereas it is highly reasonable and agreeable to the nature of our excellent constitution, that persons prosecuted for high treason … should be allowed all proper means for defence of their innocence.' **76** 6 & 7 Will. IV, c. 114: An act for enabling persons indicted of felony to make their defence by counsel or attorney. **77** See Walter Ullmann, *Law and politics in the middle ages* (London, 1975), chs. 2 and 3. **78** Hans Pawlisch, 'Sir John Davies, the ancient constitution and the civil law', (1980) 23 *Historical Journal* 689.

work, *A discoverie of the true causes*. Roman rules with respect to taxes on trade were exhaustively considered in Davies's report of the *Case of customs payable for merchandise*.[79] Of more immediate interest in an Irish context, in a passage in *A discoverie of the true causes* Davies lauded the Romans for setting their face against the emergence of patterns of legal discrimination, this through adherence to a policy of ensuring that their laws were imparted to all the peoples conquered by them:[80]

> But the Romaine State, which conquered so many Nations both barbarous and civill; and therefore knewe by experience, the best and readiest way of making a perfect & absolute conquest, refused not to communicate their Lawes to the rude & barbarous people, whom they had conquered; neither did they put them out of their protection, after they had once submitted themselves.

Davies did not say so, but this represented implicit criticism of the record of the government of the medieval lordship of Ireland.

VI

There were contradictions in Davies's outlook and the logic of individual arguments was far from impregnable either. Yet the tenor of his remarks was unmistakable and this embodied, as did the later observations of Coke, a mood that was destined long to prevail among practitioners of the law in England, and since Ireland had now been transformed, so far as legal geography was concerned, into nothing other than a cultural extension of England, this applied among Irish practitioners as well. The history of Rome might be worth studying out of antiquarian enthusiasm and for occasional guidance on the resolution of contemporary problems. But, as regards the day-to-day mechanical workings of the courts, the common law alone furnished authentic, comprehensive and reliable leadership on matters of doctrine and procedure. From acceptance of this undisputed intellectual primacy it resulted that the civil law and its progenitor, Roman law, had to be kept politely but firmly at a distance.

Not that knowledge of either of them could be dispensed with altogether in the rugged legal terrain of Stuart England and Ireland. The presence within the legal systems of both countries of non-common law jurisdictions such as admiralty and the ecclesiastical courts where a distinct cadre of legal professional practised, the so-called civilians or civil lawyers, ensured that a degree of familiarity with civil law (and through it Roman law) and with canon law remained throughout a prerequisite for a few.

For Ireland, there is little hard evidence about the awareness of civil or Roman law that actually obtained or as to any kind of practical impact these might have had for the two and a half centuries after Davies's death.[81] Nor is there satisfactory information that

79 Davies, *Le primer report*, ff. 7–17v. **80** Sir John Davies, *A discoverie of the true causes why Ireland was never entirely subdued, and brought under obedience of the crowne of England, untill the beginning of his maiesties happy raigne* (London, 1612), pp 124–5. **81** In the world of academic scholarship (political science, historical research),

would bear on possible local provision for imparting a knowledge of either. The explanation depends only in part on the meagre character of the surviving data – for instance, the paucity of Irish law books and the total absence of Irish law reports in the interval between Davies's collection and the 1780s. The truth is that basic preliminary survey work has not yet been undertaken. This being the case, the only way forward is to highlight such evidence as happens to be available, and, in addition, to indicate the lines of inquiry that might be thought helpful.

As in England, acquaintance with these supposedly alien legal traditions might actually be in demand, not only for purposes of practice in the ecclesiastical courts, but also for a variety of governmental needs. An instance of the latter is recorded in an episode of 1621, for example, when the bishop of Meath complained to James I that in Ireland too many lay impropriators had reneged on their duty to set aside proper maintenance 'for a sufficient number of godly ministers'. In response, the king wrote to the lord deputy instructing him to launch an inquiry into what might lawfully be done. To this end, he was to summon as advisers 'our learned judges and such as may be best experienced in the civil and canon law'.[82]

Instructive likewise is the establishment by Trinity College Dublin in 1668 of a professorship of laws,[83] which subsequently earned designation as a regius professorship of civil law. In view of the lack of any prior provision within the college since its foundation in 1592 for just such a professorship, the innovation plainly augured something special. To date, however, no light at all has been shed on the nature of the tasks which the first incumbent, one Henry Stiles, was supposed to, or did in fact, discharge. And very soon the professorship was doomed to become a sinecure, held *in commendam*, as it were, by a succession of professors, doubtless worthy enough in their own right but already allocated a plethora of other academic duties.[84]

In an effort to establish the true picture and thus to reduce our level of ignorance, basic library research would appear to be an essential prerequisite. A group of small-scale projects, which ought not to present immense difficulties in the way of their completion, may be briefly outlined here.

Following the adoption by the Irish parliament in 1541 of the act for the kingly title, Edward VI, on his accession, became king of Ireland as well as of England. It was thus as king of both countries that Edward lent his name to one of the more remarkable projects of pan-European Renaissance cultural sponsorship from a time long

the impact of the Roman law tradition was, of course, undeniable, though that impact appears not to have been exhaustively surveyed. An Irish interest is furnished by Archbishop Ussher's English-language legal and political tracts, certain of which make generous use of the *Corpus juris civilis*, especially the *Code*, though there are a few references to the *Digest* and the *Institutes*. See notably *The power communicated by God to the prince, and the obedience required by the subject: briefly laid down and confirmed out of the holy scriptures, the testimony of the primitive church, the dictates of right reason, and the opinion of the wisest among the heathen writers*, but, in addition, both *Of the original and first institution of corbes, herenaches, and termon lands* and *A discourse showing when, and how far, the imperial laws were received by the old Irish and the several inhabitants of Great Britain* (C.R Elrington (ed.), *The whole works of the most rev. James Ussher, D.D.*, 17 vols. (Dublin, 1864), xi, at 235, 419 and 465, respectively). **82** *Pat. rolls Ire., Jas. I*, pp 470–1. The identical complaint was aired in Thomas Ryves's *The poor vicar's plea* (London, 1620). **83** *Cal. S. P. Ire., 1666-69*, pp 654–5. **84** *The Dublin University calendar 1833* (Dublin, 1833), at pp 111–12, furnishes a succession list.

before anyone had dreamt of a European University Institute or a Eurovision Song Contest. In 1553 Edward joined the French king, Henry II, the emperor Charles V, Cosmo de Medici duke of Florence, as well as the pope, in supporting the printing in Florence that year of Taurellius's two-volume folio edition of Justinian's *Digest: Digestorum seu pandectarum libri quinquaginta ex Florentinis pandectis repraesentati*.[85] A library for Trinity College Dublin began to be assembled in 1592, another for King's Inns in 1787. Both sport a copy of Taurellius's edition, though there is some variation in the representation of Edward VI's co-sponsorship. Might there be other copies of Taurellius's edition in Ireland? Where did these two Dublin copies originate?

As a result of the exertions of the American scholar, R.S. Matteson, a large amount of information has in recent years been pieced together on what must have been at the time the biggest collection of books in private ownership in early eighteenth-century Ireland – the library of William King, successively bishop of Derry and archbishop of Dublin in the established church.[86] The collection has long since been dispersed, the lion's share, however, finding its way into the G.P.A. – Bolton library in Cashel. There survives a catalogue for the complete collection which was prepared shortly before King's death in 1729. This includes a special section devoted to books on civil law. It should not prove too onerous an exercise to identify the books listed under this heading. It might even prove possible to begin to speculate as to why King should have acquired them.

Lists of holdings of early printed books in the fields of civil and Roman law to be found today in libraries other than those already mentioned – for example, in Marsh's library in Dublin or in the library of St Patrick's College, Maynooth – could, with equal utility, and, hopefully, equal facility, also be prepared.[87] A certain amount is known about the libraries of Irish judges and lawyers from the Restoration period onwards. In some instances, catalogues or inventories are extant. These latter, too, might profitably be the object of scholarly scrutiny.[88]

In 1776 Edward Gibbon commenced the publication in six volumes of his *History of the decline and fall of the Roman empire*. It was an immediate success. Chapter 44 in the

85 Edward Gibbon unhesitatingly labelled Taurellius's edition 'splendid': Gibbon, *The history of the decline and fall of the Roman empire*, 2nd ed., 6 vols. (London, 1776–88), iv, 365, n. 92. **86** R.S. Matteson, 'Archbishop King's library: some discoveries and queries', (1974) 9 *Long Room* 7 at 12. The original catalogue, save for one section, is at Cashel; a microfilm is available in Trinity College Dublin's library. **87** Past generations of bibliophiles have not exactly encouraged the carrying out of surveys into the holdings of law books in major depositories. Beriah Botfield, for instance, in *Notes on the cathedral libraries of England* (London, 1849), dismissed the legal material then to be found in Exeter cathedral library in the following withering terms (at p. 155): 'The law books contained in this room may be very soon enumerated, as there is no interest whatever attached to the Codex Theodosianus; Corpus juris Civilis Gothofredi; Oughton's Ordo Judiciarum, in 2 vols., 4to.; Burns' Ecclesiastical Law; Blount and Jacob's Law Dictionaries; Lambard de Priscis Anglorum Legibus; Durandi Speculum Juris; Spencer de Legibus Hebraeorum, Cantab. 1685; Gibson Codex Juris Civilis, &c in 2 vols. folio; and an old edition of Blackstone's Commentaries.' The law books in Winchester cathedral library were likewise dismissed as 'a barren theme' (ibid., p. 478). **88** See W.N. Osborough, 'In praise of law books', (1986) 21 *Ir. Jurist* 326 at 352–3 for a summary of much of the available data. F.E. Ball, in his *The judges in Ireland, 1221-1921*, 2 vols. (London, 1926; repr. Dublin, 1993), ii, 28 also mentions the libraries of two Williamite judicial appointees, Henry Echlin, made a baron of the Exchequer in 1690, and Thomas Coote, made a justice of King's Bench in 1693.

fourth volume dealt at length with the history of Roman law from the time of the Decemvirs down to the reign of Justinian. Gibbon fully grasped the pivotal position occupied by Roman law in the legal history of continental Europe. It can scarcely be doubted that his account will have reawakened an interest in the topic in the English-speaking world, including Ireland. Though, in the immediately preceding years, transmission to Ireland of any kind of detailed knowledge of Roman law will most likely have come about through the education of Irish students in England and such training of Ireland's small coterie of civil lawyers as these received, the impact ultimately that Gibbon will have had should not be under-estimated. What he accomplished was to underscore the universal presence of Roman law. For the English-speaking world, Roman law had again been placed on the intellectual map.

It is worth noting that two centuries earlier the Elizabethan dramatist Christopher Marlowe had managed to put across the same sort of message, albeit obliquely, in more modest fashion and certainly with less panache. In the opening scene of *The tragicall history of Doctor Faustus* Marlowe shows us Faustus condemning the futility of all the learning he has acquired, a conclusion that prompts him to enter into his fateful compact with the Devil. When Faustus focuses his attention on the law, it is Roman law and Justinian that supply his frame of reference (understandably so, since Faustus himself was a construct of recent mid-European history and folklore):[89]

> Physic, farewell. Where is Justinian?
> *Si una eademque res legatur duobus,*
> *Alter rem, alter valorem rei*, etc.,
> A petty case of paltry legacies!
> *Exhaereditare filium non potest pater, nisi* –
> Such is the subject of the institute
> And universal body of the law.
> This study fits a mercenary drudge,
> Who aims at nothing but external trash
> Too servile and illiberal for me.

None of this is complimentary to lawyers or to legal studies anywhere: it repeats the standard attack levelled at the law by men of letters.[90] Yet this short passage, including the lines of simple Latin supposedly extracted from Justinian,[91] must have served to maintain a continuing awareness of Roman law in the minds of successive audiences present at performances of Marlowe's play. Performances in Ireland naturally would require to be taken into account. Unfortunately, it is not possible to state how many such performances there were before Irish audiences, even in Dublin, prior to 1800, say.[92]

89 *The tragicall history of Doctor Faustus*, act 1, scene 1, lines 27-36. **90** Wilfrid R. Prest, *The rise of the barristers: a social history of the English bar, 1590-1640* (Oxford, 1986), ch. 6; Osborough, 'In praise of law books', (1986) 21 *Ir. Jurist* 326, at 328-35. **91** 'Si una eademque res …': if one and the same thing is bequeathed to two people, one of them should have the thing itself, and the other the value of it. 'Exhaereditare filium …': the father may not disinherit the son unless … **92** The answer may be available in the distinguished theatre

VII

In England, starting from the early eighteenth century, recourse was again intermittently had to Roman law in formulating common law doctrine. The modern law of bailment and that of restitution, to give but two examples, were thus influenced in this way. The judges responsible, endowed with this outward-looking cast of mind, are well-known and included such figures as John Holt and William Murray, later Lord Mansfield, both of whom held office as chief justices of King's Bench.[93] Less well-known, and certainly not as highly regarded, was an early nineteenth-century chief justice of Common Pleas, William Draper Best.[94]

In Ireland, it is indisputable that the legal profession took its cue on virtually all matters of doctrine from their colleagues in Westminster Hall.[95] It may safely be inferred, therefore, that in this roundabout fashion some inkling of Roman law will likewise have begun to penetrate the collective consciousness of the profession in Ireland. Positive proof, however, is lacking. As has previously been remarked, there is a dearth of Irish law reports prior to the 1780s; corroboration from such a source for the years before is simply not to be obtained. Nor is the question of possible civilian sympathies alluded to by F.E. Ball in his thumb-nail sketches of the judicial bench in Ireland for the eighteenth century.[96] Some appointments to the Irish bench were made from the English bar, particularly in the first half of the century, and such appointees may have served as instruments of the cultural penetration we have in mind. But one career that might perhaps be worth specific examination is that of a native appointee, Robert Hellen, named to the Irish Common Pleas in 1779. Hellen, Ball recounts, had practised principally as a civilian.[97]

Towards the end of the nineteenth century, bench and bar in Ireland were, in their turn, to open texts of Roman law and even to embark on discussion of technicalities to be found there. They came to the exercise very much later than their English and Scots counterparts. But, as it is hoped will be demonstrated from the series of cases it is now proposed to examine, the resultant contribution by Irish lawyers to legal understanding in areas where the common law is still shaped by Roman law, if small in amount, is by no means lacking in interest.

Such discussion of Roman law as has occurred in the Irish courts in the nineteenth and twentieth centuries must at the outset be firmly distinguished from what consti-

historian W.J. Laurence's ms. 'Notebooks on the history of the Dublin stage', now at the University of Cincinnati library. Students of the history of theatre in Dublin might like to make it their business to find out. • As it happens, there is one major allusion to Marlowe's *Doctor Faustus* in Irish fiction – in Sheridan le Fanu's novel, *The house by the churchyard*. See the dialogue between the characters Lieutenant Puddock and Captain Devereux in ch. 62, and the futher reference in ch. 69. Le Fanu's novel, of course, is relatively late, the commencement of its publication in monthly instalments in the *Dublin University Magazine* occurring in 1861. **93** Scrutton, *Influence of Roman law on the law of England*, pp 135, 180–1; P.B.H. Birks, 'English and Roman learning in *Moses* v. *MacFerlan*', (1984) 37 *Current Legal Problems* 1. **94** See his dissenting judgment as a puisne judge of King's Bench in *Blundell* v. *Catterall* (1821) 5 B. & Ald. 268, 106 ER 1190; and his advice as chief justice of Common Pleas to the House of Lords in *Gifford* v. *Yarborough* (1828) 5 Bing. 163, 130 ER 1023. **95** See generally 'Puzzles from Irish law reporting history', below, p. 193. **96** Ball, *Judges in Ireland*, ii, passim. **97** Ball, *Judges in Ireland*, ii, 164.

tute mere embellishments of classical learning, which are also preserved in the reports. Two instances of the latter, each rather different in character, may be briefly recalled.

The first instance of embellishment of this variety is to be seen in the judgment of Crampton J in *R.* v. *Conway*, a decision of the Irish Queen's Bench in 1858.[98] Clerical intimidation was a regular feature of parliamentary elections in mid-Victorian Ireland,[99] and it was for this offence that the prosecution of Father Conway, the Roman Catholic curate at Castlebar, Co. Mayo, had been ordered by the House of Commons, following incidents stated to have taken place during the general election of 1857. In strict law, Father Conway's trial should have gone ahead at the Mayo assizes, but the Irish law officers, apprised of the state of local feeling, deemed it prudent to seek to have the venue switched to Dublin. A few years later, with the pronounced deterioration in respect for the law that marked the Irish land struggle, a statutory provision was enacted conferring broad authority to change the venue of criminal trials but, at the time of Father Conway's case, whether or not to grant a motion seeking a change of venue rested solely within the discretion of the court.

In what was undeniably a politically charged atmosphere, Crampton J sought to deflect the criticism that might be directed at the judges, whatever was decided. He did so by reminding those who might chance to read his remarks that the constitutional task set the bench was always to discharge its office regardless of popular applause, regardless equally of the fear or favour of the crown. The position was admirably summarised in the lines of Horace:[100]

> iustum et tenacem propositi virum
> non civium ardor prava jubentium
> non vultus instantis tyranni
> mente quatit solida.
>
> (The man tenacious of his purpose in a righteous cause is not shaken from his firm resolve by the frenzy of his fellow citizens bidding what is wrong, nor by the face of the threatening tyrant.)

The quotation was indeed apt, even if Queen Victoria, had she known, might have winced at being compared to an *instans tyrannus*. Even if, too, it is unlikely that the philosophy espoused by Horace will have impressed those prone to criticise the Irish judges, especially when Crampton J and his colleagues in the court of Queen's Bench granted the law officers' motion and Father Conway's trial was rearranged for Dublin.[101]

98 (1858) 7 ICLR 507. Another example of this kind of embellishment that was to find its way into the Irish law reports occurred later the same year in *Parnell* v. *Parnell* (1858) 7 Ir. Ch. Rep. 322. Here reference will be found to the plainly celebrated refusal of Master Henn in the case of *Joly* v. *Walsh* to draw up a court decree in the absence of proper proofs, a practice the master would have likened to the rough justice that Rhadamanthus administered in the underworld: 'castigatque auditque dolos subigitque fateri/ quae quis apud superos furto laetatus inani/ distulit in seram commissa piacula mortem' (Virgil, *Aeneid*, vi. 567). **99** J.H. Whyte, 'The influence of catholic clergy on elections in nineteenth-century Ireland', (1960) 75 *English Historical Review* 239. **100** Horace, *Carmina*, iii, 3. **101** A few years earlier, Sir Walter Scott had reproduced the same passage twice, albeit in abbreviated form, in his novel *The fortunes of Nigel*. There James I employs

The second instance is to be discovered in the judgment of Gavan Duffy J in *Maunsell* v. *Minister for Education*,[102] decided in 1940. In the case, the judge concluded that the principles of natural justice had been breached when a national schoolteacher, about to be made redundant in compliance with somewhat complex administrative criteria, had been given no opportunity to object. To stress the longevity of the legal rule it was his intention to call in aid, Gavan Duffy J recalled lines from Seneca's play, *Medea*:[103]

> quicunque aliquid statuerit, parte inaudita altera
> aequum licet statuerit, haud aequus fuerit.
>
> (Whoever shall have given judgment, leaving one of the parties unheard, will not have acted justly, even if his judgment in fact does justice.)

This rule the judge had earlier insisted (in English),[104]

> is long and firmly established; it is elementary justice; it applies even where the person affected has no merits; it applies though the enactment does not seem to have contemplated notice; and it applies to every body having authority to adjudicate upon matters involving civil consequences to individuals.

Maunsell and Gavan Duffy J's quotation from *Medea* are briefly adverted to in the chapter on Roman legal thought in John Kelly's masterly survey of western legal philosophy.[105]

Overlooked by Gavan Duffy J in *Maunsell*, and not mentioned either by Kelly, is the context in which, in Seneca's drama, Medea utters her protest to King Creon that she has been unfairly treated. Jason, her husband, had deserted Medea and was about to marry Creon's daughter, Creusa. Creon, anticipating (with some justification) great mischief on Medea's part, had ordered her instant banishment – the decision to which Medea had demurred in the lines reproduced in *Maunsell*. Jason intercedes, Creon relents, the sentence of banishment is deferred for 24 hours. Medea has now been given both the chance and the time to wreak her revenge. It is terrible indeed. First to die, as a result of Medea's machinations, are Creusa – Jason's intended bride – and King Creon himself. Also fated to die, again at Medea's hands, in the episode horrifically recaptured in Géricault's famous painting, are her two infant sons by Jason. In the inventory of female wickedness, Jezebel and Lady Macbeth rank very high. Medea, administrative lawyers everywhere, of both sexes, might deign to recollect, ranks higher still.

the lines to describe the character of Nigel's father, Lord Glenvarloch (ch. 5) and then, somewhat self-consciously and surely inappropriately, his own (ch. 9). In 1872, again before the statutory change was made, the same court granted a change of venue in another case where clerical intimidation was alleged, this time at the behest of the defendant. It may be significant that the defendant was the Roman Catholic bishop of Clonfert. See *The Queen* v. *Duggan* (1873) IR 7 CL 94. **102** [1940] IR 213; 93 ILTR 36. **103** Lines 199–200. **104** [1940] IR at 213. **105** J.M. Kelly, *A short history of western legal theory* (Oxford, 1992), p. 76.

VIII

A spate of law-suits on fisheries law came before the Irish courts from the 1860s onwards. One fundamental problem to surface appears to have prompted the first detailed reference to Roman law that is recorded in the modern Irish law reports. It arose in regard to navigable, non-tidal rivers and navigable, non-tidal inland lakes. Might riparian owners proportionately (*usque ad medium filum aquae*) lay claim to a right of fishery? And was such right exclusive so as to defeat any pretended entitlement on the part of the public to fish in the river or lake?

Murphy v. *Ryan* in 1868, an early dispute in this series of litigation, examined the position in relation to a stretch of the River Barrow.[106] In accordance with recognised common law doctrine, the future Irish lord chancellor, Lord O'Hagan, then sitting as a puisne judge, in the court of Common Pleas, perhaps predictably, sustained the claim of the riparian owners to exclusive rights. Lord O'Hagan manages to convey a hint even so that the result may not have represented his personal preference. A passage in his judgment draws attention to the different stance adopted by other legal systems:[107]

> The Roman law gave to the public larger privileges than the law of England, recognising their property in all rivers which had a continual flow of water, and in the fishing of them, and in the use of their banks.

Lord O'Hagan does not explicitly avow it, but this passage amounts to a précis of the legal position as set down in Justinian's *Institutes*:[108]

> Flumina autem omnia et portus publica sunt: ideoque ius piscandi omnibus commune est in portubus fluminibusque. ... Riparum quoque usus publicus est iuris gentium, sicut ipsius fluminis: itaque navem ad eas appellere, funes ex arboribus ibi natis religare, onus aliquid in his reponere cuilibet liberum est, sicuti per ipsum flumen navigare. Sed proprietas earum illorum est, quorum praediis haerent: qua de causa arbores quoque in isdem natae eorundem sunt.
>
> (Rivers and harbours are state property, so everybody shares the right to fish in them. ... The law of all peoples allows public use of river banks, as of the rivers themselves: everybody is free to navigate rivers, and they can moor their boats to the banks, run ropes from trees growing there, and unload cargo. But ownership of the banks is vested in the adjacent land-owners. That also makes them owners of the trees which grow there.)[109]

Lord O'Hagan continues his excursus in *Murphy* v. *Ryan* by tracing the impact of Roman law on contemporary civilian practice as well as on the practice of certain states in the United States. 'The same principle' [of Roman law], he thus asserts,[110]

106 (1868) IR 2 CL 143 (Common Pleas). **107** Ibid., at 149. **108** *Inst.* 2.1.2, 4. **109** Justinian's *Institutes*, transl. and with intro. by Peter Birks and Grant McLeod (London, 1987), p. 55. **110** (1868) IR 2 CL at 149.

> appears to be recognised by the modern codes of France and other continental countries which have been largely inspired by the civil law, and also by the local tribunals of several of the American states, although in others of them the common law doctrine is in full force, even in relation to great rivers like the Mississippi.

Lord O'Hagan's actual views on the merits of the common law's adoption of the riparian principle to determine fishing rights in the non-tidal, navigable river need not detain us; they may have been orthodox enough. More important to know is that pressure to extend that principle to the determination of fishing rights in the large non-tidal, navigable inland lake was to meet strident opposition within the hish judiciary in the immediate aftermath of *Murphy* v. *Ryan*. *Bloomfield* v. *Johnston*,[111] a case fought over fishing rights in part of Lough Erne, came on appeal before the Irish court of Exchequer Chamber in 1868, shortly after *Murphy* v. *Ryan* had been decided. Here, the riparian proprietor had been granted a 'free fishery' by the crown, but that, Whiteside CJ maintained, was not to be interpreted to mean a several or exclusive fishery, nor could the legal deficiency be supplied by summoning up and applying the riparian principle. In the opinion of the chief justice, that would quite unfairly lead to the bestowal upon the riparian proprietor of 'eight miles of land covered with water'.[112] O'Brien J expressed his concurrence, noting that 'the presumption that a riparian proprietor is entitled to the adjacent subaqueous soil of non-tidal waters along his land may be rebutted'.[113] He chose not to explain exactly when this might occur, but the inference appears to be: when the documentary evidence adduced pointed against it, when it would constitute cartographical lunacy, or when it could be shown that this would be manifestly inequitable in the case of a large expanse of water.

The crucial contest in this branch of law was to come in the battle over fishery rights in Lough Neagh, the largest inland lake in the British Isles, which is touched at some point by no less than five Ulster counties. In the litigation of 1908–11, *Johnston* v. *O'Neill*,[114] a majority (4–3) in the House of Lords was finally to vindicate a title based largely on early and somewhat unsatisfactory crown grants, an adjudication which was destined to be followed in turn by the Northern Ireland High Court and Court of Appeal in separate proceedings in the 1960s, *Toome Eel Fisheries (NI) Ltd.* v. *Cardwell*.[115] The grants in *Johnston* v. *O'Neill* favoured parties other than the riparian owners, so, in the view that the majority of the House of Lords took (and which was accepted by the Northern Ireland courts in the 1960s), no question of relying on the riparian principle could arise, and the status of that principle in determining rights in an inland lake, accordingly, was left unexplored. Equally, in the eyes of the majority, no question of the public conceivably possessing a right to fish in the lough – and certainly not to catch eels – throughout, for commercial reasons, the focus of piscatorial attention – could arise either.

111 (1868) IR 8 CL 68 (Exch. Ch.). **112** Ibid., at 94. **113** Ibid., at 97. **114** [1908] 1 IR 358 (Ross J); [1909] 1 IR 237 (Court of Appeal); [1911] AC 532 (House of Lords). **115** [1963] NI 92 (McVeigh J); [1966] NI 1 (Court of Appeal).

When the major nineteenth-century dispute over rights in Lough Neagh arrived before the courts in the 1870s, the applicable legal principles as well as the inferences to be drawn from the available documentary evidence seem to have been a good deal less clear-cut. *Bristow* v. *Cormican*[116] likewise was taken on appeal to the House of Lords,[117] but not on the central issue that was to be highlighted in *Johnston* v. *O'Neill.* Rather, the emphasis at all stages of the appeal – Exchequer, Exchequer Chamber, House of Lords – attached to the subordinate question as to whether the trial judge had acted properly in withdrawing from the jury the right to decide the substantive issue originally raised in the proceedings.[118] That issue was never in fact to be resolved at the time, for no new trial in *Bristow* v. *Cormican* was ever held.[119] That doubt pervaded the Irish bench at least, whilst *Bristow* v. *Cormican* wound its way up through the courts, as to the correct legal principles to apply in a dispute over fishing rights in the large inland lake, was abundantly plain. Dowse B in the court of Exchequer may be cited as an example. Unconvinced that the law was already settled, as some had claimed by pointing to *Bloomfield* v. *Johnston*, Dowse B proceeded to urge the profession, whenever the crunch issue should fall to be determined, to undertake a careful analysis of legal precedent in the United States. The differing approaches of the courts in the various states – differences first alluded to by Lord O'Hagan in *Murphy* v. *Ryan*[120] and which are neatly summarised by Whiteside CJ in *Bloomfield* v. *Johnston*[121] – encapsulated much of major comparative interest. In the relevant passage in Dowse B's judgment, the legal position governing rights in the River Mississippi was again to receive specific mention:[122]

> It may be that the English law is the common law of the Northern States and the civil law that of the Southern; but I think, irrespective of that, considerations of convenience and necessity dictated the adoption of the civil law on the subject of rivers in the Southern States, because it would have amounted to an absurdity that if a man owned a strip of land containing perhaps a quarter of an acre on the bank of the Mississippi, he should be entitled to a several fishery extending three-quarters of a mile out to the middle of the river.

Whiteside CJ in the court of Exchequer Chamber may be taken as a second example. He, too, was perplexed by the state of the legal authorities and by the guidance to be obtained from them. He made two positive contributions nevertheless. In the first place, he reiterated with some force the rejection of the riparian principle he had uttered earlier in *Bloomfield* v. *Johnston*. But, secondly, and perhaps more intriguingly, he deliberately left open the possibility that the public in the immediate vicinity of Lough Neagh might have continued as beneficiaries of some customary right to fish in the lough, a right that would date back to the time of Shane O'Neill in the sixteenth century.[123]

116 (1874) IR 10 CL 398 (Exch.); (1876) IR 10 CL 412 (Exch. Ch.). **117** (1878) 3 App. Cas. 641 (House of Lords). **118** The outcome at each stage of the appeal was a decision to the effect that the trial judge had erred. **119** See the speech of Earl Loreburn LC in *Johnston* v. *O'Neill* [1911] AC at 554. **120** (1868) IR 2 CL at 149. **121** (1868) IR 8 CL at 89–90. **122** (1874) IR 10 CL at 412. **123** (1876) IR 10 CL at 435.

In this strange interlude in the evolution of Irish fisheries law, it is obvious that Roman law doctrine proved for a while an attraction to certain members of the Irish judiciary. It is difficult otherwise to interpret Whiteside CJ's forthright opposition to the use of the riparian principle to determine fishing rights in Lough Erne and Lough Neagh. Nevertheless, it would be a serious mistake to exaggerate the significance of what actually transpired. The attack on the riparian principle ultimately achieved little, for no judicial majority could subsequently be put together in Ireland for the other, no less crucial, dimension to Roman law doctrine – recognition of the public's right to fish. Whiteside CJ, a leading protagonist in this attempted doctrinal revolution, for his part, did not fail for lack of trying. In *Bristow* v. *Cormican*, he roundly berated the denial of a public right to fish in a large inland lake, solely on the grounds that its water was not salt, as 'an arbitrary rule, repugnant to reason, convenience, and the common sense of mankind'.[124] While a few of his colleagues may have been of like mind, eschewing his choice of words perhaps, but explicitly disowning, like him, the assertion that *Bloomfield* v. *Johnston* represented unequivocal support for such denial,[125] others, we know, wholeheartedly disagreed. At the time *Bristow* v. *Cormican* was before the courts the opposition included, in the Exchequer, the formidable figure of Palles CB and, in the Exchequer Chamber, a no less formidable trio led by Lawson J.[126] It was this opposition that had gained the field by the time *Johnston* v. *O'Neill* came to be litigated in the Irish courts in 1908 and 1909, Ross J and the entire Court of Appeal then unanimously concluding, amongst other things, that *Bloomfield* v. *Johnston* was now unquestioned authority for the previously contentious proposition that the public could advance no valid claim to fish in the navigable, non-tidal, inland lake.[127] Any lingering doubts must finally have been expunged by the majority decision of the House of Lords in the *Johnston* v. *O'Neill* appeal.[128]

In the case of non-tidal stretches of rivers, Roman law doctrine with its recognition of public rights was, as we have seen, brusquely dismissed at the outset. In *Murphy* v. *Ryan*[129] Lord O'Hagan embraced the riparian principle, and this seemed set to cut off any debate. It should be noted, however, that, to judge from the tenor of remarks let fall by Dowse B, Whiteside CJ, and, possibly, even Lord O'Hagan himself, it may have been the absence within the island of Ireland of any river possessed of a width, over the portion where it was non-tidal, approaching that, say, of the Mississippi which alone ensured the retention for Ireland of the riparian principle in the determination of fishing rights in the navigable, non-tidal river. That geography should have had anything to do with so basic a question of property rights is a little odd, but the conclusion itself would seem warranted.

124 Ibid., at 434. **125** See, e.g., the judgment of Fitzgerald J in *Bristow* v. *Cormican*: (1876) IR 10 CL at 426–7. **126** (1874) IR 10 CL at 402–3; (1876) IR 10 CL at 413–14. **127** See, in particular, the judgment in the Court of Appeal of Holmes LJ: [1909] 1 IR 237 at 240–1. **128** See especially the speech of the Earl of Halsbury: [1911] AC at 568. For critical comment on the history of litigation in respect of fishing rights in Lough Neagh, see T.M. Healy, *Stolen waters* (London, 1913). **129** (1868) IR 2 CL 143.

IX

Lord O'Hagan's allusion to Roman law in the course of his judgment in *Murphy* v. *Ryan* might be viewed, of course, as little more than a jurisprudential flourish – a display of legal learning, interesting no doubt after a fashion, but scarcely vital for the resolution of the particular pressing difficulty. Similar jurisprudential flourishes were to emanate from the pens of Irish judges of later generations, though flourishes containing references to Roman law remained rare. One example was forthcoming in 1900 in a celebrated habeas corpus case, *In re O'Hara*.[130] Here the Court of Appeal cancelled an informal adoption agreement at the behest of the natural mother and returned her 11-year-old daughter to her. FitzGibbon LJ utilised the opportunity to explain the difference between the then state of the law in England and Ireland and the law in other legal systems:[131]

> English law does not recognise the power of bindingly abdicating either parental right or parental duty. Neither the Roman nor the Indian law of adoption finds place in our jurisprudence.

In retrospect, a much more significant breakthrough had occurred some years before, when for the first time, it is thought, Roman law texts were actually cited by the Irish court. In 1893 in *Spurway* v. *Spurway* Porter MR quoted to good effect the Justinianic definition of domicile:[132]

> unde non sit discessurus si nihil avocet: unde cum profectus est, peregrinari videtur.
>
> (the place from which a man won't go away unless something calls him away, and from which when he goes away he seems to be a sojourner in a foreign country.)[133]

On the particular occasion, the master of the rolls lay no claim to originality: the same text, he frankly conceded, had been recited by Lords Cranworth and Wesleydale, in *Whicker* v. *Hume* in 1858.[134] Porter MR made use of Roman law again in 1895 in *In re Lough Neagh Shipping Co.*,[135] a Chancery motion heard that year before him which dealt with the consequences of a shipping company having gone into liquidation. A complication was introduced by a number of separate commercial arrangements, which brought into play the principle of subrogation of debts. The master of the rolls deemed it helpful to stress the Roman law origins of subrogation or substitution, and quoted a text from the *Digest*:[136]

> plane cum tertius creditor primum de sua pecunia dimisit, in locum ejus substituitur in ea quantitate quam superiore exsolvit.

130 [1900] 2 IR 232. In an earlier habeas corpus case, also involving infant custody, a judge of Queen's Bench had already made some reference to Roman law: see *In re Connor* (1866) 16 ICLR 112 (per Hayes J at 124). **131** [1900] 2 IR at 241. **132** [1894] 1 IR 385 at 397. **133** C. 10.39.7. **134** 7 H.L. Cas. 124 at 160 and 164 respectively; 11 ER 50 at 64 and 66. **135** [1895] 1 IR 533. **136** At 540.

His foray into Roman law, however, proceeded no further.

Matters were gone into in rather more depth a few months later in *R.* v. *Hehir*,[137] a decision of the Irish court for Crown Cases Reserved. Here members of the court found themselves to be in disagreement over the self-same fundamental difficulty in the law of larceny that had earlier divided their English colleagues. *Hehir*, like *R.* v. *Ashwell*,[138] raised the neat question of the implications for liability of a mistaken transfer of the thing alleged to have been stolen where physical transfer of possession of it had been demonstrably consensual. For enlightenment as to the meaning of the concept of possession, both counsel and members of the court in *Hehir* were to turn to Roman law.

Counsel for the prisoner argued[139] that the *Digest* supported the line that larceny was not committed where transfer of the thing had been consensual:[140]

> qui putavit se rem attingere volente domino non tenetur furti.
>
> (He who was of opinion that he had got the thing with the consent of the owner is not to be made liable for theft.)

Gibson J, on the other hand, considered that the position under Roman law was by no means so clear.[141] An earlier text in the *Digest* seemed to him to leave the matter open, possibly even tending in the opposite direction:[142]

> apiscimur possessionem animo et corpore, neque per se animo aut per se corpore.
>
> (We are to understand the concept of possession in an intellectual sense and in a material sense, neither in the intellectual sense alone, nor in the material sense alone.)

Gibson J was satisfied that the ramifications were accepted by the common law, and hypothesised a chilling variation on a story from Genesis to press home the point:[143]

> As a general rule … legal possession imports knowledge and consent. When Joseph replaced in his brethren's sacks, without their knowledge, the price of the corn they had bought, though they had apparent dominion and control over the sacks with their contents, they were no more, before discovering it, in possession of the money which Joseph had put in by an act of trespass, than they would have been of dynamite secretly placed there.

Neither Gibson J's invocation of the Roman law on *furtum* nor his use of an arresting image, a ploy at which, during his career on the bench, he showed himself unusually

137 [1895] 2 IR 709. **138** (1885) 16 Q.B.D. 190 (Ct. Cr. Cas. Res.). **139** [1895] 2 IR at 711 (Gerald Fitzgibbon). **140** The Mommsen text (D. 47. 2. 46) reads: 'recte dictum est, qui putavit se domini voluntate rem attingere, non esse furem.' The sense, of course, is the same. **141** [1895] 2 IR at 723. **142** D. 41. 2. 3. **143** [1895] 2 IR at 724.

adept, impressed the majority of his colleagues. That majority voted for Hehir's acquittal.

X

Hehir served as a prelude to the first sustained and critical analysis of Roman law doctrine to be conducted in modern times by an Irish court. The next year, 1896, a strong Court of Appeal (Walker C, Porter MR, FitzGibbon and Barry LJJ) pondered a problem that had not apparently been previously raised in the law on donations *mortis causa*: whether a gift made in contemplation of suicide might yet, for legal purposes, constitute a valid donation. The problem was raised in this acute form by the strange business brought to light in *Agnew* v. *Belfast Banking Co. and Claney*.[144]

After her marriage to Robert Agnew on 12 May 1892 Jane Claney had gone to live with her husband at the latter's house in the country close to Bangor in Co. Down. Four days later Jane spent the night with her sister Maria, the second defendant in the subsequent law-suit, at her former residence in Bangor itself. Early the following day, the 17th, Robert called to see Jane in Bangor, and borrowed money from her to pay his rent and also for a train fare. What happened next was subsequently seen to be of central importance. On 7 May, Jane had lodged £200 in the Bangor branch of the Belfast Banking Co. and been given a receipt as proof of the deposit. On the 17th, following Robert's departure, Jane signed this receipt and handed it to her sister, accompanying the transaction with the words: 'Maria, that is yours: if anything should happen to me, that is yours in God's name.' No evidence was produced of any ill-will between Robert and Jane; it did, however, emerge that Jane had begun to think that Robert might be a wastrel, as she had told her sister that Robert 'would need a great deal to do him'.

Later on the 17th Jane rejoined her husband at his home in the country. Four days later she suddenly took ill and died. The cause of death was poison that had been self-administered. In a letter addressed to Maria and dated the 17th, Jane was found to have expressed an intention to take her own life.

The bank did not know to whom to release the £200 plus interest in Jane's account. Robert, as administrator of the estate, then commenced legal proceedings. At the trial of the action, held in the Exchequer Division before Palles CB and Murphy J, the jury indicated their wish that the money should go to Maria. The judges, however, refused to approve, ruling that Jane had not make a valid donation *mortis causa*. The case thus came by way of appeal to the Court of Appeal.

Here guidance was sought from Bracton and from the *Digest* in view of the novelty of the contention advanced on Maria's behalf. Clearly, neither of these legal authorities sought to confine the notion of the valid donation to a gift made by a person who knew at the time of the making of the gift that he or she was dying of some illness: gifts in contemplation of other kinds of death could be included. Bracton entertained no doubts on the question:[145]

144 [1896] 2 IR 204. **145** Bracton, *On the laws and customs of England* (n. 46 above), ii, 178.

> Et mortis causa donatio multiplex esse poterit, ut si quis contemplatione, vel suspicione mortis alicui dat, cuiusmodi donationes saepe fiunt ab aegrotantibus, vel ab eis qui in aciem sunt ituri, vel per mare navigaturi, vel peregre profecturi, et in se tacitam habent condicionem, ut huiusmodi donationes revocentur si aegrotus convaluerit, si miles ab acie redierit, si nauta a navigatione, et peregrinus a peregrinatione.
>
> (A gift *mortis causa*, as where one in contemplation or expectation of death makes a gift to another, may take many forms, such being often made by those who are ill, or about to enter into battle, sail over the sea, or set off on a pilgrimage, and they include the tacit condition that they are revocable if the sick man recovers, the soldier returns from battle, the sailor from his voyage or the traveller from his journey.)[146]

The discussion of the same topic in the *Digest* (where the extent of Bracton's indebtedness to it is manifest) left no doubts either:

> Paulus libro septimo ad Sabinum. Mortis causa donare licet non tantum infirmae valetudinis causa, sed periculi etiam propinquae mortis, vel ab hoste vel a praedonibus vel ab hominis potentis crudelitate aut odio aut navigationis ineundae.[147]
>
> Gaius libro primo rerum cottidianarum sive aureorum. aut per insidiosa loca iturus.[148]
>
> Paulus libro septimo ad Sabinum. haec enim omnia instans periculum demonstrant.[149]

A translation, confined to the essential points of doctrine, reads:

> It is lawful to make a gift in contemplation of death not only on account of illness but because of the risk of imminent death at the hands of an enemy or robbers or because of an impending voyage or if one is about to travel through inhospitable places. All these things signify immediate danger.

D.39. 6, the *Digest* title devoted to donations *mortis causa*, demonstrates the broad approach of Roman law in another manner. In the theory of the donation *mortis causa* the donor's intention is taken to be that he would prefer himself to the donee, should he survive the emergency; but that the donee would be preferred to his heir, should he not. The choice of illustration on the part of the compilers of the *Digest* is significant. They recall, from Homer's *Odyssey*,[150] the gift made by Telemachus to his companion Piraeus, as he ventured forth, not to die of disease or to commit suicide, but to do battle with his mother Penelope's suitors:[151] 'sic et apud Homerum Telemachus donat Piraeo.' The *Institutes* repeat the allusion to Homer.[152] Their gener-

146 Ibid., ii, 179 (Thorne's transl.). **147** D. 39. 6. 3. **148** D. 39. 6. 4. **149** D. 39. 6. 6. **150** *Odyssey*, xvii, 78f. **151** D. 39. 6. 1. **152** *Inst.* 2.7.1.

ally more compressed treatment of the entire topic includes a statement of basic doctrine in a text to which the Court of Appeal in *Agnew* were later to devote a great deal of attention:[153] 'mortis causa donatio est, quae propter mortis fit suspicionem, cum quis ita donat, ut, si quid humanitus ei contigisset, haberet is qui accepit.'

Under Roman law itself certain donations *mortis causa* might be struck down as void for immorality. Alan Watson's researches turned up the case of C. Visellius Varro whose gift to his mistress Otacilia Laterensis was set aside on these grounds.[154] The stigma attaching in the law of England and Ireland to suicide at the time Jane Agnew poisoned herself made it a simple matter for the Irish Court of Appeal to condemn Jane's gift to her sister on a similar basis. Porter MR took the point straightaway:[155]

> In my opinion, it is fundamentally opposed to the first principle of our law, or of any law which treats suicide as a crime that legal rights should be created by the intention to commit suicide to be followed by the actual commission of it.

FitzGibbon LJ accepted the public policy argument as well, concluding that a donation could not be supported 'on a danger which is so purely voluntary as to be criminal in its origin'.[156] Unlike the master of the rolls, however, FitzGibbon LJ was prepared to express an opinion on the question of the limits to a valid donation:[157]

> I must guard myself from being supposed to limit to disease the danger in apprehension of which a valid *donatio mortis causa* may be made. I see no reason to hold that a man can make a valid donation when he is about to undergo a surgical operation, but cannot do so when he is about to peril his life at the call of duty, or in the cause of humanity.

One at least of the members of the Court of Appeal was thus prepared to extend the frontiers, as sanctioned by both Bracton and the *Digest*.

Though scarcely oblivious of the public policy argument, Walker C and Barry LJ chose rather to emphasise textual difficulties. For the lord chancellor it was inconceivable that the definitions in the *Institutes* could be applied to contemplation of suicide or, indeed, death by suicide at all: the words 'quae propter mortis fit suspicionern', to his way of thinking, could not possibly apply to a person who did not apprehend death but voluntarily sought it.[158] The other crucial phrase to command attention was 'si quid humanitus ei contigisset'. Counsel for Maria Claney, in arguing for the validity of Jane's gift, had hoped to persuade the court that this phrase could be rendered in English as 'if any fatal accident should befall', a version sufficiently vague as to let in even suicide. The lord chancellor was unimpressed: the words in question seemed to him to mean 'should anything happen to him human and mortal as we are'.[159] Barry LJ took a serious view of this second textual problem too. The bulk of his short concurring opinion is devoted to demonstrating, by scholarly reference to a number

153 Id. **154** Alan Watson, *The law of property in the later Roman republic* (Oxford, 1968), p. 232. **155** [1896] 2 IR at 216. **156** [1896] 2 IR at 221. **157** Id. **158** [1896] 2 IR at 213. **159** Id.

of Latin authors, that the words 'quid humanitus' in Latin usage were nothing other than a euphemism for death.[160]

Even if the public policy argument is put to one side, the Court of Appeal seem to be insinuating that there was nothing to show that Roman law would have endorsed the course of action that had commended itself to the jury in the Exchequer Division – to treat Jane's donation as valid and hand over the £200 plus interest to her sister, Maria. In recent times, in a number of jurisdictions, suicide has been removed from the calendar of crimes.[161] To judge from what the Court of Appeal concluded in *Agnew*, this dramatic reversal in the stance of the law would by no means guarantee a different result in the unlikely event that a case on all fours with *Agnew* were again to be presented before the courts.

XI

In 1900, in *Brady* v. *Warren*,[162] a case of trespassing deer,[163] the Queen's Bench Division (Palles CB, Johnson and Boyd JJ) were also to open older legal authority to help despatch the problem presented before them. The deer had escaped from the defendant's large demesne – Warrenscourt in Co. Cork – causing damage to crops in a neighbouring farmer's fields. Liability depended on whether the defendant could be said to have 'owned' the deer. This, in turn, depended on how the deer fell to be classified. The common law, traceable back through Blackstone to Bracton, and deriving ultimately from Roman law, stipulated that wild animals that had been domesticated remained objects of ownership even if prone to wander, so long as they retained a homing instinct. Bracton formulated the legal position as follows:[164]

> si autem animalia fera facta fuerint mansueta et ex consuetudine eunt et redeunt, volant et revolant, ut sunt cervi, pavones et columbae, alia regula comprobata est, ut eo usque nostra intellegantur quamdiu habuerint animum revertendi. nam si revertendi animum habere desierint nostra desinunt esse. revertendi autem animum videntur desinere habere cum consuetudinem revertendi deseruerint.
>
> (But if wild animals are tamed and customarily go and come back, or fly away and return, as deer, peafowl and pigeons, another rule is applicable, [namely], that they are taken to be ours so long as they have the intention of returning, for if they cease to have that intention they cease to be ours. They are taken no

160 [1896] 2 IR at 223–5. **161** Suicide Act 1961 (England and Wales); Criminal Justice Act (NI) 1966, s. 12 (NI); Criminal Law (Suicide) Act 1993 (R.I.). The decision in *Agnew* v. *Belfast Banking Co. and Claney* was followed by Russell J in the English Chancery Division in 1925: *In re Dudman* [1925] Ch. 553. *Agnew's* case, however, was distinguished in another Irish lawsuit where a donation followed by suicide was held by Gavan Duffy P nonetheless to be valid: see *Mills* v. *Shields* [1948] IR 367 and, for further proceedings in the same case, *Mills* v. *Shields (no. 2)* [1950] IR 21. In none of these three later cases is any Roman law opened. **162** [1900] 2 IR 632. **163** Brady also sued in respect of damage done by trespassing rabbits, where he was not successful. **164** Bracton, *On the laws and customs of England*, ii, 43.

> longer to have the intention of returning when they lose the habit of returning.)[165]

Blackstone, in his survey of the relevant law, furnishes a short inventory of wild animals capable of being domesticated and thus of being objects of ownership simpliciter:[166] deer in a park are listed, as are hares or rabbits in an enclosed warren, doves in a dove-house, pheasants or partridges in a mew and fish in ponds or trunks.[167] The example of the trained hawk, also given by Blackstone, is utilised by him to help illustrate the additional point that Bracton in the extract above, we can see, was equally concerned to stress, namely, that the law extended possession or ownership beyond mere 'manual occupation', or, as we would phrase it, actual physical control. 'My tame hawk', Blackstone explains,[168]

> that is pursuing his quarry in my presence, though he is at liberty to go where he pleases, is nevertheless my property; for he hath animus revertendi.

In *Brady* v. *Warren*, on the evidence, a majority of the court (Palles CB and Johnson J) held that the deer in question had been domesticated, and that they had retained their *animus revertendi*, despite their adventures outside the defendant's demesne. The defendant was accordingly answerable to Brady for their depredations.

Palles CB and Johnson J both consulted the law laid down in Bracton. Palles CB, however, explored the earlier Roman law. Bracton specifically mentioned the propensity of deer to adopt the habit of going and returning. So, too, the chief baron pointed out, did Gaius in his *Institutes*.[169] Gaius, however, talked exclusively in terms of deer going into and coming back from 'the woods': 'item cervis qui in silvas ire et redire solent.' The more precise ambit to the ethological hypothesis propounded by Gaius did not appreciably affect the operation of the governing legal principle. But, properly interpreted, in the light of knowledge as to the habitats of deer under the Roman empire in the second century AD, the singularity of the passage in Gaius was vital in terms of the evidential inferences it might in the appropriate case be proper to draw:[170]

> The woods referred to were, doubtless, not land in the actual occupation of mankind, as is the plaintiff's farm here, but the wild forests beyond the resort of man, which would be the natural habitation of such deer if they returned to their original wildness. The habit of going into such woods, although accompanied by a habit of returning, involves more of a desire to become wild again than merely breaking into an adjoining farm and returning from it, as if they permanently remained in the wild forests they would be deemed to have become wild again.

165 Thorne's transl. **166** Sir William Blackstone, *Commentaries on the laws of England*, 17th ed., 4 vols. (London, 1830), ii, 391-2 (bk. 2, ch. 25). **167** On the case of fish, see the discussion of *Purcell* v. *Minister for Finance*, below, p. 53. **168** Blackstone, *Commentaries*, ii, 391-2. **169** Gaius, *Inst.* 2. 68; cf. *Inst.* 2.1 15. **170** [1900] 2 IR at 656.

Bambi scampering off to the unkempt forests of early Christian Europe, the chief baron here seems to be implying, might leave you in some doubt about his actual intentions. Bambi heading for the nicely manicured fields of the early twentieth century Cork farmer, with their oats, corn and turnips,[171] was a different proposition altogether. The chances of the defendant being able to avoid liability after this magisterial assertion were set to diminish still further when the chief baron went on to observe that 'the fact that deer are more usually domesticated now than they were in feudal times has, for more than a century and a half, been recognised as a matter of law'.[172]

XII

In 1911 in *A.G.* v. *McCarthy*[173] the Irish courts undertook another detailed examination of Roman law texts. An authoritative exposition of the doctrine of alluvion was the outcome.[174]

By the doctrine of alluvion, where land is added to the foreshore by the gradual and imperceptible action of natural causes, the owner of the foreshore adjoining the accretions acquires in the latter a good title against the crown or the state. Bracton formulated the law in the following way:[175]

> Item quod per alluvionem agro tuo flumen adiecit, iure gentium tibi adquiritur. est autem alluvio latens incrementum, et per alluvionem adici dicitur quod ita paulatim adicitur, quod intellegere non possis quoquo momento temporis adiciatur. nam et si tota dies figas intuitum, imbecellitas visus tam subtilia incrementa perpendere non potest, ut videri poterit in cucurbita et similibus. si autem non sit latens incrementum, immo apparens, contrarium erit. ut ecce vis fluminis partem aliquam ex tuo praedio detraxit et vicini praedio appulit, certum est eam tuam permanere.
>
> (Soil which a river adds to your land by alluvion becomes yours by the *jus gentium*. Alluvion is an imperceptible increment which is added so gradually that you cannot perceive how much the increase is from one moment of time to another. Indeed, though you fix your gaze on it for a whole day, the feebleness of human sight cannot distinguish such subtle increases, as may be seen in the growth of a gourd and other such things. On the other hand, if the increment is not imperceptible but apparent it will be otherwise, as where the violence of a stream has swept away a parcel of your land and attached it to that of your neighbour; it is clear that it remains yours.)[176]

As with donations *mortis causa*, the indebtedness to Roman law is obvious. The equivalent passage in the *Institutes* thus reads:[177]

171 See ibid., at 633. **172** Ibid., at 656–7. **173** [1911] 2 IR 260. **174** See Lord Wilberforce's tribute in *Southern Centre of Theosophy* v. *South Australia* [1982] AC 706 at 720. **175** Bracton, *On the laws and customs of England* (n. 46 above), ii, 44. **176** Thorne's transl. **177** *Inst.* 2.1.20–1; cf. D. 41.1 7.

> Praeterea quod per alluvionem agro tuo flumen adiecit, iure gentium tibi adquiritur. est autem alluvio incrementum latens. per alluvionem autem id videtur adici, quod ita paulatim adicitur, ut intellegere non possis, quantum quoquo momento temporis adiciatur. quodsi vis fluminis partem aliquam ex tuo praedio detraxerit et vicini praedio appulerit, palam est eam tuam permanere.

While the law laid down in Bracton and in the *Institutes* confined the operation of the doctrine of alluvion to rivers, the common law was to extend its sphere of application to include the marine foreshore. An early instance is contained in the advice furnished by Best CJ on behalf of the judges to the House of Lords in a seminal decision of 1828. In this case, *Gifford* v. *Yarborough*,[178] the dispute had centred on title to a salt-marsh 400 acres in extent which had been added to the southern shore of the Humber estuary a few miles to the south-east of Cleethorpes in Lincolnshire.[179] The doctrine of alluvion would also appear to be available today where accretions occur along the shore-line of an inland lake. Recognition of the doctrine's applicability in just such a situation was forthcoming from Carswell J in the Northern Ireland case of *Hume* v. *Tennyson*,[180] although there the suddenness of the accretions that had taken place prevented its coming into operation.[181]

To appreciate the precise contribution made by *A.G.* v. *McCarthy* to the shaping of the modern doctrine of alluvion at common law, attention has first to be drawn to one development recorded some thirty years after the decision in *Gifford* v. *Yarborough*. In 1859, in *A.G.* v. *Chalmers*,[182] the English lord chancellor, Lord Chelmsford, was faced with yet another problem concerning title to land where accretions had been joined to coastal properties. The place was in Wales – along a part of the Burry inlet on the coast of Carmarthenshire between Llanelly and Pembrey. In his decision, Lord Chelmsford expressed reservations over the applicability of the doctrine of alluvion where the accretions, though gradual, were not imperceptible at least in one sense of the word. Where the amount of land added was capable of exact measurement and was thus knowable, Lord Chelmsford appeared to hold that the doctrine could not be relied upon.

The common law position was obviously somewhat obscure when *A.G.* v. *McCarthy* surfaced in the Irish Kings's Bench Divisional Court in 1911, and an authoritative statement on the law will have been eagerly awaited. The chance to provide such a statement had, in fact, arisen some years earlier in Ireland, in 1896, in the case of *Re Hickson's Estate*.[183] Here Ross J disposed of a problem that seems to have been identical with that raised in *A.G.* v. *McCarthy* and, quite coincidentally, had emanated from the same corner of Ireland – the Dingle peninsula in Co. Kerry. All that

178 5 Bing. 153, 130 ER 1023. **179** The description of the area is taken from the report of the decision of the court of King's Bench at an earlier stage of the litigation: *The King* v. *Lord Yarborough* (1824) 3 B. & C. 91, 107 ER 668. **180** [1987] NI 139. **181** The level of Lough Neagh had been deliberately lowered in accordance with the Lough Neagh (Levels) Scheme 1955. Dramatic accretions of land subsequently occurred over a one- to three-week period. See [1987] NI at 141. **182** 4 D., G. & J. 55, 115 ER 72. **183** Briefly noted, [1911] 2 IR at 300.

happens to have been set down about the case, sadly, is a brief reporter's note to tell us that Ross J's decision was the same as that later reached by the Divisional Court in 1911, and that Justinian was among the authorities that had been opened.[184]

In *A.G.* v. *McCarthy* the contested accretions had happened along the strand at Inch, which faces out into Tralee bay on the southern side of the Dingle peninsula.[185] In the past, a series of marker posts had been inserted on the beach. In addition, evidence from maps made it possible to establish with some accuracy the actual alteration that had been effected in the shore-line.[186] Since the accretions therefore were measurable and knowable, this entailed that the doctrine of alluvion did not apply, if the views propounded by Lord Chelmsford in *A.G.* v. *Chalmers* were treated as sound.

The Irish Divisional Court unanimously reached the conclusion that they were not. Though support for Lord Chelmsford's stance was to be derived from a passage in Hale's treatise *De jure maris*,[187] the rationale underlying *Gifford* v. *Yarborough* had effectively undermined it.[188] Furthermore, the clear sense of the passages in both Bracton and Justinian's *Institutes* effectively argued against it. For Palles CB, the vital question to be determined was this: while the process of the accretion of the land and of the recession of the sea was continuing, was its progress actually perceptible by the human observer? From the evidence presented in relation to the strand at Inch, whatever about the marker posts and the maps, the chief baron concluded only one answer was possible: 'no'.[189]

Gibson J, who many years earlier had discussed the Roman law of *furtum* in *Hehir*, was again to touch on Roman law in his separate critique of the pertinent legal authorities. He had difficulty in identifying the unit or measure of time to employ to decide on any 'gradual and imperceptible' accretion:[190]

> What is the base to which the addition is to be made, and what is to be the method of observation? Is the increase to be latent at the end of a week or of a month, ... or for longer periods?

Nor was assistance, he believed, to be derived either from the *Institutes* or from the longer extract in Bracton:[191]

> According to them, latent increment is where no one can perceive how much is added at any moment of time, which would, literally understood, apply to all increments save those caused by sudden convulsions or avulsions.

For Gibson J this was too drastic a solution. He proposed, accordingly, that the terms 'gradual and imperceptible' had to be understood by the common law as referring to the faculties of average humanity, and to the transactions of everyday life.[192]

184 Id. **185** Close by there is to be found one of the Irish habitats of the natterjack toad. **186** In the original edition of the Irish Reports a map of the relevant stretch of the coast may be found between pp 264 and 265 ([1911] 2 IR); the map is not reproduced in the Professional Books reprint. **187** As acknowledged by Palles CB: [1911] 2 IR at 278 ff.; and by Gibson J: [1911] 2 IR at 299. **188** See the judgment of Palles CB: [1911] 2 IR at 278. **189** Ibid., at 293-4. **190** Ibid., at 296. **191** Id. **192** Id.

While the exact sense of Gibson J's remarks at this point is not perhaps the easiest to grasp, he appears to be accepting a range of situations where the doctrine of alluvion would not apply, and thus to be travelling part at least of the way with Lord Chelmsford. Yet, at the same time, Gibson J takes pains to express his agreement with the view of Palles CB that the mere ascertainability of the original basal line would not exclude the right of alluvion. His acceptance of this crucial rider comes in a geography lesson of somewhat inordinate length, whose tenor must raise a doubt about the existence of any significant residual difference in approach between the chief baron and himself.[193]

Gibson J was to spot an additional complication in the older authorities. Bracton stated explicitly that the doctrine of alluvion did not extend to 'agri limitati'. This was borrowed from the *Digest*[194] which, for good measure, purported to exclude 'agri assignati' as well. 'Agri assignati', the judge held, were not a troublesome category. These were lands acquired by the state and parcelled out in lots among the *coloni*[195] – an anachronistic system of land distribution, and one plainly not germane under the particular constitutional dispensation operative in Co. Kerry in the early twentieth century. 'Agri limitati', on the other hand, did pose a problem. These were lands demarcated by clear measurements and clear boundaries. The solution Gibson J advanced, in what for him was this unforeseen predicament, if it fails to carry complete conviction, testifies to the need, for practical purposes, always sharply to distinguish the position obtaining under Roman law and that under common law:[196]

> No English authority discusses 'agri limitati', but it is not improbable that the reference to marks, etc. in old books and cases is influenced, in some degree, by Bracton's exception.
>
> I do not think that either Bracton or the *Digest* in excluding alluvion in the case of 'agri limitati' – whatever that may mean – can be accepted as guides to existing English Common Law.

XIII

Within a decade or thereabouts of the handing down of the decision in *A.G.* v. *McCarthy* the constitutional dispensation underwent radical overhaul not only in Co.

193 'In some districts the sea has receded, leaving places (for example, Sandwich), once ports, now far removed from the water; elsewhere the mainland, as at Shankill and Wicklow, has been eroded and washed away. In both classes of case the original boundaries can be fixed. There is no distinction between gradual and imperceptible addition and gradual and imperceptible subtraction. Whether the original boundaries of the lands were fixed by natural objects, or by constructions, such as sea-walls, Martello towers, etc., or by measurements and maps, or by the testimony of faithworthy old witnesses, the principle governing the ownership of alluvion growing by imperceptible process of nature is the same. The Ordnance Survey, in determining boundaries, can hardly be supposed to have had the effect of depriving the subject of alluvial rights as against the Crown': [1911] 2 IR at 298. **194** In agris limitatis ius alluvionis locum non habere constat (Florentinus): D. 41. 1. 16. **195** [1911] 2 IR at 295. **196** Id.

Kerry but in twenty-five other Irish counties besides. Independence – the establishment of the Irish Free State in 1922 – saw to that. As might have been foreseen, there was a military side to the struggle to win independence, but there had been a political dimension too. And, curiously, it is within this latter context that one encounters a feature which is of special interest so far as the story of Roman law in Ireland is concerned.

It was fundamental to the policy of the revolutionary Dáil to create within the country an entire governmental apparatus that would operate effectively in opposition to the traditional apparatus maintained by the crown. A lynch-pin of these arrangements was the system of republican courts inaugurated in 1919 and fated to last until mid-1922.[197] In jurisprudential terms, the major interest of these courts probably lay in their experimental character: during a period of rapid political change, it was inevitable that a determined effort would be launched to render justice cheaper, quicker and generally more accessible. But the theorists who conceived and instituted the republican courts had another object at the back of their minds – to question, if indeed not to repudiate, the legal inheritance from England, an inheritance, which, for historical reasons, as much as from personal antipathy, they were disinclined to regard other than with mixed feelings. Whilst repudiation may have represented the long-term objective, the practicalities of day-to-day judicial administration argued strongly in favour of the adoption of a much more moderate position. The guidelines produced for the benefit of Dáil court judges, published in 1921 and known as *Judiciary*,[198] thus embodied a compromise. The law previously in force – in effect, the common law of England as modified by the statute-book – was to be retained, shorn of all excrescences 'clearly motivated by religious or political animosity'.[199] It was envisaged that the Dáil would eventually promote major law reform by means of a code, but, in the meantime, every encouragement was to be afforded those litigants and their legal representatives who sought fresh sources of inspiration for the settlement of routine law-suits. 'Pending the enactment of a Code by An Dáil', *Judiciary* accordingly stipulates,[200]

> citations may be made to any Court from the early Irish Law Codes or any commentary upon them in so far as they may be applicable to modern conditions, and from the Code Napoléon and other codes, the Corpus Juris Civilis and works embodying or commenting on Roman Law, but such citations shall not be of binding authority. Save as aforesaid, no legal text book published in Great Britain shall be cited in any court.

The practical impact of these remarkable provisions remains unclear. Whilst the ban on the citation of any British text book was total, the ban itself did not apparent-

197 David Fitzpatrick, *Politics and Irish life 1913-1921: provincial experience of war and revolution* (Dublin, 1977), ch. 5; J.P. Casey, 'Republican courts in Ireland, 1919-1922', (1970) 5 *Ir. Jurist* 321; idem, 'The genesis of the Dáil courts', (1974) 9 *Ir. Jurist* 326; Cahir Davitt, 'Civil jurisdiction of the courts of the Irish republic, 1920-1922', (1968) 3 *Ir. Jurist* 112. And see now Mary Kotsonouris, *Retreat from revolution: the Dáil courts, 1920-24* (Dublin, 1994). **198** Saorstat na hEireann, *Judiciary: rules and forms, parish and district courts* (Dublin, 1921). **199** *Judiciary*, p. 9. **200** Id.

ly extend to the citation of cases from the English law reports – as was officially explained to a Dáil court judge who had raised the point.[201] David Fitzpatrick, in his survey of the period, dubs the ban 'a ridiculous rider', and asserts that Conor Maguire who, as a Dáil land commissioner, possessed a copy of *Judiciary* probably thought so too. Maguire, who was later to become a chief justice of Ireland, Fitzpatrick reveals, went so far as to underline, and to query, this ban in his personal copy.[202] As regards the use made of early Irish law, Dorothy Macardle fills a gap in our information. In her glowing account of the courts – very different in tone from Fitzpatrick's much more critical aperçu – she recounts an episode involving one of the Dáil court judges, Judge Meredith. Meredith, who was subsequently to serve on the Supreme Court of the Irish Free State, is alleged on one occasion actually to have applied a principle derived from early Irish law. Unfortunately, however, the accompanying detail furnished by Macardle is not as complete or as enlightening as one might wish.[203]

No evidence has been presented that resort was ever had to texts of Roman law or to the Code Napoléon. Their inclusion in the guidelines is, in fact, something of a conundrum. Speculation might direct us back to the earlier discussion that had taken place in the Irish courts on possible recognition of public rights in rivers and lakes,[204] but is probably not very profitable. If the promulgation of *Judiciary* symbolised a modest resurgence of interest in the civilian tradition in Ireland, that interest was not destined to endure. In the summer of 1922, the Dáil courts were suppressed by the Provisional Government and the former crown courts were thus restored to a position of undisputed and unchallengeable hegemony within the legal system. Any flirting with continental legal ideas that may have occurred in this short revolutionary interregnum – and we cannot be certain any in fact did – was thus, abruptly, forcibly and firmly, brought to an end.

XIV

Undoubtedly, *Agnew* v. *Belfast Banking Co. Ltd.* and *A.G.* v. *McCarthy* constitute the high point in the examination of Roman law by the Irish judiciary in the modern era. In comparison, the record since the 1920s has been a trifle lacklustre.

Not that that record shows a complete blank. In the Free State High Court in 1933 Hanna J was to open up Roman law when faced with the problem of whether to admit to probate a will of July 1916, prima facie invalid in that it had been attested by but a single witness: *In the goods of Taylor*.[205] The will was that of a Dublin surgeon, Sir William Taylor, who a few months later joined the colours with a commission in the

201 The ban was on text books only; 'there is no objection to any person acting before our courts [referring to] statutes, legal reports or other matter of this kind': Assistant Minister of Home Affairs to P. Gantly, sub-registrar, North Tipperary, 19 Jan. 1992 (NA DE 10/59). I owe this reference to Mary Kotsonouris. **202** Fitzpatrick, *Politics and Irish life 1913-1921*, p. 329, n. 16. **203** 'An enlightened attitude towards women prevailed. When a woman was being tried it was customary to have a woman among the judges on the Bench. In one instance, Judge Meredith, holding that English law was retrograde in the matter before the court – the appeal of an unmarried mother for medical expenses – applied the Brehon Code and gave judgment in favour of the girl. This created an interesting link with old Irish principles of justice and preserved continuity between the old Brehon Law of Ireland and the Republican courts.' Dorothy Macardle, *The Irish republic*, 4th ed. (Dublin, 1951), p. 376. **204** See above, pp 35-8. **205** [1933] IR 709.

Royal Army Medical Corps. Whilst on leave in 1917 and just before returning to his unit in France, Sir William wrote on the front of the envelope containing his 'will' a memorandum that concerned the bequests in it, and this he dated and signed but the signature was not witnessed. Sir William survived the war, dying in 1933, and, no other evidence of his testamentary intentions then coming to light, the question arose as to whether legal effect could be given to the irregular will of 1916 and the memorandum of the following year. Hanna J held that it could, being satisfied that at the time Sir William composed his memorandum he was a 'soldier' 'in actual military service' for purposes of section 11 of the Wills Act 1837. The memorandum thus constituted a valid testamentary disposition and its effect was to incorporate Sir William's insufficiently executed will and to make the latter valid as well.

This corollary was, of course, the crucial determination and Hanna J derived comfort from the knowledge that the very point had arisen under Roman law and had been dealt with in this fashion, a state of affairs he adjudged 'very remarkable'.[206] Included in title 11 of book 2 of Justinian's *Institutes*, a title devoted to military wills, there was thus to be found the following provision:[207]

> Sed et si quis ante militiam non iure fecit testamentum et miles factus et in expeditione degens resignavit illud et quaedam adiecit sive detraxit vel alias manifesta est militis voluntas hoc valere volentis, dicendum est valere testamentum quasi ex nova militis voluntate.

Or, in the judge's own free translation:[208]

> If a man, before becoming a soldier has made his testament irregularly, and afterwards, while on service, opens it, and adds something or strikes something out, or in any other way makes his wish manifest that this testament should be valid, it must be pronounced to be so, as being, in effect, a new testament made by the soldier.

Earlier in his judgment Hanna J had supplied his own short account of the origin of the special rules for soldiers' wills:[209]

> According to the writers in Roman Law, this privilege dates from the time of Augustus, who gave it as a temporary concession. It was made a general law by Nerva and confirmed by Trajan.

Hanna J, however, did not choose to emphasise one critical difference between Roman law and the common law of the 1930s: the irregular will made by a Roman soldier whilst on active service retained its validity for only one year after the soldier's release from service.[210] Had that further rule been applied in the case of Sir William Taylor's 'will', the court would have been compelled to declare an intestacy.

206 [1933] IR at 719. **207** *Inst.* 2.11.4. **208** [1933] IR at 719. **209** [1933] IR at 718. **210** *Inst.* 2.11.3.

Another much more limited foray into Roman law is on record again for the courts in the South, in 1938. That year they were confronted by a curious problem that had arisen under the malicious injuries code (under which the local authority might be made to bear the cost of property damage maliciously inflicted), a problem set by an incident that had taken place some nineteen years earlier: *Purcell* v. *Minister for Finance*.[211]

One night in November 1919, a floating tank containing captive eels, which was suspended in the River Fergus at Aughrimtuohy in Co. Clare, had been wantonly destroyed, and the eels in it permitted to escape.[212] Whether, in the circumstances, compensation under the terms of the code was payable at all raised a barrage of intriguing legal problems, connected in the main with the true interpretation to be given to what had occurred: for example, how to define the property interest that had been violated, whether to treat the fate of the eels as a 'destruction', or even as a consequential loss which the law might deem irrecoverable. Much of the resultant deliberation in the High Court and Supreme Court is not immediately germane. It is enough to observe that, in the statement of the law dealing with proprietary rights in wild animals, birds and fish which the judges felt obliged to supply, there is regularly repeated the fundamental common law rule that once control over the wild animal is lost, it ceases to be yours.[213] In *Brady* v. *Warren*,[214] the case of the trespassing deer, Irish judges of an earlier generation had occasion, it may be remembered, to explore the rules in this same branch of law.[215]

In *Purcell's* case the Irish judges traced the rule they thus made it their business to emphasise back only so far as Blackstone.[216] But, of course, it is much older than that, deriving, via Bracton, from Roman law. The rule in the *Institutes* could not be plainer:[217]

> quidquid autem eorum ceperis, eo usque tuum esse intellegitur, donec tua custodia coercetur: cum vero evaserit custodiam tuam et in naturalem libertatem se receperit, tuam esse desinit et rursus occupantis fit.
>
> (If you catch such an animal, it remains yours so long as you keep it under your control. If it escapes your control and recovers its natural liberty, it ceases to be yours. The next taker can have it.)[218]

In *Purcell's* case it was escaping eels that provided the justification for the judiciary in the South to return in effect to the Roman law origins of common law doctrine. In 1963 it was to be diseased meat carcases that were to send one of their Northern Ireland brethren off on a not dissimilar journey: *Northern Ireland Master Butchers Wholesale Supply Association* v. *Belfast Corporation*.[219] This complex litigation featured a long-running dispute between the butchers and the corporation, in the latter's role as sanitary authority, over the profits to be made from the diseased carcases in question.

211 [1939] IR 115 (High Ct. and Supreme Ct.). **212** For further difficulties faced by owners of eel tanks during the Irish 'troubles' of the period, see *Whipp* v. *Mackey* [1926] IR 372. **213** See, e.g., in the High Court, Gavan Duffy J [1939] IR at 122, and, in the Supreme Court, Sullivan CJ at 130, Mumaghan J at 136–7 and Meredith J at 144–5. **214** [1900] 2 IR 632. **215** See above, pp 44–6. **216** Blackstone, *Commentaries* (n. 166 above), ii, 391. **217** *Inst.* 2.1.12. **218** Birks and McLeod transl. **219** [1965] NI 30.

The dispute reached the critical stage long before the onset of bovine spongiform encephalopathy, but, of course, risks associated with contaminated matter entering the human food chain had been recognised for many years. Indeed, the relevant provision in the applicable public health legislation sought to guard against precisely this eventuality. Section 132 of the Public Health (Ireland) Act 1878 thus prescribed that, where meat was seized as unsound, the matter was to be referred to local magistrates, who were empowered to order the meat 'to be destroyed or so disposed of as to prevent it from being exposed for sale or used for the food of man'.

In Belfast, up until 1931, the procedure laid down by section 132 of the 1878 Act had ordinarily been scrupulously observed.[220] Unsound carcases were mentioned to the local justices, and the latter, if satisfied that the complaint was made out, would issue a condemnation order. In 1931 the corporation elected to adopt a different tactic. Provided the butchers conceded that a condemnation order was justified, the corporation would proceed not to seek such an order but would arrange, instead, for the seized carcases to be put through a digester plant at the municipal abattoir. Consent forms authorising the 'destruction' of carcases in the absence of any formal justices' order became a regular feature of the new procedure.[221] In 1955 technological progress made it possible for diseased carcases to emerge from the digester plant in the form of melted oil and solid dry material – substances which could then be employed in the manufacture of fertilisers and animal feeding stuffs. In short, it became feasible for the corporation to make a profit from this theatre of operations in the abattoir. The master butchers, not unnaturally perhaps, sought a share in the profits. When their demand met with a rebuff, they commenced legal proceedings, in which they claimed a declaration, injunctive relief, and damages for trespass and conversion.

McVeigh J found in favour of the butchers on all contested issues. The procedure inaugurated by the corporation in 1931 was without legal sanction. The seizure of carcases where the intention had not been to apply for a condemnation order from the justices was unlawful, and amounted to trespass. Putting the carcases through the digester plant and pocketing the resultant profits alike constituted acts of conversion. Damages were awarded, based on the value that the carcases might be established to have possessed. McVeigh J summarised his general approach in the following words:[222]

> It would indeed be astonishing if the defendants or any other local authority could take possession of materials of value belonging to other people and, whilst ignoring statutory procedures, could sell them direct to outsiders and retain the proceeds. It would indeed be a strange result if the owners of the materials had no remedy in such circumstances.

220 Some doubt on the matter has to be entertained in view of earlier legal proceedings: *In re Douglas and Belfast Corporation* [1909] 2 IR 30. On that occasion Holmes LJ was to observe (ibid., at 47): 'A local authority like Belfast Corporation ought to strictly adhere to what is authorized by statute; and I am sure that it is only necessary to call attention to the matter to have it attended to for the future.' **221** 'I request you will allow the carcase of ... belonging to me, now in the municipal abattoir, to be destroyed without bringing same before the magistrates, as I admit same is unsound and unfit for human food. Signed ...': see [1965] NI at 31. **222** [1965] NI at 51.

The *Northern Ireland Master Butchers* case raised a number of abstruse points of law – for instance, the doctrine of unjust enrichment and its place in modern law, and the action for money had and received.[223] But the fundamental problem, as in *Purcell's* case, was one of classification or definition – how to regard the term 'destroy'. The term itself was present both in section 132 of the 1878 Act and in the consent forms that the butchers had come under pressure to sign following the change of procedure in 1931. If the carcases could be said to have been 'destroyed' after being processed through the digester plant, then perhaps the corporation had a sustainable defence. Eschewing an examination of the question as to what, in the light of modern science, might actually constitute 'destruction', an examination counsel had had the temerity to invite him to undertake, McVeigh J was to decide that, on a commonsense view, 'destroyed' was to be taken to mean absolute destruction. It resulted that it was not therefore sufficient destruction of the carcases for these to have been put through the digester plant which had converted them into the melted oil and solid dry material.

The applicability of the notions of trespass and conversion in this unusual set of facts and against this unprecedented background posed its own problems. It is at this stage that we glean from McVeigh J that analogies from Roman law had been investigated. Counsels' arguments are not reproduced in the report, and the judge's own reference to these developments, regrettably, is very short. That the litigation had encouraged this other, very different, intellectual inquiry is incontrovertible, as is plain from McVeigh J's remarks, marred, though these are, by one egregious misapprehension:[224]

> To clarify the concepts of trespass and conversion, and in default of illumination from the conventional legal lamps, the shadowy figures of the Roman jurists Gaius and Justinian [*sic*] with their torches still alight walked in the detention and condemnation rooms of the Corporation abattoir, no doubt much to the astonishment of those who work there – and the word on their lips was 'specificatio'.

Mention of 'specificatio' in this passage naturally opens up an enthralling prospect,[225] but an intimidating one, too, as Lord Ardmillan, a Scots judge of last century would have been the first to admit. On one remarkable occasion Lord Ardmillan was obliged to resolve a dispute concerning title to a hearse that had been constructed partly of materials supplied by A and partly of materials supplied by B.[226] The outcome in the *Northern Ireland Master Butchers* case, perhaps for some such reason, was to signal a major disappointment. 'Even if', McVeigh J was to continue, in a sentence where he contrives to kill two well-plumed birds with the same stone,[227]

223 Ibid., at 33. **224** Id. **225** See, e.g., *Inst.* 2. 25 f. **226** *Wylie & Lockhead* v. *Mitchell* (1870) 8 M 552. Lord Ardmillan identified the problem as one in specificatio and referred to 'the celebrated controversy between the Proculeians and the Sabinians'. He indicated that he did not propose 'to enter on that alarming field of juridical conflict'. He shrank in fact from 'even treading on the edge of '... that Serbonian bog,/ Betwixt Damiata and Mount Casius old/ Where armies whole have sunk.' (Milton, *Paradise Lost*, bk. ii, line 592). See (1870) 8 M at 561. **227** [1965] NI at 33-4.

> it be necessary (and it may not be) to summon up the masters of Roman law to the solution of some of the problems in this case, I do not consider that it is necessary to embark on a consideration of the laws of conservation of matter in order to solve the meaning of the word 'destroy'.

Only a few months after the handing down by McVeigh J of his decision in the *Northern Ireland Master Butchers* case, a series of incidents unfolded in the west of Ireland that would again see resort being had to Roman law in order to resolve a legal quarrel. In *Mahoney* v. *Neenan*,[228] the plaintiff alleged that between the months of July and September 1964 the Neenans had entered his land, which abutted an inlet of the River Shannon in Co. Clare,[229] and illicitly removed seaweed worth £20 from the foreshore there. He sought an injunction and damages. Both in the Circuit Court before Judge Ó Briain and at the ensuing High Court appeal before McLoughlin J he was to succeed.

Undeniably, on the facts, the Neenans faced an uphill legal struggle. If the foreshore was held to belong to Mahoney, that, seemingly, concluded the litigation in Mahoney's favour. If, as was perhaps more likely, the foreshore was held to belong to the state as successor to the crown,[230] their legal position was in no sense improved. As early as 1833, the Irish King's Bench, in a major contribution to the law on the subject, had, in effect, followed English precedent,[231] by acknowledging the extremely limited nature of the rights enjoyed by the public in regard to the foreshore. In *Howe* v. *Stawell*,[232] the King's Bench thus held that the public might cross the foreshore to fish, possibly even to collect shell-fish left by a receding tide; at common law, the rights of the public extended little further, and certainly not to collect seaweed and carry it away. In adopting this stance, the common law in both countries thus clearly rejected the very different rule, accepted by Bracton and originating in Roman law, that the sea-shore, by natural law, fell to be counted among the common property of everyone, like the air, flowing water and the sea itself:[233]

> et quidem naturali iure communia sunt omnium haec: aer et aqua profluens et mare et per hoc litera maris.

This broader outlook evinced by Roman law we have, of course, already encountered in the earlier discussion that centred on rights in rivers and lakes.[234]

In the years following the decision in *Howe* v. *Stawell* there was to be considerable litigation in Ireland over the removal of seaweed from the foreshore.[235] Many novel

228 (1965) 99 ILTR 117 (Circuit Ct.); [1966] IR 559 (High Ct.). **229** At Moyasta, Kilkee, Co. Clare. **230** As recognised under the terms of the Foreshore Act 1933. **231** E.g., *Blundell* v. *Catterall* (1821) 5 B. & Ald. 268, 106 ER 1190. **232** (1833) Alc. & Nap. 348. The case related to events that had taken place at Glannaverane Strand, on Courtmacsherry Bay, west of Kinsale, Co. Cork. The removal of the seaweed on this occasion had been a major enterprise, involving many servants and labourers. The use of carts and horses, in addition, it was maintained, had resulted in an amount of damage to the adjoining fields. **233** *Inst.* 2.1.1. The *Institutes* make it clear that the 'shore' extended landwards as far as the highest tide in winter: 'est autem litus maris, quatenus hibernus fluctus maximus excurrit.' (*Inst.* 2.1.3). **234** Above, pp 35–8. **235** See generally G.A. Lee, 'The right to take seaweed from the foreshore', (1967) 18 *N.I.L.Q.* 33. Mr Lee repre-

points fell to be determined – proof of title to the shore where title was alleged to reside in some party other than the crown (under, for example, some manorial concession);[236] the meaning of the expression 'kelp shore' in conveyancing instruments;[237] the right of tenants to remove seaweed according to the supposed custom of the estate;[238] whether unauthorised removal of seaweed could ground a claim in trover.[239] There is even a solemn adjudication by the Irish court for Crown Cases Reserved on the question of whether ungathered seaweed might be categorised as a thing capable of being stolen in the law of larceny.[240] Alcock and Napier, who reported *Howe* v. *Stawell* in 1833, appended a lengthy editorial note in which (in the style of Lord O'Hagan in *Murphy* v. *Ryan*)[241] they drew attention to differences existing between the common law and Roman law.[242] But a long time was set to elapse before, in *Mahoney* v. *Neenan*, Roman law was again to be scrutinised in determined fashion – for possible guidance on the answer to a question of practical detail, a question that had not apparently been agitated in the interim.

Erosion of the land – the opposite process to alluvion – had occurred in the inlet on the Shannon where the seaweed removed by the Neenans had been deposited. There was genuine uncertainty therefore as to who actually owned the ground from which the weed had been abstracted – whether Mahoney or the state. The argument that turned on Roman law focused on a different matter altogether. Counsel for the Neenans sought to circumvent the ruling in *Howe* v. *Stawell* (whether it applied or not) by stressing what he urged as a crucial factual difference. The Neenans, he told the court, had cut the weed at low water, this had drifted ashore with the incoming tides and had then been carried away from where it had come to rest. He attempted, in short, to establish the Neenans' proprietary rights in the seaweed under a principle of title by occupancy. 'It is further submitted', the law report's account of counsel's argument reads:[243]

> that the fact that the seaweed (a *res nullius*) had been cut by the defendants at low-water mark, and had been brought landwards by the action of the tides, gave them a *jus in rem* in the seaweed, and this right was not lost, or abandoned, even if the tides deposited the seaweed on the plaintiff's lands. The seaweed remained the property of the defendants and if, after request, the plaintiff refused to deliver it to them, he could be sued for detinue, or for damages for trover and conversion.

sented the defendants in *Mahoney* v. *Neenan*. **236** *Healy* v. *Thorne* (1870) IR 4 CL 495 (vicinity of Shennick Island, Skerries, Co. Dublin); *Brew* v. *Haren* (1874) IR 9 CL 29 (Exch.), (1877) IR 11 CL 198 (Exch. Ch.) (a case from Seafield, Barnagrosse, Co. Clare); *Hamilton* v. *A.G.* (1880) 5 LR Ir. 555 (Vice-chancellor) (title to sea-shore at Holmpatrick, Skerries, including Haven Island, Shennick Island (as in *Healy* v. *Thorne*, above), St Patrick's Island and Colte Island); *Daly* v. *Murray* (1885) 17 LR Ir. 185 (Vice-chancellor and C.A.) (shore at Evagh and Lisvody, barony of Kinalea, near Kinsale, Co. Cork). **237** *Boyle* v. *Mulholland* (1860) 10 ICLR 150 (Exch.) (Co. Louth shore of Carlingford Lough, between Bellaverty and Whitestown). **238** *Mulholland* v. *Killen* (1874) IR 9 Eq. 471 (Ch. App.) (location as in *Boyle* v. *Mulholland*). **239** *Healy* v. *Thorne* (above); *Brew* v. *Haren* (above). **240** *R.* v. *Clinton* (1869) IR 4 CL 6. The decision was in the negative. The original prosecution had resulted from incidents occurring at Ardgillan, Co. Dublin. **241** (1868) IR 2 CL 143. **242** Alc. & Nap. at 357–8. **243** *Mahoney* v. *Neenan* [1966] IR at 560.

For good measure, counsel added a reference to the passage in the *Institutes* dealing with title by occupancy, the text of which reads:[244]

> Ferae igitur bestiae et volucres et pisces, id est omnia animalia, quae in terra mari caelo nascuntur, simulatque ab aliquo capta fuerint, iure gentium statim illius esse incipiunt: quod enim ante nullius est, id naturali ratione occupanti conceditur.
>
> (Wild animals, birds and fish, the creatures of land, sea and sky, become the property of the taker as soon as they are caught. Where something has no owner, it is reasonable that the person who takes it should have it.)[245]

The nettle, conjured up in so masterly a fashion by counsel for the Neenans, McLoughlin J, however, declined to grasp. For him the Neenans' presence on the foreshore, irrespective of whose land it was, was so tainted with illegality that it was impossible, in his eyes, for them to acquire rights over the seaweed that they might later seek to exercise.[246] Left altogether out of consideration, unfortunately, as a consequence of McLoughlin J's narrow approach, is the possible recognition to be extended the principle of title by occupancy in other circumstances. What, for the sake of argument, would the legal position have been if the Neenans had approached the shore to cut weed at low water by boat? That electing such a method to gather seaweed would have worked a significant alteration in the legal complexion of the situation was pressed by counsel appearing in *Howe* v. *Stawell* as long ago as 1833.[247] Recourse to this method of gathering weed is well-established for certain coastal regions of Ireland – particularly Connemara – into modern times.[248] The hypothesis itself cannot therefore be dismissed out of hand as either fanciful or unrealistic.

A more adventurous strategy undoubtedly for McLoughlin J to have embraced would have been to confront counsel's argument head on. In *R.* v. *Clinton*,[249] the prosecution for larceny of ungathered seaweed previously alluded to, Whiteside CJ accepted the classification of such weed as a '*res nullius*', which entailed, as the outcome, that it could never be the object of larceny.[250] But was seaweed to be placed on a par with wild animals, birds and fish for purposes of the law governing title by occupancy? In 1877, in *Brew* v. *Hagen*,[251] a decision of the Irish court of Exchequer Chamber, May CJ asked this exact question. The answer he gave was a resolute negative:[252]

> I do not think that the case of seaweed cast by the action of the sea upon the foreshore and that of animals *ferae naturae* are analogous. Wild animals in a state of nature have powers of motion and volition, over which the owner of the land on which they are found can exercise no control or dominion; when they

244 *Inst.* 2.1.12. **245** Birks and McLeod transl. (p. 55). **246** [1966] IR at 564–5. **247** Alc. & Nap. at 348. **248** See, e.g., *Lee* v. *Nolan* (1901) 1 NIJR 200 (decision of sub-commissioners of Irish Land Commission on the value to be placed on the entitlement of tenants to take weed from a 'kelp shore'). **249** (1869) IR 4 CL 6. **250** Ibid., at 14–16. **251** (1877) IR 11 CL 198. **252** Ibid., at 217–18.

> have lost these characteristics, and become inanimate, they belong to the owners of the land which nurtures them, and on which they are found when dead. Seaweed is an inanimate vegetable production; if the natural agency of the winds and waves casts it upon the foreshore, and it is there left, it seems to me that it should be regarded as increment or accretion to the land on which it is found, and that it should follow the ownership of such land. I am not aware that the rule or principle of title by occupancy has ever been applied by the common law to a subject-matter of this nature ... In the case of seaweed, eagerly sought for as it is by the peasantry as a valuable manure, I think such a rule of property should not be applied, except upon the clearest proof that the law affords no other principle by which the property therein can be determined.

That looks like the last word on the question, unless it is possible to contend that, where weed is cut at low water and let drift ashore, the principle of title by occupancy might after all operate.

One final reference to Roman law may be noted. In *Adair* v. *National Trust for Places of Historic Interest or Natural Beauty*[253] Girvan J in the Northern Ireland High Court was presented with the problem of the entitlement of members of the public to collect shellfish (periwinkles and whelks) and to dig for lugworms on the foreshore of Strangford Lough in Co. Down. On the way to his eventual decision, which represented a partial victory for Adair, the judge quoted from Justinian's *Institutes*[254] to show that under Roman law 'the shore of the sea as far as the waves go at their furthest point was considered as belonging to all men'.[255]

XV

Ireland is situated at the outer rim of Europe, across seas that were traversed with genuine fear and trembling by the early navigators, Phoenician, Roman, and Viking. Unsurprisingly, it has been thought cause for wonder then that the rules of medieval canon law should once have held sway here (and, indeed, albeit in restricted form, should even have continued to do so after the Reformation).[256] That Roman law also had a role to occupy in the unfolding drama of law in Ireland, which, given the odds, is equal cause for wonderment, it has been the business of the present survey to demonstrate. Inevitably, there remain very large gaps in the knowledge that alone would help to solve a number of the problems that this exploratory report has thrown up; and, unhappily, it must be recognised that, where such gaps are attributable to the sparseness of the surviving evidence – as is the case with some of them, but by no means with all –, these gaps are unlikely ever to be filled. We have little hard information on the relationship between the law of the later Roman empire and the law in

253 [1998] NI 33. **254** *Inst.*, 2.1.1. **255** [1998] NI at 41. **256** See R.H. Helmholz in his intro. to *Canon law in Protestant lands* (Berlin, 1992), a collection of essays by various authors and edited by him, at p. 9.

force in early Christian Ireland; we cannot speak with confidence about the diffusion from the twelfth century onwards of the jurisprudence in the Justinianic compilations; we are at a loss to identify the inspiration behind the mysterious account in Irish of the origins of Roman law in Trinity College MS. 1337; we are not in a position to establish the extent to which Roman law, perhaps a commercially-oriented *ius commune*, served as a direct vehicle for the resolution of litigation in remoter regions of the medieval lordship;[257] we have not as yet started to list, let alone to evaluate, the holdings of Roman law and civil law material in the various major libraries; we are at a loss to comprehend the processes by which a revival of a working knowledge of Roman law came about in the nineteenth century; no historian of the foundation of the Irish Free State, it is believed, has yet made it his business to seek to explain the mention of the Corpus Juris and of the Code Napoléon in the Dáil court guidelines of 1921.

While in modern times the common law, prompted, no doubt, by the likes of John Davies, Edward Coke and other kindred spirits, has allotted to Roman law a pronouncedly minor role for the latter to play, it is noteworthy that the rules of Roman law have been prayed in aid by the Irish judicial bench in so diverse a range of contexts: rights affecting rivers and lakes; domicile; subrogation; 'possession' in larceny; donations *mortis causa*; alluvion; military wills; proprietary rights in domesticated animals, captive fish and shellfish on the seashore; *specificatio*; title by occupancy. It is noteworthy besides that, in a number of instances, resort should have been had to texts of Roman law – Gaius's *Institutes*, Justinian's *Digest*, Justinian's *Institutes* (especially book 2, title 1 '*De rerum divisione*' (on the classification of things)) – directly, and quite independently of Bracton and Blackstone. If, in leading cases such as *Agnew* v. *Belfast Banking Co. Ltd.* (donations *mortis causa*) and *A.G.* v. *McCarthy* (alluvion), the response of the judges to the technical challenge presented must, by any standard, be counted impressive, this, naturally, has to be balanced against other cases – the *Northern Ireland Master Butchers* litigation and *Mahoney* v. *Neenan* would be candidates – where the judicial performance, for whatever reason, is decidedly, self-evidently, something of a disappointment.

As it happens, one of the cases just cited, *Agnew* v. *Belfast Banking Co. Ltd.*, helps to clarify the proper parameters for a survey such as this. In it members of the Irish Court of Appeal opened particular Roman law texts touching on donations *mortis causa* which preserve an allusion to an episode in Homer's *Odyssey*. It is this episode which is instructive. When Telemachus quitted Sparta, summoned back to Ithaca by Athene, King Menelaus was to present him with a brace of handsome parting-gifts, a mixing bowl of silver and gold, a two-handled cup, and a richly embroidered gown. During the journey, Telemachus managed to evade an ambush set for him off the Elian coast by Penelope's suitors – and thus to escape certain death. A premonition of death was entirely natural, then, when, with Ithaca attained, Telemachus should have stridden forth, in concert with his father Odysseus, to meet the suitors for the final showdown. At this critical juncture, Telemachus chose to announce his intention to bestow upon

257 For the *ius commune*, see Helmut Coing, 'Roman law as ius commune on the Continent', (1973) 89 *LQR* 505.

Piraeus, his companion in adversity, the gifts which King Menelaus had showered upon him.[258] In the presence of evidence of this nature for the origins of legal doctrine still valid today, and as yet displaying no signs of obsolescence, it is clear that the quest Sir Henry Spelman would have us undertake to discover 'the several heads from which these laws of ours are taken', is not, in the case of the legacy of classical antiquity, to be restricted to the law of Rome.[259] Nor is it, bearing in mind, if we may, in addition, the lesson imparted by Seneca's *Medea*, to be restricted to formal legal texts either.

In south-west Scotland, possibly on the Galloway peninsula, one day in 82 AD Agricola, governor of Roman Britain, very likely watched the sun set in the western sky, rueful of the fact that, from the throw of the dice, it would not, after all, be his lot to impart the civilisation of Rome to the island that lay over the horizon. Only in a very much later era, in fact, did Roman law, in tandem with the other accoutrements of classical civilisation, finally accomplish that Olympian leap across St George's Channel and the Irish Sea. As regards Roman law – our preoccupation here – the success of the resultant transplant was a conspicuously modest affair, a consequence both of the competition from the indigenous brehon law tradition and of the political connection of Ireland to the England of the common law, the legal tradition that was eventually to prevail on the island. The actuality of the success of this transplant, however limited it was doomed to be, merits a degree of attention. A prime source of enlightenment is supplied in the law reports. In *Agnew's* case it is fascinating to discover Barry LJ conducting an Advanced Latin seminar on the meaning of a contested expression extracted from Justinian's *Institutes* – 'si quid humanitus ei contigisset'. In *Brady* v. *Warren* it is no less intriguing to see Palles CB, vexed by a phrase in Gaius's *Institutes* – 'item cervisque in silvas ire et redire solent' –, immersed in a serious disquisition on the domestication of the European deer, and managing, into the bargain, to cull from it a legal argument of apparent substance. The most vivid impression, however, is that conjured up in the inimitable language of McVeigh J. In the *Northern Ireland Master Butchers* case the proceedings took many twists and turns. At one stage, when the attention of the bar was riveted on the legal implications of the success of the new digester plant, McVeigh J tells us that he had had no difficulty at all in visualising the physical presence of Gaius and Justinian stalking the detention and condemnation rooms of the Belfast corporation abattoir. And with the word '*specificatio*' on their lips.

An alternative, or complementary, strategy should appeal to aficionados of litigation topography.[260] It is to travel in our mind's eye – or, better still, in the flesh – to some of the places where incidents occurred that precipitated the litigation in which we know recourse was to be had to Roman law. It is possible today to stand above the blockhouse down from James Fort on the Castle Park promontory that guards the entrance to Kinsale in Co. Cork and, with no great difficulty, to imagine the *Mary Leybourne* rounding the Old Head (unlike the luckless *Lusitania*), skirting East Holeopen Bay, finally coming into view and limping in to the dockside in the middle harbour for repairs after its storm-battered voyage back from Portugal, the payment of

258 *Odyssey*, xv-xvii. **259** The episode from the *Odyssey* is not referred to in *Agnew's* case. In a leading recent English authority on donations *mortis causa*, *Sen* v. *Headley*, it is: [1990] Ch. 728 at 741 (Mummery J). **260** For this species of topography, see my *Law and the emergence of modern Dublin* (Dublin, 1996), ch. 1.

the bill for which was to precipitate in the 1470s the plainly protracted quarrel over the use of Roman law in the court of Galway's sovereign. A journey to the Dingle peninsula in Co. Kerry would prove no less rewarding, for it was from here, on no less than two separate occasions at the turn of the present century, that litigation was to originate that saw the doctrine of alluvion given its distinctive modern gloss by the Irish courts. The strand at Inch provides the scenario for *A.G.* v. *McCarthy*, but it may be found more satisfying to cross from the southern side of the peninsula to the northern, to where *Re Hickson's Estate* first raised the specific problem in the law of alluvion. Walking westwards along the beach at Fermoyle, with the whole Brandon range spread out before you – Beenabrack, Ballysitteragh, Gearhane, Brandon Peak, Mount Brandon itself and, finally, to the right, the strange protuberance that is Masatiompan – it is, indeed, cause for amazement and reflection that here, across from Cloghane, in the lee of these mountains, in the presence of so marvellous a panorama, rules of Roman law worked out perhaps by anonymous Roman jurists so many centuries before should have been regarded as fit to achieve the resolution to a major Irish lawsuit – a distinctive one at that, linked, as it was, to problems of land purchase, and involving the triangular relationship of landlord, tenants and the Irish government.[261]

The teaching of Latin is in decline, possibly irreversible decline, in Irish secondary schools. Roman law, too, enjoys a precarious existence within the university law schools – a curious reversal of fortune for a subject which, following the major initiatives in Irish legal education that date from 1850, long enjoyed protected status as a compulsory subject. Whatever about the level of knowledge of Roman law possessed by today's judges and practitioners, it seems unlikely that the future will witness a stampede to open Gaius, Justinian's *Digest* or his *Institutes*, or even Bracton, in order to resolve the more abstruse legal conundrum that still contrives to surface from time to time. This state of affairs – common to many jurisdictions beside Ireland – has attracted no shortage of pessimistic utterances. Over a decade ago, for instance, Chief Justice Bray of South Australia thus bleakly declared in 'A plea for Roman law':[262]

> The forces which are turning the study of English into a study of contemporary literature and the study of history into a study of contemporary politics would like to turn the study of law into a study of contemporary sociological theory and practice. The curious unexpressed assumption that you can understand trees by dissecting fruits and ignoring roots should be energetically exposed for the barbarous fallacy that it is.

And he endorsed the views of an American critic, Christopher Lasch:[263]

> Our culture's indifference to the past – which easily shades off into active hostility and rejection – is the most telling proof of that culture's bankruptcy.

261 The litigation was crucial for the estate. The tenants were claiming rights over the foreshore at Fermoyle, created by alluvion, and made the recognition of these a precondition to agreeing to the purchase of their holdings. See [1911] 2 IR at 300. **262** (1983–5) 9 *Adelaide LR* 50. **263** *The culture of narcissism: American life in an age of diminishing expectations* (New York, 1978), p. xviii.

Chief Justice Bray had a point, but he may have painted too dismal a picture. It is arguable that there remains an indebtedness to Rome which cannot be entirely gainsaid, nor does it appear to be under specific threat. The quest for origins may hold diminishing appeal. But in the fashioning of legal logic – the assembling of precedent, the drawing of distinctions and contrasts, the imaginative deployment of allusion and analogy – and, above all, in the creation of the awareness of what makes for perspicacious expression – somewhere along the line, even if we do not know quite how, I venture to suggest, Roman law was to make a significant contribution. In innumerable contemporary legal contexts, the casuistic talents once displayed by Sabinians and Proculians, talents Zimmermann has recently insisted show more than a passing resemblance to those possessed by their common law counterparts of today,[264] are clearly still in vogue. Nowhere is this more easily discerned than in the interpretation of statutory provisions of the modern tax code. The question whether, for example, the process that pasteurizes milk or the one that ripens bananas qualifies for consideration as 'manufacturing' has to be dealt with, and a display of considerable intellectual dexterity is necessarily required in furnishing an answer.[265] And what about J cloths and nappy-liners which are, apparently, created out of huge bales of raw fabric as a result of being put in sophisticated and expensive machines which rapidly cut and fold? Is this 'manufacturing' with the various tax benefits that may accrue? Sabinians and Proculians would surely have welcomed a fellow jurist had they been privileged to read the bravura performance registered by Miss Justice Carroll in settling this very question not so very long ago:[266]

> It seems to me that the reduction in size and ease of handling combined with the inherent quality of the raw material has a utility, quality and worth which are due to, and cannot be dissociated from, the process carried out by the respondent. The fact that the process does not bring about any change in the raw material does not of itself prevent the process from being a manufacturing process. I can think of other products where the raw material is unchanged. A toothpick is part of a tree which has been cut and packaged but it has an intrinsic quality given to it by the process, namely size and convenience and being tailored to a process. Confetti is another. You can throw confetti where you could not throw bulk paper.

You can indeed.

264 Reinhard Zimmermann, *The law of obligations: Roman foundations of the civilian tradition* (Cape Town, 1990). **265** See *Cronin* v. *Strand Dairy Ltd.*, III ITR 441; *Charles McCann Ltd.* v. *Ó Culacháin* [1986] IR 196. **266** *Ó Laochdha* v. *Johnson & Johnson (Ireland) Ltd.* [1991] 2 IR 287 at 290. For a further instalment in the saga of deciding what constitutes 'manufacturing', see *Brosnan* v. *Leeside Nurseries Ltd.* [1998] 2 IR 304 (unrooted chrysanthemum cuttings subjected to process producing mature dwarfed chrysanthemums out of season).

The Irish Custom of Tracts*

Under the Irish custom of tracts,[1] a person dispossessed of livestock or other chattels was entitled to follow the trail left by the thief and, through resort to self-help, to recover what had been stolen. If the thief was not caught, the occupier of land where any trail ended was also made answerable and, by extension, was required, where restitution was not possible, to make good the victim's loss. In time, variations emerged that were designed to distribute the cost of this compensation among a range of other people deemed responsible for the occupier.

The custom had a long pedigree, and analogous customs had been in operation elsewhere from early times. 'Cattle lifting', Pollock and Maitland wrote in their *History of English law*, was 'a theme to which the Anglo-Saxon dooms and the parallel "folk laws" of the continental nations' were ever recurring.[2] They gave an illustration:

> My cattle have been driven off; I must follow the trail; it is the duty of my neighbours to assist me, to ride with me. If we catch the marauder still driving the beasts before him, we take him as a 'hand-having' thief and he is dealt with in a summary fashion; 'he can not deny' the theft.[3]

Those in pursuit were not always so fortunate actually to catch up with the marauder. Early customary law, however, evolved a further rule to meet just such an eventuality, as Pollock and Maitland went on to explain:

> Even if we can not catch a thief in the act, the trail is treated as of great importance. If it leads into a man's land, he must show that it leads out again; otherwise it will 'stand instead of a foreoath'; it is an accusing fact.[4]

Pollock and Maitland's description, based on Anglo-Saxon sources, captures the essence of the comparable Irish custom of tracts.

This Irish custom won endorsement from the Irish council in 1552 or 1553 (6 Edward VI) when it was accorded the force of law by an act of state. It came under criticism in a report presented in 1622, but, despite this, secured a temporary reprieve. Final abolition was to take place some eighteen years later, in 1640. A key ingredient,

*For help of various sorts in the preparation of this article, I should like to thank John McCafferty, Mary Robertson, Catherine Murray, Katharine Simms and Fergus Kelly. **1** Or 'tracks'. **2** Sir Frederick Pollock and F.W. Maitland, *The history of English law before the time of Edward I* (2nd. ed., 1898), repr. with new intro. by S.F.C. Milsom, 2 vols. (Cambridge, 1968), ii, 157. **3** Ibid. **4** Ibid.

it would seem, in the legal systems of later medieval and early modern Ireland, the custom escaped serious scholarly attention until 1970 when Hand and Treadwell published their edition of James I's directions of 1622 for reforming Irish law.[5] The thirty-fourth of these directions dealt explicitly with the custom of tracts as well as with the associated custom of 'kencogus law'. Hand and Treadwell's remarks on tracts are succinct and to the point. Though the following account of the custom introduces an amount of fresh material, it also represents an expansion of their original treatment. In the circumstances, it is appropriate to acknowledge their pioneering aperçu.[6]

The commissioners of 1622, responsible for the report to which reference has been made, viewed the Irish custom of tracts as 'an old, pre-conquest expedient of law and order'.[7] In this, as we have shown, they were almost certainly correct. The first concrete recognition of the custom in Ireland comes rather later even so, in the thirteenth century and towards the end of it. This is in a handbook of contemporary law and custom ascribed to Giolla na Naomh mac Duinnshléibhe Mhic Aodhagáin (*d.* 1309), who is described in the annals as ollamh of Connacht and Ireland and 'a universal master equally skilled in all the arts'.[8] The handbook is written in Early Modern Irish, and the passage in it that touches on the custom of tracts begins with these three lines, as read by D.A. Binchy and translated by Gearóid MacNiocaill:

> In t-ineth a mbertur lorg na gaidi, muna fetann lorg na gaidi do cur dibh … ic na gaidi orro fein acht munaba bothar coitinn ceatra no inadh cruaidh tirim inba doigh a falach.
>
> (The place to which the track of the stolen goods is followed, unless [the inhabitants] can disembarrass themselves of the track of the stolen goods … they are liable for making good the theft, unless it be a common cattle-track or hard ground whereby they [the tracks] may be lost.)[9]

In an important article in *Historical Studies X*, MacNiocaill furnishes a more detailed account of the custom as expounded here by Giolla na Naomh:

> Whatever place the cattle are tracked to the inhabitants of that place must show either that the tracks go on elsewhere – exception being made of a place that abounds in hard ground, with consequent loss of the trail, or of a common cattle trail – or show that the cattle were brought there against the will of the inhabitants – *force majeure* – or accept liability for the theft or make formal

5 'His majesty's directions for ordering and settling the courts within his kingdom of Ireland, 1622', eds. G.J. Hand and Victor Treadwell, *Anal. Hib.*, 26 (1970), 177-212. Hereafter cited as 'H.M.'s directions, 1622'. 6 As will more immediately appear, I am also indebted in particular to the publications of Gearóid MacNiocaill and Kenneth Nicholls. 7 See Hand and Treadwell, *Anal. Hib.*, 26, at 206. 8 Katharine Simms, 'The brehons of later medieval Ireland', in Daire Hogan and W.N. Osborough (eds.), *Brehons, serjeants and attorneys* (Dublin, 1990), p. 50 at 59; Gearóid MacNiocaill, 'Aspects of Irish law in the late thirteenth century', *Historical Studies X*, ed. G.A. Hayes-McCoy (Co. na Gaillimhe, 1976), p. 25 at 30. 9 D.A. Binchy, *Corpus Iuris Hibernici*, 6 vols. (Dublin, 1978) (hereafter C.I.H.), ii, 693 at lines 10-13; MacNiocaill, 'Irish law and the Armagh constitutions of 1297', *Ir. Jur*, vi (1971), p. 338 at 344.

> rebuttal. Similar circumstantial evidence is afforded by finding fragments of flesh in a given place, the presumption being that the stolen beast had been slaughtered and eaten by the thieves on their home ground; so too if the stolen beasts are found in an out of the way, unfrequented place. In this latter case, all the inhabitants are obliged to make oath of their innocence, whether their standing be good or otherwise; if nobody admits the theft, discarding the fear of perjury, they are held collectively liable for the theft.[10]

The custom of tracts also receives express recognition in a late thirteenth century document of ecclesiastical provenance. This is the text of an agreement of November 1297 entered into by Brian MacMathghamhna, king of Oriel – a territory largely confined to the present county of Monaghan together with part of Fermanagh – and his subordinates to order their affairs in accordance with certain constitutions recently issued by Nicholas MacMaol-Iosa, archbishop of Armagh. The then bishop of Clogher, Matha O Cathasaigh, was associated with this agreement, which explains why the latter was recorded in a register for the diocese, now lost, of which, however, substantial fragments are extant.[11] The immediate background was the promulgation in 1296 of Pope Boniface VIII's bull *Clericis laicos*, which forbade lay rulers to force churchmen to pay taxes without papal approval. Archbishop Nicholas MacMaol-Iosa profited from the reception of the bull in Ireland the following year to draw up a set of constitutions that extended the sphere of ecclesiastical liberty and to extract promises from a number of lay rulers, including those in Oriel, to abide by them.[12] The upshot was that in the diocese of Clogher the king and lords of Oriel gave a series of solemn undertakings covering generally their relationship with local churchmen. One key undertaking concerned depredations that might be practised upon churchmen. Here, in appropriate cases, the custom of tracts was made applicable. The undertaking additionally spelt out the liability of the lords of Oriel in the attendant circumstances:

> Sane si bona alicuius clerici seu ecclesiasticae personae per furtum aut rapinam auferri contingat, quoque clerici seu tenentes ecclesiarum ad terras cuiuscunque laici vestigia sic *ablatorum fuerint prosecuti, concedimus et fide *melia promittimus quod dominus illarum [terrarum] in quibus vestigia ipsa fuerint inventa de rebus sic *ablatis totaliter teneatur, nisi vestigia eadem de terris suis ad terras vicinas prosequatur, et quod tunc laicus investigans illarum vicinarum terrarum domino vestigia *ablatorum sic inventa coram testibus denunciet absque dolo, et simili modo secundus et tercius ad quorum terras vestigia ipsa devenirint facere teneantur et sic deinceps quoadusque ad auctorem furti vel rapinae finaliter deveniatur.[13]

10 'Aspects of Irish law in the late thirteenth century', *Historical Studies X*, p. 25 at 36-47. For discussion of the circumstantial evidence point in this context, see Fergus Kelly, *A guide to early Irish law* (Dublin, 1988), p. 205. **11** H.J. Lawlor, 'Fragments of a lost register of the diocese of Clogher', *Louth Arch Soc Jn*, iv (1916-20), 226; 'The register of Clogher', ed. Kenneth Nicholls, *Clogher Rec*, vii, no. 3 (1971-72), 390. **12** See further Gearóid MacNiocaill, 'Irish law and the Armagh constitutions of 1297', *Ir Jur*, vi (1971), 338; A.J. Otway-Ruthven, *A history of medieval Ireland* (London & New York, 1968), p. 135. **13** The original text as

(If the goods of any cleric or ecclesiastical person should happen to be carried off by theft or spoil, and the track of the goods so carried off is followed by clerks or tenants of churches to the lands of any layman, we grant and promise in the best of faith that the lord of these lands in which the track is found shall be entirely responsible for the stolen goods unless he follows the track from his lands to neighbouring lands, then the layman so following [the track] shall, before witnesses and without fraud, show the track of the stolen goods to the lord of those neighbouring lands, and similarly the second and third persons to whose lands the track leads are bound to do [the same], and so successively until it is finally brought to the doer of the theft or spoil).[14]

We may pause here to note three things. In the first place, there is the omission in this clause of any mention of the defences linked to the operation of the custom as recognised by Giolla na Naomh mac Duinnshléibhe Mhic Aodhagáin. Secondly, the clause contains the important stipulation as to the primary responsibility of the lord: this helps to explain the link between the custom and the species of liability for others that went under the name of kencogus law.[15] Thirdly, the clause insists that the tracker and successive individuals must be able to show, before witnesses and without fraud (*coram testibus … absque dolo*), that the trail leads elsewhere and has not come to an end. As we shall shortly discover, corrupt practice seemingly was to play its part in the sequence of events that led to the final abolition of the custom in Ireland in 1640. Against that background, these early arrangements to guarantee fair dealing are of especial interest.

Little is known of the fortunes of the custom for the next two and a half centuries. In the mid-Tudor period, however, the custom was to be given the force of law by the Irish council. This was done by means of an act of state adopted in late 1552 or early 1553, virtually in the last year of the reign of Edward VI. The text of this act of state does not survive. All we have, in fact, is a bald entry in a table of contents (which has survived) for the pertinent council book of the Irish council (which has not): 'Where the tract failith, there the goods stollen to be satisfied: [fol.] 339.'[16] This is an unfortunate situation. The act of state apparently regulated the operation of the custom, and it would have been enlightening to learn of the extent to which, if at all, the doctrinal glosses propounded by Giolla na Naomh in the thirteenth century were endorsed by the Irish council in the sixteenth.

Further potential mystery surrounds this act of state. In 1640, when repeal of the custom was decided upon by the Irish council of that time, the assumption that prevailed was that only a single act of state – presumably that of Edward VI – needed to be set aside. The possibility that there may have been two acts of state dealing with

given by Nicholls: 'Register of Clogher', at 418. The Latin text is alone reproduced in Lawlor's 'Fragments of a lost register of the diocese of Clogher' (above, n. 11), at 251-2. **14** Nicholls's translation: 'Register of Clogher', at 417, 419. **15** For kencogus, see 'His majesty's directions for ordering and settling the courts within his kingdom of Ireland, 1622', eds. G.J. Hand and Victor Treadwell, *Anal. Hib.*, 26, at 184-5. **16** 'A table to the rede counsell booke, beginning in King Henry the 8 raigne, the 24th yeare', TCD MS 843 (formerly F3.17), f. 17 (transcribed, HMC, *Haliday MSS* (London, 1897), p. 282). The date of 6 Edward VI is expressly repeated in 1617: see *Cal. S. P. Ire., 1615-25*, p. 153.

the custom needs, however, to be examined. An advisory opinion on the custom emanating from Co. Down in 1617 includes a reference to the 'old' law, as opposed, one infers, to the 'new': in other words, the impression is given that there may have been two 'laws'.[17] Again, the anonymous author of a paper on the laws of Ireland, to be dated to *c.*1610, asserts that the crucial act of state was approved when Sussex was lord deputy.[18] If 1552/3 is right, this assertion cannot also be right, for Thomas Radcliffe, Lord Fitzwalter, and, subsequently, third earl of Sussex, only became lord deputy under Mary in 1556 – which is three or four years too late.

In fact, there is no mystery. The Irish council did indeed adopt a further act of state regarding the custom and this took place early in 1557 during Sussex's lord deputyship. It is to be found among a set of 'orders taken at Dublin' which are dated 30 January 1556/7. The relevant portion of the particular order laid it down:

> that iff eny horse, cowe or other cattayll be stollen and the tracte followydd to a certeyn place and the owner or owners inhabitor or inhabitors thereof be before recorde requyred to putt the tracte oute of the grounde to them belonging and they shall refuse so to doo, they to answer the goodes.[19]

Since we lack hard evidence as to the precise content of the act of state of 6 Edward VI, the relationship between the two regulations remains unclear. From internal evidence, it would seem, however, that the act of state of January 1556/7 was exclusively concerned with a specific problem not provided for hitherto: the one that arose when the occupier of lands where the trail ended had not so much failed to put the tract on to somebody else's land but had refused total cooperation in the effective mounting of the procedures linked to the custom. The internal evidence is furnished by the residue of the order in question which continues by prescribing a sanction to be preferred against all persons guilty of a comparable sort of non-cooperation – refusal to join in the hue and cry:

> yf huyte and crye be made and the inhabitors theraboutes doo not aunswer the same, and ... yt be proved that the parties that followe the goodes susteyne losse therby, then they that did not aunswer the crye to satisfie the partie or partyes for his or ther losses so sustayned.[20]

Aside altogether from the problem of the relationship between these two acts of state, the employment of this particular constitutional mechanism to enshrine the custom of tracts within the legal system of Tudor Ireland should occasion no surprise. Under Tudor and Stuart administrations in Ireland the mechanism was commonly so employed by the Irish council to introduce major changes in substantive law. This power residing in the council was very different in character from that of issuing tran-

17 See *Cal. S. P. Ire., 1615-25*, p. 153. This advisory opinion is considered in detail below. **18** 'Lawes of Irelande', Huntington Lib., San Marino, Cal., Ellesmere MS 7042, p. 11. **19** 'Acts of the privy council of Ireland, 1556-1571', ed. J.T. Gilbert, HMC, *Haliday MSS* (1897), p. 26. The original manuscript Gilbert reports has a marginal note: 'For tractinges of stolne goodes'. **20** HMC, *Haliday MSS*, p. 26.

sient proclamations, and the relative frequency of its employment is attributable to the lengthy intervals that separated sittings of the Irish parliament (where major changes might more appropriately be made), and the need to be able somehow to bring about the minimum of desirable legal change with reasonable promptitude. Down to 1641 at least, it was generally recognised, both in London and in Dublin, that the Irish council enjoyed unfettered authority to make use of this exceptional power to initiate new law. In 1578, the then Irish lord deputy, Sir Henry Sidney, requested authority from London to convene a new Irish parliament. The English privy council turned down the request, judging it impolitic at the time in view of the contemporary controversy over cess.[21] In their reply to Sidney, they added that it was 'un-needfull', since, in their understanding, in Ireland 'many of the thinges required to pass by Parliament may be as sufficiently perfected by order of the Lord Deputy and Councell, as by statute lawe'.[22] In 1635, another lord deputy, Viscount Wentworth – the future earl of Strafford –, made haste to capitalise upon the constitutional realities, which did not have to be explained to *him*. Instructions from London to introduce a bill dealing with the subject of simony had arrived too late for him to enter it into his legislative programme. Archbishop Laud, his correspondent, was, however, told not to worry: 'I shall be able to help all well enough, by making an Act of State.' The reassurance Wentworth sought to convey could not have been couched in plainer terms. 'We uphold Acts of State here', he confided to Laud, 'very strongly and punish the transgressors against them as familiarly and roundly as we do against any Statute of them all, and by that means are they as well obeyed.'[23]

An evolution in constitutional thinking led in early seventeenth-century Ireland to acceptance of the principle that any major legal change introduced by act of state should be confirmed by act of parliament at the first available opportunity. Whatever the reason, in the case of the act or acts of state on the custom of tracts, this was never to occur. Given the surrounding circumstances, it was perhaps fitting that when abolition of the custom came about in 1640, this was to be accomplished, apparently, by another act of state.

The manuscript source 'The lawes of Irelande' asserts that confirmation of the custom of tracts was adjudged both 'fitt and necessary' at the time.[24] Other extant justifications are somewhat more illuminating. In 1612, James I, in a letter to his Irish lord deputy, Sir Arthur Chichester, indicates his approval of the custom on the basis that it had furnished an effective means of detecting thieves in a country where, through secret conveyances and combinations to conceal thefts, this was particularly difficult.[25] 'The lawes of Irelande' itself touches on one practical point, plainly of considerable importance. The custom, to work satisfactorily, demanded skill in tracking. As to that, 'The lawes' says, one needed to have no fear: the Irish were 'incredi-

21 For the controversy, see J.G. Crawford, *Anglicising the government of Ireland: the Irish privy council and the expansion of Tudor rule, 1556-1578* (Dublin, 1993), ch. 6. **22** English privy council to Sidney, 1 June 1578: *The Walsingham letter-book*, eds. James Hogan and N. McN. O'Farrell (Dublin, 1959), pp 1-2. **23** Wentworth to Laud, 18 May 1635, Sheffield City Lib., Strafford papers, vi, p. 183. **24** Huntington Lib., Ellesmere MS 7042, p.11. **25** The king to Chichester, 11 March 1612: *Cal. S. P. Ire., 1611-14*, p. 255.

blye cunning' in that they were able to find the track 'by the bruising of a grasse in the summer tyme'.[26] In 1640, the petition moved in the Irish house of lords to seek abrogation of the original act of state claims that the custom had originally been 'commodious to planters' but had long since ceased to be so for reasons that are then explained.[27]

The custom of tracts is mentioned in the 'Orders for the countie of Kilkennye' drawn up at sessions held in Kilkenny itself in the summer of 1578 and which were presided over by William Gerrard, the then Irish lord chancellor.[28] Two of these orders dealt specifically with the need to combat theft of livestock. One sought to prevent ferry-boat movements at night, cover of darkness having knowingly been utilised for the transporting of stolen cattle.[29] The immediately preceding order introduced the custom of tracts to the county, if, indeed, it had not been in force there earlier. The penalties that the order prescribed for failure to cooperate in following any trail prove to be of particular interest:

> And it is furder ordered for the better tryall out of felons and goodes stolne, that where the trace of anye cattell stolne is founde in anye towne or nier any towne that they of the towne nerest to the place where the tracke is found shall uppon request made by the towne[30] and so from place to place to everye towne, and theim to whom the tracke is offered to travell and helpe to pursue the tracke untill either the cattell be found or that the tracke canne be noe furder driven, and suche towne and pariche where the tracke shalbe lefte to bringe forthe the fellon or answere for the cattell, and that anye person that shall refuse to followe the tracke aforesayd to be punished by fyne and imprisonment, and if anye person doe resiste or refuse theim followinge the tracke, from further following therof, he to paye the valewe of the cattell stolne.[31]

The custom is alluded to again in 'Articles for the guidance of the seneschal, sheriff and justices of the peace in Co. Wexford', drawn up in the 1580s.[32] These articles, composed by the lord deputy and council, deal with a range of law and order issues. Article 12, in the only surviving version of it that we have, and possibly heavily calendared, stipulated, in blunt terms: 'Upon whose ground the track is lost he shall put it upon another, or himself answer the theft'. There is no reference in either instance to the sorts of problem that, as we shall soon discover, had surfaced in Ulster by the 1610s. Acknowledgment that the custom was set to be observed in Kilkenny in 1578 and in Wexford in the 1580s – both in south Leinster – is evidence of the custom's geographical spread, and is, naturally, useful to have.

Another initiative, of similar vintage, might have been expected to have an impact on the routine workings of the custom, wherever in Ireland the latter was actually

26 Huntington Lib., Ellesmere MS 7042, p. 10. **27** *Lords' jn. Ire.*, i, 133. See further below. **28** 'Lord Chancellor Gerrard's notes of his report on Ireland, etc.', *Anal. Hib.*, 2 (1931), at 174–80. **29** Id., 177–8. **30** Charles McNeill's note on the manuscript observes that at this juncture something appears to have dropped out. **31** *Anal. Hib.*, 2 (1931), at 177. **32** 'Calendar of the Irish Council Book, AD 1581–86', ed. D.B. Quinn, *Anal. Hib.*, 24 (1967), 91 at 162 (no. 305).

observed. This was a decree emanating from Lord Deputy Perrott for the marking of livestock. The decree ordered justices of the peace to cause

> high constables, and petty constables and overseers, to see that all manner of cattle, stud mares, sheep and lambs, be marked with iron marks or ear-marks, within ten weeks after warning by proclamation, to be made in the good towns within the shire, upon pain that every offender herein shall forfeit his cattle, stud mares, sheep or lambs, that shall be found so unmarked, the moiety whereof to be to the use of him that will give information, and the other moiety to the poor of the parish.[33]

Pollock and Maitland, in their discussion of early customary law on the retrieval of stolen livestock, saw an immediate connection between a custom such as the Irish custom of tracts and insistence on the ear-marking or branding of cattle. Being placed under the obligation of publicly exposing to the view of one's neighbours the cattle that one owned, made it a matter of notoriety that any thief was driving away what was not his.[34] So, one might suppose, would have been the outcome in Ireland, too, after the promulgation of the new decree of the 1580s. But it is surely doubtful whether so draconian an instruction as our Irish decree could have engendered widespread compliance.

For the reign of James I there are two major entries relating to the custom in the published Irish state papers – one for 1612, the other for 1617 – and both, significantly, connected with the practical mechanics of the custom in counties of Ulster.

In the spring of 1612, James I, at the behest of Sir James Douglas and other undertakers in Co. Armagh, sought to impress upon Lord Deputy Chichester the need to act forcefully across a broad spectrum of law and order problems.[35] Greater effort was required, the king wrote, 'for the safety of the undertakers and to secure them against the practices of such lewd persons as endeavour to dishearten them from proceeding any further in their plantation'. Chichester did not dissent from James's analysis. The situation in Armagh was worrying, he noted in an apostil, the level of 'stealths' for a start, which he attributed to features of the local topography: 'the woody countries of Clancan, Brazilogh, Killultagh, Killwarnan, the Brentric, the lower part of Orier and Onealan ... ever bred knaves.'

The depredations which the undertakers had suffered in the preceding winter months were of particular concern to the king. He urged resort to the custom of tracts, of which, as we have already observed, he enthusiastically approved, adding, for good measure, that, in appropriate cases of proven theft, monetary compensation might be substituted for specific restitution. Chichester's apostil shows that, in his opinion, the custom was not functioning satisfactorily and that, in any event, doubts had arisen over the practicability and the legality of arranging substitute compensation – difficulties to

33 'Orders to be observed by the justices of the peace within their several limits throughout the realm', *Desid cur Hib*, i, 20 at 23; cf. *Anal. Hib.*, 24 (1967), at 160 (no. 287). Perrott was lord deputy from 1584 to 1588. **34** *History of English law*, ii, 157. **35**.The king to Sir Arthur Chichester, 11 March 1612 (apostiled by the latter), *Cal. S. P. Ire., 1611-14*, pp 254-6.

which the king had not chosen to allude or of which he was genuinely ignorant. The relevant passage from the king's letter and Chichester's accompanying apostil need to be read together.

James wrote as follows:

> And, further, as it has always been difficult in that country[36] to find out the offenders in theft through secret conveyances and combinations to conceal them, he [the king] thinks it fit according to an order which has been long in use and practice there, that if after stealth from any of the undertakers the goods be found or by track may be proved to have come into the hands of any of the natives, or of the servitors, but then either the stolen goods or the true value of them should be restored to the undertaker, and that restitution according to this order be made to the petitioners for stealths committed upon them last winter.[37]

Chichester's memorandum was both frank and informative:

> The benefit of tracks is afforded to all, which gives more the true value; but the British undertakers are careless in keeping of their goods, and being lost, do seldom or never follow the track, but seek for restitution out of the whole county, or sundry baronies, according to their own valuation, and it has been proved unto me that one of them lost a horse or gelding, in which he demanded £15, but offered to sell him for £5 before he was stolen, and if restitution should be made after that manner, they would not care to be robbed every day.[38]

The king, under pressure from Douglas and the others, sent another instruction to his lord deputy. Chichester was to order the judges of assize to examine all orders made at the assizes 'in prejudice of the undertakers'. Chichester interpreted this instruction, surely correctly, as veiled criticism of what had transpired at the recent assizes when applotments presented there had been rendered nugatory. A second apostil has the story:

> There was £140 applotted upon the county of Armagh towards restitution of goods stolen, which the British undertakers refused, albeit the innocent as well as the offender was charged therewith, whereupon the officers forebore to levy it, as well by order from me as the judges of assize, upon the previous complaint of the country, praying to be eased of such unlawful taxations, and to hang the offenders.[39]

36 It is not clear whether James is referring to all of Ireland or just Co. Armagh. **37** *Cal. S. P. Ire., 1611-14*, p. 255. **38** Ibid. Similar views were expressed by Chichester a few months later: see Chichester to Humphrey May, 8 July 1612: 'Letter book of Sir Arthur Chichester, 1612-1614', ed. R.D. Edwards, *Anal. Hib.*, 8 (1938), 3 at 30-3. **39** *Cal. S. P. Ire., 1611-14*, p. 256.

In Chichester's eyes, the situation was thus doubly disturbing. Many victims of stealths could not be bothered to follow the tracks. They sought compensation in lieu but exaggerated the value of their claims. Moreover, it would appear that there was no legal power to force the county at large to meet the bill. A later letter of Chichester's, in July, to Humphrey May indicates that, despite his own personal reservations and under continuing pressure from the king, he again sought reparations on behalf of the undertakers from the native tenants and freeholders in Armagh, and exclusively from them.[40]

Further insight into the operation of the custom in another Ulster county – Down – may be gleaned from an advisory opinion of 1617, also in the published state papers. Entitled 'Tracks in the county of Down', this consists of an opinion of the justices of the peace and gentlemen of the county on the use, prosecution and levying of tracks.[41] The precise background to the preparation of the opinion is unknown. Fortunately for us, it nevertheless sheds light on many a dark corner.

The justices and the others start by expressing their unequivocal support for retention of the custom, the county 'being so subject to stealths'. The actual rules for following any trail are then expounded. The trail had to be taken up within twenty-four hours of the occurrence of the theft (as provided by 'the 'ould Act'). There was a limit as well on the length of any hunt: the trail was not to be pursued 'above four or five days'. At any place where the trail petered out, the inhabitants there had twelve hours' grace in which to demonstrate that the trail could in fact be followed elsewhere.[42] Where the trail led to a particular place late in the evening, the rule was to allow the inhabitants a night's grace plus six hours after sunlight the following day.[43] Any tracker endowed with the requisite expertise in tracking was to be obliged to pursue the trail until it ended; in return, such tracker was to be remunerated for so doing.[44]

The remainder of the opinion shows preoccupation with delimiting the exact locality obliged to contribute to payment in lieu (under the apparent legal dispensation that provided for this when actual restitution was impossible).[45] Only the specific townland where the trail ended was liable. To levy the charge off a barony or parishes was unacceptable, since these areas were often too large. Levying a charge on all and sundry would mean imposing a burden on someone who might not have had the opportunity to demonstrate that the trail led elsewhere, not having been advised that the following of a trail was in progress. Furthermore, to impose a general liability was at odds with the preferred policy of imposing liability only on those who were truly answerable, would interfere with the efficient operation of the custom, and would

40 Chichester to Humphrey May, 8 July 1612, *Anal. Hib.*, 8, at 32. **41** 'Tracks in the county of Down', *Cal. S. P. Ire., 1615-25*, pp 153-4. **42** 'That the track shall remain upon a place where the track was left twelve hours that the inhabitants of that place may have time to put the track forward.' **43** 'If the track be brought to any place late in the evening ... the trackers shall remain upon the track six hours the next day after it be daylight, notwithstanding they have required the inhabitants to put off the track overnight.' **44** 'If any known tracker be upon the track, the same tracker upon the reasonable hire of the several towns, shall follow the track unto the end.' **45** Chichester, it may be remembered, appears to have doubted that any credible such dispensation existed.

penalise the innocent.[46] On the other hand, where scattered dwellings had been amalgamated into 'town reeds', it was only right that all the members of any individual reed should be made answerable whenever a trail terminated anywhere within the reed.[47]

The opinion of the Down justices and gentlemen ties up one or two loose ends where human failure had made it impossible to follow the trail. Where negligence in the supervision of town cattle led to the trail being lost, the whole town was to be made amenable ('charged with that track'). Where the trail had been interfered with wilfully on the part of a specific individual, he alone was answerable unless he was a man of straw when, once again, the town assumed responsibility.[48]

An impression that lingers in the mind of any reader of this exhaustive opinion of 1617 is that at that date, in one of the counties of Ulster at least, the custom of tracts was in full working trim, was regularly availed of, and was attended with the minimum of controversy. The picture conveyed by Chichester in the two apostils attached to the king's letter of 1612 and in his later letter to Humphrey May was altogether different. Then we were in the presence of a sceptical administrator, perhaps doing his best to be fair, but nonetheless, in effect, sounding the death-knell for the custom of tracts in Ireland. What is undoubtedly of interest, in view of this conflict of evidence, is the studied omission – an omission to which Hand and Treadwell have drawn attention[49] – of any recognition accorded the custom in the detailed 'Instructions for the lord president and council of Munster, 20 May 1615'.[50] Since Chichester was still lord deputy at the time – he was succeeded by Oliver St John in 1616 – and he may be supposed to have had a hand in the formulation of these instructions, the omission itself, of course, is scarcely startling. It is worthy of note even so.

The Instructions dealt with two distinct kinds of depredation, both of which in the Ulster counties of the period would have resulted in recourse to the custom of tracts: (i) where the theft occurred within the presidency of Munster, the thief resided there and was amenable to its jurisdiction; and (ii) where the theft occurred within the pres-

46 'For the manner of levying of the track. They are of opinion that if the same should be laid upon the baronies and the parishes some of them being spacious, there would light a burden upon some whose service had not been required to put off the track, nor could within those hours be informed of any such track, and withal would be the means to slack the quick and ready preservation [prosecution] of tracks for the burden being generally laid, those upon whose lands the tracks were left, bearing but equal share, would be the more careless to put the same from their lands, who haply might be thieves, and enrich themselves upon the baronies, if that the barony should bear the track in general, these thieves may make it a practice, and therefore they hold it very reasonable that the track should be answered and satisfied the full and true value of the goods lost out of that townland where the track should be left, as is before set down.' I trust I have made correct sense of the convoluted syntax. **47** 'But in regard that a late proclamation and instructions came from the Lord Deputy for composing scattered houses into town reeds, and to be so planted, if convenience will afford, that two or three towns may build together upon the meares and meeting of their several town reeds, which being established, they think it fit, that if a track be brought to any part of those lands belonging to that town reed, that the whole town reed should bear their share alike, which will be a cause of society betwixt them to help one another, and will induce them to be the more willing to draw themselves together into town reeds.' This proclamation is not listed in the Irish proclamations given in Steele, *Tudor & Stuart proclam.* **48** 'Lastly, they hold likewise that where a track shall be foiled by the cattle of any town negligently that then the whole town be charged with that track, but if foiled wilfully by the means of any particular man, that the party so foiling the track shall answer the track if he be of ability, if not the town to answer the track, and the party to be well punished.' **49** *Anal. Hib.*, 26, at 206. **50** *Desid cur Hib*, ii, 1–36.

idency, but the thief fled with what had been stolen to somewhere else in Ireland. In both instances, it was insisted that common law procedures and remedies be exclusively utilised – as we would say today, prosecuting for the theft or suing for the conversion – and, in addition, where the thief fled out of the presidency, resort be had to 'fresh suit and prosecution', a procedure linked to the hue and cry.[51] The emphasis, markedly at variance, is unmistakable.

Thus, where the theft took place within the limits of the presidency, and the supposed thief dwelt there too, the Instructions stipulate:

> All and every his majesty's subjects ... being preyed, robbed, or spoiled ... [are to] presume not to seek their revenge by their accustomed Brehone laws, or restitution of their goods by arbitrary means, other than by complaint as aforesaid, to the lord president and council, or before the judge of assizes in their circuits, or justices of the peace in their quarter sessions, or as by his majesty's laws is appointed.[52]

And where the thief had fled outside the geographical limits of the presidency:

> If any person or persons shall, at any time hereafter, prey or spoil the inhabitants of the said province [Munster], and fly with the said spoil into any foreign part of this realm, that then and at all such times, it shall and may be lawful to the said lord president and council, and every other persons having their warrant in writing, or any two of them (whereof the lord president to be one) to make fresh suit and prosecution after all and singular such person and persons so fleeing as aforesaid into any part or place of this land out of the said province; and he and them so fleeing with the said cattle or prey, wheresoever they shall find them, to apprehend and take, and the said person and persons, and prey so taken, to bring and return into the said county, there to answer the fact according to justice, and the cattle to be restored to the owner: charging and commanding all and singular the king's majesty's officers within the said province, and the said other foreign parts, to be aiding and assisting in the prosecuting after all such felons and traitors.[53]

Taking their cue perhaps from Chichester's reservations as well as from the judges and others who appeared before them, the commissioners of 1622 on reform of the Irish legal system recommended outright abolition of the custom. The notes kept by one of their number, Sir Nathaniel Rich, show that the commissioners regarded the hue and cry, outlined in the Statute of Westminster I of 1275, and, as we have seen, certainly familiar to the Irish council, as the proper alternative offered by English common law.[54] Though most of the recommendations forwarded to London were accepted by the king and privy council there, a few were not, and the recommenda-

51 See Pollock and Maitland, *History of English law*, ii, 160-1. **52** *Desid cur Hib*, ii, at 16. **53** *Desid cur Hib*, ii, at 21. **54** See Hand and Treadwell, *Anal. Hib.*, 26, at 206.

tion urging abolition of the custom fell into the latter category. The relevant portion of the direction in the formal king's directions, authorised for publication at the end of July 1622, amounted to a temporary respite:

> And for the custome of Tracts, for which there is no law established, but are directed by Act of State, that the same, so long as they continue in use, be equally communicated, as well to the Irish as Brittish, or wholly taken away.[55]

Only in 1640, eighteen years later, was the last chapter in the history of the custom set to unfold. On 11 June, the house of lords' committee of privileges and grievances, in a report to the house, again urged outright abolition: the act of state in regard to tracts was 'thought fit to be taken away'.[56] Other grievances were dealt with in the same report. The committee thus recommended that legislation passed in the parliament of 1634–5 which imposed penalties for ploughing by the tail and for pulling wool off live sheep[57] should be put into cold storage. On the other hand, the committee urged the introduction of new legislation to compel bailiffs and informants to make good their presentments at assizes or else assume responsibility for the costs incurred.[58]

The upshot was that the house of lords nominated two of its members, Viscount Gormanstown and Bishop Bramhall of Derry, to draft a petition for presentation to Sir Christopher Wandesford, the lord deputy since the preceding April. At the outset, the grievance associated with the continued existence of tracts seems to have been tackled separately; administratively, at a later stage, the other grievances and one or two additions were to be tacked on. On 14 June, Gormanstown advised the lords that Wandesford was willing to move quickly on the issue of tracts and would welcome a delegation from the lords to attend a meeting of the Irish council fixed for 3p.m. that very day which would be considering it.[59] A committee of nine – Viscounts Gormanstown, Netterville and Kilmallock, Barons Slane, Howth and Lambert, and the bishops of Dromore and of Clogher as well as of Derry (Bramhall) – duly waited upon Wandesford.[60] The latter, we learn from an observation of Bramhall's, had earlier brought the issue before the council, but there had been 'no full resolution'.[61] The discussion that took place on the afternoon of 14 June, in contrast, was immediately productive. As Bramhall reported on the 16th, it had been resolved to embark on a consultative exercise within the localities concerned in order to determine whether there was general support for abolition. Two documents ('papers') would be forwarded in advance of the summer assizes in certain counties. Representative panels of freeholders would be summoned to vote on the two documents – one for revoking the existing act of state (it was ever assumed that a single act of state was involved), the other for retaining it. If 'the greatest number' should vote in favour of the document supporting revocation, the act of state would be revoked.[62]

55 'Order of lord justices and council, 27 July 1622', Steele, *Tudor & Stuart proclam*, II, 24–5 (no. 238); 'H.M.'s directions, 1622', direction xxxiv. **56** *Lords' jn. Ire.*, i, 118. **57** 10 & 11 Chas I, c. 15. Penalties had originally been introduced by an act of state of 1606. **58** For clarification of this suggestion, see *Lords' jn. Ire.*, i, 133 (23 October 1640). **59** *Lords' jn. Ire.*, i, 120. **60** Ibid. **61** Ibid. **62** *Lords' jn. Ire.*, i, 121.

The plan was implemented in the summer of 1640. Significantly, it involved consultation with the counties of Ulster alone – Down, Armagh, Fermanagh, Cavan, Donegal, Londonderry, Tyrone, Antrim, Carrickfergus and Monaghan.[63] Problems connected with the operation of the custom in the first two named counties – Down and Armagh – had surfaced in the recent past, as we have had occasion to note. It is also worthy of mention that Monaghan, adjacent to Armagh, formed part of the territory of Irish Oriel governed by the agreement of 1297 to which the bishop of Clogher was a party – an agreement which recognised the operation of the custom at that early date. Wandesford and the council directed the sheriffs in the ten counties to summon 'a grand panel' of all 'the British freeholders' resident there to attend the assizes and, with the judges of assize presiding, to vote on the two documents. The judges of assize were to return the results to Wandesford in Dublin.[64] A conspicuous omission, in view of the non-discriminatory language of direction xxxiv in H.M.'s directions of 1622, was the failure to involve any Irish land-holders in the consultation exercise.

The plan envisaged the presence at the summer assizes of very large panels indeed. On 16 June, Bramhall intimated that as many as 24 freeholders for each barony were to be consulted. On 29 September, Wandesford and the council referred to there having been convened 'a grand panel' of all the British freeholders, which may have amounted to the same thing.[65]

At a meeting of the council held on 29 September the result of the exercise was made known. The judges of assize who had supervised it reported in person that the number of freeholders who wanted the act of state revoked far exceeded those who preferred retention of the status quo. Wandesford accordingly announced that the new act of state would be drawn up, repealing and annulling the original one (presumably that of 6 Edward VI).[66] The last stage in the saga was enacted shortly afterwards when the house of lords, aware of the result of the consultation exercise and of Wandesford's promised course of action, formally moved that the new act of state should be promulgated forthwith.

This formal petition incorporated other grievances of the lords. It sought suspension of the statute that proscribed ploughing by the tail and pulling wool off live sheep (which we have already encountered) but, in addition, both the statute that punished the burning of corn in the straw[67] and the statute that required the wearing of English apparel.[68] Suspension of all these measures was requested by way of a quid pro quo for approval of the subsidies the Irish parliament had recently voted for the king.

The opening passage of the petition dealt with the custom of tracts and, interestingly for our purposes, rehearses the reasons that commanded themselves to the lords in 1640 for urging adoption of an unusual Irish constitutional precedent (though not previously unknown) – the repeal of one act of state by another act of state:

63 See the reply of the lord deputy and council, 29 September 1640, printed in *Lords' jn. Ire.*, i, 133–4 (23 October 1640). **64** Ibid. **65** Bramhall's report to the house of lords, 16 June 1640: *Lords' jn. Ire.*, i, 121; Reply of the lord deputy and council, 29 September 1640: *Lords' jn. Ire.*, i, 133–4. **66** *Lords' jn. Ire*, i, 133–4. **67** 10 & 11 Chas. I, c. 17. **68** 28 Hen. VIII, c. 15.

> Whereas ordinances, advisedly constituted, may afterwards more advisedly be revoked according to the alteration of the times, as the act of state to recover goods stolen upon tracts, was sometimes commodious to planters, but is now found, by costly experience, to be a shelter for thieves, a burthen to the good subjects, and an occasion of much perjury ...[69]

The lords' petition is dated 23 October.[70] It is a safe assumption that the repealing act of state was enacted by Wandesford and the council shortly afterwards, and certainly before Wandesford's own death in December. No official entry of this, however, has been found; nor is the exact text known.

The trenchant language of the house of lords' petition notwithstanding, it is not altogether clear why the custom of tracts should have been abandoned in 1640, a conclusion, as I have indicated, we must reach. Nor is it clear whether it disappeared with a bang or with a whimper. The praises of the custom had been sung as recently as *c.*1610 by the anonymous author of 'The lawes of Irelande' and as recently as 1612 by a far less shadowy personage, the king himself. And in 1617, even reading between the lines, there is nothing to indicate that a mere thirteen years from the end the justices of the peace and the gentlemen of Co. Down had ceased to be enamoured of the custom and the procedures connected with its operation.

Evidence of skulduggery may indeed have played a part. Falsely insisting the trail ended at Whiteacre, falsely refusing to acknowledge the trail led on to Blackacre: such a lack of scruple on the part of the tracker, however professional his reputation, was bound, in the nature of things, to have serious repercussions. Incidents of this kind, when they occurred, naturally lent credence to the insinuation contained in the 'Instructions for the lord president and council of Munster' of 1615 that the system of self-help validated by the custom was essentially arbitrary. We may infer that that was Chichester's view, even if he himself is only formally on record as complaining about a different manifestation of skulduggery – the presentation of grossly inflated compensation claims.

It is indeed possible that the compensation system that came in the final stages to be linked to the functioning of the custom was a major factor in its undoing. There is no indication that the difficulties which Chichester highlighted in his apostils to the king's letter of March 1612 and in his letter to Humphrey May the following July were ever properly tackled. Crucial here was surely the lack of untrammelled legal authority to determine who exactly within a specific county was liable to contribute to any compensation fund for 'stealths'. Basing a power to tax on an outdated act of state had, in any event, probably begun to be regarded as constitutional anathema.

It was anomalous, of course, that in the final years the custom was restricted in its field of operations to the counties of Ulster. Anglicisation certainly entailed the extirpation of residues of brehon law, and it made little difference that, in terms of its pedigree, the custom may not have been properly placed in that category at all. That, for whatever reason – for purposes of political posturing or otherwise –, was how the

69 *Lords' jn. Ire.*, i, 133. 70 It was also ordered to be entered in the *Lords' jn.*: ibid.

custom of tracts had come to be regarded. Tanistry and gavelkind had already had sentence of death pronounced upon them.[71] In the new Ireland, could tracts survive in isolated splendour? But there was another facet to anglicisation. Could it continue to contrive to be tolerant of a regional variation which rankled in the administrator's breast and which prevented the country from being treated as a uniform legal entity?

Sir Nathaniel Rich, in his notes on the work of the commissioners of 1622, had pointed the way forward. The approach that was required was to institutionalise the system of hue and cry which in England had been regularised in 1275. The hint was to be taken in the Irish parliament in 1635 when new legislation was enacted to bring up to date existing Irish statute law dealing with the hue and cry.[72] This contained clear-cut provisions on the levying of the tax that constituted the compensation fund on which victims of theft could call. If no thief was caught after the raising of the hue and cry, the neighbourhood where the theft had taken place was obliged, as before, to contribute to that fund. There was a sweetener, however. If only one thief out of a larger band was apprehended, the community in question could breathe again: they would not have to set up any fund.[73] At the same time, fresh stimulus was given to adjacent neighbourhoods to join in the hue and cry when any trail led into their bailiwicks. Should they, uncitizenlike, decline to become involved and join the hunt, they were liable to incur financial penalties.[74]

Neither repeal of the act of state on tracts nor revival in an Irish context of the old hue and cry secured peace and harmony in the Irish countryside. Cattle rustling and the seizure of livestock gave every appearance of remaining endemic throughout the rest of the seventeenth century. By the eighteenth century, when a measure of political peace had been restored, the island was still fated to have to contend with sporadic outbreaks of unrest of one kind or another. From the perspective of the administration installed in Dublin Castle, the challenge to property was perceived to relate not so much to cattle and other livestock being rustled (which, of course, continued) but rather to their being maliciously injured – as was notorious in the instances of houghing of cattle. And thus there came into existence a fresh body of law – dealing again with a problem generated by conditions in the Irish countryside – which wrote yet another distinct chapter in the history of Irish law. The malicious injuries code was to be born.[75]

APPENDIX

In the absence of any first-hand account from a sixteenth- or seventeenth-century Irish tracker as to how he exercised his craft, regard may profitably be had to modern illumination of the topic. Bang and Dahlstrom's classic handbook, *Collins guide to animal tracks and signs*,[76] produced principally for the benefit of zoologists and naturalists,

71 H.S. Pawlisch, *Sir John Davies and the conquest of Ireland: a study in legal imperialism* (Cambridge, 1985), ch. 4. **72** 10 & 11 Chas. I, c. 13. **73** Section 6. **74** Section 1. **75** D.S. Greer and V.A. Mitchell, *Compensation for criminal damage to property* (Belfast, 1982), ch. 1. **76** Preben Bang and Preben Dahlstrom, *Collins guide to animal tracks and signs: a guide to the tracking of all British and European mammals and birds* (London, 1974). This represents a compendium of up-to-date information on every aspect of the problems associated with the tracking of animals. It is strongly recommended for consultation.

Bang makes a number of preliminary observations that, it is safe to assume, would have been equally accepted by the Irish tracker of the early modern period, of Oriel in the late thirteenth century, too, or even by those of Giolla na Naomh's acquaintance. Many animals, Bang notes, are creatures of habit, an assertion that has obvious implications for locating any trail at the outset:

> Most animals do not move at random round their home area, but have a network of paths or runs, which they follow most of the time and which they know well so that they can take flight along them when disturbed.[77]

Animals consulted their convenience too in their movements:

> According to the local conditions these paths will always take the route that is easiest for the animals, and so they will often be full of bends, and will skirt round tree-stumps, rocks and other obstacles.[78]

Insistence in the rules drawn up for Co. Down in 1617 that the tracking of stolen livestock be commenced at the earliest opportunity or not at all attracts the effective endorsement of Bang when he writes, sagely enough, that 'Most tracks and signs only last for quite a short time, and they usually become indistinct and then disappear quite quickly'.[79]

Tracks 'are best followed when the ground is covered with snow'; ideal snow conditions for this purpose are then described.[80] The comparative rarity of snow in Ireland's winters inevitably entailed that the professional Irish tracker had ordinarily to contend with considerable difficulties on the ground when following any trail, in short, had to display that 'incredible cunning' he was reputed to possess. Here, the trackers' knowledge of the marks left behind by retreating cattle, horses, goats and sheep[81] must have played a vital role. So too, necessarily, must have their capacity to attribute the stripping of the bark off trees, where this had occurred, to goats and sheep,[82] and to identify the source and, employing a sense of smell as well as their eyesight, the freshness of whatever animal droppings they may have encountered during any pursuit.[83]

guide was originally published (in Danish) under the title *Dyrespor* in Denmark in 1972. **77** Bang & Dahlstrom, op. cit., p. 20. **78** Ibid. **79** Bang & Dahlstrom, op. cit., p. 6. **80** Id., p. 7. **81** For Dahlstrom's illustrations of these, see id., pp 73-4. **82** Id., p. 92. **83** Id., pp 169, 171, 185.

The Legislation of the Pre-Union Irish Parliament

Legislation constitutes a prime source of law in the modern legal system. (It is a trite observation, perhaps, but bears repetition nevertheless.) In today's duo of Irish jurisdictions, the Republic of Ireland and Northern Ireland, legislation thus takes its place alongside the other prime sources – decisions of the courts (the judges), writings of legal authors (the jurists), laws emanating from Europe, and, in the Republic alone, provisions of the Constitution.

Under modern constitutional dispensations, legislation is to be understood as the laws enacted by a representative assembly or parliament. In this sense, it enjoys a long ancestry in England and Ireland, but developments of major significance were required before statute law in its recognisable contemporary dress could be said to have come of age. First, the practice had to evolve of regularly summoning an advisory body – of regularly calling a parliament – to assist with the government of the kingdom, in the case of England, or of the lordship, in that of Ireland. Here, it is prudent to recall that the establishment of precise dates for many constitutional innovations is frequently no easy matter. It is plain, for example, that when the word 'parliament' itself is first encountered in thirteenth-century records, it is being employed in a wholly non-technical fashion. As regards the medieval lordship of Ireland, the first apparent use of the word relates to a 'parliament' held at Clandermot, Co. Cork, in 1234, but the earliest unambiguous reference comes thirty years later, in 1264, when we learn that the justiciar (or chief governor) consulted with a ministerial council composed of treasurer, chancellor, escheator and two others at Castledermot in Co. Kildare. Five further 'parliaments' are recorded before 1289, but the first mention of elected representatives – knights of the shire – in attendance only occurs in 1297. Two years later, representatives of the towns are stated to be present as well.[1] But change was still gradual. As late as 1345, for instance, we know that a parliament might be convened in Ireland which consisted exclusively of ministers, prelates and magnates.[2] And the picture is further confused, certainly until late in the fifteenth century, through resort to the frequent practice of summoning what was denominated a 'great council' with legislative powers, as opposed to a 'parliament'.

For a parliament to be entitled to the specific designation, the convention was eventually established, in the course of the reign of Edward III (1327-77), that representatives of the shires and of the towns had to be included. In Ireland, as in England,

1 J.A.Watt 'The first recorded use of the word "parliament" in Ireland', *Ir. Jur.*, 4 (1969), 122. **2** H.G. Richardson and G.O. Sayles (eds.), *Parliaments and councils of medieval Ireland*, i (Irish Mss. Comm., Dublin, 1947), p. xvi.

two distinct chambers were set to emerge – the upper (a house of lords) and the lower (a house of commons). Over the centuries, too, the law and practice governing parliamentary representation underwent various vicissitudes. In the history of the pre-Union Irish parliament, two crucial departures from arrangements previously obtaining may be signalled. Under Henry VIII (1509-47) the proctors, or representatives of the lower clergy, were formally excluded,[3] and early in the eighteenth century (if not before) Catholics came to be disbarred as well. The proctors never returned and Catholics only again became entitled to sit on the passing of Catholic Emancipation in 1829.[4] By then, as is well known, the parliament in College Green in Dublin had ceased to exist.

Secondly, it had also to come to be accepted that a primary function of this representative assembly was to make new laws. There were two principal aspects to this. For a start, it needs to be appreciated, as Richardson and Sayles pointed out in their classic survey of the medieval Irish parliament,[5] that that parliament transacted a great deal of business of an administrative or even judicial variety: the doctrine of the separation of powers lay very far over the horizon. Parliament's primacy as a law-maker was only established when this other business began to diminish in both quantity and importance, with administrative tasks being transferred to the nascent civil service and the judicial tasks being handed over to, or being assumed by, the likes of the court of chancery or the privy council sitting as a court of law.

But, in addition, it has to be understood that these changes occurred in tandem with another major development: the progressive surrender by the king of pretensions to a law-making power in his own right. Before parliament's primary role in the matter of the making of laws gained constitutional acceptance, the creation of a new law was the prerogative of the king (acting with his council) who would promulgate such law by means of his writ or mandate. The first 'statute', dated 1204, included in a published collection of early Irish legislation,[6] turns out, on closer inspection, to be a writ (or instruction) from the king (John, 1199-1216), conferring upon his justiciar in Ireland an entitlement to issue, for purposes of the commencement of legal proceedings, five standard common law writs on the latter's own initiative. The so-called Statute of Mortmain of 1279, a measure originally intended, it would appear, to apply exclusively in England, is revealed, by like analysis, as a writ addressed to the judges of the common bench telling them how to handle a pressing contemporary problem – the alienation of excessive amounts of land into the hands of the church.[7] 'Writs', 'mandates', 'ordinances', 'statutes': the alteration in nomenclature is both baffling and troublesome. The beginning of wisdom is to understand that the alteration reflects changes in the record-keeping practices of the medieval government clerk no less than coexistence of councils and parliaments, innovation in parliamentary procedure and the changing balance of power between the king and his subjects. An exact chronology is again impossible, as H.F. Berry, in his introduction to the collection of early

3 28 Hen. VIII, c. 12 (*Stat. Ire.*, i, 102): an act against proctors to be any member of the parliament. **4** 10 Geo. IV, c. 7: an act for the relief of his majesty's Roman Catholic subjects. The crucial provision is s. 2. **5** H.G. Richardson and G.O. Sayles, *The Irish parliament in the middle ages* (Philadelphia, 1952). **6** *Stat. Ire., John-Hen. V*, ed. H.F. Berry (Dublin, 1907). **7** The statute *de viris religiosis*: 7 Edw. I (*Stat. of realm*, i, 51).

Irish legislation alluded to above, was constrained to admit. 'At what period,' Berry wrote,

> or in what reign the king's ordinances completely yielded to the more constitutional authority of parliamentary enactment has never yet been precisely ascertained.[8]

By the time of the Reformation in the sixteenth century, parliament's central role in the enactment of legislation had come to be accepted as a key element in the evolving constitutional scheme of things. Even so, the royal prerogative remained an alternative fountain of law. Nowhere within the king's dominions was this more evidently true than in Ireland. It was under the prerogative that, in England, in 1534, ordinances for the government of Ireland were drawn up, uniquely, for the time, printed, and despatched to Ireland for observance there.[9] An even more telling example is linked to the pattern of infrequent Irish parliaments which establishes itself under the Tudors and which persists into the seventeenth century. That pattern forced adoption of the expedient of legislation in the name of the Irish lord deputy and privy council (the *alter ego* of the king) – the so-called acts of state. The crucial importance of this device in the Irish government of the period cannot be gainsaid. In 1578, at the height of the controversy over cess,[10] the English privy council advised Sir Henry Sidney, the Irish lord deputy of the day, that the calling of an Irish parliament, as Sir Henry had proposed, was 'un-needful', and proceeded to observe that

> it is thought many of the things required to passe by Parliament may be as sufficiently perfected by order of the Lord Deputy and Councill.[11]

From what is known of the detailed direction of Irish government business, both in the 1570s and for many years subsequently, the privy council in London knew very well what they were talking about, and they were indeed on safe ground. For the moment at least.

By the Restoration in 1660 the practice of introducing legislation under the protective guise of acts of state had met effective constitutional opposition in Ireland from the judicial bench.[12] The king in person, however, still retained the power to modify statute law duly adopted by his parliaments, through the exercise of his suspending and dispensing powers. These were prerogatives that William and Mary were obliged to forswear when the crown was offered jointly to them in 1689, following the flight of James II late the previous year. What exactly they gave up – itself, conversely, a

8 *Stat. Ire., John-Hen. V*, p. viii. Berry's observations are repeated by Johnston J in his judgment in *Little* v. *Cooper* [1937] IR 1 at 20. See further on these matters H.G. Richardson and George Sayles, 'The early statutes', *Law Quarterly Review*, 50 (1934), 201, 540. **9** *S.P. Hen. VIII*, ii, 207-16. **10** J.G. Crawford, *Anglicizing the government of Ireland: the Irish privy council and the expansion of Tudor rule, 1556-1578* (Dublin, 1993), pp 369-407. **11** *Walsingham letter-book, 1578-1579*, ed. J. Hogan and N.M. O'Farrell (Irish Mss. Comm., Dublin, 1959), p. 1. **12** See the letter to the duke of Ormonde, 27 Apr. 1661, quoted in L.J. Arnold, *The restoration land settlement in county Dublin, 1660-1688* (Dublin, 1993), p. 43.

measure of the victory that the English parliament had accomplished – is spelt out in detail in the relevant clauses of the Bill of Rights of 1689.[13]

Anomalies were also destined to leave their mark on the evolving shape of constitutional government. In England and Ireland alike legislative force was conventionally to be extended to parliamentary initiatives never reduced to statutory legal form, least of all one involving the attachment of any royal assent. In England, the Petition of Right of 1628 was thus regarded from the outset as possessing the undiluted force of law.[14] In Ireland, the like treatment was to be accorded the house of commons resolution of 18 March 1736 exempting pasturage from the payment of tithe (agistment tithe),[15] a resolution famously excoriated by Jonathan Swift in his verses on 'The Legion Club':

> Could I, from the building's top,
> Hear the rolling thunder drop,
> While the devil upon the roof
> (if the devil be thunder proof)
> Should, with poker fiery red,
> Crack the stones and melt the lead;
> Drive them down on every skull,
> When the den of thieves is full;
> Quite destroy the harpies nest;
> How might then our isle be blest!

The relationship of the English parliament *vis-à-vis* the parliament of Ireland has left an indelible imprint on the history of legislation in Ireland, and that relationship accordingly merits a word of explanation. At intervals, during the existence of the Irish parliament, its members would assert the claim that their parliament was the equal in every respect of its English progenitor. This occurs in 1460 in the midst of the Wars of the Roses and the rivalry between Yorkists and Lancastrians, in 1640–1 at the close, and in the aftermath, of Wentworth's controversial lord deputyship, in 1689 during the sittings of James II's Irish parliament and, with increasing frequency in the eighteenth century prior to 1782, whenever an appropriate opportunity presented itself. The precise claim most commonly urged on these occasions was Ireland's entitlement to legislative independence, in short, that the very *raison d'être* of the Irish parliament was for it alone to make laws for Ireland and, as a necessary corollary, that the English

13 1 Will. III & Mary II, sess. 2, c. 2 (*Stat. at large*, iii, 275). As is mentioned below, no Bill of Rights was ever enacted by the pre-Union Irish parliament and the extent to which the constitutional constraints imposed upon the executive power of the crown in England by virtue of the Bill of Rights operated in the Irish context is unclear. **14** L.J. Reeve, 'The legal status of the Petition of Right', *Historical Journal*, 29 (1986), 257. **15** *Commons' jn. Ire.*, iv, pt. 1, 219. (The reference is to the 2nd ed.) And see further the 'Report from the committee appointed to take into consideration the petition of Samuel Low and others, in behalf of themselves and the rest of the gentlemen land-holders in this kingdom [in regard to agistment tithe], 18 Mar. 1735/36', *Commons' jn. Ire.*, iv, pt. 2, lxv–lxx. Agistment tithe was eventually formally proscribed in the dying months of the old Irish parliament – 40 Geo. III, c. 23 (*Stat. Ire.*, xx, 338): an act to quiet and bar all claims of tythe agistment for dry and barren cattle.

parliament lacked any authority or mandate to ignore this by seeking to enact laws binding the smaller country. The language in which such constitutional claims was couched is naturally of some interest. In 1460 the Irish commons grounded its contention on the proposition that 'the land of Ireland' was and at all times had been 'corporate of itself', and, consequently, was

> by the ancient laws and customs used in the same, freed of the burthen of any special law of the realm of England, save only such laws as by the lords spiritual and temporal and the commons of the said land had been in Great Council or Parliament there held, admitted, accepted, affirmed and proclaimed, according to sundry ancient statutes thereof made.[16]

The Irish parliament's claim was to receive its definitive statement with the publication by William Molyneux in 1698 in Dublin of his important tract, *The case of Ireland's being bound by acts of parliament in England, stated*, a tract which, in fact, aspired to maintain the opposite proposition – that Ireland neither was, nor should be, so bound. Protests from Ireland then, before and later notwithstanding, the English parliament asserted, and continued to assert, a power to legislate for Ireland, if need be without the latter's consent. The Declaratory Act of 1720 – the 6th of George I[17] – enthroned this rival constitutional doctrine which, as it happens, was buttressed by more precedents and a longer practical expression than Molyneux and others who thought like him were probably prepared to concede. In 1782-3, the British parliament repealed the Declaratory Act,[18] and passed a Renunciation Act,[19] and Irish legislative independence was firmly assured.

For present purposes, it is essential to draw attention to one facet of this unusual history, namely, that down to 1782 legislation adopted by the Irish parliament and legislation adopted by the English parliament and extending to and binding Ireland were co-equal sources of statute law in Ireland. Sometimes, indeed, the word 'co-equal' is a misnomer, for the English laws operative in Ireland might prove of greater practical significance. So much can certainly be said in respect of such measures as the Treason Act 1351,[20] the various acts passed in England regulating the consequences of the Reformation in the sixteenth century and that precede their Irish equivalents, those passed in England during the Interregnum and those dealing with the consequences of the Williamite victory at the Boyne, in the middle and at the end of the seventeenth

16 *Stat. Ire., Hen. VI*, ed. H.F. Berry (Dublin, 1910), p. 645. **17** 6 Geo. I, c. 5 (*Stat. at large*, iv, 481): an act for the better securing the dependency of the kingdom of Ireland upon the crown of Great Britain. See further Isolde Victory, 'The making of the 1720 Declaratory Act', in Gerard O'Brien (ed.), *Parliament, politics and people: essays in 18th-century Irish history* (Dublin, 1989), p. 9. **18** 22 Geo. III, c. 53 (*Stat. at large*, viii, 153): an act to repeal an act made in the sixth year of the reign of his late majesty King George the First, intituled, an act for the better securing the dependency of the kingdom of Ireland upon the crown of Great Britain. **19** 23 Geo. III, c. 28 (*Stat. at large*, viii, 226): an act for removing and preventing all doubts, which have arisen, or might arise, concerning the exclusive rights of the parliament and courts of Ireland, in matters of legislation and judicature; and for preventing any writ of error or appeal from any of his majesty's courts in that kingdom from being received, heard and adjudged, in any of his majesty's courts in the kingdom of Great Britain. **20** 25 Edw. III, stat. 5, c. 2 (*Stat. of realm*, i, 319-20, 324).

century, respectively. As regards an earlier epoch one pronouncement has been even less equivocal:

> In theory Irish courts had to administer two bodies of statutes, Irish and English, but there is no question as to the far greater importance of English statutes in the reigns of the first two Edwards [i.e. 1272-1327].[21]

The inferior constitutional standing of the Irish parliament had other consequences. Between 1495 and 1782, by virtue of Poynings' Law enacted in the former year,[22] the English privy council exercised immense control over the autonomy of the Irish legislature and the freedom of action of Ireland's chief governor. The law laid down that no Irish parliament could be summoned until the Irish privy council had first certified to its English counterpart the legislative proposals it was hoping to see enacted and the latter had signified its consent, in other words, had imposed no veto. As has often been noted, these provisions were unremarkable for their time. No parliament in England could meet without the approval of the king and his council, and when it met, it still possessed no initiative, at least not before the very end of the Tudor period.[23] However this may be, the constitutional arrangements introduced in 1495 endured until 1782, and, with the passage of years, increasingly irked despite the acceptance of modifications in practice such as the acknowledgment of a right of initiation of draft legislation in the Irish commons by means of the heads of bill procedure.[24] Though the Irish statute-book starts to fill rapidly in the eighteenth century, it is clear that a very large number of legislative proposals including, undoubtedly, many desirable reforms, did not prosper, and the obvious inference to draw is that opposition within the Irish privy council or within the English, or, perhaps, the delays apparently inseparable from the scrupulous observance of the Poynings' Law procedure, will have been responsible. No Irish Bill of Rights along the lines of the English measure of 1689 or its Scots equivalent of the same year, was ever enacted. Yet we learn from the *Journals* of both the Irish house of lords and the Irish house of commons that two projects to pass an Irish Bill of Rights, intended very obviously to be taken seriously, were actually set on foot.[25]

A second act adopted by Poynings' parliament at Drogheda in 1494-5 affirmed the lower standing of the Irish legislature. At the same time it also imported an extra tranche of English statute law into the corpus of legislation deemed to be in force in Ireland. The act in question incorporated into Irish law at one fell swoop all acts of

21 G.J. Hand, *English law in Ireland, 1290-1324* (Cambridge, 1967), p. 159. **22** An act that no parliament be holden in this land until the acts be certified into England: 10 Hen. VII, c. 4 (*Stat. Ire.*, i, 44). For the background, see Richardson & Sayles, *Ir. parl. in middle ages*, ch. 17. **23** G.B. Adams, *Constitutional history of England* (New York, 1921), p. 252. **24** D.B. Quinn, 'Early interpretation of Poynings' law, 1494-1534', *Irish Historical Studies*, 2 (1941), 241; R.D. Edwards and T.W. Moody, 'History of Poynings' law, 1494-1615', *IHS*, 2 (1941), 415; Aidan Clarke, 'The history of Poynings' law, 1615-41', *IHS*, 18 (1972-3), 207; Mary Hayden, 'The origin and development of heads of bills in the Irish parliament', *RSAI Jn*, 55 (1925), 112; T.J. Kiernan, *History of the financial administration of Ireland to 1817* (London, 1930), chs. 1-3, 6. For the commons' right of initiation, see the opinion of the Irish judges on the reference to them by Lord Lieutenant Sidney in 1692, reprinted in G.E. Howard, *Miscellaneous works*, 3 vols. (Dublin, 1782), iii, 193-204. **25** See my 'The failure to enact an Irish Bill of Rights: a gap in Irish constitutional history', *Ir Jur*, 33 (1988), 392.

parliament 'late made' in England concerning 'the common and publique weal' which had not previously been introduced into Ireland.[26] The precise import of this remarkable omnibus provision has been examined both by A.G. Donaldson and, more recently, by Steven Ellis.[27] A degree of uncertainty attached both in the late 1490s and, indeed, in subsequent years as to which particular English statutes became effective in Ireland by virtue of the Irish act of 1495. That uncertainty was fated to endure: as late as 1838, for instance, a debate of exceptional quality was conducted in the United Kingdom house of lords as to the possible impact of the act of 1495 on the procedures for choosing sheriffs in Ireland.[28]

To summarise: the technical complications as to what might constitute the statute law in force in Ireland were substantial. There was the legislation enacted by the Irish parliament itself, of course, but, in addition, several species of English legislation might also be operative – legislation deliberately extending to Ireland, legislation extended by special writ, and legislation made applicable in 1495 that was both 'late made' and concerned 'the common and publique weal'.

II

It is equally important to be aware that the arrangements for preserving a knowledge of this statute law, whether of Irish or English origin, could face severe hazards. If we concentrate on the statutes of Irish provenance,[29] the position was that statute rolls only began to be kept in the reign of Henry VI (1422-71). Whilst these were reasonably complete down to 1800 (until their destruction in 1922),[30] there were certain omissions: it was known, for instance, that the roll for 1499 had been stolen and that for 1516 mutilated.[31] H.F. Berry, who between 1907 and 1914 edited the first three volumes in the early Irish statutes series, was obliged to cast his net very widely in both England and Ireland in order to locate the texts of measures enacted by the Irish parliament before the start of the statute rolls or even later where it was evident that lacunae existed in the official sources.[32] The first printed edition of Irish statutes – a selection going back to the reign of Henry IV (1399-1413) – was only produced in

26 An act confirming all the statutes made in England: 10 Hen. VII, c. 22 (*Stat. Ire.*, i, 56). **27** A.G. Donaldson, 'The application in Ireland of English and British legislation made before 1801' (unpublished Ph.D. thesis, Queen's University Belfast, 1952), pp 174-84; S.G. Ellis, 'Parliament and community in Yorkist and Tudor Ireland', in *Parliament and community* (*Historical Studies XIV*), eds. Art Cosgrove and J.I. McGuire (Belfast 1983), p. 43. For a judicial airing of the problem see the remarks of Kennedy CJ in *R. (Moore)* v. *O'Hanrahan* [1927] IR 406 at 422-4. **28** *Hansard 3*, xliii, cols. 989-1043: 25 June 1838. See especially the earl of Mulgrave at col. 1012, Lord Brougham at cols. 1022-3 and Lord Plunkett at col. 1043. For the political background, see D.S. Johnson, 'The trials of Sam Gray: Monaghan politics and 19th century Irish criminal procedure', *Irish Jurist*, 20 (1985), 109. **29** The introduction to *The statutes of the realm*, 11 vols. (London, 1810-28) contains a helpful synopsis of the manner in which, in the medieval period, English legislation applying in Ireland was promulgated and publicised: *Stat. of realm*, i, intro., p. xlv. **30** A single statute roll, that for the session 28-9 Henry VIII, survived the conflagration at the Public Record Office in 1922. **31** Quinn, op. cit., note 33 below, at 49. **32** See Berry's preface to *Stat. Ire., John-Hen. V* and *Stat. Ire., Hen. VI.*

1572. It is a fair assumption that prior to that anything approaching a detailed acquaintance with the totality of native statute law must have been a rarity.

Reliance on the statute rolls, on copies of individual enactments and on transcripts entered into books maintained for reference purposes by clerks in the exchequer, for instance, with attendant proclamations as appropriate, was no satisfactory basis for government intent not only on preserving a proper record of statute law but also on spreading an awareness of its content. The invention of printing in Europe in the second half of the fifteenth century pointed the way forward: to arrange for the printing of the statutes in an edition of sufficient size to satisfy estimated official and professional need. In the case of Ireland, what was a trifle unusual, though by no means unprecedented, was the length of time it took to accomplish a project which, from the government's point of view, it is hard to believe could not have been regarded as other than eminently desirable.[33]

The question of printing an edition of the Irish statutes first appears to have been broached in 1537. That year, one of the Irish judges, Thomas Luttrell, in a representation to Anthony St Leger, recently chosen to inquire into the state of Ireland, and destined three years later to commence a long stint as lord deputy, urged the latter to support an initiative. 'Fewe or none', Luttrell wrote, could have knowledge of the statutes passed in Ireland 'because they be kept in the Tresaurye, and no bookes made of them'. Many individuals, Luttrell insisted, had in consequence broken the law 'for ignoraunce'.[34] If Luttrell hoped for swift action, he was disappointed. Though the question was re-examined intermittently thereafter, it was only in the late 1560s that action at long last seemed probable. Sir Henry Sidney, lord deputy at the time, was an enthusiast as was Sir William Cecil in London. An edition of Scottish statutes was brought out in 1566 and the following year Cecil forwarded a copy of it to Sidney.[35] Two years later, the claim that the failure to print the Irish statutes had caused the latter to be turned 'into oblivion' seems finally to have stung the government into action.[36] The Irish privy council, with assistance from the Irish judges, made a selection of statutes from the then extant rolls and other available sources and sent the selection to the English privy council for approval. This was forthcoming, and in 1572 the first printed edition of the Irish statutes appeared from the well-known London printing-house of Richard Tottell.[37] Though a great deal of effort had gone into the production of this volume, the latter itself did not sell well, and in 1573 the English privy council, anxious to dispose of the stock still on their hands, wrote to their Irish counterpart, urging the adoption of a scheme under which copies of the edition

> maye apon reasonable prices be disposed in the Corporate townes Seneshalshipps and other Jurisdiccions of that Realme, so that the learned men and other people of the countery maye have most notice of the same.[38]

33 See generally D.B. Quinn's survey, 'Government printing and the publication of the Irish statutes in the sixteenth century', *Proceedings of the Royal Irish Academy*, 49 (1943), sect. C, 45. **34** *S.P. Hen. VIII*, ii, 509–10. **35** Quinn. 'Publication of Ir. statutes in 16th century', 53. **36** Ibid., 53–5. **37** *In this volume are contained all the statutes from the tenthe yere of King Henry the sixt, to the xiii. yere of … Queene Elyzabeth made and established in … Irelande* (London, 1572). **38** Quoted, Quinn, 'Publication of Ir. statutes in the 16th century', 56.

A unique copy of the 1572 edition survives in Cambridge University Library.

That the 1572 edition of the Irish statutes was a selection only, and by no means definitive, was recognised from the outset. James I (1603–25) was aware of this, and made use of the knowledge to upbraid his Irish council during the Irish parliament of 1613 to 1615, a parliament over the preparations for which we learn from Sir Edward Coke James took a great deal of care.[39] Under the Poynings' Law procedure the English privy council had received from its Irish equivalent the draft of a bill designed to repeal existing statute law that discriminated against the native Irish. James complained to Dublin that the draft contained no listing of the precise measures scheduled for repeal. The omission, the king declared,

> as in all cases of weight, was no better than walking in darkness, so much more in this case, for that it was informed unto us, that the printed Booke of Statutes of Ireland, which wee have in this Kingdome, is no perfect register of all the Actes of Parliament there, but that there may be many publique Acts in the Records there, not printed in the sayd book.[40]

The criticism was heeded. The two statutes repealing discriminatory laws, one passed in the reign of James I, the other in that of Charles I, both listed the exact measures it was intended to set aside.[41]

The royal rebuke was also taken note of by Sir Richard Bolton, who brought out the next important edition of Irish statute law in Dublin in 1621.[42] Bolton, recorder of Dublin at the time but who was to become chief baron in 1625 and lord chancellor in 1639, started his collection in the reign of Edward II, well over a century earlier than the edition of 1572. Bolton made much of the difference, writing in his epistle dedicatorie (or preface) of his discovery that

> many good Statute-lawes, of force in this Kingdome, were neuer hitherto imprinted, and … that, for want of imprinting, many others are perished and lost, in those troublesom and miserable times of rebellion, which haue beene in this Kingdome.[43]

39 *Case of the parliament of Ireland* (1613) 12 Co. Rep. 110; 77 Eng. Rep 1386. **40** *Acts of the privy council, 1615-1616*, p. 79. **41** Act of repeale of diverse statutes concerning the natives of this kingdom of Ireland, 11, 12 & 13 Jas I, c. 5 (*Stat. Ire.*, i, 441); an act for repeale of divers statutes heretofore enacted in this kingdome of Ireland, 10 & 11 Chas. I, c. 6 (*Stat. Ire.*, ii, 153). These two acts were in turn removed from the statute book by the Statute Law Revision (Ireland) Act 1878. It is unfortunate that, in consequence, the grandiloquent Jacobean prose of the prelude to the operative words of repeal in the earlier statute is a good deal less likely to be encountered nowadays. Its section 5 prescribed (in part): 'And for as much as there is no better means to settle peace and tranquilitie in this kingdome, being now inhabited with many worthy persons borne in his Majestie's said several kingdoms, than by abolishing and abrogating of the said several lawes, and by giving them free libertie to commerce and match together, that so they may grow into one nation, whereby there may be an utter oblivion and extinguishment of all former differences and discorde betwixt them …' **42** *The statutes of Ireland beginning the third yere of K. Edward the second and continuing untill the end of the parliament, begunn in the eleventh yeare of … King James, and ended in the thirteenth yere …*, ed. Sir Richard Bolton (Dublin, 1621). There is a good entry on Bolton in the *Dictionary of national biography*. **43** Ibid., epis-

But if Bolton made certain additions, these amounted to little enough, and the effective 'canon' of early Irish legislation was that established by the edition of 1572. It was this canon with such additions as were made by Bolton that, in respect of the medieval and early modern period, directed the work and dictated the choice of Francis Vesey, the barrister who edited the next important collection of Irish statutes, the first folio edition, that began publication in 1765.[44]

With the establishment of the Irish Record Commission in 1810, the prospect of the production of a definitive edition of all the traceable early Irish statutes was brought much closer.[45] Preliminary research was undertaken, but in 1824 the plan was abandoned, largely, one presumes, on grounds of expense. By then, however, definitive editions of both the English and Scottish statute books had been published,[46] and the abandonment of the Irish project attracted the anger of contemporaries. In 1854, J.T. Gilbert, describing the situation in regard to the early Irish statutes, complained that

> upwards of 1,200 were still unpublished, though the ancient legal institutes of England, Scotland and Wales have long since been published at the public expense.[47]

The opening of the Irish Public Record Office in 1867 led to a revival of the project, but it was only in 1901 that Treasury sanction was ultimately obtained. Since then four volumes of an early Irish statutes series have been published by the Record Office (now the National Archives): *John-Henry V*, ed. H.F. Berry (1907); *Henry VI*, ed. Berry (1810); *1-12 Edward IV*, ed. Berry (1914); *12-22 Edward IV*, ed. J.F. Morrissey (1939). A final volume covering the reigns of Richard III, Henry VII and Henry VIII is, after many delays, now scheduled to appear in the near future. Here, many lacunae are to be anticipated.[48] Pending the appearance of this final volume in the early Irish statutes series, reference may be made to a helpful guide and lists prepared by D.B. Quinn, as supplemented by S.G. Ellis.[49]

tle dedicatorie. **44** *The statutes at large, passed in the parliaments held in Ireland from the third year of Edward the second A.D. 1310, to the first year of George the third AD 1761, inclusive*, ed. Francis Vesey, 8 vols. (Dublin, 1765). Vol. viii of this edition was an index volume. Research has shown (C. Benson and M. Pollard, ' "The rags of Ireland are by no means the same": Irish paper used in the Statutes at Large', *Long Room*, 2 (1970), 18) that three further volumes were produced in this first folio edition, making a total of 11 volumes published between 1765 and 1782. **45** Margaret Griffith, 'The Irish Record Commission, 1810-1830', *IHS*, 7 (1950-1), 17. **46** The English (and from 1707, British) statutes down to 1713 (*Stat. of realm*) were published in nine vols. between 1810 and 1822 (though the edition was only completed with the publication of index vols. in 1828), the Scottish statutes from 1424 to 1707 in eleven vols. between 1814 and 1824. **47** J.T. Gilbert, *History of the city of Dublin*, 3 vols. (Dublin, 1854-9), i, p. xiv. **48** Prior to the destruction of the public records in 1922 transcripts had been made of only a fraction of the statute rolls then extant for the period in question. The statute roll for 28-9 Henry VIII survived, as has already been noted. Otherwise, inevitably, there are many gaps. **49** D.B. Quinn, 'The bills and statutes of the Irish parliaments of Henry VII and Henry VIII', *Anal. Hib.*, 10 (1941), 71; S.G. Ellis, 'Parliaments and great councils, 1483-99: addenda and corrigenda', *Anal. Hib.*, 29 (1980), 96. These two surveys contain information as to where the texts of individual statutes not printed in any official collection but reproduced elsewhere may actually be found. For legislation enacted at Poynings' parliament at Drogheda in 1494-5, they thus both take account of the material printed in Agnes Conway, *Henry VII's relations with Scotland and Ireland 1485-1498* (Cambridge, 1932): see in that vol. the appendices and ch. 7 (by Edmund Curtis). One additional discovery may be here recorded.

Under the Commonwealth (1649-60), the Irish parliament was suppressed. Representatives from Ireland sat in the parliament in England, and that assembly passed acts and ordinances that had direct immediate effect in Ireland.[50] On the restoration of Charles II in 1660, the Irish parliament was revived, and in 1678, to meet the need that had arisen in the interval, a second edition of Bolton's collection of 1621 was published. This 1678 edition contained all subsequent acts of the Irish parliament down to and including those passed during the session 17 & 18 Charles II. The edition thus included the texts of the Act of Settlement of 1662 (14 & 15 Chas. II, sess. 4, c. 2; *Stat. Ire.*, ii, 239) and of the Act of Explanation of 1665 (17 & 18 Chas. II, c. 2; *Stat. Ire.*, iii, 2), adding immeasurably, of course, to its utility but also to its bulk. Though a reprint was put in hand in 1723, this contained no additional statute law at all. In the interim a new departure in the arrangements for printing the Irish statutes had been introduced, and it is to these that we must now turn.

III

The office of king's printer in Ireland had been inaugurated late in the reign of Elizabeth I (1558-1603).[51] The first patents created a commercial monopoly, and, whilst from the end of the seventeenth century it became impossible for the holder of the office to prevent others from setting up as printers in Ireland, the king's printer still retained the sole and exclusive right to undertake government printing, the statutes included. After the Williamite wars, and as sessions of the Irish parliament became much more frequent, the king's printer instituted the practice of printing at the close of each parliamentary session the statutes enacted during it. These sessional collections

The full text of the act of 1495 for cancelling records done in the name of Edward VI (the title Lambert Simnel took when he was crowned in Christ Church cathedral, Dublin, on 24 May 1487) is set down in W.M. Mason, *History and antiquities of the cathedral church of St Patrick near Dublin* (Dublin, 1820), p. 343, n. 1. The act is 10 Hen. VII, c. 14 in Quinn's listing (see above); the chapter numbers do not correspond with those employed in the official printed editions, e.g., *Stat. Ire.* The act in question reads as follows: 'Item, prayen the comens, that in consideracion of the great and dampnable abusion and errour that was of late had in the coronynge of the Ladde withyn the land of Irelande, contrary to their naturall duyties and allegeaunce, and over that, dyd kepe courtees parliamentes, and made styles and processe in the Laddes name; that it be ordeigned, enacted and establisshed by auctoritie of this present parliament, that all and every maner recordes, processes, stiles, pardons, lyveries, actes, and ordenaunces of counseill, and all maner actes, kept, made, had, and don, in the said Laddes name bee cancyllyd, revoked, adnulled, and demyd void, and of noon effect in lawe, and who soever person or persons don kepe counseill or recyve any of the said recordes, processes, stiles, pardons, lyveries, or any other actis or ordenauncez as before is specified, after a certeyn proclamacion ther uppon to be made, that then, he or they that so to do, be demyd, be the same auctorite, traytour attaynted. [signed] Le Sr Deputic le voit.' **50** W.R. Scott, 'Members for Ireland in the parliaments of the Protectorate', *Journal of the Royal Society of Antiquaries of Ireland*, 23 (1983), 73; *Acts and ordinances of the Interregnum 1642-1660*, eds. G.H. Firth and R.S. Rait, 3 vols. (London, 1911), passim, but see especially ii, 494-5, for the text of an ordinance of 25 Dec. 1650 applying recent English legislation to Ireland. **51** M. Pollard, 'Control of the press in Ireland through the king's printer's patent, 1600-1800', *Irish Booklore*, 4, no. 2 (1980), 79; J.W. Hammond, 'The king's printers in Ireland, 1551-1919', *Dublin Hist. Rec.*, 11 (1950-1), 29, 58, 88.

were printed in black type, the type that featured in the various editions of Bolton's statutes. The departure had its teething problems. Andrew Crooke, who held the office of king's printer from 1693 to 1731, by no means gave universal satisfaction, for instance. In 1725, he was formally rebuked by the Irish house of lords for his tardiness in producing the then outstanding set of sessional statutes and also for printing sets on paper of inferior quality.[52] The reprimand was repeated in identical terms in 1730.[53] (Interestingly, in 1717, Crooke had also been officially rebuked for errors in the printed text of a lord lieutenant's speech.)[54]

Over time, these new arrangements proved much less of a boon than had been predicted. The succession of supplementary volumes, 'of different Sizes and in different Types, without Indexes or any aid to find the Contents or even the Titles', Francis Vesey tells us in 1765,[55] made the business of discovering what Irish statute law actually was fraught with difficulty. A not dissimilar problem, as it happens, was described by all those who in earlier epochs had been associated with projects for printing the statutes. In 1621, Bolton, for one, assures us that, from experience, he had found

> that the printed books of those Statutes which were formerly printed, are so few, that there bee not sufficient to furnish only the practisers and Iudges of the Law; so as both the comon people, and some of the professors of the Law, yea the Iudges themselves, did want the ordinarie meanes to attaine to the knowledge of the Statute-lawes.[56]

Bolton went on to observe that, in these circumstances, those who wished to familiarise themselves with the *ipsissima verba* of Irish statutes were 'constrained verie often, to have recourse to the Parliament Rolls'.[57] What is interesting as respects the same problem, identified as such by Vesey for the first half of the eighteenth century, is that there is some evidence, admittedly slight, that recourse was then had to a quite different method of resolving it: the Irish practitioner or layman would infer that an English statute on the relevant topic, the text of which was more readily accessible, necessarily applied in Ireland as well, even though, in strict constitutional logic, it might not, or, most decidedly, could not.[58] Whether the passing by the English parliament of the Declaratory Act of 1720 could have contributed to this atmosphere of legal confusion it seems impossible, at this remove in time, either to affirm or to deny, at least not until

52 *Lords' jn. Ire.*, ii, 854: 7 March 1725. **53** *Lords' jn. Ire.*, iii, 143: 13 April 1730. **54** *Lords' jn. Ire.*, ii, 550: 30 August 1717. **55** In his 'advice to the reader' at the start of vol. i of the 1st folio ed. of 1765-82 (note 44 above). **56** *The statutes of Ireland*, ed. Bolton (1621), epistle dedicatorie. **57** Ibid. Others, in later years, in various circumstances would also consult the 'authentic text'. In preparing the 1st folio ed., Vesey did ('advice to the reader' in vol. i); in preparing the revised ed. of 1885, W.F. Cullinan did; in checking a possible error in the printed text of a statute of 1751, Bushe CJ did (*Charters* v. *Sherrock* (1831) Alc. & Nap. 17); in seeking an explanation for the failure of the Statute of Jeofailles of 1542 to prescribe the minimum period that the Irish law student was obliged to attend a London inn of court, all those wrestling with the particular problem – a blank at the critical juncture in the printed text – have (see conveniently Colum Kenny, *King's Inns and the kingdom of Ireland: the Irish 'inn of court', 1541-1800* (Dublin, 1992), pp 40-8). **58** For an instance of this involving Jonathan Swift, see Joseph O'Carroll, 'Contemporary attitudes towards the homeless poor', in David Dickson (ed.), *The gorgeous mask* (Dublin, 1987), p. 64 at p. 66.

a great deal more research is undertaken into the Irish legal system in the eighteenth century.

The speed with which decisions taken in April 1762 led to the appearance three years later of the early volumes of the first folio edition of the Irish statutes must, in retrospect, be adjudged nothing other than remarkable. On 17 April Boulter Grierson, the then king's printer, reported that he had virtually exhausted his stock of statutes – of what he termed 'the statutes at large' but six sets were left.[59] Three days later, the house of lords supported the idea of a complete reprint and by the 27th the plan had acquired official sanction and the lord lieutenant, the earl of Halifax, had made the necessary government order.[60] Possibly in the light of the earlier difficulties with Andrew Crooke, it was arranged that Lord Chancellor Bowes and the other judges should choose the paper, the size of the resultant volumes (folio) and the type face to be used (common type). Grierson was confirmed as printer and was personally responsible for at least the first eight or nine volumes of the edition. Francis Vesey, appointed editor, was a graduate of Trinity College, Dublin, who had been called to the English bar in 1748 and to the Irish three years later. In 1766 Vesey became a master in chancery in Ireland and later still he was to edit a set of English nominate law reports, *Cases argued and determined in chancery in the time of Lord Chancellor Hardwicke, 1746-1755* (London, 1771), a set best known to legal antiquarians as Vesey, senior. At the time of his appointment Vesey may thus have enjoyed a certain reputation within the Irish legal profession.[61] Vesey was to justify what he was about on grounds with which we are already familiar – the difficulty of keeping track of the various sessional volumes which supplemented the later editions of Bolton. These volumes, he wrote in an 'advice to the reader',

> were become too numerous for use; and even those so dispersed, that at the present complete sets are with difficulty to be procured, to answer the purposes of justice, especially at the assizes held in the several counties.

Other decisions taken at the outset had a bearing on the finances of a major printing contract and were designed to reassure Grierson. Nobody wanted the fate that had apparently overtaken the edition of 1572 to be repeated. Thus it was agreed that each member of the house of lords and house of commons would be supplied with a complete bound set, and payment for these was guaranteed.[62] Grierson's bill came to over £10,000, nearly £4,000 of which had been paid on account before the residue was finally approved for settlement early in 1768.[63] Initially, 200 sets were supplied to members of the house of lords, and 310 to members of the house of commons. New members were entitled to their sets as well: 80 additional 9-volume sets were thus

59 *Commons' jn. Ire.*, vii, 162. **60** *Lords' jn. Ire.*, iv., 252, 261. **61** *Alumni Dublinenses, 1593-1860*, eds. G.D. Burtchaell and T.U. Sadleir (Dublin, 1935), p. 839; *King's Inns admission papers, 1607-1867*, eds. Edward Keane, P.B. Phair and T.U. Sadleir (Irish Mss. Comm., Dublin, 1982), p. 490; *The gentleman and citizen's aimanack (by John Watson, bookseller) for 1766* (Dublin, 1766), p. 50. **62** *Lords' jn. Ire.*, iv, 252: 20 Apr. 1762. **63** *Commons' jn. Ire.*, viii, pt. 2, app. cxc (Grierson's itemised account properly notarised and presented to parliament); id., viii, pt. 1, 203, 222: 25 Nov. 1767, 4 Feb. 1768.

supplied in 1770 at a cost of £1,525;[64] 23 additional sets in 1772 for £437;[65] 19 additional sets in 1774 for £361;[66] 17 additional sets in 1776 for £323;[67] 86 additional sets in 1778 for £1,635;[68] and another 35 additional sets in 1780 for £665.[69] After the death of Boulter Grierson in 1771, these payments were made to his widow, Mary – Mary Hay from 1772, following her re-marriage – who held the king's printer's patent in trust for her son George, until the latter came of age. Grierson's itemised bill confirms that a small number of these sets were earmarked for presentation purposes. One such set was sent to the king, George III, for example. These various presentation sets were to be lavishly bound and constitute crucial evidence bearing on the skill and proficiency of the Dublin bookbinders of the period.[70]

The first folio edition was brought up to date by the appearance of a ninth volume in 1767. Before two more volumes completed the series several years later, the pattern had re-established itself whereby supplementary volumes were produced containing the statutes enacted at successive parliamentary sessions;[71] in all instances, the relevant authorisations are faithfully recorded in the *Lords' journals*. To the consternation of many, the pattern was duplicated in another less welcome respect: black type continued to be employed rather than the more legible common type of the Vesey edition,[72] upon which, indeed, as we have seen, the judges in 1765 had insisted. By 1782, two final volumes in the 'Vesey' edition – volumes x and xi – had made their appearances.[73] But two years later, the stock was reported to be exhausted, and the decision was reached to proceed to a fresh edition which would include, in the same format, all Irish statutes down to the time of publication.[74] Editorial responsibility was entrusted, first, to a recently qualified barrister, James Goddard Butler,[75] and, then, following the latter's death in the early 1790s, to another barrister, William Ball, who also produced the two index volumes in the series, volumes viii and xxi.[76] This second folio edition

64 9 Geo. III, c. 1 (*Stat. Ire.*, x, 1), s. 7 (actually £1,525 13*s*. 4*d*.). **65** 11 & 12 Geo. III, c. 1 (*Stat. Ire.*, x, 65), s. 7 (actually £437 5*s*. 9*d*.). **66** 13 & 14 Geo. III, c. 1 (*Stat. Ire.*, x, 333), s. 16 (actually £361 4*s*. 9*d*.). **67** 15 & 16 Geo. III, c. 8 (*Stat. Ire.*, x, 681), s. 17 (actually £323 4*s*. 3*d*.). **68** 17 & 18 Geo. III, c. 1 (*Stat. Ire.*, xi, 3), s. 17 (actually £1,635 1*s*. 6*d*.). See, too, *Commons' jn. Ire.*, ix, 344: 11 Nov. 1777. **69** 19 & 20 Geo. III, c. 1 (*Stat. Ire.*, xi, 303), s. 14 (actually £665 8*s*. 9*d*.). **70** Noel Kissane (ed.), *Treasures from the National Library of Ireland* (Dublin, 1994), features at p. 32 volume vii in a presentation set of the first folio (Vesey's) edition. A description of the bookbinding is supplied: 'Handsome binding of morocco (goatskin), dyed red. Central lozenge an overlay of white leather which is stuck on and cut away in centre to reveal the ground morocco, here stained royal blue. Decoration and gilding of bindings were done with a range of tools, mainly brass stamps, each with a feature such as a bird or flower. The leather was first painted with white of egg (glair) which acted as an adhesive: the tools were then treated and used to press on gold leaf in the required patterns. Borders were generally put on by a roller with a continuous pattern.' In 1927 King George V returned to the then Irish government from the Royal Library at Windsor one of the less lavishly produced later presentation sets: *Irish Law Times & Solicitors' Journal*, 61 (1927), 166. **71** *Commons' jn. Ire.*, x, 262–3: 20 Nov. 1781. **72** Ibid. **73** Benson & Pollard, 'Ir. paper in the Statutes at Large', 18. **74** *Lords' jn. Ire.*, v, 531: 14 May 1784. Sec, too, *Lords' jn. Ire.*, vi, 121–2: 21 May 1787. **75** According to *King's Inns adm. papers*, p. 67, Butler had only become a member of the Irish bar in 1780. He is there described as the son of John Butler, Dublin Castle. There is no record of his having attended Trinity College, Dublin or either Oxford or Cambridge. **76** Ball became a member of the Irish bar in 1775: *King's Inns adm. papers*, p. 19. He had graduated B.A. from Trinity College in 1769: *Alumni Dublinenses*, p. 37. For Ball's criticism of the adequacy of the sole index vol. in the 1st folio ed. – also numbered vol. viii – see his note 'to the reader' at the start of *Stat. Ire.*, viii, at pp 2–3.

embraced 21 volumes, and spanned the period from 1310 (where Bolton and Vesey had also started) down to the extinction of the Irish parliament in 1800. It was brought out by the king's printer of the day, Boulter Grierson's son, who, like his grandfather and uncle, king's printers too in their time, also, confusingly, bore the same Christian name of George.

In 1794, this George Grierson also commenced publication of an octavo edition of the statutes as a speculative venture. Aimed, one assumes, very largely at the local legal profession, this edition omitted all spent and repealed statutes, which had been kept in both folio editions, though printed there in smaller type. The octavo edition also excluded all prefatory matter, nor was, for example, the listing of private statutes contained in the principal index volume, volume viii of the second folio edition, to be retained. The last volume in this octavo edition, volume xii, appeared in 1801. A simplified index volume, based nevertheless on William Ball's magisterial work for the second folio edition, was finally supplied in 1828 by Richard Nun, a 43-year-old barrister of some twenty years standing, who subsequently became a judge and a QC,[77] and who was to write, in conjunction with J.E. Walsh, a well-regarded treatise on *The powers and duties of justices of the peace in Ireland* (Dublin, 1841). In this index volume, Nun provides in the initial 'advertisement' a useful table of correspondence for the octavo and folio editions.

Prior to the eighteenth century we have tantalisingly few glimpses, at least in the more readily accessible sources, of the actual economics of copying, and later, of printing, the Irish statutes. In 1455, two clerks, James Prendregast and James Cruys, were paid the sum of 40*d.* to make a copy of all statutes enacted by the Irish parliament between the eighth and thirty-third regnal years of the then king, Henry VI. The copy was commissioned for consultation by the three Irish common law courts, king's bench, common pleas and exchequer. That at the time these courts lacked such a copy had, according to a commons' complaint, caused the relevant statutes to be 'out of memory and unknown, and it is not the better for the making thereof (*hors del memory & nemy convz & il nest pas le melior pr la fesaunce de* –).[78] Quinn assembles useful data on the topic for the Tudor period in his important article that traces the background to the decision to print the Irish statutes in 1572.[79] In 1661, in the immediate aftermath of the Restoration, we learn that a Dr Sterne was paid £50 for overseeing the printing of the acts and other 'declarations of this parliament', though no other details are to hand.[80]

There is much more information so far as the first folio edition is concerned. Not only is the text of Boulter Grierson's bill extant[81] but there is also available the report of the committee of the house of commons appointed to scrutinise it and who finally, early in 1768, passed it for payment.[82] The committee had plainly pressed Grierson for

77 *King's Inns adm. papers*, p. 368. Nun had graduated B.A. from Trinity College in 1804: *Alumni Dublinenses*, p. 625. He subsequently became, in 1829, assistant barrister (judge) for Co. Tyrone (*Watson's or the gentleman's and citizen's almanack … for 1830* (Dublin, n.d. [1830]), p. 90) and, in 1844, a QC (*The Dublin almanac and general register of Ireland for 1845* (Dublin, n.d. [1845]), p. 124). **78** *Stat. Ire., Hen. VI*, pp 311–12. **79** Quinn, 'Publication of Ir. statutes in the 16th century', passim. **80** *Lords' jn. Ire.*, i, 272: 27 July 1661. **81** *Commons' jn. Ire.*, viii, pt. 2, app. cxc. **82** *Commons' jn. Ire.*, viii, pt. 1, 203, 205: 25 Nov. 1767, 4 Feb. 1768.

much more explanatory material than he had originally divulged. Their probing revealed that Grierson's overheads had been increased by circumstances they were prepared to accept lay beyond his control – the loss of 100,000 sheets attributable to mildew and the difficulties caused by the scarcity of paper in the country between May 1763 and August 1764. The question of paper indeed looms large in the committee's deliberations. Careful scrutiny of Custom House records in respect of the importation of paper at the time, and carried out recently, has shown that the paper employed by Grierson for the first folio edition in all likelihood originated in Holland and France in addition to Ireland. For the second folio edition, paper originating in Holland and England as well as in Ireland was very probably used.[83]

In subsequent years, the achievement of economies increasingly engaged the attention of the commons and further committees were set up at regular intervals.[84] In 1781, one such committee urged the abandonment of the practice of printing the statutes in both black letter and common type and recommended that the same quality of paper should be used throughout.[85] The recommendations contained in a second report the following year covered new ground: not only was black letter type to be abandoned, but members of the commons and lords should henceforth enjoy an entitlement merely to be supplied with sheets of the statutes only and not bound volumes, and members who lost their copies should have to pay for replacements themselves.[86] Whilst black letter was indeed to be jettisoned, it is not clear what action, if any, was taken on strength of the committee's two other proposals.

With the appearance of the second folio edition well under way, and completion almost in sight, and one year after the revised octavo edition was started, a further strategy was adopted to tackle the general overall problem. In 1795, the Irish parliament passed an act 'for the better promulgating the statute law of this kingdom'.[87] Citing, as justification, 'the inconveniences' that had arisen 'from the statute law of this kingdom not being sufficiently known' – by now, of course, an exceptionally well-worn refrain – the act proceeded to encourage grand juries the length and breadth of the country to acquire copies of the statutes. It did so by giving them authority to purchase one complete set for use of the assizes and two copies of statutes of successive parliamentary sessions for use at quarter sessions. What impact this may have had, and whether, on grounds of cost, the grand juries that chose to exercise their new powers, preferred the octavo to the folio edition, are not easy to determine.

Payments to the three individuals involved in the editing of the first and second folio editions – Francis Vesey, J.G. Butler and William Ball – are helpfully recorded in the *Lords' journals*. In 1771, Vesey petitioned for payment. Lord Annaly, the then chief justice of king's bench, reported favourably on Vesey's work, and recommended a sum of £1,000.[88] Butler's petition of 1787 revealed that he had already been paid, possibly in advance, £500 for the work expended on the first five volumes of the second folio edition. Butler then sought an extra £300 in respect of a further six volumes, which

83 C. Benson and M. Pollard, '"The rags of Ireland are by no means the same": Irish paper used in the Statutes at Large', *Long Room*, 2 (1970), 18, passim. **84** e.g., *Commons' jn. Ire.*, x, 161: 9 June 1780. **85** *Commons' jn. Ire.*, x, 262–3: 20 Nov. 1781. **86** *Commons' jn. Ire.*, x, 383: 24 July 1782. **87** 35 Geo. III, c. 46. **88** *Lords' jn. Ire.*, iv, 607, 622: 21 Dec. 1771, 4 Mar. 1772.

would seem to have been approved.[89] His widow, Jacobina, presented a supplementary petition in 1792 for work completed on another two volumes and for work left unfinished on three more. Her late husband, she argued, had expended infinite labour on the entire project, neglecting his legal practice and causing injury to his health. She was now in distressed circumstances. It was eventually decided to recommend a payment of a further £500 to Mrs Butler.[90] Somewhat mysteriously, William Ball would appear to have fared best of all. In 1800, for his work on the concluding volumes of the edition from where Butler had left off and for that on the massive index volume (on which he claimed he had worked six hours a day for eight years) a sum of £4,000 was recommended.[91] Whether this amount was intended to cover the last two volumes, the collection of statutes for 1799 and 1800 (volume xx) and its slim accompanying special index (volume xxi) is not altogether clear.[92]

IV

If we leave to one side the specialist volumes in the early Irish statutes series published by the Public Record Office since 1907, the last composite edition of the statutes of the pre-Union Irish parliament was the so-called revised edition brought out in 1885 under the aegis of the Irish Office at Westminster. The editor was William Fitzpatrick Cullinan, whose background and career, as it happens, share a certain affinity with that of Trollope's Phineas Finn. The son of a doctor from Ennis, Co. Clare, Cullinan was called to the English bar after an education that took in both Trinity College, Dublin and Cambridge. He subsequently became legislative draftsman in the Irish Office around 1877.[93] Cullinan employed as the model for this single-volume edition the 18-volume edition of the *English statutes revised 1235-1878* which had begun to appear from 1870 on. Cullinan's volume was two years in preparation.

Long after the passing of the Acts of Union in 1800,[94] judges, practitioners, government officials and, doubtless, many others besides continued to sense the need for an edition of the pre-Union Irish statutes which supplied the full text of such statutes as were still in force and which simultaneously took account of the various repeals wrought both by the pre-Union Irish parliament itself and, after the Union, by the United Kingdom parliament. Employing the volumes of the first folio edition together with the supplementary volumes for succeeding years from the second as the template, this is exactly what Cullinan made it his business to produce. He was also to

89 *Lords' jn. Ire.*, vi, 121-2: 21 May 1787. **90** *Lords' jn. Ire.*, vii, 66, 69: 24, 30 Mar. 1792. **91** *Lords' jn. Ire.*, viii, 343: 24 Feb. 1800. Ball's note 'to the reader' (*Stat. Ire.*, viii, 1-5) details the claim and explains his *modus operandi*. **92** It may be significant that Ball was later to be pressed to ensure that all who were entitled to receive the main index volume (vol. viii) did in fact do so. See *Lords' jn. Ire.*, viii, 543: 1 Aug. 1800. This was the very day that the Irish Act of Union received the royal assent. **93** *Alumni Cantabrigienses*, ii – 1752-1900, ed. J.A. Venn, 6 vols. (Cambridge, 1940-54), ii, 196; *Records of the honourable society of Lincoln's Inn, ii: 1800-1893* (London, 1896), p. 315; *Thom's Irish almanac and official directory for the year 1878* (Dublin, 1878), p. 132. **94** An act for the union of Great Britain and Ireland, 39 & 40 Geo. III, c. 67 (*Stat. at large*, x, 613); an act for the union of Great Britain and Ireland, 40 Geo. III, c. 38 (*Stat. Ire.*, xx, 448).

exclude statute law adjudged to be but local in character, though this presented difficult problems of classification as he was to explain. A key feature of the resultant volume was likewise copied from the contemporary multi-volume edition of the *English statutes revised.* This was the inclusion of a chronological table listing all Irish statutes from 1310 onwards contained in the two folio editions which the revised edition of 1885 itself excluded as having been repealed or otherwise spent, together with a short statement as to the exact warrant for that exclusion. The preparation of these lists will not have been anything other than arduous and, to those persons who might seek to chart the later fortunes of some specific earlier Irish statute, the availability of so comprehensive and authoritative a check-list constitutes a priceless asset.

Cullinan did not scrupulously observe his own injunction – to exclude every statute that was clearly spent or had been expressly repealed. To furnish some indication, however slight, of the nature of the statutes excluded and of the historical interest necessarily attaching to a selection of these, plainly proved irresistible. The question, at bottom, was one of editorial judgment and the approach of Vesey and Bolton to the similar difficulties they faced in their day was not uninstructive. In 1765 Vesey felt obliged to apologise for the sheer size of the end-product. He was aware, he declared in his 'advice to the reader',

> that the inserting expired or repealed Acts at large, would increase the Bulk of this Collection; but it is hoped the Public will dispense with that Inconvenience, as they may afford light, and be useful for the construction of subsisting Laws; and will remain curious and authentic Documents in the Public History of this Kingdom.[95]

In 1621 Bolton, faced with the problem of whether to exclude statutes which, though not expressly repealed, had certainly fallen into disuse, was to argue in much the same vein. Bolton had approached the senior judiciary for advice. 'The said Iudges & Master of the Rolls', he then reported, had advised

> that those Statutes that had beene formerly printed, and were not expressly repealed, should be printed againe, and that for two reasons; the one, lest peraduentre any should vnadvisedly taxe me of partialitie, that matters of greater moment were omitted, and matters of lesse consequence published: and the other was, that although the said Statutes be out of vse, or determined at this day, yet the same may well serve for an historical Vse; whereby the iudicious Reader may partly discerne both the State of the Church and commonwealth in those times.[96]

Like considerations plainly weighed with Cullinan, so much so in fact that not only was he to provide us with the full text of five statutes of 'historical interest' in an

95 *Stat. Ire.*, i (1765 ed.), address to the reader. **96** *The statutes of Ireland*, ed. Bolton (1621), epistle dedicatorie.

appendix, but we have a separate index to all the acts 'relating to the settlement of the kingdom'.

V

One final cautionary word requires to be uttered. Regrettably, perhaps, the revised edition of 1885 cannot be regarded as an entirely foolproof guide to the statutes of the pre-Union parliament still in force in either Irish jurisdiction today. Individual pre-Union statutes or individual provisions of such statutes have continued to suffer legislative repeal at intermittent intervals. An instance of such legislative spring-cleaning occurs in 1885 itself when the section in the Irish Statute of Jeofailles 1542 (33 Hen VIII, sess. 2, c. 3) that imposed mandatory attendance by Irish law students at a London inn of court, a provision once stigmatised as this 'badge of servitude' laid on the Irish nation, was repealed by the Barristers Admission (Ireland) Act of the same year.[97] The revised edition went to press before this particular repeal was accomplished, so the terms of the unrepealed statutory provision were reproduced in it.

Shortly before the appearance of the 1885 edition, two major statute law revision acts repealed a considerable quantity of pre-Union Irish legislation, an exercise which, coincidentally, enabled the size of the resultant single volume to be kept within manageable limits. (Sleuths will detect, however, that, initially at least, a two-volume edition seems to have been in contemplation.) These were the Statute Law Revision (Ireland) Act 1878,[98] which covered statutes adopted between 1310 and 1781, and another act bearing the identical title the ensuing year,[99] which dealt with the period between 1535 and 1800. Omnibus repealing legislation of this genre continued in vogue after two distinct Irish jurisdictions came into existence in the 1920s. In the case of Northern Ireland, further repeals of pre-Union statute law were thus brought about by fresh legislation passed at Westminster in 1950 and 1973. The Statute Law Revision Act 1950,[100] in the part of the act dealing with Northern Ireland, repealed Irish statutes passed between 1477 and 1800. The later Statute Law Revision (Northern Ireland) Act 1973[101] dealt with the period spanning the years 1635 and 1795. In the case of the Republic, comparable but by no means identical, and, in some instances in fact, more radical, refurbishment was achieved by measures enacted by the Oireachtas in 1962 and 1983, respectively. The Statute Law Revision (Pre-Union Irish Statutes) Act 1962[102] covered the years 1459 to 1800 – and, incidentally, has not escaped judicial criticism.[103] The Statute Law Revision Act 1983,[104] in a part devoted to the legislation of the pre-Union parliament, dealt with a much longer period, 1236–1796, and thus officially, for the first time, acknowledged the existence of Irish statute law contained in the Public Record Office's published series of early Irish statutes.[105]

97 48 & 49 Vict., c. 20. **98** 41 & 42 Vict., c. 57. **99** Statute Law Revision (Ireland) Act 1879: 42 & 43 Vict., c. 24. **100** 14 Geo. VI, c. 6. **101** 1973, c. 55. **102** No. 29 of 1962. **103** See the judgment of Kenny J in *Browne* v. *Fahy*, unreported, High Court, 5 Oct. 1975. **104** No. 11 of 1983. **105** In modern times, probably the first occasion upon which any Irish court extended recognition to the content of early Irish statute law occurred in 1818 when the Court of Delegates decided the appeal in the case of *The deanery of St*

There is a subsidiary consideration. In 1975, in an *obiter dictum*,[106] Kenny J of the Irish High Court doubted the continued applicability in modern circumstances of an unrepealed Irish statute of 1634, the Act against maintenance, embracery, &c. and against the unlawful buying of titles.[107] This presents the question of whether a doctrine of desuetude is applicable in either Irish jurisdiction today so as to deprive older statutes of legal validity and effect where they are obviously not tailored to modern conditions. Such a doctrine has been formally recognised in Scotland.[108] In Ireland, however, the point must be adjudged moot.[109] In 1955, the then Irish attorney-general, Mr McGilligan, advised the government that English forcible entry statutes of 1381 and 1391,[110] extended to Ireland under the terms of Poynings' Act 1495, were obsolete and incapable of modern application and enforcement.[111] In 1986, Keane J of the Irish High Court drew a blue pencil through portion of a section in an act of the United Kingdom parliament, the Petty Sessions (Ireland) Act 1851,[112] which prohibited petty sessions, the equivalent of today's district court hearings in the Republic, from being conducted in licensed premises.[113] The prohibition was located in an exception to section 8 of the act which enabled petty sessions to be conducted in a building other than a properly designated courthouse so long as appropriate administrative procedures were observed. Institutional reforms introduced at the end of the nineteenth century – the removal of grand juries from local government – had, however, made it impossible for these administrative procedures to be activated let alone followed. Accordingly, the prohibition, the ban, in all circumstances, on the employment of licensed premises despite the exception, could not be given effect to either. Neither the administrative ruling of 1955 nor the judicial of 1986 involved a decision on the modern-day validity of any statute of the pre-Union Irish parliament. But the considerations each raises are clearly of general application.[114]

Patrick's: Ponsonby v. *Pomeroy* (Mason, *History of St Patrick's cathedral*, p. 473n; J.C. Erck, *An account of the ecclesiastical establishment subsisting in Ireland* (Dublin, 1830), p. 286). The admission of proxy votes at the election by the cathedral chapter of the dean was, on one view, forbidden by a decree of the Lateran Council of 1215, but only if the deanery could be ranked sufficiently high in the Irish ecclesiastical hierarchy. The Delegates relying, *inter alia*, on the provisions of the Irish statute 14 Edw. IV, c. 5 (*Stat. Ire., 12-22 Edw. IV*, pp 197-203), held that the deanery could be accorded the necessary high rank. • The legislatures in the Republic and in Northern Ireland have also been kept busy repealing early English statute law made applicable in Ireland by virtue of Poynings' Act 1495: see, for example, for the Republic, the Mortmain (Repeal of Enactments) Act 1954 (No.32 of 1954), and for Northern Ireland, the Mortmain Repeals Act (NI) 1960 (1960, c. 20). The two lists of repealed English statutes contained in these measures are largely, but not completely, identical. **106** *Browne* v. *Fahy*, unreported, 5 Oct. 1975. **107** 10 Chas. I, sess. 3, c. 15. **108** A.L. Diamond, 'The repeal and desuetude of statutes', *Current Legal Problems*, 28 (1975), 107. **109** G.W. Hogan, 'Statutory interpretation – the doctrine of desuetude', *Dublin Univ. L. J.* 9 (1987), 136. **110** 5 Ric. II, stat. 1, c. 7 (*Stat. of realm*, ii, 20); 15 Ric. II, c. 2 (*Stat. of realm*, ii, 78). **111** The thrust of the advice was revealed by Desmond O'Malley, Minister for Justice, in the course of the passage through the Seanad (the Irish Senate) of the measure that became the Prohibition of Forcible Entry and Occupation Act 1971 (No. 25 of 1971): *Seanad Debates*, vol. 71, cols. 336-40 (18 Aug. 1971). Senators Mary Robinson and John Kelly, amongst others, had suggested that fresh legislation in the area was superfluous, a proposition Mr O'Malley was to reject. **112** 14 & 15 Vict., c. 93. **113** *The State (Feeley)* v. *O'Dea* [1986] IR 687. **114** I am grateful to Paul Brand for reading and criticising an early draft.

Letters to Ireland: Professional Enlightenment from the English Bench

Correspondence passing between the English judicial bench and Ireland constituted one of the mechanisms through which the tenets of the common law came to be observed in the latter. As regards its importance in enabling the common law to put down firm roots, such correspondence naturally cannot be placed on a level with other better known and longer recognised mechanisms associated with the reception in Ireland of the common law – the extension to Ireland of the institutional framework of English law, the similar extension of the system of writs for the initiation of litigation, the forwarding of English legislation for observance in Ireland and the introduction of the supervisory appellate jurisdiction exercised by the English court of King's Bench. Yet the role this correspondence may have occupied in the transmission to Ireland of knowledge pertaining to law generally as well as to legal technicalities should not be underestimated, to be dismissed out of hand or in cavalier fashion. The inventory of items of this correspondence passing between England and Ireland, extending from the thirteenth to the twentieth century, and which is presented in the following pages, is designed to demonstrate that the importance of these 'letters to Ireland' by no means diminished as over the centuries the constitutional and legal relationship of the two countries continued to evolve. There is, as will be seen, ample evidence to support that assessment.

Some years ago in the pages of the *Irish Jurist*, Paul Brand first drew attention to the significance of such letters to Ireland in the context of his own immediate concern, the story of the transplantation of the medieval common law into Irish soil.[1] Careful scrutiny of a legal manuscript found in one of the London inns of court yielded an early instance of guidance being offered by a prominent member of the judiciary in England in response to a query forwarded from Ireland. Whilst the identity of the author of the query was unknown, that of the respondent was clearly shown – Ralph de Hengham, the holder of high judicial office in England, first as Chief Justice of the King's Bench, 1274-90, then as Chief Justice of the Bench (later known as Common Pleas), 1301-9. The date of the composition of Hengham's response was uncertain but fell between the earliest and latest dates just given.

A dispute had broken out in Ireland over the right of presentation to a church in Moygarban, probably the modern Magorban near Cashel in Co. Tipperary. It raised a point of law relating to the form of pleadings to be employed in an assize of darrein presentment.[2] One Walter of Stanton, claiming title to make the presentation of rector

1 Paul Brand, 'Ralph de Hengham and the Irish common law', (1984) 19 *Ir. Jur. (ns)* 107; reprinted with an additional postscript in idem, *The making of the common law* (London and Rio Grande, 1992), p. 465. **2** This

to the church, was suing the prior and convent of Athassel, who had advanced the defence known as the exception of plenarty. This exception, not infrequently met with in a hearing of a darrein presentment, amounted to the contention that there was no vacancy in the ecclesiastical benefice to which the plaintiff sought to make the presentation and that the entire proceedings in consequence were misconceived. In short, that there was already an incumbent installed and in possession and that there was no vacancy, whether due to death or resignation.

Raising the exception did not end matters, however, for whenever this occurred, the defendant would normally have to produce prima facie evidence that the ecclesiastical benefice was, in fact 'full', in the shape of letters of institution and of admission. The judge would then seek from the local bishop a certificate in confirmation since the question as to whether or not a church was vacant was acknowledged as lying exclusively within the latter's cognisance as ordinary. Even then injustice could creep in where, for example, a religious house had wrongfully obtained the advowson and was thus quite improperly in a position to raise the exception of plenarty – precisely the allegation levelled by Walter against the prior and convent of Athassel. Whether a change needed to be made to the pleadings customarily demanded when such were thought to be the circumstances had been the subject of contradictory rulings in England between 1262 and 1274. Hengham's Irish correspondent sought advice on the correct doctrinal stance to adopt. In his reply, Hengham attempted to provide the necessary enlightenment, finally ranging himself on the side of the school of thought that held that, in such circumstances, and despite the passage of years, further particulars would have to be produced:

> In consimili casu vidi diversa judicia. Quia dominus Martinus de Lytebirii statim cum viri religiosi allegassent plenitudinem ecclesie a longinquo tempore statim sine ostensione quod aliquid haberent de patrono vel episcopo adjudicavit mandari episcopo quod super hoc inquiretur. Et Ricardus de Midd' statum suum reputans insufficiens sentivit et dixit quod nisi ostenderet quod ecclesia illa esset plena ad presentacionem veri patroni vel quasi per admissionem alicujus ordinarii vel quasi quod ecclesia fuit vacans et oporteret ulterius respondere quia hae sunt interroganda – a quo plena, a quo tempore, ad cujus presentacionem et ad cujus ordinarii admissionem. Et si hae sunt interroganda tunc erit ad ea respondenda quod dixi superius quamvis propter magnam vim quia in isto brevi de possessione non est distinguendum de vero patrono vel vero ordinario. Sed ostensis supradictis mandatum erit episcopi.[3]

The outcome to the dispute over the advowson at Magorban is unknown.

Brand later located in a second manuscript dated to *c.*1281[4] what appeared to be the answer of a second justice to the same Irish conundrum regarding the appropriate procedure to be followed on an assize of darrein presentment.[5]

was the remedy introduced by Henry II and designed to deal expeditiously with violations of rights of advowson, or presentation to ecclesiastical benefices. **3** Lincoln's Inn, MS. Miscellaneous 738, ff. 70r–70v. **4** Cambridge University Library, MS. L1.4.18, ff. 142v–43r. **5** Brand, *The making of the common law*, p. 470.

In the sixteenth century another problem of ecclesiastical law – of a very different stamp and one unimaginable in the Anglo-Irish lordship of the thirteenth or fourteenth century – again prompted recourse to the English judiciary for help.

On this occasion, the problem revolved around the validity of a lease of lands at Tallaght (Tavelaugh) belonging to the archdiocese of Dublin. Prior to the Reformation, leases of lands belonging to the archdiocese required for their validity the consents of the dean and chapter of the two Dublin cathedrals, Christ Church (the priory of the Holy Trinity) and St Patrick's. In November 1546, however, Henry VIII ordered the dissolution of St Patrick's, empowering the then Irish lord deputy and lord chancellor to receive from the dean and chapter the surrender of the cathedral church itself, its revenues and estates and all its possessions.[6] The dissolution subsequently proceeded with the support of the incumbent dean, Edward Bassenet, but it did not command anything like universal assent. Leaving aside the possibly ambiguous attitude of George Browne, the new Protestant archbishop of Dublin (1535–54), it was plain enough that he had given no licence to the dean and chapter to dissolve themselves, an omission that was to be the focus of attention in the later litigation. As for the chapter itself, evidence extracted by W. Monck Mason, the early nineteenth century historian of St Patrick's, from a source no longer extant, revealed that they had been coerced into giving their consents: Dean Bassenet, so it is alleged, imprisoned the precentor, the treasurer, two archdeacons, and fifteen prebendaries until their approval was forthcoming.[7] The cathedral was later restored in 1554 in the reign of Philip and Mary.[8] In the interval between dissolution and restoration, however, a lease had been made of the lands at Tallaght, apparently by Archbishop Browne. The lease was in favour of Sir Raulf Bagnal from whom one Roger Brereton, the party in possession in the mid-1560s, derived his interest.[9] The lease had been drawn up in proper form, but it had been consented to by the single dean and chapter in existence in Dublin at the time, that of Christ Church.

In 1567 Adam Loftus was translated by Queen Elizabeth from Armagh to Dublin where he remained the Protestant archbishop until his death in 1605. He immediately involved himself in a campaign that had seemingly already got under way to overturn Browne's lease of the lands at Tallaght, and thus to secure these lands for the benefit of the church, if not for himself. There were two principal planks in Loftus's argument:

(i) that the dissolution of St Patrick's had been unlawful since the licence of the archbishop had not been obtained; and
(ii) that the lease of the Tallaght lands had been invalid since the consent of a second cathedral chapter was essential and that had not been secured.

6 W. Monck Mason, *The history and antiquities of the collegiate and cathedral church of St Patrick's near Dublin* (Dublin, 1820), p. 150. **7** The allegations were to be found in the pleadings of one Quartermass, the churchmen's attorney, suing in their name for an 'amoveas manus' after the cathedral was restored in the reign of Philip and Mary: Monck Mason, *History of St Patrick's*, pp 150, 162. In this suit, the churchmen sought the return of the moveable possessions of the cathedral dispersed at the time of the dissolution. **8** Monck Mason, *History of St Patrick's*, p. 155ff. **9**. *Cal. pat. rolls Ire., Hen. VIII-Eliz.*, p. 494.

The Dublin churchmen's quarrel with Brereton is first mentioned in an entry in the Irish patent rolls for 1565, two years before Loftus became archbishop of Dublin. Loftus, however, whilst archbishop of Armagh, his previous post, had also held the deanery of St Patrick's *in commendam* and was known to have resided in Dublin. It is thus not unlikely that he was an active protagonist in the controversy with Brereton even at this earlier date. In 1565 it was baldly recorded that Lord Deputy Sussex had been involved somehow in the controversy, had come out against Brereton and had ordered the latter to surrender the lease to the archbishop to be cancelled.[10] The archbishop referred to is presumably Hugh Curwen, Browne's successor and Loftus's own immediate predecessor. Sussex further ordered that Brereton should, by way of compensation, be given a £10 yearly pension, 'out of the lordship of Tavelaughe' and payable on the font in Christ Church cathedral.[11]

From the surviving evidence, it is not easy to piece together what happens next. It is probable, however, that Brereton was not satisfied, and was not to be bought off in this fashion. That he subsequently succeeded in defending the validity of the post-dissolution lease in proceedings before the ordinary common law courts is very likely: coverage of the later English stage in 'the proceedings' set down in Dyer's Reports[12] shows that at some indeterminate stage the Irish judges had indeed examined the question. Worryingly, from the standpoint of legal certainty, the Irish judges, according to Dyer, had been 'of divers opinions', although 'the greater part' thought the lease was valid and so bound the archbishop.[13]

Sir Henry Sidney succeeded the earl of Sussex as lord deputy in 1566 and the task descended to him accordingly to find a way out of the imbroglio over the Tallaght lease. Late in 1568 or early in 1569, he adopted the expedient of asking the advice of the judges in England on the two central issues raised by Loftus – the validity of the dissolution of St Patrick's cathedral in the absence of the archbishop's licence, and the validity of the lease that lacked on its face the concurrence of the second cathedral chapter. In what capacity Sidney chose to pursue this course of action is unfortunately not made explicit. It is not impossible that *Archbishop of Dublin* v. *Brereton* had itself already been considered by the Irish privy council board acting judicially (rather than by the common law courts) but agreement had not been forthcoming, and Sidney hoped that in this fashion he could break the deadlock. Quite independently, however, as chief governor, he may have felt it incumbent upon him to secure the best available legal advice so as to be in a position to terminate, somehow or other, an unedifying protracted quarrel. Two other factors may have entered into Sidney's calculations – that an important matter of state was involved, albeit obliquely (the validity of the temporary suppression of St Patrick's); and that one of the protagonists (Loftus) was a long-standing member of the privy council and a doughty champion of the new state church as well as of episcopal privilege, and thus a force to be reckoned with.

10 Ibid. **11** Ibid. **12** *Archbishop of Dublin* v. *Brereton*, 3 Dyer 232b, 73 Eng. Rep. 633. Though Dyer spells the name of the defendant differently, this is clearly the case in which our Brereton is Loftus's adversary. **13** Ibid.

Sidney's channel of communication appears to have lain through the English privy council who then passed on his request for guidance to the English judges.[14] The latter examined the issues at stake, reached certain conclusions and expressed these in a letter returned to Sidney on 13 May 1569. This letter, in a modernised rendering, will be found in the printed calendar of Irish patent rolls.[15] The text of the original entry made there was copied into the St Patrick's manuscript known as the '*Dignitas Decani*'.[16] It is this latter version which is set out now:

> Aftir our due comendations unto your good Lordship. Wheras we conceived Lettres from your L: with a case therin conteyninge these wordes, Wheras for the space of IIIIe yeres and moe in the Citie of Dublin, there have bene two Churches accompted Cathedralls both, either havinge a severall Chapiter, Deane and Seale, the consents of bothe, and the Seales of both hath bene accustomed to be had and putt to everie Graunte made of any thinge apperteyninge to the Archbusshopp. The last yere of Kinge Henry theight the one [of two] Churches, namelie St Patricks with the consent of the Dene and the moest parte of the Chapiter of the same in their Chapter House did yelde and geve upp without thassent of the Busshopp into the Kings possession the said Church with all things therto belongings, to him his Heires and Successors. Whether this was a lawful Dissolution or Surrender, or no, is the first Doubt, onelie for that the Busshopp consented not to it: Then the same Busshopp in King Edwards reigne and before the restitution of St Patricks made a Lease with the consent of the Deane and Chapiter of the other Churche, named Cristischurche onelie; for that in deede St Patricks was in all opinion and apparance dissolved; the Preistis excluded; the Lands dissipated, and the Church converted to Lay uses; whether this Lease there made be good to bynde the Successor or no, is the secound Doubte; by which your Lordshipp's Lettre, we were requested for that some difficultie and doubt grewe upon the said case befor your L: to send you our Oppynions and Resolutions therin; whereby your L: mighte be the bettir satisfied and directed of your Judgement to be geven in that behalfe.
>
> Theis be therfor to signifle unto your L. that we have not onelie herde the mattir and cause debated by Learned Counsaill both on the behalfe of the Archbusshopp of Dublin, and also on the behalfe of Roger Brereton; betwene whom we understand the matter doth rysse in question before your L: But also have at severall tymes made speciall meetings and conference among our selves towchinge the said matter; and in end with deliberate consideration doo think upon the case, That forasmouch as it semeth to us by the same case for any thinge that we have yett herde to the contrarie that the Graunt surrendered or given upp of the Church of St Patricks, and of all things thereto belongings was

14 The English privy council registers between May 1567 and May 1570 are missing: *Acts of the Privy Council of England, 1558-70*, p. 351. **15** *Cal. pat. rolls Ire., Hen. VIII–Eliz.*, pp 529-30. **16** *The 'Dignitas Decani' of St Patrick's Cathedral, Dublin*, ed. N.B. White (Irish Manuscripts Commission, Dublin, 1957).

> and is a lawfull and perfect dissolution or surrender of the said Churche, and of the Corporation and Chapter therof; And that by reason therof there remayned not any Chapter to the said Busshopp, but onely the Deane and Chapter of Christ Churche, which was still in Esse; at which tyme this Lease was made and confirmed by the said Deane and Chapter; We take it, that the Lese made afterwards by the Archbusshopp by and with the onelie assent of the said Deane and Chapter of Christis Churche to be good and effectuall in the Law to bynd in succession, for that the Corporation of the Deane and Chapter of St Patricks was then dissolved, and had no beinge.[17]

The judges' letter ends with a remarkable passage in which, politely but firmly, they convey to Sidney a preference for not having been asked to give their advice in the first instance. It is an early expression of an argument heard more regularly and more distinctly in the eighteenth century when the judges and writers combined to work out more coherent notions of what the independence of the judiciary actually meant. What the five signatories (the chiefs of the three common law courts – Robert Catelyn (Queen's Bench), James Dyer (Common Pleas) and Edward Saundier (Exchequer) – and two puisnes – Thomas Carus (Queen's Bench) and John Walshe (Common Pleas))[18] seem to be insinuating is that, as a matter of principle, they were not in favour of furnishing the executive, or anyone else, with an advisory opinion on any question that might come before them in open court in the ordinary way:

> And albeit that it hathe bene seldome sene that our Opinions are used to set forthe in writinge, but onely in souch Judiciall places [as we] were called unto; Wheras Judges we speke judicially, yet consideringe your L: place of service, and good zeale to direct causes accordinge to the comon Lawes of this Realme, We thought it good to advertise your L: of our oppinions, hopinge that We shall not be often troubled with the lyke: Reservinge nevertheless our Liberties upon further mattier to be shewed hereafter in this case, as reason is: And so commytt your L: to the tuition of thalmightie, who ever presarve the same with encrease of honor.[19]

The judges signed as Sidney's 'verie lovinge Frendis' and wrote from 'Serjaunts Inne in Fletestrete'.

Citing no authority, Monck Mason says the English judges were divided on the issues on which Sidney had sought guidance.[20] This is not inconceivable, but even if division took place, the fact that puisne barons of the Exchequer do not seem to have participated in these conclaves at Serjeants' Inn until after 1579,[21] entails that only nine judges would have been eligible to participate; and, of these nine, five, including, as we have seen, the chiefs of the three courts, had found against Loftus and in favour of

17 Ibid., pp 147-8. **18** For thumbnail sketches of each of these judges, see Edward Foss, *The judges of England*, 9 vols. (London, 1848-64), v, 471-4, 479-85, 537-9 and 542-3. Catelyn, Dyer and Saundier (Saunders) are in *D.N.B.* Dyer is associated with reports that go under his name. **19** *'Dignitas Decani'*, p. 148. **20** *History of St Patrick's*, p. 150. **21** Foss, *The judges of England*, v, 409.

Brereton.[22] It is instructive too that Loftus, in the efforts he subsequently made to have the views of the English judges superseded, at least in the version of these efforts we have, alludes not at all to divisions or to majorities and minorities.[23] It seems probable that Monck Mason may have confused the state of judicial opinion in Ireland, where there was division – the authority for which is in Dyer[24] – and the state of judicial opinion in England.

The conclusions arrived at by the English judges were straightforward and crisply expressed. The original post-dissolution lease was valid, only one cathedral chapter having been 'in esse' at the time of the demise and confirmation. No doubt whatsoever attached either to the validity of the dissolution itself. In later centuries both Jonathan Swift, another dean of St Patrick's, and Monck Mason were to assail the reputations of both Henry VIII and Dean Bassenet over what actually transpired early in 1547,[25] but under Elizabeth and her judges there was to be no retrospective annulling through the medium of judicial opinion of the incontrovertible historical record: the corporation and church of St Patrick's had been '*per donum et sursum-redditionem Decani et Capituli, legitime dissolutum et determinatum, etiam absque consensu Archiepiscopi*'.[26]

Loftus seems to have travelled to London himself in March 1569 to make representations to Sir Robert Cecil over the business of the Tallaght lease.[27] Defeated at the hands of the English judges two months later, he by no means threw in the towel. In a letter to Cecil the following August he complained that he had not had 'favour in the controversy with Brereton that was meant' – an intriguing throw-away of a remark. He went on to solicit a letter from Cecil addressed to Lord Deputy Sidney that he, Loftus, might have the purchase of Brereton's 'interest'.[28] The affair thereafter sinks without trace. It could be that Loftus was more successful in gaining part remission of the first fruits of his archbishopric, a concession he was also diligently hoping to extract at this juncture.[29] A final irony may or may not have been communicated to Loftus before his death in 1605. That year the judges in England were to decide that the lease by which they themselves occupied Serjeants' Inn in Fleet Street – the address from which Chief Justice Catelyn and his colleagues had forwarded their reply to Sidney – was itself invalid.[30]

At first glance, the sole seventeenth century instance of professional guidance from the English bench to feature in the present inventory possesses extremely dubious credentials. In strict legal form, a report signed by all twelve common law judges and addressed to the king, William III, it bears on its face no obvious indication that

22 One of the missing signatories, Richard Weston, a puisne in Common Pleas, was the brother of Robert Weston, Irish lord chancellor, 1567–73. **23** *Cal. S. P. Ire., 1509–73*, p. 416: Loftus to Cecil, 15 August 1569. **24** 3 Dyer 232b. **25** Monck Mason, *History of St Patrick's*, p. 150. **26** Quoted, ibid. **27** *Cal. S. P. Ire., 1509–73*, p. 405: Sir W. Fytzwylliams to Cecil, 19 Mar. 1569. **28** Ibid., p. 416: Loftus to Cecil, 15 August 1569. **29** Loftus's efforts in this regard were to be crowned with success: *Sidney State Papers, 1565–70*, ed. Tomás Ó Laidhin (Irish Manuscripts Commission, Dublin, 1962), p. 130: Queen to Sidney, 17 May 1570; *Cal. S. P. Ire., 1509–73*, p. 432: Loftus to Cecil, 2 July 1570. **30** *Holloway* v. *Watkins*, Cro. Jac. 51, 79 Eng. Rep. 43; *Foss, The judges of England*, v, 285. The premises originally belonged to the dean and chapter of York and had been seized by the Crown – wrongly, the judges held in 1605 – under powers given by statute for the suppression of chantries in the reign of Edward VI.

it may have been intended to be transmitted to Ireland for possible use there. Yet, just such an interpretation is indeed warranted, given the unusual background against which this advice of the judges had first been solicited, a background which will shortly be unfolded. In this connection, it is also worthy of note that whilst, as might be anticipated, the judges' report survives in English state papers – and is printed in the series *Calendar of State Papers, Domestic*[31] – the text of it was available in Dublin to G.E. Howard when he published his miscellaneous literary and prose works in 1782, for the report will be found there too.[32]

The English judges' report of 22 June 1693 signalled the culmination of a contemporary constitutional debate, a debate which had seen the Irish executive at odds with the Irish legislature.[33] At the Irish parliament convened in October 1692, the House of Commons objected to two measures which the recently appointed lord lieutenant, Viscount Sydney, had brought forward and which he wished to see passed into law. The measures in question were 'money bills', and the commons claimed that they had the sole and exclusive right to initiate these, adding that, in their estimation, precedent was firmly on their side. Whilst one of the new measures proposed by Sydney, a new tax on beer, was let through,[34] the other, which sought to impose certain other taxes for twelve months, was rejected *tout court*. Sydney was aghast at this challenge to the right of the Irish executive (the privy council and himself) to initiate financial legislation for Ireland, and on 3 November he reprimanded the commons and ordered that this protest be formally entered in the parliamentary record. Constitutionally, the procedure for initiating Irish legislation was regulated from the time of Henry VII by Poynings's Law and an amendment to that measure dating from the reign of Philip and Mary.[35] Sydney maintained that the votes, resolutions and proceedings of the commons violated both and were also contrary to 'continued usage and practice ever since'. They represented, besides, a gross invasion of the prerogatives and rights of the crown. Sydney concluded:

> We the Lord Lieutenant as well to assert the rights of their majesties [King William and Queen Mary], and the rights of the crown of England, (Whereof we are and ever will be most tender) in transmitting such bills under the great seal of England to be considered of in parliament, as to discharge the trust reposed in us, and prevent the inconveniencies which may hereafter happen, in case these votes and resolutions of the House of Commons should be made publick, or remain on their Journals, without any contradiction or animadversion, have thought it necessary, this day, in full Parliament to protest.[36]

31 *Cal. S. P. dom., 1693*, p. 191. **32** G.E. Howard, *Miscellaneous works*, 3 vols. (Dublin, 1782), iii, 205. There is a transcription, in addition, in the Robinson MSS (Gilbert collection): see note 46 below. **33** See generally J.I. McGuire, 'The Irish parliament of 1692', in Thomas Bartlett and D.W. Hayton (eds.), *Penal era and golden age: essays in Irish history, 1690-1800* (Ulster Historical Foundation, Belfast, 1979), p. 1; T.J. Kiernan, *History of the financial administration of Ireland to 1817* (London, 1930), pp 113-20. **34** *Commons' jn. Ire.*, ii, pt. 1, p. 28. **35** 10 Hen. VII, c. 4; 3 & 4 Phil. & Mary, c. 4. **36** *Lords' jn. Ire.*, i, pp 477-8.

Sydney prorogued the parliament the same day. A fresh parliament was not to meet again until August 1695, although so long an intermission was envisaged by no-one as likely at the time.

In the wake of a sequence of events unparalleled in the history of the local parliament, Sydney took action to bolster his position. Early in February 1693, the Irish judges were directed to examine the contentions that had been advanced by the House of Commons.[37] Responding swiftly, in a lengthy and illuminating opinion presented to Sydney on the 14th, the judges – eight in all[38] – in effect supported the lord lieutenant's stance.[39] In the first place, they denied that the commons possessed the so-called 'sole right' to prepare heads of bill for raising money. Secondly, they affirmed that the chief governor and council retained the prerogatives Sydney claimed: to prepare money bills; to certify and to transmit these to the monarch and privy council in England with a view to their being returned under the English great seal and thereafter forwarded to the Irish commons; and all this applied even though the heads of such bills had not had their first rise in the commons.

In preparing their report for Sydney, the Irish judges undertook a careful examination of Irish parliamentary records and also of the dates entered on the transmisses of various proposed measures forwarded in the past to England. From this, they deduced that many money bills had been initiated when parliament had not actually been sitting, thus warranting the necessary inference that these had been initiated by the privy council. And this remained the picture even after the adoption of the amendment to Poynings's Law under Philip and Mary, a major constitutional change which for the first time enabled draft bills to be forwarded to the English privy council whilst parliament was actually sitting. (Previously, all measures proposed for adoption had to be cleared in advance of the summoning of parliament itself.) It was true, the judges went on to concede, that the commons had prepared bills and heads for money and other purposes, but this practice was to be viewed 'as remembrances by way of humble advice and not in point of right'. It was impossible, accordingly, to accept as a matter of correct constitutional interpretation that the Irish executive had lost the power of initiating financial legislation. A sweetener was added for the benefit of the commons: the state of affairs that their researches had revealed the judges adjudged 'no inconveniency', since the commons could always reject any bill.

The Irish privy council adopted the judges' report the day it was presented, 14 February.[40] Enclosing a copy in a letter to the earl of Nottingham, the secretary of state, on the 20th, Sydney warned that he was far from convinced that this would be the end of the affair. 'Notwithstanding all this', he reported:

37 *Cal. S. P. dom., 1693*, p. 28: warrant by lord lieutenant and council, 6 February 1693. **38** The chiefs of the three courts, Richard Reynell (King's Bench), Richard Pyne (Common Pleas), John Hely (Exchequer), and five puisnes, John Lydon and Henry Echlin (King's Bench), Richard Cox and John Jeffreyson (Common Pleas) and Standish Hartstonge (Exchequer). The only signature missing was that of the second puisne in the Exchequer, Richard Ryves. He, however, had died early in 1693: F.E. Ball, *The judges in Ireland, 1221-1921*, 2 vols. (London, 1926), ii, 60. **39** Howard supplies a printed text: idem, *Miscellaneous works*, iii, 192. And see too City of Dublin Public Libraries, Pearse St., MS. 39 (Gilbert coll.), pp 139-50. **40** *Cal. S. P. dom., 1693*, p. 35.

> there are some here that say they will never quit the point, and that they would rather be taxed by parliament in England. What is to be expected from these gentlemen in the House of Commons may easily be imagined.[41]

These self-same 'gentlemen' Sydney had earlier castigated as 'a company of madmen'.[42]

As the prospect of a resumed parliamentary sitting came nearer and English parliamentarians in tandem with their Irish allies continued their attack on the Irish executive on a broad front and with increasing vehemence, the tone of Sydney's letters to Nottingham in turn became perceptibly more frenetic. On 17 March, with the political temperature still close to boiling-point, Sydney, in virtual desperation it would seem, asked for the clearest possible instructions from London. Specifically, the lord lieutenant wanted to know precisely how he was to conduct himself should it be decided to resume the parliament in April, a contingency that, somewhat surprisingly, still appears to have been on the cards even at this late date. In that event, he wrote to Nottingham, 'it will be necessary' for the king:

> to give his orders … as to whether any notice shall be taken of the votes of last session, touching their claim to have money bills begun in the house of commons, what is to be done with them if they attack the Lord Chancellor, the Speaker, or any others that have appeared in His Majesty's interest, what bills should be presented to them, how to proceed if they receive them, and what to do if they reject them.[43]

Sydney was destined to be recalled in June, three months later. Confidence in his statecraft had probably been shattered by the self-evident deterioration in the Irish political situation, a deterioration due in no small measure to Sydney's own ill-advised actions. Before then, in March, and to create breathing-space, a lifeline of sorts was thrown. In a letter sent to Sydney by Nottingham on the 18th, and which will have crossed with Sydney's own letter of the day before, the secretary of state brought the lord lieutenant two items of intelligence.[44] First, the plan to reconvene parliament in the immediate future had been dropped: Sydney was instructed rather to continue the prorogation for a further six weeks. (Nottingham added that September was now thought the likeliest early sitting date, but, as has already been indicated, this parliament was later to be dissolved and the next parliament was not actually to meet again for over two years.) The second piece of news concerned another decision that may have seemed a trifle unorthodox: the English judges were also to be invited to explore the constitutional claims of the Irish commons. 'His Majesty has ordered', Nottingham wrote:

> that as soon as the judges shall come from their circuits, they shall meet and consider the claims of the House of Commons relating to money bills; for

41 Ibid., p. 38. **42** *Cal. S. P. dom., 1695 and addenda*, p. 213: Sydney to Nottingham, 17 October 1692. **43** *Cal. S. P. dom., 1693*, p. 69. **44** Ibid., p. 71.

> though the judges of Ireland have made the matter plain, yet the opinion of the judges here will strengthen and add weight to it, and it can be resolved what measures should be taken in the money bills to be passed when parliament sits.

The English judges were duly commissioned and duly met. Their report, presented to the king on 22 June, and bearing the signatures of all twelve common law judges, led by Chief Justice Holt of the King's Bench,[45] was in the following terms:

> The opinion of all the judges of England about the sole and undoubted right of the commons of Ireland to prepare heads of money bills ...
>
> In obedience to your majesty's commands, signified by the right honourable the Lord Keeper of your great seal of England, requiring us to consider an act of parliament, made in Ireland, 10 Henry VII intituled, An act that no Parliament be holden in this land, until the acts be certified into England; and an act of Parliament made there, 3d and 4th Philip and Mary, intituled, An act how Poinings shall be expounded and taken; we thereupon certify to your majesties our opinions in writing, under our hands in the particulars following:
>
> 1 Whether it is the sole and undoubted right of the commons of Ireland, in parliament assembled, to prepare heads of bills for raising money?
>
> 2 Whether the Lord Lieutenant and council may not prepare and certify bills for raising money, to their majesties and council of England, to be returned under the great seal of England, and afterwards sent to the commons, unless the heads of such bills have first their rise in that house?
>
> We have met together and considered the same, and we are thereupon of opinion,
>
> 1 That it is not the sole and undoubted right of the commons in Ireland, in parliament assembled, to prepare heads of bills for raising money.
>
> 2 That the Lord Lieutenant may prepare and certify bills for raising money, to your majesty and council of England, to be returned under the great seal of England, and afterwards sent to the commons, albeit the heads of such bills have not their first rise in that house.[46]

The reference to the English bench in 1693 was not the first occasion upon which an English king had solicited the advice of his judges on a difficulty linked to Poynings's Law and the Irish parliament. In 1613, James I had sought judicial clarification of several key phrases in Poynings's Law itself. The reference of 1613 preceded the summoning of an Irish parliament later that year – the first for nearly three decades – and the clarification that the judges were able to pass on to the king will be found

45 Aside from Holt, the signatories were G. Treby (chief justice of Common Pleas), R. Atkins (chief baron) and the following puisnes – W. Dolben, W. Gregorie, G. Eyre (King's Bench); E. Nevil, J. Powell, T. Rokeby (Common Pleas); and W. Letchmore, J. Turton and J. Fowell (Exchequer). **46** The printed text in Howard, *Miscellaneous works*, iii, 205, and the transcription in the Pearse St. library (note 39, above), MS. 39, pp 151–2, furnish the names of all twelve signatories; these are not given in *Cal. S. P. dom., 1693*, at p. 191.

reproduced in the pages of Coke's Reports.[47] But one remarkable aspect of the reference of eighty years later sufficed to place it in a class all its own. It followed hard on the heels of the reference of the identical questions to the Irish judicial bench, which that bench had answered at great length in their report to Sydney of February 14. Nottingham, as secretary of state in London, had seen that report and accepted that this 'made the matter plain'.[48] The sole justification he could light on for seeking a second report from the English bench was his contention that this would 'strengthen and add weight to it'.[49] That choice of words, it is obvious, left little room for manoeuvre to the English judges, least of all any of them tempted to distance themselves from the stance earlier adopted by their Irish counterparts.

No allusion is made to it and it cannot therefore be firmly established but, nevertheless, it is very probable that the English judges were supplied with a copy of the earlier Irish report of February. As to their own report of June, whatever weight the verdict it enshrined may have added to that arrived at previously by the judges in Ireland did not derive from any fresh evidence or novel contention advanced: the report itself amounts to nothing more than a bland recapitulation of the two major conclusions set forth in the Irish report. On any view, the soliciting of this second report was an unusual tactic. The explanation for it is to be found in the contemporary political situation in both Ireland and England. Nottingham will have gathered from Sydney's letters to him that a sizeable number of senior practitioners in Ireland had come out against the lord lieutenant's interpretation of the constitution. Sydney told Nottingham on 6 November 1692, for instance, that the then prime serjeant, Serjeant Osborne, and 'almost all the rest of their Majesties' counsel' had supported the commons' claim.[50] (He had, for good measure and to show who was in charge, then proceeded to dismiss Osborne from his post, as well as an ally, the third serjeant, Serjeant Broderick.)[51] If the English judges could be depended upon to deliver the goods, this would demonstrate, it may very well have been argued in London, that trouble-makers such as Osborne, Broderick and others of like mind, were, legally speaking, out on a constitutional limb or, to put it in cruder political terms, on a hiding to nothing.[52]

But it is far from fanciful to infer that there may not have been other considerations besides. William III and his advisers in London will almost certainly have come to appreciate that in both England and Ireland the Irish bench was perceived as being too close, politically, to Sydney. The evidence, indeed, was there for all to see. After the prorogation of November, various members of the Irish bench had elected to accept knighthoods from Sydney,[53] a controversial move that prompted the taunt that the elevation was 'for intellectual services rendered' (as a cynical twentieth century citation might have phrased it). Against such a background, any opinion that the Irish judges might have chosen to proffer on a contentious constitutional question was likely to be

47 *Parliament in Ireland*, 12 Co. Rep. 110, 77 Eng. Rep. 1386. **48** *Cal. S. P. dom., 1693*, p. 71: Nottingham to Sydney, 18 March 1693. **49** Ibid. **50** *Cal. S. P. dom., 1695 and addenda*, p. 217. **51** Ibid., p. 218: Sydney to Nottingham, 9 November 1692. **52** On the role of Osborne and Broderick in orchestrating opposition to Sydney, see McGuire, 'The Irish parliament of 1692', at p. 13. **53** Ball, *The judges in Ireland*, ii, 11, 54, (Richard Cox), 57 (Henry Echlin and John Hely), 59 (John Jeffreyson and Richard Pyne).

viewed as lacking the rigour and detachment due from a truly independent judiciary, now in the process of being identified as a vital landmark in the constitutional landscape. In short, the opinion will have been bruited abroad that the Irish judicial bench was compromised.[54] The soliciting of a second report can thus be seen as an option selected not only to help isolate elements in the Irish legal fraternity but also to help calm the political turmoil in both London and Dublin, linked in part to the belief that the Irish bench had overstepped the mark, turmoil that was, if anything, threatening to get even worse. Though strictly a report addressed to William III, the English judges' opinion of 22 June 1693 assuredly also qualifies as another 'letter to Ireland'.[55]

So far as one can tell, Sydney had not personally pressed for this additional lifeline, though doubtless he was happy enough to have it extended to him. It did not, however, fall to Sydney to extract any political advantage from the English judges' opinion of June, for, as we have seen, even before the opinion was presented to the king, he himself had been recalled. A succession of lords justices was to govern Ireland until Capel's appointment as lord deputy in 1695 and the Irish parliament, as has already been remarked, did not in the event reconvene until the same year.

Sydney may have won the constitutional argument in 1692-3 but, as the years rolled by, it became plain that this had counted for little more than a Pyrrhic victory. For a while, admittedly, it did indeed look as if the pronouncement on the respective roles of executive and legislature in regard to money bills, adopted by Sydney and endorsed by judicial opinion on both sides of the Irish Sea, might prevail. As J.L. McCracken has pointed out:

> The commons' claim to an exclusive right to initiate revenue bills was not consistently maintained: in 1703, 1713, 1715, and 1727 revenue bills prepared and transmitted by the council in England were accepted and passed by the house.[56]

On the other hand, as things turned out, there was to be a repeat performance of the events of the autumn of 1692 in November 1769 during the Townshend viceroyalty when, once again, the commons proceeded to reject another money bill on the self-same grounds that the measure had not taken its rise in the commons.[57] By then, however, it had become abundantly plain that the evolution in eighteenth century Irish constitutional practice had swung round to the view propounded by the commons in 1692. As a sop to what remained of constitutional theory and by way of

54 It is not unconnected that a rumour apparently was spread of a plan actually to impeach the judges. *Cal. S. P. dom., 1693*, p. 121: Sydney to Nottingham, 5 May 1693. **55** In 1713, in the dispute over the Dublin mayoralty election, Queen Anne's administration was again to seek two sets of advice over the legality of a retiring lord mayor's supposed prerogatives. One set of advice was provided by the Irish judges, the second by the queen's law officers and other counsel in England. See *Calendar of the ancient records of Dublin*, eds. Sir J.T. and Lady Gilbert, 19 vols. (Dublin, 1889-1944), vi, 526-7. **56** 'The political structure, 1714-60', in T.W. Moody and W.E. Vaughan (eds.), *A new history of Ireland – iv: eighteenth century Ireland, 1691-1800* (Oxford, 1986), p. 57 at p. 65. **57** R.B. McDowell, *Ireland in the age of imperialism and revolution, 1760-1801* (Oxford, 1979), pp 225-7; Thomas Bartlett, 'The Townshend viceroyalty, 1767-72', in Bartlett & Hayton (eds.), *Penal era and golden age*, p. 96.

a sort of gentleman's agreement, the Irish commons continued to tolerate the practice of allowing the privy council to draw up a supply bill as the cause for summoning each fresh parliament.[58] That aside, it was incontrovertible that the commons did indeed now possess a general right to initiate any kind of money bill. The commons, despite a series of reverses, had come into its own.

The 1693 reference to the English judges raised an issue of high politics; so too, although less conspicuously, did the earlier reference of 1569. In complete contrast, a request for assistance from the same quarter which is documented for 1725 related to decidedly much more mundane business. On this occasion, the request was addressed to the recorder of London from his Dublin counterpart, John Rogerson. The son of the Sir John Rogerson, the Dublin lord mayor after whom a stretch of the quays along the River Liffey is named, Rogerson had been made recorder of Dublin in 1714, holding that office concurrently with other posts he held successively, first that of solicitor general and then that of attorney general. Disappointed in the representations he made to become lord chancellor in 1725, Rogerson was fated to be elevated two years later to the Irish King's Bench as chief justice.[59]

One Offleman had succeeded in an action upon a promissory note heard in the Dublin courts probably early in 1725. An appeal was taken by way of a writ of error but, in the result, the judgment in favour of Offleman was affirmed. In the interim, before a decision on the writ of error was pronounced, separate proceedings (on a *scire facias*) had been commenced in the recorder's court before Rogerson against two individuals who had gone surety for the defaulter, a man called Hunt. In these proceedings, counsel for Offleman moved for judgment in his favour on the basis of the recent outcome in the related principal suit. To such a course being adopted exception was taken on the grounds that the issuance of the writ of error sufficed to remove the associated proceedings before the recorder from his cognisance altogether. Rogerson overruled the objection and decided in Offleman's favour. Before doing so, however, he took the precaution of sounding out his counterpart in London, as O'Callaghan's note of the case discloses:

> The defendants becoming bail for Hunt at the suit of Offleman in an action upon a promissory note, judgment was for Offleman, and a *scire facias* was brought on the recognisance to which demurrer and joinder in demurrer [were made]. Before judgment on the *scire facias*, error was brought of the principal judgment which was affirmed. I moved for judgment on the *scire facias*, and Rogerson, recorder of Dublin, having consulted Thompson, recorder of London, gave judgment for the plaintiff and said that there being a suit commenced on the recognisance they became distinct records, and that the writ of error could no more remove the proceeding on the *scire [facias]* than it could remove judgment on the *scire facias* if such had been given.[60]

58 Declan O'Donovan, 'The money bill dispute of 1753', in Bartlett & Hayton (eds.), *Penal era and golden age*, p. 55 at p. 58, n. 3; J.G. Simms, 'The establishment of protestant ascendancy, 1691–1714', in Moody & Vaughan (eds.), *New history of Ireland – iv*, p. 1 at p. 2. **59** Ball, *The judges of Ireland*, ii, 107–8, 199–200. **60** *Offleman* v. *Kennedy and Dover, Manucaptors of Hunt*, 9 Sept. 1725 in the Tholsel before Rogerson, 'Cases

The details of a second eighteenth century instance of help proffered by the English bench are tantalisingly incomplete. Significantly, perhaps, it emerges, however, that the dispute that had surfaced concerned some aspect of criminal law. In Hilary term, 1788, one of the king's serjeants, Serjeant Adair, argued unsuccessfully for the acquittal of a murderer on a writ of error returnable before the King's Bench. Adair's argument was couched in 'very extraordinary terms', according to our informant, the marquis of Buckingham, who had just commenced his second stint in office as Irish lord lieutenant the previous November.[61] Adair, so we are told, had expressed 'his particular anxiety for the credit of the criminal justice in Ireland' and had also alluded – in menacing terms as Buckingham saw it – to the remedy the defendant would be forced to seek should the court rule against him:

> he pointed out a remedy (in the teeth of the judicature bill) in case the court shall give judgment in defiance of his objections.

The King's Bench, then presided over by Lord Earlsfort,[62] was not impressed by Adair's impassioned plea or threat of further proceedings; rather, they overruled him *una voce*.

Unhappily, the precise focus of the immediate controversy does not appear as this was of no particular interest to Buckingham. A detail divulged in the relevant letter to his brother in London[63] is, however, of some interest to us here. Apparently, Lord Earlsfort, after announcing the decision of the King's Bench, produced – and produced, Buckingham implies, in the body of the court – a letter which, in the lord lieutenant's words, gave 'the unanimous opinion of the English King's Bench on the same side'. Thus was Adair routed, so it was triumphantly announced.

A further reference of another moot point of criminal law occurred not long after. Fixing a precise date presents a difficulty, something that was to be explained judicially very much later, in 1882.[64] The reference itself was made in the course of the case of a Major Campbell who was tried for murder. This trial took place some time between 1783 and 1816.

On the other hand, unlike for 1788, we know a great deal about the actual circumstances that led to the eliciting of guidance from the English bench. A problem had arisen concerning the practice to be followed over the admissibility in evidence of a dying declaration. For such declaration to be admissible, it was common ground that it had to be shown that at the time the declaration was made the declarant had no hope of recovery. Was this vital issue to be ruled on by the trial judge or could it be left to the jury to resolve? As with the form of the pleadings in darrein presentment when the exception of plenarty was raised – a problem in the medieval common law

from the common place book of Cornelius O'Callaghan' (Extracts from Mr Gore's notes): City of Dublin Public Libraries, Pearse St., MS. 36 (Gilbert coll.), pp 437–8. **61** HMC, *Fortescue MSS.*, i, 302: marquis of Buckingham to W.W. Grenville, 6 February 1788. **62** The former John Scott, later raised to a viscountcy (1789) and an earldom (1793) and known as Lord Clonmell. **63** W.W. Grenville, prime minister (as Lord Grenville), 1806–7. **64** By Baron Fitzgerald in *The Queen* v. *Colclough* (1882) 10 LR Ir 241 at 257. This was a decision of the Irish Court for Crown Cases Reserved.

we have examined earlier – English authority was again inconsistent. One precedent of 1789 had been content to leave the issue to the jury; further precedents of 1790 and 1792 had ruled unequivocally that the issue was to be decided by the judge.

At the trial of Major Campbell, the presiding judge followed the earlier English precedent of 1789. A case was stated for the twelve judges, under the informal procedure that then prevailed for their convening, a procedure which anticipated the later establishment of the Court for Crown Cases Reserved.[65] When they eventually met, the judges resolved to seek the advice of their English confrères on the point of law in dispute. The latter, so we are told:

> unanimously concurred that the course taken was not the right one, and that the judge ought to have decided the question himself.[66]

The Irish judges themselves then endorsed that view.

Charles Kendal Bushe held the office of chief justice of the Irish King's Bench for nineteen years, from 1822 to 1841; in the eighteenth century only Lord Annaly had held the office for longer. During Bushe's extended tenure two well authenticated requests for information and advice addressed by him at the behest of the Irish bench to his English counterparts are on record: the first to Chief Justice Abbott (the later Lord Tenterden) in 1826 and the second to Lord Chief Justice Denman in 1838.

In Hilary term 1826, the Irish judges, possibly at Bushe's own suggestion, embarked on a review of their limited jurisdiction to hear criminal 'appeals', the jurisdiction that had been invoked, for example, in the Major Campbell case. From before the end of the preceding century, the judges travelling circuit had adopted the convention of 'reserving' moot points of criminal law for resolution by all the superior court judges meeting in Dublin. In 1826 discussion centred on two practical questions:

(i) whether counsel should be heard when the judges met to consider these 'reserved cases'; and
(ii) how the conclusions reached by the assembled judges were to be communicated.

The judges decided that, before taking any action, they would find out how things were handled in England. Bushe accordingly wrote to his English equivalent, Chief Justice Abbott. The episode and the outcome are dealt with succinctly by Jebb in his *Crown and Presentment Cases*:

> For the purpose of ascertaining the English practice, Bushe CJ wrote to the lord chief justice of England, who informed him of the particulars of that practice. The summary of it is that if the judge who reserved the case thinks it of such a

65 11 & 12 Vict., c. 78. **66** 10 LR Ir at 257. In the *Colclough* case, the accused, the stamp distributor in the Queen's Bench Division, had been charged with uttering forged documents. The right of the trial judge to rule on the sufficiency of the evidence adduced by the prosecution became the focus of attention, and provided the pretext for Fitzgerald's historical excursus which led him back to the Major Campbell case.

> nature that counsel should argue it, it generally is argued by one counsel on each side; the argument is in open court, but the judges do not deliver any opinion in court; the opinion is made known by the judge who presides at the next assizes or sessions, as in cases where counsel are not heard.[67]

The reply satisfied Bushe and his colleagues who thereupon resolved to follow the English practice in both respects.

Bushe's correspondence with Lord Denman in 1838 dealt with a split of opinion within the Irish bench in the wake of the passage of the reform bills in 1832: over the issue of whether the self-same meetings of the Twelve Judges convened to tackle reserved criminal cases could, in effect, be constitutionally convened to settle disputed questions on the registrability of electors arising under the new parliamentary franchise. In Ireland different judges had offered different interpretations, an unhappy spectacle to which Baron Smith had drawn early attention in the controversial grand jury charge he delivered in October 1833 at the Dublin city commission, which precipitated a parliamentary debate engineered by Daniel O'Connell.[68] A majority on the bench, sensing the need for uniformity, admitted the competence of the Twelve Judges to hand down binding judgments, even at the price of being forced to abandon preferred individual interpretations. A minority, consisting of Baron Richards and Mr Justice Perrin, was adamantly opposed, challenging head-on the pretensions of any majority to deliver binding declarations.

A climax appears to have been reached in Hilary term 1838, as Jebb, who is again our source of information, reveals:

> In consequence of a doubt which had been raised as to the extent to which an individual judge, upon circuit, ought to consider himself bound by the opinion and decision of the majority of the twelve judges upon questions reserved from circuit for their consideration in Queen's Bench Chamber, it was resolved at a meeting of the judges, on the 11th of February 1838 that the English practice upon this subject should be ascertained.[69]

Chief Justice Bushe thus once more took up his pen to write to his English counterpart, now Lord Denman who had succeeded Lord Tenterden as English chief justice in 1832.

Bushe wrote from his country estate in Co. Kilkenny a letter, which in the version that is extant is dated 8 February, three days before the date Jebb gives for the meeting of the judges in Dublin. The sole specimen to hand of the precise language in which an Irish correspondent craved assistance on legal questions from England, Bushe's letter, sadly, must be adjudged something of a disappointment. A longwinded epistle, cover-

67 *Resolution of the 12 Judges of Ireland as to hearing Counsel on Reserved Cases:* Robert Jebb, *Cases, chiefly relating to the criminal and presentment law, reserved for consideration and decided by the twelve judges of Ireland, from May 1822 to November 1840* (Dublin, 1841), p. 1. **68** Robert Day, Grand jury charges (4 MS. vols, Royal Irish Academy), iv, 348 at 349 (pasted-in newspaper cutting); Ball, *The judges in Ireland*, ii, 272. **69** *In the matter of decisions upon reserved cases:* Jebb, *Crown and presentment cases*, pp 234–5.

ing the essence of the problem admittedly, it yet fails to help concentrate Denman's mind on the specific topic he was supposed to be addressing. 'My lord', Bushe wrote:

> At the desire of the judges of Ireland, I take a liberty, which I am sure your lordship will forgive, as connected with the administration of justice. With a view to the right of the parties in the particular instance, and in order to establish, as far as may be, uniformity of decision, we have been in the habit of reserving, upon circuit, cases of difficulty arising in the Crown Court, or in our jurisdiction (I believe, peculiar to Ireland) of judges of appeal, as judges of assize, from the decisions of assistant barristers in the several counties, and in the following term each judge who has done so, sends to each other judge, with a view of obtaining the advice and assistance of his brethren, a written statement of the facts of the case, and the questions arising from them; and the chief justice, by notice, assembles the judges for the purpose of taking such references into consideration; at which meeting, if the judges consider it proper, or if the parties require it, a day is fixed for the argument of the case by counsel at both sides, and such argument is heard in public; and after the argument, the judges, among themselves and not in public, either on the same day, or on a subsequent day, fixed for the purpose, discuss the case; and if there be a difference of opinion each judge, beginning with the junior, states the reasons for his opinion; and according to what appears to be the opinion of the majority, the conviction, if in a criminal case, is held to be good or bad; or if in an appeal case the judgment of the assistant barrister below is to be affirmed or reversed, and the necessary steps are taken by the judge, who reserved the case, for communicating the decision to the proper officer. So far, I believe, there is no substantial difference between the proceedings in England and Ireland; but it has recently become necessary in this country, from some differences of opinion upon the subject, to ascertain to what extent such a resolution by the judges, when not unanimous, is obligatory upon, or ought to influence such of the judges as constituted the minority, and for that purpose it is our wish to be apprised of what is understood among the English judges upon that subject, and to learn whether a judge, who was in such minority, would consider himself at liberty, upon the ensuing circuits, to rule contrary to the decision, and according to his own original opinion; or whether he would treat the decision as binding upon him, until overruled by higher authority, or reviewed or altered upon a subsequently reserved case.[70]

In ending his letter, Bushe did not hide the fact that the matters he had aired were now regarded as ones of considerable practical importance in Ireland. In the circumstances, he begged for the favour of an early reply and before his colleagues departed on the spring assize circuits.

70 Bushe to Denman, 8 February 1838, quoted, John Alcock, *Observations concerning the nature and origin of the meetings of the twelve judges for the consideration of cases reserved from the circuits* (Dublin, 1838), pp 2–3.

Denman obliged, forwarding to Bushe on 13 February a one paragraph reply:

> I am honoured with your lordship's letter, inquiring whether the judges of England, on their circuits, hold themselves bound by the opinion of the whole body of the judges on Crown Cases reserved; and I have no difficulty in stating that each of us does hold himself so bound, whether or not his own opinion agreed with that of the majority, or whether or not the case may have been argued by counsel.[71]

Prompt, undoubtedly, Denman's reply was, but it is plain, even making allowances for confusion attributable to the cumbersome fashion in which the Irish chief justice had presented his query, that Denman had failed to grapple with the specific difficulty peculiar to Ireland on which Bushe had sought clarification. Irish variation having affected Irish practice the way it had, it was perhaps inevitable that such would be the outcome. Bushe wanted guidance on what to do about registry cases, and here Denman could furnish no meaningful assistance at all.

The exchange of letters with Denman was to settle nothing: if the purpose behind the approach to England was to gain backing for precedential authority to be accorded majority decisions, it failed lamentably. When the crunch issue of the interpretation of the law on the registrability of electors again came before the Irish judges at their Easter term meeting on 30 April, Baron Richards and Mr Justice Perrin stood firm, reiterating their opposition to the idea that rulings of individual judges were amenable to this form of 'appeal' and could thus by a majority determination be set at nought.[72] Denman's obvious support for the principle of collegial uniformity the two dissenters dismissed as totally unwarranted in the context of Irish electoral law, and, by extension, totally inapplicable as well. The division of opinion within the Irish judiciary was set to continue as the quarrel itself rumbled on. In 1841 the minority secured a fresh convert: that year Maziere Brady, raised to the bench as chief baron of the Exchequer in 1840, in a reasoned judicial opinion, chose to align himself with the views propounded by Richards and Perrin in 1838.[73] The quarrel itself was only to be brought to an end when resort was eventually had to parliamentary action. This came in 1850 when explicit powers were for the first time bestowed upon the Twelve Judges to entertain appeals in registry cases.[74] The episode teaches the important lesson, novel to this inventory, that recourse to England for enlightenment might prove no panacea at all when the Irish legal situation was markedly different and the local judiciary were themselves hopelessly divided.[75]

Lord Denman's reply to Bushe in 1838 was brief to the point of terseness. It is not obvious, for instance, that he understood the need to explore the subtleties and complexities of Ireland's embryonic system of appeals before sitting down to compose

71 Denman to Bushe, 13 February 1838: Alcock, op. cit., p. 4; Jebb, *Crown and presentment cases*, p. 235. **72** *In the matter of decisions upon reserved cases*: Jebb, *Crown and presentment cases*, p. 235. The majority, on the occasion of the vote, consisted of the two chief justices, Bushe himself and Doherty, Chief Baron Joy, the puisne judges, Moore, Johnson, Burton, Torrens and Crampton and the puisne barons, Pennefather and Foster. **73** *In re Larkin*, 4 Ir LR 46. **74** 13 & 14 Viet, c. 69: see ss. 58, 74 and 79. **75** See further Desmond Greer, 'Lawyers or politicians? The Irish judges and the right to vote 1832–1850', in Caroline Costello (ed.), *The Four Courts: 200 years* (Dublin, 1996), p. 126.

his response. In stark contrast, in 1905, in the single twentieth century exchange of correspondence between the two benches to be included here, Lord Alverstone, a successor of Denman's in the post of English chief justice, went to inordinate lengths to contrive to be as helpful as possible. The explanation for this may have lain, in part at least, on this side of the Irish Sea. The Irish King's Bench Division, the referring court, had gone to a deal of trouble to prepare a memorandum for Alverstone to reply to. As a matter of courtesy, the latter very probably felt under an obligation to respond in kind.

A board of conservators had launched a prosecution against a mill-owner for polluting a river. The summons, framed under s. 80 of the Irish Fisheries Act 1842,[76] charged him with causing deleterious matter to be discharged into the river in question. In contention was the identification of the exact stage at which the deleterious character of the matter placed in the river required to be ascertained. The justices who heard the summons interpreted s. 80 in a particular manner, as a consequence of which the prosecution was dismissed. The board of conservators appealed, but Judge Orr, the chairman of quarter sessions, accepted the views of the justices and affirmed the dismiss. Judge Orr, however, then adopted a mode of proceeding which until then, apparently, had been unknown in Irish quarter sessions practice. Despite the acquittal, he stated a case for a higher court, an initiative which entailed that when the acquittal was duly brought before the King's Bench Division by way of certiorari, that court would necessarily have before it the question of the correct interpretation of s. 80. At the consequent hearing before the King's Bench Division, a majority (Lord O'Brien CJ, Palles CB and Gibson J)[77] resolved that on the principal point of law, the interpretation of s. 80, both the justices and Judge Orr had been in error. The stage at which the deleterious character of the matter discharged required to be ascertained was at the very moment it entered the river and not, as the two lower courts had maintained, at some moment subsequent to that. It followed, accordingly, that the grounds set out in the case stated by Judge Orr as justification for the acquittal were bad in law.[78]

Judge Orr's initiative in stating a case was applauded but now that a majority of the court was about to decide that both the acquittal and its confirmation rested on an erroneous interpretation of law, bafflement stared the King's Bench Division in the face, bafflement over the powers of disposal that were available to them. Could they, for example, without further ado, remit the case to the lower court, enabling, in effect, the prosecution to be reopened? Uncertain that they possessed any such power, the judges, having reserved judgment after hearing argument on 27 October and 4 and 10 November 1905, resolved to seek assistance from London. A memorandum with accompanying letter was thus drawn up and sent to Lord Alverstone.

The latter replied with a detailed memorandum on 1 December. The King's Bench Division announced their judgment on 16 January 1906. Though, as we have seen, they were divided on the interpretation of the critical section in the act of 1842, they were agreed that Lord Alverstone's memorandum was invaluable and should be

76 5 & 6 Vict., c. 106. **77** Madden and Wright JJ dissented. **78** *The King* v. *Justices of Antrim* [1906] 2 IR 298.

placed on the records of the court and printed in the Irish Reports. What by the early years of the twentieth century was probably regarded as the adoption of a wholly exceptional strategy was doubtless thought warranted by members of the court because of the novelty of the predicament in which the court had found itself. And arranging a wide circulation for Alverstone's remarks could, in the light of all the attendant circumstances, be defended on a somewhat similar line of reasoning.

Lord Alverstone's memorandum was cast in the following terms:

> A simple answer to the questions enumerated at the end of the Memorandum enclosed in the letter of The Lord Chief Justice of Ireland, of November, will not, in my opinion, give exactly the information which appears to me to be desired. I will, however, answer the questions in the first instance, and then add some supplementary observations which will, I trust, cover the ground of the inquiry.
>
> 1. In the case of an acquittal by Quarter Sessions, subject to a case stated, if, in the opinion of the Court, upon such case the accused ought to have been convicted, the Court, when acting under its Common Law jurisdiction, would have quashed such acquittal.
> 2. If the acquittal was quashed, the Court did not remit the case to Sessions to proceed to determine the appeal, treating it as open and undetermined; the only judgment pronounced was one confirming or quashing the order or conviction appealed against. The decision in the case of *Rex* v. *Bloxam* has been followed in subsequent cases; but, for the reasons which I will state in my Memorandum, that case has little, if any, direct bearing upon the point under discussion.
>
> A copy of the order in *Rex* v. *Bloxam* is sent herewith.
>
> I desire to supplement the answers which I have given to the questions, specifically submitted to me, by a few observations.
>
> The practice of stating cases from Quarter Sessions at Common Law, as apart from statute, has arisen, as the framers of the Memorandum are well aware, out of the ancient direction in the Commission to the parties to take the opinion of the Judge of Assize. Owing to the inconvenience of that course, there arose the practice of stating a special case for the opinion of the Court of King's Bench.
>
> Prior to the Judicature Act of 1894, it had become the settled practice of the Court of King's Bench not to consider or express an opinion upon a special case, unless the order or conviction appealed from finally disposed of the matter.
>
> The cases of *R.* v. *Kesteven* ([1844] 3 QB 801), *R.* v. *Marton cum Grafton* ([1847] 10 QB 971), *R.* v. *Sutton Coldfield* ([1874] LR 9 QB 153), and *R.* v. *Skinner* [1884], are instances of the application of this rule, and many other cases may be found, although, as appears from the reports, attempts had been made from time to time to induce the Court of King's Bench to interfere, and entertain a case which only dealt with the matter interlocutorily.

> The Rule of Law is, in my opinion, correctly stated at p. 175 of Short and Mellor's Crown Office Practice.
>
> I send herewith a note of the case of *R.* v. *Skinner* in 1884, which is not reported.
>
> I may further point out that the argument based upon this principle is clearly stated in the judgment of Lord Cairns in the case of *The Overseers of Walsall* v. *London & North-Western Railway Co.*, at pp 39-42 of 4 App Cas, and accepted by him as one of the grounds of his judgment in that case.
>
> The fact that the Court of Queen's Bench was, in consequence of this well-established principle, fettered in its action and unable at times to do full justice, had been pointed out on more than one occasion; see, among others, the note in *Reg.* v. *Skinner*; and it was mainly in consequence of this result that sub-sect. 2 of sect. 2 of the Judicature Act, 1894, was passed to enable the Court of Queen's Bench to make the order which the Court of Quarter Sessions might have made, or to remit the case, if necessary, for a re-hearing.
>
> Side by side with this jurisdiction of the Court of King's Bench there was the jurisdiction to quash by certiorari, and to compel a re-hearing by mandamus on various grounds, which it is not necessary here to discuss. *Rex* v. *Bloxam* ([1834] 1 Ad & E 386) was an instance of the exercise of that kind of jurisdiction. It followed *R.* v. *Ridgway* ([1822] 5 B & Ald 527), and it has not been infrequent when rules for a certiorari have been granted, if there has not been a proper hearing, to direct a hearing by mandamus, or otherwise, or at times to order cases to be re-stated if the point was not sufficiently raised.
>
> These authorities in no way affect the principle upon which the Court of King's Bench acted before the Statute of 1894, in cases stated by Sessions, where no application had been made for a certiorari.[79]

Acting in accordance with Lord Alverstone's information and advice, the King's Bench Division then reached certain predictable conclusions, admirably summarised in the headnote to the report of *The King* v. *Justices of Antrim* in the Irish Reports:

> When a court of quarter sessions acquits a defendant, and makes the acquittal subject to a case stated, wherein the reasons on which the quarter sessions acquitted are set forth, and such acquittal is brought up into the King's Bench Division by writ of certiorari, there is jurisdiction, under the Common Law, in the King's Bench Division to inquire into the sufficiency of the reasons so set forth, and if such reasons be found insufficient, the King's Bench Division will quash the order of quarter sessions. But the jurisdiction of the King's Bench Division in Ireland is confined to affirming or quashing the order of quarter sessions. There is no jurisdiction analogous to that which prevails in England under the Supreme Court of Judicature Act, 1894, section 2, to remit the order

79 [1906] 2 IR at 309-11. The footnotes to Lord Alverstone's memorandum, giving further details on the cases of *R.* v. *Bloxam* (1833) and *R.* v. *Skinner* (1884), have been omitted.

> with the opinion and direction of the court for rehearing and determination of the court of quarter sessions.[80]

If these proceedings of 1905-6 were thought to have brought to light a lacuna in Irish law, it is noteworthy that no immediate remedial steps were set in motion. It is possible to contend that there was no lacuna in fact and that *The King* v. *Justices of Antrim* ignored previous Irish authority which showed, contrary to what Lord O'Brien and his colleagues maintained, that the superior court did possess the power to remit after the prosecution had secured the quashing of an order of dismissal made by the lower court. Such a point of view had been expressed by Chief Justice Lefroy in *R.* v. *Thompson* in 1855.[81] 'It would seem to me extraordinary', Lefroy there declared:

> that a course should be set down for certiorari, and the court should adjudge that the justices were wrong, and set aside their decision, and, notwithstanding, that it should be necessary to wait for the issuing of a mandamus to order the parties to proceed. It really seems incidental to our jurisdiction that we should be able to order justices to proceed rightly.[82]

However this may be, in today's two Irish jurisdictions provision has been made by law enabling the superior court both to quash and to remit. In Northern Ireland, article 64 in the County Courts (NI) Order 1980[83] thus stipulates:

> upon the hearing of any appeal ... (including an appeal by way of case stated), the appellate court may –
> (d) where the appeal is by case stated, amend the case stated or remit it, with such declarations or directions as the appellate court may think proper, for hearing and determination by the county court or for re-statement or amendment or for a supplemental case to be stated thereon.

In the Republic, rule 26(4) of Order 84 of the Rules of the Superior Courts 1986 enshrines a comparable formula:

> Where the relief sought is an order of certiorari and the court is satisfied that there are grounds for quashing the decision to which the application relates, the court may, in addition to quashing it, remit the matter to the court, tribunal or authority concerned with a direction to reconsider it and reach a decision in accordance with the findings of the court.[84]

The latter rule, it has recently been affirmed, was a restatement of existing law and signalled no new departure.[85] However, this remains a notoriously tricky branch of law and the caution the King's Bench Division displayed in 1905-6 was thoroughly understandable and conveyed another lesson worth heeding.[86]

80 [1906] 2 IR at 298-9. **81** 7 Ir. Jur. 124. **82** Ibid., at 126. **83** SI no. 397 of 1980 (NI no. 3). **84** SI no. 15 of 1986. **85** *Sheehan* v. *Reilly* [1993] 2 IR 81. **86** For assistance in unravelling many of the complica-

Ireland witnessed the first adventure of the common law.[87] Throughout the centuries of the resultant close connection with England, however, the workshops of the common law remained firmly based at Westminster.[88] This side of the Irish Sea, any leanings towards intellectual irredentism, an acknowledged manifestation of the new common law in twentieth century Commonwealth jurisdictions,[89] were unimaginable and were never in vogue either.[90] Cultural dependency was accepted as a fact of life and within the climate of opinion that it engendered the conduct of the local governing élite – both in the original Anglo-Norman lordship and in the later all-island kingdom – was in certain particulars entirely predictable. When legal problems surfaced that were seen to require recourse to the oracles of the law for the best advice going, it was only natural that that élite should have had recourse to where those oracles were to be located. Invariably, that meant turning to London and challenging the judicial talent to be found there.

From the short inventory presented here, it will be seen to have emerged that the enlightenment being cultivated by means of correspondence was enlightenment on a bewildering array of topics. A process of random selection indeed might even appear to have been at work. Topics referred to the English bench might embrace puzzles in substantive law – on the form of the pleadings to be employed in a possessory assize such as darrein presentment, for example, or on the rules to apply *vis-à-vis* the admissibility in evidence at a murder trial of a dying declaration. In such areas of lawyers' law, the formulating of the initial inquiry and its subsequent transmission to England might naturally infer a degree of ignorance on the part of the inquirer, someone who should, if a truly competent legal professional, have known the answer himself. Yet, the drawing of such an inference could be quite illegitimate: in the case of both of the illustrations just given, the relevant law in the home of the common law itself – at two widely separated historical periods, as it happens – was in a state of considerable confusion. Seeking clarification from the experts felt to be close to the centre of things, on further reflection, might be seen to be both eminently intelligible and eminently intelligent. Failure to act in that manner indeed might rather invite criticism.

A number of the inquiries directed to the English bench touched on the small print of the common law and originated in problems that emerged in the course of ongoing court proceedings. With regard to these, one point merits emphasis. Difficulties in communication with England necessarily delayed the receipt of any guidance solicited from that quarter, but it has to be borne in mind that lawsuits in the medieval period and very much later, too, could prove long-drawn-out affairs and the time factor, in consequence, may not therefore have constituted quite the disincentive to

tions, see Kevin Costello, 'Certiorari followed by remittal', (1993) 3 *ICLJ* 145. **87** The phrase was coined by the late Mr Justice Johnston: W.J. Johnston, 'The first adventure of the common law', (1920) 36 *LQR* 9. **88** '... it is at Westminster and Lincoln's Inn that the officinae legum Angliae – the workshops for the manufacture of authoritative judge-made law – are only to be found. At the Four Courts we import that article; we do not manufacture it': Lord Justice Christian in *Hone* v. *Blanchi* (1877) 11 *ILTSJ* 586 at 589. **89** See, e.g., *Invercargill City Council* v. *Hamlin* [1996] AC 624 (observations on development of the common law in New Zealand). **90** There were common law variations between England and Ireland in the medieval period, however; for these, see G.J. Hand, *English law in Ireland, 1290-1324* (Cambridge, 1967), ch. 9, 'The custom of the land of Ireland'.

soliciting guidance as might otherwise have been supposed. Other inquiries were inspired by no particular difficulty aired in the courts. Here chief governors and judges alike took the initiative in seeking elucidation of some point of general principle or practice that struck them at the time as worth seeking. The decision of the Irish judges in 1826, when engaged in plans to reform the handling of reserved criminal cases, to approach Chief Justice Abbott in London to learn what they could from him about contemporary English practice, furnishes an apt illustration. Less frequently, doubt on some point of general principle or practice might register in the course of ongoing legal proceedings as well. Here, equally, recourse to London for elucidation of what needed to be elucidated might be had. Forwarding to Lord Alverstone in 1905 the list of queries on the powers of disposal available to a superior court when quashing an acquittal on certiorari – the problem raised in *The King* v. *Justices of Antrim* – provides an excellent example.

The broader the question on which the considered advice of the English bench was requested, the greater the risk, inevitably, that the latter would be accused of trespassing into the political domain. We do not know the sentiments of Chief Justice Holt and his colleagues over the instruction to them in the spring of 1693 to advise on a burning constitutional issue of the hour – the claim of the Irish commons to the sole and exclusive right to initiate money bills. Nor do we know how they regarded the receipt of this instruction after the Irish judges, as they will almost certainly have been aware, had reported on that very question and, more to the point, had reported on it in a determined and unambiguous fashion. It is by no means impossible that some discomfort was caused and that such judicial discomfiture, scarcely minimised by the embarrassment actually suffered when complying with similar instructions received later, ultimately precipitated expressions of forthright opposition from the judges to the constitutional acceptability of continuing to make their services available to the executive in this way. Whilst, plainly, it would be unwise to antedate the attaining of a crucial stage in the emergence of the concept of an independent judiciary, it is remarkable that as early as 1569, in *Archbishop of Dublin* v. *Brereton*, Chief Justice Catelyn and his brethren, in responding to Lord Deputy Sidney's request for advice on the validity of the lease at Tallaght, should have chosen to indicate no small degree of unease over ever being pressed for that advice at the outset.

Most of the inquiries addressed to London touched on questions of lawyers' law, but a minority either possessed considerable political content or were passed on, it would seem, very largely for political motives. As a means for coping with Archbishop Loftus over the affair of the lease at Tallaght, 1569, and as a means for facing down Baron Richards and Mr Justice Perrin for their intransigence over the handling of registry appeal cases, 1838, this last suggestion offers an explanation for the transmission that is quite plausible. The complex interlocking at constitutional, legal and political levels between Ireland and England is nowhere shown to better advantage than in one of the 'letters' in the present inventory – the advice of the English judges presented in June 1693 on the sole and exclusive right to which the Irish commons lay claim. It has been contended that the requisitioning of this advice and the publicity later accorded to it were very likely designed to fulfil a dual political purpose in Ireland – to enhance the reputation of a beleaguered local judicial bench but also to silence that bench's truculent opponents, opponents including the two erstwhile king's serjeants, Serjeants Osborne and Broderick. That some legal victory secured across the Irish Sea, it was fondly imagined, could play perhaps even a vital role in calming incipient turmoil as well as in settling the occasional political score, is illustrated once more in 1788 when in the King's Bench, on the hearing of the writ of error in the murder case, Lord Earlsfort relished finding himself in a seemingly impregnable position when he was able to brandish in Serjeant Adair's face a letter from the English King's Bench expressing complete concurrence with the stance of the Irish court.

It is to an Irish lord lieutenant, the marquis of Buckingham, that we owe these graphic details. (For those with a vivid imagination, they conjure up a picture not so very different from that conveyed by Neville Chamberlain in the aftermath of Munich: the excitement is over, now let us get back to the ordinary grind.) On the other hand, it is a matter for extreme regret that Buckingham deigns to furnish us with so little solid information on the precise background to events. We remain totally in the dark as regards the gist of Serjeant Adair's particular complaints. We are similarly ignorant as to what the English King's Bench had actually written (apart from the fact that they had agreed with Lord Earlsfort and his colleagues). Even the identity of the signatory in London, had it been noted, would have been of more than passing interest. This is because, in the early months of 1788, when the events in the Irish King's Bench described by Buckingham unfolded, we still lie within the interregnum demarcated by Lord Mansfield's withdrawal from active participation in the work of the English King's Bench (1786) and his eventual resignation two years later (June 1788), when he was succeeded, not by Francis Buller, Mansfield's preferred candidate, but by Lord Kenyon, 'a vastly inferior lawyer'.[91]

Future investigation may unearth answers to these and other questions suggested by the events that occurred at the old Four Courts in February 1788 and that prompted a reference to them in Buckingham's correspondence with his brother. (Research into the Dublin newspapers of the period might conceivably bear fruit.) If this came about, it would be most welcome. Also welcome, indeed much more obviously so, would be the discovery of other letters from the English judicial bench conveying further professional enlightenment, clear candidates for inclusion in an extended inventory. Such additional items of correspondence would help to clarify whether the pattern to the eliciting of advice from the English judges hesitantly pieced together in the preceding pages is in every respect warranted, or might require modification.

91 *DNB*, s.v. Buller, Francis.

Ecclesiastical Law and the Reformation in Ireland

Deviation from the Roman norm was the charge exhibited against representatives of the Celtic church, and to which they were obliged to respond, at the synod of Whitby in 664: the Celtic church calculated the date of Easter on a different basis, maintained a different form of tonsure and sanctioned a mode of episcopal consecration that differed too. 'All who served the One God,' King Oswy is made to declare in Bede's account of the occasion, 'should observe one rule of life.' Thirty years earlier, Pope Honorius I had been much more blunt: the Celtic churchmen were 'not to imagine that their little community isolated at the uttermost ends of the earth had a wisdom exceeding that of all the church ancient and modern throughout the world'.[1]

In the eighth-century Irish canons the authority of Rome was acknowledged,[2] as inferentially it had been too by the outcome at Whitby, but the condition of the native church was to continue to arouse anxieties in Ireland and within the wider church. In the twelfth century – and it is no coincidence that the same century was also to see the arrival of the Anglo-Normans in the country – the reformers finally grasped the nettle. In the estimation of the reformers, four particular mischiefs by then demanded attention in the Irish church: the customary law and practice of marriage, hereditary church offices, lay control generally, and the lack of a diocesan and parish structure. A series of synods that stretch from Cashel I (1101) to Cashel II (1171-2), responding to what was regarded as an internal crisis but prompted at the same time by the teachings of the continental reform movement, set out to tackle this difficult agenda.[3]

It took time for the decisions reached at Whitby in the seventh century to win acceptance within the entire Celtic church. The implementation of the twelfth-century reforms was equally gradual and resistance to certain of them was prolonged and, to a degree, successful. The conservatism of Irish churchmen and Irish society, reflected in the retention of older ecclesiastical structures, must thus be reckoned with in any survey of the church in Ireland up to the reformation and indeed even beyond. There existed unusual features in the medieval and early modern Irish church which neither the anglicizing stance of Henry II at the synod of Cashel II, nor the endeavours of churchmen of both nations in succeeding centuries managed to supersede. The system of church discipline, created by the medieval canonists, applied in Ireland and was thus available to assist 'in the advancement of Christ's kingdom' there as much as elsewhere

1 Kathleen Hughes, *The church in early Irish society* (London, 1966), ch. 10. **2** Hughes, *Ch. in early Ir. soc.*, p. 124. **3** Hughes, *Ch. in early Ir. soc.*, ch. 24.

in western Christendom. Confronted by the peculiar problems endemic in the medieval lordship of Ireland, however, even the most determined of churchmen were forced to concede that there were limitations to what it was possible to achieve through reliance upon this instrument.

At the synod of Cashel II Henry II gained the assent of the Irish clergy to the proposal that thereafter divine offices should be celebrated in every part of the country according to the forms and usages of the church of England. If liturgical uniformity resulted, there was much other unfinished business.[4] Since mid-century, recognition of a quartet of archbishops had been secured through the bestowal of four pallia – for Armagh, Dublin, Tuam and Cashel –, a pattern of dioceses was taking shape, but a network of parishes had still to be constructed.[5] A method of appointing bishops through election by cathedral chapters had to await the ordering of the chapters themselves.[6] The basis upon which, in the decades ahead, arrangements would be made for church lands to be held in feudal tenure of the king likewise remained to be resolved. Significantly, many of the eventual grants were without obligation of military service, from the church's point of view a distinct advantage, and one that has been attributed to developments occurring in canon law between 1066 and the later twelfth century.[7] A final task, no less vital in the civilizing mission of the new political order and of the canon law itself, related to the establishment of ecclesiastical jurisdiction and in particular to the creation of an indigenous system of ecclesiastical courts.

II

As to the latter, it is reasonable to suppose that, within a short time of the consolidation of the Anglo-Norman invasion, ecclesiastical courts based on the English model had been erected in the various dioceses that came within the Anglo-Norman sphere of influence. It is also reasonable to suppose that these courts applied virtually the same law as that applicable in the equivalent courts in England, namely, the canon law of the medieval church as amplified or modified by local church decrees, and subject to the identical restrictions imposed by the king there, namely, his delimitation of jurisdictional competence, a delimitation that was ultimately to become enforceable in the royal courts by means of the writ of prohibition.

Both must remain largely suppositions, however, for evidence bearing on the exercise of ecclesiastical jurisdiction during the first hundred years of the medieval Irish lordship is sparse. The Dublin diocesan manuscript known as Archbishop Alen's regis-

4 A.J. Otway-Ruthven, *A history of medieval Ireland* (London, 1968), ch. 4. 5 A.J. Otway-Ruthven, 'Parochial development in the rural deanery of Skreen', *RSAI jn.*, xciv (1964) 111; K.W. Nicholls, 'Rectory, vicarage, and parish in the western Irish dioceses', *RSAI jn.*, ci (1971) 53. 6 G.J. Hand, 'The medieval chapter of St Mary's cathedral, Limerick', in *Medieval studies presented to Aubrey Gwynn, S.J.*, eds. J.A. Watt, J.B. Morrall, F.X. Martin (Dublin, 1961), p. 74. 7 Otway-Ruthven, *Med. Ire.*, p. 128. See further G.J. Hand, *English law in Ireland 1270-1324* (Cambridge, 1967), pp 175-6.

ter supplies the name – Master W. de Trewell – of the diocese's ecclesiastical court judge or official of the 1250s.[8] The same register summarises correspondence of the ensuing decade that passed between Pope Urban IV and the bishop of Dromore on the subject of church courts.[9] From as early as the 1220s Sir John Davies in the seventeenth century cites a record of a law-suit in which the competence of the archbishop of Dublin to pronounce judicially on a matter of bastardy is highlighted.[10] These occasional glimpses but, more especially, the survival of records from the royal courts for the later years of the reign of Edward I and the first half of that of Edward II, transcribed and published in the *Calendars of justiciary rolls, 1295-1303, 1305-07, 1307-14* (Dublin, 1905-56), would indicate nevertheless that the suppositions mentioned above are not wide of the mark.

The evidence from the justiciary rolls that bears on the shape of ecclesiastical jurisdiction in Ireland at the turn of the fourteenth century has been rehearsed before,[11] but, in view of the dearth of records from the church courts of the period, merits repetition. By 1300 it is clear that the procedure regulating the appointment of bishops was now identical as between Ireland and England; the right of sanctuary, too, was admitted, as indeed had been the case in Celtic Ireland; and benefit of clergy could now, as in England, be claimed by the felonious clerk. Concerning the latter, procedures were in place to determine whether benefit of clergy had been properly claimed, to regulate delivery of the clerk to his bishop and to regulate supervision of the clerk's purgation. In the domain of private law, it is equally clear that the church courts possessed an unchallenged competence in matrimonial and testamentary litigation. The justiciary rolls from 1295 to 1314 record conflict, however, over the question of jurisdictional competence in specific areas: cases of advowson (title to benefices),[12] cases of defamations,[13] cases involving lay chattels and cases connected with tithe. Elaborate exposition of the accepted legal rules governing the resolution of such conflict in law-suits touching lay chattels and tithes is to be found in a string of cases which had originated in the Munster dioceses of Cloyne, Cork and Limerick as well as in the Leinster dioceses of Dublin and Kildare.[14] The contemporary importance of the courts Christian is indicated in other ways. In 1303, in Cork, an advocate was successfully sued in the royal courts for reneging on a promise made to his client to start proceedings for divorce in the church court.[15] In a case from 1307, again in the royal courts, a woman charged the archdeacon of Limerick with taking a bribe – twelve gallons of wine – to institute a charge against her of adultery under ecclesiastical law.[16] A year later, in the course of what sounds like a faction feud in Waterford, one group of youths sought refuge, during a lull in the pitched battle, actually inside the bishop's court next to the church.[17]

8 *Calendar of archbishop Alen's register* c.*1172-1534*, ed. Charles McNeill (Dublin, 1950), p. 76. **9** *Reg. Alen*, p. 92. **10** Sir John Davies, *A report of cases and matters in law resolved and adjudged in the king's courts in Ireland* (Eng. transl. of lst ed. of 1615; Dublin, 1762), pp 145-6. Further details of this sparse history are collected in G.J. Hand, *The church in the English lordship 1216-1307* (Dublin, 1968). **11** J.A. Watt, 'English law and the Irish church: the reign of Edward I', in *Med. studies presented to A. Gwynn*, p. 133. **12** *Cal. justic. rolls, Ire., 1307-14*, p. 107. **13** *Cal. justic. rolls, Ire., 1305-07*, p. 424; *Cal. justic. rolls, Ire., 1307-14*, p. 102. **14** *Cal. justic. rolls, Ire., 1295-1303*, pp 93, 96, 194, 297, 394, 458 (lay chattels); *Cal. justic. rolls, Ire., 1307-14*, pp 94-5 (tithe). **15** *Cal. justic. rolls, Ire., 1295-1303*, p. 459. **16** *Cal. justic. rolls, Ire., 1305-7*, p. 450. **17** *Cal. justic. rolls, Ire., 1307-14*, p. 140.

The series of the seven Armagh archiepiscopal registers, covering with some intermissions the years from 1361 (Archbishop Sweteman) to 1543 (Archbishop Cromer), contains most of the extant information put together from the standpoint of the ecclesiastical court administrator.[18] Proper analysis of the registers to establish their significance in terms of medieval canon law still awaits its historian, though a useful start has been made with the marriage litigation they record.[19] The registers however would appear to show – to emphasize one point that is certainly germane – that jurisdictional conflict between royal court and church court had been broadly settled. That conflict nonetheless was never far from people's thoughts. The church courts could run foul of the borough courts too, as an earlier recorded controversy from 1267 confirms,[20] and it is surely noteworthy that in two separate places in Archbishop Alen's register the jurisdictional boundaries are exhaustively delineated.[21]

Where the church court enjoyed exclusive competence, the rules of the medieval canon law, and the existence of a right of appeal to Rome, resulting in the nomination of judges delegate to proceed to hear such appeals, naturally affirmed the canonists' central role. No study of the work of papal judges delegate in Ireland is available but it seems probable that the exact contribution they were in a position to make to advance the canon law in Ireland may have been seriously limited by two major constraints – the regularity with which, like many other churchmen in medieval Ireland, they were forced to adopt the role of arbitrator rather than judge, and the extent to which, certainly in the last two centuries before the reformation, the focus to their involvement was concentrated on contested appointments to benefices. In this latter connection, it is important to mention that it was royal exasperation over this kind of judicial activity that provoked the enactment of the group of pre-reformation statutes directed at the pretensions of the papacy. It is also worth remarking that it was from this assemblage of pre-reformation statutes of praemunire and provisors, and not from any Tudor act of ecclesiastical supremacy, that the Irish state, early in the reign of James I, chose its artillery when it had embarked upon its campaign to coerce recusants into acceptance of the tenets of protestantism.[22]

The precise role papal judges delegate filled in Ireland in expounding or spreading an awareness of canon law may be obscure, but it is 'not open to doubt', as J.A. Watts has expressed it, 'that Ireland came under the powerful sway of this highly articulate legal system'.[23] Rulings on questions referred from Ireland entered into the canon law of the church.[24] Provincial legislation and synodal decrees too came to be treated as sources of law that were no less important.[25]

18 See *Registrum Iohannis Mey, the register of John Mey, archbishop of Armagh, 1443-1456*, eds. W.G.H. Quigley and E.F.D. Roberts (Belfast, 1972), intro. **19** Art Cosgrove, 'Marriage in medieval Ireland', in *Marriage in Ireland*, ed. Art Cosgrove (Dun Laoghaire, 1985), p. 25. **20** *Reg. Alen*, p. 129. **21** *Reg. Alen*, pp 93-4, 288-90. **22** The proceedings against Robert Lalor, discussed below, were thus taken under a statute of praemunire of the reign of Richard II. **23** *The church in medieval Ireland* (Dublin, 1972), p. 131. **24** Watt, *Ch. in med. Ire.*, pp 132-3. **25** Aubrey Gwynn, 'Provincial and diocesan decrees of the diocese of Dublin during the Anglo-Norman period', in *Archivium hibernicum*, xi (1944) 31; C.R. Cheney, 'A group of related synodal statutes of the thirteenth century', in *Med. studies presented to A. Gwynn*, p. 114; and see generally Gwynn's survey, with its focus on the Red Book of Ossory, in his *Anglo-Irish church life: fourteenth and fifteenth centuries* (Dublin, 1968), p. 38.

No university existed in the medieval Irish lordship, and continuance of respect for the canon law tradition was principally assured through the attendance of students from Ireland at Oxford and Cambridge, and on the continent – Paris, Bologna, Vienna, Trèves, Cologne, Rome.[26] The association of lectors with intellectual activity in the late medieval monastic houses, an association confirmed by the Irish annals and papal letters alike, suggest that some effort was expended on imparting a knowledge of canon law locally. Canice Mooney, indeed, was to go so far as to say, of these and other associations, that 'it is clear ... that it was possible without ever leaving Ireland to pursue courses in letters, in civil and canon law, that were considered adequate for promotion to the priesthood and other ecclesiastical offices'.[27] The level of understanding possessed locally of the rules of canon law is another matter. Crucial evidence would be furnished by what is known of books of canon law in actual circulation. Unfortunately, in the case of Ireland, this evidence is meagre in the extreme. Copies of the writings of Panormitanus and of the *Summa* or *Repertorium utriusque juris* of Peter of Brescia are alluded to in the will of Dean Alen of St Patrick's cathedral, Dublin, in 1505.[28] Details also survive as to the canon law holdings of two late medieval Irish libraries – that at the Franciscan friary at Youghal, Co. Cork, and that at St Mary's cathedral, Limerick. In the second case the information comes from an inventory made in 1631,[29] and the source is not therefore totally reliable. The catalogue at Youghal[30] was drawn up in 1491 by Br William O'Hurrily, 'lest perchance, by carelessness, or neglect, or which is worse want of conscience, [the books] might be completely destroyed and no memorial of them remain'. Br William's catalogue reveals that the Youghal Franciscans then owned copies of the *Decretum* of Gratian, the *Decretals* with additions, Panormitanus in five volumes, the *Liber Sextus* with the *Clementines*, the *Lectura super Sextum Decretalium* of Dominicus de San Geminiano, and the *Commentaria in Quatuor Libros Sententiarum*, together with the text in two printed paper volumes, of St Bonaventure.

III

Of the fortunes of the canon law, indeed of ecclesiastical jurisdiction itself, in the areas of Ireland outside English control, and thus free of the limitations imposed by royal authority and common law alike, little can be said with confidence. Since these areas expanded geographically in the fourteenth and fifteenth centuries, the lack of clear information is especially unfortunate. The general division into dioceses accomplished in the twelfth century had been followed by the creation of a parish network with

26 Canice Mooney, *The church in Gaelic Ireland: thirteenth to fifteenth centuries* (Dublin, 1969), pp 25-6. **27** Mooney, *Ch. in Gaelic Ire.*, p. 25. **28** There is some uncertainty as to whether Alen's will actually took effect: see the discussion in *Register of wills and inventories of the diocese of Dublin in the time of archbishops Tregury and Walton 1457-1483*, ed. H.F. Berry, RSAI extra vol. for 1896-7 (Dublin, 1898), p. 199. On Dean Alen himself see Gwynn, *Anglo-Irish church life: fourteenth and fifteenth centuries*, pp 75-6. **29** BL Add. Ms. 4793, f. 121. I owe this reference to Mr William O'Sullivan. **30** James Coleman, 'A medieval Irish monastic library catalogue', in *Bibliographical Soc. of Ireland*, ii (1925) 111.

which it should be presumed that even in Gaelic Ireland a system of payment of tithe will have been linked. Even if this actually occurred, the impact in the fourteenth century and later of a decline in English political authority could, it would seem, have occasioned a return to previous tradition where an alternative structure of financial support for the native clergy was assured through the payment of a variety of customary dues and through the rental from termon lands, and all underwritten by coarb and erenagh.[31] Though the extent to which there may have been a reversion to such a system of financial support for the clergy may be contested, there is one feature of conditions in Gaelic society in the later middle ages, of importance to the church, on which historians are in broad agreement. That society was marked by a fragmentation of political authority which made the identification of the secular arm upon which the church might wish to depend, for the pursuit of church tenants defaulting on rent, for the caption of excommunicates or for any other purpose, fraught with difficulty. Furthermore – a matter of no less concern to the church – even where the secular arm was correctly identified, its effectiveness in coming to the aid of the church, given all the attendant circumstances, may have been problematic.[32]

If the kind of ecclesiastical jurisdiction exercised in Gaelic Ireland by bishop, vicar-general or official is likely therefore to have been, qualitatively, considerably different from that acknowledged to subsist within the *ecclesia inter anglicanos*, it would be a mistake to deduce from the fact that so few records have survived that that jurisdiction was of little practical importance. One example from the area of marriage litigation should serve to make the point. In Gaelic Ireland it was incontestable that concubinage and clandestine marriage were practised on a wide scale but, equally, the source of intelligence is almost invariably church archives which reveal the persistence of individual endeavour to stamp out both. That the laity protested is manifest from the petitions of the women presented to Archbishop Colton in the course of his visitation of the diocese of Derry in 1397.[33] That the clergy spearheaded the movement of protest is clear not only from the history of the question but also from the frequency with which archbishops of Armagh would issue commissions to surrogates to hear matrimonial litigation arising *inter hibernicos*. There is an instance of this around 1530 when Cormac Roth, Archbishop Cromer's vicar-general, granted to Seneskyn McDywin, cleric of Armagh, authority to decide alone all matrimonial causes, should his colleague, Master Eugenius McGynosa, be negligent.[34] From this admittedly incomplete picture the inference is none the less warranted that, whilst the teaching of the church may not have been sufficiently influential to prevent the continuation of traditional marital and sexual practice, its impact may have been strong enough to persuade the leaders of Gaelic society that it was worth their while to attempt to clothe their activities in canonical respectability.[35]

The Armagh registers disclose a steady trickle of appeals to the archbishop from litigants in the dioceses of Clogher, Clonmacnoise, Derry, Down, Kilmore and Raphoe.

31 For assistance with these difficult matters see Mooney, *Ch. in Gaelic Ire.*, pp 10-16. **32** See, generally, Katharine Simms, 'The archbishops of Armagh and the O'Neills, 1347-1471', in *Irish Historical Studies*, xix (1974) 38. **33** Art Cosgrove, 'Marriage in medieval Ireland', pp 37-8. **34** 'Archbishop Cromer's register', ed. L.P. Murray, *Louth arch. soc. jn.*, ix (1937-40), at p. 129. **35** Cosgrove, 'Marriage in medieval Ireland', p. 33.

Disputes between churchmen and over church lands are prominent, but there is evidence too for the exercise of ecclesiastical jurisdiction in testamentary causes and even in civil suits generally. Archbishops of Armagh and their vicars-general appear to have been particularly determined to uphold the exercise of ecclesiastical jurisdiction as such. In a well-publicised case from 1413 a Maguire is pronounced excommunicate for interfering with the attendance of clergy at a bishop's court,[36] and two of the invocations of the secular arm mentioned in Archbishop Cromer's register for the years 1527 to 1530, naming Conosius Maguire and Fergal O'Boyle, captains of their nations, respectively, were expressly designed to secure physical protection for two ecclesiastical court litigants, one who was appealing direct to Rome from a decision of the bishop of Clogher and the other who was appealing to the archbishop from a decision of the bishop of Kilmore.[37]

A third invocation of the secular arm, dated 1527 and inspired by the need to secure the caption of an excommunicate, was addressed to another captain of his nation, Conosius O'Neill.[38] It was with the O'Neills, the most powerful secular authority within the Gaelic dioceses of the province of Armagh, that successive archbishops were on several occasions obliged to compromise. Both sides came to appreciate the mutual benefit to be derived from a *modus vivendi*. In the 1440s the archbishop secured a notable victory when the then O'Neill allowed him to conduct visitations and to attend to routine church administration. The relationship was never smooth, however, and understandings and agreements could all too easily break down.[39]

IV

However fascinating the history of the *ecclesia inter hibernicos* remains, at the outset of the protestant reformation in Ireland interest naturally switches back to the *ecclesia inter anglicanos*. It was within this latter division of the Irish church that the reformation was planned to have the more immediate repercussions. Certainly, it was upon the people living within the English sphere of influence, an area destined to increase in size in the course of the sixteenth century as English power itself revived, that it might have been anticipated the programme of change linked to the reformation would have had the more major impact. A new ecclesiastical order did in fact come into existence bound up with which were a number of structural and doctrinal changes; but the course that the reformation ran in Ireland was unique, bequeathing a legacy probably more distinctive and thus more significant in its political, rather than in any narrow legal, sense.

The Irish lordship was not involved in the manoeuvring that signalled a progressive hardening of relations between Henry VIII and the papacy from 1527 to 1534.

36 H.J. Lawlor, 'A calendar of the register of archbishop Fleming', *Proceedings of Royal Irish Academy*, xxx (1912-13), sect. c, p. 94 at pp 152-3. This entry is reproduced in E.D. Atkinson, *Dromore: an Ulster diocese* (Dundalk, 1915), at p. 32. **37** 'Archbishop Cromer's register', *Louth. arch. soc. jn.*, ix (1937-40), 126. **38** 'Archbishop Cromer's register', *Louth. arch. soc. jn.*, viii (1933-6), 344. **39** Simms, 'The archbishops of Armagh and the O'Neills, 1347-1471', in *Irish Historical Studies*, xix (1974) 38.

Henry's determination to jettison Queen Catherine and the difficulties to which that gave rise did coincide with a period of unrest in Ireland that found expression in the Kildare rebellion of 1534. Its suppression did not exactly tempt any local politician to question the motives of a Tudor monarch when at the first Irish parliament to be convened thereafter, that which sat in 1536 and 1537, an agenda of reformation-style legislation was brought forward. This collection of laws, in general a reflection of what had been processed shortly before for England, judged in purely ecclesiastical terms, possessed far-reaching implications. While Henry experienced some difficulty in securing acceptance of all the items on the agenda – the first Irish proposal for the suppression of the minor monastic houses provoked opposition and the clerical proctors made such a nuisance of themselves in the king's eyes that their right to sit in parliament was brusquely terminated – the overriding impression that the sources convey is that this initial agenda of reformation legislation was greeted with indifference. There was certainly no effective challenge to the king's claim to supremacy in the ecclesiastical sphere. That the reformation in Ireland throughout has something of a lacklustre appearance might perhaps have been predicted: although Lollards had been known in Ireland, there was no tradition of dissatisfaction with the medieval church, no sermon like Dean Colet's of 1512 (so far as is known), no causes célèbres such as had punctuated the recent history of England and Scotland, all of which had ensured a modest swelling in the ranks of the new 'protestants' on the larger island.

If the package of reformation statutes introduced by Henry and reintroduced, after the Marian interlude (1553-8) which witnessed a partial repeal, by his second daughter, Elizabeth, triggered little opposition, neither was it greeted with marked enthusiasm. It would be wrong to say that Ireland was merely hedging its bets. Tradition had more to do with it: the Anglo-Irish were reluctant to envisage the church without the pope but nor could they contemplate a political structure without the English sovereign, 'the custodian,' as Brendan Bradshaw has remarked, 'of social and political stability, and the guarantor of their legal privileges and status over the Irish.'[40] The truth of the matter would seem to be that Ireland could have gone either way – protestant or catholic. That, eventually, in Ireland, the counter-reformation was to achieve one of its more celebrated successes owes not so much to internal opposition to reformation legislation or even to the liturgical changes which, admittedly in Ireland's case, were long delayed, but to a deterioration in English political management which made adherence to the tenets of counter-reformation catholicism not just emotionally more comfortable but a symbolic political gesture.[41] It was no idle flourish that prompted Nicholas Canny to entitle a seminal discussion of his on the period, 'Why the Reformation failed in Ireland: une question mal posée': the question was inappropriate because in its own terms the reformation in Ireland did not fail, at least not at the start.[42]

40 'The opposition to the ecclesiastical legislation in the Irish reformation parliament', *Irish Historical Studies*, xvi (1968-9), p. 285 at p. 303. **41** For up-to-date treatment of an Irish historical problem of considerable complexity Ciaran Brady will be found a helpful guide: 'Conservative subversives – the community of the Pale and the Dublin administration, 1556-86', in *Radicals, rebels and establishments: Historical studies, XV*, ed. P.J. Corish (Belfast, 1985), p. 11. **42** N.P. Canny, 'Why the reformation failed in Ireland: une question mal

By the end of the sixteenth century even so the vast majority of the population in Ireland professed catholicism, a position subsequently to be modified, and then only in part, in respect of the planted northern counties of Ulster. In the meantime, however, the Dublin government had come under the control of an English administration in which protestantism and loyalty had begun to be thought of as equivalents, new English administrators had come to predominate, and the risky enterprise had been embarked upon of seeking to buttress, if sometimes only fitfully, with such instruments of law and of persuasion as lay at their disposal, a church establishment based four square on anglicanism.

Anglicanism was still the predominant sect within Irish protestantism, but in Ireland protestantism itself was, and remained, a minority cult. The position in England was different, but the English administration in Ireland chose to ignore the fact: in relation to religious questions and issues of church and state they could scarcely conceive that what had been set aside and reordered in England should not likewise be set aside and reordered for Ireland. Legislation followed, parrot-fashion, in Ireland in its reformation parliament of 1536-7: against the authority of the pope, asserting the king's supremacy over the church, redirecting the payment of first fruits, regulating ecclesiastical appeals, conferring the pope's faculty jurisdiction elsewhere.[43] Most of this is repealed under Mary but under Elizabeth the pattern is re-established – she becomes supreme governor of the church and with her there arrives, as in England, liturgical change insisted upon by an act of uniformity.[44] Under Henry the monastic houses had been suppressed and their lands seized, again under legislative authority (1537-42) modelled on earlier English precedents.[45] Significantly, the first order for the suppression of an Irish monastic house – the priory of Augustinian canonesses at Graney – was issued in 1535 on the strength of the English act of supremacy, two years before its Irish variant had been enacted. So striking an instance of the extra-territorial exercise of English executive power would intimate that for Ireland there was to be no escape from Henry's reformation plans. Nor was there to be. The constitutional implications of such precipitate action, in derogation, seemingly, of the prerogatives of the Irish parliament, nevertheless, merit scrutiny. The conclusions of R.D. Edwards on the point are impeccable: 'The Tudor government regarded parliament in Ireland as a means of securing public endorsement for a policy already approved in England, and already operating in Ireland without reference to any necessity of securing the prior sanction of the Irish parliament'.[46] Edwards here pinpoints the existence of two legislatures –

posée', *Journal of Ecclesiastical History*, xxx (1979) 423. **43** 28 Hen. VIII, cc. 13 (act against the authority of the bishop of Rome), 5 (act authorising the king, his heirs and successors, to be supreme head of the church of Ireland), 8 and 26 (act for first fruits and act for the first fruites of abbeyes, priories, and colledges), 6 (act of appeales), and 19 (act of faculties). For the sequence of events see, apart from Bradshaw (n. 40, above), R.D. Edwards, 'The Irish reformation parliament of Henry VIII, 1536-7', *Historical Studies, VI*, ed. T.W. Moody (London, 1968) 59. **44** 2 Eliz. I, c. 1 (act restoring to the crown, the auncient jurisdiction over the state ecclesiasticall and spirituall, and abolishing all forreine power repugnant to the same); 2 Eliz. I, c. 2 (acte for the uniformity of common prayer and service in the church, and the administration of the sacraments). **45** 28 Hen. VIII, c. 16 (act for the suppression of abbyes), 33 Hen. VIII, sess. 2, c. 5 (act for the suppression of Kylmaynham and other religious houses). **46** Edwards, 'The Irish reformation parliament of Henry VIII, 1536-7', at p. 64.

the English and the Irish – with overlapping geographical competence. It was not a neat arrangement and, as will be demonstrated later, was productive of needless complication – and some uncertainty – in the arranging of the affairs of the Irish church in the wake of the reformation.

V

The story of ecclesiastical law in Ireland in the immediate aftermath of the reformation is inextricably linked with that of the new protestant church establishment.[47] It is best examined under two headings: changes in the courts that applied the rules of ecclesiastical law and doctrinal innovation within these rules. In both contexts, the influence of England was paramount, but minor variations nevertheless did ultimately emerge. The element of continuity in court structures and matters of doctrine before and after the reformation must equally be surveyed.

A reshaping of ecclesiastical jurisdiction was authorised by the two acts of supremacy, the Henrician and the Elizabethan, and by the Henrician acts of appeals and of faculties. Elizabeth's position in particular as supreme governor of the church made possible the creation of a series of commissions given a special but wide-ranging brief to prosecute ecclesiastical causes. The first such commission in Ireland was set up for Co. Westmeath in 1561, a second for the province of Armagh followed in the succeeding year. Both were given standard powers 'to visit, reform, redress, order, correct and amend errors, heresies, schisms, abuses, offences, contempts and enormities' punishable under the new ecclesiastical dispensation.[48] A further commission was set up for the entire country in 1564,[49] and its terms served as the model for successive such commissions set up in 1593 and again, in the reign of Charles I, in 1635. There was little omitted from the inventory of powers bestowed upon these all-Ireland commissions: they were specifically enjoined to punish heresy and sedition, enormities in church, absenteeism from church, adultery, fornication and simony; they were to ensure acceptance of the oath of supremacy and compliance on the part of the clergy with the Henrician act of 1537 which made the English 'order, habit and language' mandatory; they were to seek out catholic literature, copes, vestments and crosses, and to force lay impropriators to attend to the repair of churches. The commission of 1593 was utilised principally against catholic recusants, that of 1635 against presbyterians and both, in consequence, became politically expendable. Published decrees of the commission of 1564, straddling the years 1570–2, relate exclusively to cases of adultery, including the case of a bishop of Cork deprived and punished for this offence in 1570.[50]

A more enduring structural change resulted from the disappearance of papal judges delegate as a consequence of the enactment of the Irish act of appeals. Such judges dele-

47 On the immediate fortunes of the new protestant church establishment see Alan Ford, *The protestant reformation in Ireland, 1590–1641* (Frankfurt, 1985; new edition, Dublin, 1997). **48** Rowley Lascelles, *Liber munerum publicorum Hiberniae*, 2 vols. (London, 1852), i, 181–2. **49** *Calendar of patent and close rolls of chancery in Ireland, Henry VIII to 8 Elizabeth I*, ed. James Morrin (Dublin, 1861), pp 489–90. **50** J.T. Gilbert, *A history of Dublin*, 3 vols. (Dublin, 1854–9), i, 114, 213–15.

gate had been part of the fabric of the legal system of medieval Ireland, and their activities are exhaustively listed in papal archives and Irish diocesan and royal court records.

The Irish act of appeals of 1537,[51] like its English counterpart of two years before, prohibited the taking of any further appeals in ecclesiastical causes to Rome. An appeal to a commission or court of delegates appointed under royal authority was instituted instead. The precise procedure envisaged by the Irish statute differed, however, and was curious in the extreme.[52] The Irish litigant might petition for the appointment of delegates before either the Irish lord chancellor or the English. Where the approach was made locally, the Irish lord chancellor, before naming any commission of delegacy, had to secure the agreement of two out of the following four office-holders: the chief justice of king's bench, the chief justice of common pleas, the master of the rolls and the under-treasurer. Where the Irish litigant made his approach to the English lord chancellor, the latter enjoyed a free hand, and could appoint either English delegates or Irish delegates. This dual appeal procedure lasted until 1782.

For the period 1572 to 1601 details of 51 different commissions of delegacy appointed by the Irish lord chancellor may be extrapolated from the printed Elizabethan fiants. The single largest category of case embraced matters of clerical discipline and disputed appointments at parish level and in cathedral chapter – 18. Next come matrimonial cases – 16. There were 7 testamentary cases, 2 tithe and 1 defamation. Insufficient information is available as to the nature of the remaining cases.[53]

Another post-reformation innovation, the court of the prerogative and faculties, derived its authority from both the act of supremacy and the act of faculties. The enactment of the latter statute[54] led in Ireland to the appointment of royal commissioners to administer locally the powers previously enjoyed by the papacy in granting faculties and dispensations.[55] The exact ambit of these powers remained contentious and indeed was to be the focus of attention in a major law-suit which is reported in Davies' reports of 1615.[56] In the Elizabethan era the commissioners of faculties had major responsibilities in relation to restructuring within the church: they would inquire into title to hold benefices, sanction deprivations and license pluralities.[57]

In 1571, during a period of intense innovation in the Irish judicial system, Elizabeth extended the work of the commissioners by attaching the prerogative jurisdiction. Such a jurisdiction to handle problems of testate and intestate succession in respect of wealthier decedents had been successfully asserted in England by archbishops of Canterbury since as long ago as the reign of Edward I. No comparable jurisdiction had ever existed in Ireland. The Elizabethan act of supremacy now facilitated the making of a change that one imagines was considered overdue.[58]

51 28 Hen. VIII, c. 6. **52** S. 2. **53** Calendar to fiants of the reign of Elizabeth 1, for 1570 to 1601, in *12th* to *22nd Reports of the deputy keeper of the public records in Ireland* (Dublin, 1880-90). **54** 28 Hen. VIII, c. 19, repealed by 3 & 4 Phil. & Mary, c. 8 (act repealing estatutes, and provisions made against the see apostolique of Rome, sithence the twentieth year of King Henry the eighth, and also for the establishment of spiritual and ecclesiastical possessions and hereditaments conveyed to the laity), but revived by 2 Eliz. I, c. 1. **55** *Liber. mun. pub. Hib.*, ii, 79-80. **56** *The case of a commenda*, Davies' reports, p. 185. **57** Ford, *Protestant reformation in Ire.*, 1st ed., pp 22-3. **58** Herbert Wood, *A guide to the records deposited in the public record office of Ireland* (Dublin, 1919), p. 222.

For over fifty years a succession of royal patentees exercised the combined functions of commissioners of faculties and judges of the prerogative. This ended in 1622 when James I, as part of his policy to bring the church in Ireland into line with that in England, established a court of the prerogative and faculties and conferred the nominal judgeship of the court upon the primate, the Church of Ireland archbishop of Armagh, and his successors in perpetuity.[59] Fresh patents of Charles I[60] confirmed the arrangement which survived until, first, in 1857, the court of probate was created and, second, in 1869, the Church of Ireland was itself disestablished.

The commissions for ecclesiastical causes, the court of delegates and that of the prerogative and faculties all represented a break with the past. Continuity, however, was in evidence too as is borne out by what is known of the diocesan courts. In the case of Dublin, the survival of a formulary for its consistorial court, to be ascribed to the 1580s, testifies to the uninterrupted functioning of ecclesiastical jurisdiction in the very heart of the Pale itself.[61] Corroboration for this comes in information on the provenance of appeals scheduled for hearing before Irish delegates which is to be found in the Elizabethan fiants. No less than 28 of the 51 authorised commissions of delegacy for which there is data between the years 1572 and 1601 were intended to deal with Dublin appeals. The court in question was in almost every instance the Dublin consistorial; two cases at most may have involved the archbishop's metropolitical jurisdictions.[62]

The fiants also constitute an invaluable source of information on the position elsewhere. Insufficient detail is forthcoming in a number of cases, but, in relation to the rest, three appeals apiece would appear to have been in contemplation from Meath and Cashel, two from Armagh (one of which concerned a decision of the dean in a lawsuit of 1580 between 'Hugh Maganeis' and 'Sophronia O'Nele'),[63] two from the united diocese of Waterford and Lismore (one of which arose from a decision of the archdeacon of Lismore), and one appeal from each of the dioceses of Ardfert, Killaloe, Leighlin, Limerick and Tuam. Other snatches of information enable the list to be extended. In December 1585 the bishop of Ossory, Nicholas Walsh, was murdered in his own home. The assailant, one James Dullard, is named in the printed state papers but these do not explain the circumstances. Canon Leslie's research revealed, however, that the bishop had been instrumental in opening proceedings in his own court against Dullard for adultery.[64]

59 *Cal. pat. rolls, Ire., Jas. I*, pp 543–5; *14th Report of the commissioners appointed to inquire into the duties, salaries and emoluments of the several officers, clerks, and ministers of justice, in all temporal and ecclesiastical courts in Ireland: judge or commissary of the court of prerogative and faculties*, H.C. 1826 (68), xvii, 1, at pp 15–19; Joshua Cunningham, *Forms and precedents used in the ecclesiastical courts of Ireland* (Dublin, 1830), pp 364–9. **60** *Cal. pat. rolls, Ire., Chas. I*, p. 166; Cunningham, *Forms and precedents*, pp 370–2 (patent of 2 Chas. I). *Supplemental report to the 19th report of the commissioners appointed to inquire into the duties, salaries, and emoluments of the several officers, clerks, and ministers of justice, in all temporal and ecclesiastical courts in Ireland: court of prerogative and faculties*, H.C. 1830 (518), xv, 413, p. 6 (418) (patent of 8 Chas. I). **61** *'Registrum diocesis Dublinensis': a sixteenth century precedent book*, ed. N.B. White (Dublin, 1959). Cf. Archbishop Alen's statutes for the Dublin consistorial court, 1530: *Reg. Alen*, pp 274–5. **62** *Fiants Ire., Eliz., 1570–1601*. **63** Fiant no. 3647. **64** J.B. Leslie, *Ossory clergy and parishes* (Enniskillen, 1933), pp 14–15.

Many dioceses are left unaccounted for in this survey. Is it conceivable that ecclesiastical courts continued in uninterrupted fashion there too? The lack of evidence is particularly marked for dioceses situated within Gaelic Ireland whose pre-reformation history has already been noted, but wherever it is manifest, this lack naturally invites the inference that in many areas ecclesiastical jurisdiction was non-existent or had broken down. Whilst some caution is warranted, for the reasons that have been set out above, it would seem not improbable that the situation on the ground in a number of dioceses made the effective exercise of ecclesiastical jurisdiction well-nigh impossible. Many dioceses for the major part of Elizabeth's reign were in a derelict state and lacked a resident or indeed any bishop. Even where there is proof that a consistorial court existed, political and other factors may have militated against regular recourse to it. A fiant for 7 July 1584 evokes the atmosphere very well.[65] It conferred authority to appoint a commission of eight (not a commission of delegates) 'to hear and determine the questions moved by Johanna Carvill alias Carrwell alias Bourke, as to her marriage with the late John Bourke, baron of Letrym, the legitimacy of her children and to grant to her the administration of his goods'. It continues with the recital that Johanna 'dare not for fear of life proceed in the local bishop's court, that a former commission had been rendered abortive by the unexpected death of the baron and subsequently by the attitude of Hugh or Ullick, earl of Clanrickard, and of Johanna Butler, alleged wife of the said baron.' There is a further consideration connected with the creation of the various regional and national commissions for ecclesiastical causes. If consistorial courts were a common phenomenon and in a healthy condition, why, it is legitimate to ask, should the appointment of such supplementary commissions have been deemed necessary in the first place?

Reliable information on the entire position is first set forth in an official survey carried out in 1622. That year commissioners, appointed to inquire into the condition of the established church in Ireland, sought returns from all the archbishops and bishops as to the state of their respective dioceses. One question required the churchmen to describe the current arrangements within their several bailiwicks for the exercise of ecclesiastical jurisdiction. A number of the returns that were forwarded to Dublin suggested that nothing was amiss.[66] Ecclesiastical courts were held regularly, the name of the official or judge was given, together, in appropriate instances, with a brief note of his qualifications and even of his remuneration. Some of the officials were laymen, some clergy. It was common too for the bishops in their answers to explain that in the remoter areas of their respective dioceses different arrangements obtained. Returns along these lines were presented for the following dioceses: Armagh, Clogher, Clonfert, Derry, Down and Connor, Dromore, Elphin, Kildare, Killaloe, Kilmore and Ardagh, Meath and Raphoe.

65 Fiant no. 4479. **66** What follows is based principally on Marsh's Library, Dublin, Ms. Z 3.1.3, and Trinity College, Dublin, Ms. 550. The return of the bishop of Dromore (Ms. Z 3.1.3, pp 120–5) is printed in E.D. Atkinson, *Dromore: an Ulster diocese*, pp 127–32. The return of the bishop of Killaloe (Ms. Z 3.1.3, pp 63–4) is printed, in a much more comprehensive version, in Philip Dwyer, *The diocese of Killaloe from the reformation to the close of the eighteenth century* (Dublin, 1878), pp 147ff.

Other diocesan returns, recently examined and perhaps imperfect copies,[67] yielded no salient information at all: those for Ardfert, Cashel, Cork Cloyne and Ross, Ferns, Leighlin and Limerick. More eloquent, possibly, than this negative evidence, are the observations which the bishops of Derry and of Kilmore and Ardagh add to the effect that rival ecclesiastical jurisdiction was being exercised and rival ecclesiastical courts kept by 'the popish authorities', 'to the great dishonour of god, hindrance of religion and shame of the government,' as Dr Downham, bishop of Derry, phrases it.[68] Specific accusations included a charge that in his diocese no less than four different officials or judges made a practice, for small rewards, of divorcing married couples and of letting them marry again.[69]

The existence of a rival catholic system of ecclesiastical jurisdiction would appear equally to have been established in the proceedings brought against Robert Lalor in 1606 and reported at length in Davies' reports.[70] Lalor is described as catholic vicar-general of the dioceses of Dublin, Kildare and Ferns. Among the charges levelled against him under the statute of praemunire were that he had instituted priests, granted dispensations for non-payment of tithe and in respect of marriages within the prohibited degrees, and pronounced divorces. Documentary proof was tendered, but while Lalor may have been correct in his contention that he personally had never held a court, there is something lame, possibly bogus, about his allied contention that the documents in question were designed to be employed as precedents merely and had not actually been composed by him. Understandably, in the wake of the reports from the bishops in 1622, the king's directions for the church drawn up the same year urged the rigorous enforcement of the Elizabethan act of supremacy directed at exercises of ecclesiastical jurisdiction by the catholic clergy.[71] In 1630, however, Bishop Bedell of Kilmore was complaining again of exercises of ecclesiastical jurisdiction by catholics, his specific gravamen then being the use of the weapon of excommunication against persons resorting to the official, that is, Church of Ireland ecclesiastical courts.[72]

Against a historical vacuum and in the face of catholic opposition the survival of the ecclesiastical courts of the state church can be counted a remarkable achievement which may be due, more than it has been possible to show, to solid pre-reformation tradition. Other factors which receive considerable publicity in the Irish sources prior to 1641 again emphasize the extent of the achievement though from a quite different perspective: these are allegations of vexatious proceedings, too frequent court sittings, procedural irregularities, oppressive fees and general corruption.[73] Both sets of king's directions in 1622, those for the courts and those for the church, purported to tackle

67 See previous note in respect of the return from the bishop of Killaloe. **68** TCD Ms. 550, pp 188–209. **69** Richard Mant, *History of the church of Ireland from the reformation to the revolution*, 2 vols. (London, 1840), i, 403. **70** *The case of praemunire, or the conviction and attainder of Robert Lalor priest, being indicted upon the statute of 16 Ric. II, cap. 5*: Davies' reports, p. 230. **71** Orders and directions concerning the state of the church of Ireland and the possessions thereof, free schools, and other endowments, and lands given to charitable uses, for and concerning other things tending to the advancement, of true religion and maintenance of the clergy in the said realm: Trinity College, Dublin, Ms. 808 (F. 2.1), direction 33. **72** Bishop Bedell to Archbishop Laud, 1 April 1630, quoted Mant, *History of Ch. of Ire.*, i, 436. **73** *Advertisements for Ireland, c.1623*, ed. George O'Brien, RSAI extra vol. for 1923 (Dublin, 1923), p. 54; R.B. Knox, *James Ussher archbishop of Armagh* (Cardiff, 1967), pp 90–4; *Commons' jn. Ire.*, 17 June 1640.

criticisms of this kind,[74] but Bishop Bedell's difficulties with his chancellor in Kilmore in the 1630s and the Irish house of commons' remonstrance on the entire question presented in June 1640 show that it was no simple matter to arrange a solution.[75] The anonymous author of *Advertisements for Ireland*, composed circa 1623, having recited the predictable litany of complaints, yet accepted the need for ecclesiastical jurisdiction, suitably reformed. Irish marriage customs feature yet again in the calculations of the reformer:

> Many of the British inhabitants there and natives keep two wives at once in divers places, and the mere Irish ordinarily, after a private contract, or sometimes without any condition but liking both sides, cohabit with single women in public as their wives and never solemnize any other marriage with them, and thereupon their issue, that by common report were held legitimate in their father's lifetime, after his death are found to be bastards, and that amongst the chief men of rank. And in this way they exceed most nations, which proceeds from the corruption and negligence of the clergy's officers there that wink at this upon private compositions.[76]

VI

Legislation of the Irish parliament of 1537 provided, as in England, that, notwithstanding the break with Rome, the law regulating the exercise of ecclesiastical jurisdiction was, in the main, to be carried over:

> All and every archbishop, bishop, archdeacon, commissarie and official, and every of them, shall and may use and exercise in the name of the king only all such canons, constitutions, ordinances and sinodalls provincial, being already made for the direction and order of spirituall and ecclesiastical causes, which be not contrarient, nor repugnant to the king's lawes, statutes, and customes of this land, nor to the damage and hurt of the king's prerogative royal, in such manner and forme as they were used and executed before the making of this act, till such time as the king's highness shall order and determine according his lawes of England.[77]

The final clause clearly alludes to the planned revision of English ecclesiastical law which Henry VIII had set in motion a few years before. Though the revision was undertaken, no official action resulted,[78] and ecclesiastical law in England as well as in

74 'His majesty's directions for ordering and settling the courts within his kingdom of Ireland 1622', eds. G.J. Hand and V.W. Treadwell, *Analecta Hibernica*, xxvi (1970) 177 at pp 210–12 (directions 44 and 47); King's directions for the church (n. 71, above), directions 29 and 30. **75** Knox, *James Ussher*, pp 90–4; *Commons' jn. Ire.*, 17 June 1640. **76** *Advertisements for Ireland*, p. 54. **77** 28 Hen. VIII, c. 13 (act against the authority of the bishop of Rome), s. 10. **78** R.H. Helmholz, *Roman canon law in reformation England* (Cambridge, 1990), pp 35–6.

Ireland after the reformation retained very much the flavour of the pot pourri that it had already assumed. A conservative approach predominated. Introducing the Irish Manuscripts Commission edition of the *Registrum diocesis Dublinensis*, J.A. Watt observed that the formulary demonstrated that, 'despite the magnitude of the religious changes in the sixteenth century, on the institutional level there was substantial continuity between the late medieval and the Elizabethan periods'.[79] Continuity remained the dominant theme despite the interruptions of the Cromwellian interlude in the middle of the seventeenth century. In this area, as in a number of others, the restoration era lived up to its name, the general mood being best caught by the preface prefixed at the revision of the Book of Common Prayer in 1662:

> Common experience sheweth, that where a change hath been made of things advisedly established, no evident necessity so requiring, sundry inconveniences have thereupon ensued; and those many times more, and greater, than the evils, that were intended to be remedied by such change.

In Ireland, as in England, the reformation ipso facto naturally worked a repeal of an amount of pre-existing legal doctrine. In purely theological terms, a new ecclesiastical order – anglicanism – had been brought into being. Less of a departure from the old faith than some of the other contemporary manifestations of protestantism – it preserved an episcopacy and adhered to conventional models of ecclesiastical jurisdiction – anglicanism nonetheless represented a new beginning of sorts. Jeremy Taylor, future bishop of Dromore, was in no doubt as to the extent of the divergence from Rome when, early in 1660, he corresponded with a fellow of Trinity College, Dublin, who had sought his advice on the composition of a library of anglican theology. Taylor recommended 66 books in all. In introducing one category, Taylor was to write:

> There remains now her [i.e. anglicanism's] doctrine to be learned, that you may know what shee is pro sensu, as what she is pro cultu and her doctrine is contained in the common prayer booke, in the church catechisms, in the 39 articles and in the booke of homilies.[80]

In doctrinal terms, the church of Ireland had aligned itself closely with the Church of England. Elizabeth's act of uniformity of 1560[81] insisted upon the use of the Book of Common Prayer, and there are references to this in the patents of the various Irish commissions for ecclesiastical causes. In 1567 there followed the issuance in Dublin of *A brief declaration of certain principal articles of religion*, twelve in all.[82] Orders were given that this *Declaration* was to be read publicly by the clergy on their induction and twice thereafter. The *Declaration* set forth the leading doctrines of the church as belief in a

79 *'Registrum diocesis Dublinensis': a sixteenth century precedent book*, ed. N.B. White (Dublin, 1959), intro., p. v. **80** Colin McKelvie, 'Jeremy Taylor's recommendations for a library of Anglican theology (1660)', *Irish booklore*, iv, no. 2 (1980) 96 at p. 101. **81** 2 Eliz. I, c. 2 (act for the uniformitie of common prayer and service in the church, and the administration of the sacraments). **82** W.D. Killen, *The ecclesiastical history of Ireland*, 2 vols. (London, 1875), i, appendix I.

triune God and in the truth of the bible; it acknowledged the royal supremacy, and included a protest against the mass as a propitiatory sacrifice capable of securing the release of souls from purgatory.

None of this constituted any serious divergence from the stance previously adopted by the English church. The failure, however, to extend immediate recognition to the *Thirty-nine articles of religion* adopted by the English bishops and clergy at the convocation in London in 1562 opened up the prospect of a doctrinal split at a later date. The extent to which the Church of Ireland's own articles of religion adopted by the Irish bishops and clergy at the convocation in Dublin in 1615[83] can be said to contain doctrinal differences remains controversial.[84] Unlike the English collection of articles, the Irish collection numbers a staggering 104 and, whilst some of these repeat word for word the content of several of England's 39, and in the case of a few, precedents are to be found in other English formularies, a proportion plainly betray an independence of outlook. The 16th of the Irish articles touches on predestination and its language exactly mirrors that employed in the 17th of the English: 'The godlike consideration of predestination and our election in Christ, is full of sweete, pleasant, and unspeakable comfort to godly persons.' The 52nd opposes to the practices of the Roman church the injunctions of the bible. The philosophy evinced by equivalent English articles is similar but the language in the Irish article has no parallel there:

> All worship devised by mans phantasie, besides or contrary to the scriptures (as wandring on pilgrimages, setting up of candles, stations, and iubilies, pharisaicall sects and fained religions, praying upon beades, and such like superstition) hath not onely no promise of reward in scripture, but contrariwise threatnings and maledictions.

The acknowledgment of the king's supremacy and rejection of the claims of the pope is presented in identical terms in the 57th to 59th articles. The 63rd to 66th articles touch on the duty to one's neighbour. Acceptance of clerical marriage (the 64th article) and rejection of the anabaptists' doctrine of community of property (the 65th) have their counterparts in the English articles. The 66th, however, which proclaims that faith is to be kept even with heretics and infidels, stands apart. The 63rd again has no counterpart in the English formulary:

> Our duty towards our neighbours is, to love them as ourselves, and to do to all men, as we would they should do unto us; to honour and obey our superiours, to preserve the safety of men's persons, as also their chastitie, goods and good names; to beare no malice nor hatred in our hearts; to keep our bodies in temperance, sobernes and chastitie; to be true and iust in all our doings; not to covet other men's goodes, but labour truely to get our owne living, and to doe our dutie in that estate of life unto which it pleaseth God to call us.

83 Killen, *Eccl. hist. Ire.*, i, appendix III. **84** Knox, *James Ussher*, ch. 2.

A notable omission from the Irish articles of 1615 – and thus helping to impart their puritan flavour – was any mention, such as is to be found in the 36th article of the English articles, of the three ecclesiastical orders of deacon, priest and bishop, or of the procedures for consecrating bishops. The desideratum of a 'correspondence between the churches of England and Ireland' that was 'more entire and accurate' was pressed by Bishop Bramhall before the Irish convocation of 1634 as the major reason for setting them aside in favour of the English.[85] The 1st canon of the Irish canons of 1634 was the outcome: it simply adopts the Thirty-nine articles en bloc.[86] Thirty years later Jeremy Taylor applauded Bramhall's success in securing their acceptance (and the suppression in effect of the native articles of 1615),

> that they and we might be populus unius labii, of one heart and one life, building up our hopes of heaven on a most holy faith, and taking away that shibboleth which made this church lisp too undevoutly, or rather in some little degree to speak the speech of Ashdod, and not the language of Canaan.[87]

The Irish canons of 1634 are closely modelled on the English canons of 1603. The 47th to 55th canons deal with the law of marriage: marriage within the prohibited degrees (canon 47), parental consent for those marrying under 21 (canon 48), marriage by licence (canons 49-52), and matrimonial causes generally (canons 53-5). The 56th canon adopts the English definition of bona notabilia in the context of the law on testate and intestate succession administered in the court of the prerogative and faculties. The 57th to 60th canons deal broadly with procedural questions in ecclesiastical court litigation. A group beginning with the 61st elaborate upon the power of churchwardens to initiate proceedings for various kinds of sexual and moral delinquency.

The provisions in the canons of 1634 touching on marriage and marriage law and delimiting the jurisdiction of the prerogative court in succession cases had an effect that endured. The Cromwellian regime that was to be installed in Ireland in little more than a decade's time proceeded to abolish episcopacy and all its works.[88] Though the canons generally enjoyed something of a revival at the restoration their importance as a source of law received a blow at the end of the century from which they were destined never to recover. In a series of law-suits, commencing late in the century and culminating in the celebrated judgment of Lord Hardwicke in *Middleton* v. *Crofts* in 1736,[89] the English judges made it plain that church canons, unless reflective of accepted pre-reformation law or unless implemented by legislation in parliament, could no longer be treated as capable of binding the laity. A single clear exception was admitted: the post-reformation definition of bona notabilia. Edward Bullingbrooke and Arthur Browne, eighteenth-century writers on ecclesiastical law in Ireland, regarded the decision in *Middleton* v. *Crofts* as determinative of the identical point in Ireland.[90]

85 Quoted, J.T. Ball, *The reformed Church of Ireland 1537-1886* (London, 1886), p. 117. **86** *Constitutions and canons ecclesiasticall* (Dublin, 1635), canon 1. **87** Quoted, Ball, *Reformed Church of Ireland*, p. 117 n. **88** T.C. Barnard, *Cromwellian Ireland: English government and reform in Ireland 1649-1660* (Oxford, 1975), chs. 5 and 6. **89** 2 Atk. 650; 26 Eng. Rep. 788. **90** Edward Bullingbrooke, *Ecclesiastical law, or the statutes, constitutions, canons, rubricks, and articles of the Church of Ireland*, 2 vols. (Dublin, 1770), i, intro., pp iii-vi; Arthur Browne,

After the reformation alterations in the rules of ecclesiastical law thus continued to be made by churchmen sitting as a legislature in convocation. The role of parliament was equally significant; indeed, in view of the trend represented by *Middleton* v. *Crofts*, it will cause no surprise to learn that, ultimately, it became very much more so. Apart from the institutional changes that the legislation of the Irish reformation parliament of 1536–7 either required or facilitated, many other matters of detail were actually the subject of regulation, precisely as had occurred too in England. The act of faculties, in making arrangements for the transfer elsewhere of the pope's authority to grant faculties and dispensations, sets limits on the authority being transferred: it was only to be employed 'for causes not being contrary or repugnant to the holy scriptures and laws of God',[91] a restriction, interestingly, which is examined in some detail, though not, unfortunately, so as to produce great enlightenment, in one of the cases reported in Davies' reports.[92] Court fees in probate cases were dealt with in another act passed by the Irish parliament in 1537.[93] Later legislation of 1542 returned to the topics of the prohibited degrees in the law of marriage and of the law of tithe generally.[94] On none of these occasions is there any sense that parliament was stepping outside its area of competence. In 1586, however, a rather different impression is created: that year the Irish parliament passed measures aimed at perjury and forgery but it is expressly stipulated that neither is to apply to proceedings in, or connected with, the ecclesiastical courts.[95]

After the restoration the parliament moved swiftly to again assert its dominance. In the ecclesiastical sphere, legislation is enacted not only to validate marriages celebrated in accordance with the laws of the Cromwellian regime, but also to prohibit any cleric from holding benefices in both England and Ireland and to bring to an end the payment of customary church dues, a system which represented yet a further survival from Ireland's Gaelic past.[96] Catholics were prohibited from exercising rights of presentation in the established church under any advowsons they might have chanced to acquire.[97] Later, the laws regulating succession and the administration of estates were modernised. In the eighteenth century, it was parliament that enacted the penal laws directed at catholics and it was parliament that became the regular forum for amendment of the law of tithe.

The importance of statute law as a source of the post-reformation ecclesiastical law of Ireland cannot be gainsaid. At the same time, a warning extended by Arthur Browne in 1799 deserves to be heeded: 'The confused heap of statutes in Ireland, on

A compendious view of the ecclesiastical law, 2 vols. (Dublin, 1799), ii, appendix, p. 94. **91** 28 Hen. VIII, c. 19, s. 2. **92** *Case of a commenda*, Davies' reports, p. 185 at pp 205–6. **93** 28 Hen. VIII, c. 18 (act for the proofe of testaments). **94** 33 Hen. VIII, c. 6 (act for marriages); 33 Hen. VIII, c. 12 (act for tythes). **95** 28 Eliz. I, c. 1 (act concerning willfull perjurie), s. 5; 28 Eliz. I, c. 3 (act against forging of evidence & c.), s. 11. **96** 17 & 18 Chas. II, c. 3 (act for the confirmation of marriages); 17 & 18 Chas. II, c. 10 (act for disabling of spiritual persons from holding benefices, or other ecclesiastical dignities in England or Wales, and in Ireland at the same time); 17 & 18 Chas. II, c. 13 (act concerning tythings, oblations and mortuaries). **97** 17 & 18 Chas. II, c. 2 (act for the explaining of some doubts arising upon an act intituled, An act for the better execution of his majestie's gracious declaration for the settlement of his kingdom of Ireland, and satisfaction of the several interests of adventurers, soldiers and other his subjects there, and for making some alterations of and additions unto the said act, for the more speedy and effectual settlement of the said kingdom), s. 158.

ecclesiastical law, ought to rescue from blame the man who at any hazard endeavours to extricate the clergy out of their confusion.'[98]

It is necessary to refer to what is a somewhat complex topic at this juncture, for within its contours lies part of the solution to the problem of the extent to which Irish post-reformation experience matched England's, a problem which, as will be shown, is not divorced either from the question of fidelity to pre-reformation law and practice. The confusion to which Arthur Browne rightly drew attention is not primarily connected with the reformation itself at all but rather with the perplexing nature of the relationship between the parliament of Ireland and that of England. Although, by the time of the reformation, constitutional opinion tended towards the view that major legal changes for Ireland could only derive validity from their enactment as statute law by the Irish parliament, the English parliament still purported to pass legislation expressly extending to Ireland, some of which was never actually reenacted by the local legislature.[99]

It has previously been seen that two years before the enactment by the Irish parliament in 1537 of its own act of supremacy, orders had issued from the king in England for the suppression of an Irish religious house, on the strength of the English act of supremacy. The English act of dispensations was given like extra-territorial effect,[100] again before the adoption of the Irish act of faculties. Even when the counterpart Irish legislation was enacted, problems could still arise. The act of faculties furnishes an example. This legislation would appear to confer some degree of recognition on the previously enacted English act of pluralities, but how much is obscure, and, in the absence of express Irish legislation, remained so. As late as the 1860s Archdeacon Stopford was to declare that, prior to the passing of an act of the United Kingdom parliament in 1850 which finally laid the matter to rest, the position that arose where an Irish cleric took a second benefice was regulated in theory by the third Lateran council – the first benefice only becoming void on the cleric's actual presentation to the second or following actual deprivation.[101]

Particular difficulties arise from the fact that no Irish parliament sat during the reign of Edward VI (1547-53). No Irish legislation was thus introduced at the time to confirm the system of ordination for deacons and priests and for appointing and consecrating bishops, nor for the suppression of chantries, the prohibiting of the purchase and sale of ecclesiastical offices, and the setting up of a dual system of penalties for non-payment of tithe; and such legislation never was. Yet the evidence from certain later enactments of the Irish parliament manages to convey the impression that, in violation of strict constitutional principle, some at least of this corpus of legislation started to be regarded as being in force in Ireland. This is Browne's view, for instance, with regard to the statute of Edward VI prescribing the dual system of penalties for subtraction of tithe.[102]

98 Browne, *Compendious view of the ecclesiastical law*, ii, preface, p. ii. **99** Though scarcely devoid of parti pris, Molyneux's examination of this topic remains essential reading: William Molyneux, *The case of Ireland's being bound by acts of parliament in England stated* (Dublin, 1698). **100** 25 Hen. VIII, c. 21 (Eng.) (acte for the exoneracion frome exaccions payde to the see of Rome). **101** E.A. Stopford, *A hand-book of ecclesiastical law and duty, for the use of the Irish clergy* (Dublin, 1861), p. 83. **102** Browne, *Compendious view of the ecclesiastical law*,

There are other conundrums. In 1547, in the first year of Edward VI, the legislation enacted by the English parliament to regulate the appointment and consecration of bishops purported to abolish, for both England and Ireland, the issuance of the congé d'élire as a stage in the process, and to make all such appointments donative in the king by letters patent.[103] In 1560 the Irish parliament reenacted the abolition of the congé d'élire,[104] but no mention is made of the purported earlier abolition for Ireland thirteen years before. Nor do these complications receive any mention in proceedings in the English king's bench in 1621 concerned with the validity of certain leases made by a sixteenth-century bishop of Ossory, the legality of whose mode of appointment came into question.[105] By then, as it happens, England had long since reverted to the status quo ante: the Elizabethan statute, 8 Eliz I, ch 2 (1566), had again made the appointment of bishops elective in each cathedral chapter, however fictitious such apparent freedom was to prove or remains. Whether the abolition of the congé d'élire in Ireland actually effectuated a significant alteration in the pre-existing canon law was destined to be disputed by senior prelates of the established church during the reign of James I. [106]

In 1622 the patent settling the court of the prerogative and faculties in Ireland gave to the judge the power of attachment. Legislation enacted in England in 1641 forbade the exercise by any ecclesiastical court judge of any such power. Ireland is nowhere mentioned. Nevertheless, over time, according to Browne, this statutory prohibition came to be regarded as disposing of the matter in Ireland as well.[107]

VII

There had been innovation in the system of courts but some continuity as well. There had been changes in the content of ecclesiastical law; but, whilst the amount that was altered doubtless increased as parliament chose to become more and more involved, a solid core of doctrine remained that had its roots in the canon law of the medieval church. The guardians of this strange amalgam of legal thought, the judges and practitioners in the ecclesiastical courts, will have professed the new religion. How prepared were they even so to discharge their task? And how well in fact did they do so?

Nearly a century had elapsed since Henry VIII's Irish reformation parliament sat before steps first appear to have been taken to specify the qualifications of the judges in the ecclesiastical courts. The matter is dealt with in both sets of king's directions for 1622 and again in the Irish canons of 1634. The king's directions for the courts required bishops to appoint 'honest and sufficient officials'; parish clergy were to be engaged for the purpose, 'not at all or sparingly unless upon case of necessity'.[108] The

ii, appendix, pp 96-7 (following Bullingbrooke). **103** 1 Edw. VI, c. 2 (Eng.) (acte for the election of bisshoppes, and what seales and style they and other spirituall persons exercising jurisdiction ecelesiasticall shall use). **104** 2 Eliz. I, c. 4 (act for the conferring and consecrating of archbishops and bishops within this realme). **105** *O'Brian* v. *Knivan*, Cro. Jac. 552; 79 Eng. Rep. 473. **106** Knox, *James Ussher*, pp 30-2. **107** Browne, *Compendious view of the ecclesiastical law*, ii, appendix, p. 98. **108** King's directions for the courts (n. 74 above), direction 44.

directions for the church stipulated that any appointee should be a professor of civil law in possession of a degree of bachelor or doctor of law or a man 'of significance' who had been a proctor for at least five years.[109] The 23rd and 76th canons in the canons of 1634 varied these requirements: any appointee had to be at least 26 years of age, 'learned in the civil and ecclesiastical laws', and either a bachelor or master of arts. Both canons insisted that any appointee be 'reasonably well practised', the 76th canon (which dealt with the choice of chancellors separately) adding that such person should likewise be 'well affected and zealously bent to religion, touching whose life and manners no evil example is had'.

These various provisions may have gone some way to answer the complaint of the author of *Advertisements for Ireland* that too many of the holders of office in the ecclesiastical courts were inspired by mercenary motives.[110] Little is known about the individuals who can be identified as having served as judges of the ecclesiastical courts in the first century after the reformation, and any conclusions to be drawn from the information that is available must necessarily be tentative – whether as to their mercenary bent, intellectual ability or any distinctive contribution they may have made to ecclesiastical law in Ireland.

Levack supplies short biographies of two civilians who passed part of their careers at least in Ireland: Ambrose Forth and Thomas Ryves.[111] Of these two, Ryves is undoubtedly the more interesting figure. It was in 1616 that Ryves, a protégé of Sir John Davies and a kinsman of the latter's wife, succeeded to the judgeship of the prerogative and faculties. He was instantly immersed in a political struggle, which he was eventually to lose, to retain the faculty jurisdiction. In the face of opposition from a faction within the Irish episcopate against Ryves' appointment, Davies wrote in support of his protégé to London. Few of the commissioners appointed to execute the functions of the court of prerogative and faculties, Davies confided to Sir Thomas Lake, were 'so well qualified as this gentleman, who was bred in Winchester, New College in Oxford, and has studied law in the best universities of France, and has extraordinary ability of wit, elocution and all manner of learning'.[112] Davies was soon dead and his encomium did not prevent the transfer of the court of the prerogative and faculties to the primate in 1622. Ryves nevertheless was to continue in the king's service. What Davies said about him would seem warranted, certainly by reference to one of the books Ryves was to write, *The poore vicar's plea*, which represents a moving appeal for the redistribution of wealth within the Irish church.[113]

In 1622 the curtain is drawn back to afford a glimpse of another ecclesiastical court judge, Winter Bridgeman, chancellor of the diocese of Killaloe at the time. The details on Bridgeman are to be found in the return forwarded by John Rider, bishop of Killaloe, to the commissioners who were then inquiring into the state of the Irish church including the exercise of ecclesiastical jurisdiction. Bridgeman was a native of England, had spent three years as a scholar at Lincoln College, Oxford, and four years

109 King's directions for the church (n. 71 above), direction 29. **110** *Advertisements for Ireland*, p. 54. **111** B.P. Levack, *The civil lawyers in England, 1603-41* (Oxford, 1973), pp 231 and 267. **112** Davies to Lake, 20 Dec. 1615: *Cal. S.P. Ire., 1615-25*, p. 106. **113** Thomas Ryves, *The poore vicar's plea, declaring that a competence of meanes is due to them out of the tithes of their severall parishes, notwithstanding the impropriations* (London, 1620).

as a student at the Inner Temple. A competent common lawyer, he had subsequently become 'addicted to ye study of ye civill lawes wherein he doth excell'. He had been thirty years in Ireland and was a JP for Co. Clare: he lived at this day, Rider adds, 'in ye execution as well of that office, as of my jurisdiction upright, without scandall, grievance or complaint'.[114]

That a considerably larger number of competent individuals were available in Ireland to assist in the despatch of ecclesiastical litigation is indicated in a letter of 1638 from Strafford, the lord deputy. Strafford had been pressing Lord Keeper Coventry in England to make use of his power to appoint Irish delegates to hear Irish ecclesiastical appeals. The legislation demanded only that such delegates be 'discreet and well-learned'. Coventry, in response, asked for a list of names, and Strafford supplied thirty-five, the customary 'mix' for the period of prelates, civilians and common lawyers.[115]

The likelihood must be that the torch of learning that was kept lit by a Forth, a Ryves, a Bridgeman or any of Strafford's thirty-five, had been originally ignited outside Ireland, in England. Trinity College, Dublin was founded in 1592 but had no role to play in the professional training of post-reformation Irish canonists and civilians, certainly not before the end of the seventeenth century and even that date may be too early. A single law degree is known to have been conferred by the College in the first quarter century of its existence. The College's neglect of this area of training was regretted by at least one of its early provosts, William Bedell. Bedell served as provost between 1627 and 1629 before his translation to be bishop of Kilmore. In 1628, in a letter to Archbishop Ussher, then vice-chancellor, he confided that mistakes had been made:

> I suppose it hath been an error all this while to neglect the faculties of law and physick, and attend only to the ordering of one poor colledge of divines; whereas with a little more labour and a few priviledges attained, a great many more good wits might have been allowed to study, and seasoned with piety, and made instruments for the bringing in learning, civility and religion.[116]

For the eighteenth century there is some evidence of a falling away from the standards set by the directions of 1622 and the canons of 1634. The position in regard to the calibre of delegates would equally appear to have declined, making necessary the mounting in the late 1720s of an initiative, the details of which, sadly, are not available, to improve a knowledge of the canon and the civil law. This particular initiative would appear to have been taken by Marmaduke Coghill, judge of the prerogative and faculties at the time.[117] Authors of Irish treatises published in the middle of the nineteenth

114 Philip Dwyer, *The diocese of Killaloe from the reformation to the close of the eighteenth century* (Dublin, 1878), p. 147. **115** Lord Deputy (Strafford) and Council of Ireland to Lord Keeper Coventry, 30 June 1638 (H.M.C. *Various collections*, 3 (1904) 182–3). Strafford's interest had been engaged by a case in which two clergymen had successfully established their right to claim tithe of fish, only to be robbed of the spoils of victory when an appeal was brought before English delegates, the law-suit dragged on and legal fees soared. Strafford to Archbishop Laud, 27 Nov. 1637: *Strafford's letters*, ed. Knowler, ii, 136. **116** Quoted, *Dublin University calendar, 1833*, p. 43. **117** Mant, *Hist. of Ch. of Ire.*, ii, 409.

century, for their part, also paint a gloomy picture. Not untypical is W.R. Miller who introduces his guide to Irish probate practice in the following terms:

> In the numerous ecclesiastical courts scattered broadcast over every part of the country, and many of them presided over by gentlemen not of the legal profession, and without any pretensions to legal requirements, this most important branch of the administration of justice was, for ages, permitted not to flourish, but, unfortunately, to fade.[118]

Such late evidence is evidence from a quarter that is certainly suspect – Miller presumably was concerned to supply reasons for practitioners to purchase his book – but nevertheless it raises the distinct possibility that for some length of time the state of the ecclesiastical courts in Ireland had been other than healthy.

The question remains: how far back in time is it legitimate to travel? Evidence in relation to the practitioners appearing in the courts would be relevant, but such evidence is slender, and little assistance is to be derived from it. It is a curious coincidence even so that an outburst directed against the advocates in the Irish ecclesiastical courts finds its way into Archbishop Alen's register whilst a century later one of the Irish church canons of 1634 directs its attention at the rowdiness of proctors.[119] That the stream of Irish ecclesiastical law is unlikely to have continued to flow pure and uncorrupted is suggested by a detail revealed by Arthur Browne: in Ireland, certainly at the time he wrote, the end of the eighteenth century, and probably by virtue of an arrangement of long standing, common lawyers were permitted to appear as advocates in the ecclesiastical courts, though they were not allowed to sign pleadings. 'In that kingdom,' Browne relates, 'the common lawyer is not much distinguished from the civilian: multiplicity of business has not produced division of labour.'[120]

The post-reformation Irish ecclesiastical law tradition was to generate a small indigenous literature. It is so miniscule that it is a virtual certainty that the serious practitioner will have had to rely on pre-reformation English treatises, such as Lyndwood's *Provinciale*, or post-reformation ones, such as Swinburn's *A briefe treatise of testaments and last willes*. Nor can texts of medieval canon law be ignored. That these continued to circulate is clear: in 1683 an archdeacon of Limerick included in his will, in a bequest of books to Trinity College Dublin, two volumes of the *Decretals*.[121]

In the early years procedural works predominate. The *Registrum diocesis Dublinensis*, to which attention has already been drawn, is a book of forms compiled for the use of the official of the Dublin consistorial court in the 1580s.[122] The period after the restoration sees the drawing up of rules of court for the various jurisdictions of the Irish legal system. A set of rules governing the practice and procedure of the Irish ecclesiastical

118 W.R. Miller, *The practice of the court of probate in Ireland* (Dublin, 1863), preface, p. v. Cf. the preface to W.H. Kisbey, *The law and practice of the court for matrimonial causes and matters* (Dublin, 1871). **119** *Reg. Alen*, p. 275; *Constitutions and canons ecclesiasticall* (Dublin, 1635), canon 79. **120** Browne, *Compendious view of the ecclesiastical law*, ii, 131 n. **121** J.D. White, 'Extracts from original wills formerly preserved in the consistorial office, Cashel', *Kilkenny Archaeological Society Transactions*, new series, ii (1858–9), p. 317. **122** *'Registrum diocesis Dublinensis': a sixteenth century precedent book*, ed. N.B. White (Dublin, 1959).

courts was produced in 1682, and survives in a manuscript copy in the library of King's Inns in Dublin. The first printed treatise deals with procedural questions as well: *Praxis Francisci Clerke*, edited by Thomas Braden, dean of Ardfert, and published in Dublin in 1666.[123]

It is plain that in Ireland in the immediate aftermath of the reformation a knowledge of canon law was preserved. A number of precedents contained in the *Registrum diocesis Dublinensis*, *c.*1580, carry glosses, giving citations from the various books of canon law, with an occasional reference to Roman law. Classical medieval canonists retained their standing as well: thus in the same collection Panormitanus (1386-1445) is cited twice, Innocent IV (*d.*1254) once, Lanfrancus de Oriano (*d.*1488) three times, and the *glossae ordinariae* twice.[124] That, in addition, the rules of canon law themselves were actually put into effect is confirmed, above all, by Sir John Davies' Irish law reports which were published in Dublin in 1615. No less than five of the eleven cases recorded by Davies touch directly on questions of ecclesiastical law, questions, plainly, of substantial contemporary importance – *the case of proxies*, *the case of the dean and chapter of Ferns*, *the course of trial of legitimation and bastardy*, *the case of a commenda* and *the case of praemunire* – and of these five, *proxies*, *the dean and chapter of Ferns* and, especially, *a commenda* bristle with pertinent quotations of the canon law and from the canonists. In *proxies*,[125] a complicated suit involving a claim by the crown for back payment of episcopal procurations, the right to which the crown had acquired, from the owner of the lands of a dissolved religious house, both parties to the suit place reliance upon the views of the sixteenth-century Italian canonist, Lancelotti (1522-90) (*Institutiones juris canonici* (1563)) as to when proxies were payable and as to their quantum. Lancelotti is to the fore again in *dean and chapter of Ferns*[126] where it was eventually resolved that an episcopal lease of the 1580s lacked validity because, for purposes of its ratification, the cathedral chapter had not been properly convened nor had it properly voted. In *a commenda*,[127] another complicated suit connected with the legality of a faculty granted to the bishop of Ossory in 1591 by the then commissioners of faculties, Archbishop Adam Loftus of Dublin and Ambrose Forth, to hold a benefice within his diocese in commendam, a very great deal of learning is deployed on the whole subject of dispensations – dispensations from popes, bishops and kings. There are a large number of citations from the *Decretum* and the *Decretals* and from the writings of Joannes Andreae (1270-1348), Pierre Rebuffus (1487-1557) (*Praxis beneficiorum* (1564)) and Ludovico Gomez (*Commentaria in regulas cancellariae apostolicae judiciales* (1543)). The subject-matter of the actual dispute – whether the bishop, by virtue of the faculty, had been made perfect incumbent of the particular vicarage – naturally prompted recourse to material of this kind. Nevertheless, the sheer amount that is actually referred to, as Davies in his account of the case clearly insinuates, must have owed much to the two civil lawyers involved in the presentation of the arguments, Oliver Eustace, for the king, and Dr John Haly, for the defendants.

123 Clerke had been a proctor in London in the late sixteenth century. See further Helmholz, *Roman canon law in reformation England*, pp. 128-31. **124** *Reg. dioc. Dubl.*, intro, p. v. **125** Davies' reports, p. 1; Hans Pawlisch, 'Sir John Davies' law reports and the case of proxies', *Irish Jurist*, xvii (1982) 368. **126** Davies' reports, p. 116 (*the case of the dean and chapter of Fernes, or de capitulariter congregatis*). **127** Davies' reports, p. 185.

Much later in the seventeenth century, two causes célèbres, the forced marriage of the daughter of Sir James Ware (1668) and the deprivation of Lemuel Mathews, archdeacon of Down (1694), provoked an interesting small literature where again a great deal of technical knowledge of canon and ecclesiastical law is on display.[128]

Indigenous treatises devoted to this branch of law in Ireland had to wait until the eighteenth century. Then ample amends were made by Edward Bullingbrooke, with his *Ecclesiastical law ... of the Church of Ireland* (1770) and by Arthur Browne, with his *A compendious view of the ecclesiastical law* (1797–9).

128 For the case of the marriage of Mary Ware, see, e.g. Dudley Loftus, *The case of Ware and Sherley* (Dublin, 1669). For an account of the Lemuel Mathews saga, which includes an exhaustive listing of the contemporary literature, see G.T. Stokes, *Some worthies of the Irish church* (London, 1900), pp 235–9.

The Regulation of the Admission of Attorneys and Solicitors in Ireland, 1600–1866

The rules governing admission to the lower branch of the legal profession form an integral part of the system of statutory control exercised over it that remains a feature of the law in the two jurisdictions of modern Ireland.[1] This system of control may be traced back to legislation enacted in medieval and early modern England. In a recent survey of the lower branch in England, C.W. Brooks has recalled that one post-restoration reader at the inns of court claimed that attorneys were dealt with in more regulatory statutes than any other occupational group in the realm.[2] Mention of two will suffice here. The ordinance De Attornatis et Apprenticiis of 1294 stipulated that the judges should appoint a limited number of qualified men to act as attorneys. The much-rehearsed statute 4 Henry IV, c. 18, passed by the English parliament in 1402, is more detailed, and at the same time a model of succinct expression:

> For sundry damages and mischiefs that have ensued before this time to divers persons of the realm by a great number of attornies, ignorant and not learned in the law, as they were wont to be before this time; it is ordained and established, that all the attornies shall be examined by the justices, and by their discretions their names put in the roll, and they that be good and virtuous, and of good fame, shall be received and sworn well and truly to serve in their offices, and especially that they make no suit in a foreign county; and the other attornies shall be put out by the discretion of the said justices; and that their masters, for whom they were attornies, be warned to take others in their places, so that in the mean time no damage nor prejudice come to their said masters. And if any of the said attornies do die, or do cease, the justices for the time being by their discretion shall make another in his place, which is a virtuous man and learned, and sworn in the same manner as afore is said: and if any such attorney be hereafter notoriously found in any default of record, or otherwise, he shall forswear the court, and never after be received to make any suit in any court of the king …[3]

Remarkably – and it is eloquent testimony to the enduring strength of the common law – reliance was placed on the words of the statute of Henry IV in the Irish court of exchequer as late as 1844, when A.R. Symes, the law reporter and former barrister, sought, by way of special concession, an abridgement of his period of apprenticeship

1 Solicitors Act 1954, Solicitors (Amendment) Act 1960; Solicitors (Northern Ireland) Order 1976. 2 C.W. Brooks, *Pettyfoggers and vipers of the Commonwealth: the 'lower branch' of the legal profession in early modern England* (Cambridge, 1986), p. 19. 3 *Stat. realm*, ii, 138–9.

and to be admitted an attorney much sooner than was customary.[4] In applications of this kind it doubtless helped to be in a position to demonstrate that the bench had long retained a discretion to act which moreover was expressly sanctioned by statute. Fortunately, other evidence exists to show that the statute 4 Henry IV, c. 18 was recognised as having legal effect in Ireland, and at a considerably earlier date. The explanation is standard in the case of medieval English statute law: the statute became operative under the provisions of Poynings' Act of 1495 (10 Henry VII, c. 22) which extended to Ireland the generality of the pre-existing statute law of England. Thus John Merick, in a collection published in Dublin in 1617 of English statutes which he reckoned applied in Ireland, includes 4 Henry IV, c. 18. Edward Lee does likewise in his guide of 1734; so too do Bullingbrooke and Belcher in their abridgement of 1754. There is also reference to the statute in the preface to a practitioner's manual brought out by Gorges Edmund Howard in 1759.[5]

Mention in the writings of Howard, inclusion in compendia of statute-law brought out in the seventeenth and eighteenth centuries and resurrection for purposes of an isolated lawsuit in the nineteenth hardly constitute compelling proof however that the statute 4 Henry IV, c. 18 continued throughout to have significant practical impact. The question is an instructive one to air at the outset. Although the statute of Henry IV had the capacity to provide the sinews of the regulatory framework for the admission of attorneys at the point where this survey commences in 1600, if the statute actually did so then or in subsequent years corroborative evidence in either respect is wholly lacking. In a petition to parliament of 1858 the recently founded Law Society deals cursorily with the law determining entry to the solicitors' profession that antedated the passing of the seminal Irish act of 1733. Before that date, the petition recalls,

> the right to exercise the profession of attorney-at-law in Ireland was attained by persons binding themselves to, or placing themselves in the office of, some admitted attorney for a certain period, and afterwards applying to one of the courts of law in Ireland for liberty to practise as an attorney in such court.[6]

Baron Pennefather of the Irish court of exchequer is the author of another foray into history in his judgment on Lyons' controversial application to be admitted an attorney that came before the courts on several occasions between 1834 and 1839:

> Before the statute of the 7 Geo. II, c. 5, Ir. [the act of 1733], this court and the other superior courts in Dublin exercised, under certain regulations, the power

4 *In re Symes* (1844) 7 Ir Eq R 339. 5 John Merick, *A compendious collection and breefe abstract of all the auncient English-statutes ... which now are in force within this kingdome of Ireland ...* (Dublin, 1617), p. 53; Edward Lee, *The statute-law of Ireland common-placed ...* (Dublin, 1734), p. 24; Edward Bullingbrooke and Jonathan Belcher, *An abridgement of the statutes of Ireland ...* (Dublin, 1754), p. 28; G.E. Howard, *A compendious treatise of the rules and practise of the pleas side of the exchequer*, 2 vols. (Dublin, 1759) i, p. xx. 6 Daire Hogan, *The legal profession in Ireland 1789-1922* (Dublin, 1986), p. 15.

> of admitting attornies as their own officers, to discharge the duties of the respective courts. It was thought right, however, by the legislature, that certain rules should be laid down by legislative enactments, reserving to the superior courts the power of exercising their original jurisdiction in such cases as, in their discretion, it might seem fit so to do.[7]

On the historical perception of rules and procedures on entry to the profession these two extracts are illuminating both as to what they say and as to what they omit. In the latter connection, the absence of any express reference to Henry IV's legislation is noteworthy.

Two explanations for this neglect of the early legislative precedent may be tentatively advanced. The first is indicated by Brooks when assessing the evidence for England.[8] Until the mid-sixteenth century, he argues, the available information shows that the regime envisaged by the act of 1402 was in regular use. Thereafter the pattern alters, as a result, Brooks maintains, of changes in the general procedures of the common law courts. These changes were linked to the rise in influence of the prothonotaries and their clerks. It is Brooks' contention, in the case of the court of king's bench for instance, that by the late sixteenth century the majority of attorneys were not admitted in the fashion contemplated by Henry IV's statute: this was for the simple reason that, in a technical sense, so many had become clerks of the chief prothonotary of the court. In chancery the early dominance of the six clerks and their underclerks had brought about a concentration in their hands of functions the equivalents to which elsewhere fell to be carried out by attorneys – thus leaving a residue of functions to be performed by a motley group of practitioners who were to acquire in the course of time the denomination of solicitors. Only in common pleas, ultimately, were the attorneys destined to remain independent of clerks and their underclerks and to discharge tasks of the traditional procedural variety on behalf of their several clients. The inference one is invited to draw from these disparate developments is that the manner in which the English system of courts chose to evolve rendered the act of 1402 an increasingly unsatisfactory instrument for the purpose for which it had been originally engineered. Falling first into disuse, the act sank eventually into oblivion.

A second possible explanation is of a different calibre, being confined to circumstances peculiar to Ireland: it is concerned generally with the matter of the knowledge of past law possessed by subsequent generations of administrators and judges in the country. The contention being put forward is that reliable, rounded knowledge of the actual content of Irish law in previous centuries was invariably a commodity in short supply. The absence of what today would be termed adequate library resources – the unavailability of copies of Irish and English statutes for instance – must be counted a principal cause. But there were other problems and technical complications too that made it difficult to discover not only what the law had been in the past but also more seriously what it amounted to in the present.[9] With facilities for the proper practice of

7 *In re Lyons* (1839) 1 Ir Eq R 267 at 272. **8** Brooks, *Pettyfoggers and vipers*, p. 19f. **9** Consider for instance

the profession so depressing, exactitude on matters of indigenous legal history was neither encouraged nor indeed did it come to be expected. The upshot deserves to be contrasted with the much-vaunted durability of the common law: precise historical recollection could not and did not survive.

Whatever the explanation, a void opened up and to one facet of this void special attention needs to be drawn. A certain vagueness came in time to surround the practical operation of the rules governing admission to the lower branch of the legal profession in Ireland. The date at which this vagueness first manifested itself is not immediately obvious. More germane to the present purpose is to observe the long-term consequences flowing from it. A concomitant of any intelligible regime for controlling the admission of attorneys and solicitors (indeed, the admission into any profession) was the furnishing of answers to such questions as who had the authority to sanction entry, what the requirements on entry were and how exactly entry was to be effectuated. Answers to these questions were vital and they were in fact to emerge, but they emerged somewhat haphazardly. What occurred was that at intermittent intervals and in varying circumstances a succession of initiatives was taken. Some new 'rule' was the outcome in each instance. The authors of these initiatives fell into one of four groups. First, there were the two parliaments, the English as well as the Irish. Secondly, as also might have been anticipated, there were the judges. From a study of their involvement however it is helpful to distinguish between the three roles that members of the judiciary filled: that as judges simpliciter (sitting in court, deciding matters arising there), that as draftsmen of rules of court (for the courts to which they were attached), and, finally, that as benchers of their inn of court (in effect, of the society of King's Inns). Third, there were sundry senior court officers. And fourth, there were the masters of apprentices (ordinarily court clerks or attorneys themselves) who prescribed the terms of the indentures of apprenticeship.

Over time, the outcome of this sequence of haphazard regulatory initiatives was the transformation of the regime on admissions into a world of almost byzantine complexity. Development tended to take this direction in particular because of the relative infrequency with which any attempt was made to relate each successive initiative to the pre-existing rules. This world survived far into the modern period undoubtedly alike constituting a discouragement to the fainthearted and posing a trap for the unwary. That it survived the length of time it did appears, superficially, something of a puzzle, given that from the 1770s onwards at least the trend was perceptibly towards the 'professionalisation' of the lower branch.

It is this modernizing movement that culminates in major changes in the 1860s. In 1860 itself the decision is reached to introduce written examinations.[10] Six years later parliament transfers important regulatory functions to the new representative profes-

this defence by Edward Lee of his decision to include within the body of statute law in force in Ireland certain post-Poynings' Act English legislation. The prose is awkward but the sense is plain (*The statute-law of Ireland common-placed*, p. vii): 'Some English statutes made since Poynings's law, tho' Ireland, not expressly mentioned, yet in regards they (to particular purposes) bind the people of Ireland, are here set down, some of which see in title, Egyptians, petitions, etc.' And see generally my 'In praise of law books', *Ir. Jur.*, xxi (1986), 326 at 351. **10** Hogan, *Legal profession in Ireland*, pp 109–11.

sional body, the Law Society.[11] Together, these two events may be said to mark the birth of the modern Irish solicitors' profession. By comparison, the removal of the remaining vestiges of the distinction between solicitors and attorneys which followed a decade later as one of the consequences of the enactment of the Judicature Act is a minor footnote.[12]

The persistence of the confusion and obscurity which the reforms of the 1860s and later were designed to expunge is exemplified by an episode that took place in the rolls court in the early 1830s, to which some publicity has already been accorded.[13] In the course of a lawsuit a dispute surfaced as to whether a solicitor, prior to the receipt of his professional licence, was obliged to subscribe an oath, traditionally subscribed by all attorneys at the period, not to permit any person to practise in his name.[14] A solicitor named Smith claimed not to have subscribed any such oath and he was criticised in consequence in open court by the then master of the rolls, Sir William McMahon. Sir William considered that the oath was both appropriate and prudent. But was the subscribing of it legally mandatory? Smith had investigated the matter and he was satisfied that he had been entitled to decline to subscribe it. A rule of court of 1791 merely required the presentation of a certificate signed by the senior master and by the registrar that the aspiring solicitor was a fit and proper person; there was no mention of an oath. Sir William was forced to admit he had made a mistake and apologised. Happily, the solicitor left on record an explanation of how this abuse of insisting on an unnecessary oath had originally come to be perpetrated:

> Many gentlemen do not wish to take the same trouble to inform themselves, but prefer applying to some of the subordinate clerks in the six clerks' office, who have an interest in making a mystery of the manufacturing of solicitors, and in this way I can account for the introduction of the objectionable and unnecessary clause, through the ignorance of some clerk who had obtained some hearsay notion of the oath taken by attorneys (originally framed in reference to the then popery acts), of which the present version is a clumsy imitation.[15]

II

In the absence of hard data, the arrangements that governed the admission of attorneys in Ireland in 1600 can only be matter for speculation. It is legitimate to infer, however, that a system of apprenticeship operated and that some test, however cursory, preceded formal admission to the pertinent common law court, king's bench, common pleas or exchequer. Who administered that test remains problematic.

Parliamentary intervention, redolent of the statute 4 Henry IV, c. 18, continued in England. In 1605 an act superimposed a degree of specificity upon the existing rules

11 Attorneys and Solicitors (Ireland) Act, 1866: 29 & 30 Vict., c. 84. **12** Supreme Court of Judicature (Ireland) Act, 1877: 40 & 41 Vict., c. 57. **13** Hogan, *Legal profession in Ireland*, p. 99. **14** *Birch* v. *Oldis* (1831) Glascock 351. **15** At 355-6.

regulating the entry of attorneys there: the latter were to be brought up in the courts or to be well practised in the soliciting of causes and to be found by their dealings to be skilful and of an honest disposition.[16] No equivalent Irish act ensued: sittings of the Irish parliament were still relatively infrequent at this time. To move on several years, it would seem, to judge from an entry in the Irish commons' journal for 1641, that some kind of legislative initiative, of which, however, the details do not survive, was at that stage in contemplation.[17] Under the Commonwealth, it is true, specific measures were adopted to drive catholics out of practice.[18] But otherwise there was no formal intervention in the field in Ireland.

Matters were not left as before, however – whatever that might have involved – for significant modifications were effected in other ways in the Ireland of the seventeenth century. These originated in the activities of the Irish inn of court, the society of King's Inns, which had been revived in 1607, and in the increasing preparedness of the Irish courts of law, certainly from around 1670 onwards, through the drawing up of rules of court to proceed to regulate both the admission and the activity of attorneys.

In 1806 Bartholomew Duhigg, the first historian of King's Inns, contended that the right of the benchers to regulate the lower branch through insistence on compulsory membership was first asserted in 1793.[19] The claim cannot be supported. Hogan has explained that the new rules of 1793 merely enshrined 'an old obligation which, with effect from the first day of Hilary term 1794, was enforced with a new vigour'.[20] The testimony of the Black Book of King's Inns too is unchallengeable. Attorneys were amongst the categories of legal practitioner admitted to the Inns on the latter's revival in 1607. And in 1629 there occurs the first recital of a crucial new rule to the effect that no one was to be admitted an attorney in any of the courts of Dublin unless he had first been admitted to membership of the society. A corollary adopted at the same time obliged existing attorneys who were not already members of the society to present themselves for admission early in the next ensuing Hilary term; otherwise they were to be struck off. Every attorney was equally required to keep one week's commons at the society in each law term.[21] This basic rule was restated in 1656, in 1683 and again in 1710. The restatement of 1683 went further: it insisted that proof of the payment of the Inns admission fine (originally in the case of attorneys set at 13*s*. 4*d*., and shortly to be raised to £2 13*s*. 9*d*.) had to be presented as a preliminary to admission as an attorney in any of the common law courts.[22]

The unequivocal character of the rule on compulsory membership of the Inns notwithstanding, the pages of the Black Book reveal that there were many defaulters among the ranks of attorneys. Membership had been made compulsory for barristers too and lists of defaulters in both categories were ordered to be brought forward in

16 3 Jas. I, c. 7; Robert Robson, *The attorney in eighteenth century England* (Cambridge, 1959), p. 53. **17** *Commons' jn. Ire.*, i, 252: 10 July 1641. **18** Colum Kenny, 'The exclusion of catholics from the legal profession in Ireland, 1537-1829', *IHS*, xxv (1987), 337 at 349. **19** Bartholomew Duhigg, *History of the King's Inns* (Dublin, 1806), p. 459. **20** *Legal profession in Ireland*, p. 22. **21** T. Power, 'The "Black Book" of King's Inns: an introduction with an abstract of contents', *Ir. Jur.*, xx (1985), 134 at 180 (Black Book, ff. 181r-181v). **22** Ibid., pp 167 (f. 116r (1656)); 165 (f. 87v (1683)); 208 (f. 329r (1710)).

1629, 1663, 1674, 1698 and 1704. The entry for 1698 singled out attorneys who 'never pay any respect to the courts where they are sworn but live in the country' and unfairly monopolised assize business.[23] Failure to pay for commons and to contribute to the fund for pensioners was another regular complaint – in 1657, 1663, 1667 (when the complainant is one Abigail Swift, the widow of the recently deceased steward), 1698 and 1704.[24] To meet this latter problem a rule adopted in 1710 required all new members, attorneys included, to lodge a bond with the treasurer of the Inns and to provide sureties that they would at all times observe the rules of the society.[25] Denial of the right to practise was the standard sanction, though a less draconian form of punishment appears to have been in force around 1704.

The prominent position occupied by the society of King's Inns in the scheme of regulation is indicated by other evidence. An Irish statute of 1715 which conferred rights of practice in the assize courts on attorneys who had been admitted to the superior courts in Dublin stipulated that such attorneys should first have paid their 'commons and other duties to the stewards of the Inns'.[26] A second revival of King's Inns towards the end of the eighteenth century brought a spate of new rules of court that reaffirmed yet again the obligation of prior membership of the society. In 1789, four years before the benchers adopted the regulation to which Duhigg took such grave exception, the court of common pleas insisted, as a preliminary to entry, on proof of payment of one's admission fine to the society.[27] In 1785 king's bench followed suit: where common pleas had been content with a receipt however, they demanded a certificate.[28]

III

There was nothing novel about compulsory membership of the Inns being dealt with in this fashion in the rules of the various courts themselves. The existence of this further mode of regulation was expressly acknowledged by Baron Pennefather in 1839,[29] and the legacy itself went back to 1671, the date of the first set of rules of court for the Irish common law courts thought to have survived. This set emanated from common pleas and began with a re-assertion of the Inns' own contemporary regulations: existing attorneys were to become members of the Inns prior to the start of the next ensuing Michaelmas term; new attorneys would in future be obliged to become members of the Inns in the course of the same law term in which they were admitted to practice; all were to attend commons at the Inns one week in each term at least.

23. Ibid., pp 180 (ff. 181r-181v (1629)), 186 (f. 197r (1663)), 195 (f. 258v (1674)), 202 (ff. 282r-283r (1698)), 206 (ff. 319r-319v (1704)). **24**. Ibid., pp 168 (ff. 120r-121v (1657)), 186 (f. 197v (1663)), 190 (f. 209v (1667)), 202 (ff. 282v-283r (1698)), 206 (ff. 319r-319v (1704)). **25** Ibid., p. 208 (f. 329r). **26** 2 Geo. I, c. 11 (an act for reviving and amending an act intituled an act for recovery of small debts in a summary way, before the judges of assize), s. 12. **27** Order of 22 June 1789: R.S. Moore and T.K. Lowry, *A collection of the general rules and orders of the courts of queen's bench, common pleas and exchequer of pleas in Ireland* (Dublin, 1842) (hereafter *Moore & Lowry*), app. 1, p. 61. **28** Rules and orders of the court of queen's bench in Ireland, lxxxvii (20 June 1795): *Moore & Lowry*, p. 138. **29** *In re Lyons* (1839) 1 Ir Eq R 267 at 272.

There was one additional requirement: each attorney of the court was to notify the steward of the Inns of his place of residences.[30]

The common pleas rules of 1671 touched on many other facets to the work of the court's attorneys. Rule iii in a group headed 'concerning attorneys and officers', for example, prescribed what had to be done to preserve one's right to practise in court.[31] Of most interest however is the information the rules furnished as to the regime then in force that governed entry to the profession. A period of apprenticeship 'of 5 years at the least' was prescribed; so too were the categories of possible master and the mode of conduct of the 'moral examination' of apprentices. All these matters were dealt with in rule vi of the group headed 'concerning attorneys and officers':

> That none be admitted an attorney of this court, unless he hath served or shall serve by the space of 5 years at the least, as a clerk to some judge, serjeant at law, practising counsellor, attorney, clerk or officer of one of his majesty's courts at Westminster or Dublin unless his master die or give over his practice, and he also upon examination be found of good ability and honesty for such employment and that sufficient proof, to be put into writing, be made of such service upon a desire of admittance, and filed with the clerk of the warrants without fee, and taking the oath of supremacy in open court; that every minister and officer of this court shall in like manner take and receive the said oath, according to the statute made in the second year of Elizabeth upon his admission into his office, ministry or service.[32]

A complementary group of rules, headed 'concerning the better preservation of order among the officers and clerks', completed the picture:

> rule i That the court do once in every year, in Michaelmas term, nominate and appoint three or more able and credible practitioners in the court, to continue for the year following, for these purposes following:
>
> rule ii That they, or any two of them, examine such persons as desire to be admitted attorneys, and appoint convenient times and places for the same; and in order thereunto, that such persons as shall desire to be admitted attorneys, first attend the prothonotary with his proof of service, then to repair to the persons appointed to examine attorneys, and being approved, to be presented to the court with his approbation, and then to be sworn in open court, unless some just exception be against him.
>
> rule iii That they give information to the court from time to time upon their oaths, of breaches of order, and miscarriages of officers, attorneys and clerks.[33]

30 Rules and orders of his majesty's court of common bench in Ireland, of Trinity term, in the 22nd year of King Charles II – concerning attorneys and officers, i: *Moore & Lowry*, app. I, pp 4–5. **31** *Moore & Lowry*, app. I, p. 5. **32** *Moore & Lowry*, app. I, p. 6. **33** *Moore & Lowry*, app. I, p. 9.

Unfortunately, no evidence appears to be available as to the manner in which any of the rules from either of the two groups operated in practice. The dearth of any data at all for the other common law courts is another serious lacuna.

IV

The major legislative intervention in the affairs of the lower branch in Ireland that starts to unfold at the end of the seventeenth century has to be set in the context of contemporary political events. In Ireland the victory of William III over James II at the Boyne in 1690 ushered in an era of penal laws where religious affiliation was the yard-stick of political loyalty. The class that had suffered during the short reign of James made it their business, once the tables had been turned and their fortunes had revived, to ensure that none other than loyal protestants should taste political power or hold legal or administrative office. The 'protestantising' of the Irish legal profession was a direct outcome, a policy carried through in respect of the lower branch by legislative measures spanning the years 1691 to 1733 and which were effectively in force until 1792. This chapter in the story of Irish law has been related before but not always so as to underline the impact of the policy on entry to the lower branch.[34]

An act passed for Ireland by the English parliament in 1691 served as the harbinger of what was to follow. A fresh test of political reliability was imposed on all aspirants to public office in Ireland, a category broad enough to include barristers, attorneys and clerks of the courts. Such aspirants were required to subscribe the oath of allegiance and the oath of abjuration and to make the declaration against transubstantiation.[35] The only test of loyalty demanded by the common pleas rules of 1671 was preparedness to subscribe the oath of supremacy that went back to the reign of Elizabeth.[36] Clearly, the English act of 1691 displayed features that were bound to cause offence to catholic practitioners. One category alone was exempted: those (lawyers included) who managed to bring themselves within the terms of the religious concessions contained in the articles of Limerick and later, by extension, of Galway too.

The English act of 1691 was aimed at many others besides attorneys. The Irish act of 1698 on the other hand boldly proclaimed itself 'an act to prevent papists being solicitors'.[37] The preamble set forth a justification for the passing of so severe a measure,[38] and the act itself inserted, by way of addition to the earlier proofs of loyalty, on the giving of an undertaking to educate one's children as protestant. The two oaths, the declaration and the undertaking were expressed to be required of all persons seeking 'to act as solicitor in any court of law or equity, or as agent or manager in any cause or suit in law or equity, or as seneschal, or solicitor in all or any of the courts or offices in this kingdom'.[39]

34 Kenny, 'The exclusion of catholics', *IHS*, xxv (1987), 337; T.P. Power, 'Conversions among the legal profession in Ireland in the eighteenth century' in Daire Hogan and W.N. Osborough, eds., *Brehons, serjeants and attorneys* (Dublin, 1990), p. 153; Hogan, *Legal profession in Ireland*, pp 14-15. **35** 3 Will. & Mary, c. 2 (an act for abrogating the oath of supremacy in Ireland and appointing other oaths). **36** Concerning attorneys and officers, vi: *Moore & Lowry*, app. I, p.6. **37** 10 Will. III, c. 13. **38** See Power, 'Conversions among the legal profession', at p. 154. **39** 10 Will. III, c. 13, ss. 1 and 2. Exceptions applied in the case of solicitors

The provisions contained in a further act of 1707 were designed to strengthen the act of 1698.[40] Penalties were increased, 'reputed papists' as well as 'papists' simpliciter were brought within its scope; and the courts and activities that were prohibited to catholics were individually listed: the four courts in Dublin, the courts of the Tipperary palatinate, 'any court of record in this kingdom', any ecclesiastical or admiralty court and service as clerk in any sheriff's office or in any commission issued by a court of equity.[41] Section 3 enabled informers to interrupt legal proceedings and intimate to the presiding judge their suspicions regarding the religious persuasion of any practitioner present in court. Failure by such practitioner to subscribe the necessary oaths and pass the other tests that had been prescribed compelled the judge to treat the former as a 'popish solicitor convict'. The act shut out catholics from apprenticeship; it also deprived solicitors who benefited from the terms of the articles of Limerick of their right to continue in practice unless they subscribed the oath of abjuration.[42] As these and other penal law measures progressed through the Irish parliament, a number of petitions were presented on behalf of individuals who sought special concessions. These were presumably catholic attorneys and solicitors: such petitions for instance were received from Oliver Weston in 1704 and 1707 and from Francis Glascock, Robert Ridge and Peter Daly, all in 1707.[43]

A further turn of the screw occurred in 1727. Legislation adopted that year was aimed at legal practitioners who were either converts to protestantism or born of popish parents. It stipulated that aspirant barristers and attorneys falling within either category should adduce proof that they had been protestants for at least two years prior to applying for admission.[44] The judges of the court of common pleas adopted a rule of court two years later to guard against the risk that the 1727 measure might become a dead letter. An additional affidavit was demanded of all aspirant attorneys falling within either of the suspect classes. The examiners of apprentices were additionally enjoined to 'enquire into these particulars and certify how they find the same'.[45]

There was legislation yet again in 1733.[46] Henceforth aspirant attorneys and solicitors had to demonstrate that they had been protestants from the age of 14 or for at least two years before commencing their apprenticeships.[47] Section 6 facilitated conviction on charges connected with breach of the act by describing the tasks then commonly understood to be performed by the Irish solicitor and which accordingly were forbidden to catholics. It is an invaluable contemporary check-list. Any person would be deemed to be acting as a solicitor who

> draws, dictates or abbreviates, pleadings or transcribes or abbreviates any depositions or other evidence in order to be made use of in any suit either at law or

pursuing their own lawsuits (s. 3) and such solicitors as fell within the terms of the articles of Limerick (s. 4). **40** 6 Anne, c. 6: an act to explain and amend an act intituled, an act to prevent papists being solicitors. **41** Ss. 1 and 2. **42** Ss. 6 and 8. **43** *Commons' jn. Ire.*, ii, 431 (22 Feb. 1704) and 508–9 (25 July 1707). **44** 1 Geo. 11, c. 20: an act for regulating the admissions of barristers at law, six clerks, and attornies, and of other persons, into offices and employments; and for preventing papists practising as solicitors; and for further strengthening the protestant interest in this kingdom. **45** Order of Michaelmas term, 3 Geo. II, 1729 (Lord Chief Justice Reynolds, Mr Justice Gore and Mr Justice Bernard): *Moore & Lowry*, app. I, p. 47. **46** 7 Geo. II, c. 5: an act for the amendment of the law in relation to popish solicitors; and for remedying other mischiefs in relation to the practitioners in the several courts of law and equity. **47** S. 2.

in equity or takes upon himself the direction or management in any cause or suit or the defence thereof in the said Four Courts, or any of them, wherein he is not a party, nor concerned in interest.

Over the plight of catholic would-be practitioners vain protests continued to be mounted. One such protest was presented to the Irish commons in 1734 from a group headed by Sir Edmund Butler, bart., and including William Purcell of Crumlin, John Reilly of Dublin, two Dublin merchants Francis Lynch and Augustus Clark, and a Dublin brewer, one Richard Mathews.[48] No other details are available.

V

The act of 1733 had a dual importance. It served to strengthen the existing legislation aimed at preventing catholics from entering the legal profession. But the majority of the act's provisions constituted, in effect, as Baron Pennefather recalled in 1839,[49] the first indigenous statutory framework for detailed regulation of the lower branch to be adopted in Ireland. This framework duplicated much of what was already prescribed by the common pleas rules of 1671, and it would be misleading to deduce from its adoption at this time the existence of any new-found determination to advance professional standards. Equally, however, the decision to cast in a statutory mould an approximation to the best in contemporary practice cannot be dismissed as bereft of significance. The principle of the exercise of statutory control over the workings of the lower branch had been reasserted and this was to have major long-term implications.

An English act of 1729 was the immediate inspiration.[50] That act had laid down, as had the Irish common pleas rules of 1671, an apprenticeship period of five years: the Irish act of 1733 introduced an identical clause. The inventory of categories of master at liberty to take apprentices that the act went on to furnish represented a change from those authorised under the terms of the common pleas rules of 1671: henceforth these were to be only six clerks in chancery, attorneys or licensed solicitors. Such masters could possess an English qualification or an Irish: in short, the Irish apprentice could enter into indentures with an English master. Prior to admission, the apprentice had to procure an affidavit that he had completed his period of service and this had to be presented in the appropriate court and filed in the manner prescribed.[51] The indentures had to be registered by each master, although it was the apprentice himself who was obliged to pay the fee, fixed by statute at one shilling.[52] The size of the profession was also an object of concern: in an attempt to keep numbers down the maximum number of apprentices any master could have simultaneously was fixed at three for attorneys and solicitors and at six for six clerks in chancery.[53] A further clause dealt with the problem that could arise where a master died before the five-year

48 *Commons' jn. Ire.*, iv, 137 (3 April 1734). **49** *In re Lyons* (1839) 1 Ir Eq R 267 at 272. **50** 2 Geo. II, c. 23 (Eng.): an act for the better regulation of attornies and solicitors. **51** 7 Geo. III, c. 5, s. 2. **52** S. 3. **53** S. 9.

period of apprenticeship had concluded.[54] Section 7 inaugurated a system for licensing solicitors. Aside from the standard requirements as to religious persuasion, no particular criteria were laid down or restrictions envisaged. Publicity however was to be accorded to the names of those licensed as solicitors for the whole of the law term next ensuing.[55]

Though the extent to which these various arrangements represented a true departure can be exaggerated, it is undeniable that a degree of structural reform within the lower branch was being attempted. Simultaneously, deliberate cultivation of new traditions of professionalism may have been projected. In this latter regard, the drawing up in 1740 by the three judges of the court of common pleas – Lord Chief Justice Singleton, Mr Justice Gore and Mr Justice Lindsay – of the terms of a fresh professional oath that was ordered by them to be subscribed by every attorney of the court prior to admission is of more than passing interest. Statute law had originally demanded the subscription of the oath of supremacy; at the outset of the penal law era this had been superseded by the oath of allegiance and the oath of abjuration. From scrutinising the terms of the supplementary oath of 1740 (that was ordered to be administered in open court by the prothonotary or his clerk), it is plain that the preoccupation of its authors was with matters of a different sort:

> You shall do no falsehood or deceit, nor consent to any to be done within this court, and if you shall know of any to be done, you shall give notice thereof to the lord chief justice, or other his brethren justices of this court, that it may be reformed.
>
> You shall delay no man for lucre or malice.
>
> You shall increase no fees, but you shall be contented with the old accustomed fees.
>
> You shall plead no foreign plea, nor sue any foreign suits unlawfully to the hurt of any man, but such as shall stand with the order of the law and your own conscience.
>
> You shall seal all such process as you shall sue out of this court, with the seal thereof, and see the king's majesty and chief justice discharged for the same.
>
> You shall not wittingly or willingly sue or procure to be sued any false suit, or give aid or consent to the same, on pain to be expelled this court for ever.
>
> And further, you shall truly use and demean yourself in the office of an attorney within this court according to your learning and discretion. So help you God.[56]

In certain respects, the wording of this oath follows that prescribed by the English court of common pleas in the late Tudor period and which is reproduced by Brooks:[57] the Irish common pleas oath of 1740 cannot therefore pretend to be original. Similar if somewhat shorter oaths were administered to attorneys on their admission to prac-

54 S. 14. **55** S. 8. **56** Order of Hilary term, 14 Geo. II, 1740: *Moore & Lowry*, app. I, p. 50. **57** Brooks, *Pettyfoggers and vipers*, p. 119.

tise in the other courts, whose provenance is equally likely to have been English. One of these, that used in the Irish court of exchequer in the middle of the nineteenth century, is reproduced by Plunkett:

> You and each of you shall well and truly and faithfully behave yourselves in the office of attorney in this her majesty's court of exchequer; you shall do no falsehood or rasure or cause or consent to the doing of any; nor to the rasing of any records, pleadings, writings or memoranda of this court, whereby the court of the queen or her subjects may be hindered or prejudiced, and if you know of any to be done shall give speedy knowledge thereof to the lord chief baron or the barons of this court, that thereby the same may be redressed and reformed. You shall delay no man for lucre or malice, and rightfully and truly you shall do unto all men in that which belongeth you to do by reason of your place and office of an attorney.[58]

The practice of administering such oaths fell into disuse after the enactment of the Judicature Acts in the 1870s. Plunkett did not mourn their passing. 'The young attorneys', he wrote, 'who stood up in open court to repeat these oaths on the threshold of their professional careers might have been excused if they had reflected like Carlyle – "Where we are we know; where we are going no man knoweth".'[59] On the publicising of the terms of the new common pleas oath of 1740, comparable heterodox opinions may have been expressed, though these are not now traceable. Apart altogether from the question of its practical efficacy, the oath itself deserves to be probed into a little further. The terms of it strongly indicate one line of inquiry that is surely worth pursuing. Those terms are redolent of ideas of contemporary professional virtue. Is it conceivable that the oath's judicial progenitors could have planned to launch an assault on the phenomenon of professional vice?

This is not the place to attempt a survey of the virtues and vices of attorneys and solicitors in eighteenth-century Ireland, either individually or collectively. Research has not advanced sufficiently to enable even a start to be made. Yet some mention of the matter in a brief sketch is warranted: questions of professional ethics are a focus of concern in the regime governing entry to any profession that is worthy of the name. They were a focus of concern in the regulations relative to attorneys in the common pleas rules of 1671, and the character of aspiring attorneys remained throughout the particular preoccupation of the examiners deputed by each court, more especially after the reforms of 1773.

Occasional glimpses reveal individual members of the lower branch going about their daily routine. From these it is a reasonably safe conjecture that the majority led unremarkable lives. Though the redoubtable Gorges Edmund Howard is a witness to the contrary, it is also a reasonably safe conjecture that in the process that majority helped to maintain, even to consolidate, rough and ready standards of professional

58 E.A. Plunkett, 'Attorneys and solicitors in Ireland' in *Record of the centenary of the charter of the Incorporated Law Society of Ireland, 1852-1952* (Dublin, 1953), p. 38 at pp 64-5. **59** Plunkett, loc. cit., p. 65.

respectability. A few achieved a modicum of fame. Elizabeth Bowen in her family history, *Bowen's court*,[60] left a pleasing vignette of the Dublin attorney Richard Chester, her forebears' mid-century family confidant, factotum and general legal adviser. Staying in Dublin but passing down the years, there was William Deane, a solicitor in whose honour a medallion commemorating his prominence in contemporary scientific pursuits was struck by the celebrated Dublin medallist, William Mossop, in 1785;[61] Archibald Hamilton, too, an attorney who flourished at the turn of the nineteenth century, and who is to be espied in his dual extra-curricular roles of impress officer for Ireland and council member of a prominent charity, the Sick and Indigent Roomkeepers' Society.[62]

But black sheep flourished as well. The penal laws directed at catholic landholding which were maintained in full vigour between 1704 and 1778 provided scope for collusion, fraud and general sharp practice on a grand scale. From the scattered pieces of evidence surviving, such vices were undoubtedly practised by a number of attorneys that it remains possible to identify. Two of those who can be named – Daly and Franks – were both attorneys in the court of exchequer. Exchequer attorneys were far and away the largest group and the explanation for any relative predominance in the ranks of villainy is probably to be found in that circumstance rather than in any procedure peculiar to the exchequer court which could have facilitated the perpetration of abuses.[63]

Aside from the temptations held out by the penal laws, there was the lucrative side to the work of an attorney retained by a large landed family. This could have proved the undoing of William Beauman, admitted in 1794. He had kept estate papers, title deeds and counterparts of tenant's leases as a lien on costs incurred by him in connection with lawsuits undertaken at the family's behest and as security for loans advanced to them. The pack of cards came tumbling down in 1828, nearly thirty years after the commencement of the first in a series of intricate and seemingly interminable lawsuits, when Beauman was ultimately ordered to surrender all the various documents. Suspiciously, six years later, Beauman himself was struck off.[64]

The severest strictures directed at any identifiable eighteenth-century Irish attorney were probably those pronounced on Thomas Kenney by Chief Baron Yelverton in

60 Elizabeth Bowen, *Bowen's court* (2nd ed., London, 1964; repr. London, 1984), pp 174-82. The vignette is based on letters sent by Chester between the early 1760s and the mid-1770s. Chester was admitted an attorney of the court of exchequer in 1756: *King's Inns admission papers, 1607-1867*, eds. Edward Keane, P.B. Phair and T.U. Sadleir (Dublin, 1982), p. 84. **61** Deane's scientific interests lay principally in the establishment of works to make bottles and window glass. At his death in 1793 he bequeathed both his chemical apparatus and his planetarium to Trinity College, Dublin. See further William Frazer, 'The medallists of Ireland and their work', *RSAI Jn.*, xvii (1886), 443 at 448. Deane was admitted an attorney of king's bench in 1732 (*King's Inns admission papers*, p. 126) and was subsequently licensed as a solicitor. A.E.J. Went's *Irish coins and medals* (Dublin, 1978) reproduces Mossop's commemorative medallion. **62** Archibald Hamilton, 'A treatise on impressing', *Ir. Jur.*, viii (1973), 117; Deirdre Lindsay, 'The Sick and Indigent Roomkeepers' Society', in David Dickson (ed.), *The gorgeous mask: Dublin, 1700-1850* (Dublin, 1987), p. 132 at p. 136. Hamilton was admitted an attorney of the court of exchequer in 1796: *King's Inns admission papers*, p. 208. **63** See 'Catholics, land and the popery acts of Anne', below, p. 230. **64** *Gifford* v. *Hart* (1804) 1 Sch & Lef 386; *Lansdowne* v. *Beauman* (1828) 1 Molloy 89; *King's Inns admission papers*, p. 29.

1796. Kenney had elected to sue a client called Browne, an erstwhile sailor, for reneging on a bargain he was convinced was lawful and proper. Yelverton was astounded at Kenney's conduct which he condemned out of hand as

> a complete tissue of imposition from its commencement to its determination. It is a case which originated, continued and ended in fraud. It is the case of an attorney obtaining from his client pending the cause an unconscionable bargain, without any consideration – for extraordinary acts of friendship never performed – services never done – or, if done, more than amply rewarded.[65]

VI

Irrespective of whether the act of 1733 or the oath of 1740 truly displayed a commitment to a new professional ethos, the refrain itself was taken up by the Irish house of commons in the ensuing decades. In 1749 and again in 1764 initiatives were brought forward for the better regulation of the lower branch. The heads of bill of 1749 were approved but were swiftly lost to sight. Those of 1764 were approved, progressed to the bill stage but thereupon they too were doomed to sink without trace. Intriguingly, in the process, the title of the measure had been altered. The original heads of bill had been expressed to be 'for better regulating agents, receivers and attornies'; the bill that emerged was entitled merely a measure 'for better regulating stewards, agents and receivers'.[66]

The refrain had also been taken up by that self-appointed scourge of his own profession, G.E. Howard. Howard devoted the major part of the preface to his treatise on the pleas side of the exchequer, published in 1759, to criticism of the Irish attorney's profession mid-century. The profession was overcrowded and too many attorneys enjoyed insufficient annual income. Nor could it harbour any delusion that it was 'learned': a preponderance of recent entrants were 'hackney clerks' and educational attainments in Latin, mathematics and the rudiments of book-keeping were all depressingly low. Howard took particular exception to the statutory reform under which Latin was replaced by English as the language of record for the courts, castigating it as 'a deadly stroke to learning'. There was a further evil over which Howard 'would fain have drawn a veil': the profession's over-indulgence in alcohol. He repeated the reputation that the Irish profession had come to enjoy amongst the members of the English: 'they seemed to them to do nothing but walk the courts the whole morning, and to devote whole evenings to the bottle.'[67]

These abortive parliamentary initiatives and the scattershot from Howard can scarcely be dignified as a 'campaign'. The result nevertheless in 1773 was a legislative measure that gave the reformers much of what they were seeking. The statute, 13 &

65 *Kenney* v. *Browne* (1796) 3 Ridg P C 462 at 521. **66** *Commons' jn. Ire.*, v, 66, 68, 69, 80; vii, 285, 294, 329, 330. **67** G.E. Howard, *A compendious treatise of the rules and practise of the pleas side of the exchequer in Ireland*, 2 vols. (Dublin, 1759), i, preface, passim.

14 Geo. III, c. 23, 'an act for the better regulation of the admission and practice of attornies' underwent only minor modifications during its ninety-year existence. It was to prove of singular importance in connection with entry requirements through its insistence that for the last three years of the stipulated five-year period of apprenticeship the aspiring attorney would have to attend for two terms at the least in every year at the Four Courts in Dublin.[68]

The reasons for the change were itemised in sections 1 and 6. There existed, section 1 declared,

> a frequent practice among the inferior class of attornies of the said courts to take apprentices of low education, whose circumstances or condition of fortune frequently induce them to be guilty of mean and improper practices to the dishonour of the profession, and to the great injury and damage of their clients and the public in general.

Section 6 portrayed the legislature's anxieties no less vividly. It cited the 'many inconveniences and mischiefs' that had frequently arisen and daily arose,

> by reason that persons, who have been legally admitted attornies of the courts, but who afterwards resided entirely or for the most part in the country, do there in like manner take apprentices from amongst the lower class of the people without education as aforesaid, or any means of subsisting themselves, and cause them to be sworn attornies of the said courts, where it often happens they never after appear, but become common barreters or promoters of suits especially amongst labouring and industrious poor people, to the impoverishing and ruin of them and their families.

Howard in 1759 had attributed the new practice of attorneys taking up residence in the country to their comparative penury. Whatever the reason, movement into rural areas did take place and the countryside perhaps inevitably came to be treated as a new theatre of operations. The development was not always to the liking of the local gentry. A not untypical attitude perhaps was captured in a newspaper advertisement, later to achieve a degree of notoriety:

> To be let, from the 1st November, 1779, the house and demesne of _____ situated near the town of H_____d, in the co. of Galway. There is a rookery on the lands, good sportage, and *not an attorney* within 12 miles on any side. – Apply to _____ etc.[69]

Where the gentry's fears over the development may have been largely indeterminate, Howard's were clear-cut and forcibly expressed. He dreaded the promotion of a need-

68 13 & 14 Geo. III, c. 23, s. 6. **69** Reproduced in Oliver J. Burke, *The history of the lord chancellors of Ireland from A.D. 1186 to A.D. 1874* (Dublin, 1879), pp 205–6.

less litigiousness and the collapse of an established social peace. 'From their poverty', many attorneys, Howard wrote,

> are under a necessity of settling in the country, to the absolute ruin and oppression of the lower kind of people, and the embroiling of whole countries. In short, it is letting out a drove of wolves and tygers to devour mankind; for it is unknown, what mischiefs an evil-inclined attorney can produce, and create in the neighbourhood he dwells in; he has this advantage of the rest of mankind, that he can torment, perplex, and impoverish, without being himself at any cost or expense, nay, sometimes to his gain and profit.[70]

The thrust to section 6 was plainly influenced by perceptions such as Howard's; whether the principal remedy envisaged by parliament – compulsory attendance at the courts in Dublin – would make any difference remained to be seen.

Section 4 of the act represented another attempt to contribute to the solution of the immediate difficulty. It restated in an expanded form the task of the examiners deputed by each court to vet all aspirant attorneys: these examiners were to enquire into the morals and qualifications of the latter and to report accordingly. The innovation was no dead letter, for the names of the first five common pleas examiners appointed for this purpose under the terms of the act are preserved in an order of that court made in Trinity term 1774. Apart from the prothonotary (the hon. Barry Barry) or his deputy (Hector Graham), these were to be the following practising common pleas attorneys: William Lane, Crosdail Moloney, John Carroll and William Lyster.

Several other aspects of entry procedure were touched on. Section 5 stipulated that all apprentice-applicants had to furnish their names, those of their master and their parents, and also details of their place of residence. Two matters were left entirely to the discretion of the judges. Section 7 acknowledged their right to grant exemptions from the rule of compulsory attendance in court. Section 9, re-echoing perhaps a provision to be found in the statute 4 Henry IV, c. 18, confirmed the possession by the judges of all three common law courts of a broad dispensing power. Nothing, the wording of the section ran, was to prevent the judges or the barons respectively from conducting their own examination into the character and qualifications of such persons as applied,

> or from admitting or refusing to admit such persons in such manner and with discretion, as the said judges and barons respectively have heretofore in that behalf lawfully used.[71]

Section 9 thus retained in the judiciary the power to regulate a large number of matters. It was under section 9 that the judges of the several courts purported to act when allowing suppliants to abridge the period of their apprenticeship. Predictably, as will be demonstrated, use of section 9 for such purposes was to prove extremely

70 Howard, *A compendious treatise* ..., i, preface, p. iv. **71** *Moore & Lowry*, app. I, p. 55.

contentious. It was under powers implicit in the same section too that the judges promulgated and later varied the rules that governed the admission in one common law court of an attorney already admitted to practice in either of the remaining two. But section 9 could be utilised for the promotion of some more immediate educational objective and on at least one occasion there is evidence that this happened. In Easter term 1782 the judges of the court of common pleas – Lord Chief Justice Paterson, Mr Justice Lill and Mr Justice Hellen – drew up the following order:

> The judges observing that inconveniences have frequently happened (which must necessarily increase if not prevented) by clerks having neglected to learn to write and read the court and text hands,
>
> To remedy which, they give public notice, that the officers and examiners appointed by law to certify the qualifications of clerks, previous to their being admitted attornies, shall require if such clerks can read and write the court and text hands well, and shall certify the same.[72]

It is known that the judges, in their capacity as benchers of King's Inns, discussed the same problem in that forum at this time.[73] It is not improbable therefore that the judges of king's bench and the barons of the exchequer adopted a stance identical to that of their colleagues in common pleas on this particular educational difficulty.

The act of 1773 spawned one major controversy. In 1781 attorneys with offices in Cork presented a petition to the Irish house of commons, seeking the exemption of their apprentices from the rule contained in section 6 that made a period of attendance at the courts in Dublin mandatory. The petitioners averred:

> that on account of the great trade and business carried on in the city of Cork it is absolutely necessary that there should be at all times attornies resident in the said city to advise and conduct the affairs of the merchants, traders and others, and also to conduct and manage suits at law in the court of record of the said city where causes of very great consequence, particularly relative to trade, are carried on and determined, and petitioners flatter themselves that they have conducted the business of the said city for a number of years past with credit and advantage to their clients and the public.

They continued:

> That for the well conducting their business, it is necessary, and has been the custom, time out of mind, to take apprentices who have been heretofore constantly admitted attornies of some or one of the superior courts of law but that on account of [the act of 1773] the petitioners labour under great difficulties in getting their apprentices admitted attornies of the said superior courts,

72 *Moore & Lowry*, app. 1, p. 57. 73 Colum Kenny, 'The history of the King's Inns Dublin, to 1800', (unpublished Ph.D. thesis, University of Dublin 1989), pp 255–6.

> although the petitioners conceived that by the preamble of the said act it was merely intended for attornies residing in the country parts of this kingdom and not practising in the profession, and not meant to extend to attornies residing and practising in large cities.[74]

The Cork attorneys' petition was presented in December 1781 and initially appears to have met with a degree of support. However, when the heads of a bill were brought forward to give the Cork attorneys the concession they had sought, a group of Dublin attorneys counter-petitioned that it would be wisest to make no change. It was their contention that the act of 1773:

> hath already been attended with the most essential advantages to the public and been the means of preventing many exceptionable and improper persons from being admitted members of that profession.

They concluded 'that a variation from, or repeal of any part of the said act ... would be of the most dangerous consequences to the community'.[75] This may have been hyperbole but it clinched the argument. Matters for the moment were allowed to rest.

The adoption by the benchers of King's Inns of new rules in 1793 reopened the same broad issue. Rule vi prescribed that any attorney applying to take apprentices should state 'his place of abode, and whether he attends the courts in Dublin or not'.[76] An inference that it became possible to draw from this form of wording was that attorneys who were not resident in Dublin might not be permitted by the benchers to take any apprentices at all – plainly, from the point of view of attorneys resident in Cork and elsewhere, a retrograde step. Two Cork attorneys tested the waters in 1795. According to Duhigg, the benchers discussed the issue at length and, on being satisfied that for the final years of their articles, the apprentices in question would be in attendance at the courts in Dublin as the act of 1773 insisted should be the case, approved the application. In 1802 however, for reasons that are not immediately apparent, the benchers contemplated a shift of position: they declined to give any decision on a number of applications presented to them, referring the issue to a sub-committee of five.

The impasse drew forth the wrath of Duhigg whose *History of the King's Inns* was published four years later, before, apparently, that impasse had been resolved. Duhigg made no secret of his view that the rules of 1793 in more than one particular were ultra vires. He contended that it was intolerable if rule vi conferred legitimacy on the course of action followed by the benchers in 1802 in regard to the applications from Cork: the outcome of the delay was that 'no apprentices can be taken by Cork residents, whereby that ancient city may be said to lye in a state of legal blockage'. The Cork attorneys had not acquiesced lightly either in this sinister turn of events. Their memorial to the benchers went over much the same ground as the earlier petition addressed to the Irish house of commons in 1781. According to Duhigg's summary, that memorial stated:

74 *Commons' jn. Ire.*, x, 273: 7 Dec. 1781. **75** *Commons' jn. Ire.*, x, 315: 5 Mar. 1782. **76** The rules are set out in an appendix to Duhigg's *History of the King's Inns*, at p. 581.

> Cork to be a city opulent, commercial and populous. That there are generally thirty resident attornies, who are all admitted of the superior courts; the greater number of whom served apprenticeships to attornies resident in Cork. That there is a court of record which sits once a week, the jurisdiction of which is unlimited in personal actions. That quarter sessions sit to try misdemeanours weekly, whereby apprentices have an opportunity of practical improvement in civil and criminal business. That much conveyancing is done in the city of Cork, which they go through with the assistance of their apprentices, but except resident attornies are permitted to take apprentices, it will be impossible to do.

It has not been possible to establish when exactly the impasse was finally resolved.[77]

VII

Legislation of 1792, the statute 32 Geo. III, c. 21, set aside the restraints and disabilities to which catholics had been subject and henceforth entry to either branch of the legal profession in Ireland was in effect open to all. Promotion of catholic barristers to the rank of king's counsel or appointment of catholics to judgeships still had to await Emancipation in 1829 and advancement of a catholic to the lord chancellorship further legislation in 1867.

The early 1790s inaugurated a number of important if little publicized changes which also helped to shape the future development of the lower branch. For instance, the common law courts set out to improve supervision of the attorneys attached to each through a system of registration of names and addresses.

It is not easy to establish what degree of supervision of this latter type had existed previously. Under the act of 1773 apprentices had had to supply their names and addresses, and the names of their masters as well. The benchers too through the assumption by them of the power to vet the taking of apprentices by attorneys would have amassed an amount of this kind of ephemeral information in addition. The common pleas rules of 1671 insisted that all of its attorneys who wished to be regarded as in active practice had to make a personal appearance in court every term not later than the seventh day. Common pleas attorneys were also obliged to take 'dwellings in some convenient place' and to inform the steward at King's Inns where their 'chambers and habitations' were.[78] The requirements of the other courts in these latter respects are not known.

Starting in 1791, the exchequer of pleas introduced a novel system of registration that the other courts were to copy. Henceforth a book would be kept in the office attached to the court and in it each attorney would be obliged to enter up his place of

77 The foregoing account is based on that supplied by Duhigg in his *History of the King's Inns*, at pp 550–5.
78 13 & 14 Geo. III, c. 23, s. 5: rule vi of the general rules of King's Inns of 1793 (Duhigg, *History of the King's Inns*, p. 581); *Moore & Lowry*, app. I, p. 5.

residence. King's bench made provision to similar effect in 1798 (repeating the rule in 1803), and common pleas in 1799. The exchequer of pleas required its attorneys to enter their place of residence in the city of Dublin; king's bench and common pleas insisted on a place of abode that fell geographically 'within the Circular Road'.[79] Proximity to the Four Courts therefore was made not only virtuous but imperative. All these various provisions undoubtedly conditioned members of the lower branch to the routine of regularly entering up their names and addresses in an official register. From the perspective of government, such conditioning must have enabled the introduction of the requirement of an annual practising certificate that was to occur shortly to proceed with comparative smoothness.

It is not improbable that these new provisions stemmed from decisions arrived at earlier by the judges acting in their role as benchers of King's Inns. Other regulations promulgated directly by the judges in this latter capacity had an even more fundamental impact. Rule v of the general rules of the Society issued in 1793 altered yet again the requirements in regard to prospective masters: only attorneys – and Irish attorneys at that – it stipulated, could take apprentices. In the century and more that had elapsed since 1671 it is possible, through study of the alterations in these requirements, to chart the stages in the process by which the Irish lower branch was to be given certain of its distinctive characteristics.

First, the profession became exclusively 'Irish'. The common pleas rules of 1671 and the act of 1733 had expressly contemplated the possibility that an apprenticeship might be served with an English master in England. Plainly at this stage recruitment of persons born in England and undergoing training there was both sanctioned and welcomed. Few obstacles even would appear to have been placed in the way of more senior English expatriates who wished to transfer to Ireland. The case of Richard Goodenough happens to be documented; how many similar such cases there were must await future investigation. Goodenough served as under-sheriff of London at the time of the Popish Plot and was instrumental in securing the conviction and execution for treason of Cornish, the sheriff. Cornish's innocence soon after appearing, Goodenough was himself imprisoned. There is mention of this unsavoury customer in Gilbert Burnet's *History of his own time* and Dean Swift, in his copy of that book, notes that, following his final release, Goodenough retired to Ireland where he practised as an attorney. This latter detail is confirmed by the *King's Inns admission papers* which record both Goodenough's membership of the society (unfortunately, undated) and his death in December 1708.[80]

Entry into the Irish profession for English expatriates was made much more difficult following the adoption of the statutory requirement in 1773 that each apprentice should spend part of his apprenticeship in attendance at the courts in Dublin. Nor did rule v of the King's Inns rules of 1793 signal any relief. The notion that the English practitioner might somehow insinuate himself into the ranks of the Irish profession – as easily perhaps as Goodenough had done – was not immediately abandoned howev-

79 *Moore & Lowry*, app. II, p. 38 (exchequer of pleas); pp 153-4 (king's bench); app. I, p. 66 (common pleas).
80 Gilbert Burnet, *History of his own time* (Everyman ed., London, 1979), pp 235-6; *King's Inns admission papers*, p. 192.

er. And it appears to have been only in 1863 that the Irish Law Society first successfully objected in an Irish court to the association of an English attorney with an Irish lawsuit.[81]

Concentration of apprentices in the hands of attorney-masters was a development of no less significance. The prospect that an apprentice might enter into articles with, in effect, a member of the bar was terminated by statute in 1773. Articles entered into with a court officer simpliciter (a six clerk) were similarly forbidden under the terms of the King's Inns rules of 1793.[82] Rule v thus represented the culmination to an evolutionary trend, one doubtless assisted by changes in legal procedure and in the Irish legal system generally, which reflected an adherence to the virtues of specialisation and of a more pronounced division of labour. It read shortly and simply:

> That no person shall be admitted a member of this society, in order to his becoming an attorney, who has not served twenty whole terms as an apprentice, to an attorney, a member of this society.

Rule vii of the same rules of 1793 governed the procedure for the admission of aspiring attorneys to the Inns. It again was an innovation:

> That before any attorney's clerk or apprentice shall be admitted into this society, in order to his being sworn an attorney, he shall be examined publicly in the dining-hall of the society in the presence of the benchers and the society, then there assembled, by the same officers who now examine such persons, and by any other member of the society there present, who may think fit to do so.

A further rule, rule viii, obliged a master who refused a favourable reference to give his reasons. Rule vi, as we saw earlier, appeared to sanction the refusal of the benchers to let attorneys based in Cork take apprentices. Neither escapes Duhigg's bitter censure.[83] Over rule vii the invective is even more uncontrolled:

> If this dominion over attornies was ancient and legal, still truth ought to accompany its enforcement. The preceding mummery was never intended for serious exhibition; without a character, how could it be enforced? Yet legal practicers have been hitherto such tame and voluntary vassals, that there seems no law or usage necessary to consecrate their servitude.[84]

Aside from the legislation of 1792, the principal emphasis to legislative intervention at this period related to financial matters. Stamp duty was leviable on each set of indentures of apprenticeship from 1790 onwards.[85] The provisions stipulated that portion of

81 *Scovell* v. *Gardner* (1863) 16 ICLR 84n. **82** On the position of apprentices to six clerks see *In re Lyons* (1839) 1 Ir Eq R 267. Six clerks were only finally barred from practising as solicitors and attorneys themselves in 1823: 4 Geo. IV, c. 61, s. 12. The office itself was abolished in 1836: 6 & 7 Will. IV, c. 74. **83** On rule viii Duhigg commented, 'There is not a scintilla juris scripti aut inscripti to warrant this innovation': *History of King's Inns*, p. 586. **84** *History of King's Inns*, p. 585. **85** Hogan, *Legal profession in Ireland*, p. 126.

the income was to be transferred to King's Inns. After 1866 attorneys ceased to be obliged to become members of the King's Inns but portion of the stamp duty was still transferred to the Inns. The continuance of this arrangement soured relations between the Law Society and the Inns in the last third of the nineteenth century.[86]

The rules of the common law courts had long laid down what had to be done by an attorney to be permitted to continue in practice and to continue to enjoy the privileges of an attorney. A new – and in the eyes of members of the profession – an unwelcome development was the introduction of the requirement that each attorney and solicitor obtain a practising certificate annually and that this be paid for.[87] The requirement first surfaced in England in 1785. It appears to have been introduced in Ireland in 1806,[88] though it is commonly asserted that introduction did not occur until 1816.[89] Different rates applied, depending on the number of years the attorney or solicitor had been in practice: qualified practitioners with less than three years' experience paid at the lower rate of £3. The higher rate was £8. Although it can scarcely have been anticipated, this financial levy was destined to leave a mark on practice and procedure generally with regard to the system of admitting attorneys in the common law courts.

In 1715 statute made admission as an attorney in any one of the common law courts a prerequisite to the exercise of any right to practise as an attorney in regard to civil business at the assizes.[90] In 1851 a similar monopoly was conferred on attorneys with respect to the assistant barrister's courts (the future county courts).[91] In the light of such statutory concessions it remained anomalous that admission as an attorney in one common law court bestowed no right to practise in the other two. That the anomaly actually existed is amply confirmed by a glance at the Dublin almanacks for the 1760s. These give names of all Dublin attorneys with an indication of the court or courts by which they had been admitted. The vast majority are identifiable as attorneys of one court alone and within that majority the preponderance is invariably of attorneys attached to the court of exchequer. Very few indeed had been admitted in more than one court and there is no record that any had been admitted in all three. Within a generation, however, as another glance at the Dublin almanacks will show, the pattern had changed: by 1802 for instance there was a sizeable number of attorneys who had been admitted to practice by all three courts and that number was to increase with the passage of the years.[92]

The act of 1773 had effectively restated the existing law that admission as an attorney was admission to practise in a single common law court. Already however a slight

86 Charles Gamble, *Solicitors in Ireland 1607-1921* (Dublin, 1921), pp 44 et seq. **87** There was a not unimportant quid pro quo: the establishment of the conveyancing monopoly. **88** By s. 24 of 46 Geo. III, c. 64: an act to repeal the several duties under the care of the commissioners for managing the duties upon stamped vellum, parchment, and paper in Ireland, and to grant new and additional duties in lieu thereof; and to amend the laws relating to the stamp duties in Ireland. **89** See ss. 65-8 of 56 Geo. III, c. 56: an act to repeal the several stamp duties in Ireland, and also several acts for the collection and management of the said duties, and to grant new stamp duties in lieu thereof; and to make more effectual regulations for collecting and managing the said duties. **90** 2 Geo. I, c. 11, s. 12. **91** By s. 13 of 14 & 15 Vict., c. 57: an act to consolidate and amend the laws relating to civil bills and the courts of quarter sessions in Ireland, and to transfer to the assistant barristers certain jurisdiction as to insolvent debtors. **92** See Watson's *Dublin Almanack* for the years 1762 and 1802 respectively.

modification was in operation whereby an attorney admitted to one court could practise in another with the consent of an attorney of that other in regard to any lawsuit of which the latter had carriage. So much is clear from rules of court drawn up by both common pleas and exchequer in 1776 which sought to terminate the modification and which indeed appeared to accord better with the philosophy espoused by section 8 of the 1773 act. By 1786, however, common pleas had again changed its mind, reverting to the status quo ante.[93]

The court of king's bench seems to have done most to enforce the rigour of the 1773 act. A rule adopted in 1775 affirmed that 'for the better and more regular manner of carrying on business' attorneys from other courts who desired to practise in king's bench would have to be admitted in the ordinary fashion. Another rule the following year stressed that any such attorneys could not expect to be exempted from the scrutiny of the court's own examiners, and a further rule of 1784 even went so far as to lay down the period of notice that had to be given by attorneys from other courts who sought admission.[94]

The introduction of annual practising certificates on a permanent basis from 1816 onwards meant that these various arrangements now assumed a different complexion. The certificate was a certificate to practise in the court to which one had been admitted as an attorney; it did and could not confer any right to practise in all. If the individual practitioner sought such a right he would have to seek admission in all three courts and pay three times over for the privilege, i.e. for three practising certificates. This financial impediment to the emergence of a single, comprehensive right of practice became increasingly difficult to defend in the face of the emergence within the legal system of a general rapprochement between all the courts. In a show of obduracy each maintained a different stance on the procedures associated with the striking off of an attorney prior to his call to the bar;[95] with equal stubbornness each adhered to a different time-table for the swearing in of attorneys in each law term.[96] But the substantive law they all recognised was virtually the same and rules of procedure became very similar too, especially under the impetus of legislation of 1831 which authorised the three courts to draw up uniform rules of court, the so-called 'general rules' of the epoch preceding the Judicature Act.[97]

Individual attorneys continued to fall foul of the strict legal position. In a succession of cases reported in the 1830s it is commonplace to read of an attorney who had been admitted in common pleas and exchequer alone seeking to move an execution in king's bench in the name of an attorney of that court and with the latter's consent.[98] This was of course a fraud on the Stamp Act of 1816 as the court in question did not hesitate to point out. The serious side to such manoeuvres was that proceedings handled by the technically unauthorised risked being dismissed as a nullity. In 1833 the

93 *Moore & Lowry*, app. I, pp 56 and 58: orders of 19 June 1776 and Michaelmas term 1786 (common pleas); app. II, p. 38: order of 26 June 1776 (exchequer). **94** *Moore & Lowry*, pp 124 (rule of May 1775), 125 (rule of 25 June 1776), 135 (rule of 29 Nov. 1784). **95** See *In re Smith* (1838) Crawf & Dix 611. **96** *Moore & Lowry*, p. 233. The data there supplied presumably represents the then current situation in 1842. **97** By s. 5 of 1 & 2 Will. IV, c. 31: an act to improve the administration of justice in Ireland. On rapprochement between the courts, see further below, pp 263–5. **98** E.g., *Murphy* v. *Rafferty* (1837) 5 Law Rec. ns 148.

court of exchequer, when faced with clear evidence of the perpetration of just this kind of abuse, reacted with remarkable equanimity, and charity: it elected to excuse the practitioner involved on grounds of his youth and of the fact that he did 'a lot of business'.[99]

The law on this contentious question had been changed in England in 1815 but no equivalent measure was immediately forthcoming for Ireland. To the average member of the Irish lower branch at the time it must have seemed that somewhere there was a determination to add insult to injury when in 1836 the benchers adopted a new rule that henceforth any future applicant to take apprentices had to be not only an attorney admitted in all three common law courts but a solicitor in addition. The following year the benchers contemplated a retreat.[100] In fact the pressure to bring Irish law into line with that in England on the financial side to the question was now proving irresistible. Finally in 1840 the overdue legislative reform was enacted. Where the practitioner paid stamp duty on securing his admission to practice in any one of the four superior courts (chancery and the three courts of common law) he would be entitled to be admitted to the three others without the payment of any additional duty.[101]

VIII

Another facet to the benchers' decision of 1836 and to the remedial legislation of four years later deserves to be noted: both contributed in different ways to the achievement of a merger of the ranks of attorneys and solicitors and thus in a sense anticipated the joint educational programme of the 1860s and the final union proclaimed by the Judicature Act of 1877. Historically, admission to the ranks of solicitor had been organised very differently – where it was organised at all. Their separate story can be briefly recounted.

In the common law courts the attorneys oversaw the critical procedural stages in litigation. A residue of tasks, in particular the drafting of documents, came to be discharged, not only in relation to common law litigation, but also in relation to that in the equity courts, chancery and equity exchequer, by a practitioner with the different title of solicitor. Solicitors were not covered by the regulatory legislation of the medieval and early modern periods. Though lawyers of multifarious descriptions 'solicited' causes in the various courts, no legal training of any kind was insisted upon – there appears to have been no apprenticeship system, for instance – and the attack on a number of them as 'sundry varlets' which Brooks records for the England of 1577[102] may indeed have been thoroughly deserved.

The first attempt to regulate them occurs at the start of the eighteenth century and is linked exclusively with the penal laws directed at catholics. A formal licensing system was introduced in 1733. Thereafter, no one could practise as a solicitor in any of the

99 *Dinnon* v. *Aubrey* (1833) 1 Law Rec. ns 38. **100**. Hogan, *Legal profession in Ireland*, p. 97. **101** 3 & 4 Vict., c. 79: an act to amend the law relating to the admission of attornies and solicitors to practise in the courts of law and equity in Ireland. **102** Brooks, *Pettyfoggers and vipers*, p. 26.

four courts, who, in addition to satisfying the requirements as to religion, had not served the minimum of a five-year apprenticeship.[103] That apprenticeship was described in identical terms to that demanded by the same legislation of the aspiring attorney. It appears to have been envisaged that the ranks of solicitors should be filled in much the same way as the ranks of attorneys themselves. In 1791 this in fact was insisted upon in a chancery rule drawn up that year which is of considerable significance. This rule provided:

> That no person shall presume to practise as a solicitor of the court of chancery, who shall not have been first duly sworn and admitted an attorney of his majesty's court of king's bench, common pleas or exchequer, and who has not a fixed place of residence in the city of Dublin, and that from and after the last day of Hilary term 1791, no such attorney shall be allowed to practise as a solicitor of the said court, unless he shall first obtain a certificate, signed by the senior master and the registrar of the court, or his deputy, that he is a fit and proper person to be admitted a solicitor of the court and that he has a fixed place of residence in the city of Dublin ...[104]

What constituted another important structural reform in the Irish legal profession in the 1790s was almost certainly the achievement of Clare, the lord chancellor. Unlike certain other of his initiatives of the period, this particular change was to endure. And, unsurprisingly, as a result, the numbers of solicitors showed a marked increase.

Administratively, there came to exist the temptation to treat solicitors on a par with attorneys. Over the matter of the oath that convention was to dictate solicitors should subscribe, this was a mistake as, it will be recalled, a solicitor with the name of Smith managed to persuade Sir William Mc Mahon, the master of the rolls, in the case of *Birch* v. *Oldis*. (Smith firmly relied on the text of the 1791 chancery rule.)[105] In other contexts, the perceived equivalence of function was close enough to the mark. And the decision to apply the rules on the annual practising certificate to each attorney and solicitor willy-nilly made sound sense. Efforts continued to be made nonetheless to emphasise the distinctiveness of the role of the solicitor. In a case in 1824 an attorney with the name of Barrett was discovered to have used the name of a solicitor called Tobin in defending a suit in equity. The court was not prepared to ignore what had been done. The manoeuvre flouted the rule of 1791 on attorneys becoming solicitors; it constituted, moreover, a fraud on the Stamp Act.[106] The next year the lord chancellor had occasion to point out that only a solicitor recognised as such by the court would be entitled to costs in any equity suit.[107] Plainly one ignored these demarcation rules at one's peril.

The comparison with the predicament of attorneys seeking without proper authority to maintain a presence in all three common law courts is striking. Even the expe-

103 7 Geo. II, c. 5, s. 7. **104** H.G. Hughes, *Practice of the court of chancery in Ireland* (Dublin, 1837), pp 429–30: rule of 1 Jan. 1791. **105** *Birch* v. *Oldis* (1831) Glascock 351. **106** *Lawrence* v. *Sharp* (1824) 1 Hogan 85. **107** *French* v. *Morgan* (1825) 1 Hogan 230.

rience of shared misfortune therefore had a levelling tendency. As occurred in relation to attorneys, the benchers' resolution of 1836 and the reform of the law on the annual practising certificate served to bring much closer the emergence of a unified lower branch. Within a few short years only the notaries public, the licensed conveyancers and the proctors of the ecclesiastical courts failed to fit neatly into the pattern of what was unfolding.

IX

In 1821 parliament sanctioned a reduction in the period of apprenticeship from five years to three for graduates of the three universities of Oxford, Cambridge and Dublin (Trinity College).[108] This move, whilst it connoted a welcome preoccupation with the educational attainments of aspiring attorneys (a preoccupation that was to intensify as the century progressed) by no means commanded universal support at the time. A London practitioner told the house of commons select committee in 1821 for instance that it could not be claimed that a university education was absolutely necessary for the profession of an attorney or a solicitor.[109] Three years earlier an attorney in the north of England had been asked to advise a Mrs Munby of York whether she should consider sending her son to university as a first step to his becoming an attorney. In forthright terms he had pronounced against: 'It would not only defeat all that you had planned for his future introduction into business; but would most probably be ruinous to him.'[110] She was urged instead to send her offspring to a respectable academy.

Parliament pressed ahead regardless. The resultant legislation contended that the present five-year period of apprenticeship, a feature of both English and Irish statute law, was from its undue length likely to deter the graduate and that it was expedient that entry to the profession should be facilitated 'in consideration of the learning and abilities' requisite for the taking of a university degree.[111] The concession was surrounded by a number of restrictions set out in section 3: in order to profit from it the arts graduate had to acquire his degree within six years of matriculation, the law graduate within eight; and indentures had to be entered into within four years of graduation.

The act of 1821 was not well drafted. On one reading, section 3 seemed to say that law graduates obtaining their degree within eight years of matriculation were to be excluded from the concession – the reverse of what was intended. An act passed in 1822 sought to rectify the error.[112] The terms of this short remedial act were themselves unsatisfactory however, for the measure conveys the unmistakable impression that a uniquely English problem was being attended to. The explanation for this of course lay in the fact that the draft of the bill of what became the act of 1821 had orig-

108 1 & 2 Geo. IV, c. 48: an act to amend the several acts for the regulation of attornies and solicitors. **109** Hogan, *Legal profession in Ireland*, p. 92. **110** Quoted in Robert Robson, *The attorney in eighteenth century England* (Cambridge, 1959), p. 45. **111** 1 & 2 Geo. IV, c. 48, s. 1. **112** 3 Geo. IV, c. 16: an act to amend an act, made in the last session of parliament, for amending the several acts for the regulation of attornies and solicitors.

inally contemplated the conferment of the new privileges on graduates of the universities of Oxford and Cambridge alone and that it was only at an advanced stage that the bill's scope was widened to embrace graduates of the university of Dublin. Further legislative provision in 1827 gave the act of 1821 retrospective effect so as to confer an entitlement to claim admission on persons graduating before 1821 who had served three years' apprenticeship in the interim.[113] This entitlement, however, was expressly limited to persons seeking admission to the profession in England: no equivalent statute appears to have been deemed necessary or desirable for Ireland. In 1851 the general scheme of concessions in favour of graduates, originally confined in the case of Ireland to graduates of Trinity College, was extended to cover graduates in arts and law of the new Queen's Colleges at Belfast, Cork and Galway.[114]

The year 1851 witnessed the introduction of another major concession, this time in favour of the undergraduate student. Apprenticeship was reduced from five years to four for two categories of student: those studying simultaneously for a university degree and those pursuing simultaneously a course of recognised study extending over two years at either Trinity College or the Queen's Colleges.[115]

These various concessions in favour of graduates, undergraduates and persons pursuing a prescribed course of university education represented a major shift in attitude by the profession. The particular concessions were to become part of the permanent educational arrangements governing entry to the lower branch. They also signalled the start of the involvement of the Irish universities in professional legal education which was destined to become a dominant feature in the twentieth century. As is about to be demonstrated, in the early years the judges were to place interesting glosses upon certain of these concessions, generally acting under the broad discretionary powers conferred upon them by section 9 of the act of 1773.

X

Considerable light is shed on the actual procedures governing the entry of attorneys and solicitors in the pages of Irish law reports from the late 1820s onwards, the precise point when local law reporting becomes both more comprehensive in coverage and more avowedly professional in tone. A short résumé of this body of case-law will not therefore be out of place.

One group of cases examines diverse aspects of the law on indentures of apprenticeship. The technical legal position was that at the same time as the apprentice was bound to his master his indentures had to be enrolled and the stipulated stamp duty paid. A flexible stance would apparently be adopted however where, due to the negli-

113 By s. 5 of 7 Geo. IV, c. 44: an act to allow, until the tenth day of October 1826, the enrolment of certain articles of clerkship; to prevent attornies and others from being prejudiced in certain cases by the neglect to take out their annual certificates; to prohibit the stamping articles of clerkship after a certain time; and to extend the period for taking out certificates after matriculation at the universities. **114** By s. 1 of 14 & 15 Vict., c. 88: an act for amending the several acts for the regulation of attornies and solicitors. **115** 14 & 15 Vict., c. 88, s. 2.

gence of some clerk of the master's, for instance, the indentures had not been enrolled in the prescribed office at the prescribed time: the apprentice would not be placed at a disadvantage. One such case was referred to the court of king's bench in 1835 and the judges there, having first called for a report on what had occurred from their examiners, had no compunction over granting, three years after the apprentice had first been bound, a motion for the enrolment of his indentures *nunc pro tunc*.[116]

By contrast, where stamp duty had not been paid, altogether different considerations generally would seem to have applied. In a case of 1830 from king's bench the judges there, it is true, chose to be remarkably lenient. Stamp duty had not been paid until the five-year period of apprenticeship had all but expired. The court heard that the apprentice in question very shortly after he had been bound had got embroiled in an equity suit which had drained him of every shilling and he had only lately enjoyed the fruits of ultimate success. The court went on to grant a *nunc pro tunc* motion despite an initial reluctance to do anything of the sort.[117] In the exchequer a much more hostile attitude was evinced towards comparable applications presented there even when it was arguable that the apprentice himself was not at fault. In a case from 1828 the apprentice had given his master the money to pay the stamp duty but the latter had applied it to his own purposes and the prescribed duty was only finally paid a year later: the court refused an application to antedate the commencement of the period of apprenticeship to 1823.[118] In a similar case heard in 1842 the barons of the exchequer again refused the relief sought. Baron Pennefather pointed out that apprentices could themselves ensure that they were not defrauded – and their entry into the profession accordingly delayed – by seeing to it that the stamp duty was actually paid before the indentures were signed. Baron Lefroy was perturbed that the master involved, William Barlow, solicitor to the Ordnance at the time, should in such fashion have managed to deceive both the apprentice, one William Fry, and the latter's father, a military officer. He advised the father to take steps against Barlow either before the court or before the benchers of King's Inns.[119] Whereas in the king's bench case of 1828 the court indicated that they were satisfied that the applicant had not sought to evade the Stamp Act, by 1834 the exchequer had refused to accept that this was in any way germane.[120]

Departure, illness or death of a master during the currency of an apprenticeship occasioned a number of difficulties. A fresh master had to be found, one who was at liberty to take another apprentice, that is, was still within quota, in appropriate instances the erstwhile master's consent to the reassignment was required, and in all cases that too of the benchers of King's Inns, following the adoption by the latter of a rule to that effect.[121] In a case from 1832 where the master had simply disappeared and it was not known if he would ever re-appear, the court was successfully applied to for consent to a reassignment in principle.[122] In a further case from 1839 the apprentice's first master had died in July of the previous year and the apprentice had only managed

116 *Anon.* (1835) 2 Law Rec. ns 140. **117** *Anon.* (1830) 4 Law Rec. 258. **118** *Anon.* (1828) 2 Law Rec. 36. **119** *In re Fry* (1842) Long & Town 679. **120** *Ex p. Kinder* (1834) 1 Jones 43. Kinder was four and a half years into his apprenticeship when he vainly endeavoured to secure a *nunc pro tunc* ruling in his favour. **121** On the importance of obtaining the benchers' permission see e.g. *Anon.* (1828) 2 Law Rec. 74 and *Stewart* v. *Davis* (1847) 11 Ir LR 34. **122** *In re William Hitchcock* (1832) 5 Law Rec. 222.

to find himself a new master by the middle of the November following. He applied successfully to the court of exchequer to be given credit in respect of the 'lost months'.[123]

Eight years later the same court was faced with a more difficult problem in *Stewart v. Davis*.[124] The brothers Davis were attorneys and partners. James operated the Belfast end of the practice, and lived there; William resided in Dublin. Stewart was apprenticed to James and was based in Belfast. James died during the currency of Stewart's apprenticeship. William decided to move to Belfast to manage the practice from there, but since he already had the maximum number of apprentices allowed, Stewart had to be re-assigned. Stewart's family proposed the name of another Belfast attorney, Suffern. William, however, demurred, suggesting rather an attorney in Dublin called Cusack. It emerged from further contact between the parties that William would not consent to the option that Stewart be placed with Suffern unless he received a payment of £100. Stewart's family in turn sought a partial refund out of the £195 they had earlier paid over to James when Stewart had been apprenticed to him.

It is not easy to explain the conduct of William Davis and the barons of the exchequer, once they had been made familiar with the evidence in the case, did not find it easy either. The Belfast end to the practice had been operated separately and no part of the £195 paid to James had ever found its way into William's pocket. William admittedly was concerned to provide for his brother's widow and his many children.

In the result the barons of the exchequer ordered William to reassign Stewart's indentures; they also required the examiner to report on the refund, if any, properly payable to the Stewarts. Chief Baron Pigot elected not to take his leave of the brothers Davis and the financial arrangements of their firm without a few parting shots. 'Theirs', he observed,

> was a partnership conducted as most are, one partner residing in a populous town in the country, and the other in town (Dublin); both take a share in the apprentices bound to each; one partner dies, then the other partner becomes the owner of the entire concern, taking the benefit of, what may perhaps be the most beneficial portion of the partnership property, the depending suits; he therefore must take the benefit cum onore, and, therefore, with regard to the liability to refund a portion of the fee taken on the apprenticeship of the son of the petitioner, it is but just that he should bear the burthen, if the officer should hold that it ought to be refunded.[125]

With respect to the period of apprenticeship itself, the rules on attendance at the courts in Dublin – the rules that had provoked the remonstrance from the attorneys of Cork – underwent some further elaboration. The statute of 1773 insisted on two terms attendance in each of the last three years of the apprenticeship. In Crowley's case the king's bench admitted the apprentice despite the fact that he had kept two terms in his third year, none in his fourth and four in his fifth and last. Ill-health was the explana-

123 *In re Powell* (1839) 1 Ir Eq R 328. **124** (1847) 11 Ir LR 34. **125** 11 Ir LR at 43.

tion and on that basis the ordinary rules were waived as indeed the statute itself expressly authorised.[126]

The question whether master and apprentice were obliged to keep the same terms in attendance at the courts in Dublin was raised in John Julian's application in 1832. Julian had graduated from college in 1829 and was entitled therefore to be admitted after a three-year apprenticeship. His master, one Pollock, and Julian had not kept the same terms in Dublin. Pollock had frequent business down the country and it was Pollock's son who had been in attendance with Julian. It was a misapprehension, the court of exchequer ruled, that master and apprentice had to attend together. Indications to that effect to be found in a book of precedents containing a standard affidavit of an apprentice to ground admission as an attorney were not warranted by law.[127]

In relation to the conduct of the apprentice during the currency of his apprenticeship a variety of problems surfaced. First, there arose, prior to the intervention of parliament in 1851, the question of the acceptability of concurrent university study. The question arose in this way. The act of 1821 had introduced the concession of a reduced period of apprenticeship for the university graduate. Might it be possible for the undergraduate to claim the benefit of the same concession? The point of statutory interpretation involved was authoritatively settled by the court of exchequer in Carmichael's case in 1831. The conclusion accorded with the more intelligent reading of the clause: the concession was directed at graduates alone and the corollary entailed that graduation had to precede apprenticeship. Carmichael had become apprenticed early in his undergraduate career, and the barons of the exchequer, perhaps somewhat inconsistently in view of the interpretation they had just placed on the act of 1821, permitted an abridgement of the period of apprenticeship to occur. Chief Baron Joy yielded one hostage to fortune when, in support of his decision, he observed:

> It is true that the order of time may be of importance; but it is nevertheless the duty of the court, to support the respectability of the profession, and to encourage those who have had a collegiate education.[128]

The possession of a university degree remained a factor in a number of cases falling outside the scope of the act of 1821 where abridgement of the customary period of apprenticeship was to secure court sanction. But in the case of undergraduates, the actual decision in Carmichael's case can be counted something of an aberration. Once the matter of statutory construction had been settled the courts seem to have been determined to set their minds against further concessions. Archibald Colville, another apprentice flush from success in concurrent undergraduate study which had earned him a degree, sought in 1838 the immediate concession that had been accorded Carmichael a mere seven years before, only to receive this reproof from Baron Richards:

126 *In re John Crowley* (1827) 1 Law Rec. 168; 13 & 14 Geo. III, c. 23, s. 7. **127** *In re John Julian* (1832) 5 Law Rec. 315. For the remarkable reply of the author of the book of precedents, W. Stewart, see ibid., at 317. **128** *Ex parte Thomas Carmichael* (1831) 1 Hayes 138.

> As the applicant was going on with his college course and learning his profession at the same time, the statute is clear on that point, and according to that the apprenticeship must commence after taking out a degree.[129]

It was a lesson that had to be repeated more than once before the four-year period of apprenticeship for undergraduates was introduced in 1851 and all transitional difficulties were disposed of.[130]

Blotting one's copy-book by means of concurrent undergraduate study was easy enough to identify. Other blemishes in the careers of prospective attorneys were much harder to pinpoint. Three affairs, spanning the years 1827 to 1849, were the subject of special reports by the 'moral examiners' which were then in turn evaluated by the courts. In the case of Bamfield in 1827, the examiners reported against his admission as an attorney of the court of common pleas. Whilst an apprentice he had acted in his master's name and had been privy with others to extorting a bond from a person whose arrest he had contrived when so acting. The court of exchequer had even gone so far as to issue an attachment against him. The chief justice, Lord Plunket, endorsed the findings of the examiners: as guardians of the public interest, the judges were obliged to be careful; moreover, Bamfield had added to his villainy by making payments out of moneys that belonged to his wife and family.[131]

Dowling whose case was adjudicated upon in 1835 was more fortunate. Here again it was alleged that an apprentice had in fact acted as an attorney. For good measure, details of a number of alleged disreputable transactions were furnished. The moral examiners investigated the general background, found that Dowling had perhaps been imprudent but did not recommend against his admission. The Law Society who had taken an interest in the proceedings were not so hesitant: they opposed Dowling's admission outright. Taking their cue rather from the conclusions of the examiners, the barons of the exchequer nevertheless decided to admit Dowling.[132]

The affair of William Coates in 1849 disclosed a somewhat unusual but perhaps not unparalleled situation. A man of some wealth, he appears to have been brought in to help rescue a failing practice. Technically the apprentice, Coates seemed to possess more power than his master, certainly in regard to money matters. Objecting to Coates' admission, a Mr Kenny alluded to these financial arrangements – those evidenced by one document in particular – and also brought forward an undifferentiated complaint against Coates for sharp practice. Though plainly they did not like what they uncovered during their examination of the firm, the moral examiners once again did not recommend against admission. The Law Society did not appear before the examiners, but when the matter was aired again before the barons of the exchequer they both put in an appearance and announced their opposition to Coates' admission. A great deal of detail is gone into at all stages of the investigation into Coates and his master's practice. Eventually, the barons by a majority decided to admit Coates.[133]

129 *In re Archibald Colville* (1838) 6 Law Rec. ns 121. Compare *In re Collum* (1839) 1 Ir Eq R 278, where a graduate of three-years standing was permitted an abridgement even though he had commenced articles before he became a graduate and had not been bound de novo. **130** *In re Foot* (1855) 4 ICLR 499. **131** *In re Bamfield* (1827–8) 1 Law Rec. 12. **132** *In re Dowling* (1835) 3 Law Rec. ns 198. **133** *In re Coates* (1849)

Baron Richards lodged a strong dissent. The deed at the centre of the controversy, he declared,

> makes the apprentice the master; enables him to deny him a pair of shoes to his feet, clothes on his back, or a shilling in his pocket. With this deed before me, I cannot think service under it such service as the law requires.[134]

At the heart of all these controversies, including that associated with the status of the undergraduate student, was the fundamental question of what a legal apprenticeship was for and what was supposed to be happening in the course of it. Unfortunately, the notion of apprenticeship itself was rarely delineated with anything approaching precision, not even where – alas, too infrequently – individual indentures of apprenticeship from the years before 1866 have survived and their texts can be studied.[135] Presence in an office, attendance in court, gradually, from experience, from watching others or as a result of personal instruction, learning 'the tricks of the trade': no contemporary, invited to put flesh on the bones, would have been likely to have been more specific than that. This recurring vagueness about an element so crucial to the whole process of securing entry to the profession made it possible of course for markedly different attitudes to be manifested towards applicants for entry whose personal circumstances diverged from those of the normal run of candidates. Nowhere were these attitudes to prove more contradictory than in the case of applicants for admission who whilst apprenticed to the traditional type of master simultaneously held down a job as salaried clerk to an officer of the court. Apart from the biblical-sounding question as to whether such individuals could satisfactorily serve two masters at the same time, concern was inevitably expressed at their possession of an independent source of income. A further factor that entered into the equation was the circumstance that such individuals almost certainly did manage to acquire, from the strange routes their careers had assumed, considerable knowledge of the law and the practice of the courts: could that, consistently with the standards that the lower branch sought to espouse, actually be held against anyone?

The suppression of a range of court offices in the 1820s and '30s threw a number of such salaried clerks out of a permanent job, and the issue of their admission into private practice became acute. Eventually one of their number, Timothy Lyons, after several rebuffs, managed in 1838 to persuade Lord Plunket, by this stage lord chancellor, that there was no insuperable opposition to his admission as a solicitor. Exchequer soon followed suit, sanctioning Lyons' admission as an attorney of that court a few months later.[136]

Throughout the Law Society had opposed the application not because, they hastened to say, they were against Lyons personally but because he belonged to

> a class of persons whose admission ... would do away with the general rule against mock apprenticeships and leave the profession open to those mischie-

13 Ir LR 235. **134** At 245. **135** Irish indentures from 1790 and 1865 are quoted in Hogan, *Legal profession in Ireland*, p. 108. **136** *In re Timothy Lyons* (1837) 6 Law Rec. ns 116n, (1838) 1 Dr & Walsh 327, (1839) 1 Ir Eq R 267.

> vous consequences which must ever ensue from the admission into it of incompetent and irresponsible persons.[137]

Their objection in short was grounded on the belief that a person who held down two jobs at the same time was necessarily a risky investment. Lyons indubitably could not be regarded as having followed the normal route in his apprenticeship. None of this special pleading prevailed with Lord Plunket. Lyons had had a responsible job as clerk to one of the six clerks in chancery; he could not but have acquired a sound grasp of the law and of the practice of that court. As to other possible grounds of objection, the lord chancellor was content to observe that Lyons was a young man who had 'acted with the greatest propriety', was 'of unimpeachable moral character', and had 'applied himself with the utmost diligence to the duties of his profession, meritoriously endeavouring at the same time to give assistance to a family depending upon him'.[138]

It is not known how many members of the group of ex-salaried clerks to which Lyons had belonged sought, and were granted, admission as attorneys and solicitors in the wake of Lyons' final success after a struggle lasting five years. Perhaps not very many. It seems probable even so that the Law Society would not have lightly abandoned the fight against what they had chosen to label 'mock and colourable' apprenticeships.

Applications to abridge the normal five-year period of apprenticeship were probably already in contemplation when the Irish parliament chose to confirm the dispensing power of the judges in enacting section 9 of the act of 1773. They were destined to become comparatively frequent, so frequent in fact that special rules of court were drawn up to regulate the manner of their presentation. Contemporaneously with the promulgation of section 9, G.E. Howard had expressed his concern lest the power bestowed by it might not be 'too indulgently exercised'.[139] As events were to show, that concern was soundly based.

The case-law from the late 1820s onwards amply demonstrates that exercise of this dispensing power could be requested for any one of a number of different reasons. It might be called in aid to secure the regularisation of the position of some apprentice where his indentures had not been enrolled, or stamp duty paid, at the specified time. Most commonly however it was resorted to in order to obtain the sanction of the court to the abridgement of the length of an individual apprenticeship. One instance is recorded of the court sanctioning such an abridgement in order to facilitate an apprentice on the point of emigrating to Australia.[140] But the background in the overwhelming majority of such applications was very different: another member of the apprentice's family already an attorney would have died and the application for an abridgement presented by the apprentice would be designed to enable him to succeed to the family practice with the least possible delay.

Succession to an uncle, brother or brother-in-law might be sought in this fashion, but it was the death of a father that precipitated most of the applications.[141] In cases

137 1 Dr & Walsh at 331. **138** 1 Dr & Walsh at 334. **139** *Moore & Lowry*, pp 232-3: king's bench rule of 26 Nov. 1832; Hogan, *Legal profession in Ireland*, p. 96 (quoting Howard). **140** *Ex parte Bushe* (1854) 4 ICLR 434. **141** Death of uncle: *In re Jameson* (1834) 3 Law Rec. ns 72. Death of brother: *Ex parte Carmichael*

recorded from before 1835 the courts seem to have been prepared to sanction an abridgement by as much as four years. Thereafter, however, they seem to have insisted that at least three years had to be served before application could be made. At the same stage too they drew the line at sanctioning an abridgement that would have enabled anyone to become an attorney under the age of 21.[142] So far as the actual merits of the individual application were concerned, years of service in the attorney-relative's practice prior to formal apprenticeship created a favourable impression, as did the possession of a university degree. Support from within the profession was also likely to prove of assistance. A remarkable degree of support from this quarter was forthcoming at the hearing of White's application in the exchequer in 1829: every attorney and barrister in practice on the particular circuit expressed themselves in favour, after White's father had died, leaving a widow and nine children. The circumstances of this particular application elicited an instructive observation from Baron Smith:

> I would be disposed to lay most stress on the petition of the solicitors who pray that a rule might be relaxed which had been adopted to protect them and who therein show they would willingly give up the emoluments they would otherwise receive if this young gentleman was not now admitted. The compassion of the case can have nothing to do with it.[143]

Compassion indeed does seem to have had little to do with it. Even after the courts had appreciably stiffened the requirements for an abridgement, it is plain that their principal concern was to attempt to achieve, by means of the exercise of this power they possessed, protection of the interests of the clients of what were so many one-man practices.

The case-law also sheds welcome light on an aspect to admission procedures that has so far escaped scrutiny: the position with regard to members of the bar who endeavoured to become attorneys. Transfers of this sort occurring at any stage after the differences between the two branches of the profession took final shape are almost impossible to quantify. Duhigg asserts that in the middle of the eighteenth century a sizeable number of attorneys switched to being barristers,[144] but information in respect of traffic proceeding in the opposite direction is virtually non-existent. For the early nineteenth century however it is possible to detect the emergence of what may indeed be a new pattern: the barrister seeking to become an attorney in order to take over some family practice that would, following the death of some close male relative, almost certainly otherwise have gone under.

In the cases of Symes and McNally reported at length in 1844 and 1853 both barristers sought admission as attorneys following the deaths of their respective brothers. The

(1831) 1 Hayes 138; *In re McNally* (1853) 3 ICLR 518. Death of brother-in-law: *Ex parte Fitzgibbon* (1830) 1 Hayes 139n. Death of father: *In re White* (1829) 3 Law Rec. 34; *In re Nolan* (1833) 1 Law Rec. ns 199; *In re Armstrong* (1834) 3 Law Rec. ns 72; *In re Charles Hughes* (1838) 6 Law Rec. ns 120; *In re Mulhall* (1861) 12 ICLR app. xxi. **142** *Ex parte Robinson* (1838) 2 Jones 622. **143** 3 Law Rec. 34. **144** Duhigg, *History of King's Inns*, p. 313.

cases had different outcomes but on both occasions the barons of the exchequer announced at the outset that they were obliged to follow a ruling of long standing made by the benchers that no barrister could be admitted an attorney until he had first been disbarred and then entered into indentures of apprenticeship. Only then could any question of the abridgement of the period of apprenticeship be entertained. This latter represented a concession which the Law Society, in observations addressed to the court over Symes' application, were clearly loath to accept. 'It is very important,' they declared, 'that all should enter into the profession of attorney on nearly equal terms; that one should not have to undergo great expense and a long preparation, which another is spared'.[145]

Over Symes' application the barons of the exchequer stood their ground and admitted Symes almost at once. He had in fact been exceptionally well qualified. A graduate who had served in the office of the assistant clerk of the rules in the court of queen's bench, he had been in the chambers of a distinguished Lincoln's Inn conveyancer, Mr Malins, and had been in practice at the Irish bar for seven years. In addition, in conjunction with Jebb, Symes had brought out a set of reports of Irish queen's bench decisions.

McNally's application presented in 1853 looked remarkably similar. He had been in practice at the bar for twelve years. Prior to that he had been in the chambers of an eminent pleader, Mr Molyneux. McNally sought another swift transfer after his brother, an attorney, had been killed in a railway accident. The attorney general of the day appeared on behalf of the Law Society in order yet again to oppose an application for a major abridgement in the period of apprenticeship. Once more however the barons of the exchequer were unimpressed and they voted to authorise McNally's admission. On this occasion, however, the instinct of the Law Society proved sounder. Five months after admitting McNally the barons of the exchequer vacated their order on the strength of evidence of disreputable conduct on McNally's part which had subsequently come to light. His undoing was a series of financial dealings with his brother's widow – there had been assigned to him the costs due the brother at the time of the latter's death and all of the widow's interest in the outcome of lawsuits that had then been pending.[146]

The basic rule governing applications in this area – that there had to be disbarment and then a period of apprenticeship – was regularly operated on a number of subsequent occasions. Publicity over its terms could still be required however as the circumstances of Hilliard's application in 1858 made clear.[147]

A last group of cases focus on the final stages of the process of gaining entry to the lower branch: the filing of the application to be admitted an attorney by the pertinent court. The act of 1773 and accompanying rules of court had set the requirements: notice had to be given in all the common law courts, though admission was being sought in only one; and notice had to be served by the prescribed date in the preceding law term. The judges were consistent in their insistence that these requirements be

145 *In re Symes* (1844) 7 Ir Eq R 339 at 342. **146** *In re McNally* (1853-4) 3 ICLR 518 (decision to admit) and 576 (vacating of order). **147** *Ex parte Hilliard* (1858) 7 Ir Ch R 63.

scrupulously observed. An aspiring common pleas attorney who had omitted to post his notices in the other two courts experienced this rebuke from Torrens J in 1839: 'The attorneys of the other courts are entitled to notice as well as those of this court. It would be going behind their backs to admit this gentleman.'[148] Seven years earlier, in 1832, the exchequer refused to excuse an aspiring attorney who had posted his notices late, after the law term in fact had terminated: 'For aught we know a hundred persons might have been in attendance during last term to oppose his admission.'[149] In a second common pleas case, heard in 1831, where yet another aspiring attorney had omitted to post his notices in the regular fashion, Mr Justice Moore touched on somewhat different considerations, in moving the rejection of the application for special treatment:

> I own I have a strong difficulty in assisting any apprentice who is not strictly regular in everything required, when I consider, that from the records of the King's Inns, there is an average application of 130 persons to be admitted, in every year. For their own sakes, apprentices should wish the utmost strictness to be attended to.[150]

XI

An element in the litigation summarised in the foregoing survey was the increasingly important contribution registered by the society which had been founded in 1830 specifically to advance the interests of members of the lower branch. The Law Society with its headquarters in Dublin was to grow perceptibly in influence and prestige as the century advanced, a high point being reached in 1852 when the society was granted its charter.[151]

In its formative years the Law Society came to hold a 'watching brief' in those cases where application was made to the courts for an abridgement of the period of an apprenticeship: the various applications of Lyons in the 1830s and the applications involving barristers like Symes and McNally furnish instances. Simultaneously, the society sought to apply pressure to the judges and to the benchers of the King's Inns on a range of topics connected with the maintenance of standards and the well-being of the professions of attorney and solicitor generally, pressure that, naturally in the course of time, was to extend to mooted reforms of the rules governing entry. By 1835 the courts had recognised the right of the Law Society to be heard to object to an application for admission as an attorney. Four years earlier they had listened too when the society took the initiative in proposing that two attorneys convicted of felony should be struck off the rolls. In 1863 the society scored a victory that was as complete as it was symbolic when the Irish courts upheld its contention that an attorney who had merely qualified in England should not be permitted to appear in an Irish lawsuit.[152]

148 *Anon.* (1839) Smythe 87. **149** *Ex parte Black* (1832) Hayes 206n, following *Ex parte Thompson* (1831) Hayes 206. **150** *Anon.* (1831) 4 Law Rec. 187. **151** Hogan, *Legal profession in Ireland*, ch. 7. **152** *In re*

Equally critical was the adoption of the new rule by the benchers in 1843 – again as a result of pressure – that copies of memorials of all persons seeking to be apprenticed to attorneys should also be lodged with the society.[153] Baron Pennefather spelt out a crucial corollary four years later: an attorney who had voluntarily got himself struck off and who sought re-admission would first have to give notice to the Law Society.[154] 'He ought', the baron insisted,

> to give them the same notice as a person seeking originally to be admitted; as though this applicant may be most correct and proper in his conduct, still he has been after a long time out of the control of the court as one of its officers, and a person might have done something in the meantime which would render it desirable that he should not be again admitted.

Prompted by developments in England, the Law Society from the beginning pressed the benchers for reforms in the system of education for aspiring attorneys and solicitors.[155] Apprenticeship, attendance at the courts in Dublin, possession of a university degree, exposure to scrutiny by the moral examiners, recital of a solemn oath, membership of King's Inns: none of this, so it was contended, quite reflected the proper image the profession now held of itself or guaranteed that the correct decisions on the admission of individual candidates were assured. The remedy was thought to lie in a two-tiered system of written examinations – an intermediate examination to be sat by all aspiring apprentices and a final to be sat during the concluding stage of apprenticeship. Change along these broad lines was introduced in England in the 1830s, but the benchers in Dublin were not satisfied that this constituted the right way forward. Thus was battle joined.

In the early 1830s the attorneys and solicitors of Ireland had made common cause to challenge an interpretation on the impact on the level of their fees of the Irish currency change introduced in the previous decade.[156] It is not impossible that from the lessons learned then there evolved the instinct for concerted effort and passion for unrelenting politicking that become such conspicuous features in a new, more assured and less self-effacing generation of practitioner. The claim advanced by this generation that it was motivated exclusively by the best interests of the profession may have been dismissed out of hand by certain contemporary critics, though equally it would have delighted earlier critics such as Howard and Duhigg who had regularly upbraided Irish attorneys for their pusillanimity. However this may be, a series of developments, some of them, interestingly and perhaps paradoxically, the achievement of the judiciary, undoubtedly helped to buttress this claim, which was advanced, first of all, by informal groupings and then after 1830 more publicly by the Law Society. In 1828 the then lord chancellor, Sir Anthony Hart, denied that under Irish law any attorney could be exempted from arrest for debt, in refusing a claim for the issuance of a writ of protec-

Dowling (1835) 2 Law Rec. ns 198; *In re Michael White, In re Jeremiah O'Brien* (1831) Glascock 55; *Scovell* v. *Gardner* (1863) 16 ICLR 84n. **153** Hogan, *Legal profession in Ireland*, p. 115. **154** *Anon.* (1847) 10 Ir LR 111. **155** Hogan, *Legal profession in Ireland*, ch. 8. **156** *Case of Solicitors and Attorneys* (1835) Lloyd & Goold temp. Sugden 349.

tion in favour of the particular attorney.[157] Over twenty years previously, in 1807, in another symbolic break with the privileged era of past years, the courts adopted a new general rule to the effect that attorneys litigating in a personal capacity would have to pay the same fees as other litigants.[158]

The battle fought by the Law Society to induce the benchers to introduce written examinations was greeted with final success in 1860. Six years later legislation terminated the rule that members of the lower branch were obliged to become members of King's Inns and, in acknowledgement of the new role of the Law Society, transferred to that body certain functions connected with the regulation of the affairs of the lower branch. To preserve a degree of continuity with earlier arrangements, however, the benchers were confirmed in their role as supervisors of the programme of education for aspiring attorneys and solicitors.[159] This programme, despite the significant reforms of 1860, continued to attract an amount of criticism[160] but the Law Society only became master in its own house when this residual link with the benchers was finally sundered in 1898.[161]

Throughout the course of this warfare over the perceived educational needs of the lower branch, the Law Society laid regular emphasis on its own respectability and on its commitment to the interests of the profession. Three years before parliament passed the act of 1866, thus endorsing the reforms of 1860, the members of the Irish court of queen's bench had seized the opportunity to express a view on the position of the attorney in the Ireland of the period, a view against which educational controversies both then and in later years deserve to be set. An attorney engaged by the defendant in a pending lawsuit changed sides, provoking the client in question to lodge a protest over the attorney's conduct in a frank letter that he despatched to the Law Society. Was the occasion a privileged one or was it not? A majority of the court had little difficulty in deciding that privilege attached. A passage in Mr Justice Hayes' concurring judgment touched on weightier matters to which the circumstances of the litigation had tempted him to give voice. The upshot is a picture of the lower branch at a time when one radical departure had recently been inaugurated and policies designed to 'professionalise' the profession in all its aspects were plainly in the ascendant:[162]

> The good conduct of the profession, collectively and individually, is one of the most precious possessions of the public, and one of the best guarantees of public liberty and safety. It is to our attorney that we confide the inmost secrets of our heart, in confidence that they will not be betrayed; and it is from our attorney that we expect the advice which is to regulate our conduct in the most important concerns of life. The profession of an attorney is not then to be compared with other, the ordinary callings and avocations in life, and the laws which

157 *Anon.* (1828) 1 Molloy 76. **158** *Moore & Lowry*, app. I, p. 76. **159** 29 & 30 Vict., c. 84: an act to amend the laws for the regulation of the profession of attorneys and solicitors in Ireland, and to assimilate them to those in England. **160** Mark S. O'Shaughnessy, 'On legal education in Ireland', *JSSISI*, vi (1871–6) 124 at 152 et seq. **161** 61 & 62 Vict., c. 17: an act to amend and consolidate the laws relating to solicitors and to the service of indentured apprentices in Ireland. **162** *Hamerton* v. *Green* (1863) 16 ICLR 77 at 99.

> regulate that profession very clearly demonstrate that; for while other professions and businesses are allowed, in a great measure, to regulate themselves, very special enactments apply to the attorney.

There is much more in similar vein.

Puzzles from Irish Law Reporting History

The preface dedicatory to Sir John Davies's Irish law reports of 1615 starts with a short account of the successful transplantation of the common law to Ireland. Much of the credit is there accorded to King John: he made the first division of shires, erected courts of justice and published the laws of England. 'Briefly,' Davies writes, King John 'did order and settle the government heere in all pointes according to the Modell of the commonwealth of England'.[1] An uninterrupted sequence of legal records for the lordship of Ireland extending from the reign of John down to that of Henry VI bore testimony, Davies continues, to the magnitude of John's achievement. There were pipe rolls, 'containing the charge of the revenue, both Certaine & casuall'; plea rolls, encompassing both common pleas and pleas of the crown; parliament rolls; charters; patents; commissions; and inquisitions. Davies had seen what survived up to the turn of the seventeenth century and he was impressed, terming it 'as faire and authentique' an archive as any he had glimpsed in England.[2] It was a remarkable inheritance since, as Davies indicates, embezzlement and careless maintenance had already exacted a fearful toll and, indeed, though Davies would plainly have been disturbed at the prospect, were fated to continue to do so.

There was one conspicuous omission from Davies's inventory of surviving record material – the indigenous law report. Davies emphasises the point:

> Howbeit during all the time that the lawes of England haue had theire course in Ireland, which is nowe full foure hundred yeares, there hath not been any Report made and published of any Case in lawe, argued, or adiudged in this Kingdome: but all the arguments and reasons of the iudgements and resolutions given in the Courts of Ireland, haue hitherto beene utterly lost, and buried in oblivion.[3]

Thus is one puzzle identified. Prior to the seventeenth century there are no Irish year books or any other kind of law reports.

Before proceeding to try to furnish an explanation, it is necessary to fault Davies for a degree of exaggeration. Some indication, albeit slight, of the mental processes informing the decisions of the Irish courts may actually be derived from quarters Davies chooses not to mention: (i) indigenous court records (where these survive);[4] (ii)

1 Sir John Davies, *Le primer report des cases & matters en ley resolues & adiudges en l.s. courts del roy en Ireland* (Dublin, 1615), preface dedicatory, f. 1. **2** Ibid., f. 1v. **3** Ibid. **4** The major collections available in print are the following: (i) *Calendar of the justiciary rolls of Ireland, 1295-1303*, ed. James Mills (Dublin, 1905); *Calendar of the justiciary rolls of Ireland, 1304-07*, ed. James Mills (Dublin, 1914): *Calendar of the justiciary rolls*

records of Irish cases that went on appeal to the English King's Bench and are preserved in either English court records or English year books and sometimes in both. Correspondence passing between the English and Irish judicial benches as another source of illumination is not to be ignored either.[5]

Yet, in the main, Davies has the better of the argument. Any species of law report of Irish judicial decisions is totally lacking from the thirteenth to the sixteenth century and that entails, as Davies rightly saw, that a very great deal indeed has been lost. This might not have mattered so much had the official archive of which Davies speaks in such fulsome terms itself managed to survive. Unfortunately, this was not what was to happen: the explosion and fire at the Dublin Four Courts complex, where the Irish Public Record Office had the ill luck to be located, in the summer of 1922, at the outset of the Civil War, worked considerable destruction. It should be remembered besides that there had been substantial losses of other Irish public records in the intervening centuries as well.[6]

In most countries during the middle ages, and even more recently than that, systematic law reporting represented the exception rather than the rule. For Davies, even so, the non-existence of any Irish law reports partook of the nature of a mystery. That lack, he writes

> seemeth to me the more straunge, because there haue beene within this Realme, in euery age since the raigne of King John, men sufficiently learned in the lawes, who have deriued theire learning out of the fountaines of lawe in England, the Innes of Court ... And therefore they might haue beene induced to imitate the learned men of England, who from the Norman Conquest downewards, did continually preserue the memory of such notable cases as did from time to time arise, and where argued and ruled in the Courts of Iustice in

of Ireland, 1308-14, ed. Herbert Wood and A.E. Langman and revised by M.C. Griffith (Dublin, n.d. [1956]); S.G. Ellis, 'The Common Bench Plea Roll of 19 Edward IV (1479-80) in the Public Record Office of Ireland', *Analecta Hibernica*, 31 (1984), 19. (ii) *The register of John Swayne, archbishop of Armagh and primate of Ireland, 1418-39*, ed. D.A. Chart (Belfast, 1935); *Registrum Iohannis Mey: the register of John Mey, archbishop of Armagh, 1443-56*, ed. W.G.H. Quigley and E.F.D. Roberts (Belfast, 1972); *The register of Milo Sweteman, archbishop of Armagh, 1361-80*, ed. Brendan Smith (Dublin, 1996); (iii) Historical Manuscripts Commission, *Egmont MSS*, vol 1, part 1 (1905), pp 1-60 (Irish court of castle chamber decrees, 1573-1630); (iv) Edmund Curtis, 'The Court-Book of the Manor of Esker and Crumlin, 1592-1600', *Journal of the Royal Society of Antiquaries of Ireland*, 59 (1929) 45, 128; *Journal of the Royal Society of Antiquaries of Ireland*, 60 (1930) 38, 137; *Court book of the liberty of Saint Sepulchre within the jurisdiction of the archbishop of Dublin, 1585-90*, ed. Herbert Wood, extra vol. of the Royal Society of Antiquaries of Ireland for 1930 (Dublin, 1930). Other collections survive both in original manuscript and in transcription. **5** See, for example, Paul Brand, 'Ralph de Hengham and the Irish Common Law', *Irish Jurist*, 19 (1984) 107; and, more generally, 'Letters to Ireland: Professional Enlightenment from the English Bench', above p. 101. **6** For an overview of the fate of the Irish public and legal records see 'In Search of Irish Legal History: A Map for Explorers', above, p. 1. Additional information on the destruction of records of clerks of the crown and peace will be found in the *32nd Report of the Deputy Keeper of the Public Records in Ireland* (Dublin, 1900), appendix, schedule 3, p. 96, which is conveniently summarised in ch. 4, 'Grand juries and the presentment system', of Peter O'Keeffe and Tom Simington's *Irish stone bridges: history and heritage* (Dublin, 1991). For an account of the records that survived up to the time of the 1922 explosion and fire, see Herbert Wood, *A guide to the records deposited in the Public Record Office of Ireland* (Dublin, 1919).

> England, by reducing the same into bookes of Reports, which may bee called, not improperly, the Annalles of the lawe.[7]

Davies investigates the mystery no further in his preface, abandoning this Irish historical conundrum in favour of a batch of topics almost certainly of greater interest to a contemporary English audience: the vaunted excellence of the common law; the value of Law French; the propaganda directed at uncertainty and delay in the law; the explosion in litigation; the nobility of the lawyer's calling; the barrister and his honorarium.

The precise historical question Davies raises is much easier to formulate than to answer. Furthermore, any answer must, to no small extent, be speculative in nature. It is surely correct, however, in the putting together of that answer, to have regard to the salient characteristics of the legal system that existed in the lordship of Ireland, especially in the later middle ages.[8]

The first of these characteristics to merit emphasis is the alteration that took place in the scale of activity of the common law courts in the lordship. It is clear that the effective area of operation for these courts was much diminished from the fourteenth century onwards, as English power in Ireland itself weakened and the Pale was reduced in size. Furthermore, in respect of the geographical areas where the common law might have been expected to continue to hold sway, it is evident that considerable resort was being had to arbitration and even that reliance was being placed upon mixed or hybrid systems of law.

Second, there would appear to have taken place a change in the nature of legal business transacted before the common law courts. Because of the dearth of legal records and of other independent sources of information, the evidence is necessarily sparse. What there is bears the connotation that the common law courts came in time to process in the main a routine diet of scarcely exhilarating lawsuits of straightforward debt and trespass.

Third, there had been the lack of a fixed base for the common law courts from the start of Anglo-Norman settlement in the twelfth century. It is startling to discover that it was only under the Tudors that the courts finally managed to secure a permanent home in Dublin. In the interim there had occurred a long sojourn in Carlow for certain of the courts in the second half of the fourteenth century; and recent research has shown that the Irish King's Bench was regularly itinerating until well into the sixteenth century.

Fourth, the 'professional leadership' manifested by the courts in London in relation to all manner of things remained unchallenged; that leadership, in short, was treated as one of the facts of Irish legal life. Throughout the middle ages there is recorded for the

7 Davies, *Le primer report* (above, n. 1), preface dedicatory, f. lv. 8 In what follows, my indebtedness to all those who have laboured to shed light on the legal system of the lordship and of the kingdom of Ireland between the twelfth and seventeenth centuries should be apparent. I acknowledge especially the work of F.E. Ball, H.G. Richardson, G.O. Sayles, A.J. Otway-Ruthven, G.J. Hand, Paul Brand, Steven Ellis, C.A. Empey, Katharine Simms, J.G. Crawford and Colum Kenny. Not to be omitted either is M.J. Blake, the editor of *Blake family records, 1300-1600* (London, 1902), an important collection of medieval and early modern muniments deriving in the main from the Galway area.

Irish courts no inclination whatsoever on their part to diverge from what was viewed as acceptable doctrine or an acceptable mode of proceeding by the courts in England. The king, the English privy council and the English King's Bench were in any event endowed by contemporary constitutional doctrine with sufficient authority to neutralise any displays of separateness that the Irish courts might have felt tempted to manifest. Law reporting enjoys close connections with legal education. In the case of Ireland, an equally critical factor – reflective again of the approval of the hegemony of London – was the lack of any local inn of court until the reign of Henry VIII. Even when King's Inns was established in Dublin in 1541 the dominance of London was reflected in the requirement, embodied in a statutory provision adopted by the Irish parliament in the same year, that candidates for admission to the Irish bar had to attend for their education at one of the London inns of court. Not until as late as 1850 did King's Inns become involved in the provision of legal education locally; and only in 1885 was the statutory requirement of attendance at the London inns dropped.[9]

Fifth, there is the uncertain calibre of the typical holder of judicial office in the Irish common law courts. This is a relevant consideration because initiatives in reporting are likely to be linked in some fashion not only to perceptions of the needs of the profession but also to the encouragement and support of the judicial bench. For the greater part of the sixteenth century and back into the later medieval period, appointments to the Irish bench were monopolised by sons of gentry families from the Pale with a background of education, in a number of instances, at the inns of court in London. The evidence for corruption within this group, while incontrovertible, is by no means exceptional. Other evidence, no less regularly adduced, testifies to the judges' general mediocrity and lack of knowledge of the law, and is strangely, and significantly, at odds with the broad historical encomium in their favour pronounced by Davies in the preface to his reports.[10]

Given the meagre and contradictory evidence, prudence dictates that the intellectual attainments of Ireland's judges of, say, the later Tudor era should not be too harshly regarded. At the same time, however, and for the same reason, it must remain within the bounds of possibility that these attainments contributed in some degree to the state of affairs in relation to Irish law reporting that baffled Davies: the need to embark on the enterprise may have lain beyond the judges' comprehension and the enterprise itself not have commanded their sympathy. The seed, in short, could have fallen on ground that was exceptionally stony.

The opportunity that existed in the lordship of Ireland for decision-making only on a modest scale and only in a small geographical zone and only by a beleaguered judiciary of unproven reputation who, we happen to know, lacked until the later sixteenth century any permanent headquarters risks being dismissed as a chimera; perhaps, as the authority of the English government in Ireland revived under the Tudors, with all that that meant for the Irish legal system, as a progressively unaccept-

9 Statute of Jeofailles (An acte touching mispleading and jeofailles), *Stat. Ire.*, 33 Hen. VIII, sess. 2 (1541–2), c. 3; Barristers (Ireland) Act, 1885, 48 & 49 Vict., c. 20. **10** Paul Brand, in his seminal article 'Ireland and the Literature of the Early Common Law', *Irish Jurist*, 16 (1981) 95, raises a number of issues that disincline one to become too dismissive of the calibre of the local legal profession.

able one. Yet, when it is recalled that that opportunity presented itself in a context where the professional hegemony of London continued in every respect to be conceded, it is hard to resist the conclusion that the conjunction of that further factor was bound, throughout the medieval and early modern periods, to have proved fatal to the development of a tradition of interest in indigenous law reporting.

Whatever the explanation for the non-appearance of any Irish law reports prior to 1615, a deep-rooted aversion to the very thought of Irish law reporting appears to have persisted. Davies cheerfully concludes his preface dedicatory by expressing the hope that his collection of cases might be the first of several. The exercise had been undertaken 'principally for the use and benefit of our Practisers heere in Ireland', but there had been another object in view:

> to moue and incite others in this Kingdome, by this first example, which doth onely open and shew them the way, to performe the like service heereafter to posterity.[11]

Davies's expectation were doomed not to be realised. Irish lawsuits were still to proceed by way of appeal to the English King's Bench and later to the English or British House of Lords, and it is possible to discover accounts of a proportion of these in the English nominate reports for the seventeenth and eighteenth centuries. Reports of single lawsuits brought before the Irish courts begin to be printed too: the genre expanded and though these accounts were often variable in quality, to the Irish legal historian at least, collectively, they furnish critical enlightenment.[12] But, leaving aside ten Irish cases gathered into an appendix to Gilbert's *Equity Cases* published in 1734, and leaving aside the specialist material included in Howard's *Popery Cases* of 1775,[13] there was to be no collection of Irish law reports published between that of Davies in 1615 and that of G.W. Vernon and J.B. Scriven in 1787.[14]

Focusing on one obvious consequence of this prolonged hiatus, R.B. McDowell observes that 'the paucity of Irish law reports for the era makes it difficult to assess the quality of the judiciary',[15] but there are many other implications – for example, the extraordinary handicap that that paucity creates in the way of charting the development of common law doctrine in Ireland and the loss of a prime source of information on local social and economic conditions.[16]

11 Davies, *Le primer report* (n. 1 above), preface dedicatory, f. 11v. **12** For listings see Paul O'Higgins, *A bibliography of Irish trials and other legal proceedings* (Abingdon, 1986). **13** G. Gilbert, *Reports of cases in equity, argued and decreed in the courts of chancery and exchequer, chiefly in the reign of George I ... to which are added, some select cases in equity heard and determined in the court of exchequer in Ireland* (London, 1734) (25 Eng. Rep. 1-188); G.E. Howard, *Several special cases on the laws against the further growth of popery in Ireland* (Dublin, 1775). **14** G.W. Vernon and J.B. Scriven, *Reports of cases determined in the King's Courts, Dublin with select cases in the House of Lords of Ireland, 1786-88* (Dublin, 1787-9). **15** In *New history of Ireland – iv, Eighteenth-century Ireland, 1691-1800*, ed. T.W. Moody and W.E. Vaughan (Oxford, 1986), p. 706. For an assessment of the Irish judges' approach to the interpretation and enforcement of the eighteenth-century penal laws see 'Catholics, Land, and the Popery Acts of Anne', below, at pp 234-5. **16** In regard to the last point, one thinks, for instance, of the telling use made of the English nominate reports by Douglas Hay in his 'Poaching and the Game Laws on Cannock Chase': Douglas Hay et al., *Albion's fatal tree: crime and society in eighteenth-century*

A second puzzle is thus encountered: why are there no published collections of Irish law reports between the beginning of the seventeenth century and the end of the eighteenth? The mystery in this instance deepens when it is borne in mind that in the eighteenth century in Ireland printing became relatively commonplace; the country therefore was not without a facility to the effective lack of which, prior to 1615, the non-existence of law reports then might, in part at least, have been attributed. Naturally, even so, cost, in the absence of' express demand, could have represented an insurmountable barrier to the emergence of the entrepreneur reporter or editor.[16a]

In a brief discussion of the question, McDowell opts to lay stress on a rather different factor – the indifference of the Irish legal profession and the fact that that profession lacked a tradition of intellectual rigour. The non-existence of reports, he writes,

> together with the fact that few legal works of value by Irish men were produced in Ireland during the eighteenth century suggests that the Irish bar was distinguished for forensic skill and 'rhetorical elegance', rather than for profound learning and an interest in the principles of jurisprudence.[17]

The argument has weight. A similar line of reasoning was employed earlier in what is advanced above as an explanation for the non-existence of Irish reports prior to 1615. The leopard never changes his spots. Why, it might be asked, in respect of the issue of extending support to the idea of native law reports, should either the Irish bench or the Irish bar quite perversely have chosen to do so? As against this, so far as part of McDowell's argument is concerned, it might be claimed that his stance is unduly severe. The writings of two members of the Irish legal profession of the latter half of the eighteenth century, F.S. Sullivan and Arthur Browne,[18] are not perhaps of the highest standard, but they transcend the mediocre and it is difficult, in consequence, to accept, not at least without the detailed examination that the question merits but which has not so far been accorded to it,[19] McDowell's somewhat perfunctory dismissal of the profession's publishing record and thereby of its intellectual aspirations. Admittedly, in legal-cultural terms, eighteenth-century Dublin by no means rivalled eighteenth-century Edinburgh. How far, in this particular domain, the Irish capital fell short of 'the Athens of the North' is the bone of contention.

England (London, 1975), ch. 5. **16a** Lord Mountmorres's explanation – the lack of an Irish law of copyright – is not wholly convincing: *The history of the principal transactions of the Irish parliament, 1634-66*, 2 vols. (London, 1792), ii, 154. **17** *New history of Ireland – iv* (n. 16 above), p. 707. **18** F.S. Sullivan, *An historical treatise on the feudal law, and the constitution and laws of England, with a commentary on Magna Carta* (London, 1772); Arthur Browne, *A compendious view of the civil law*, 2 vols. (Dublin, 1797-9). **19** James Lyne, in the preface to the reports known as *Wallis by Lyne* (see n. 32 below), published in 1839 but recording decisions handed down between the 1760s and the 1780s, advances a much more sympathetic view of the profession. In almost all of the cases he edited, Lyne writes (preface, p. vii), 'is exhibited more learning and reference to authority than is generally supposed to have characterised the arguments at the bar during that period. Ingenious advocacy, and strong original views, are no more than what might be expected from the distinguished men whose names appear as counsel in the following pages; and in many instances it has been an ungrateful task to abridge and consolidate the arguments, which in the manuscripts are given separately and at length.' On Irish legal publishing of the period see Paul O'Higgins's short pioneering survey, 'Law Printing in Eighteenth-Century Ireland', *Law Librarian*, 17 (1986) 93.

Why the hiatus had occurred in the production of Irish law reports and why that hiatus had lasted the length of time it did was investigated by Vernon and Scriven in the introduction to their reports of 1787. The answer they furnish is obviously pertinent, though this is not to deny the force of McDowell's point of view. The caveat is warranted, for Vernon and Scriven, anxious to secure a market for their reports, were unlikely, in their preliminary remarks, to direct a broadside at their contemporaries that charged either them or their predecessors with intellectual uncouthness; unsurprisingly, we find that they eschew anything of the sort.

In furnishing an explanation for the non-existence of Irish reports, Vernon and Scriven placed emphasis on two distinct factors. First, in contrast to the position as they understood it to exist in England, a dearth of business in all the Irish central courts had produced a marked division of manpower within the local legal profession, which in turn had set serious obstacles in the way of the enterprise of producing law reports:

> The number of courts is the same here as in England; the business transacted in them considerably less: to account for this, we need only reflect on the comparative extent, population and commerce of the two countries. The natural consequence of this deficiency of business, was, that individuals, eminent in their profession, did not find sufficient employment to attach them to a particular court; so that they were obliged to appear in different courts, according as the causes they were engaged in happened to be called on; and thus the course of practice continues at this day. Hence frequently it may be, that a counsel hears no more of a cause than his own argument, or at the utmost not sufficient to enable him to make a tolerable report of it.[20]

The ramifications spread into the area of what today would be termed restrictive practices within the barristers' profession. 'To this practice too', Vernon and Scriven add, 'may be attributed the employment in each case of a greater number of counsel than in England, in order to guard against interruptions from their absence.'[21] Returning to their main theme, the two authors conclude that the difficulties of reporting under these circumstances might appear sufficient to deter anyone from the undertaking.[22] Close familiarity with the working methods of the eighteenth-century Irish bar would alone warrant concurrence with the views expressed by Vernon and Scriven. That these views constitute part of the explanation nonetheless happens to be corroborated by Howard in the preface to his *Popery Cases*. Howard mentions explicitly the difficulty Vernon and Scriven were later to emphasise: in assembling cases to include in a collection of reports, that of following a case through from start to finish and of being certain that one was seised of the right case when pursuing its progress through the various stages of proceedings in court.[23] Further corroboration naturally would be welcome.

20 Vernon and Scriven, *Reports* (1790 ed.), preface, pp vii–viii. For assistance with the publishing history and distinct editions of these reports, see O'Higgins, *Bibliography* (n. 12, above), pp 58–9. **21** Vernon and Scriven, *Reports* (1790 ed.), preface, p. viii. **22** Ibid. **23** Howard, *Popery Cases* (n. 14, above), preface, pp iii–v.

The second factor identified by Vernon and Scriven was of a wholly different character: opposition on political grounds. Individuals, the authors reveal, had objected to the undertaking of such a work in Ireland, basing that objection on the conviction that decisions of the courts in England – the home of the common law – should alone be entitled to be committed to print and thus be preserved for future guidance.[24] Nearly 150 years before, Catholic and Protestant factions in the country had clashed over this very question of how best the fortunes of the common law in Ireland could be assured, though the focus to the quarrel then had been different – whether the establishment of an inn of court in Ireland with responsibilities for legal education should be encouraged – but the underlying issue was identical.[25] In 1642 the Catholics of the Confederation of Kilkenny favoured the plan, seeking a need to instil in the gentry of Ireland a knowledge of the law, 'to the end the laudable laws of England may not die amidst the disasters of these times'.[26] The Protestants, however, were less than enthusiastic and firmly opposed to the suggestion that, as a corollary, the requirement of compulsory residence in London for the prospective Irish barrister be abandoned. The sojourn in London constituted a means to be civilised 'after the English customs', and enabled students to become familiar with, and to love, the English language and the English nation. In order to preserve the law in its purity in Ireland the best strategy lay in ensuring that students continued to draw 'from the original fountain' and to see 'the manner of the practice of that in the same great channels where his majesties courts of justice do flow most clearly'.[27] In concluding their remonstrance attacking the Catholics' plan, the Protestants did not mince their words, '[T]he separation of the kingdoms in that place of their principal instruction where their foundations in learning are to be laid', they argued, would give rise to danger:

> a degenerate corruption in religion and justice may haply be introduced and spread with much more difficulty to be corrected and restrained afterwards by any discipline to be used in Ireland.[28]

An upsurge of nationalist sentiment among the lawyers of late eighteenth-century Ireland worked a transformation which led to the fears of the Irish Protestants of the 1640s being in effect dismissed as largely illusory. Compulsory residence at a London Inn was to stay but there was now no objection in principle, so it was averred, to the appearance of a collection of Irish law reports. Vernon and Scriven trod warily, nevertheless, appealing to reason and choosing their words with care. Those opposed for political reasons to the publication of a set of Irish reports advanced considerations which, they asserted, 'do not seem warranted to the extent in which they are applied'. It was common ground that, in the normal course of judicature, 'the Decisions in England must ever have their due weight in our courts, as far as they apply'. But differences had opened up between the law in England and

24 Vernon and Scriven, *Reports*, preface, p. viii. **25** Colum Kenny, *King's Inns and the kingdom of Ireland: the Irish 'inn of court', 1541-1800* (Dublin, 1992), ch. 5. **26** Ibid., p. 121. **27** Ibid. **28** Ibid.

the law in Ireland, and where such differences obtained English decisions offered no assistance whatsoever. Was the Irish practitioner to be deprived of access to some relevant judicial precedent merely because of an allegedly flawed pedigree – a provenance exclusively and obdurately Irish? Vernon and Scriven reckoned not, indicating that a majority within the contemporary profession were now of like mind, and equally contemptuous of so preposterous a proposition. Where English decisions do not apply, they wrote,

> as must frequently happen from time to time, in cases peculiar to this country, it seems unquestionable that the determinations of such in our own courts should be generally known, and rescued from oblivion. The great number of statutes confined to this country, the tenures that are peculiar to it, and the rules of practice which each court prescribes to itself, afford abundant matter to justify a compilation of this nature.[29]

Facilitating sound decision-making in the area of practice – an area of enduring concern to the profession – was to be emphasised in a final parry:

> To evince that such a work is necessary, we have only to appeal to the experience and observation of the profession. In numberless instances, and cases of importance, counsel are obliged to refer to memory for determination of which more permanent traces are not to be found. In matter of practice, upon which so much of the business of a court depends, the inconvenience is more frequently, and more sensibly felt. For these reasons we are not without hopes that this publication will be acceptable to the profession …[30]

In their remarkable preface Vernon and Scriven highlighted the inferiority complex of certain of their contemporaries. But they neither chastised nor rebuked. The tone they observed throughout was both moderate and by no means stridently nationalistic. In the evolution of law in Ireland in the future, English and Irish judicial precedent might be expected serenely to co-exist, hardly belligerently to jostle. It was right that this should be so. There existed many branches of law where the masters of the common law in England would remain influential. But there existed certain areas of law in Ireland – Vernon and Scriven identified three – where occupants of the Irish bench might be expected (indeed, would be obliged) to leave their imprint too. The debate rehearsed and the essential signposts erected, the way now lay open for Vernon and Scriven's successors as compilers of collections of Irish law reports to set about their appointed task energetically with all professional opposition either tamed or silenced.

In the history of Irish law reporting, the question of the relationship of English law to Irish law, a central question which Vernon and Scriven had started to explore,

29 Vernon and Scriven, *Reports*, preface, p. ix. **30** Ibid. For an attack directed at the fallibility of counsel's memory, see the judgment of Power B in *Faris, custodee* v. *Faris* (1794) Ir. Term Rep. 109 at 123.

was not destined to fade from view. As we shall see, the identical question was to be resurrected in dramatic fashion in the 1870s. To locate the third puzzle, however, it will be necessary, rather than to move forwards, to retrace our steps. Its essential nature is indicated by the length of the gap – some 172 years – in Irish law reporting between the appearance of Davies's reports and those of Vernon and Scriven. During this long period it is known that *English* law reports circulated widely in the country.[31] But the question forces itself upon us: how did the local legal profession, and in particular bench and bar, actually manage in the absence of published *Irish* reports? Were there no manuscript collections of native cases and did not these circulate?

The quick answer is that manuscript collections did exist and that there is evidence for the circulation of some of them. How in practical terms these collections, and such dissemination of them that it is possible to prove occurred, may actually have helped the profession to manage is, however, and unfortunately, not so easy to fathom.

One of the more celebrated of these collections was the set of notes kept by John Wallis, KC, of decisions handed down in the Irish Chancery and in the other superior courts during the years when Lord Lifford was Irish lord chancellor (1767–89). These notes finally came into the hands of a descendant of Wallis's, W.J. Alexander of Lincoln's Inn, who made them available to James Lyne, another prominent Dublin barrister but of a later generation, whose father had known Wallis and to whom, in fact, Wallis had first entrusted his notes. Lyne, deservedly remembered for his *Treatise on leases for lives renewable for ever* (Dublin, 1837), then set about preparing the collection for publication. Many cases on the penal laws were omitted and counsel's arguments were frequently considerably abridged. The reports, recognised ever since by their designation of *Wallis by Lyne*, were eventually published in Dublin in 1839.[32] No other manuscript collection of eighteenth-century Irish cases was to be transformed in this way: *Wallis by Lyne* remains unique.

It may be found of assistance at this point to furnish a list of manuscript collections of Irish law reports known to exist today. Necessarily in the nature of a progress report on discoveries registered to date, this inventory nonetheless conveys a fair picture of the sort of material that has survived, as well as intimating the chances for doctrinal elucidation that study of its content may ultimately engender. The extant collections are dispersed among various repositories: in London, in the British Library and in Lincoln's Inn Library; in New York, in Columbia University Library; in Belfast, in the Public Record Office of Northern Ireland; and in Dublin, in the National Archives (formerly the Public Record Office of Ireland), in King's Inns Library and in the Pearse Street Public Library.

31 The proof is furnished by extensive reference in all the surviving law report material, in parliamentary debates and in the published treatises (especially those of Howard) as well as by the data to be gleaned from various catalogues and inventories of lawyers' libraries. 32 *Reports of select cases argued and determined in the High Court of Chancery in Ireland, principally in the time of Lord Lifford …*, edited from the original notes of the late John Wallis, KC, by James Lyne (Dublin, 1839), preface, pp v–vii.

Period covered	*Description of collection*
1686–88	Notes of cases by Thomas Nugent, Baron Riverstown (lord chief justice of King's Bench, 1687–90)[33]
1716–34	Notes of cases in the Irish Chancery and the Irish Exchequer by Henry Singleton (lord chief justice of Common Pleas, 1740–53)[34]
*c.*1716–*c.*1730	Cases from the commonplace book of Cornelius O'Callaghan (member of the Irish bar, dies 1759)[35]
1730–72	Cases from the collections of the Hon. Richard Annesley (member of the Irish bar, 1770)[36]
1732–40	Notes of cases in the Irish Exchequer by John Wainwright (baron of Exchequer, 1732–41)[37]
1768–74	Notes of cases by Edmund Malone (judge of Common Pleas, 1766–74)[38]
1779–84	Notes of cases by James Hewitt, Viscount Lifford (lord chancellor, 1767–89)[39]

The above list is confined to collections that predate the modern cycle of reporting which commences with Vernon and Scriven's reports in 1787. Collections of a comparable kind continued to be compiled in Ireland in the nineteenth century. These later collections vary in one major respect, in that they tend to reflect activity over a much wider range of jurisdictions: in addition to the superior courts, there is coverage, for instance, of the assistant barrister's court (later the county court), the insolvent debtors' court and the magistrates' court.[40]

It is clear that the later collections of decisions of the superior courts enjoyed a degree of circulation. The manuscript reports of Robert Day, a puisne judge of the Irish King's Bench from 1798 to 1818, are cited in Hudson and Brooke's reports (1827–8).[41] In 1868, in a major examination of the right of an alien to commence proceedings in the Irish courts in respect of real property situated in the country, the decision was founded on a judgment from 1836 of Lord Chief Justice Bushe which

33 National Archives of Ireland (formerly PROI), CO. 1776. **34** Columbia University Library, MS Singleton, 71; Henry Singleton, *A brief catalogue* (London, 1937), item no. 71. **35** Pearse Street Public Library Dublin, Gilbert Collection, MS Robinson, 36 ('Extracts from Mr Gore's Notes'), pp 411–73; Douglas Hyde and D.J. O'Donoghue, *Catalogue of the books and manuscripts comprising the library of the late Sir John Gilbert* (Dublin, 1918), p. 955. Several entries in this collection are undated: hence the uncertainty about the precise span of years that is covered. **36** Public Record Office of Northern Ireland, D 1854/4/2,/4,/7; see typescript calendar of contents of Annesley papers in the Search Room which supersedes the descriptive account of a less comprehensive collection given by R.C. Singleton in *Analecta Hibernica*, 16 at p. 354ff; *Report of the Deputy Keeper of the Records for the Years 1960-1965* (Belfast, 1968), p. 191. **37** British Library, MSS Add 19851–58. Only eight volumes now survive of the eleven that originally comprised this collection: P.B. Phair, 'Sir William Betham's Manuscripts', *Analecta Hibernica*, 27 (1972) 60. **38** Lincoln's Inn Library, LI Misc. 391 (Wedderburn MSS, vol. XIV); J.H. Baker, *English legal manuscripts* (Zug, 1975), p. 109. The attribution is the present author's. **39** King's Inns Library, uncatalogued. **40** The relevant coverage will be found in collections that are located in the King's Inns Library, the Library of Trinity College, and the Public Record Office of Northern Ireland, respectively. **41** See, e.g., 1 Hudson & Brooke 308.

existed in manuscript only and which had been lent to the court by John Brook, QC.[42] In England as late as 1906, in a case concerned with the right to withdraw the licence of a notary public, the English master of faculties relied on a manuscript account of a judgment rendered by his Irish equivalent in 1860, Judge Keatinge.[43]

There is clear evidence, too, for the circulation of manuscript collections predating Vernon and Scriven. A preoccupation of the Irish bench and bar for upwards of a generation after the publication in 1775 of Howard's *Popery Cases* – the reliability of this compilation of penal law decisions – was to precipitate remarks that in the present connection are of the utmost interest. A marginal note to the report of *Dillon* v. *Dillon* in one of the volumes in the Hon. Richard Annesley collection of decisions observes that the report of the same case in Howard was extracted 'from hence and revised by LC'.[44] This illuminating detail is unlikely to have been added much after 1775. In regard again to the genesis of the Howard volume an amount of absorbing detail is to be gleaned from exchanges between counsel during the hearing of an appeal in the Irish House of Lords in 1794. In argument in *Barnewall* v. *Barnewall*, Prime Serjeant Fitzgerald launched an attack on Howard (who had died eight years earlier in 1786) and on his book. Arthur Wolfe, the attorney general, in reply, declined to offer any defence of Howard's character but, as to the worth of *Popery Cases*, forcefully maintained that 'every man conversant in the subject' could vouch for the authenticity of what Howard recorded. A fascinating résumé then ensues. 'The cases in that book, down to the year 1752', Wolfe explains,

> were printed from a manuscript, which was handed about from one lawyer to another, the late Mr Malone, Mr Harwood, and others. Howard, who was an active busy man, had an inclination to publish a collection of Popery Cases, and the vanity to pass for the author of them; he obtained a copy of the manuscript, and the cases subsequent to 1752, he procured from gentlemen of distinction; some from Mr Radcliffe, others from Mr Ridge, etc, and these gentlemen did carefully collate the cases before they were published. The case of *Ambrose* v. *Heffernan* was taken by a gentleman of the bar, who is still existing, and he reported the case with all possible accuracy, so that as to the authority of the cases, it is idle to say they were not decided.[45]

Evidence for circulation also derives from an examination of the legal manuscripts once in the possession of Christopher Robinson, who held office as a puisne judge of the Irish King's Bench from 1758 to 1787.[46] At some period in Robinson's career he acquired a collection of miscellaneous legal material that included notes of cases

42 *Davies* v. *Lynch* (1868) IR 4 CL 570, following *Jack d. Peoples* v. *Buchanan* (1836). **43** *In re Champion*, [1906] P. 86, following *O'Brien* v. *Bennett* (1860). **44** PRONI, D. 1854/4/7. What the letters 'LC' might stand for is anyone's guess. **45** 3 Ridgeway's P.C. 24 at 37 (the prime serjeant's attack) and at 45 (the attorney general's detailed response). The excerpt from the attorney general's response is reproduced in J.W. Wallace, *The reporters arranged and characterised with incidental remarks*, 4th ed. (Boston, MA, 1882), p. 551n. **46** F.E. Ball, *The judges in Ireland, 1221-1921*, 2 vols. (London, 1926), ii, pp 169-71 and 210 for details of Robinson's career.

expressed to be from Cornelius O'Callaghan's commonplace book spanning the years *c.*1716 to *c.*1730 and which are listed in the inventory given above. Notes of other cases either were made by Robinson himself or were transcribed for him, and the marginal annotations which are extensive throughout his manuscripts convey the unmistakable impression that Robinson regarded his collections as the working tools of a meticulous lawyer; they were not being set in aspic as objects of antiquarian interest alone. Nor would it appear to be accidental that, with the passage of years, Robinson came to acquire amongst his judicial brethren a reputation as the infallible oracle on the law and practice of an earlier generation.

Study and analysis of the eighteenth-century manuscript collections of Irish legal decisions have barely begun. The insight such scrutiny is likely to furnish into the local legal system of the period is self-evident. For instance, questions such as the frequency with which English precedent is cited and the manner in which reference to previous Irish authority is handled – to proceed no further down the list of possible questions – can definitely be answered. The practical uses to which the several collections may have been put are also deserving of attention. Naturally, the precise motivation behind the making of each compilation would, wherever this is feasible, first need to be established: a compilation undertaken as an educational exercise by a young bar student is different from one intended to serve as a thesaurus for an ambitious or conscientious practitioner, and different again from one embarked upon to provide a simple record, or for purposes of personal edification. Establishing motivation may not always be simple, and first impressions can mislead: James Lyne, in introducing John Wallis's reports to the public in 1839, indicated that he was unable to satisfy himself whether Wallis had ever intended to publish his collection or had merely compiled it for purposes of private reference.[47]

The final puzzle from Irish law reporting history to be examined here surfaces in the late 1870s. It will be necessary, first, however, briefly to survey the developments of the intervening years. Whilst the modern cycle of Irish reports commenced with Vernon and Scriven in 1787, coverage of the decisions of the superior courts was to remain erratic down to the 1830s, and even thereafter serious lacunae occur: cases that clearly merited being reported were somehow overlooked. With the breaking at the end of the eighteenth century of the taboo against native law reports, a profusion of nominate Irish reports made a belated appearance. Some of these attained a high standard, and all of them, conveniently for those who may wish to find out more, are now comprehensively listed by O'Higgins.[48] Approval of these developments is appropriately signalled by the instructive decision of 1840 in which Sir Michael O'Loghlen, the master of the rolls, upheld a claim to copyright in respect of a law report. The case, *Hodges and Smith* v. *Walsh*, deserves to be more widely known, not least because the reporter who reports it, with an eye to securing a niche in history himself, appends a note in which he expresses at some length his concurrence, predictably enough, with Sir Michael's forthright determination.[49]

47 Wallis by Lyne (n. 32 above), preface, p. v. **48** O'Higgins, *Bibliography* (n. 12 above), part 2, pp 13-60. **49** (1840) 2 Ir Eq Rep 266. The case is briefly cited in C.G. Moran, *The heralds of the law* (London, 1948),

Not everything continued to give satisfaction, however, and in the mid-1860s a movement in favour of altering the arrangements for law reporting in Ireland resulted in the establishment of the Irish Law Reporting Council. Two matters in particular are likely to have rankled. First, there was the enduring question of cases that escaped being reported altogether. In the early years of Ireland's nominate reports it was forgivable that a case from 1786 might be included in a set of reports ostensibly devoted to the decisions of 1794 or a case from 1817 in a set covering 1833 (provided each, of course, was adjudged to be of sufficient importance and thus deserving to be rescued in this manner from the prospect of almost certain oblivion).[50] It was likewise understandable that, before a proper standard of law reporting had been achieved, which reduced avoidable omissions to a minimum, authors of legal texts wishing to do justice to their respective specialist themes, should have insisted that they had no alternative but to include a collection of selected cases as an appendix – as Arthur Browne (civil law: matrimonial, probate and admiralty), J.C. Erck (ecclesiastical law) and John Finlay (tithe; landlord and tenant)[51] all do – or to incorporate into the substance of their works decisions of the courts that are otherwise unrecorded – a strategy adopted both by Howard and by James Lyne.[52] What was tolerated at the start, however, was later perceived as reflecting no credit on the profession; indeed, rather, the reverse.

Equally grave, in the estimation of the reformers, will have been the inferior calibre of certain of the reports, themselves the product of a succession of haphazard entrepreneurial initiatives. Many of the new reports, as has already been remarked, attained the highest standard; but others fell seriously short. The plagiarist and his modus operandi had been exposed to public gaze in 1840 in *Hodges and Smith* v. *Walsh*. More embarrassment occurred in subsequent years, in 1864, for instance, when the Irish Court for Crown Cases Reserved handed down its critical judgment on confession evidence in *R.* v. *Johnston*.[53] In this case, the precedential value of earlier Irish decisions in the area of confessions was carefully analysed and much unfavourable comment directed at the apparent absence of any provision for checking and authenticating the remarks of the judges.

The Irish Council of Law Reporting was set up in 1867, two years after its English counterpart. Daniel, in his *History and origin of the law reports*, makes clear the indebtedness of the Irish to those who had launched the earlier English innovation.[54]

p. 59. **50** *R* v. *Reily* (1784), a case dealing with the constitutional duties of sheriffs, is included in Ridgeway, Lapp and Schoales's Irish Term Reports of 1794, at p. 204. *A.G.* v. *Flood* (1817), a case touching on mortmain and where the focus was on an attempt, finally ruled unsuccessful, to endow a professorship of Celtic, is included in Hayes's Reports of 1833, at p. 611; it is there stated that the text of the proceedings including the judgments was made available by Serjeant Greene and Harstonge Robinson, Esq. **51** Arthur Browne, *A compendious view of the civil law*, 2 vols. (Dublin, 1797-9); J.C. Erck, *An account of the ecclesiastical establishment subsisting in Ireland* (Dublin, 1830); J. Finlay, *A treatise on the law of tythes in Ireland* (Dublin, 1828), *A treatise on the law of renewals in respect to leases for lives renewable for ever in Ireland* (Dublin, 1829). O'Higgins's *Bibliography* supplies further details of the contents of all of these books (at pp 359, 365-7), with the exception of Finlay's book on tithe. **52** E.g., G.E. Howard, *A compendious treatise of the rules and practice of the pleas side of the exchequer in Ireland* (Dublin, 1759); James Lyne, *A treatise on leases for lives renewable for ever* (Dublin, 1837). See further O'Higgins's *Bibliography*, part 8 (pp 357-85), passim. **53** (1864) 15 ICLR 60. See further J.D. Jackson, 'In Defence of a Voluntariness Doctrine for Confessions: *R.* v. *Johnston* Revisited', *Irish Jurist*, 21 (1986) 208. **54** W.T.S. Daniel, *The history and origin of the law reports* (London, 1884), pp 294-5.

Conceived in the spirit of the new-found professional ethos common on both sides of the Irish Sea, and aimed more especially to tackle the problems with which Irish law reporting was thought to be beset, the Irish council enjoyed a short honeymoon period when no criticism of its performance is recorded. The calm was rudely shattered a decade later, however, when a series of unprecedented and ferocious criticisms began to be directed at the council and its reports. What was even more extraordinary was the identity of the critic: Jonathan Christian, a distinguished member of the Irish judicial bench. Thus is the final puzzle introduced: what lay behind Christian's venomous and no-holds-barred one-man campaign?

Christian was appointed a puisne judge of the court of Common Pleas in 1858, moving on to become the lord justice of appeal in Chancery in 1867. His judgment in *In re Tottenham's Estate* in the following year caused a mild sensation.[55] The substance of Christian's criticisms – one was levelled at the practice of judicial patronage in Ireland – but more particularly the manner in which these were expressed ensured that the case lingered long in the folk memory of the Irish bar.[56] It is plain enough that the longer Christian remained on the bench, the more irascible his temperament became. In asides in court, in his published judgments and in letters to the newspapers, he made it transparently obvious that he did not suffer fools gladly. Unfortunately, perhaps, for Christian, his view of the world led him to place too many of its denizens within the latter category – not only trimmers and politicians (a predictable allocation) but also, more seriously, colleagues on the Irish bench and even his superiors in the House of Lords. Unsurprisingly, Christian was regarded as having gone much too far on one occasion, when a meeting of the Irish bar was convened to protest about his conduct. Unusually, for an Irish, or any, judge, he earned the distinction of being rebuked from the floor of the House of Commons on separate occasions by both Disraeli and Gladstone.[57]

Christian had earlier savagely assailed plans to reform Irish land law and the Irish system of courts, but his concentrated attack of the years 1877 and 1878 on the competence of the Irish Council of Law Reporting and on the quality of their law reports attained new heights – or, depending on one's point of view, plumbed new depths – in the art of judicial denigration. This remarkable episode has already been recounted by the late V.T.H. Delany,[58] but there was one facet to the controversy to which Delany did not choose to draw attention and this omission warrants a fresh examination here.[59]

A not untypical specimen of the violent language employed by Christian occurs in the course of the judgment he delivered in the case of *Hone* v. *Blanchi* in November 1877:

55 (1868) IR 3 Eq 528. **56** See, for example, the judgment of Kennedy CJ in *R. (Moore)* v. *O'Hanrahan*, [1927] IR 406 at 428. **57** Ball, *The judges of Ireland*, ii, 309-10, 359-60; Daire Hogan, 'Arrows Too Sharply Pointed: The Relations of Lord Justice Christian and Lord O'Hagan, 1868-1874', in John McEldowney and Paul O'Higgins (eds.), *The common law tradition: essays in Irish legal history* (Dublin, 1990), p. 61; V.T.H. Delany (see next note). **58** V.T.H. Delany, 'Lord Justice Christian and Law Reporting', *NILQ*, 12 (1956-8), 46. **59** What follows is based largely on the blow-by-blow and extremely detailed account furnished in the pages of the volumes of the *Irish Law Times and Solicitors' Journal* (*ILTSJ*) for both 1877 and 1878 (vols. 11 and 12, respectively).

> In the whole vast ocean of printed matter, since the days of Caxton, I venture to say that there could not be found within an equal space such a mass of utterly worthless rubbish as makes the staple of the eleven Equity volumes of the Irish Reports.[60]

Several months earlier Christian had used language only marginally less opprobrious, and to this, not unnaturally, the Council of Law Reporting had felt compelled to respond. Charge was met by counter-charge: battle was well and truly joined. Christian, for his part, was to bring forward allegations of negligence, mistake, suppression and of failing to consult with the judiciary. The council, in turn, defended its mode of operations, sustained the contentions of its reporters and denied everything.[61] The dispute attracted attention in the columns of the press in Dublin and much further afield. Where one organ of opinion would rebuke Christian for his 'ribald persiflage' or his 'untimely zeal', another would discover in his 'unmistakable honesty of purpose a redeeming virtue'.

Christian relented not at all. So disenchanted did he become with the performance of the council that he forbade publication of his judgments in the Irish Reports. Those that were actually published, many of which, like *Hone* v. *Blanchi*, continued his vendetta against the council, are in consequence only to be found in the pages of the *Irish Law Times and Solicitors' Journal*. In August 1877, a few months before *Hone* v. *Blanchi*, a high point was reached when the Dublin satirical magazine, *Zoz*, devoted a full-page cartoon to the whole sorry affair.[62] The embers of the controversy had not died down when, late in 1878, it was announced that Christian had resigned, on grounds of his increasing deafness. The former lord justice of appeal died in 1887.

From the barrage of accusations directed by Christian at the council, two in particular warrant attention. It was Christian's firm belief, first, that an alteration in the system of remunerating reporters had precipitated a serious deterioration in the quality of the reports in Ireland. Christian lamented:

> The truth is – and the sooner and the wider it is acted upon the better – these reports are the merest sham. Law reporting was respectable in Ireland so long as it was in the hands of enterprising and private publishers, and so long as the reporters were paid, not by salaries, but according to their work; but it has withered lamentably – nay, utterly, under the ridiculous aping of the great modern system of London.[63]

A second accusation, linked to the vexed issue of the selection of cases for reporting, is ignored in Delany's otherwise balanced and attractively written synopsis of the quarrel. The gap is regrettable, for the accusation, as it happens, constitutes a further important chapter in the debate initiated by Vernon and Scriven on the proper rela-

60 *ILTSJ*, 11 (1877), p. 586 at p. 593. **61** See *A statement by the Council of Law Reporting in Ireland in reply to the observations made by the Lord Justice of Appeal in Chancery on July 17, 1877*, with an appendix of correspondence (Dublin, 1877). **62** 'The Martyred Christian', cartoon by 'Spex' (John Francis O'Hea), *Zoz*, 4 August 1877. **63** *Mackey* v. *Scottish Widows' Fund and Life Assurance*, *ILTSJ*, 11 (1877), p. 358 at p. 360.

tionship of law in Ireland to law in England. It will be recalled that, in their contribution to that debate, the two early editors had sought to demarcate branches of Irish law where English precedent should continue to hold sway and other branches, such as statute law, property law and practice, where, because of the unique character of the indigenous legal rules, English precedent offered no guidance and Irish precedent should be permitted to develop and to be regarded as authoritative. Though they themselves are unlikely to have seen it in quite this light, in effect Vernon and Scriven here make an important concession in favour of those of their contemporaries opposed to the launching of any set of Irish reports *tout court.* However this may be, there is no evidence even so that in the intervening years what was implied for the practice of Irish law reporting by that concession – that it was right that the flow of English doctrine into many branches of Irish law should continue uninterrupted, and unimpeded by rival Irish doctrine – had been in any sense observed. The philosophy that had come to inform the practice of law reporting in the country, certainly by the time that Jonathan Christian went public on the question, was, rather, to report any case that was adjudged to be worth reporting. Nor is there a scintilla of evidence to indicate that the Irish judicial bench favoured subscribing to any kind of self-denying ordinance whereby they would deliberately decline to advance general common law doctrine and abandon intellectual labour of that elevated species exclusively to the courts in London. They conceded, naturally, as they were obliged to do, that the store of Irish judicial precedent was at the same time ever likely to remain of much more modest proportions.[64]

From the stance adopted by Christian during the quarrel of 1877–8, it looks far from unlikely that he would actually have favoured drawing up just such a self-denying ordinance and even recommending it for approval. 'It has long been an opinion of mine', Christian exclaims, in *Hone* v. *Blanchi*, in a passage remarkable even for him for its bluntness,

> that general law reporting in Ireland is a radical mistake; and for two reasons – first, if conducted on a respectable scale, it would not pay – the market is too limited – and the pretension could result in nothing but some miserably stunted product like that which is now exposing us to the derision of the stranger; secondly, it *ought not* to pay, as it would have no intrinsic value, for, constitu-

64 A good example is to be found in the judgment of Barry LJ in *Pirrie* v. *York-street Flax Spinning Co.* [1894] 1 IR 417 (a patent case connected with the Ulster linen industry): 'It is much to be regretted, for the sake of our country, that we have in the Courts here so little practical experience in the administration of patent law and the application of its principles. As evidence of this state of things, I may state the fact that this is only the third occasion, during the many years I have been on the bench, in which a patent case has ever been submitted to my judicial consideration. On the other hand, in England, as the necessary outcome of its exhaustless activity in commerce and manufacture, and the vast and varied fields which it affords for industrial enterprise, the law of patents constitutes a distinct, extensive, and most important branch of our jurisprudence, attracting to it largely, sometimes almost exclusively, the study, attention and advocacy of most eminent members of the bar, having attached to it a special class of practitioners, known as patent agents (who require and possess the most varied knowledge and acquirements), and having for itself a special literature, which, in very voluminous tomes, records patent cases independently of the volumes in which the ordinary decisions of our tribunals are reported.' (at p. 478.)

> tionally speaking, the decisions of Irish courts on points of general law lack the quality of binding authority.[65]

Warming to his theme, Christian then imparts what, doubtless, he regarded as a few more home truths:

> When one wants to know what is the law of Ireland on a point of general jurisprudence, there is always a previous question – What is the law of England; that is, by the Constitution, and has been, at least since Poynings' law, the relation to each other, in things legal, of the countries. But it is at Westminster and Lincoln's Inn that the *officinae legum Angliae* – the workshops for the manufacture of authoritative judge-made law – are only to be found. At the Four Courts we import that article; we do not manufacture it.[66]

Unabashed and undeterred, Christian proceeded to lead evidence to bolster another contention of his – a contention not unconnected – namely, that Irish case-law was held in low esteem in England. His adversaries repudiated this dismal verdict, drawing attention rather to a number of instances where the record showed Irish cases had been acclaimed in England. At this juncture the conflict between the antagonists degenerates into the bare recital of lists of cases from opposing inventories.

Our fourth and final puzzle – why Lord Justice Christian chose to mount his ferocious assault on the standard of Irish law reporting of his day – can be approached in one of two different ways. From what is known of Christian and of his general attitudes, it is tempting, in the first place, to posit an explanation that would otherwise almost certainly be viewed as quite far-fetched. It is incontrovertible that Christian was contemptuous of the abilities of a number of his judicial colleagues,[67] and it is implicit that he saw little benefit accruing to Irish law – or law anywhere for that matter – from the appearance of the judgments of these colleagues in print. Changing the ground-rules for the reporting of judicial decisions in Ireland – a course of action which, as we have seen, Christian strongly supported – would thus have bestowed what Christian might well have counted the inestimable boon of denying his brethren an outlet for their intellectual pretensions. It is an extreme thesis, probably deserving to be dismissed from consideration accordingly, but there is some evidence that can be adduced in favour of it.

The second approach involves taking the statements Christian uttered on the question of law reporting literally at face value. Driven by the conviction that there was a wrong needing to be set right, Christian finally spoke his mind at length and in detail. For doing so, we can at least feel grateful to him: the message he chose to convey could not have been plainer even if excessive resort to hyperbole forces one to become a trifle uneasy over its immoderate tone and, in consequence, over its precise merit. In Christian's estimation, the workshops for the manufacture of authoritative judge-made law were located comprehensively and exclusively in London. This was not by divine

65 *ILTSJ*, 11 (1877), p. 586 at p. 589. **66** Ibid. **67** See Hogan, 'Arrows Too Sharply Pointed'.

providence; it was a fact of life. And it was equally a fact of life that branch offices did not even exist in Ireland: at the Four Courts 'the article' was imported, it was not manufactured. Seen in this light, the dispute between the two sides in 1877-8 over the practice of law reporting in Ireland now assumes a more serious complexion. This was no dialogue of the deaf, fit only to be ignored or otherwise relegated to obscurity. Issue had been joined and a fundamental difference of attitude over the law and over its future evolution in Ireland revealed in all its nakedness to public view.

Differences of perception in regard to these matters were by no means unprecedented: the disputants of 1877-8 did not fail to air arguments that had been aired on other occasions in the course of the modern legal history of Ireland. The first puzzle investigated here, investigated from the perspective of the year 1615, concerned the question as to why Ireland had produced no early law reports or year books. The second, investigated from the perspective of' the year 1787, concerned that as to why the country produced no law reports between 1615 and then. If a major element in the explanation is – as the excerpts quoted above from Christian, our single nineteenth-century witness, invite us to hold – that down the centuries the lawyers of the common law tradition in Ireland consistently believed, or consistently believed in sufficient numbers, that the vital legal workshops for all general Irish purposes were physically located outside the country, then we have managed to solve at one fell swoop our first two puzzles.

What we have identified as the preferred solution to the fourth puzzle – that Christian believed in the intellectual dependency of Ireland in matters of jurisprudence and felt compelled to remonstrate with those who chose to close their minds to what he regarded as self-evidently true – touches on the same broad theme of the relationship of the two legal systems, the Irish and the English. The suggested solution to this final puzzle merits further consideration. At the very least, it would appear legitimate to inquire into how much actual favour Christian's views – both on the proper mission of Irish law reporting and on the future of Irish law – may have enjoyed amongst his contemporaries.

The matter is not easy to assess. One possible significant piece of evidence dates from 1873. That year the Irish judiciary had been faced with the prospect, contained in the Supreme Court of Judicature Bill brought forward by Gladstone's administration of the day, of the abolition of the appeal from Ireland to the House of Lords. They had reacted with undisguised horror and, in writing to the government in protest, alluded amongst other things to the need to preserve a tribunal which, they argued, contributed 'largely to the maintaining of uniformity in the administration of a common jurisprudence'.[68] Whilst the sentiment undoubtedly favoured retention of political union, it by no means did so either in the terms or in the language Christian would later choose to enunciate. In particular, support is conspicuously lacking for any notion that Ireland should be regarded as an intellectual dependency of England in

68 *Copy 'of the Resolutions of the Irish Judges in reference to the Supreme Court of Judicature Bill, as the same were transmitted to the Chief Secretary for Ireland, together with the letter of Baron Dowse which accompanied the same'*, HC 1873 (273), liv, 335.

matters of jurisprudence and should hasten to reconcile herself to that fact. We do not have the considered views of the more celebrated Irish judges of the last quarter of the nineteenth century on these weighty issues, neither those of Christopher Palles who in 1874 commenced his long tenure on the bench nor those of Gerald FitzGibbon or Hugh Holmes, whose preferment came later, in 1878 and 1887, respectively. Yet it is easy to imagine what those views would have been: each one would assuredly have dismissed Christian out of hand.[69]

A doubt nonetheless lingers: might Christian even so have articulated an attitude that was shared albeit by a small minority of his contemporaries? Caution in approaching the question is advised, for, turning to a similar state of affairs alleged to have existed within the confines of Irish fiction (another compartment, if a rather different one, met with in the intellectual history of the island), we find the claim being advanced, almost certainly correct, that Ireland lacked a recognisable literary culture prior to 1800, the year which saw the publication of Maria Edgeworth's *Castle Rackrent*.[70] The observation underscores the value of attempting to quantify the support for, and the opposition to, Christian's much-trumpeted belief in the intellectual dependency of Ireland, a belief that was, admittedly, articulated by him relatively late in the nineteenth century. If Christian did in fact misread the situation – as seems not improbable – it would be useful nevertheless to establish when the situation itself had changed; when, to express it in plain language, members of the judicial bench in Ireland had come to think of themselves in every way the equals of their counterparts in England.[71]

Solving one ingredient of our third puzzle – making sense of the surviving eighteenth-century manuscript reports – remains a formidable challenge to the Irish legal historian. As the work unfolds, it is possible that enough will emerge to enable an answer to be proffered to a fifth puzzle that these pages have willy-nilly brought into focus as well: when can we date the first manifestations on the Irish judicial bench of the possession by them of the sense of a confident, all-embracing and independent indigenous legal tradition?

69 Much can be inferred from the judgments delivered by the members of the Irish Court for Crown Cases Reserved in the important rape case of *R.* v. *Dee* (1884–5) 14 LR Ir 468. **70** See, e.g., Barry Sloan, *The pioneers of Anglo-Irish fiction, 1800–1850* (Gerrards Cross and Totowa, 1986), p. 240. **71** If intellectual history is viewed as a unity – perhaps an unwarranted assumption – a later observation of Sloan's is not without interest in the present context (*Pioneers of Anglo-Irish fiction*, at pp 243–4): 'The best English novels of the period introduce a much wider range of interests, and generally contain more complex and profound explorations of character and morality, than their Irish counterparts. This locates a key thematic difference between nineteenth-century fiction in the two countries, for the Irish were only beginning to answer questions of national identity which were well-established certainties for the English, which they felt no need to debate endlessly.'

Catholics, Land and the Popery Acts of Anne

From 1704 until 1778 – for the greater part of the eighteenth century in fact – a rigorous legal code sought to emasculate the rights of catholics in Irish land. Comparable legislation existed in England too but that in force in Ireland contained a number of features designed to render the latter more effective. In addition, there was the crucial difference, to which attention has often been drawn, that Ireland's penal laws in matters of religion (of which the present code formed so prominent a part) were directed at the religious majority and not, as in England or in France (in which last country sides were switched), at a religious minority.

If the precise sequence of events behind the framing of the vital clauses of the Irish code remains obscure,[1] the motivation behind the code's promulgation is plain. There is retaliation for wrongs suffered in the past and there is an attempt to secure the avoidance of any repetition of these wrongs in the future. Contemporary judicial understanding proceeded along such lines. Sir Richard Cox, chief justice of the Irish queen's bench, was to declare in 1714:

> Too many of them [the papists] think we are incorrigible rebels and have no title to our lands nor much to our goods; and consequently if they had opportunity would think it meritorious to deprive us of both.[2]

Cox went on to regale his audience, the County Kilkenny grand jury, with a series of predictable references – references to 'the woeful experience' of 'our ancestors' 'in the barbarous and bloody rebellion of 1641' and to the act of attainder passed by James II's 'sham' Irish parliament of 1689 that had been aimed even at women and children, even at 'some who had never seen the kingdom'. At the other end of the chronological spectrum, nearly sixty years later, in 1771, another member of the bench, Lord Annaly, then chief justice of the Irish king's bench, talked in similar vein:

> If we consider the situation of this kingdom at that time, the intention of the legislature will appear pretty clearly to be, to prevent papists acquiring any more landed property than what the statute allows them. The act [of 1704] was made by many of those persons who had suffered so severely during the short reign of James the second, and by the disturbances which afterwards followed, and who do not seem to want resentment for the injuries they suffered, nor a desire

1 J.G. Simms, 'The making of a penal law (2 Anne, c. 6) 1703-4', *IHS*, 12 (1960-1) 105. See also the English statutes 1 Anne, c. 26 and 7 Anne, c. 29. **2** Quoted in W.P. Burke, *The Irish priests in the penal times 1660-1760* (Waterford, 1914), p. 192.

> to free their posterity from the like inconveniencies, by lessening the popish interest in this kingdom.[3]

Judicial acceptance of, or acquiescence in, such explanations is significant on its own account. In addition, however, that acceptance was to colour the approach of successive generations of Irish judges to the resolution of various problems of statutory construction arising under the code. The latter fell to be categorised, the judges tell us, not as *penal*, in which case a rule of strict interpretation would have been warranted, with consequential benefit to catholics, but rather as *remedial*, where a rule of liberal interpretation was required, with consequential harm to them. As one lord chancellor expressed it in 1726, 'tho' this is a penal law, yet it is not to be construed as other penal laws, for it is a remedial law also, and made to prevent a mischief from the increase of papists in this kingdom'.[4] That view was regularly repeated. There is a particularly forceful expression of it by Mr Justice Robinson, a judge of the Irish king's bench, in 1759.[5]

In retrospect, it is remarkable that the assault unleashed on the economic power of the catholic should have concentrated exclusively on the latter's interests in land. Throughout, catholics remained at liberty to acquire wealth from involvement in commercial activity. A corollary entailed that money bequeathed by a protestant to a catholic stayed immune from legal scrutiny, a rule that the Irish exchequer affirmed in court proceedings in 1768.[6] In their endorsement of that decision in the ensuing appeal, the British house of lords (which was to play a major role in the evolution of the jurisprudence of the code) accepted that any rule to the contrary 'would be most impolitic in a commercial country'.[7] But to contemporaries there was no mystery about the reasons for the focus to the code:

> The possession of land and social and political power were so closely intertwined that the obvious way of weakening catholicism was to prevent the amount of land in catholic ownership increasing and offering the catholic landowner the choice between conformity and the fragmentation of his estate.[8]

The code, directed so comprehensively at the right of the catholic to enjoy, inherit and purchase land constituted, from the outset, a formidable legal edifice. When every allowance is made for the relaxations occurring later, that is what, essentially, down to 1778, it remained.

The code itself is located in separate groups of clauses in two statutes enacted by the Irish parliament in the reign of Queen Anne, the statute 2 Anne, c. 6 of 1704, 'an act to prevent the further growth of popery', and the statute 8 Anne, c. 3 of 1709, 'an act for explaining and amending an act intituled an act to prevent the further growth of popery'. Some degree of familiarity with both will prove helpful.

3 *Lessee of McCarthy* v. *Hanly*, Howard 196. 4 *Ogle* v. *Archbold*, Howard 14. 5 The laws were to be regarded 'as remedial and constitutional …, made for the preservation and security of the protestant interest and establishment in this kingdom' (*Tomlinson* v. *Farrell*, Howard 121 at 154). 6 *Gilbert* v. *Cusack*, Howard 176. 7 Ibid. 8 R.B. McDowell, *Ireland in the age of imperialism and revolution 1760-1801* (Oxford, 1979), p. 177.

Section 3 of the measure of 1704 contained the inducement to the eldest son of the catholic freehold owner to conform to the established protestant church. Electing to do so, from the moment he had completed the prescribed formalities (no light requirement), such son became entitled to the reversion of the land in fee, a reversion burdened admittedly by the incumbrances of debts already incurred and by the cost of making provision out of the estate for any brothers or sisters by way of maintenance or the raising of portions. At the same instant the convert's catholic father was metamorphosed into a mere tenant for life. The conforming eldest son was given a statutory right to maintenance and such right section 8 also extended to other children electing to conform. Froude anathematised these provisions as 'an encouragement to the disobedience of children',[9] as any Victorian parent perhaps would have felt obliged to do, yet the combination of the burden represented by prior incumbrances and of that of finding support for brothers and sisters may have caused tentative converts among eldest sons to think again and postpone action. Even where the convert pressed ahead regardless, sought his pound of flesh, and family dissension broke out, culminating, as it was wont to do, in some expensive, protracted and unpleasant family lawsuit, victory, should the convert attain it, could regularly prove, if more than Pyrrhic, considerably less than total. This would appear to be the apt verdict to give on an episode left on record in the history of the O'Conors of County Roscommon. In the 1750s, Hugh, a younger son of Denis O'Conor, having conformed, made the attempt, as his brother Charles was later to put it, 'to wrest ... the poor plank that brought my father to shore after the great wrecks of the family fortune in 1698'. A protestant family, the Frenches, held mortgages on portion of the O'Conor inheritance, however, and the O'Conors who remained catholic had the grim satisfaction to learn after the standard gruelling, costly and prolonged lawsuit, that the claim of the Frenches was to be given precedence over the claims of Hugh, 'the apostate and perjurer'. Hugh, nevertheless, did reap some financial benefit.[10]

Another major family quarrel, over a maintenance claim and much else besides, that broke out earlier in the century between the Blakes of Menlogh, County Galway, resulted, after two lengthy hearings in the Irish chancery and an appeal in the principal lawsuit to the house of lords, in final victory for Thomas Blake, the conforming eldest son, and defeat for Sir Walter, the catholic father. If the account of this affair in the law reports is to be credited, the father had been so incensed at his son's change of religion and marriage to a protestant that he stopped at nothing in his efforts, ultimately adjudged forlorn, to deny that son any of the family wealth. Undeniably, here, too, the resultant sequence of interconnected lawsuits involved both Thomas and Sir Walter in substantial financial outlay, a topic of mutual recrimination, it would seem, even during the hearing of the house of lords appeal.[11]

9 J.A. Froude, *The English in Ireland in the eighteenth century*, 3 vols. (London, 1872-4), i, p. 368. **10** *The O'Conor papers: a descriptive catalog and surname register of the materials at Clonalis house*, eds. G.W. and J.E. Dunleavy (Madison, 1977), pp xi, 28, 44. **11** *Blake* v. *Blake* (1724) 5 Brown 747, 2 Eng. Rep. 369. Thomas survived his father by one year: *Blake family records 1300 to 1600*, ed. M.J. Blake (London, 1902) p. 152. Ironically, the validity of Thomas's conformity certificate of 1716 came to be doubted and was to be the subject of prolonged judicial investigation a century later (*Loveland* v. *Lynch* (1814) 2 Dow 324, 3 Eng. Rep.

Section 7 of the act of 1704 tackled one aspect of inheritance. Any catholic who took property by devise, descent, gift, remainder or trust had six months in which to conform to the established church. Failing that, for the rest of his life or until he should change his mind, the interest was transferred to the nearest protestant relative.

A different aspect to inheritance was dealt with by section 10, in terms from which there was to be no escape. In a significant departure from contemporary practice, this section set aside, so far as catholic families were concerned, the common law rule of inheritance by primogeniture, replacing it with a species of gavelkind. Where a catholic held land in fee simple or fee tail and had not disposed of it during his life for good consideration, the new dispensation, inaugurated by this gavelling clause, envisaged descent in equal shares to all the sons and, in default of male issue, descent in equal shares to all the daughters. Section 10, besides introducing a rule of fragmentation, also effectively signalled the legislative abolition of the testamentary freedom of the catholic landowner,[12] a freedom which his protestant compatriot, in complete contrast, continued to enjoy.[13] Articles in catholic family settlements that bore on their face no trace of conflict with the philosophy of the gavelling clause might manage as before to pass muster.[14] Furthermore, where property was handed on from generation to generation as a result of a succession of fathers begetting only sons, it was possible for a large landholding to remain in catholic ownership, a piece of good fortune that was to befall the Kenmare estate, for instance.[15]

Section 12 regulated one matter outstanding. The gavelling clause did not come into force where an eldest son conformed within three months of his father's death.

Fresh acquisitions of land, like continuing enjoyment and inheritance of it, were equally the object of legislative restriction. 'Every papist', another critical section, section 6, stipulated,

> shall ... be disabled to buy and purchase in his or their own name or in the name of any other person or persons to his or her use or in trust for him or her, any manors, lands, hereditaments, or any rents or profits out of the same or any leases or terms thereof, other than any term of years not exceeding 31 years, wherein a rent not less than two thirds of the improved yearly value at the time of making such leases of the tenements leased, shall be reserved and made payable during such term.

All such species of acquisition were declared to be null and void.

The second popery act, the statute 8 Anne, c. 3, set out to strengthen the earlier act in a number of different ways. Section 3 concentrated on the financial relationship between a catholic parent and conforming children: in bringing any doubt on the matter to an end, it confirmed that the court of chancery possessed a continuing discretion to revise upwards the level of any such children's maintenance. Section 11 stiff-

881; see also *Macnamara* v. *Lynch* (*c.*1800), Rowe 489). **12** See *Burke* v. *Morgan* (1717) 5 Brown 365; 2 Eng. Rep. 734. **13** Confirmed by 2 Anne, c. 6, s. 13. **14** See *O'Fallon* v. *Dillon* (1804) 2 Sch. & Lef. 3. **15** *The Kenmare manuscripts*, ed. E. MacLysaght (Dublin, 1941), p. xi.

ened the formal requirements that governed conformity to the established church, 'to show the sincerity of the party'.[16] Section 27 brought miscellaneous kinds of collateral security within the range of interests in land that catholics, under the provisions of section 6 of the act of 1704, were disabled from acquiring.

More significantly, section 27 also recast the enforcement machinery for the entire code. The section introduced the protestant discoverer. The act of 2 Anne had been content, like its earlier English counterpart,[17] simply to declare the purchases of land and the forms of lease prohibited to catholics null and void. The act of 8 Anne, however, borrowing an innovation from an English act of the preceding year which had dealt with forfeited Clanricard land in Ireland,[18] conferred *locus standi* on any protestant whatsoever to sue in respect of all property transactions forbidden to catholics. Assuming the discoverer was in a position to establish 'a discoverable interest' and to adduce proof of the prohibited transaction, the prize flowing from success at law was very great: the land or lease was to be adjudged his to enjoy for the duration of the particular interest it had been intended wrongfully to convey.

The discoverer clause represents, alongside the gavelling clause, one of the more unusual elements in the entire code. Given the rudimentary character of the existing enforcement machinery recognised by Irish law, the transfer, in a penal law context, to the domain of civil litigation of a figure better known to the criminal courts, if not unprecedented either in the history of Irish law or, to go back much further in time, in the history of Roman law, was not altogether a surprise. Mr Justice Robinson of the Irish king's bench, in observations made in 1771, thought as much. 'The inserting the discovery clause in 8 Anne', he noted in a judgement delivered that year, it was universally believed 'would animate our popery laws'.[19] And so, he reckoned, it had: whereas in the years between 1704 and 1709 only 36 'conformists' had been recorded, for the ten-year period after 1709 that number had jumped to 150. The verdict appears unassailable.[20] Yet for the years following 1709 it needs to be understood that the history of the discoverer and of discoveries was destined to evolve in a welter of contradictions. The result was a degree of confusion which helps to explain why, for so long a period, both the Irish judges and Irish legal profession manifested a marked reluctance to describe and to admit what was actually afoot. Ultimately, the responsibility devolved upon Lord Redesdale, the English equity practitioner and politician appointed to succeed Clare as Irish lord chancellor in 1803, to begin the process of clarification and demystification, a process by then long overdue, which even today it may not be safe to regard as altogether complete.

A range of procedural and evidential issues was disposed of by section 30. Their importance, in view of what was to follow, can scarcely be disregarded either. The section sanctioned the employment of the expeditious bill of discovery and imposed procedural and evidential handicaps on defendants as a class. In salient part, it provided as follows:

16 The phrase is that of counsel for the respondent in *Carroll* v. *Vicars* (1731) 5 Brown 396; 2 Eng. Rep. 754. **17** 11 & 12 Will. III, c. 4 (Eng.). **18** 7 Anne, c. 29. (Eng.). **19** *Lessee of McCarthy* v. *Hanly*, Howard 196 at 210. **20** *The convert rolls*, ed. E. O'Byrne (Dublin, 1981), p. xiii.

> be it further enacted ... that it shall and may be lawful for any protestant or protestants to prefer one or more bill or bills in his majesty's high court of chancery or chancery of the exchequer, against any person or persons concerned in such sale, lease, mortgage or incumbrance, and against all persons privy to such trust or confidence for papists ... and to compel such person or persons to discover and detect such trusts and confidences, and to answer to all matters and circumstances relating thereunto, as by such, bill or bills shall be required; to which bill or bills no plea or demurrer shall be allowed, but the defendant shall answer the same at large upon oath; which answer shall be good evidence against the defendant in actions to be brought upon this act, as in such cases are usual, and that all issues, to be tried in any action or suit founded upon this act, shall be tried by none but known protestants.

As befits a legislative creation that advanced on so broad a front, the two acts of Anne contained miscellaneous additional clauses on a host of subsidiary matters. A conspectus of the complexities of early eighteenth century Irish land law is thus gratuitously furnished. The sort of extra matter dealt with is best exemplified by reference to three more sections in the act of 2 Anne. Not only did this measure extend the disabilities imposed by an earlier act of 1697[21] on the so-called constructive papist, a protestant inter-marrying with a catholic (s. 5), it also banned catholics from acting as guardians (s. 4) and repeated[22] the transfer to the crown of all rights of ecclesiastical patronage wherever a catholic came to be possessed of an advowson (s. 5).

The impact on catholics of the provisions contained in the two acts of Anne, at once so extensive and so detailed, was potentially major. There existed another grouping in Irish society, however, who were not left unaffected either – the lawyers. In 1789 Lord Earlsfort, the then chief justice of the Irish king's bench, noted that when the popery acts of Anne were in force they constituted 'the principal topic and source of emolument in the profession'.[23] The importance of the code in contemporary legal practice and the interest shown in it by both branches of the profession were highlighted in other ways: the case-law that grew up furnished the incentive for the publication by G.E. Howard in 1775 of the single collection of Irish law reports of any substance to appear between 1615 and 1790[24] and explains the predominance of Irish material appearing under the heading 'papist' in Tomlins's much expanded, rearranged second edition of Brown's *Parliament cases*, published in 1803.[25] An explanation for this state of affairs is not hard to supply. The words of the code itself and recognition of the existence of omissions from it were soon seen to raise a battery of technical problems, the answers to which, judged in strict legal terms, were not always straightforward or wholly predictable. Might, for instance, the eldest son of a deceased catholic father go

21 9 Will. III, c. 3. **22** Cf. 17 & 18 Chas. II, c. 2, s. 158. **23** *Earl Fauconberg* v. *Birch*, 2 Ridgeway 147 at 161. **24** G.E. Howard, *Several special cases on the laws against the further growth of popery in Ireland* (Dublin, 1775). **25** Josiah Brown, *Reports of cases upon appeals and writs of error in the high court of parliament from 1701 to 1779*, 2nd ed., with notes and many additional cases brought down to 1800 by T.E. Tomlins, 8 vols. (London, 1803). The 1st ed. of Brown's *Parliament cases*, 4 vols. (London, 1779-81), contains far fewer Irish popery act cases but does include one – on a contested guardianship – not to be found in the 2nd ed.

through the motions of conforming to the established church and thus prevent the activation of the gavelling clause even though he was a lunatic?[26] Or would it be licit to probate a will made by a testator, an avowed protestant at the time, and divide the inheritance according to his instructions, even though there might be evidence to suggest that he had later died a catholic?[27] Did, for example, the entitlement of a discoverer to have decreed to him the particular discoverable interest vest at the moment of the exhibiting of the bill of discovery or rather at that of the pronouncement of the decree in his favour?[28] And what test of conformity, it might have been solicited, was properly applied in the case of a protestant discoverer one of whose parents was demonstrated to have been a catholic?[29] There were problems too with a conflicts of law or constitutional flavour. For instance: were the rights of a discoverer in relation to Irish interests made discoverable under the provisions of English legislation determined by English law or determined by Irish law?[30] And there were problems of a transitional nature. Did an interest vested in possession by virtue of a power created prior to 1704, but only exercised subsequently, constitute a discoverable interest?[31] Issues of retrospection loomed large too.

It became the business of the Irish lawyer to find the answer to these and a host of other questions that were raised. Where doctrinal clarification of matters of central importance was needed an emerging consensus within the profession might suffice. Thus it came to be tacitly accepted that the only species of judgement debt capable of constituting an incumbrance on the estate of a catholic for purposes of the gavelling clause in section 10 of the act of 1704 was one that met the most stringent of standards: at the very least the original transaction had to be shown to be bona fide and the parties at arm's length.[32] This was a critical determination in view of the importance of the judgement debt in the credit economy of Ireland of the period and indeed for long afterwards. In similar fashion, the decision to regard interests vesting in possession under the terms of catholic family settlements as falling within the range of 'discoverable interests' appears, at the outset at least, to have owed little to any preceding judicial enlightenment:[33] such acquisitions amounted to 'purchases' within the land lawyer's understanding of that technical term of art, and came to be universally so regarded.

Unsurprisingly, in a litigious age, many other matters of central importance were by way of contrast probed in depth in the courts. Two puzzles linked to leases of land will serve as examples. First, did a lease in favour of a catholic satisfying the requirements on duration and rent laid down by section 6 of the act of 1704 but which was

26 *Butler* v. *Butler* (1773) Howard 265. **27** This conundrum was posed by Serjeant Eyre during the hearing of an appeal in the English king's bench on a writ of error from the Irish king's bench in *Rice* v. *Oatfield* (1738) 2 Strange 1095; 93 Eng. Rep. 1054. **28** *Rives* v. *Roderick* (1729) Howard 49. **29** *Clarke* v. *Parsons* (1754) Howard 98. **30** *French* v. *Daly* (1727) Howard 27; cf. *Woodley* v. *Bernard* (1753) Howard 117. **31** *Stone* v. *Rice* (1721) Howard 71. **32** *Earl Fauconberg* v. *Birch* (1789) 2 Ridgeway 147. If it were seriously arguable that any species of judgement debt constituted a recognised incumbrance, Lord Earlsfort CJ asked (at 161): 'can it be imagined that papists during that whole period naturally wishing to exercise every act of dominion over their property, to gratify their pride, their affections, their resentments, should never have ventured to bring this question into the courts?' **33** But see *Farrell* v. *Crosbie* (1773) Howard 256, and the reference back to *Stone* v. *Rice* (1721) Howard 71.

expressed to commence at some future date, constitute a discoverable interest? A decision of the British house of lords in 1719, on an appeal from the Irish exchequer in the case of *Cusack* v. *Bulkley*,[34] held that it did, but confusion somehow persisted and a few years later it was only on the receipt of the unanimous opinion of the Irish judges that the legal position was quite clear that the Irish house of lords was dissuaded from introducing the heads of a bill that would have finally dispelled all doubt.[35] Predictably, in two cases dealt with in 1729, leases otherwise satisfying the terms of section 6 but expressed to commence, in the first case, in one month's time and, in the second, in five months' time were both held to be discoverable.[36] Thereafter, for many years, this particular issue seems to have lain dormant. In 1772, however, in the proceedings in *Windis* v. *Power*,[37] it was decided to challenge an interpretation that by then had been accepted for over fifty years. Counsel chose his ground well: the lease in favour of the catholic tenant in the case satisfied the express requirements of section 6, it had been made eight years earlier and it had entered into force only two months after it had been made. Counsel went on to dissect the language of section 6 and to assail *Cusack* v. *Bulkley*. Practical considerations too were urged: it was an inconvenience on both sides that no long lease with a catholic tenant could be drawn up until the very day on which the lease was stated to commence. In his peroration counsel did not forbear to address an appeal to the court's inherent sense of justice:

> It would at this day be a most severe construction of this statute of 2nd of Anne to give a poor man's interest after eight or ten years' possession to a common informer where the least under-value in point of rent is not even suggested by the bill, and is absolutely denied by both the answers; and where from the shortness of the reversion (but two little months) it was manifest that neither this unfortunate papist or his landlord had the least intention of evading or eluding the law.[38]

The lord chancellor, Lord Lifford, was not unmoved by these arguments: it was, he admitted, 'a hard case'.[39] The force of precedent was too great, however, and he felt compelled to grant a decree in favour of the protestant discoverer. (Happily, for the tenant, the British house of lords was prepared to adopt a markedly different stance).[40]

A second critical question, not, apparently, exhaustively or comprehensively examined on any occasion prior to 1770, concerned voidable leases and the rights, if any, capable of being created under them. Might a catholic in possession of a lease voidable as a discoverable interest yet be acknowledged to be at liberty to pass a valid sub-lease to a protestant so as to enable good title to be made on an ejectment? The matter arose at the assizes in Clonmel, County Tipperary, when Lord Chief Justice Clayton answered the question in the negative. A bill of exceptions was then argued in the king's bench in Dublin early in 1771.[41] Howard prints judgements for each of the three

34 5 Brown 369; 2 Eng. Rep. 737. **35** See *Gardner* v. *Plunkett* (1728) Howard 61. **36** *Gardner* v. *Plunkett*; *Skellen* v. *Kearney* (1729) Howard 64. **37** Howard 217. **38** At 228. **39** At 230. **40** Howard 357. **41** *Lessee of McCarthy* v. *Hanly*, Howard 195.

judges: Lord Chief Justice Annaly, Mr Justice Robinson and Mr Justice Henn. Only one unsatisfactory Irish case was found to be germane but a large number of English decisions on comparable difficulties were to hand and the thrust of these, coupled with the philosophy stated to underlie the first of the two popery acts, confirmed, in the estimation of the court, that Lord Chief Justice Clayton's approach had been impeccable. The court reserved its special scorn for the pragmatic argument that, since the lands in contention had passed into the hands of a protestant and this was 'the end and intention of the act', it would be best to leave things as they were.[42] Mr Justice Robinson saw deeper objections:

> The other construction [to the effect that a valid sub-lease could have been granted] would make papists the land jobbers of the kingdom; they would be constantly buying lands in order to sell them again; it would multiply parties so much that discoverers in the courts of equity never could hear their causes; the papists might convey to three hundred persons, who then must all be brought before the court; if one in thirty should die, when could the causes be heard?[43]

Mr Justice Henn agreed but it is noteworthy that, alone of the three, he hesitated: evidence existed to show that actions for debt had been brought in respect of rent due under discoverable leases and he was aware that such actions had succeeded.[44] To the modern lawyer, familiar with the Latin tag 'ex turpi causa non oritur ius' ('from a base consideration no legal right can arise'), such inconsistency naturally remains bewildering.

A third question of doctrinal significance under the code and of general application proved troublesome and prompted regular recourse to the courts: the question of the precise requirements that had to be satisfied before conformity of the catholic convert to the established church could receive official endorsement and the disabilities otherwise attaching could for legal purposes be disregarded. Proven conformity secured the lifting of disabilities and the consequential conferment of privileges in each of the stated contexts: conformity of the eldest son, conformity of the other children, conformity to defeat the operation of the gavelling clause, conformity of the convert spouse. The requirements themselves differed and the time within which the various stipulated acts had to be performed could differ too. Moreover, sight should not be lost of the fact that the act of 1709 introduced more stringent requirements 'as the strongest ties which human policy could invent', to confirm the sincerity of the conversion:[45] in addition to the rules regarding the bishop's certificate (as to conformity itself) insisted upon by the act of 1704, the later measure demanded the presentation and enrolling of a second document (the sacramental certificate).

The vexed question of whether there had been compliance with the conformity requirements contained in the two popery acts surfaced in a number of cases litigated many years after the main body of the code had been dismantled. In 1804, in one of these lawsuits, Lord Redesdale let drop the trite observation that 'one of the ill conse-

42 At 204 (Lord Annaly CJ). **43** At 213. **44** At 214. **45** *Carroll* v. *Vicars* (1731) 5 Brown 396 at 402.

quences' of the acts of Anne had been the inducing of a 'pretended conformity'.[46] The risk naturally had been identified from the beginning, and in the circumstances it is scarcely cause for amazement that the courts – both the Irish courts and the British house of lords – should have paused to examine with such scrupulous care as they plainly did the precise credentials of the supposed convert and, in particular, the actual certificates tendered by him or her as proof of conformity. For so long as the conformity rules applied, in fact for the duration of the code itself, it is incontrovertible that on virtually every occasion when a problem arose, the judicial approach to the relevant issues of substantive law was extremely strict.

In 1725 the then Irish lord chancellor handed down a decision that represented a breach in the ranks,[47] but this aberration was swiftly disowned in a series of cases where insistence on strict compliance was reaffirmed. In one case, a husband and wife seemed set to lose everything where the convert wife took too long to complete the prescribed formalities.[48] In a second, *Vicars* v. *Carroll*, an exchequer case of 1728, the outcome had been similar.[49] The protestations of counsel had again availed nothing. He had invited the court to sympathise with the plight of 'a number of good protestants and honest subjects who had the misfortune to be born of popish parents' should they forfeit everything as a result of an insistence upon strict compliance.[50] There was mention of the presumed legislative intent and of the emergence of anomalies caused by differences in the quality of legal advice, in another passage in counsel's speech:

> Nor could it ever be the intention of the legislature to disable a good and fair protestant because he did not to a day perform the requisites of the said second act, or, as may be said, because he turned protestant without the advice of counsel how he should turn.[51]

Against this background of settled doctrine, the legal challenge mounted in the *cause célèbre* of *Tomlinson* v. *Farrell* (1758-61)[52] must by any standard be counted both remarkable and reckless.

On 26 November 1741, before he had attained the age of 21, a member of the O'Farrell family, variously referred to as Edward or Roger, embarked upon the exercise of conforming to the established church. (At some stage he was also for good measure to drop the 'O' of his surname.) In a Church of Ireland church in Dublin he made the required declaration that he regarded himself as a protestant and renounced the errors of Rome. A few days later the appropriate certificate was forthcoming from the archbishop of Dublin and this was filed early in December in the rolls office of the Irish chancery. In May 1742 Farrell received communion according to the rites of the established church, securing the appropriate sacramental certificate shortly thereafter. On 26 May Farrell produced, proved and filed this second certificate in the court of king's bench, the same day subscribing the necessary further declaration and

46 *Butler* v. *Moore* (1804-5) 2 Sch. & Lef. 249 at 262. **47** *Evans* v. *Quin*, cited in *Vicars* v. *Carroll* (1728) Howard 33. **48** *Rives* v. *Roderick* (1729) Howard 49; the sequel is to be found in *Roderick* v. *Osborn* (1731) Singleton 92. **49** Howard 33. **50** At 42. **51** At 38. **52** The accounts of this important case in Howard and Brown need to be read in tandem: Howard 121; 5 Brown 438 (2 Eng. Rep. 782).

taking the oath of abjuration. On 23 August he finally filed in the rolls office a third certificate testifying to the fact that he had previously taken the oath of abjuration and subscribed the declaration. For purposes of any calculation to be made subsequently, the critical dates were 26 November 1741 and 26 May 1742, a period of exactly six calendar months but rather more than six lunar months (which expired on 13 May 1742) if the calibration was to be made by reference to lunar rather than to calendar months.

Twelve years later, in 1754, Farrell, now in business as an attorney and – it would appear – possessed of none too scrupulous a business character, purchased at a knock-down price the manor of Mornine in County Longford. A year later Tomlinson exhibited his bill of discovery, alleging that at the time Farrell had acquired Mornine he was disqualified on the grounds that in 1741 and 1742 he had not completed the prescribed formalities for conforming within the stipulated period of six months. According to standard common law doctrine, that period fell to be reckoned in terms of lunar months. In short, Farrell, it was asserted, had filed 13 days late.

Tomlinson v. *Farrell* was argued at length, first in the Irish chancery, then in the Irish king's bench where the vital factual issues had been ordered to be tried and where the illuminating judgements of Lord Chief Justice Caulfield and Mr Justice Robinson which Howard prints were delivered, and finally in the British house of lords. Each tribunal insisted on strict compliance. Lunar months had been in contemplation and attorney Farrell had filed too late. The upshot was that Mornine was decreed to Tomlinson. Several years afterwards, Mr Justice Robinson looked back with pride to his judgement in the case.[53] At the time he had proffered this defence of the stance of the judges:

> The legislature has required the removal of the disability, by solemn acts of notoriety, for taking or keeping their family estates; and it would, in my opinion, be unreasonable to suppose, against the letter of the law, an intention to leave converts looser as to acquiring new property; which in the common course of things must be a more likely means of continuing and keeping up a landed interest.[54]

Language of this sort plainly influenced the British house of lords who had not yet learned the art of disowning Irish judicial precedents in the penal law sphere, though this was to change with noted alacrity in the years ahead. It did not impress the Irish parliament, however, who moved swiftly to initiate a major legislative change, a development which will be pursued later. In one respect the decision in *Tomlinson* v. *Farrell* was demonstrably incongruous and parliamentary interference therefore no surprise: the decision marked a divergence from a tradition in Irish equity jurisprudence reaching back to the early years of the century under which laches or delay was viewed in far less serious a light. The context admittedly was different: whether an obstacle exist-

53 In *Lessee of McCarthy* v. *Hanly* (1771) Howard 193 at 213. **54** *Tomlinson* v. *Farrell* (1759) Howard 121 at 134.

ed to the renewal of a lease for lives where the lives had fallen in and no one had remembered in time to replace them. A new equitable doctrine, the legacy of Chief Baron Gilbert, held that in such circumstances there was no insuperable obstacle to renewal.[55] Attorney Farrell might legitimately have complained that what was sauce for the lessee ought, in the ordinary course of events, and if justice existed in this world, likewise to have been regarded as sauce for the convert.

The challenge presented by the need to furnish doctrinal clarification of the substantive law of the code resulted, as we have seen, almost uniformly, in the reaffirmation of its stark anti-catholic bias. But there was another facet to the endeavours of the eighteenth century Irish legal mind in the penal law sphere, a facet to which similar prominence requires to be accorded. 'The acts', wrote Froude at the end of last century, 'were not, as a whole, carried out with the triumphant recklessness of a dominant faction'.[56] So far as the land law clauses in the two popery acts of Anne are concerned, this judgement is sound. Two factors, in equal proportion, contributed.

T.E. Tomlins notes in his report of the Irish penal law case of *Woodley* v. *Cue* decided in 1757 that in the same fashion as the medieval churchman learnt to evade the statute of mortmain, the Irish catholic became equally adept at evading the clauses in the two acts of Anne.[57] The assessment is broadly true: the years immediately following the adoption of the two acts witnessed the elaboration, by a succession of legal advisers, of a range of devices deliberately tailored to circumvent the effects of the legislation. The ingenuity so conspicuously and so frequently on display says much about the professionalism of the eighteenth century Irish lawyer, whether attorney or barrister, a breed that now perhaps for the first time emerges into the light of day. That so much intellectual effort should have been expended on the attempt, sometimes proved vain but more commonly successful, to secure a form of insurance, adjusted to the needs of the individual catholic family, possesses of course its negative aspects. Nor should a blind eye be turned to the unsavoury personalities inhabiting this legal underworld of surreptitious contrivances. Here were to be encountered the sharks, a collection of Uriah Heeps Irish-style, who were only too eager, lured on by the prospect of financial gain, to batten on to the catholic and also, too, the protestant, who had been caught unawares and found themselves ensnared in the toils of the law.

That legal advice was canvassed by members of the catholic landowning class once it became clear that the popery bill of 1703 was about to be enacted into law is undeniable. A flurry of activity took place in the weeks leading up to 23 March 1704, the very day the act of 2 Anne, c. 6 came into force. The better view remained that pre-1704 family settlements were generally left unaffected by the new act, but it is noteworthy, when matters were reviewed later, that in the second act of 1709 the Irish parliament should have chosen to give retrospective effect to the earlier ban on new settlements in violation of the act of 1704 so as to catch all settlements drawn up between 1 January and 23 March that year.[58]

55 For a useful summary of these developments, see the judgement of Lord Lifford, lord chancellor, in *Boyle* v. *Lysaght* (1787) Ridgeway 384 at 403–8. **56** Froude, *English in Ireland*, i, p, 374. **57** 5 Brown 421; 2 Eng. Rep. 770. **58** 8 Anne, c. 3, s. 6.

Predictably, the act of 1704 had proscribed the use of the trust device to enable both freehold and leasehold interests to continue to be enjoyed by catholics: the prohibition was clear-cut but its effectiveness was to be considerably curtailed, as we shall learn, once standards of proof came to be altered. The act of 1709 followed this up with a ban on annuities charged on estates which previously it had been contended were 'only personal and not real inheritances' and so not comprehended within the terms of the prohibition on the purchase of lands and tenements (s. 1). The same section of the 1709 act, in another move to check evasion, purported equally to outlaw the taking by catholics of a range of collateral securities including mortgages.

Devices successfully employed to circumvent the operation of the two acts ranged from the simple and straightforward to the much more sophisticated and complex. Pressure might be applied to younger sons to induce them to abstain from exercising their rights under the gavelling clause: there is plenty of evidence from recorded lawsuits that this occurred regularly. Where it was appreciated that a thirty-one year lease had been granted to a catholic tenant on terms that were too favourable and that the entire arrangement accordingly constituted a discoverable interest, one solution, when some protestant discoverer was rumoured to be on the prowl, was for landlord and tenant collusively to fabricate a successful action in ejectment, enabling the first lease to be replaced with a second.[59] A supply of leases with different starting-dates and expressed to be in favour of a protestant lessee might equally prove advantageous,[60] though here, very clearly, security was a paramount consideration: it would never do if a trunkful of fabricated legal documents should come to light in the attic.

Marriage law offered temptation for other forms of manoeuvre. In the case of *Rives* v. *Roderick* in 1729 the defendant had exhibited a bill of discovery in respect of two leases then in possession of Osborn, a catholic.[61] Three weeks later he married Osborn's daughter, Elizabeth. (Unfortunately for Roderick, he then failed to ensure that Elizabeth completed the formalities required of a convert spouse within the time prescribed). *Gooding* v. *Palmer*, decided the same year, is the reverse side of the coin.[62] Here a husband would seem to have gone to inordinate lengths to repudiate marriage to a catholic wife, thereby escaping from the category of 'constructive papist', defeating the plaintiff's bill of discovery and saving his inheritance. A church court had earlier upheld the validity of this particular mixed marriage, but Palmer successfully appealed against that decision to the court of delegates. Gooding protested that Palmer and his 'wife', 'by agreement and contrivance', had prevailed upon the delegates to pronounce their definitive sentence against the marriage. He invited the lord chancellor to launch a fresh investigation into the entire matter, but the latter declined.

Rives v. *Roderick* almost certainly involved resort to one singular device regularly utilised as a means to thwart the operations of the penal land law code: the collusive discovery.[63] The scale on which collusive discovery was practised is impossible to quantify. The supposedly collusive discoverer certainly makes an early appearance in

59 *The Kenmare manuscripts*, p. 186, where details of such a ruse resorted to on the Kenmare estates in 1758 are given. **60** See *Woodley* v. *Cue* (1757) 5 Brown 421; 2 Eng. Rep. 770. **61** Howard 49. **62** Howard 47. **63** See also the sequel, *Roderick* v. *Osborn* (1731) Singleton 92.

the reported cases. In the Blake litigation from the 1720s, already referred to, Sir Walter sought to trump his son Thomas's bill of discovery against him with an ace in the shape of a second bill of discovery ostensibly brought in the name of one John Murrey: Thomas, however, successfully moved his interpleader to prevent the hearing on the second bill from going ahead first, the court being satisfied that Murrey was acting in fact on behalf of Sir Walter.[64] *Ryland* v. *Green*, from the 1730s, is essentially a dispute between two discoverers.[65] Green was first in the field but died. The son unsuccessfully sought from the court permission to exhibit a bill of revivor. Ryland, an attorney, who had likewise exhibited a bill of discovery in respect of the identical subject-matter, an equity of redemption conveyed to a catholic named Fitzgerald, was alleged by Green junior to have been acting in conjunction with Fitzgerald and as a trustee for him.

There is an explanation of the collusive discovery and related legal matters from Lord Redesdale, in a passage in a judgement of his of 1804.[66] Relieved from the burden of concealing the truth which, for some reason best known to themselves, previous generations of Irish judges had elected to assume, and determined to admit the light into a number of dark corners, Lord Redesdale offers in this vignette very considerable insight. The passage merits extended quotation:

> In consequence of the acts of Queen Anne, if any conveyance were made of an estate to a papist, into whatever hands the estate might afterwards come, the tide was always in peril from a protestant discoverer; and the titles of many persons, protestants as well as papists, were liable to be thus impeached. They could not by themselves cure this defect in their titles; but were compelled for that purpose to set up some other person as a discoverer, who might obtain a decree against them founded on the defect, and then by conveyance make good their defective title. The courts therefore properly held that a protestant discoverer might be a trustee for a third person; and generally that third person was the person bona fade entitled to the estate, if the blot had not existed. This principle was proceeded on in so many instances, that it would perhaps have tended to set afloat half the titles in the kingdom, if it had been held that a protestant discoverer could not be so set up, though manifestly in collusion with the person in possession, whose title he was to impeach. But to prevent evasion by this contrivance of the popery laws, if a protestant discoverer held in trust for a papist, the estate was again subject to discovery, and might be decreed to a new claimant; but not so, if he held in trust for a protestant. Thus the courts seem to have determined through a long course of decisions: the case of *Dillon* v. *Dillon*[67] proves this: and I think the question must be considered as quite at rest, and the law must be deemed to allow of setting up a protestant discoverer as a mere instrument, like the common vouchee in a common recovery, to complete the assurance of land.[68]

64 *Blake* v. *Blake* (1724) 5 Brown 747; 2 Eng. Rep. 369. **65** (1738) 5 Brown 403; 2 Eng. Rep. 759. Earlier stages in this important lawsuit are recorded at Singleton 272 and 452. **66** *O'Gorman* v. *Comyn* (1804) 2 Sch. & Lef. 136. **67** (1772) Howard 231. **68** 2 Sch. & Lef. 144.

Lord Redesdale's remarks open up a vast prospect. It appears possible that a good crop of discoveries, perhaps even the majority, may ultimately have had little to do in any strict sense with the enforcement of anti-catholic laws. They constituted rather episodes in a conveyancing exercise as dull and uncontentious as the identification of the common vouchee in a common recovery, with which indeed Lord Redesdale establishes a parallel. Where, however, in a proportion of cases at least a genuine protestant discoverer presented himself, clever strategy might ordinarily have ensured that little was hazarded: through, for instance, the precautionary selection of some compliant protestant trustee to be held in readiness as a powerful legal adversary should the need arise. If the trustee held on behalf of a catholic, as must frequently have been the case, that interest was discoverable (though, as we shall see, court decisions were to make it increasingly difficult to prove it). Where a second trust intruded, the genuine discoverer was faced with instant defeat.

Some of the consequences of these developments may be briefly itemised. First, individuals went into business as professional discoverers. Second, bills of discovery themselves became marketable commodities.[69] Third, the courts appear to have thought better of the decision in *Ryland* v. *Green* and began to authorise the issuance of bills of revivor where the first discoverer had died before judgement but had taken the precaution of assigning his rights to another party.[70] That reversal of stance can certainly be interpreted as a minor effort to invigorate an anti-catholic code but another, equally plausible, and less emotive explanation is to hand – practical convenience.

The second factor that contributed to the relative ineffectiveness of the various legal provisions, incontestably an achievement that fell well below expectation, has hitherto been largely ignored. There is little indication prior to the 1770s that, in regard to the penal land law code, the judiciary were prepared to modify their interpretation of matters of substantive or symbolic importance. But in relation to less visible controversies, over matters of procedure and equitable doctrine for instance, the evidence of the records confirms that there were limits, limits based on the profession's general understanding of what was right and proper and lawful, beyond which the judiciary were not prepared to travel, not even on behalf of the cause of anti-popery which on occasion was heralded as close to sacred and which some of them at least may have found congenial enough. In the modern era the evolution of legal rules has enjoyed a momentum uniquely its own, a momentum, naturally, never totally isolated from the influence of the prevailing cultural milieu but equally by no means subservient to it. Plant a new code of law in a legal environment the product of many centuries' growth, and it is highly probable that that code will not prosper in quite the fashion intended: qualifications will be attached, modifications made, distinctions drawn, usually for the avowed purpose of ensuring that not too much violence is inflicted on settled and professionally understood modes of doing business. This was to

69 PRONI, *The penal laws (education facsimiles 101-120)*, no. 110. This is a facsimile of a conveyance of Rowland Kane's interest in certain lands in County Fermanagh to Hugh Montgomery, 27 April 1742. Montgomery had paid 5*s*.; the interest concerned lands in relation to which Kane had recently exhibited a bill of discovery. **70** See the typically full entry under the heading 'revivor, bill of' in *Jacob's law-dictionary* (for reference see n. 118 below).

become increasingly obvious in the practice of the courts with regard to the interpretation and application of the critical provisions of 2 Anne, c. 6 and 8 Anne, c. 3.

A significant judicial gloss, for instance, was to be read into the bald statement contained in section 30 of the latter statute that no pleas or demurrers would be permitted to bills of discovery. An attorney was destined not to succeed with a claim to legal professional privilege under an imagined exception to this provision – an adjudication made at a preliminary stage in the case of *Ryland* v. *Green*[71] – but might there not exist some factual situations where it was essential, in order to preserve an appearance of justice, to admit certain other exceptions? To that question the Irish judges were to give a clear affirmative answer. In *Gooding* v. *Palmer*, in 1729, the Irish chancery refused to sanction a fresh inquiry into the defendant's marital status; in so doing, the court in effect allowed the latter's plea that that issue was foreclosed by a definitive sentence of the competent ecclesiastical court.[72] *Redford* v. *Butler* in 1769 furnishes another illustration.[73] This case examined the scope of the section 30 prohibition in a context to which it had been extended: bills of discovery linked to the statutory proscription of foreign enlistment.[74] The defendant, Lord Dunboyne, who had earlier enlisted for foreign military service, was nevertheless in possession of a royal pardon and on the strength of this opposed the bill of discovery. Section 30 said nothing about this precise case which led Dunboyne's counsel to protest that even so some form of modification was imperative. The Irish lord chancellor agreed and allowed Dunboyne's plea and demurrer: otherwise, merely for the plaintiff to suggest that the defendant had been in French service might suffice to secure the defendant's title.

In the practical evolution of the two acts of Anne chancery and equity exchequer played the crucial role since it was before these courts that bills of discovery could alone be exhibited. The jurisdiction of the two courts was not coextensive. Only chancery was authorised to review financial relationships within the family whenever an eldest son conformed, or whenever children generally conformed. Both courts, however, exercised a jurisdiction in equity and that entailed that they possessed the power to prevent the unscrupulous from deriving benefit from the strict letter of the law. Both situations are worth exploring: the undutiful conforming son and the practice of fraud.

It is evident that the lord chancellor's aid was frequently sought in the readjustment of financial relations within a family consequent upon the conformity of the eldest son. In a case from 1743 concerning the Archbold family, there were nine other brothers and sisters, and for the purpose of maintenance and the raising of portions, the lord chancellor authorised the sale of the stipulated one-third of the inheritance. The report supplies details, not always otherwise forthcoming, on the careers of the other members of this catholic family: a sister was a nun abroad, a brother a priest abroad, a second brother a merchant in Spain and other brothers again abroad in military service.[75]

71 (1733) Singleton 272. **72** Howard 47. **73** Howard 181. **74** Under 19 Geo. II, c. 7: 'an act for the more effectual preventing his majesty's subjects from entering into foreign service; and for publishing an act of the seventh year of King William the Third, intituled, an act to prevent foreign education'. **75** *Archbold* v. *Archbold* (1743) Howard 38.

The chancellor's jurisdiction was entirely discretionary, affording him the opportunity to investigate all the family circumstances and enabling him to award a decree grounded on his personal conception of what was just and reasonable. Throughout the existence in force of the relevant legal provisions, a parade of reprobate conforming eldest sons was doomed to be given short shrift. Froude reports Cusack's case from 1705.[76] There is more detail available in *Fitzpatrick* v. *Fitzpatrick*, decided in 1745.[77] Here the conforming son had made an imprudent marriage and had remained undutiful. The chancellor awarded as maintenance the lowest defensible minimum: not for him the placing of the prodigal on his elevated biblical pedestal.

As we have seen, the incidence of collusive discovery assumed major significance in eighteenth century Irish conveyancing. The practice bordered on fraud. Deliberate fraud, on the other hand, was different from pragmatic fiction, and was perceived to constitute a hazard and would appear to have been firmly rebuffed from the beginning. Quantification of the amount of deliberate fraud inspired by the two popery acts of Anne is now impossible. It may be thought a useful exercise nevertheless to present an inventory of manifestations of this form of wrongdoing of which a record of sorts survives.

One episode is concerned with a thirty-one year lease, granted some time in the 1720s by Sir Gerald Aylmer to one of his catholic tenants, Patrick Plunkett. The lease was expressed to commence in a month's time, and was, therefore, discoverable. A discoverer, one Gardner, obtained a decree from chancery in his favour. But matters did not end there. Aylmer subsequently set on foot his own inquiries and was satisfied that what had happened was that Plunkett had conspired with Gardner to extricate himself from what he had come to regard as a hard bargain: in other words, a catholic tenant had resorted to fraud to secure a benefit for himself under the penal land law code. Howard reports that Aylmer's own suit alleging fraud against both Plunkett and Gardner was later compromised.[78] In a similar case very soon afterwards, the lessor of another lease fit to be impugned on the basis that it was granted to a catholic and was expressed to commence in future would appear to have orchestrated the ensuing lawsuit to avoid his own lease, setting his brother-in-law up as the discoverer.[79]

In the 1770s, an attorney called Daly was active in handling claims on behalf of creditors against an already heavily incumbered catholic estate, managing at the same time to line his own pocket in the process. An associated lawsuit brought to a final conclusion in 1804 enabled the then chancellor, Lord Redesdale, to castigate the conduct of Daly as iniquitous and to repudiate the conduct of the barons of the Irish exchequer court who in the 1780s had handed down a series of decrees that had in effect favoured Daly. The extraordinary outcome in this early nineteenth century litigation was that Lord Redesdale went on to allow claims based on articles contained in a catholic family settlement dated 1764, almost certainly of no legal effect at that particular date.[80]

76 Froude, *English in Ireland*, i, p. 373. **77** Howard 90. **78** *Gardner* v. *Plunkett* (1728) Howard 61. **79** *Skellen* v. *Kearney* (1729) Howard 64. **80** *Kennedy* v. *Daly* (1804) 1 Sch. & Lef. 355.

A proctor from Kerry with the surname Blennerhassett is identified as yet another villain in the draft of a bill that it had been intended to exhibit in the exchequer and which survives in the Kenmare family papers.[81] Blennerhassett, it would seem, had given erroneous advice when two catholic brothers approached him for his help in connection with obtaining a grant of administration over their deceased father's estate. He had then turned the tables on both, and engaged a succession of discoverers and a disreputable attorney in the exchequer called Franks to further harass them with legal proceedings, 'all of which actings and doings', the brothers mournfully recite in their bill, 'are contrary to equity and good conscience'. It is not known if matters were taken any further. One detail merits comment. The identification in these obscure sources of two professional miscreants, the attorneys Daly and Franks, hints at the possibility – it can be put no higher than that – of the more regular perpetration of abuses in the Irish court of exchequer.

The scope of the two popery acts of Anne began to be narrowed in a number of respects from the early 1760s. On the legislative front, the affirmation by the British house of lords of the decisions of the Irish courts in *Tomlinson* v. *Farrell* served as the catalyst. That affirmation provoked an immediate reaction, since insistence on strict compliance with the requirements on conformity left in an exposed legal position not merely the supposed convert himself but also the protestant purchaser deriving title from him. A series of enactments, commencing in 1761, was designed to supply the remedy. The first in the series, 1 Geo. III, c. 13, 'an act for quieting the possession of protestants deriving under converts from the popish religion', sought, as its title indicates, to protect from challenge any interest held by a protestant derived from a convert who had failed to complete the stipulated requirements. Provided the convert had filed the bishop's certificate and had continued to profess the protestant religion, the protestant deriving title from him secured protection. This same act was also intended to protect the position of the convert who had failed to comply with the conformity requirements. Such a convert was given extra time in which to complete the formalities – up to 25 March 1763. In the interval, provided no lawsuit had already been commenced, claims were frozen and protection was accorded. Later legislative measures repeatedly extended the time within which the convert could complete the formalities for conformity.[82] Where a lawsuit was pending and the matter was not, therefore, covered by legislative enactment, repetition of the result in *Tomlinson* v. *Farrell* remained a foregone conclusion.[83]

Other legislative responses to the furore occasioned by *Tomlinson* v. *Farrell* proved of equal importance. In 1761 the 'act for the security of protestant purchasers'[84] protected the protestant purchaser for full value even though the land acquired had been, prior to purchase, vulnerable to seizure on the various grounds spelt out in the two popery acts: such purchases, it was declared, were 'not to be impeached for disability or forfeiture'. Further legislation, introduced two years later and confirmed

81 Exchequer bill (draft) in the case of *Ferris* v. *Blennerhassett*, n.d. but probably 1730s or '40s: *The Kenmare manuscripts*, pp 341–2. **82** 3 Geo. III, c. 26, s.3 (until 1 Dec. 1765); 5 Geo. III, c. 15, s. 5 (until 1 Dec. 1767); 7 Geo. III, c. 20, s. 7 (until 1 Dec. 1768). **83** As in *Nugent* v. *Nugent* (1762) Howard 136. **84** 1 Geo. III, c. 12.

in 1773, outlawed residual challenges based on stale claims: henceforth, no claim affecting an interest acquired over twenty years before and based on an alleged prior violation of the popery acts was cognisable in the Irish courts.[85] All these measures were designed to consolidate the protestant landed interest. Yet they represent an important relaxation in the two popery acts of Anne, for in the process the sweep of both measures was being appreciably reduced.

Proof of a growing awareness of the inconvenience of the legislation and perhaps also of its dubious worth is supplied by decisions of the courts subsequent to 1761, principally those of the British house of lords. Most of these decisions concern procedural matters but there is at least one major reversal of pivotal doctrine prior to the commencement in 1778 of the process of legislative dismantling.

Collusive discoveries were linked with trusts in favour of catholics: it was the existence of the latter and the calculation that they would prove effective that precipitated resort to the collusive discovery. For the true protestant discoverer and indeed for the courts too, a critical question throughout concerned the method of adducing proof of the existence of such trusts. Debate on the issue long regarded as controversial was finally brought to an end by the decision of the British house of lords in 1762 in the case of *Low* v. *Espinasse*.[86] The plaintiff-discoverer sought to have decreed in his favour a lease granted to Espinasse by the dean and chapter of Christ Church, Dublin, on the grounds that Espinasse held as a trustee for catholics. In his contention, parol evidence was enough: to go further and to insist on written proof of such trust 'would be a certain means of furnishing an evasion of the act'. The barons of the Irish exchequer agreed but the house of lords upheld Espinasse's appeal, Lord Mansfield insisting that the trusts in contemplation of the two popery acts lay within the scope of the Statute of Frauds and proof in writing was required.[87]

A further pro-catholic, and anti-penal law, bias may be detected in developments in another area of procedural complexity: post mortem proof as to the religion in which a man died. It was one thing for a catholic to convert to protestantism: it was a different thing altogether, in the eyes of the law, for such a convert to have relapsed and died a catholic, since then the various statutory disabilities once more began to operate.

Early case law betrayed little opposition to evidence of such matters being given, and given orally. In 1729, the British house of lords affirmed a decision of the Irish chancery where the central issue was the religious persuasion at the moment of death of a Sir George Maxwell. The circumstances of the case were a trifle unusual: Sir George had been born and bred a protestant but was nonetheless rumoured to have died a catholic.[88] (The principles applied by the courts extended equally to such a case.) Another lawsuit, centring on a Sir Robert Maxwell, had a similar result, the Irish chancery authorising a bill to perpetuate testimony as to Sir Robert's religious persuasion – it was alleged he had died a catholic – ten years after his death.[89]

85 3 Geo. III, c. 12; 13 & 14 Geo. III, c. 25. The prohibition on the launching of stale claims is judicially considered in *Kelly* v. *St. George* (1771) Howard 193. **86** Howard 142. **87** 7 Will. III, c. 12. **88** *Close* v. *Ross*, cited in *Rice* v. *Oatfield* (1738) Andrews 222; 95 Eng. Rep. 372 **89** *Close* v. *Hamilton* (1729) Howard 30. It is not impossible that these two cases are in fact the same. On bills to perpetuate testimony see again

The question arose again in 1738 in *Rice* v. *Oatfield*, an ejectment action originally tried in the Irish king's bench: had Edward Rice, at the time he had granted a lease, been competent to do so?[90] Rice had conformed in 1716 but it was contended that he had relapsed prior to his death four years later. Counsel argued strenuously that proof of Rice's relapse needed to be strict – say, proof of proceedings under the provisions of the act of 1695 'to restrain foreign education' for relapsing:[91] it would be perilous to rely on oral evidence. Neither the Irish king's bench nor the English, to which an appeal from the former was brought, were convinced. For both courts the difficulty lay in the belief that it would have been virtually impossible to enforce the relevant statutory provisions unless oral evidence was permissible.

At some stage the Irish equity courts effected a significant reform, by refusing to adjudicate on the question of religious status themselves and directing rather that it be tried as an issue in the common law courts. New problems then arose regarding the circumstances in which it was proper to direct an issue on the question and the challengeability of any such direction. Between 1760 and 1767 the British house of lords offered substantial enlightenment on both problems.

The conundrum posed by the first of the cases, *Swan* v. *Dr Stephen's Hospital*, concerned the religious persuasion at the time of his death in 1752 of Edward Cusack of Athboy and Dublin.[92] Cusack in his will had made a gift over in favour of the hospital, the interest that Swan set out to discover and secure for himself, convinced that Cusack had died a catholic. Since the hospital, in strict law, was a protestant charity, counting among its governors the Irish lord chancellor who, with perfect rectitude, withdrew from the case, it smacked of oddity, as the hospital's counsel was swift to point out, that a catholic, if indeed Cusack had been one, should have chosen to endow it:

> though popery may admit works of charity as well as faith, they are rarely employed out of the pale of their own church, and still more rarely to counterwork the increase of that persuasion, in favour of one with which it is at perpetual enmity.[93]

The question presented to a specially constituted court was whether chancery should direct an issue to be tried in common pleas as to Cusack's religion at the time of his death. The matter had already been the subject of investigation by an examiner, who had heard the testimony of witnesses in Dublin, and evidence had also been taken on commission in the country. It appeared that Cusack performed the role of 'an ostentatious protestant' all his life. Nevertheless, Swan had assembled an impressive team of witnesses who were, so he maintained, in a position to tell a different story. The specific contentions were that Cusack had been present several times at mass 'seeing it sometimes through a window', that he kept company with catholics and catholic

the entry under that heading in *Jacob's law-dictionary*. **90** Howard 77; 2 Strange 1095 (93 Eng. Rep. 1054); Andrews 222 (95 Eng. Rep. 372). **91** 7 Will. III, c. 4, s. 6. **92** Howard 136; 5 Brown 429 (2 Eng. Rep. 776); Burke, *Irish priests*, p. 246. **93** 5 Brown at 436 (H.L.).

priests, especially one Plunkett, that he helped to rebuild mass-houses, and that he permitted mass to be celebrated in his coach-house. It was also claimed that, in addition to a niece, the priest Plunkett had been in attendance upon him the evening of his death; it was finally urged as significant the circumstance that Cusack had directed that his body should lie uninterred one night in a common barn.

Counsel for the hospital had his own answer to many of these allegations. One witness had come forward who was prepared to testify that Cusack had been seen going on crutches to the protestant church in Athboy 'when troubled with gout and scarcely able to stand', and then receiving the sacrament. There was a curious explanation for the presence of Plunkett in Cusack's house on the evening of his death: Plunkett, the niece and Cusack constituted a threesome at cards. Other evidence furnished an innocent explanation for controverted acts of Cusack. The latter had conversed with priests but only 'in the way of business and in the common acts of good neighbourhood'. Counsel felt the evidence on his side was sufficiently strong to enter a protest against any decision to direct an issue, particularly since, as he contended, it was wrong in principle to bring a man's religion to public trial six years after he was in the grave.

The Irish chancery (Baron Dawson, Mr Justice Marshall and Master Walker) reckoned that Swan had an arguable case and directed that an issue be tried. Overturning this procedural ruling in the British house of lords, Lord Hardwicke indicated that different circumstances might have yielded a different result:

> Had the estate been left to private persons, for charitable purposes generally, he should have suspected a concealed trust, and perhaps for superstitious uses. But being left to a public charity and parliamentary trustees there could be no room for such suspicion.[94]

Nor could Lord Hardwicke resist a thrust at the motivations of Swan. At the hearing in the Irish chancery, counsel for the hospital had condemned a possible victory for Swan on the grounds that a wresting back by the latter of the estates from the hospital would amount to an inversion of the law in order to destroy the very interest that the law was designed to preserve. Lord Hardwicke took this as his cue: 'The respondent might style himself a protestant discoverer, but he was in reality only a common informer.'[95]

In the affair of Edward Cusack, the house of lords chose not to preclude the possibility, in appropriate circumstances, of a directed issue. Five years later, when the same broad question was agitated, the eventual outcome makes it difficult to see if any circumstances whatsoever could conceivably thereafter have warranted a reference to the common law courts. In *Meade* v. *Hobson* the nephew of Dr John Meade surfaced as a protestant discoverer, and attempted to have the will of his uncle set aside on the grounds he was a catholic and sought to be decreed as his uncle's heir-at-law.[96] The nephew was able to produce witnesses to show that the testator, despite his career at

94 Howard at 139. **95** Ibid. **96** Howard 154; 5 Brown 446 (2 Eng. Rep. 787).

the Bar and having fulfilled certain of the requirements on conformity, had continued to attend catholic services. Again, a formidable body of testimony appears to have been available and although counsel for the defendant sought to stigmatise these witnesses as 'but a few illiterate, superannuated persons, of the lowest class of people', they could have been speaking the truth. The barons of the exchequer obviously decided they might have been doing so too, for they directed that an issue be tried at law. To the perhaps equal consternation of the nephew and of the barons of the exchequer, the house of lords again set aside the Irish court's procedural direction.

Where the protestant discoverer failed to secure an order for a directed trial, he might yet remain at liberty to pursue the question on his own initiative in the common law courts. A time limit was applied, usually of 12 months. If matters had not progressed any further by the time a year had elapsed, the bill of discovery stood dismissed. In 1765, in a case connected with the religious profession of the late Lord Kinsale, the Irish lord chancellor refused to direct an issue, and when the year had expired and the option extended had not been taken up, dismissed the bill of discovery. In the resultant appeal, concluded in 1767, the British house of lords, in the last of this trio of cases, promptly affirmed the lord chancellor's conduct of the litigation and his dismissal of the claim.[97]

In regard to the post mortem proof of religious affiliation the salient rules had undergone very substantial alteration. In the earlier period oral evidence was received and bills to perpetuate testimony allowed. Later the equity jurisdictions preferred to refer the question to the common law courts. Later still, not even that option appears to have been encouraged. In relation to trusts in favour of catholics, proof via the Statute of Frauds always remained a possibility. In the rather different context of post mortem proof of religious affiliation, legal evolution appears to have determined that proof was effectively to be shut out altogether. Plainly, a form of legal latitudinarianism was in the ascendant when the law precluded the discoverer from adducing proof on the religious convictions of the decedent from whom the chosen victim derived his interest.

It remained for the house of lords to upset one pivotal doctrine of substantive law. As we have seen, it had long been established – by judicial decision and judicial opinion – that leases in favour of catholics otherwise lawful but expressed to commence at some future date nevertheless constituted discoverable interests. In 1772, in *Windis* v. *Power*, despite the forceful arguments of counsel in favour of relaxing the rule, the Irish lord chancellor affirmed it.[98] Later the same year, the house of lords reversed that decision, thus setting at nought legal doctrine that had prevailed in Ireland for over fifty years.[99]

Windis v. *Power* inaugurated a major departure. The decision delighted Howard who singles it out for special praise in editorial matter contained in his *Popery cases*.[100] It is worth noting that this reversal of doctrine was the achievement of the house of lords, who had glimpsed an opportunity and taken it. In general, the Irish bench at this

97 *O'Grady* v. *Kinsale* (1767) 5 Brown 456; 2 Eng. Rep. 794. **98** Howard 217. **99** Howard 357. **100** Howard 296.

period, in stark contrast, appears to have shown little enthusiasm for initiating modifications at any level. The exceptions amount to very little. Mr Justice Henn, we know from Howard, was tempted to dissent in *Lessee of McCarthy* v. *Hanly*, but in the end forbore to do so.[101] Three years earlier, in 1768, the then Irish lord chancellor, Lord Lifford, had come closest to supporting an Irish judicial reappraisal with his frank avowal of a different approach to the canons of statutory interpretation applicable to the code:

> It is not for me to consider whether these laws are penal or remedial, nor to animadvert upon them; I must take them as they are; they are the laws of the land, and as such it is my duty to see them executed. In giving my opinion upon the present point, I shall have no regard to private feelings of individuals or sects; I shall inquire what was the meaning and intent of the legislature, which is the only solid rule of construction.[102]

But if this held out the promise of a new approach amongst the Irish judges, any such approach was decidedly slow to materialise. Within the Irish Bar, on the other hand, there appears to have existed genuine awareness of the movement in favour of relaxation, considerable professional support for it and, undoubtedly too, a desire to translate that support into concrete legal changes. An extract from the argument of counsel in the *Windis* case itself evokes the intellectual climate within elements of the Irish Bar on the eve of major legislative reforms. The same extract furnishes a useful check-list of modifications that had been made to the code and perceived by contemporaries as such:

> These laws were made at a time when it was thought to be impossible that a papist could be a good subject to a protestant prince; but a long state of probation since these laws should soften such opinions; and accordingly the modern constructions on these acts of parliament are much more lenient than the ancient; for instance, formerly where an interest was decreed to a discoverer, an account of the profits from the commencement of the discoverable interest was also decreed to him, but now the account is only from the filing of the bill; formerly a gavelling claim was held not to be barred by the statute of limitations, but now it is held to be within that statute; formerly a trust for a papist, denied by the answer, might be proved by parol; and now it is held to be within the Statute of Frauds, and must be in writing; and many other cases might be cited, if necessary.[103]

In 1778, the torch passed from the British house of lords and the Irish Bar back to the Irish parliament. That parliament had been invited at intermittent intervals in the 1760s and 1770s to introduce certain modifications in regard to mortgages and longer leases but, with the exception of a law enacted in 1772 enabling catholics to take 61-

101 Howard 195 at 214. **102** *Ambrose* v. *Heffernan* (1768) Howard 165 at 173. **103** *Windis* v. *Power* (1772) Howard 217 at 227.

year leases of bog-land, nothing had been accomplished.[104] Now the formal process of dismantling the edifice of the penal land law code was to begin in earnest. It was to be a long-drawn-out process.

The first major act, that of 1778,[105] enabled catholics to take leases for up to 999 years, deprived the conformity of an eldest son of any practical meaning and in effect repealed the gavelling clause.[106] The second major act, that of 1782, placed catholics on a virtually identical footing with protestants in regard to all matters connected with the purchase and disposition of land.[107] At this stage, two differences remained: disabilities still attached to a convert who relapsed[108] and a catholic still had to take a certain oath before he could derive the benefit of the new legislation.[109] The oath as such remained mandatory until Emancipation in 1829.[110]

Throughout the period of the dismantling of the various rules, legislative – and thus legal – uncertainty was commonplace. Even Emancipation itself did not quite lay all this uncertainty to rest. If it is only in a case decided in 1845[111] that the then Irish lord chancellor, Sir Edward Sugden, finally and stylishly disposed of perhaps the last technical question arising from the dismantling of the two popery acts of Anne in the land law sphere, it is clear that in the years between the courts – and, therefore, the legal profession as well – had been preoccupied with the need to find answers to a vast range of consequential problems. In one major dispute that surfaced in 1789, *Earl Fauconberg* v. *Birch*, the judges of the Irish king's bench signified their intention to reach the answer to a critical question arising on the interpretation of the two popery acts, untrammeled by the consideration that the acts themselves were no longer in force.[112] That attitude was certainly defensible. At the hearing of the resultant appeal, however, the Irish house of lords, now flexing its muscles following the grant to it of exclusive appellate jurisdiction in 1782,[113] threw discretion to the winds, dissociated itself from the views of king's bench, and admittedly on the strength of the views expressed by the advising judges from the other two common law courts of common pleas and exchequer, reached its own verdict.[114]

These various later decisions both in Ireland and, following the act of union, in the United Kingdom house of lords, are not always easy to reconcile. The repeal of the clauses in the two popery acts of Anne is sometimes understood to have given the courts a liberty it would not otherwise have possessed, sometimes not. The subject-matter of the litigation is beguiling too; in the presence of early nineteenth century discussion of certificates of conformity and post mortem proof of religious affiliation, the fascination is that of the *déjà vu*.

One substantial benefit that accrues from a study of this later body of case-law is the insight frequently to be gained from it into the legal practices existing when the

104 11 & 12 Geo. III, c. 21: 'an act to encourage the reclaiming of unprofitable bogs'. **105** 17 & 18 Geo. III, c. 49: 'an act for the relief of his majesty's subjects of this kingdom professing the popish religion'. **106** Ss. 1, 6 and 2. **107** 21 & 22 Geo. III, c. 24: 'an act for the further relief of his majesty's subjects of this kingdom professing the popish religion'. **108** 17 & 18 Geo. III, c. 49, s. 10. **109** 17 & 18 Geo. III, c. 49, s. 3; 21 & 22 Geo. III, c. 24, s. 16. **110** 10 Geo. IV, c. 7 ('an act for the relief of his majesty's Roman Catholic subjects'), s. 23. **111** *O'Connell* v. *O'Callaghan* (1845) 7 Ir. Eq. Rep. 596. **112** 2 Ridgeway 147. **113** 21 & 22 Geo. III, c. 49: 'an act for redress of erroneous judgments, errors and decrees'. **114** 2 Ridgeway 147 at 174.

popery acts themselves were in operation. A second benefit is the encounter with one fresh problem that legally and politically comes to the fore as the old penal code begins its retreat into the background: the problem of the validity of catholic charitable trusts. This serves as the herald of the nineteenth century with its novel assortment of legal and other riddles that were to distinguish, and to dominate, the relations of catholics and of the catholic church with the post-union state.[115]

This account of the impact of the two popery acts of Anne on the catholic landed interest of eighteenth century Ireland has been penned with two distinct audiences in mind. The lawyer, hopefully, might aspire to glean something of how the penal land law code operated in practice, of what the role and function of the legal profession were in relation to it, even of the contribution the code made to canons of statutory interpretation or to the development of the doctrines of Irish equity.[116] The historian, for his part, might equally wish to glean something of how the resolutely cumbersome machinery of this unique and universally denigrated eighteenth century Irish code was actually deployed – what exactly the rules of that code were, how the doctrine of the courts came to strengthen or to modify statute-law, the undeniable importance of a number of vital procedural rulings, and such like matters.[117] Naturally, the jargon of eighteenth century Irish law – talk of the directed issue, bills of revivor, bills to perpetuate testimony, proof in accordance with the Statute of Frauds, entitlement to mesne profits, actions in ejectment, interpleaders, the court of delegates – does not exactly facilitate the comprehension of that law by members of either audience. Though I have done my best to unravel these difficulties, I sense that for some that best may not have been good enough.[118]

In advancing what represents merely an interim report on a historical problem of vast dimensions and considerable complexity, I am only too cognisant of the risks that have been taken and of the avenues that remain unexplored. It will be apparent that so far as surveys of the case-law are concerned considerable reliance was perforce placed on Howard. Howard, however, is something of an enigmatic figure. His contemporaries accused him of plagiarism, an indictment that surely sticks. There are two schools of thought respecting his accuracy, obviously a much more critical concern. Perhaps the majority regard him as reliable but a minority, aware of the defects of *Popery cases* by comparison with the standard set by contemporary English nominate reports, do raise doubts. And when the doubters include such magisterial figures as Lord Redesdale and Lord Eldon it is certainly prudent at least to preserve an open mind.[119]

115 See J.C. Brady, *Religion and the law of charities in Ireland* (Belfast, n.d. [1966]). **116** '[W]ithin the country today, one would be hard-pressed to locate the person equipped to perceive that, for example, the relationship between equity and the penal laws of the eighteenth century directed against Catholics … represented … [a] challenge to contemporary scholarship': W.N. Osborough, 'Scholarship and the university law school', *Dublin Univ. Law Jnl.*, 7 (1985) 1 at 24. **117** 'The penal laws have loomed large in historiography … [y]et they are little studied either as a corpus of legislation or in their impact. As a body of laws, their motivation and results alike are more complex than often suggested': L.M. Cullen, 'Catholics under the penal laws', *Eighteenth-century Ireland*, 1 (1986) 23 at 36. **118** Giles Jacob, *The law-dictionary*, 2nd ed. by T.E. Tomlins, 2 vols. (London, 1797), is an indispensable tool in the unravelling of these and other legal complications. **119** *Barnewall* v. *Barnewall* (1794) 3 Ridgeway 24 at 37 (Fitzgerald, prime serjeant), 45 (Wolfe, attorney-general); *Macnamara* v. *Lynch* (*c.*1800) Rowe 489 at 495 (Lord Kilwarden, chief justice, the

In strict legal terms, much that is obscure remains. Careful perusal of the various collections of printed appeals to the British house of lords may yet yield a few answers,[120] and the same can be claimed of Irish documentation bearing on appeals from the Irish king's bench to its English counterpart. Legal documents associated with eighteenth century transactions in Irish land languishing unread and undigested in collections of family papers that happen to have survived offer a different path forward toward further enlightenment.

APPENDIX

Legal source material: an explanatory table

Andrews	George Andrews, *Reports of cases argued and adjudged in the court of king's bench, 11-12 George II. 2nd ed. With notes and references down to Michaelmas term, 31 George III, by G.W Vernon* (London, 1791).
Brown	Josiah Brown, *Reports of cases upon appeals and writs of error in the high court of parliament from 1701-1779. 2nd ed. With notes and many additional cases brought down to 1800 by R.E. Tomlins*, 8 vols. (London, 1803).
Dow	P. Dow, *Reports of cases upon appeals and writs of error in the house of lords*, 6 vols. (London, 1814-19).
Eng. Rep.	*The English Reports*, 178 vols. (Edinburgh and London, 1900-32.)
Howard	G.E. Howard, *Several special cases on the laws against the further growth of popery in Ireland* (Dublin, 1775).
Ir. Eq. Rep.	*Irish Equity Reports*, 13 vols. (Dublin, 1839-52).
Ridgeway	William Ridgeway, *Reports of cases upon appeals and writs of error in the high court of parliament in Ireland, since the restoration of the appellate jurisdiction. With notes*, 3 vols. (Dublin, 1795-8).
Rowe	R.R. Rowe, *Reports of interesting cases, argued and determined in the king's law courts of England and Ireland, the houses of parliament, and military courts, with a treatise on martial law, also abridgements of the several tithe acts from 33 Henry VIII to 4 George IV* (Dublin, 1824).
Sch. & Lef.	John Schoales and Thomas Lefroy, *Reports of cases argued and determined in the high court of chancery in Ireland, during the time of Lord Redesdale*, 2 vols. (Dublin, 1806).
Singleton	Henry Singleton, 'Notebook of cases argued and adjudged in the high court of chancery and court of exchequer in Ireland 1716-34 , Ms. Columbia University Library.
Strange	Sir John Strange, *Reports of adjudged cases in the courts of chancery, king's bench, common pleas and exchequer from Trinity term 2 George I to Trinity term 21 George II. 3rd ed. With notes and additional references to contemporary reporters and later cases by Michael Nolan*, 2 vols. (London, 1795).

former Arthur Wolfe, attorney-general); *Loveland* v. *Lynch* (1814) 2 Dow 324 at 330; 3 Eng. Rep. 881 at 883-4 (Lords Redesdale and Eldon). **120** A useful guide to this source-material has been furnished by Louis MacRedmond: 'Irish appeals to the house of lords in the eighteenth century', *Anal. Hib.*, 23 (1966) 245.

The Irish Legal System, 1796-1877

The passing of the Supreme Court of Judicature (Ireland) Act in 1877, a contemporary observer pronounced, 'closed one great cycle' in the legal history of Ireland[1] – an assessment thoroughly warranted since the Act in fact did just that. Choosing a date for the commencement of the cycle to which our witness alludes is, however, problematic: no two individuals would be likely to settle on an agreed candidate. The appearance of *The Four Courts: 200 years* has the merit of focusing attention on the possible credentials of the year that saw the opening of the new Four Courts. However artificial and idiosyncratic a choice it must at first sight appear, the year 1796 turns out, paradoxically, to constitute, if no true commencement of any cycle, a not altogether inappropriate point of departure. This survey of the Irish legal system will accordingly straddle the years 1796 and 1877, laying emphasis on the major changes that were to occur over that eighty-year span.

I

No legal system exists in temporal isolation: in order to appreciate the significance of what comes after it is always a help to understand something of what has gone before. In casting light on the earlier decades of eighteenth-century Ireland, it is obviously dangerous to simplify. Two specific features, even so, stand out in stark relief, each fated to leave its mark on Irish law. First, the movement for constitutional reform inspired by a nascent nationalism. At the start, the movement encountered but meagre success – as in the episode orchestrated by Swift, leading to the withdrawal in 1725 of Wood's patent. But, finally, in 1782, the movement was to achieve its greatest triumph, the long-sought panacea of legislative independence and the assorted boons that that was fancied to bring with it. Secondly, the presence upon the statute-book of the code known to historians as the penal laws. This collection of measures, designed to impose, and to maintain, civil disabilities on Catholics and Dissenters alike, was, in the estimation of both the legal profession and of the population at large, clearly of far greater practical importance. The code's successive promulgation, sometimes fitful enforcement and eventual gradual unscrambling wrote key instalments in the political evolution of the country at the time.[2] The code also generated a huge amount of liti-

1 J.M. Lowry, *The Supreme Court of Judicature (Ireland) Act 1877* (Dublin, 1878), p. iii. **2** See *Catholic Ireland in the eighteenth century: collected essays of Maureen Wall*, ed. Gerard O'Brien (Dublin, 1989); T.P. Power and Kevin Whelan (eds.), *Endurance and emergence: Catholics in Ireland in the eighteenth century* (Dublin, 1990).

gation and legal business generally,[3] a phenomenon which persisted until well into the next century.

A narrow if, arguably, more acceptable definition of a legal system visualises the latter principally in terms of the structure of the several courts, of their powers and of the arrangements for their functioning. So far as the Irish legal system of the eighteenth century understood in this limited sense is concerned, the image the evidence projects is of a system, intent, almost to the exclusion of anything else, on forwarding a process of consolidation. Under the countrywide pattern of assizes, the judges travelled their respective circuits to despatch criminal and civil business in all thirty-two counties. For the first time in Ireland, this assize system was to operate over a protracted period in a manner approximating to the norm. There were no interruptions occasioned by rebellion and civil war – both conspicuous in the preceding century. The absence of these intermissions lured some into entertaining the foolish belief that such misfortunes were relics of the past, misfortunes never to be encountered again. One alteration in the scheme of things, minor in scale and restricted geographically, might serve as an exemplar of this commitment to a programme of consolidation. Communication difficulties had long prevented the assize judges from including the county of Kerry in the extreme south-west in their regular itineraries more than once a year. In 1695, the lord deputy and council ordered that henceforth Kerry was to receive a visitation from the judges twice a year, as had become the invariable practice elsewhere.[4]

Not too far away, some twenty years later, the hold of central government was again poised to be similarly strengthened, albeit in quite different circumstances and in a totally different fashion. In 1715, the second duke of Ormond was attainted for his Jacobite sympathies, whereupon the Irish parliament proceeded to abolish the duke's palatinate of Tipperary and to order the suppression of its various courts.[5] To judge from the wealth of record material which, as part of the process of integrating the palatinate into the ordinary system of judicature, was then ordered to be transferred to Dublin,[6] this was no trivial, inconsequential affair.[7]

Appearances to the contrary notwithstanding, some more radical innovativeness within the legal system did take place, though it is necessary to journey lower down the judicial hierarchy to locate it. Manor courts experienced a boost in their fortunes, a trend accelerated by a succession of statutory provisions that gave them additional powers.[8] To modern eyes, it seems a strange development: doubts about the adequacy of the courts' procedures, coupled with their irregular distribution throughout the country, scarcely identified them as the aptest of vehicles for servicing routine litigation, let alone any anticipated upsurge in it. In the corporate towns, too, a comparable strategy is discernible to provide convenient forums for the handling of small debt

3 See 'Catholics, land and the Popery Acts of Anne', above, p. 213. 4 Proclamation of lord deputy and council, 9 Dec. 1695: Robert Steele, *A bibliography of royal proclamations of the Tudor and Stuart sovereigns, 1485-1714*, 2 vols. (Oxford, 1910), ii, p. 161 (no. 1312). The journey into Kerry for the assizes at Tralee remained arduous in 1704: S.J. Connolly, *Religion, law and power: the making of Protestant Ireland, 1660-1760* (Oxford, 1992), pp 41-2, 58. 5 2 Geo. I, c. 8. 6 Herbert Wood, *A guide to the records deposited in the Public Record Office of Ireland* (Dublin, 1919), pp 261-3. 7 See further V.T.H. Delany, 'The palatinate court of the liberty of Tipperary', (1961) 5 *American Journal of Legal History* 95. 8 See, e.g., 25 Geo. III, c. 44.

claims. This was achieved by means of the erection and spread of the so-called courts of conscience, courts finally to be glimpsed open to suitors in places as far distant as Derry and Kinsale. A third innovation can be dated more precisely – to the very year of 1796 itself. Nine years before, a new breed of judge had been associated with the standard work of justices at quarter sessions – in effect, a criminal law remit.[9] In 1796, these 'assistant barristers' as they were first called – an accurate designation since they were chosen from among the 'barristers' and their task was to 'assist' – had conferred on them fresh powers to hear civil suits as well.[10] A ceiling on the value of each claim presented was insisted upon, but it was the choice of mechanism that is both instructive and prophetic: the assistant barristers were made competent to adjudicate on 'civil bills'. The assize judges had pioneered this simplified method of launching civil litigation in the country in the preceding century.[11] That method now became more widely and more freely available. For Ireland, the year 1796 thus represents a turning-point in rendering justice more accessible.

Other changes, restricted to the last years of the century, are a direct reflection of the constitutional 'revolution' of 1782-3, or can trace their origins back to it.

Arrangements *vis-à-vis* judicial appeals, for instance, were all to be drastically reshaped. The appellate jurisdiction of the Irish House of Lords had been taken away by the British statute, the Dependency of Ireland Act 1720, otherwise known as the Sixth of George the First.[12] In 1782-3 the jurisdiction of the Irish House of Lords was to be restored.[13] Nor did Ireland's civilian jurisdictions remain unaffected. As regards Admiralty, the same year – 1783 – that the Irish parliament re-established the court on a fresh basis, it insisted that future appeals from the court should be referred to Irish delegates.[14] Five years later, the ecclesiastical courts were dealt with in similar style. Under legislation dating from the Reformation, appeals from the Irish ecclesiastical courts could be carried before delegates appointed by the Irish lord chancellor or by delegates appointed by his English counterpart.[15] In the course of the eighteenth century, the English chancellor manifested an increasing reluctance to appoint delegates to hear Irish appeals. In 1788, the Irish parliament responded to the invitation implicitly conveyed by this alteration in practice by itself taking matters a vital stage further: it outlawed altogether any recourse in future to the lord chancellor in London.[16] Six years further down the road, in another symbolic break with the past, the then Irish chancellor, John Fitzgibbon, introduced an additional appellate tier in this sphere of judicature. In *Goodwin* v. *Giesler*[17] he sanctioned the issuance of a commission of review that enabled an earlier decision of delegates confirming the admission of a will to probate, to be re-opened to scrutiny. No such commissions of

9 27 Geo. III, c. 40, s. 15. **10** 36 Geo. III, c.25, s. 6. **11** D.S. Greer, 'The development of civil bill procedure in Ireland', in John McEldowney and Paul O'Higgins (eds.), *The common law tradition: essays in Irish legal history* (Dublin, 1990), p. 27. **12** 6 Geo. I, c. 5 (GB). See further M.S. Flaherty, 'The empire strikes back: *Annesley* v. *Sherlock* and the triumph of imperial parliamentary supremacy' (1987) 87 *Columbia Law Review* 593; Isolde Victory, 'The making of the 1720 Declaratory Act', in Gerard O'Brien (ed.), *Parliament, politics and people: essays in eighteenth-century Irish history* (Dublin, 1989), p. 9. **13** 22 Geo. III, c. 53, 23 Geo. III, c. 28 (both GB); 21 & 22 Geo. III, c. 49. See further Andrew Lyall, 'The Irish House of Lords as a judicial body, 1783-1800', (1993-95) 28-30 *Irish Jurist* 314. **14** 23 & 24 Geo. III, c. 14. **15** The Irish Act of Appeals: 28 Hen. VIII, c. 6. **16** 27 & 28 Geo. III, c. 32. **17** (1794) Ir. Term Rep. 371.

review, it is thought, had been previously authorised in Ireland. Thus did the beneficiary of this ruling, one William Goodwin, 'a working shoemaker' living 'in obscurity at a remote distance from Dublin', who otherwise seemed fated to lose rights of succession, gain another day in court.[18]

Grattan's parliament may have accomplished little enough. But besides these structural changes, which helped advance what might be termed an indigenous jural homogeneity, it was also to prove successful on one other front: in the pressure it applied to secure an increase in the number of judges. In 1783, the number of these in each of the three superior common law courts – King's Bench, Common Pleas, and Exchequer – was raised from three to four, producing a total complement of twelve. F.E. Ball recalls, a little unkindly perhaps, that two of the barristers elevated as a result – Samuel Bradstreet and Alexander Crookshank, raised to places in King's Bench and Common Pleas respectively – had earlier, as members of the Irish Commons, vigorously opposed the idea of any increase at all when this was first mooted.[19] What 'had made them see the error of their ways', Ball suggests, was the alteration in the tenure of the Irish judges to 'good behaviour', recently effected by the Act of 1782 'for securing the independency of the judges',[20] but no less decisive had been an increase in salary.[21] A third critic of the move, John Scott, the future Lord Clonmell and chief justice of King's Bench, had warned in 1781 that to augment the size of the judiciary would play havoc with the existing system of assize circuits: the five circuits, drawn up originally in the 1610s,[22] could accommodate nine judges; they could not satisfactorily cater for twelve. Whether an actual need arose or the risk of judicial under-employment, after due study, was found to require attention, in 1796 a new sixth assize circuit was to be added. Carved out of the Leinster Circuit, and known thereafter as the Home Circuit,[23] the new circuit provoked a somewhat acerbic note from Ball:

> The first judges to preside on it were two distinguished respectively for hypochondria and seniority, Carleton and Kelly, and during the ninety years that the circuit existed, infirm and senior judges found a refuge upon it.[24]

II

In November 1796, the lord chancellor, the twelve judges and sundry court officials – many of the latter bearing titles doomed for extinction in the 1830s, '40s and '50s[25] – moved into spacious quarters at the new Four Courts. Undoubtedly, these were a substantial improvement on what had been available to them at the old venue beside Christ Church.[26] As we have seen, two changes to the legal system coincided with the

18 For commissions of review, see too *Von Stentz* v. *Comyn* (1849) 12 Ir. Eq. Rep. 662 and G.I.O. Duncan, *The High Court of Delegates* (Cambridge, 1971), ch. 4. **19** F.E. Ball, *The judges in Ireland, 1221-1921*, 2 vols. (London, 1926), ii, p. 168. **20** 21 & 22 Geo. III, c. 50. **21** Ball, *The judges in Ireland,* ii, p. 168. **22** John McCavitt, '"Good planets in their several spheares" – the establishment of the assize circuits in early seventeenth century Ireland' (1989) 24 *Irish Jurist* 248. **23** Ball, *The judges in Ireland*, ii, pp 173-4, 182-3. **24** Ibid., ii, 183. **25** See, e.g., 6 & 7 Will. IV, c. 74, 7 & 8 Vict., c. 107. **26** Colum Kenny, 'The Four Courts at Christ Church, 1608-1796', in W.N. Osborough (ed.), *Explorations in law and history: Irish Legal History*

transfer: the creation of the Home Circuit and the conferment of civil bill jurisdiction on the assistant barristers. Fresh challenges, as it happens, were in the immediate offing. Less than two years later, the United Irish Rising of 1798 and the manner of its suppression precipitated a host of questions in regard to such matters as martial law, acts of indemnity[27] and habeas corpus.[28] Several of these questions were unprecedented, none were easy to solve, and all lent a sharp focus to the rapport – and sometimes, ironically, to the lack of it – between the judiciary, on the one side, and the executive in Dublin Castle and the military authorities, on the other. Danger was to stalk the land too, and not just in the shape of the duelling pistol, an accessory with which a proportion of the more prominent lawyers of the period were plainly not unfamiliar.[29] The fate that was to befall Arthur Wolfe, Viscount Kilwarden, Clonmell's successor as chief justice of King's Bench, will have occasioned more than a mere frisson of alarm. In 1803, in the course of Emmet's abortive, short-lived rebellion, he was to be dragged from his coach in the heart of Dublin and done to death.[30] It was not to be the last such atrocity in the annals of the judiciary in Ireland.

The Act of Union between Great Britain and Ireland [31] predates Emmet's rebellion. Coming into force on 1 January 1801, this novel constitutional dispensation could not but have a major effect on the Irish legal system.

One short-term consequence was patently detrimental. Under the Union 'engagements' barrister MPs voting for the Union had been given the promise of appointment to judicial office to fill future vacancies. To Fitzgibbon's evident distaste, these engagements were kept and individuals of dubious attainments were indeed to gain preferment.[32] Implementation of the policy was to present its own difficulties, as Ball explains:

> Within four years of the passing of the Act of Union no less than six barristers were raised to the bench solely because they had supported the measure in the Irish parliament. Not one of the six was free from objection on the ground either of brieflessness, or of acrimony, or of youth, and within a year from the appointment of the last of the six, two of them were arraigned, one in the English King's Bench for libel, and the other in the house of lords for tyrannical conduct.[33]

Ball's allusions are to Robert Johnson and Luke Fox, made puisnes in Common Pleas in 1801 and 1800, respectively. Nearly a generation was to elapse before the bench was to regain a measure of its former prestige.

On the bonus side, the exposure of the inadequacies of Ireland's law and legal system to the scrutiny of the United Kingdom parliament is to be reckoned a signal

Society discourses, 1988-1994 (Dublin, 1995), p. 107. **27** See, e.g., Paul O'Higgins, '*Wright* v. *FitzGerald* revisited', (1962) 25 *Modern Law Review* 413. **28** On habeas corpus practice during this eventful period, see R.R. Rowe, *Reports of interesting cases…* (Dublin 1824), passim. **29** James Kelly, '*That damn'd thing called honour': duelling in Ireland, 1570-1860* (Cork, 1995), pp 162-3. **30** Ball, *The judges in Ireland,* ii, pp 243-4. **31** 39 & 40 Geo. III, c. 67 (GB), 2 July 1800; 40 Geo. III, c. 38, 1 Aug. 1800. **32** Ball, *The judges in Ireland,* ii, p. 234f. **33** Ibid., ii, 235.

advantage. In an age of reform, the Irish input into the changes proposed and actually accomplished was disappointingly slight: a disinclination to cooperate on the part of a generation of politicians increasingly mesmerised by a single *idée fixe* may have been partly to blame. If a number of the changes introduced also fell short of the ideal, it is indisputable that, on the whole, Ireland was the beneficiary of a huge amount of progressive legislation. With the gathering momentum in favour of jettisoning the Union, an increasingly reluctant beneficiary maybe, but a beneficiary nevertheless.[34]

Article 8 of the Treaty of Union addressed itself to the legal system, guaranteeing to continue the status quo subject to two caveats, the second of which touched on the question – long contentious in the eighteenth century – of appellate jurisdiction. 'All laws in force at the time of the Union', the article declared,

> and all the courts of civil and ecclesiastical jurisdiction within the respective kingdoms, shall remain as now by law established within the same, subject only to such alterations and regulations from time to time as circumstances may appear to the Parliament of the United Kingdom to require; provided that all writs of error and appeals depending at the time of the union or hereafter to be brought, and which might now be finally decided by the House of Lords of either Kingdom, shall from and after the union be finally decided by the House of Lords of the United Kingdom.

Indigenous jural homogeneity remained in place for the civilian jurisdictions. As regards appeals from the Irish ecclesiastical courts, no post-Union statutory modifications were to be made to the regime established in 1788: appeals continued to be carried before Irish delegates until the ecclesiastical courts themselves were abolished on the disestablishment of the Church of Ireland in 1871.[35] Article 8 of the Treaty went on to deal separately with the Irish court of Admiralty and appeals from that court. The latter, as laid down by the act of 1783, were to continue to go before Irish delegates. This arrangement prevailed until 1867. Then, in a general reordering of matters pertaining to the court, there was substituted the Court of Appeal in Chancery with a further right of appeal to the English Privy Council. Alternatively, the dissatisfied litigant could appeal directly to the Privy Council, and thus leapfrog over the intermediate Irish appeal court.[36]

III

After 1801, the House of Lords served as the final appellate court for Irish litigants in the vast majority of cases. The merit of the arrangement, copperfastened as it was by article 8 of the Treaty of Union, might be thought to call for further comment.

34 Cf. J.C. Brady, 'Legal developments, 1801–79', in W.E. Vaughan (ed.), *A new history of Ireland – v: Ireland under the Union, 1–1801–70* (Oxford, 1989), p. 451. **35** See below, pp 256–7. **36** 30 & 31 Vict., c. 114, ss. 90, 91.

No assessment is available on the performance of the British House of Lords as the final court of appeal for Ireland over the years 1720 to 1782. The Lords' 1779 decision in *Bateman* v. *Murray*[37] on the renewal of leases for lives, in which strict conditions for such renewal were laid down, appears an aberration, forcing, as it did, immediate legislative reversal by the Irish parliament through the Tenantry Act passed the same year.[38] On the other hand, as regards the penal laws, it is clear that the Lords, in marked contrast to the Irish judges, were, on several occasions, prepared to adopt a liberal approach to their interpretation and enforcement.[39] But none of this advances the discussion very far.

Nor is it any easier to propound firm conclusions on the performance of the Lords in London when their authority to hear Irish appeals was restored in 1801. It is probable that the Irish judges will have been dismayed by decisions such as *Pluck* v. *Digges* (1832),[40] where the Lords insisted that retention by the landlord of a reversion was essential to create the relationship of landlord and tenant, and *Gray* v. *The Queen* (1844),[41] where, again overruling the lower Irish court, they maintained that a person accused of felony was still entitled to twenty peremptory challenges of jurors even when the felony was not capital. Both adjudications, the Irish bench might have argued, flew in the face of 'local conditions on the ground', with which they would have regarded themselves as naturally more familiar.

In addition, pronouncements on a range of questions with a more obviously political content were unlikely to have given universal contentment or been greeted with universal applause. Evidence is unmistakable that the Lords did indeed walk a judicial tight-rope, and the inference is certainly there to be drawn that the Lords were very well aware of what they were about. Their decision, for example, in *Malone* v. *Knox* (1838),[42] effectively to uphold the issuance of writs of rebellion from the Irish Exchequer over the non-payment of tithe, may be contrasted with another decision, rather more celebrated, six years later, to allow a writ of error and throw out conspiracy charges against Daniel O'Connell and others (1844).[43]

R.B. McDowell has argued that, to judge from the number of appeals lodged by Irish suitors, the provision of the appeal to London, reintroduced in 1801, would seem to have given broad satisfaction.[44] In 1874, Lord Justice Christian saw no reason to dispute such a verdict. 'The contentment of Ireland' with the House of Lords as its court of last resort, he protested, had been 'boundless'. Speaking from his own 'varied experience of nearly forty years', he had 'never heard a murmur against it'.[45] Other judges besides Christian are likely to have offered guidance on the question, their views over the decades being transformed into the accepted wisdom within a pro-Union profession, unchallenged and unchallengeable. It is possible, of course, that in

37 5 Bro. P.C. 20; 2 Eng. Rep. 506. **38** 19 & 20 Geo. III, c. 30. **39** See 'Catholics, land and the Popery Acts of Anne', above, at p. 231f. **40** 5 Bligh N.S. 31; 5 Eng. Rep. 219. **41** 11 Cl. & Fin. 427; 8 Eng. Rep. 1164. See further D.S. Johnson, 'The trials of Sam Gray: Monaghan politics and nineteenth century Irish criminal procedure', (1985) 20 *Irish Jurist* 109. **42** 4 Bing. (N.C.) 574; 132 Eng. Rep. 910. **43** *O'Connell* v. *The Queen*, 11 Cl. & Fin. 155; 8 Eng. Rep. 1061. See further Ian Holloway, '*O'Connell* v. *The Queen*: a sesquicentennial remembrance', (1995) 46 *NILQ*. 63. **44** R.B. McDowell, *The Irish administration, 1800-1914* (London, 1964), p. 105. **45** Jonathan Christian, *The coming final court of appeal for Ireland* (Dublin, 1874), p. 3.

support of their stance, the Irish judiciary may genuinely have been impressed by the quality of legal scholarship that, from time to time, but by no means always, the House of Lords could display on the hearing of an Irish appeal. On any view, their performance on the bothersome question of the power to appoint clerks of the peace – *Harding* v. *Pollock* (1829)[46] – and that on the equally vexed question of Presbyterian marriages – *R.* v. *Millis* (1844)[47] – must be counted impressive. Such considerations go part of the way at least to explain the vigour with which, in 1873, the Irish judges sought to abort the plan, recently brought forward by Gladstone's administration, to abolish the appeal to the Lords altogether by substituting an appeal to a very differently constituted court of last resort.[48] Emotional commitment and personal identification with the Union and what it was deemed to represent cannot, naturally, be left out of the equation either. Christian, for instance, displayed both traits, which is no surprise since he had long come to regard the House of Lords as the sole reliable guardian of the doctrinal soundness of Irish law.

In 1856, a parliamentary paper included the staggering intelligence that a British lord chancellor, engaged in the hearing of an Irish appeal, had had to be lent overnight a textbook on Irish land registration law.[49] So understandable a precaution which, to a lawyer at least, may not sound so very odd or disturbing, does nonetheless raise the issue of the availability to the final appellate court of appropriate Irish legal expertise. Reflection on the outcome in cases such as *Pluck* v. *Digges* or *Gray* v. *The Queen* raises the issue too. At an intelligent guess, counsel are unlikely to have let slip the opportunity to educate the Lords on matters relevant to Ireland and its legal system considered germane to the disposal of the particular appeal, matters of which the Lords either lacked knowledge or professed actual ignorance. Nevertheless, counsel and, conceivably, even the Lords themselves might have viewed it a distinct advantage had Irish expertise been more immediately and more authoritatively accessible, present, in short, from within the body of the House of Lords itself.

Some years after the enactment of the Appellate Jurisdiction Act of 1876,[50] the convention was introduced which saw a member of the Irish bench being regularly translated to serve as a lord of appeal in ordinary, the first appointment, in 1882, being that of Lord Fitzgerald. Prior to that, there were a number of peers who had had professional experience in Ireland and who were thus in a position to assist in this fashion with the judicial work of the House – probably more peers than is commonly realised. Lord Redesdale, Irish lord chancellor from 1802 to 1806, with a reputation as an equity lawyer,[51] served in just such a capacity for a number of years following his return to England. So, too, did Lord Manners, who had held the Irish seals from 1807 to 1827. Lord Plunket, another Irish chancellor (1830-4; 1835-41), though eligible to occupy the same role, did not apparently choose to do so.[52] Sir Edward Sugden, later ennobled as Lord St Leonards, who, in the course of a distinguished career, served

46 6 Bing. 25, 130 Eng. Rep. 1189; 3 Bligh N.S. 161, 4 Eng. Rep. 1300. **47** 10 Cl. & Fin. 534; 8 Eng. Rep. 844. **48** McDowell, *The Irish administration,* p. 105. The plan was later dropped. For the background see Christian's polemical pamphlet, *The coming final court of appeal.* **49** McDowell, *The Irish administration*, p. 105. **50** 39 & 40 Vict., c. 59. **51** Schoales and Lefroy's reports, 2 vols. (Dublin, 1806) concentrate exclusively on Redesdale's decisions when he held the Irish seals. **52** Christian, *The coming final court of appeal*, p. 6.

both as Irish chancellor (1834-5; 1841-6) and as English (February-December 1852), actively participated in the judicial work of the House. So, too, did Thomas O'Hagan who, following statutory removal of the relevant religious disability,[53] became Irish chancellor in 1868, serving in that capacity until 1874 and again in 1880-1, and who was elevated to the peerage as Baron O'Hagan of Tullahogue in 1870.[54] For *Duke of Devonshire* v. *Neill*,[55] the Munster Blackwater several fishery case resolved by the Lords in 1882, O'Hagan was still on hand to furnish an amount of useful and enlightening Irish historical data that helped to buttress the final decision.

Equal familiarity with aspects of Irish history stood Mr Justice Willes in excellent stead when delivering advice for the Lords in an earlier Irish appeal connected with a different several fishery, on the Shannon, in Limerick: *Malcomson* v. *O'Dea* (1863).[56] Willes hypothesised the presence of Norsemen in Limerick before the tenth century, and went on to draw a crucial inference from that. Willes, the son of a Cork doctor and educated at Trinity College Dublin, had followed a professional career in London, being raised to the English bench as a judge of Common Pleas in 1850. His participation in the hearing of the appeal in *Malcomson* v. *O'Dea* was by no means unusual since, prior to 1876, it was frequent practice for the Lords to summon the English common law judges to give them advice; nor did the passing of the Appellate Jurisdiction Act bring the practice to a halt, the self-same judges being summoned to offer advice as late as 1898. (The Irish common law judges never appear to have been invited to fill a comparable role.) It has been pointed out that no less than nine individuals elevated to the English bench in the reign of Queen Victoria were of Irish extraction.[57] Whatever about the rest, Willes – acknowledged to have been one of the more learned jurists of the century – did not hesitate to make use of knowledge of the land of his birth.[58]

It is possible to exaggerate the value of the availability to the House of Lords of special knowledge possessed by the likes of a Willes or an O'Hagan. Many problems brought before the Lords for solution presented little or nothing in the way of local colour: Irish law to a considerable extent – and certainly in key areas of private law (land law excepted) – was identical with English. Moreover, as regards potentially controversial business – less frequently aired than might be supposed – initial ignorance on the part of the Lords or of advising common law judges, and geographical distance too, may have conferred hidden benefits. Such a combination of factors could have helped to promote, among all participants in the hearing of Irish appeals, that judicious frame of mind, so essential, in the calculations of contemporaries, to the resolution of a proportion of them if that resolution was in Ireland to command anything close to respect.

53 30 & 31 Vict., c. 75. **54** McDowell, *The Irish administration,* p. 106. It should be noted that O'Hagan's role in the House of Lords as a legislator may have been the more important. **55** 8 App. Cas. 135. **56** 10 H.L.C. 593; 11 Eng. Rep. 1155. **57** A.W.B. Simpson (ed.), *Biographical dictionary of the common law* (London, 1984), s.v. Willes, James Shaw (entry by R.F.V. Heuston). **58** See further R.F.V. Heuston, 'James Shaw Willes', (1965) 16 *NILQ* 193.

IV

The 1st of August 1800 is the day that the Irish parliament's Act of Union received the royal assent. The same day like assent was given to a second statute which signified another institutional innovation. This was the creation of an intermediate court of appeal.[59] In Ireland, the Court of Exchequer Chamber had hitherto enjoyed a low profile. It was now re-established and given clearly defined and much broader powers. Whether its revitalisation at this precise juncture as part of the Union package of measures owes more to a desire to retain an amount of legal business for the Four Courts, or needs to be viewed rather as an intelligent attempt to filter appeals that would otherwise needlessly arrive before the House of Lords by a more direct and more expeditious route, need not perhaps detain us: carried over by article 8 of the Treaty of Union, the new court instantly secured its place in the sun. Composed of the twelve judges of the Irish common law courts, the refashioned Court of Exchequer Chamber was made competent to hear writs of error from all four superior courts: Chancery in addition to the three courts of common law. A quorum was set at nine.[60] In many instances, direct appeals to the House of Lords were not ruled out: writs of error not being obtainable to mount appeals from the equity sides of Exchequer and Chancery, appeals in such cases went straight to London.

The court was to survive until 1877. Additional jurisdiction was conferred in 1850 when steps were taken to enable it to review decisions of assistant barristers on the registrability of voters under the franchise.[61] This modest change brought to an end a wrangle that had divided the judges since 1832. A majority held that such decisions were properly reviewable by all the judges meeting in informal conclave. Mr Justice Perrin and Baron Richards, however, believed otherwise, and their stance was later to receive the firm backing of Chief Baron Brady in 1841: *In re Larkin*.[62] It may be a coincidence, but it is worth noting that just before the statutory change, in 1849, Baron Richards, the principal protagonist of the minority viewpoint, had been seconded from the Exchequer to help launch the new Incumbered Estates Court.

Other legislation affecting the work of the Court of Exchequer Chamber was introduced in the 1850s. In 1857, it was laid down that thenceforth the court, when hearing an appeal, should be made up exclusively of judges drawn from the two common law courts other than the third from which the appeal was being brought.[63] An appeal from Common Pleas – to give that example – fell from this time on to be determined by the combined benches of Queen's Bench and Exchequer, and by them alone: Common Pleas judges would thus no longer participate in the hearing of appeals from themselves. The new dispensation, modelled on an identical provision to be found in a statute of 1830 which reconstructed England's equivalent court,[64] reflected new canons of judicial propriety. It was, however, to pose its own problems, as we shall shortly discover.

59 40 Geo. III, c. 39. **60** Ibid., s. 2. **61** 13 & 14 Vict., c.69, ss. 58, 74, 79. **62** 4 ILR 46. See further D.S. Greer, 'Lawyers or politicians? The Irish judges and the right to vote, 1832–50', in Caroline Costello (ed.), *The Four Courts: 200 years* (Dublin, 1996), p. 126. **63** 20 & 21 Vict., c.6. **64** 11 Geo. IV & 1 Will. IV, c. 70, s. 8.

A second change introduced in 1856, the year before, was aimed at regularising appeals from the two extant equity jurisdictions. The equity side of the Exchequer had recently been abolished,[65] and the two courts concerned were thus Chancery and a post-Union innovation (to be dealt with shortly), the court of the master of the rolls. A second intermediate court of appeal was established, to be known as the Court of Appeal in Chancery, which was given exclusive carriage of appeals from the two courts mentioned, except from the petty bag side of Chancery, and, subject, as one might have anticipated, to a final appeal to the House of Lords.[66] The court was composed of the lord chancellor, a lord justice of appeal – a new judicial post – and any common law judge invited by the lord chancellor to serve. Later, appeals from the refashioned court of Bankruptcy and Insolvency, the new court of Probate, the Landed Estates Court, the court of the vice-chancellor (all to be dealt with below) and, as we have already seen, also from Admiralty were to be brought within the purview of the court in addition.[67] In the run-up to the Judicature Act, the Court of Appeal in Chancery was to have a stormy passage. Jonathan Christian, the sole lord justice of appeal, who had been promoted to the position from Common Pleas in 1867, turned into a veritable Ishmael on the bench, contemptuous of his colleagues' abilities and ever-ready to heap derision and worse on all those unfortunate enough to come within distance. A principal target of Christian's splenetic abuse – which scarcely helped matters – was none other than Lord O'Hagan. O'Hagan, as lord chancellor, was Christian's regular colleague on the court from 1869 to 1874. Any day the court announced its intention to deliver judgment, barristers would flock to the court-room, in the expectation that, with luck, they might see yet further sparks fly.[68]

A third appellate tribunal was set to materialise in Ireland in 1848: the Court for Crown Cases Reserved.[69] (As the designation implies, to dub the tribunal 'appellate' is, in strict law, a trifle misleading.) Charting the genesis of the new court is not free of difficulty. At some date, certainly before the passing of the Act of Union, the judges of Ireland's common law courts began to meet informally to settle between themselves moot questions of criminal law. Such questions would be reserved by the presiding judge at the assizes and referred for further consideration by the full bench back in Dublin. At one period, we know the junior judge was required to maintain a book in which such problem cases were regularly entered up. By an extension of the practice, decisions of the recorder of Dublin on criminal matters and those of the assize judges on the fiating of grand jury presentments were similarly made reviewable, within the same circumscribed limits. Whether, after 1832, rulings of the assistant barristers on the registration of voters could, with equal legitimacy, be referred to meetings of the twelve judges triggered the dispute which, as we have had occasion to note, divided

On the background to this change in England, see Sir William Holdsworth, *History of English law*, i (7th ed., revised, London, 1956), pp 242-4. **65** See below, pp 252-3. **66** 19 & 20 Vict., c. 92. **67** 20 & 21 Vict., c. 60, s. 29 (Bankruptcy and Insolvency appeals); 20 & 21 Vict., c. 79, s. 45 (Probate appeals); 21 & 22 Vict., c. 72, s. 41 (Landed Estate Court appeals); 30 & 31 Vict., c. 44, s. 6 (by implication – appeals from the vice-chancellor); 30 & 31 Vict., c. 114, s. 91 (Admiralty appeals). **68** See generally Daire Hogan, 'Arrows too sharply pointed: the relations of Lord Justice Christian and Lord O'Hagan', in J.F. McEldowney, and Paul O'Higgins (eds.), *The common law tradition: essays in Irish legal history* (Dublin, 1990), p. 61. **69** 11 & 12 Vict., c. 78.

the bench and was to last down to 1850. During Charles Kendal Bushe's tenure as chief justice of King's Bench (1822-41), initiatives were taken to formalise proceedings. If the referring judge approved, hearings of 'reserved cases', were to be held in open court with appearances from counsel on both sides.[70] The Act of 1848, which erected Courts for Crown Cases Reserved in both England and Ireland, emphasised the need for still greater formality and thus to introduce, as the preamble to the measure phrased it,

> a better mode than that now in use of deciding any difficult question of law which may arise in criminal trials in any court of oyer and terminer and gaol delivery.

The reforms introduced in Ireland at Bushe's behest in 1826 owed a great deal to information on current English practice supplied to Bushe at the time by his English counterpart.[71] As regards questions of substantive criminal law, however, the post-1848 reconstructed court soon manifested a remarkable independence of outlook, reflected in rulings such as *R.* v. *Burke* in 1858[72] (collateral questions and the linguistic competence of witnesses) and *R.* v. *Johnston* in 1864[73] (confessions). The Irish court was later to go to the lengths of actually departing from precedents established by its English counterpart, but not, it is thought, on any occasion prior to 1877. Examples are furnished by *R.* v. *Dee* in 1884[74] (consent in rape) and *R.* v. *Hehir* in 1895[75] (larceny).

All the common law judges were constituted members of the Court for Crown Cases Reserved. A quorum was fixed at five, of whom one had to be the chief of one of the common law courts.[76]

V

The eighty or so years that separate the opening of the new Four Courts and the passing of the Judicature Act saw the erection of a number of new courts of first instance. Scarcely was the ink dry on the Treaty of Union than the first of the progeny came into being: the court of the master of the rolls.[77] By the eighteenth century the office of master of the rolls in Ireland had become a sinecure.[78] In 1801, the holders of the sinecure having first been bought out, the office was transformed into a fully-fledged court of chancery and Sir Michael Smith, the third baron of the Exchequer, was

70 Robert Jebb, *Cases, chiefly relating to the criminal and presentment law, reserved for consideration and decided by the twelve judges of Ireland, from May 1822 to November 1840* (Dublin, 1841), p. 1. **71** Ibid; see also above, pp 116-20. **72** 8 Cox C.C. 44. **73** 15 ICLR 60. See further J.D. Jackson, 'In defence of a voluntariness doctrine for confessions: *The Queen* v. *Johnston* revisited' (1986) 21 *Irish Jurist* 208. **74** 14 LR Ir. 468; the court dissented from *R.* v. *Barrow* (1868) LR 1 CCR 156. **75** [1895] 2 IR 709; the court dissented from *R.* v. *Ashwell* (1885) 16 QBD 190. **76** 11 & 12 Vict., c. 78, s. 3. **77** 41 Geo. III, c. 25. **78** For details of the history of the office in Ireland before 1800 see R.W. Greene, *A report of the proceedings upon an information in the nature of a quo-warranto, at the suit of The King against Waller O'Grady* (Dublin, 1816), passim.

promoted to fill it.[79] The sharing of chancery business that thus came about ordinarily generated few difficulties, but there was to be a clash of opinion in 1827 between one of Smith's successors in the post, Sir William McMahon, and the then lord chancellor, Sir Anthony Hart, when the latter sought to regulate the entitlement of the former to hear petitions without reference to himself.[80]

A second additional chancery judge was sanctioned in 1867.[81] Known as the vice-chancellor, he, like the master of the rolls, sat in his own court. Hedges Eyre Chatterton who, as law officer, had carriage of the legislation that created the new post was himself to be elevated to occupy it.[82] England saw the appointment of the first of its vice-chancellors in 1813. Two more positions with the same title were added in 1842, producing a complement of three vice-chancellors in England prior to the adoption of the Judicature Act there.[83] In Ireland, in contrast, Chatterton was destined to serve out his time as the country's sole vice-chancellor: when he retired in 1904, the post was to be abolished. In 1885 Chatterton experienced the remarkable distinction of having a street in a red-light district of Dublin named after himself by the city council. This was in retaliation for Chatterton's refusal as vice-chancellor to permit Sackville street to be renamed O'Connell street: *Anderson* v. *Corporation of Dublin*.[84]

The year 1821 saw the establishment of the Court for the Relief of Insolvent Debtors.[85] Permanent commissioners in bankruptcy were appointed in 1836 and 1837,[86] thus superseding the earlier practice under which individual commissioners had been appointed on an ad hoc basis. A court combining functions in both areas was constituted in 1857, to be known after 1872 simply as the Court of Bankruptcy.[87] Walter Berwick was a noted bankruptcy judge of those years. Promoted after a stint as an assistant barrister in Munster where he had taken an interest in juvenile delinquency, Berwick died in the horrific Irish mail disaster at Abergele in north Wales in August 1868.[88] The fountain in Grand Parade in Cork was erected by Berwick in 1860 'in remembrance of the great kindness shown to him by all classes' during his twelve years' service as judge in the city.

A major innovation of 1848, peculiar to Ireland, represented a concrete response to one recurring practical difficulty. Many landowners in Ireland had got themselves hopelessly into debt and the land, as a consequence, was burdened with innumerable incumbrances, so much so that the transferability of land itself – a desideratum in the political ideology of the day – was seriously impeded. To facilitate the sale and transfer of the estates in question, the government established a special court, the Incumbered Estates Court, to be replaced in 1858 by the differently entitled Landed Estates Court given even broader powers. Lord Justice Christian explained the background very well in the remarkable exordium to his judgment in *In re Tottenham's Estate* (1869):[89]

79 Ball, *The judges in Ireland*, ii, pp 236-8. **80** Brady, 'Legal developments, 1801-79', p. 468. **81** 30 & 31 Vict., c. 49, s. 4. **82** Ball, *The judges in Ireland*, ii, p. 302. **83** Holdsworth, *History of English law*, i, pp 442-5. **84** (1884) 15 LR Ir. 410. See further my *Law and the emergence of Dublin: a litigation topography for a capital city* (Dublin, 1996), ch. 5 and appendix. **85** 1 & 2 Geo. IV, c. 59. The library of Trinity College Dublin holds a collection of the judgments of Peter Burrowes, one of the early judges of the court. **86** 6 & 7 Will. IV, c. 14; 1 Vict., c. 48. **87** 20 & 21 Vict., c. 60; 35 & 36 Vict., c. 58. **88** (1868) 2 *Irish Law Times and Solicitors' Journal* 427-8. **89** IR 3 Eq 528.

> The Incumbered Estates Act was passed at an abnormal time, with certain objects, and the first and indispensable necessity was this – to sweep from the land of Ireland, at one stroke, that *incubus* of complicated title and incumbrance which had been a terror or a snare to intending purchasers, and by which a large part of this island was practically withdrawn from the land market.[90]

In implementation of these objectives, the principal task undertaken by the courts was straightforward enough:

> Where any land, or lease of such, was subject to encumbrances the value of which exceeded half the net rent, the encumbrancer on such land or lease could apply to the court for the sale of such land or lease for the purpose of discharging the relevant encumbrances.[91]

Endowing the judges of the courts in question with, as Christian was later to phrase it, 'the whole administration of incumbered estates, the investigating of their titles, the sales of them and the distribution of their purchase moneys',[92] constituted a significant departure, not least because the courts themselves became, as Christian again put it, 'the main feeder of Equity in a country where great commercial controversies, company adjustments and such like, were comparatively unknown'.[93] The departure was significant for another reason of course: the relevant acts of parliament establishing the two courts were controversial, necessarily involving as they did a substantial measure of interference with property rights.[94]

The legislative scheme envisaged that bidders for property that was placed on the market by either of the courts should be given an indefeasible title. Ordinarily, indeed, this is what they obtained, but, as Kennedy CJ was sapiently to remind conveyancers in 1930, circumstances could still exist where even a Landed Estates Court conveyance might not be conclusive as to title.[95] The sale of estates under the aegis of the courts was customarily preceded by the issuance of attractively illustrated prospectuses. A collection of these has recently been published.[96] Apart from the aesthetic pleasure it gives, the volume in question examines the work of both courts afresh and contains a great deal of interesting local history.

VI

Legislation wrought several modifications in the jurisdiction of the various superior courts. Two major modifications will alone be noted here.

In 1850, following in the wake of a similar reform introduced for England,[97] legislative enactment transferred the equity jurisdiction of the Irish Exchequer to

90 Ibid., at 547. **91** Brady, 'Legal developments, 1801-79', pp 456-7. **92** Christian, *The coming court of final appeal*, p. 38. **93** Ibid. **94** See further the judgment of Christian LJ in *In re Tottenham's Estate* (1869) IR 3 Eq 528 at 547-48. **95** *Moore* v. *A.G.* [1934] IR 44. **96** M.C. Lyons, *Illustrated incumbered estates, Ireland, 1850-1905* (Whitegate, Co. Clare, 1993). **97** 5 Vict., c. 5.

Chancery.[98] It was a curious tactic in many respects since, at the start of the century, the equity side of the Exchequer handled an immense amount of business.[99] The extinction of the equity side of the English court is discussed in a helpful monograph by Bryson,[100] but it is not immediately apparent why the equity side of the Irish court should have met the identical fate. The preamble to the pertinent Act in 1850 is far from enlightening: it merely states that the reform was adjudged expedient.

The reconstitution of the Irish court of Admiralty by act of parliament in 1867 was accompanied by a number of changes to the court's jurisdictional remit.[101] Article 8 of the Treaty of Union had confined the Irish court to an instance jurisdiction. Though there is some evidence that the court in the past had on the rare occasion exercised a jurisdiction in prize,[102] its authority to do so seems to have been grounded on a misapprehension, and the legislation of 1867 once again expressly disavowed any intention to confer such a jurisdiction upon the Irish court. The Act went on to clarify existing doubts about the court's powers in certain other areas – damage done both by and to ships, necessaries and material men, seamen's wages and maritime contracts – and to give the court new spheres of competence – in relation to such matters as damage to goods carried on board ship, towage, disputes over the ownership of ships and marine mortgages.[103] The serving admiralty judge, Thomas Frederick Kelly, was not retained in office. Instead, John Fitzhenry Townsend secured appointment under the new dispensation; he was to die in harness at the ripe age of 82 in 1893.[104] The sequence of events in 1867 rankled with Judge Kelly as he made plain in a farewell address delivered to admiralty practitioners late that year. 'I have a right,' he declared, 'to feel indignant at the mode in which my retirement has been effected, and the almost merciless manner in which I have been treated'.[105] When, in 1830, Sir Jonah Barrington was finally removed from the very office to which Kelly some years later was to be appointed, he too mouthed not dissimilar sentiments, but then, in Sir Jonah's case, the track record was very far from clean: he had been guilty of malversation of court funds, moneys raised from the sale of two derelicts. (Kelly's record, as it happens, was not entirely whistle-clean either.)

VII

Probably the most dramatic changes of all took place lower down the judicial hierarchy with a general widening of jurisdiction, and a consequent accumulation of powers by assistant barristers and justices of the peace. To the civil bill jurisdiction possessed by the former, originally conferred in 1796, there was to be added – by a long series of legislative enactments – a jurisdiction that embraced such matters as ejectment, replevin, the registrability of voters, insolvency, probate and administration and suits

98 13 & 14 Vict., c. 51. **99** Ball, *The judges in Ireland,* ii, p. 281. For the origins of the equity side of the Exchequer, see Wood, *A guide to the records in the Public Record Office of Ireland*, p. 107. **100** W.H. Bryson, *The equity side of the exchequer* (Cambridge, 1975). **101** 30 & 31 Vict., c. 114. **102** Walter Boyd, *The law and practice of the high court of Admiralty of Ireland* (Dublin, 1868), p. 14. **103** See 30 & 31 Vict., c. 114, ss. 27-47 for the details. Boyd, op. cit., pp 11-30 is a useful guide. **104** (1893) 22 *ILTSJ* 67, 77. **105** Quoted, (1867-68) 1 *ILTSJ* 622.

in respect of the occupation and ownership of land – the series terminating in the devolution of a general equity jurisdiction in 1877.[106] A comparison between two practitioners' manuals, Napier (1836) and Carleton (1878),[107] indicates at a glance the comprehensive character of this extension of jurisdiction. Down the years, the status of holders of the office of assistant barrister was to be increased as, too, was the salary. In 1877 holders of the office were given a new title: henceforth they were to be called 'county court judge'.[108]

No less remarkable was the development of petty sessions and the increase in the powers of justices of the peace. Around 1820 justices in Co. Cork appear to have begun the practice of regularly meeting as a group to deal mainly with minor criminal infractions. The idea spread, government took it up, and in the years 1823 and 1824 a pattern of countrywide petty sessions was installed. To begin with, there was difficulty in finding enough suitable persons to serve as JPs in remoter parts of the country but, in time, and with patience, even this hazard was to be overcome. Two important consolidating and amending statutes passed in mid-century – the Summary Jurisdiction (Ireland) Act 1850 and the Petty Sessions (Ireland) Act 1851[109] – convey very well the flavour of the wide powers that had then come to be possessed by JPs.

An impressive succession of manuals was to be produced, each one designed to assist justices, many of whom possessed no special legal training, in the discharge of their functions both as individuals and as participants in the work of petty and quarter sessions. One of the more celebrated of these manuals was the two-volume work published by Nun and Walsh.[110] Richard Nun was the assistant barrister for Co. Tyrone and John Edward Walsh much later in his career (1866) was to win appointment as master of the rolls. In terms of its interest, the rationale the authors supply for the book in their preface plainly transcends the immediate stated objective:

> There is perhaps, no part of our legal system in which a wider difference exists between the state of the law in England and Ireland than in that portion of it, the administration of which devolves upon the magistracy. The obvious consequence of this is, that the English works, treating of the office of a justice of the peace, numerous as they are, are of little or no practical utility to a justice in Ireland, while similar works adapted to the law in this country are comparatively few.[111]

From 1836 onwards, stipendiary magistrates, confined originally to Dublin, began to be deployed throughout the rest of the country,[112] and one of their functions was to

106 56 Geo. III, c. 88 (ejectment); 7 & 8 Geo. IV, c. 69 (replevin); 2 & 3 Will. IV, c. 52 (registrability of voters); 14 & 15 Vict., c. 57 (insolvency); 20 & 21 Vict., c. 79 (probate and administration); 33 & 34 Vict., c. 46 (occupation and ownership of land); 40 & 41 Vict., c. 56 (equitable jurisdiction). **107** Joseph Napier, *Digest of the civil bill and manor court statutes, with a copious commentary* (Dublin, 1836); J.W. Carleton, *The jurisdiction and procedure of the county courts in Ireland* (Dublin, 1878). **108** 40 & 41 Vict., c. 56, s. 3. **109** 13 & 14 Vict., c. 102; 14 & 15 Vict., c. 93. **110** Richard Nun and J.E. Walsh, *The powers and duties of justices of the peace in Ireland, and of constables as connected therewith; with a copious collection of statutes and forms*, 2nd ed., 2 vols. (Dublin, 1844). **111** Ibid., i, p. vi. **112** 6 Will. IV, c. 13, s. 31.

assist in the work of petty sessions. Again, no especial legal knowledge was demanded and, indeed, a preponderance of those appointed 'resident magistrates' or 'RMs' were retired army officers. Relations between the RMs and the superior courts, who exercised surveillance over the entire magistracy, largely by means of *certiorari*, were not always the most amicable. A doubtless apocryphal remark concerning one RM and attributed to Richard Dowse (made a baron of Exchequer in 1872) has Dowse say of the RM in question that he 'could no more state a case than compose a Greek ode'. Equally unrestrained criticism of the nineteenth-century Irish magistracy and Irish magisterial law is not exactly unknown in the modern era either. As regards summary jurisdiction in pre-independence Ireland, one future chief justice was to declare, that 'if Ireland had a complaint', it was 'that that jurisdiction was exercised too summarily'.[113] That much said, it is clear from surviving records that a great deal of criminal and civil business was despatched by petty sessions efficiently and conscientiously.[114] In the seventeenth century the inauguration of the assize system on a national basis undoubtedly made justice more accessible; it certainly promoted greater familiarity with it.[115] A similar verdict can be uttered on what was to be accomplished by the assistant barristers' and petty sessions courts in the course of the nineteenth.

VIII

In the last twenty years prior to the passing of the Judicature Act two sets of courts were to vanish from the Irish legal landscape: the manor courts and the ecclesiastical courts.

The former had experienced an increase in activity in the course of the eighteenth century but by the 1840s it is apparent that they were falling into disuse. In part, this was due to the attractiveness of their competitors, the assistant barristers' courts and petty sessions, the latter of which were also to take business away from the courts of conscience. But other factors, too, contributed. Seneschals – the judges who presided in the manor courts – were appointed by lords of the manor. Certain of these, however, possibly because of the availability of rival forums, would omit to make appointments whenever vacancies arose. More significant perhaps, the legal profession came to regard with ill-disguised antipathy the fashion in which the manor courts functioned. In 1841, in a case involving the court in Belfast, the Queen's Bench emphasised its inability to intervene even though the seneschal there had blatantly exceeded his powers: *Bracegirdle* v. *Waring*.[116] Difficulties over mounting effective control on account of an erratic appeal system were not the whole picture: the procedures actually employed by the courts were also to attract condemnation.[117] In 1848, for instance, in *Costelloe* v. *Hooks*,[118] a case touching on the conduct of affairs by the seneschal of the

113 *Melling* v. *O Mathghamhna* [1962] IR 1 at 46, per Ó Dálaigh J (as he then was). **114** See further Desmond McCabe, 'Magistrates, peasants and the petty sessions courts, Mayo, 1823 -50', (1985) 5 *Cathair na Mart* 45, and Penny Bonsall, *The Irish RMs: the resident magistrates in the British administration in Ireland* (Dublin, 1997). **115** McCavitt, '"Good planets in their several spheares" ', passim. **116** Jebb & Bourke 12. **117** See generally on these matters, Napier, *Digest of the civil bill and manor court statutes*. **118** 11 ILR 294.

manor court in Newry, the Queen's Bench stigmatised the device of attachment of goods to initiate proceedings as not only unwarranted but also unlawful. Crampton J, a participant in the decision, was not content to leave matters there, adding, in a postscript, that he only wished the legislature had deprived the manor courts of all jurisdiction long ago.[119] The quietus came a decade later in 1859, when an act of parliament suppressed them totally.[120]

Despite the litany of complaints, it is impossible even so not to sense that something may have been unwisely dispensed with when the manor courts were abolished. In 1837, in evidence to a select committee, a seneschal from west Cork praised the achievement of the three courts over which he presided. 'The people', he observed,

> are invariably pleased with being able to tell their story in Irish and to address the jury through me and to tell their story as they like themselves.[121]

His encomium touched on other matters besides, of no less interest:

> The jury are conversant with their little manners, customs and bargains much better than gentlemen and all that; I do think that many of them would come to a better and fairer decision than almost any magistrate at least more satisfactory to the parties.[122]

The official ecclesiastical courts were set to disappear as a result of clearly focused political opposition. The courts themselves were linked formally to the Anglican Church of Ireland, and, by the same token, the disestablishment of that church in 1869[123] – to date from 1 January 1871 – meant the abolition of the courts on the appointed day.[124] By then the only important jurisdiction remaining in the old consistorial courts lay in the sphere of family law, and arrangements were swiftly made by statute to transfer that jurisdiction to a new secular tribunal, the Court for Matrimonial Causes and Matters.[125] The critical legislation preserved one point of contact with the immediate past, the new court being obliged to apply the relevant principles and rules in a manner 'as nearly as may be conformable' to those 'on which the ecclesiastical courts of Ireland have hitherto acted and given relief'.[126]

Earlier in the century, a series of measures had effectively whittled down the once extensive jurisdiction possessed by this group of courts. Pressures that led, first, to the introduction of tithe composition (1823)[127] and, then, to that of tithe rent-charge (1838)[128] ensured finally the removal from the purview of the ecclesiastical courts of all matters concerned with the payment of tithe, a branch of law which, in the latter half of the eighteenth century and into the earlier years of the nineteenth, had proved irremediably contentious. (The common law courts, and especially Exchequer, shared

119 Ibid., at 304. **120** 22 Vict., c. 14. **121** Quoted, McDowell, *The Irish administration*, p. 118. **122** Ibid. On manor courts in Ulster, see further W.H. Crawford, 'The significance of landed estates in Ulster, 1600–1820', (1990) 17 *Irish Economic and Social History* 44, and see, too, more generally, T.C. Barnard, 'Lawyers and the law in later seventeenth-century Ireland', (1993) 28 *Irish Historical Studies* 256 at 271–2. **123** 32 & 33 Vict., c. 42. **124** Ibid., s. 21. **125** 33 & 34 Vict., c. 110. **126** Ibid., s. 13. **127** 4 Geo. IV, c.99. **128** 1 & 2 Vict., c. 109.

jurisdiction in this area; they too, it can safely be claimed, will scarcely have objected to the loss of unwelcome political attention.)[129]

Further inroads into the jurisdiction of the ecclesiastical courts affected testate and intestate succession, a jurisdiction shared between the consistorial courts in the case of less wealthy decedents, and, in that of the more wealthy, as readers of le Fanu's *The house by the churchyard* and familiar with the plight of Doctor Sturk's widow may recall, the euphoniously entitled Court of the Prerogative and Faculties. In 1857, in conjunction with similar action taken at the time for England, a new secular court of Probate was established to which the relevant jurisdiction and powers of both the consistorial courts and the Court of the Prerogative were transferred. The assistant barristers' courts too shared in the distribution of business.[130] Among the higher echelons, continuity of personnel was preserved. Richard Keatinge, who had been named judge of the Prerogative in 1843, thus carried on as the new judge of the Court of Probate, serving in that capacity until retiring in 1868.[131] When Admiralty was reconstituted in 1867, Judge Kelly, as we have seen, was not to be so fortunate.

With the loss of jurisdiction by all these courts, the need to appoint delegates to attend to resultant appeals markedly declined. The final end for delegates, too, came with Disestablishment itself.

Ecclesiastical courts under that designation were, of course, to survive Disestablishment. They survive today where any church, as a voluntary association recognised by the State, has chosen to erect such courts and has continued to maintain them.[132] The marriage tribunals of the Roman Catholic church furnish the most obvious example.

IX

A last forum merits rather more than a cursory glance: the board of the Irish privy council. A court 'of great antiquity', as McDowell puts it[133] and as Crawford's recent monograph on the Tudor period confirms,[134] the privy council in the nineteenth century was reduced to tackling a more modest but still varied 'judicial' agenda. It had long taken seisin of appeals under the ministers' money legislation of 1665,[135] and this continued.[136] Nineteenth-century legislation was to confer upon it express authority to entertain appeals in relation to both tithe composition (1823)[137] and incumbered

129 *Knox* v. *Gavan* (1836) 1 Jones 190, a decision of the Court of Exchequer, attracted a degree of such publicity. See further my 'Executive failure to enforce judicial decrees: a neglected chapter in nineteenth century constitutional history', in McEldowney & O'Higgins (ed.), *The common law tradition*, p. 85. **130** 20 & 21 Vict., c. 79. S.58 defines the assistant barristers' share of the spoils: they could deal with estates where the personalty was valued at under £200 and the realty under £300. The former consistorial courts' jurisdiction was tied to the decedent's wealth being exclusively located within the diocese. **131** (1876) 10 *ILTSJ* 113. **132** For discussion of such matters see, e.g., *The State (Colquhoun)* v. *D'Arcy* [1936] IR 641. **133** McDowell, *The Irish administration*, p. 106. **134** J.G. Crawford, *Anglicizing the government of Ireland: the Irish privy council and the expansion of Tudor rule, 1556-1578* (Dublin, 1993). **135** 17 & 18 Chas. II, c. 7. The council's jurisdiction was founded on the wording of s. 1. **136** See, e.g., *Petition of the parishioners of St Peter's and St Kevin's parishes* (1828) 1 Law Rec. 298. **137** 4 Geo. IV, c. 99, ss. 29, 30. See, too, 2 & 3 Will. IV, c. 119,

estates (1849),[138] neither mere trifles. An account from 1827 of the privy council's hearing of a tithe composition appeal possesses unusual interest. *Parishioners of Timoleague* v. *Fergusson*[139] reveals the then lord lieutenant, the marquess of Wellesley, presiding, with judicial and ecclesiastical members of the council also in attendance. Among the barristers present for what is a hearing in open court was one 'D. O'Connell', who, at Wellesley's invitation, was deputed to interpret the evidence of a principal witness, a witness who was an Irish-speaker. The latter related how a churchwarden, one of the local publicans, had advanced the time of the crucial 'vestry' meeting called to fix the level of the rector's composition for tithe, and how, after the meeting was over, the rector had ordered punch to be served to everyone there. The privy council, after an adjournment, ordered the tithe commissioners to undertake a re-assessment.[140]

Though later in the century the privy council was to be given additional powers to hear complaints against all manner of administrative decisions,[141] its involvement in more mainstream judicial business appreciably diminished. Problems raised by tithe composition were soon enough disposed of. Ministers' money was finally phased out in the 1850s,[142] so complaints under that head also became a thing of the past. Significantly, when, in 1858, the Landed Estates Court replaced the Incumbered Estates Court, it was provided that thereafter appeals were to be transferred to the recently established Court of Appeal in Chancery.[143] Again, in 1870, it was laid down that appeals under the Landlord and Tenant (Ireland) Act of that year were to be brought before an entirely new creation, the Court for Land Cases Reserved.[144] The inferior standing of the Irish council within the constitutional scheme introduced by the Union is best exemplified by an innovation dating from 1867 when the Irish court of Admiralty was reconstituted. As we have already noted, Irish delegates were supplanted as the final court of appeal. Instead, appeals were to be carried before the English privy council in London.[145]

One other facet to the council's range of activities deserves notice. Certainly as late as Emmet's rebellion in 1803 the council customarily exercised important police functions – ordering the apprehension of suspects, the members of the council even interrogating the latter themselves. When exactly this practice died out is unclear, but a sequence of reforms in the area of policing, culminating, in 1836, in the creation of a countrywide force, the Irish Constabulary, will have contributed to its final abandonment. Both this constabulary, renamed the Royal Irish Constabulary in 1867, and the Dublin Metropolitan Police were in the course of time to develop detective and special branches. It is likely that the privy council will have been only too willing to surrender the powers it had previously exercised in the broad area of policing to the new professionals.

ss. 8, 9, 10. The arrangements were continued for a limited period after the introduction of tithe rent-change: see 1 & 2 Vict., c. 109, ss. 13-14. **138** 12 & 13 Vict., c. 77, ss. 51, 52. **139** 1 Law Rec. 103. **140** The appellants might have been better advised to let sleeping dogs lie, since the commissioners set the composition at an even higher figure. For further proceedings in the affair, which finally proved abortive, see 1 Law Rec. 577. **141** McDowell, *The Irish administration*, pp 106-7. **142** 17 & 18 Vict., c. 11; 20 & 21 Vict., c. 8. **143** 21 & 22 Vict., c. 72, s. 41. **144** 33 & 34 Vict., c. 46, s. 24. **145** 30 & 31 Vict., c. 114, s. 91.

X

Police reform may be counted among the longer-term processes at work that were set to transform the Irish legal system as the nineteenth century advanced. So, too, may the emergence of a more pronounced professional ethos within the membership of the Irish legal profession itself. This last became apparent in three distinct major contexts: in the establishment of new representative bodies, in provision for legal education and in the publishing of legal texts.

The curious episode of the King's Inns charter (1792-3), when the benchers of King's Inns were forced to surrender the charter they had earlier persuaded the king to grant, indicated that what at the time was the profession's sole governing body could no longer afford to ignore expressions of outright opposition to it. Both the obtaining of the charter itself and the composing of the draft bye-laws made under it can be interpreted as moves to reform the profession, but suspicion of the benchers' motives was universal and deep-seated: their grandiose plans were perceived rather as a smoke-screen behind which unwanted and uncalled-for controls were to be imposed. At the conclusion of the affair, new bye-laws were nevertheless introduced, and though these dropped the educational features in the draft bye-laws they replaced, were to confirm the hegemony of the benchers as the profession's sole governing élite.[146]

Long unquestioned, from the second quarter of the nineteenth century onwards that hegemony of the benchers was increasingly to come under attack. The first major inroad into the powers previously wielded by them came in 1830 with the establishment of the Law Society of Ireland. Among the society's stated objects were those to improve the law and to reform legal education, and also

> to preserve the rights and privileges of attorneys – to promote useful communication and good feeling amongst the members of the profession – fair and honourable practice – and to adopt such measures as may be best calculated to ensure respectability and advantage to the public.[147]

The society received its royal charter in 1852 under the name of the Incorporated Law Society of the Attorneys and Solicitors of Ireland.[148]

The Bar were not untouched by the criticisms that the new solicitors' representative body came to level at the benchers; but they were much slower to take effective action themselves or to agree precisely on what needed to be done. For their part, the benchers contrived to improve their image with new guarantees being given over representation within their ranks, but continuing controversy as regards library facilities and other bread-and-butter issues eventually helped to convince the doubters that a new system of representation for barristers was needed as well. The seizing of the crucial initiative was long delayed and it was only in 1897, twenty years after the adoption of the Judicature Act, that the General Council of the Bar came into being.[149] The

146 Colum Kenny, *King's Inns and the kingdom of Ireland: the Irish 'inn of court' 1541-1800* (Dublin, 1992), ch. 9; Daire Hogan, *The legal profession in Ireland, 1789-1922* (Dublin, 1986), pp 20-2. **147** Hogan, *The legal profession in Ireland*, pp 93-4. **148** Ibid., p. 113. **149** Ibid., pp 60-5.

benchers thereafter were still to retain important powers, not least in relation to the education of students reading for the Bar.

Developments in education for those working to join either branch of the profession proceeded slowly and were frequently accompanied by a great deal of rancour. The Dublin Law Institute, founded in 1839 by a barrister, Tristram Kennedy, and designed to fill a major educational lacuna, proved short-lived when the benchers of King's Inns who had originally extended to Kennedy their financial support, later chose to withdraw it.[150] Whether this reversal in the benchers' attitude should be attributed to the malign influence of Sir Edward Sugden, Lord Plunket's successor as lord chancellor in 1841, or whether more general considerations lay behind it, is not immediately obvious. Whatever the explanation, one consequence of the rebuff had important long-terms effects: this was the appointment in 1846, at Irish instigation, of a parliamentary select committee to survey arrangements for legal education then in place within the entire United Kingdom.

The report of the select committee, chaired by the Irish MP, Thomas Wyse, represents a milestone in the history of legal education in both Britain and Ireland. Having taken into account a mass of evidence, much of it supplied from Ireland, the committee concluded that the existing arrangements were woefully inadequate and that drastic action was needed.[151] The benchers of King's Inns were at long last galvanised into action. In 1850 the benchers reached agreement with the board of Trinity College to combine their joint resources: both would appoint a number of professors to give lectures on legal topics. Attendance at the two sets of lectures was made compulsory but aspirant barristers still did not have to pass any examinations. In 1864, in a curious twist, they were given the option of either attending the lectures or passing examinations. Only, eventually, in 1872 were the benchers to insist that aspirant barristers had to do both.[152] The insistence that they should also enrol as students of one of the London inns of court – another grievance that permeates much nineteenth-century discussion of legal education in Ireland – was only to be abandoned outside our period in 1885.[153] The fact that thirteen years earlier self-contained, indigenous educational structures *vis-à-vis* the Irish Bar had been put in place naturally facilitated the dropping of the requirement that Irish law students were to 'keep their terms' and 'eat their dinners' in London.

Improvements in educational provision for the solicitors' profession were among the stated objectives of the Law Society when it was established in 1830:

> to adopt such measures as may be best calculated to prevent the apprenticing or admission of uneducated and improper persons, and to prevent unqualified persons from qualifying.[154]

So far as educational reform was concerned, the main difficulty the Society faced was attributable to the fact that decisions in this area lay within the hands of the benchers

150 Colum Kenny, *Tristram Kennedy and the revival of Irish legal training* (Dublin, 1996), passim; Hogan, *The legal profession in Ireland*, pp 104–5. **151** Ibid., pp 105–9. **152** Ibid., pp 109–11. **153** 48 & 49 Vict., c. 20. **154** Hogan, *The legal profession in Ireland*, p. 94.

of King's Inns and for nigh on a generation the latter saw no need to introduce any changes at all. The agreement of 1850 with Trinity College, for instance, was designed exclusively for the benefit of aspirant barristers. Finally, however, in 1860, as a result of persistent lobbying, the benchers agreed to inaugurate for entrants to the solicitors' profession both a preliminary examination (in Latin, History, Arithmetic, Bookkeeping, Geography and English Composition) and a final examination. The benchers also instituted a professorship of law 'specially adapted to the wants of that branch of the profession'. Thereafter, lectures were to be given to solicitors' apprentices. In 1866 the Law Society took over responsibility for education of the solicitors' branch of the profession, subject, in the last analysis, to the overall control of the judges. In 1898, even this last link was cut.[155]

The growth of professionalism was mirrored likewise in the appearance of an Irish legal literature.

In the eighteenth century Irish legal authors had been a comparative rarity. The publication in 1772 of F.S. Sullivan's *Historical treatise on the feudal law,*[156] a text based on the lecture course Sullivan had given at Trinity College, marks him out as an exception. But, perhaps significantly, the book was produced both posthumously and in London and the specifically Irish content is meagre enough. Another Trinity professor, Arthur Browne, focused on Ireland's civilian jurisdictions – the ecclesiastical courts and admiralty – in a major work, published in Dublin in 1798-9. His *Compendious view of the civil law*[157] sought to combine historical scholarship – also Sullivan's forte – with a great deal of up-to-date practical guidance, and the portion that treated of admiralty law in particular was found of immediate utility by practitioners, not least, apparently, by practitioners in the United States.[158]

B.T. Duhigg in his *History of the King's Inns* (1806)[159] aimed to produce another volume of enduring historical worth. Unfortunately, however, though Duhigg's history contains a great deal of invaluable information, his treatment of a number of episodes in the fortunes of the Inns is flawed, and he is in many other respects unreliable.[160] Thereafter the emphasis in Irish legal writing seems to have been concentrated on the production of treatises and manuals that possessed more obvious practical value and that could be relied on, accordingly, both to sell copies and to reimburse author and publisher on their outlay. In one respect, however, Duhigg did manage to set a trend. In the years ahead, many legal authors in Ireland, like Duhigg himself, were to be drawn from the ranks of assistant barristers. This is true of James Lyne, a lawyer with scholarly inclinations, who in 1837 produced probably the best Irish text on the problem that had surfaced in *Bateman* v. *Murray*[161] – leases for lives.[162] Richard Nun,

155 Ibid., pp 110-11, 130. **156** F.S. Sullivan, *An historical treatise on the feudal law, and the constitution and laws of England; with a commentary on Magna Charta, and ... illustrations of many of the English statutes* (London, 1772). **157** Arthur Browne, *A compendious view of the civil law, being the substance of a course of lectures*, 2 vols. (Dublin and London, 1798-9). **158** J.S. Sweeney, 'The admiralty law of Arthur Browne', (1995) 26 *Journal of Maritime Law and Commerce* 58. I am grateful to Professor Sweeney for furnishing me with a copy of his excellent survey of Browne's contribution to admiralty learning. **159** B.T. Duhigg, *History of the King's Inns* (Dublin, 1806). **160** Colum Kenny, 'Counsellor Duhigg – antiquarian and activist', (1986) 21 *Irish Jurist* 300. **161** (1779) 5 Bro. P.C.20. See above, p. 245. **162** James Lyne, *A treatise on leases for lives renewable for*

whom we have already met, was another assistant barrister, and so too was that most prolific of Irish legal authors, John Finlay (?1781–1856). In 1830 Finlay had no less than five law books in print: on the duties of churchwardens and parish officers; on game and inland fisheries; on tithe; on leases for lives; and on landlord and tenant.[163] Finlay was neither a Pothier nor a Story, and two of these texts are slender enough. But considerable learning informs them all, and the text on the law of tithe, with its meticulous attention to detail, its inclusion of case-material not to be found anywhere else, and its historical understanding of tithe itself makes it an excellent place to begin for anyone seeking to familiarise themselves with the intricacies of this most vexing and vexatious of topics.

The treatises and manuals produced would vary immensely in the choice of subject-matter no less than in the skill with which they were written or the professionalism with which each one was presented.[164] The pace of legislative reform and the accumulation of fresh case-law ensured that the substance of much Irish law could change very quickly, and texts purporting to tackle 'hard law' were prone to obsolescence in a dishearteningly short space of time. Though a few second editions were prepared, a common fate to befall many authors was eventually to be superseded by a new author and a new book. In many instances, however, the profession was obliged to make do with a text, acknowledged as the leading authority in the field but recognised at the same time to be out of date, and to be relied on, in consequence, with considerable circumspection. At the same time, much Irish law was identical with that in England – tort law and commercial law are examples. Here, it must not be forgotten, treatises and manuals of English provenance held sway and continued to do so.

As regards the provision of primary source materials, the first edition of the Irish statutes at large (1765) represented a major breakthrough.[165] Irish law reporting itself only finally came of age over twenty years later with the appearance in 1787 of the reports of Vernon and Scriven.[166] Ridgeway, Lapp and Schoales and a whole succession of nominate reports then follow, very much later after nominate reports had materialised in England. Of variable quality undoubtedly, and, strangely to modern eyes, with each report or set of reports concentrating for the most part on the doctrinal elaborations offered in a single specific court, these volumes bore eloquent testimony to the growth of the new professional ethos. And the pretence was soon dropped that the sole justification for publishing Irish law reports was to ensure that adequate illumination was directed at areas of the law where Ireland materially differed from England. A

ever (Dublin, 1837). **163** *The office and duty of church warden and parish officer in Ireland* (Dublin, 1827); *A treatise on the laws of game and inland fisheries in Ireland* (Dublin, 1827); *A treatise on the law of tythes in Ireland, and ecclesiastical law connected therewith* (Dublin, 1828); *A treatise on the law of renewals in respect to leases for lives renewable for ever in Ireland, with the cases and decisions thereon* (Dublin, 1829); *A treatise on the law of landlord and tenant in Ireland* (Dublin, 1830). **164** For an account of the phenomenon viewed in a broader common law perspective, see A.W.B. Simpson, 'The rise and fall of the legal treatise: legal principles and the forms of legal literature', (1981) 48 *University of Chicago Law Review* 632. **165** See 'The legislation of the pre-Union Irish parliament', above, at p. 93f. **166** See generally for what follows 'Puzzles from Irish law reporting history', above, p. 193.

brew not so very dissimilar from what was being served up in England now came to be served up in Ireland as well.

In 1867, two years after England had again set the precedent, there was established the Irish Council of Law Reporting, and the system of private, nominate reports and the semi-official system that succeeded it both came to an end. The new council soon fell out with Jonathan Christian, the lord justice of appeal; or, rather, it should be said, Christian fell out with them. In November 1877, contemporaneously, that is, with the passing of the Judicature Act, Christian launched a venomous assault on the Irish reports of his day:

> In the whole vast ocean of printed matter, since the days of Caxton, I venture to say that there could not be found within an equal space such a mass of utterly worthless rubbish as makes the staple of eleven Equity volumes in the Irish Reports.[167]

By this stage, however, the exaggeration and the scabrous tone were well-recognised Christian hall-marks, and certain colleagues are likely to have preferred to ignore both him and his remarks whatever an embarrassed and infuriated Council of Law Reporting may have sensed was the appropriate response for them. Yet, as ever, Christian did have a point. On the recurring question of how much any system of law reports should actually bother or essay to report, Christian had an uncomplicated stance. He was a minimalist. Can it be said that he was wrong?

XI

A third process at work, increasingly in evidence as the century wore on, was the rationalisation of the machinery of justice operative at higher court level. Practice and procedure were to be reformed, simplified and standardised; the functions and tasks discharged by what, historically, had been four distinct superior courts were to be gradually assimilated. The whole process was to lead finally to the passing by parliament of the Judicature Act in 1877. Thereby was that great cycle in the history of law in Ireland, alluded to by the commentator quoted in our opening remarks, to be brought to an end.

The deployment of crown prosecutors and crown solicitors to handle criminal prosecutions before the assize courts and quarter sessions signalled an innovation in criminal practice of paramount importance.[168] As regards civil litigation, insistence on the issuance of a simple writ of summons to initiate a lawsuit, by way of substitution for the many other methods previously allowed, constituted a reform of no less striking significance. Many other procedural changes involving the conduct of civil litiga-

167 *Hone* v. *Blanci* (1877) 11 *ILTSJ* 586 at 593. And see, too, above, pp 207-12 and V.T.H. Delany, 'Lord Justice Christian and law reporting', (1956-58) 12 *NILQ* 46. **168** See further Desmond McCabe, '"That part that laws or king's can cause or cure": crown prosecutions and jury trial at Longford assizes, 1830-45', in Raymond Gillespie and Gerard Moran (eds.), *Longford: essays in county history* (Dublin, 1991), p. 153.

tion were to be implemented. All form part of an exceedingly tangled story, one sometimes connected with the extinguishing of various exotically-entitled court offices – six clerk, prothonotary, filacer, exigenter, chief remembrancer is scarcely an exhaustive inventory[169] – and sometimes not.

Changes sanctioned by statute in the 1850s presaged more major reforms similar in character that were to come later. These related to the powers traditionally exerciseable by the common law courts, on the one hand, and by Chancery and the other equity jurisdictions, on the other. Two such powers, historically denied the former but regularly employed by the latter – to order discovery and to issue injunctions – were bestowed upon the common law courts by statute in 1856.[170] Two years later, movement in the opposite direction occurred when Chancery was authorised to award damages and also itself to determine contested issues of fact, powers it, too, had previously lacked.[171]

Rapprochement between the common law courts and Chancery was not the only pressing question: rapprochement between the three common law jurisdictions of King's or Queen's Bench, Common Pleas and Exchequer, predictably enough, was placed on the agenda as well. At the close of the eighteenth century, each of the three enjoyed a separate identity. In the course of the next half century or so, that identity was to be whittled down to the point where abolition of all three courts and their incorporation, together with Chancery, in a single unified high court structure must indeed have come to appear the intelligent path to pursue.

In succession law, the jurisdiction of the common law courts and the ecclesiastical courts overlapped, and doctrinal differences between the two sets of courts were not unknown. The risk that comparable differences between the common law courts themselves might also emerge could not naturally be prevented, but that risk undoubtedly receded in the nineteenth century and from an early date. For a start, a sense of collegiality was clearly promoted by the involvement of the benches of all three courts in the work of the various appellate tribunals – Exchequer Chamber (1800), the meetings of the twelve judges that foreshadowed the creation of the Court for Crown Cases Reserved (1848), even the Court of Appeal in Chancery (1856), where, it will be recalled, any common law judge might be asked to serve. Under previous dispensations, the only opportunities the several judges had available to them for actual cooperation was when they shared the burden of assize duty. The camaraderie that this will have engendered is unlikely to have had quite the same overall impact.

Various other developments drew the three courts closer and closer together. The reform, simplification and standardisation of rules of procedure played their part. So, too, somewhat more obliquely, did the abandonment of a rule of particular concern to the attorneys. From 1816 the possession of a practising certificate became a permanent requirement, as did the payment of the appropriate stamp duty. For many years, an attorney who wished to practise in more than one common law court had, however,

169 For the disappearance of these offices, see 6 & 7 Will. IV, c. 74, 7 & 8 Vict., c. 107 and 13 & 14 Vict., c. 51. **170** 19 & 20 Vict., c. 102, ss. 55, 81. **171** 21 & 22 Vict., c. 27, ss. 2,3; s. 8 of the same measure extends these provisions to Ireland.

to apply for a second or even a third practising certificate, and pay the obligatory duty on each occasion. The burden of this financial outlay irked as indeed did the inconvenience of the rule itself, but it was only finally in 1840 that a remedy was propounded. Then legislation laid it down that where the practititoner had paid stamp duty on securing his admission to practice in any one of the four superior courts (Chancery and the three courts of common law), he would be entitled to be admitted to the three others without the payment of any additional duty.[172]

The Process and Practice (Ireland) Act of 1850[173] signalled a much more dramatic advance. Citing the inconvenience that arose

> from the unequal distribution of business amongst the... superior courts of common law, whereby one is often insufficiently employed, while the others are unduly pressed, to the great delay and injury of suitors and detriment of justice,

and concluding that it was 'expedient to adopt means to equalize the business of the said courts, so far as the same can be effected',[174] the Act went on to install the necessary arrangements. The offices where process was initiated were consolidated. Writs for the commencement of 'personal actions' were to be rotated between the three courts. There was abolished the rule of medieval origin entitling a defendant, who claimed a privilege to be sued in a particular court, to present a plea of abatement. Further provision was made to enable any common law judge to try issues and make orders in chamber as regards business depending in any one of the three courts. The so-called consolidated nisi prius chamber was erected simultaneously.[175]

Outside the area of personal actions, the three common law courts still retained a portion of their former distinct identity. Common Pleas and Queen's Bench continued to handle all cases of advowson – disputes over title to benefices – until Disestablishment rather than the Judicature Act destroyed their monopoly. The equity courts – Chancery and the courts of the master of the rolls and of the vice-chancellor – preserved their separate identity too. But further reform was suggested, and, in the Victorian manner, a major inquiry was undertaken. The outcome was a set of recommendations that argued for radical structural reform. Such reform was introduced for England and Wales by the Judicature Act of 1873.[176] Exigencies of the parliamentary time-table, changes of government and criticism from the Irish judiciary on points of detail contributed to the four-year delay before similar legislation was eventually enacted for Ireland in 1877. Of the prolonged debates that accompanied passage of this measure through parliament, F.H. Newark was to observe, not altogether unfairly, that these 'turned almost wholly on the question of how much work could be got out of the Irish judges for how little money'.[177]

172 3 & 4 Vict., c.79. See my 'The regulation of the admission of attorneys and solicitors in Ireland, 1600-1866', above, at p. 177. **173** 13 Vict., c. 18. **174** Ibid., s. 31. **175** Ibid., ss. 31, 38, 39, 26 and 27-9, respectively. **176** 36 & 37 Vict., c. 66. See further Brady, 'Legal developments, 1801-79', pp 471-2. **177** F.H. Newark, *Notes on Irish legal history* (Belfast, 1960), p. 27.

XII

As regards the Irish legal system, the Supreme Court of Judicature (Ireland) Act of 1877[178] clearly entailed a new beginning. Within a unified 'Supreme Court' structure there was first of all to be found a new 'High Court'. This court was composed of five divisions reflecting the areas of competence occupied by the former superior courts now scheduled to be abolished.[179] Chancery, Queen's Bench, Common Pleas and Exchequer all had a division each; Probate and Matrimonial – relative newcomers to the legal system – shared a division between them. Further rationalisation followed in subsequent years. Thus the Common Pleas Division was to be integrated with the Queen's Bench Division in 1887, the Exchequer and the Probate and Matrimonial Divisions being merged with the latter as well in 1897. The court of Bankruptcy and that of Admiralty, both previously left out of the reckoning completely, were wound up also in 1897, their respective spheres of competence being incorporated within the Queen's Bench Division too.[180] In 1877 the new Chancery Division had had associated with it the work of the Landed Estates Court, but this could not compare with the amount of variegated judicial business which, as a result of these far-reaching changes, came to be inherited by the Queen's Bench Division. 'And so', as F.H. Newark was to express it,

> the century came to an end with the High Court in the position which it retained up to 1921 – a court of two divisions, the Chancery Division and the Queen's/King's Bench Division.[181]

The Irish Act of 1877, like its England counterpart of 1873, prescribed 'the fusion' of law and equity.[182] Every branch of the Supreme Court was thus empowered to recognise, and to adjudicate upon all rights, legal and equitable, that might arise in the progress of a cause. Considerable store was set by this portentous announcement. 'No longer', one commentator wrote,

> will an unfortunate suitor be tossed like a shuttlecock across the hall of the Four Courts from Equity to Common Law and Common Law back to Equity until his patience and money are exhausted.[183]

As was well known, in a number of contexts the rules followed by the equity and common law courts were at variance. A statutory inventory was thus drawn up which proceeded to set down the doctrinal position that was to obtain in those situations where reconciliation between conflicting rules seemed called for. The inventory disclaimed any intention to be exhaustive. In residual contexts not dealt with in the inventory, it was provided that the rules of equity were to prevail.[184]

178 40 & 41 Vict., c. 57. **179** Ibid., s.4. **180** 50 Vict., c. 6, s. 2; 60 & 61 Vict., c. 66. **181** Newark, *Notes on Irish legal history*, pp 28–9. **182** 40 & 41 Vict., c. 57, ss. 27, 28. **183** Lowry, *The Supreme Court of Judicature (Ireland) Act 1877*, p. iii. **184** 40 & 41 Vict., c. 57, s. 28 (11).

The Judicature Act in no way affected the House of Lords, being merely content to confirm its position as the court of final appeal.[185] The preceding year, as it happened, the judicial work of the House had already attracted the attention of the legislature. The Appellate Jurisdiction Act of 1876[186] had introduced two major changes. First, it gave the force of law to the constitutional convention that only peers with appropriate judicial expertise were to participate in the hearing of appeals. Secondly, to assist with the hearing of such appeals, it made provision for the appointment of lords of appeal in ordinary – the law lords. It was under this provision that, as we have already had occasion to remark, Lord Fitzgerald was to be translated from the Irish Queen's Bench Division in 1882.

The Act of 1877 did, however, make radical alterations to the system of intermediate appeals. Here a new Court of Appeal was erected, the second constituent court, alongside the High Court, of the new Supreme Court.[187] To make way for it, the Court of Exchequer Chamber, the Court of Appeal in Chancery and the lesser-known Court for Land Cases Reserved were all abolished. (The Court for Crown Cases Reserved was left unaffected.) The new court at the outset had a membership of seven – two lords justices of appeal (new posts) and five ex-officio judges: the lord chancellor, the master of the rolls, the chief justice of the Queen's Bench Division, the chief justice of the Common Pleas Division and the chief baron of the Exchequer Division. The ex-officio component was later reduced to three, on the suppression of the Common Pleas Division in 1887 and the retirement in 1916 of Christopher Palles, the last chief baron. It was laid down that no member of the court was to sit on an appeal from any judgment or order made by himself at first instance whether sitting alone or with other judges.

Earlier plans for appellate jurisdiction had drawn criticism from the entire Irish bench in 1873, and had inspired Christian to write, in the following year, his bitter pamphlet, *The coming court of final appeal for Ireland*. These plans had envisaged substituting for the House of Lords as the court of last resort throughout the United Kingdom a very differently composed final court of appeal which would, like the court of appeal that eventually materialised for Ireland, have contained a strong ex-officio element. Christian objected since he considered it wrong in principle that the projected court of final appeal, perhaps sitting as an Irish division in Dublin, should be so disproportionately weighted in favour of the ex-officio element. Personal antipathies clearly lay behind Christian's broad line of attack. Christian, as we already know, had little respect for O'Hagan, the then Irish lord chancellor, and he demurred at the prospect of someone he regarded as an intellectual lightweight serving automatically on the projected new court. Christian simultaneously sought to open up the discussion. Appalled at the prospect of a 'debasement in the quality of the final utterances of the law',[188] Christian asked what was the point of establishing any appellate tribunal unless those with the power of appointment recognised the need to secure the services of individuals of the highest intellectual calibre. It would not do at all, he declaimed, if the performance of the appeal court was markedly less impressive than that of the

185 Ibid., s. 86. **186** 39 & 40 Vict., c. 59. **187** 40 & 41 Vict., c. 57, s. 23. **188** Christian, *The coming court of final appeal for Ireland*, p. 8.

court of first instance. Here, Christian took an emphatically gloomy view of the shape of things to come. In his judgment in *In re Tottenham's Estate* in 1869[189] he had slipped in some blunt remarks on the manner in which in Ireland party political considerations had dictated exercises in patronage.[190] The refrain was picked up in his pamphlet of 1874 where, not for the first time nor indeed the last, Christian was to call a spade a spade. There was no certainty at all, Christian contended, that governments would choose intelligently when they appointed future lords chancellor. Recent surveys, based on an examination of a wealth of original correspondence, would tend to confirm Christian's main complaint that party politics had in fact come to exercise an unacceptable degree of influence on the filling of Irish judicial vacancies.[191] The practice was not to be viewed as something that came to an end when the last of the Union 'engagements' was finally honoured. Christian's misgivings were not, therefore, entirely misplaced. Far from it.

Nevertheless, the trend of future events was to suggest that Christian's fears to a large extent had been groundless. As we have seen, the Judicature Act, as passed for Ireland, retained the House of Lords as the final court of appeal, and, incidentally, thus preserved intact the arrangement contained in article 8 of the Treaty of Union. As regards the composition of the intermediate Court of Appeal, the government did not withdraw the proposal, originally advanced for the court scheduled to replace the House of Lords, that the lord chancellor should serve ex-officio. But successive governments do indeed appear to have taken very seriously the question of who to appoint to fill the two positions of lord justice – the more permanent, and, increasingly, the more influential, component in the membership of the court. Christian himself moved to the new Court of Appeal early in 1878, though he was not to serve there for any length of time, announcing his resignation from the bench the following November. Perhaps to mollify him, he had been joined on the new court by Rickard Deasy, long a member of the court of Exchequer, whom Christian identified in his pamphlet of 1874 as the person who should have been made lord chancellor in 1868. 'There is not a gentleman in Ireland', Christian had written at the time,

> Catholic, Episcopalian-Protestant, Presbyterian, or Free-thinker, but would have acclaimed the appointment of that practised equity lawyer, approved judge and true gentleman, Baron Deasy.[192]

Gerald FitzGibbon succeeded Christian on the court late in 1878. When Deasy died in 1883, his place was taken by Charles Robert Barry, and the resultant vacancy, after Barry's death in 1897, was filled by Hugh Holmes. These men all shed lustre on the new court, which swiftly earned a considerable reputation for itself throughout the common law world.

189 IR 3 Eq 528. **190** Ibid., at 573. **191** Daire Hogan, '"Vacancies for their friends": judicial appointments in Ireland, 1866-67', in Hogan & Osborough (eds.), *Brehons, serjeants and attorneys*, p. 211; Colum Kenny, 'Irish ambition and English preference in chancery appointments, 1827-1841: the fate of William Conyngham Plunket', in Osborough (ed.), *Explorations in law and history*, p. 133. **192** Christian, *The coming court of final appeal*, pp 25-6.

The Court of Appeal in Chancery had commonly sat as a two-man court, a practice that was far from ideal, not least, of course, during the period 1868 to 1874 when O'Hagan and Christian served together upon it. The rules governing the composition of the new Court of Appeal made it possible to avoid, if not entirely to eradicate, the classic problem of an evenly divided appellate tribunal.

A further difficulty that had engulfed the former Court of Exchequer Chamber since 1857 was also resolved by the new two-tiered structure. It may be recalled that, under a reform introduced in 1857,[193] the maximum number of judges that could sit in Exchequer Chamber was reduced to eight – the full complement of judges from each of the common law courts not involved in the hearing of the case at first instance. Should the Court of Exchequer Chamber divide narrowly on the merits of some appeal – say by 4 votes to 3, on an attendance of 7 – the distinct possibility arose that if the court from whose decision the appeal was brought had held unanimously the other way, the decision of the Chamber itself would not command respect – representing a mere 4 votes against 7 among the common law judges. This is exactly what occurred in *Wallace* v. *Seymour* in 1871[194] and again in *Wright* v. *Tracy* in 1873-74.[195] As Black J was to recall many years later, upsets of this kind could cause no end of trouble.[196] The arrangements for the new Court of Appeal ensured that problems of this particular variety at least would never surface thereafter.

193 20 & 21 Vict., c. 6. **194** IR 6 CL 196, 219, 343. **195** IR 7 CL 134; IR 8 CL 478. **196** See *Jameson* v. *Squire* [1948] IR 153, at 165-6.

Law in Ireland, 1916-1926*

The political convulsion in Ireland eighty years ago affected the local legal system at two levels; it altered the fabric of the court system in the country and it furnished special problems for the legal system to solve. A convulsion of the kind Ireland then experienced could have been expected to leave its imprint. It does not, however, follow that every task facing a legal system in an era of revolution possesses – or is thought by the partisans of that era to possess – a political connotation; it depends on the character of the revolution and, at bottom, on the outlook of the participants in the revolution. In Ireland's case, in the years which stretch from the Rising to the Boundary Agreement, a functioning court system managed throughout to process an amount of routine litigation which was devoid of political interest and incapable of arousing political controversy. The present survey largely ignores this element in the legal history of these years but its importance, nonetheless, must not be underestimated. The steadfastness of this court system was itself to play a critical role in influencing in the South in 1922 the political decision on the future of the court system there.

Changes in the fabric of the system of courts which an imaginary chronicler of the established court system would have been able to record were startling. From 1920 to 1922 the established system was confronted by the rival system of the Irish Republic. In 1921 it witnessed the drastic geographical curtailment of its jurisdiction with the creation of the new court system for Northern Ireland. In 1922 its Dublin centre, the Four Courts, was destroyed. In 1924 judges, continued in office since 1922 by the Government in the South, resigned to be succeeded by a fresh team at the moment when a novel court system was inaugurated. Two years later, in 1926, the permanence of the new political order was confirmed when the split between the legal professions North and South culminated in the establishment of a separate Inn of Court for Northern Ireland. And finally our chronicler would have been bound to set down some of the other consequences of the upheaval: how the conditions under which courts sat to transact their business were affected, how the machinery of the criminal law, including the police and assize systems, broke down; how resort to litigation was influenced by legal restriction, social pressure and the common belief, which proved on some points to be accurate, that litigation was fruitless anyhow; how, too, the court

* For assistance of various kinds in the preparation of this article (including permission to make use of manuscript material) the author would like to thank, in Dublin, the Hon. Mr Justice J. Kenny, Professor R. Dudley Edwards, Messrs C. Gavan Duffy, B. Farrell and C. Kenny, Misses M. Neylon and E. Semple; in Belfast, Mr K. Boyle; in London, Sir J. Molony, QC. The article is based on a public lecture given at Queen's University, Belfast in November 1971.

system was circumvented by the decision of Governments to establish special commissions to which there was entrusted the disposal of emergency legal work.

The emergence in 1920 of a second system of courts was the major development.[1] Early in 1919 the First Dáil approved the establishment of national arbitration tribunals which, since their jurisdiction depended on consent, were not technically unlawful; something similar had been attempted by O'Connell during the Repeal agitation of the 1840s and by the Land League in the 1880s. In the summer of 1920, following adoption by the Dáil of a programme for superseding British institutions, these tribunals were abolished and a full-scale court system substituted. The system, comprising parish and district courts, circuit courts and a Supreme Court, attracted a considerable amount of the business previously transacted before petty sessions, the county court and even the High Court in Dublin. Sittings were held throughout the country – including the North – but, prior to the Truce in July 1921, often only with difficulty. The British view was that the courts, unlike the earlier arbitration tribunals, were illegal and therefore liable to be suppressed and their personnel seized and, in fact, courts were broken up and a circuit court judge, among others, imprisoned. The period in which the courts flourished was, it is generally agreed, that between the Truce of 1921 and the outbreak of civil war a year later. Their work was primarily civil but no attempt was made to duplicate the politically non-contentious jurisdictions of the Crown courts in matters such as probate and workmen's compensation; nor did they possess a licensing jurisdiction. Qualified legal practitioners and law graduates manned the senior courts.

The nature of the revolution of which the Dáil courts were part helps to explain their oddest feature – the fact that they were not intended as a complete replacement for the existing structure of Crown courts. Dáil policy was to make use of available institutions and procedures where no sacrifice of national scruples was involved: the Dáil, for example, availed of British electoral machinery in the elections of May 1921; it did not set up its own machinery. Apart from serving as a training ground for future judges of the Free State, the only other legacy of the Dáil courts was the creation in the Free State in 1924 of the circuit court jurisdiction. So limited an impact raises the question of the precise significance of the courts in the legal history of the period. It would seem that they are more important to political history. Any lawyer must note the limitations on the effectiveness of the courts: the enforcement of their decrees could not always be guaranteed and their existence was too short to permit the emergence of a comprehensive jurisprudence. (Enforcement of the decrees of Crown courts could not always be guaranteed either.) As regards the second complaint, the fault scarcely lay with the courts and their judges. If fault there was, it lay with the pro-

1 Casey, 'Republican Courts in Ireland 1919-1922', (1970) 5 *IJ* (n.s.) 321; Davitt, 'Civil Jurisdiction of the Courts of the Irish Republic 1920-1922', (1968) 3 *IJ* (n.s.) 112; Maguire, 'The Republican Courts', in the *Capuchin Annual for 1968* (originally published in *The Western People* newspaper, 2 April 1966); Hanna, *The statute law of the Irish Free State 1922-8* (1929), pp 30-3; Curran, *Under the receding wave* (1970), pp 125-32. For a contemporary account, brief and derogatory, see 'I.O.', *The administration of Ireland 1920* (1921), pp 90-2 and 144. These earlier studies have recently been complemented by Mary Kotsonouris, *Retreat from revolution: the Dáil courts, 1920-24* (Dublin, 1994).

Treaty Government for deciding, in 1922, to end the courts. The Government gave its reasons in a decree suspending sittings of the Dáil Supreme Court,[2] and it is in the light of these reasons that its action may be judged:

> It has been considered necessary by the Cabinet of Dáil Eireann to suspend sittings of the Supreme Court. There are many reasons for this decision. The Courts which were instituted as a war measure by the Dáil were devised to supply tribunals acceptable to the Irish people whilst other courts were functioning under the British Government. These former British Courts are now in Irish hands under the terms of the Treaty. They are now Irish courts, and the necessity for duplication no longer exists. Great inconvenience has been caused by the existence of two sets of Courts and competition between them has tended to bring the administration of justice in Ireland into disrepute. In many cases, a plaintiff selected for his proceedings the Court which, for political or other reasons, would be an unfavourable venue for his opponent, whereupon the latter set the other Court in motion to restrain the proceedings so commenced, and try to force the plaintiff out of the Court he had selected. These injunctions had become a subject of public amusement. It must be remembered that the Courts which have been taken over by the Irish Government are complete in their machinery, more especially in relation to estates, companies, contracts, partnerships, lunacy proceedings and the taking of accounts generally. The absence of such machinery has been a glaring and fundamental defect in the old Dáil Courts. The decree of Dáil Eireann under which these Courts were constituted endowed them with jurisdiction in limited classes of cases only. They were given no express criminal jurisdiction; no licensing jurisdiction, and no powers with regard to many other important matters. During the war with England they assumed jurisdiction in matters which were purposely omitted from their express authority. This was unlawful according to the decree of Dáil Eireann, but was an expedient which enabled a certain amount of legal business to be transacted until the Irish people regained control of their own affairs. The justification for continuing a system in so large a measure irregular and unlawful, has now disappeared. The Government elected by the Irish people has a complete judicial system in its hand for which it is paying. There is no reason, therefore, why the Government should not get the value of the public money which is being expended on the staffs and personnel of these Courts. When the Constitution has been finally settled by the Irish Parliament there must necessarily be a reorganisation of the judicial system according to the requirements of the Irish people. In the meantime, the Government proposes to do away with unnecessary duplication and to let the people have the full advantage of the Judiciary and staffs for which the people are paying, and which have complete machinery for dealing with all kinds of cases.

2 (1922) 56 *ILTSJ* 172.

Whatever the criticisms levelled at the Government then and later over its decision, the timing and the reasons, the judges of the former Crown system seized an early opportunity of expressing the predictable opinion that the Government, in acting as it had, had acted wisely.[3] They had been asked by a disappointed Dáil Land Court litigant to grant a writ of prohibition to prevent the execution of a decree of the Court. They refused, on the grounds that the writ did not issue against an unlawful court, but went on to comment adversely on the terms in which the decree in question had been drawn up, by a future chief justice, as it happened.[4] Not all Irish barristers shared the critical outlook of the judges of the old regime. In the summer of 1920 a meeting of the Irish Bar voted that it was professional misconduct in a barrister to appear before a Dáil court but by November another resolution was presented, questioning the right of those assembled at the earlier meeting to have voted as they had. Significantly, the discussion on this second resolution was adjourned *sine die*.[5] An eminent KC even then was involved in sittings of the Dáil Supreme Court as indeed was a professor of law at University College, Dublin.

Two ceremonies are the symbols of the second major development in the legal system, the creation of a new court system and judiciary for Northern Ireland and the resulting split in the Irish legal professions: one, in 1921, the swearing in of Sir Denis Henry as Lord Chief Justice at Portrush, County Antrim;[6] the other, in 1926, the inauguration by Sir William Moore, Henry's successor, of the new Inn of Court at Belfast.[7]

The plan in the Government of Ireland Bill for two court systems had encountered opposition from Irish lawyers. Thomas Molony, the Lord Chief Justice, pointed to the cost and inconvenience in a letter to the Chief Secretary in which he studiously declined to act as an adviser. The Dublin-based Law Society, representing the solicitors, launched a vigorous, but vain, campaign against the plan.[8] The Society was right not to be convinced by the argument that the High Court of Appeal for Ireland, provided for in the Bill, would help maintain legal uniformity North and South, a matter over which its members from the future Border counties might have been expected to be most perturbed,[9] for that Court, as events turned out, lasted barely a year.[10] Its Dublin members feared especially the loss of their business as agents for Belfast solicitors and the Society as a whole the implications of a reduction in membership and in the catchment area for solicitors should solicitors in the North set up their own society. The Northern solicitors acted, in fact, with remarkable speed, the Incorporated Law Society for Northern Ireland coming into existence in 1922.

Implementation of the judicial provisions in the Government of Ireland Act proceeded swiftly. The High Court of Appeal was set up and the establishment of the

3 *R. (Kelly)* v. *Maguire and O'Sheil* [1923] 2 IR 58, 57 ILTR 57. **4** The late Conor Maguire. **5** (1920) 54 *ILTSJ* 152 and 273. **6** (1921) 55 *ILTSJ* 204. **7** (1926) 60 *ILTSJ* 18; Resolution signed by the Lord Chief Justice, representatives of the Court and members of the legal profession concerning the establishment of an Inn of Court for Northern Ireland: PRONI D. 166. **8** Letter to Ian Macpherson, Chief Secretary, 9 February 1920 (Thomas Molony Papers, London); (1920) 54 *ILTSJ* 125; (1921)55 *ILTSJ* 302. **9** Cf. the remarks of Serjeant Hanna in argument before the Judicial Committee of the Privy Council in *Hull* v. *McKenna, Freeman's Journal* v. *Fernstrom* and other cases [1926] IR 402, (1923) 57 ILTR 173. **10** It was established by the Government of Ireland Act 1920, ss. 38 and 42 and abolished by the Irish Free State (Consequential Provisions) Act 1922 (session 2), s. 1, sch. 1, para. 6.

Border necessitated some redrawing of assize circuits, county court divisions and petty sessions districts.[11] In the South, an established administrative machine was on hand to oversee the innovations. In the North that machine had first to be built up, for, in its case, the innovations, properly understood, represented the creation of an entirely new court system and not merely piecemeal reform. Sir Denis Henry had to assemble his team of judges, then secure temporary premises for the new Supreme Court. There were delegations to meet: one complaining about the closing of the Armagh district registry, another opposing the original plan to site the Supreme Court permanently at Stormont. Henry died in 1925 and thus did not live to see the opening of the North's Royal Courts of Justice on their present site. The search for that site, with its eminently Irish pedigree as the old potato market, was not the least of the practical difficulties that followed the decision to set up a new court system in Northern Ireland.[12]

Late in 1921 William Moore of the North's new Court of Appeal travelled to Dublin to help smooth out difficulties that had arisen regarding the transfer of pending litigation between the two court systems.[13] There was irony, then, in that, following Henry's death, it fell to Moore, as the new Lord Chief Justice, to preside at the ceremony in January 1926 which inaugurated the new Inn of Court of Northern Ireland. This broke the last of the important professional links with the South.

Come what may, Sir John Ross, the last lord chancellor, confided in an audience of Bar students in 1921, the King's Inns, at that time the only Irish Inn of Court, would never be split.[14] Five years later it had occurred. In retrospect, the split – in view of political feelings – may seem to have been inevitable but other professional organisations in Ireland did manage to remain united. Sir William Moore, at the 1926 ceremony, provided a rationalisation for the secession but preserved a discreet silence as to the actual reasons for it.[15] These lay in the suddenly worsening relations between the majority of Benchers in Dublin and the Benchers on the Northern Committee of Fifteen set up in 1922.[16] Under an arrangement concluded in 1921 the Northern Benchers were not empowered to award the degree of barrister-at-law and were obliged to admit to practice before the Northern Ireland courts all those called in Dublin. From the autumn of 1924 they sought greater independence but, as yet, there was no talk of secession. A critical stage, however, was reached when the Dublin Benchers decided in January 1925 to admit to practice the Free State Minister for Justice, Kevin O'Higgins. The latter had sat no Bar examinations (though earlier in his career had passed his final solicitor's examinations). The Northern Benchers vehemently opposed the Dublin decision on O'Higgins and let it be known that O'Higgins would not be admitted to practice in the North. After an acrimonious correspondence with Dublin, the Northern Benchers found themselves still thwarted in their attempts to exercise

11 Order in Council of 5 January 1922 under the Supreme Court of Judicature (Ireland) Act 1877 rearranging the circuits in Southern Ireland: 1922 S.R. & O. no. 43; Sir A. Quekett, *The Constitution of Northern Ireland*, ii (Belfast, 1933), p. 78; art. 4 of the Government of Ireland (Adaptation of Enactments) (No. 1) Order 1922: 1922 S.R. & O. no. 77. **12** (1921) 55 *ILTSJ* 213; (1922) 56 *ILTSJ* 242; (1924) 58 *ILTSJ* 32, 63. **13** (1921) 55 *ILTSJ* 240, 274, 314. **14** (1921) 55 *ILTSJ* 269. **15** (1926) 60 *ILTSJ* 20. **16** On the split, the entries for 1925 in the *Minute book of the King's Inns 1917-1928* are an invaluable source of information.

autonomous powers and, as a result, they decided to secede. Among the new arrangements introduced for Northern Bar students following the founding of the new Inn,[17] the most significant was the insistence that henceforth they should join an English Inn. This meant a return to 'eating dinners' in London, a practice once castigated by Edward Carson as 'one of the badges of servitude on the Irish nation'.[18] Another consequence of the secession was at the time equally contentious. No sooner had the Northern Benchers given notice of their decision than Hugh Kennedy, the Free State Chief Justice, launched a campaign to make a knowledge of the Irish language a compulsory requirement for future students of King's Inns.[19]

A court, in order to function, requires somewhere to sit. In Ireland between 1920 and 1922 this basic need could not always be satisfied. Dáil courts, it has already been related, were, in the period before the Truce, often only held under conditions of difficulty. The position with regard to the Crown courts was scarcely much different. Establishment of the Dáil courts had coincided with a transfer of allegiance on the part of most local authorities and the latter, in order to prevent sittings of Crown courts, would lock and bolt the doors of the court-houses in their areas.[20] Bolder tactics prevailed as well and court-houses were frequently attacked and set on fire.[21] The result was that, even where a court-house had not been destroyed, makeshift arrangements had commonly to be adopted.[22]

The most celebrated architectural catastrophe, as well as the aptest symbol of the deterioration in law and order (though the curfew would also have qualified), was the destruction of the Four Courts at the outset of the civil war in 1922.[23] The Four Courts was not the only legal edifice in Dublin to suffer ruin: shortly before the Truce of 1921 the Customs House had been set on fire and severely damaged.[24] Nor was it the first time that the Four Courts had been the scene of military action: this had happened during the occupation in the Rising of 1916. Portion of a report prepared by the Registrar of the King's Bench on 3 July 1922, following the evacuation of the building, leaves a vivid impression of how much more extensive the damage was on that occasion:[25]

> A large number of bound volumes of records lie in the basement of the King's Bench offices where a great amount of water has got in. The volumes are of importance. It is proposed that they should be removed to the Castle immedi-

17 The financing of the new Inn was assisted by the Finance (Stamp Duty) Act (NI) 1926, s. 3. **18** Hyde, *Carson* (1953), p. 16. **19** The result was the Legal Practitioners (Qualification) Act 1929 (IFS). The move was predicted in 1922: *Memorandum on the position of the Southern Irish judges under the Treaty and the Irish Constitution* (1922), p. 6 (copy in Thomas Molony Papers). **20** (1920) 54 *ILTSJ* 181, 211 and 236. **21** (1920) 54 *ILTSJ* 130, 134, 206 (petty sessions and county court-houses). **22** Power to authorize the holding of courts where the ordinary court-houses were destroyed was given by reg. 17 of the Regulations under the Restoration of Order in Ireland Act 1920 made on 13 August 1920: 1920 S.R. & O. no. 1530. Cf. the County Court (Amendment) Act 1923 (IFS). **23** (1922) 56 *ILTSJ* 100, 103 and 161. **24** The Customs House fire had the inevitable effect on the dispatch of routine legal business: (1921) 55 *ILTSJ* 135, 146 and 302. **25** Report by C.P. Curran, copy in the Hugh Kennedy Collection, University College, Dublin. For a further account of the devastation from the same witness, see Curran, 'Figures in the Hall' (of the Four Courts) in the *Record of the centenary of the Incorporated Law Society of Ireland 1852-1952* (1953), p. 74.

> ately. They can be taken out through a window in the cellar. One float and four men could carry out this work. They would enter from Chancery Lane gate and would only require to go in for a short distance. The Board of Works are ready to supply the float and men but require passes.

An equally vivid picture is created by the Provisional Government's following appeal to the public:[26]

> The explosion caused by the reckless action of the irregular forces in the Four Courts has destroyed a vast quantity of public records of all kinds. It has come to the notice of the Government that fragments of some of the records, partly burned, were blown to other districts, and that some of them may have been picked up by members of the public. It is very important that all such fragments be restored to the public custody. The Government, therefore, appeals to everyone who may find, or know of finding of, documents of title deeds, accounts, books, census returns, or legal records of any kind, to carefully preserve the same, preferably in envelopes, and to deliver same up to the Government at an office which will be opened for the purpose and announced in a few days.

The most serious loss at the time of the destruction of the Four Courts was that of the historical material stored in the adjacent Public Records Office, a loss which has had serious repercussions for the writing of Irish legal history.[27]

Until the Four Courts was rebuilt the superior courts of the Irish Free State were for most of the time housed in Dublin Castle. The Castle premises were not available before the spring of 1923, however, and, in the interim, judges, practitioners and clients fitted as best they could into temporary accommodation at King's Inns. In this period the civil war was at its height. High Court judges featured in a list of those to be shot,[28] and the security arrangements, coupled with the cramped conditions, made the transaction of court work an unpleasant business.[29] The Munster assizes of 1920, especially those held in Cork, had earlier introduced some of the judges to the personal risks that could attach to the discharge of judicial office;[30] and it was in Cork again, in the spring of 1922, that the Recorder faced a new threat, one soon faced by his colleagues as well.[31] The local IRA adjutant announced that the Recorder would only be permitted to hold his court if he confined himself to the hearing of workmen's compensation and malicious injuries claims. Rather than oblige, the Recorder, with the approval of the practitioners present, adjourned the sitting.

26 (1922) 56 *ILTSJ* 164. **27** Newark, *Notes on Irish legal history* (1960), p. 4. **28** White, *Kevin O'Higgins* (1948), ch. 8; O'Sullivan, *The Irish Free State and its senate* (1946), p. 100. **29** Commented on by O'Connor MR in *R. (Childers)* v. *Adjutant-General of the Forces of the Irish Provisional Government* [1923] 1 IR 5, 56 ILTR 183. **30** There was a post mortem on the Cork assizes in *R.* v. *Murphy* [1921] 2 IR 190, 55 ILTR 98. For Limerick, see (1920) 54 *ILTSJ* 167. Rows between the judges and the military authorities over the provision of a guard at assizes, 1919-21, are dealt with in a letter of Sir T. Molony, ex-Irish LCJ, to Sir W. Moore, NI LCJ, June 1929 (draft in Thomas Molony Papers). **31** (1922) 56 *ILTSJ* 115 and 150.

The episode was symptomatic of the many difficulties with which the conduct of litigation could be attended. First, there were the restrictions introduced by Government on the right to commence certain forms of litigation. When the Provisional Government succeeded to office in 1922, an announcement was made ordering the courts to discontinue the hearing of malicious injuries claims pending the establishment of special machinery outside the court system to handle them. Claims still in the pipe-line, it was also ordered, were to be handled in similar fashion.[32] Martial law conditions in 1920 and 1921 had had similar repercussions. The Crown courts remained open[33] but they found themselves obliged to decline to hear, for example, claims alleging wrongful destruction brought against the military authorities.[34] In the same period the military authorities issued an order forbidding the commencement, without their consent, of any malicious injuries claim in which the injury was alleged to have been the work of Crown forces.[35] Secondly, there was the existence, between 1920 and 1922, of two court systems. While this offered a choice to the litigant, it in fact produced a collapse of confidence which social pressures to use one or other system did little to restore.[36] Thirdly, pre-trial procedures were seriously affected. Writs and briefs were stolen or seized by the IRA and, doubtless, by others as well. Crown forces, too, engaged in similar acts of banditry and their seizure, in a raid shortly after 'Bloody Sunday', of briefs and other legal documents from the offices of a solicitor representing a Republican prisoner produced a protest from the Irish Bar.[37] In addition, effecting the service of legal documents became difficult especially during the Civil War period. Orders for substituted service were made with increasing frequency but dislocation of postal deliveries meant that notice of proceedings might not be received in time or at all.[38] The judges sought from the Provisional Government promises of military protection for process servers and others but the Government's military strength could be over-extended and such protection, it would seem, was not always forthcoming.[39]

Even where a decree was obtained from a Crown or Dáil court, it could not be relied on as final. In the legislation dealing with the winding-up of the Dáil courts, provision was made for the winding-up commissioners to re-examine all decrees made by a court of either system in default of appearance against a defendant who, on political grounds, had refused to appear before the court.[40] Another law, again operative with retrospective effect, made decrees in malicious injuries claims arising between

32 Public notices of 20 January and 11 February 1922, the texts of which are given in the fifth edition of Bolton's *Criminal Injuries (Ireland) Acts 1919-20* (1922). **33** Proclamations of 12 December 1920 and of 1 January and 14 April 1921: 'I.O.', *The administration of Ireland 1920*, pp 407-10; (1921) 55 *ILTSJ* 106. **34** *Higgins* v. *Willis* [1921] 2 IR 386, (1921) 55 *ILTSJ* 110; *Vaughan* v. *Willis* (1921) 55 *ILTSJ* 145. **35** *R. (Garde)* v. *Strickland* [1921] 2 IR 317, (1921) 55 *ILTSJ* 104; proclamation of 14 April 1922, (1921) 55 *ILTSJ* 106; Macardle, *The Irish Republic* (4th ed. 1951), p. 434. **36** For an application to a Dáil Court to stop its hearing a matter which was the subject of proceedings before a Crown Court, see (1922) 56 *ILTSJ* 61. **37** (1921) 55 *ILTSJ* 83, 100 and 175. **38** (1922) 56 *ILTSJ* 56, 150 and 204. **39** The position is exhaustively examined in *Irish Agricultural Wholesale Society* v. *St Enda's Cooperative Society* [1924] 2 IR 41, 58 ILTR 14. The Superior Courts could order substituted service under the then Order 9, r. 5 but special legislation was needed for the county courts: County Courts (Amendment) Act 1923 (IFS). See, too, the Enforcement of Law (Occasional Powers) Act 1923 (IFS). **40** Dáil Eireann Courts (Winding-Up) Act 1923, s. 26 (IFS). See, too, *Hanrahan* v. *Stapleton* (1928) 62 ILTR 11.

1919 and 1921 which had been uncontested by the relevant local authority liable to be set aside.[41] Later legislation provided for the setting aside of any decree made on a claim arising between 1921 and 1923.[42]

The accession to power of the Provisional Government in January 1922 was not accompanied by any immediate dismissal of the judges of the old regime, though resident magistrates were quickly removed.[43] The proclamation of 16 January bought time:[44]

> And we do hereby direct that all Law Courts, Corporations, Councils, Departments of State, Boards, Judges, Civil Servants, Officers of the Peace, and all Public Servants and functionaries hitherto acting under the authority of the British Government shall continue to carry out their functions unless and until otherwise ordered by us, pending the Constitution of the Parliament and Government of Saorstat na Eireann, and without prejudice to the full and free exercise by that Parliament and Government, when constituted of all and every its powers and authorities in regard to them or any of them.

The terms of this proclamation, no less than the specific reference in the Anglo-Irish Treaty of December 1921 to judicial pensions,[45] plainly envisaged that many of the judges would in fact retire, and this, indeed, occurred in 1924 when, of the judges of High Court standing or above, only two, the Master of the Rolls, Charles O'Connor, and the Land Judge, Mr Justice Wylie, transferred to the new judiciary. (There were other transfers at county court level and two of the Dublin stipendiaries became district justices.)[46] Until then, the civil war conditions which prevailed for most of the period may have diverted the judges from reflecting overlong on the ironic overtones to their impending fate: disappearance at the behest of a group of erstwhile enemies of the Crown whose political authority over its own enemies they were meanwhile required to assist in establishing. With the politicians of the new regime there were bound to be disagreements: there certainly were over patronage[47] and probably over the Dáil courts and the protection of court officers. The politicians, for their part, would have looked askance at a group of men who had 'put their names to orders suppressing national, political and even literary organs', who, in so doing, would have, as Hugh Kennedy, himself destined to be Chief Justice, expressed it, early in 1922,[48] lost any reputation for independence and had, as a result, come to represent 'poison itself in the well of justice'. Some expressed themselves even more strongly.[49] Fortunately for all

41 Provided for in the appointment of the Compensation (Ireland) Commission 1922. **42** S. 2 of the Damage to Property (Compensation) Act 1923 (IFS). **43** (1922) 56 *ILTSJ* 206. **44** (1922) 56 *ILTSJ* 15. **45** In Art. 10. **46** For the new appointments of 1924, see (1924) 58 *ILTSJ* 144 (Supreme Court and High Court), id., 203 (Circuit Court, District Court (in part)). **47** (1923) 57 *ILTSJ* 159; memo. of J.A. Costello to H. Kennedy arising out of a move by Molony LCJ to appoint a court stockbroker, 27 October 1922: Hugh Kennedy Collection, University College, Dublin. **48** Letter of H. Kennedy to E. Duggan, Minister for Home Affairs in the Provisional Government, January 1922, copy in the Hugh Kennedy Collection. **49** E.g., G. Gavan Duffy, in a letter to General R. Mulcahy, Minister for Defence in the Provisional Government, 28 July 1922, explaining his reasons for resigning from the Dáil Cabinet over the issue of suspension of Dáil Court sittings: 'It is not right to abolish our own courts until we have combed out the

concerned, the experience of common danger and a modicum of personal tact ensured that the requisite amount of co-operation was forthcoming.

In the Free State in May 1924 Kennedy,[50] after a short spell as Attorney-General, replaced Thomas Molony as Chief Justice and inaugurated the new court system enshrined in the Courts of Justice Act. The character of the ceremony, in striking contrast to that of an Irish lord chancellor's levée, betokened a change in social convention. Kennedy spoke first in Irish and then, in English, invited the gathering to reflect with him for a moment on the meaning of the day, when, as he phrased it, the silence of the Gael was, for the first time in hundreds of years, broken in the courts of law of the Pale.[51] The new system, nonetheless, was less different from the old than might be supposed.[52] A reduction in the size of the judicial establishment made it cheaper to run; court officers were given a career structure within the civil service; the grand jury went and with it the system of trying criminal cases on assize: henceforth the trial of the more serious criminal offences was to be confined to a Central Criminal Court sitting in Dublin. The ending of the assize system also meant that appeals from the new Circuit Court, the replacement court for the old county court, were no longer a rehearing but became an appeal on the note. The innovation was not a success and the appeal by way of rehearing was to be reintroduced in 1937.[53] Other major changes in the court system were the creation of a Court of Criminal Appeal and the substitution of a fully professional magistracy for the old petty sessions courts. Most controversy at the time was provoked by the plans for the Circuit Court. This centred on the merits of the proposal to confer on the Court more extensive jurisdiction than had been enjoyed by the old county court. Lord Justice James O'Connor and Hugh Kennedy argued in public on the proposal. In a letter to the Dublin newspapers O'Connor opposed it on two principal grounds: it would force a businessman to sue his debtors in a local forum and thus expose him to the risk of forfeiting credit locally, and it would cause the decentralisation of the Bar which would, in turn, threaten the independence of the profession itself. Kennedy replied to these and other criticisms.[54] It was not the last altercation between the two men. In 1929, Kennedy, as Chief Justice, was to consider an application by O'Connor to be re-admitted to the rolls of Irish solicitors.[55]

A legal system is not merely a system of courts, and no survey of law in Ireland from 1916 to 1926 can ignore what for the legal system were two changes of consequence produced by the political convulsion: the creation, in 1921 and 1922, of two local legislatures which at once set about making use of powers not possessed in Ireland since the passing of the Act of Union. For a while both legislatures gave the appear-

worst of the judges whose corruptness forced us to set up Civil Courts, men who have repeatedly proved themselves crooked on this very subject of Habeas Corpus.' G. Gavan Duffy Papers, Dublin. **50** For a brief biographical sketch see Curran, *Under the receding wave* (1970), p. 118. **51** (1924) 58 *ILTSJ* 151. **52** The changes made were, for the most part, introduced by the Courts of Justice Act 1924. This act adopted recommendations of the Committee on the Judiciary appointed in January 1923 (57 *ILTSJ* 33). For the Committee's Report see Horan, *The Courts of Justice Act 1924* (1924), p. 79ff. See further Hanna, *The statute law of the Irish Free State 1922-28* (1929), pp 17-30. For criticism that the changes were so limited see Ó Síocháin, *The criminal law of Ireland* (5th ed. 1966), pp 4-8. **53** Courts of Justice Act 1936, ss. 37-8. **54** (1923) 57 *ILTSJ* 255. **55** See *In re the Solicitors (Ireland) Act 1898 and Sir James O'Connor* [1930] IR 623, 64 ILTR 25; Gerard Hogan, 'Chief Justice Kennedy and Sir James O'Connor's Application' (1988) 23 *IJ* (n.s.) 144.

ance of competing in a programme of statutory reform: legislation modelled on the English Criminal Evidence Act 1898, for instance, was introduced in quick succession by the two parliaments, in Northern Ireland in 1923 and in the Free State the following year.[56] But, in addition, and at least of equal significance, both in the North and in the South, the government and the legislature, no less than the judiciary, were henceforth to function within the limits prescribed by a written constitution.[57] Set beside these larger developments, such problems for the Free State courts as those resulting from the conferment of legal status on the Irish language[58] or from the phasing in of a new court system[59] must assume lesser importance.

Not all the problems which the Irish legal system was required to resolve, as has already been remarked, had their origins in contemporary politics. An examination of those which gave rise to litigation in the Crown courts is confirmation. The Dáil courts acquiesced in the formers' administration of probate and hearing of workmen's compensation claims and transacted an amount of routine litigation themselves. Much legal business, then, suffered little interruption. In the North, any interruption was rare and in the South, even at the height of the Civil War, the courts continued to sit. A corpus of case-law thus continued to be built up in the various branches of law, especially in tort, workmen's compensation, national insurance, land purchase, landlord and tenant, and succession. Nor was the criminal law ignored: there were useful innovations in sentencing law and practice[60] and the law reports include two decisions of the Court for Crown Cases Reserved on procedural matters connected with the crime of murder (proof of the corpus delicti[61] and the qualifying age for hanging[62]). And there was a lengthy legal battle fought by a woman in defence of her right to appointment as petty sessions clerk.[63]

It is true that the legal system had recently been faced with a group of special problems created by political developments occurring outside Ireland. The outbreak of World War I had been followed by the adoption for the entire United Kingdom of elaborate legislation designed to meet the needs of a war-time economy.[64] Rents and mortgage interest rates were pegged, contracts could be set aside and controls over the price, and supply of foodstuffs[65] and over land use were introduced.[66] The

56 Criminal Evidence Act (NI) 1923, Criminal Justice (Evidence) Act 1924 (IFS). The early legislative programme of the Free State Government is the subject of Mr Justice Hanna's *The statute law of the Irish Free State 1922-28* (1929). Information on the early legislative programme of the Northern Ireland Government is provided, interstitially, in Quekett, *The constitution of Northern Ireland*, especially vol. 3 (1946). **57** In the Free State by the Constitution of 1922, for the background to which see Farrell, 'The Drafting of the Irish Free State Constitution – I, II, III', (1970-1) 5 *IJ* (n.s.) 115 and 243, 6 *IJ* (n.s.) 11; in Northern Ireland, by the Government of Ireland Act 1920, on which see Quekett, op. cit., vols. 1-3 and Calvert, *Constitutional law in Northern Ireland* (1968). **58** (1922-5) 56 *ILTSJ* 261; 57 id. 68; 58 id. 246 and 316; 59 id. 21. **59** (1924) 58 *ILTSJ* 229 and 280; *Hartney* v. *Tighe* (1924) 58 ILTR 109. **60** *R. (Higgins)* v. *Dublin Metropolitan Justices* [1917] 2 IR 45, 50 ILTR 210 (appeal against reformatory school sentence); *McClelland* v. *Brady* [1918] 2 IR 63, 52 ILTR 4; *O'Donoghue* v. *Morris* (1918) 52 ILTR 25 (Probation of Offenders Act 1907). The period also saw expansion in the use of the Irish recorded, or suspended, sentence. **61** *R.* v. *McNicholl* [1917] 2 IR 557, 52 ILTR 150. **62** *R.* v. *Fitt* [1919] 2 IR 35, 53 ILTR 7. **63** *Frost* v. *R.* (1917-20) 51 ILTR 146; 52 *ILTSJ* 315; 54 *ILTSJ* 104. **64** Under Increase of Rent and Mortgage Interest (War Restriction), Courts (Emergency Powers) and Defence of the Realm legislation. **65** 'Magistrates' Decisions under the Food Regulations', (1918) 52 *ILTSJ* 19. **66** For an example of local litigation, see *Rooney* v. *Department of*

introduction of conscription in England also presented some special legal difficulties in Ireland.

From 1919 the Irish legal system began to be dominated by the need to find solutions for problems exclusively local in origin and of considerable political content. At first, and to some extent, even later, the answers were clear – the issuance of mandamus against a corporation (Dublin) for refusing to permit the proper audit of books;[67] or comfortably abstruse – the scope of the tort of false imprisonment (this in the aftermath of the shootings of the policemen at Soloheadbeg, Co. Tipperary),[68] the defence of act of state in an action in tort,[69] whether it was defamatory to say of someone that he was an informer.[70] But, as guerilla war succeeded political unrest and civil war, in its turn, the months of truce, the problems set were more fundamental, to some extent, unprecedented, and their solution, in consequence, more difficult. Furthermore, even before peace was restored, fresh constitutional arrangements raised certain legal questions requiring prompt replies.

The breakdown in law and order led to a concentration on two broad themes: that of justice for participants in violence (issues of human liberty) and that of compensation for victims of it (primarily economic issues). The latter might have been left exclusively to the courts to attend to; it virtually was in Northern Ireland but certainly not in the Free State.[71] The former would never at any time in any modern state be their exclusive concern. Nor was it in the Ireland of 1919 to 1923 and beyond: when law and order broke down the use of an entire governmental machine to attempt to restore it could not be unexpected.

The first of the two themes had earlier been introduced by the Rising itself. Two distinct procedures were employed to deal with those concerned. Casement faced a State trial in London,[72] an arrangement made possible by the character of the charge laid against him. Pearse, Connolly and the others were tried in Dublin by court-martial after due proclamation had been made suspending their right, as civilians, to claim jury trial.[73] Over the opposition of the Irish Government, legislation of 1915, common to the whole United Kingdom, had established such a right for the duration of the World War and it could only be taken away if due proclamation were made in the event of invasion or, as it was put, 'other military emergency'.[74] Before the Rising the Irish Government came to the conclusion that an event of such a kind would amount to such an emergency[75] and the King presumably acted on good advice when he signed,

Agriculture and Technical Instruction for Ireland [1919] 1 IR 302, 53 ILTR 49 and 189 and later proceedings between the same parties: [1920] 1 IR 176 and (1924) 58 ILTR 83. **67** (1920) 54 *ILTSJ* 311. For proceedings against a Dublin ratepayer who refused to pay his rates suspecting that the proceeds were being transferred to Dáil Eireann by Dublin Corporation, see (1921) 55 *ILTSJ* 52. Local authorities were later granted immunity in respect of such actions: Local Authorities (Indemnity) Act 1923 (IFS). **68** *Connors* v. *Pearson* [1921] 2 IR 51. **69** *Pedlar* v. *Johnstone* [1920] 2 IR 450, 54 ILTR 29 and 55 ILTR 173; [1921] 2 AC 262. **70** *McKiernan* v. *Coulson* (1920) 54 *ILTSJ* 305. Cf. *Mawe* v. *Pigott* (1869) IR 4 CL 54. **71** The reference, in the case of Northern Ireland, is to the emergency variation in the ordinary system of paying for claims (through the rates). The variation was even greater in the case of the Free State. **72** *R.* v. *Casement* [1917] 1 KB 98. **73** (1916) 50 *ILTSJ* 125. **74** Defence of the Realm (Amendment) Act 1915. For the Irish Government's attitude, see *Royal commission on the rebellion in Ireland: minutes of evidence and appendix of documents* (Cd. 8311; 1916), p. 25 (evidence of Augustine Birrell, Chief Secretary). **75** *Royal commission on the rebellion … minutes, etc.*, p. 6.

on 26 April 1916, the actual proclamation. But certain legal authorities expressed a contrary opinion.[76] That they should have done so was not altogether surprising, for it was a time when the validity of Government proclamations was often questioned even within Government itself: the Irish and English law officers, for example, had recently given conflicting views on the legality of an Irish Government proclamation on the importation of arms into Ireland.[77] The matter was not pursued with regard to any of the leaders of the Rising – Sir John Maxwell scarcely left the opportunity – but it was touched on in *R.* v. *Governor of Lewes Prison, ex parte Doyle*,[78] the case of one of the captured rank and file who, following court-martial and sentence, was transferred to an English prison. Counsel expressly reserved the point but Viscount Reading LCJ assumed there was nothing in it and Darling J agreed, in forceful language: 'It appears to me to be incongruous that, before the echoes of this rebellion have died away, we should meet here solemnly to consider such points as have been made.'[79]

Doyle's principal complaint differed from that of Dublin solicitors on access of legal advisers to captured Volunteers;[80] it was that his court-martial had been held in camera. The court dismissed the complaint. Again, it was Darling J who employed the more colourful language:

> There was, perhaps, more substance in the complaint that the trial of the prisoner took place in camera ... The trial took place in barracks when the rebellion in Ireland was still going on. The ruins in Dublin were still hot cinders ... It would be grotesque, in circumstances such as those – martial law having been proclaimed – to do what would be equivalent to inviting the public to come and hear witnesses give evidence against rebels with whom a great many of that same public sympathised. It was perfectly notorious that any persons who were recognized as having given evidence might very shortly afterwards have been made to suffer for having assisted to restore law and order.[81]

Questions of justice for participants in violence were explored more fully in succeeding years in the context of four law and order issues.

Republicans in the Anglo-Irish War and members of the anti-Treaty IRA in the Civil War, if caught in the field or suspected of having committed one of a number of offences, faced the prospect of trial by a military court. Control of the proceedings of these courts became an issue. Granted that the courts were empowered to pass sentences of death, it was an inevitable development.

The result was a celebrated series of applications to the ordinary courts to prevent executions from being carried out.[82] Invariably, the lawyers sought writs of habeas

76 (1916) 50 *ILTSJ* 125. **77** *Royal commission on the rebellion ... minutes, etc.*, p. 72. The confused legal position is explored in *Hunter* v. *Coleman* [1914] 2 IR 372, 48 ILTR 227. See, too, *Report of the royal commission on the circumstances connected with the landing of arms at Howth on 26th July, 1914* (Cd. 7631; 1914-6), pp 8-9. **78** [1917] 2 KB 254. **79** At p. 273. **80** (1916) 50 *ILTSJ* 128 and 318. **81** [1917] 2 KB 274. **82** There was irony in this. Early in 1920 the Irish judges had been asked to man special courts which would sit without a jury; they had refused. Jones, *Whitehall diary* (ed. Middlemas), vol. 3 (1971), pp 19 and 33. See generally Colm Campbell, *Emergency law in Ireland, 1918-1925* (Oxford, 1994).

corpus or prohibition. In *Whelan's* case[83] it was claimed that the military court had not included anyone of the required legal ability and had, therefore, been improperly constituted; in *Murphy's* case,[84] that it had failed to observe the rules of evidence. Neither claim affected the outcome, as the ordinary courts declined to interfere. In the second case, judicial disapproval of a similar failure at the court-martial of certain of the mutineers from HMS *Bounty* was explained away; no excess of jurisdiction was involved. In both cases the principle *omnia praesumuntur rite esse acta* was applied. A later attack raised a more fundamental point: the trial jurisdiction of the ordinary courts, it was claimed, could not be ousted so long as these continued to sit. In reply, the judges said that the fact that they were able to continue to sit was irrelevant: so long as a state of war or armed rebellion existed, as, in their view, it did, their jurisdiction was indeed ousted.[85]

A further argument was tried. Both the Defence of the Realm Regulations and the Restoration of Order in Ireland Act 1920 provided for trials to be conducted by regularly constituted courts-martial. With the intensification of hostilities, however, the British military authorities, acting under residual powers, dealt with captured Republican prisoners through summary military tribunals, rather different from the formal courts-martial envisaged by the 1920 Act. In *Egan* v. *Macready*,[86] the Master of the Rolls, Charles O'Connor, later to win appointment to the Free State Supreme Court in 1924, accepted the argument that the military authorities were not entitled to act in this fashion. He held (probably wrongly) that the actions of the authorities fell to be justified under the prerogative. Ordinarily, they might be so justified but the exercise of prerogative powers in the relevant domain had, he thought, been effectively limited by an earlier exercise of legislative power, in the enactment of the Restoration of Order in Ireland Act.

The aftermath of the case is as important as the decision itself.[87] General Macready refused to order the release of the particular Republican prisoners, O'Connor threatened to commit Macready for contempt, and Macready, in turn, to arrest O'Connor. In the end, the Government ordered compliance with O'Connor's decision, but Macready presumably obtained from the Government their approval for the issue by him of a remarkable Special Order of the Day to the officers in his command, bluntly telling them to ignore O'Connor and his view of the law:

> Special Order of the Day by General Rt. Hon. Sir C.F.N. Macready, G.C.M.G., K.C.B.
>
> GHQ Ireland, Parkgate,
> Dublin. Monday Aug. 15, 1921.
>
> On the 26th July 1921, the Master of the Rolls, Ireland delivered judgment and issued a writ of habeas corpus in the case of two men under sentence of death in the Martial Law Area.

83 *Whelan* v. *R.* [1921] 2 IR 310, 55 ILTR 135. **84** *R.* v. *Murphy* [1921] 2 IR 190, 55 ILTR 98. **85** *R.* v. *Allen* [1921] 2 IR 241, 55 ILTR 107; *Re Clifford and O'Sullivan* [1921] 2 AC 570, 55 ILTR 153. **86** [1921] 1 IR 265, 55 ILTR 197. **87** (1921) 55 *ILTSJ* 192 and 206. See further Heuston, *Essays in constitutional law* (2nd ed., 1964), pp 158-61.

> The Military Authorities, in pursuance of the well known principle that in an Area where Martial Law applies Writs of Habeas Corpus do not run, refused to comply with the Writ. On this the Master of the Rolls directed Writs of Attachment to be issued against the Commander-in-Chief, the Military Governor of the Martial Law Area, and other Officers.
>
> Subsequently, by Order of the Government, the two men under sentence of death were released.
>
> On the 10th August the matter was raised in the House of Commons and the Lord Privy Seal, answering for the Government, stated that:
>
>> This action in releasing the two men was based solely upon the existing situation in Ireland, and the importance at the present time of avoiding conflict between the Civil and Military Authorities. The releases were not due to any decision given by a Civil Court in Ireland; Civil Courts have no power to overrule the decisions of the Military Courts in the Martial Law Area in Ireland. The decisions of the Military Officer Administering Martial Law in Ireland will be upheld.
>
> In view of the prominence given in the Press to the above cases, and in order that Officers both now and hereafter who are, or may be, called upon to administer Martial Law may know their powers in regard to interference by Civil Courts, the Commander-in-Chief wishes the above facts to be made known throughout the Command.
>
> C.F.N. Macready, General.

It is worth remarking that O'Connor's decision came a fortnight after the Truce of 11 July 1921. The Truce, however, expressly reserved the British position in regard to courts-martial.[88]

Nor was this all. In the Civil War period the same argument that had produced the order for Egan's release was pleaded in the legal proceedings which were undertaken to save the life of Erskine Childers.[89] And the judge before whom the point was made was again O'Connor. In his judgment, O'Connor admitted that his approach in the earlier case may have been wrong – it had certainly not been supported by any of his judicial colleagues – but, treating it as correct, as he felt he ought, there existed, he thought, one crucial difference in law between the circumstances prevailing in the summer of 1921 and those of the autumn of 1922. The Westminster-enacted Restoration of Order in Ireland Act had, in the interim, become a dead letter. It had become so because a Provisional Government had acceded to office in Ireland and was henceforth solely responsible there for the maintenance of order. The legislation was spent – *cessante ratione legis cessat lex ipsa* – and, in consequence, the right of Government in Ireland to establish informal military tribunals, such as the one which had tried Childers, was again untrammelled by any legislative control.[90]

88 *Arrangements governing the cessation of active operations in Ireland which came into force on 11th July 1921* (Cmd. 1534; 1921). **89** *R. (Childers)* v. *Adjutant-General of the Forces of the Irish Provisional Government* [1923] 1 IR 5, 56 ILTR 183. **90** Childers was shot while an appeal was pending.

In the circumstances, it is strange that in the following spring, the spring of 1923, the Free State Government was still treating the 1920 Act as being in force. It persuaded the British Government to use powers under the Act to order the English and Scottish police to arrest anti-Treaty Republicans then resident in Britain and secure the transfer of these Republicans to the Free State for internment there. In *R. (ex parte O'Brien)* v. *Home Secretary*[91] the Court of Appeal in England did not take long to point out the illegality of the entire proceedings.[92]

There was an echo of the argument between O'Connor and Macready in a further episode from the Civil War period. This was an earlier episode which had, as well, some bearing on the decision to end the Dáil courts. On 19 July 1922 Count Plunkett, father of one of the anti-Treaty Irregulars captured on the fall of the Four Courts, sought and obtained, on behalf of his son, from Diarmuid Crowley, a Dáil court judge sitting in Dublin, a conditional order of habeas corpus, returnable on 26 July, against the Governor of Mountjoy Prison and the Minister for Defence. On 25 July, Crowley was informed that the authority of Dáil courts sitting in Dublin had been withdrawn. Nonetheless, the next day, the 26th, he held his court and when the Governor and Minister made no return to the writ, held them in contempt and ordered their arrest. The order was not obeyed; indeed, the only reaction to the affair was the resignation from the Dáil Cabinet of George Gavan Duffy, the Treaty signatory and later High Court judge. At another sitting in August Crowley granted an application for mandamus against Eoin MacNeill, speaker of the Dáil, ordering him to summon it. This order, likewise, was disobeyed. Shortly afterwards, Crowley was arrested by Provisional Government forces and spent about a week in military custody. The situation had irony. Crowley was the Dáil circuit judge who, in 1920, had been imprisoned by the British for his judicial activities then.[93]

Internment was the second principal issue. Until 1920 the basis for it was provided by regulation 14B of the Defence of the Realm Regulations. Proof of hostile origin or association had first to be shown. The circumstances of Casement's landfall at Banna, Co. Kerry on Easter Saturday 1916 convinced the Irish Government that the necessary proof had at last been furnished, whereupon they resolved to intern the Sinn Fein leadership.[94] This particular decision came too late but other internment decisions in later years were successfully implemented.

The basis for internment was changed under the Restoration of Order in Ireland Act 1920. Regulation 14B remained in force but was crucially amended so as to extend internment to any 'person who is suspected of acting or having acted or of being about to act in a manner prejudicial to the restoration or maintenance of order in Ireland'.[95]

91 [1923] 2 KB 361. **92** Chandler, 'Praemunire and the Habeas Corpus Act considered in connection with the Irish Deportees and the case of Ex Parte O'Brien', (1924) 24 *Col. L. Rev.* 273; 'The Independence of the Executive of the Irish Free State', (1923) 57 *ILTSJ* 227; 'Habeas Corpus when the Custody is Uncertain', 57 *ILTSJ* 233. The Restoration of Order in Ireland (Indemnity) Act 1923 set up a special tribunal to compensate the internees; for details of the awards made by the tribunal sitting in Glasgow, see 57 *ILTSJ* 248. See, too, the *Report of the committee appointed to review the provisions of the Restoration of Order in Ireland Act 1920 and of the regulations made under that Act* (Cmd. 2278; 1924-5). **93** Casey, 'Republican Courts in Ireland 1919-1922', (1970) 5 *IJ* (n.s.) 321, 339-40. **94** *Royal Commission on the rebellion ... minutes, etc.*, pp 36-7 (evidence of Lord Wimborne, Lord Lieutenant). **95** Sch. to the

In April 1922 these extended powers were replaced, so far as Northern Ireland was concerned, by the Special Powers Act (Northern Ireland) which was destined to remain the legal basis for internment there. In the South developments were different. The new political leaders, many of whom had been interned by the British, were especially sensitive on issues of human liberty; their sensitivity, indeed, is reflected in the Free State Constitution of 1922. Civil War, however, caused even them to change their minds. The decision did not have to be taken at once, for, until the summer of 1923, the courts in the Free State held the country to be in a state of armed rebellion and that, in consequence, what the military did – which was what mattered – could not be the subject of judicial challenge.[96] On 1 August 1923, however, the courts held, so far as Dublin was concerned, that this was no longer the case, and so the ordinary legal protections of individual liberty again existed.[97] To meet continued danger to itself, the Free State Government on the same day introduced a power of internment, in the Public Safety (Emergency Powers) Act. A succession of such measures followed, for each piece of Southern legislation, unlike the North's Special Powers Act, was in fact to be of temporary duration. The validity of the succeeding measures in the South was in each instance attacked,[98] but only once, in the case of the first Act, with success. It was said that the Oireachtas, in enacting the legislation, had omitted to follow the prescribed constitutional formula to give it immediate validity; the argument was a sound one and, when the courts upheld it, a fresh Act was instantly passed to cure the defect.[99] Both North and South, in the cases, respectively, of *O'Hanlon*[100] and *O'Connell*,[101] internment legislation was challenged on the grounds that it lay outside the powers of the respective legislatures. Dodd J, in upholding, in *O'Connell's* case, the right of the Free State legislature to enact such a law and affirming that such a law was a law for peace, order and good government, could, perhaps, have been speaking of the Special Powers Act too:

> In a land of settled Government the liberty of the subject is the prevailing note. In a land unsettled and turbulent the duty of the legislature is to contrive as far as may be to reconcile personal liberty with safety to the person and property of the citizens.[102]

Numbers of those interned were high and posed a problem for the various penal and military authorities. To provide the necessary accommodation, special internment camps were opened and, in Northern Ireland, even a prison ship was brought into

Regulations under the Restoration of Order in Ireland Act 1920 made on 13 August 1920: 1920 S.R. & O. no. 1530. **96** *R. (Beaumont)* v. *Military Governor, Wellington Barracks* (1920) 56 *ILTSJ* 222 and 230; *R. (Childers)* v. *Adjutant-General of the Forces of the Irish Provisional Government* [1923] 1 IR 5, 56 ILTR 183; *R. (Johnstone)* v. *O'Sullivan* [1923] 2 IR 13, 57 ILTR 17 (Ronan LJ diss.); 57 *ILTSJ* 153 (various cases in June 1923). **97** *R. (O'Brien)* v. *Governor of the Military Internment Camp and the Minister of Defence* [1924] 1 IR 32. **98** E.g., *R. (Murphy)* v. *Military Governor of Mountjoy Prison* (1924) 58 ILTR 1. **99** *R. (O'Brien)* v. *Governor of the Military Internment Camp and the Minister of Defence* [1924] 1 IR 32. **100** *R. (O'Hanlon)* v. *Governor of Belfast Prison* (1922) 56 ILTR 170. **101** *R. (O'Connell)* v. *Military Governor of Hare Park Internment Camp* [1924] 2 IR 104, 58 ILTR 49. See, too, *R. (Burke)* v. *Governor of Mountjoy Prison* (1924) 58 ILTR 106. **102** [1924] 2 IR 104, 116.

service. Space was also made available in the ordinary prisons but this could then aggravate the problem of accommodating ordinary prisoners.[103] The political fervour and sense of camaraderie of those detained in the various prisons and internment institutions made the maintenance of security and discipline no easy task. Escapes and rioting were commonplace.[104] So too was the hunger-strike, and what was to be done with those who resorted to it raised a third law and order issue. The problem had first been faced when the suffragettes refused food to call attention to the issue of votes for women. This had been a problem in Ireland (in 1912) no less than in England.[105] The Government's decision in the case of suffragettes had been to exercise temporary release powers in order to avoid the stigma of being held responsible for any death.[106] Equal leniency was not extended to Republican prisoners and detainees, and the inevitable tragedies resulted, those of Thomas Ashe[107] and Terence MacSwiney from the pre-Treaty period being the most notable. The *Report of the Irish Prisons Board for 1917-8* details the change in policy.[108] At first a programme of forcible feeding was supported, as the Report discloses:

> As regards the expedient known as 'hunger-striking', the legal view of the responsibility of the prison authorities, based on a judgment of Lord Chief Justice Alverstone in an action by an ex-suffragette prisoner against the Home Secretary in 1909,[109] was that in the case of voluntary starvation by sane prisoners for the purpose of obtaining their release or other privileges, forcible feeding was a necessary duty of the Prison authorities to keep such persons alive, if possible, and that this duty was not performed by offering them food at frequent intervals. Prisoners on hunger-strike were accordingly fed.

But later, as the *Report* again reveals, it was announced in Parliament that even forcible feeding would not be attempted. As a result, the following notice was placed in every prisoner's cell:

> All persons committed to prison are informed that they will not be able, by wilful injury to their bodily health caused by refusal of food, or in any other way, to procure their release before discharge in due course of law.[110]

103 In the early years of Northern Ireland its Ministry of Home Affairs encountered other difficulties too: the law provided for the detention of convicted offenders in a variety of institutions, convict prison, borstal, criminal lunatic asylum, inebriates' reformatory, but none of the appropriate Irish institutions were physically situated north of the Border. See Osborough, 'Partition and the Northern Borstal Boy 1921-7', 1 *Dublin Univ. L. Rev.* 28. **104** *Report by the rt. hon. Mr Justice Dodd of the proceedings at the inquiry directed by the Special Commission (Belfast Prison) Act 1918* (Cmd. 83; 1919); Kenny J conducted an inquiry into escapes from Cork and Dublin prisons in 1919 (53 *ILTSJ* 82 and 119) and Ross J into escapes from Mountjoy in 1920 (54 *ILTSJ* 142). **105** Ó Broin, *The Chief Secretary* (1969), pp 60-3. **106** Prisoners (Temporary Discharge for Ill-Health) Act 1913. **107** The death of Ashe led to proceedings designed to ensure that prisoners in Mountjoy testified at the inquest: (1917) 51 *ILTSJ* 254. The future Governor-General of the Irish Free State, T.M. Healy, represented Sinn Fein at it. **108** *40th report of the General Prisons Board, Ireland, 1917-18* (Cmd. 42; 1918), pp v and vii. **109** *Leigh* v. *Gladstone* (1909) 26 TLR 139. **110** *40th report of the General Prisons Board, Ireland, 1917-18*, p. vii.

The authorities, nonetheless, continued to vacillate.[111]

Policing, the fourth issue, was no new issue. If its prominence in the period owed much to she state of the country, it owed something too to the fact that proposals on the police had been contained in the Home Rule bills and in the report of the abortive Irish Convention of 1917.[112]

From 1919 to 1922 a Republican police force functioned.[113] Accounts of the two other forces in existence before the Treaty are, however, rather easier to put together. In the history of the Dublin Metropolitan Police two incidents stand out: the dismissal of the deputy commissioner for attempting to seize the arms landed at Howth in July 1914, a step which was followed by the resignation in sympathy of the commissioner himself;[114] the shooting of a constable on duty near the Castle in the early moments of the 1916 Rising. Set the two incidents together and one can grasp something of the difficulties under which police work, more especially that set the Royal Irish Constabulary, was to be carried out. In the years after 1916 political meetings and politically-inspired violence continued to place a strain on the DMP. Being an unarmed force, it had, on occasion, to be withdrawn from the streets of Dublin; some of its members were deployed on political work, and the force did not entirely escape the attention of the gunman. The force survived the Treaty, and amalgamation with the Garda Síochána in 1925[115] appears to have been a matter of administrative convenience. The last years of the RIC were less fortunate.[116] Members of the force were made legitimate targets for the gun at the start of the Anglo-Irish War: the Soloheadbeg shootings[117] only heralded what was to come. In nationalist circles members of the force had been socially accepted – commonly some relation served in it – but, as the political and military situation changed, presenting the opportunity of striking 'the final blow for Irish freedom', views changed, too. Each man in the RIC came to represent a detested Government: 'the eyes and ears of the enemy', it was said. Police reorganisation contributed to the worsening relations between nationalist opinion and the RIC. To support the force's weakening resources as well as to release troops for other duties, the British Government recruited extra manpower, the 'Black and Tans' and 'Auxiliaries' for use in the South and a special constabulary raised among Ulster Protestants for use in the North. All were destined to enter the folklore of repression. Meanwhile, the RIC appeared increasingly in the firing-line as barracks were besieged by flying columns and local opinion reacted, predictably, to the programme of reprisals on which Crown forces, as a whole, appeared to have embarked. Sir John Ross summarised the disastrous finale: 'It was only when the

111 *41st report of the General Prisons Board, Ireland, 1918-19* (Cmd. 687; 1920), p. vi (lenient rule), p. vii (severer rule from 24 November 1919). See, too, Jones, *Whitehall diary*, vol. 3, pp 15-6, 36-7. **112** *Report of the proceedings of the Irish Convention* (Cd. 9019; 1918), pp 117-35. **113** There are a few details in Hogan, *The four glorious years* (1951), pp 80-1. **114** *Royal commission on the rebellion ... minutes, etc.*, p. 92; *Report of the royal commission on the circumstances connected with the landing of arms at Howth on 26th July, 1914* (Cd. 7631; 1914-16). **115** Police Forces Amalgamation Act 1925 (IFS). See, too, *Cahill* v. *A.-G.* [1925] IR 70, 59 ILTR 29. **116** See, generally, Hawkins, 'Dublin Castle and the Royal Irish Constabulary (1916-1922)', in Williams (ed.), *The Irish struggle 1916-1926* (1966), p. 167; 'I.O.', *The administration of Ireland 1920*, ch. 10. **117** Breen, *My fight for Irish freedom* (1924), ch. 5. For legal sequel see *Connors* v. *Pearson* [1921] 2 IR 51 and *O'Connell* v. *Tipperary C.C.* [1921] 2 IR 103, 54 ILTR 62 and 157.

enemy systematically applied their cruelties to their families and relatives in unprotected places that the splendid line at last wavered and broke – but they endured all that flesh and blood could stand.'[118] In 1922 the RIC was dissolved.[119] Some of its members transferred to the Garda Síochána in the South or the Royal Ulster Constabulary in the North or to other police jobs abroad. Palestine was popular. Others, again, were content to retire on pension.[120]

Dissolution of the RIC was followed by the creation, in the South, of a new unarmed force which, despite certain inauspicious beginnings, soon enjoyed a fair measure of public support.[121] In Northern Ireland fate was not so kind. Politics was to dictate too much the kind of task which the RUC would be asked to undertake. Its effect on the origins and structure of the force had already been dangerous: in the campaign, late in 1921, for the transfer of responsibility for the RIC in the North to the Northern Ireland Government; in the under-representation of Catholics; in the composition of the special constabulary with which it was associated; in the ending of the 'mutiny' among 'A' special constables on their disbandment in 1925, and in the solution of other administrative problems with which the Inspector-General, as head of the force, had so soon to wrestle.[122] The Craig-Collins pact of March 1922[123] was designed not only to end IRA activity and sectarian rioting in the North but also to develop a new police on a community basis, enabling it to enjoy wide public support. Both Irish Governments bore responsibility for the pact's collapse.[124] The Provisional Government was unable, or unwilling, to bring IRA activity to a halt and Collins's later dealings with de Valera were viewed, in the North, with profound suspicion. The good faith of the Northern Ireland Government was doubted equally soon. There was the dispute over the date from which the pact was to be fully effective; more seriously, the absence of full moral backing for the work in Belfast both of the Catholic Police Advisory Committee and of the associated Conciliation Committee; and of equal importance, perhaps, the uncertain quality of the talents of Dawson Bates, the Minister of Home Affairs.[125] At this time relations between the two Irish Governments were bad. Their suspicion of each other over the specific matter of how to secure peace in the North had especially serious implications. It meant that when the pact collapsed, as a result of seemingly uncontrollable political forces, an opportunity had been lost for creating, even in the short term, a police structure in the North with full community support.

Lisburn in County Antrim was one of several Northern towns which was witness to sectarian disturbances. From it there is recorded at this period a strange incident, the significance of which perhaps only a lawyer could have begun to understand. In

118 Ross, *Pilgrim scrip* (1927), p. 255. **119** Constabulary (Ireland) Act 1922. **120** For a later instance of litigation see *Egan and Others* v. *A.-G.* [1929] 2 Ch. 244; [1930] 1 Ch. 238; [1931] AC 113. **121** Commission on the Garda Síochána, *Report on remuneration and conditions of service*, Prl. 933 (1970), pp 23-5; White, *Kevin O'Higgins* (1948), ch. 9; 17 *Dáil Debs*. 701; (1924) 58 *ILTSJ* 270. **122** *Interim report of the departmental committee of inquiry on police reorganisation in Northern Ireland* (Cmd. 1; 1922); Clark, *Guns in Ulster* (1967); *Northern Whig* newspaper, 16 December 1925; 4 *H.C.Debs. (NI)* 66. **123** The text is given in Quekett, *The constitution of Northern Ireland*, vol. 3, p. 185. **124** Kevin Boyle, 'The Tallents report on the Craig-Collins pact of 30 March 1922', (1977) 12 *IJ* (n.s.) 148. **125** For Dawson Bates's supposed role in the 'Wickham circular' affair of November 1920, see Jones, *Whitehall diary*, vol. 3, p. 173.

licensed premises which had been burnt out over a year before and which had been abandoned since, there was to be seen standing, exposed to the elements, a publican inviting custom for his establishment.[126] In these years the problems facing the licensed trade were considerable; in certain parts of the country, for example, the annual licensing sessions had not been held and publicans were in understandable confusion about their legal position.[127] The Lisburn publican's predicament was rather different. His intention was to seek a renewal of his licence at the pending sessions, but, to secure it, he knew he had to show that he had carried on business during the year; hence his bizarre conduct. No other alternative lay open to him if he wished to protect his livelihood. He had lodged a malicious injuries claim in respect of the destruction of his premises. But slowness, at one level of the legal system, in processing that claim had left him unable to rebuild those premises and re-commence business in them within the year. And that delay, for which he had been in no respects to blame, meant that he risked provoking, at another level of the same legal system, the loss of his livelihood.

Arrangement of proper compensation for those suffering personal injury as well as property damage – the second broad theme of legal administration – rarely required the resolving of the complex tangle in which the Lisburn publican was embroiled. But the problems which confronted judges and Governments in this connection, nonetheless, were legion, for the dominant subject-matter of litigation was the malicious injuries claim. No litigation statistics, indeed, are so eloquent of the history of the country. A glance at the law reports in confirmation is scarcely needed, for the numbers of killed and injured were high and the amount of devastation colossal. As regards property damage, the camera recorded much of it, and other evidence is still to be seen in the debris scattered through the Irish countryside, from the shells of the family mansions, such as that of the Tighes at Inistioge in Co. Kilkenny, to the gutted coastguard blocks everywhere.[128]

Two principal questions faced the judges over compensation, under the malicious injuries code, for property damage: could compensation be given for consequential loss, i.e., for loss of production as well as destruction of physical assets, and could it be given in respect of damage inflicted by Government military and police? Sir James Campbell, lord chancellor until 1921 (and then, as Lord Glenavy, first chairman of the Free State Senate) answered the first of the questions in the affirmative and that view was reflected in the legislation of 1920. His successor, Sir John Ross, however, was not so sure and there has remained, in consequence, some uncertainty as to the precise position in law, an uncertainty which explains how courts North and South of the Border have arrived at opposite conclusions.[129] The judges were also divided on the second and more troublesome question. Two distinct situations arose. First, there was

126 *R. (Dudgeon)* v. *Antrim County Court Judge* (1920) 56 ILTR 134. **127** *R. (Slevin)* v. *Chairman of Longford Quarter Sessions* [1923] 2 IR 79 and 109, 57 ILTR 65. See s. 4 of the Licensing (Removal of Licences) Act 1923 (IFS). **128** In the preface to the 5th ed. of Bolton's *Criminal Injuries (Ireland) Acts 1919-20* (1922) the author wrote: 'Since the issue of the last edition the Four Courts have been destroyed, the greater portion of one side of Upper Sackville Street has been laid in ruins, while throughout the country the loss of human life and the toll of injury and destruction to property of all kinds remains yet to be ascertained.' **129** Miers, 'Compensation for Consequential Loss Under the Malicious Injuries Code' (1971) 6 *IJ* (n.s.) 50.

the case where, for example, the police were besieged in their barracks and the relief party, in dislodging the besiegers from premises opposite, destroyed the latter.[130] Some judges thought that the 'malice' necessary for the success of the owner's claim against the local authority could be supplied from the actions of the besiegers and that the damage could, in such circumstances, be said to have been caused by the besiegers. However, in an important decision, the High Court of Appeal for Ireland refused to agree, dismissing such an approach as both unrealistic and unwarranted.[131] Secondly, there were the cases where the military or police embarked on reprisal raids. Again, the judges differed. Some awards were made on the basis that Crown forces had caused malicious damage[132] but in one reported instance – and there were probably others – Mr Justice Dodd set aside such an award.[133] He took the view that what had been done could be justified in the interests of the King's peace and that, therefore, in law, there could be no malice. Not unexpectedly, any doctrine which denied compensation to the victim of any Crown raid or attack was expressly set aside in the emergency rules covering entitlement to compensation in the South for property damaged between January 1919 and the Truce in 1921.[134]

Where the compensation money was to come from soon assumed primary importance.[135] The rates could never have borne the cost and the matter became the responsibility of central government. In Northern Ireland it was arranged that both compensation funds for the Northern Government and compensation awards to actual claimants would be made available in instalments.[136] Much more damage was done in the Free State area and the Government there was forced to be less than generous. Changes were made to the rules on entitlement, sometimes, as was noticed earlier, with retrospective effect. Pre-Truce awards and claims were scrutinised by a joint British-Free State Compensation Commission,[137] and claims arising between the time of the Truce and spring 1923, by the Free State Minister for Finance.[138] Awards in respect of the latter group of claims, of which there were many more, could be made in part in Free State bonds and made conditional on the claimant's agreeing to rebuild in Ireland. Southern loyalists, some of whom had been intimidated into leaving the country, fought against what they considered to be restrictions on their right to full

130 An example is *Mahony* v. *Kerry C.C.* (1921) 55 *ILTSJ* 313. **131** *McKnight* v. *Armagh C.C.* [1922] 2 IR 137, 56 ILTR 7 and 57. **132** *Tralee U.D.C.* v. *Kerry C.C.* (1921) 55 *ILTSJ* 117; cases at Newtownbutler quarter sessions: 55 *ILTSJ* 164. Cf. *Tyler* v. *Cork C.C.* [1921] 2 IR 8, 54 ILTR 201. The issue was, predictably, politically sensitive. For British Cabinet discussion on one episode see Jones, *Whitehall diary*, vol. 3, pp 50–2. **133** *Fitzpatrick* v. *Fermanagh C.C.* (1921) 55 *ILTSJ* 180. **134** In the warrant of appointment of the Compensation (Ireland) Commission (Cmd. 1654; 1922). Provision to similar effect is contained in s. 15(10) of the Damage to Property (Compensation) Act 1923 (IFS) and s. 2 of the Damage to Property (Compensation) (Amendment) Act 1933 (IFS). An analogous problem had been highlighted by the Easter Rising in 1916: (1916) 50 *ILTSJ* 120 and 124. **135** Miers, 'Paying for Malicious Injuries Claims', (1970) 5 *IJ* (n.s.) 50. **136** Circular to Northern Ireland local authorities from the Ministry of Home Affairs, 23 February 1922 (text in Bolton's *Criminal Injuries (Ireland) Acts, 1919-20* (5th ed. 1922)). **137** *Letter to the Provisional Government of Southern Ireland on compensation for malicious injuries in Ireland* (Cmd. 1736; 1922); *Warrant of appointment of the Compensation (Ireland) Commission* (Cmd. 1654; 1922); *Summary of the terms of an agreement between His Majesty's Government and the Government of the Irish Free State relating to compensation for damage to property in Ireland, and papers relative thereto* (Cmd. 2445; 1924-5). **138** Damage to Property (Compensation) Act 1923 (IFS).

compensation. Their pressure groups, such as the Irish Claims Compensation Association and the Southern Irish Loyalists' Relief Association, however, made little headway; nor was much gained by the sympathetic speeches and journalism of the former lord chancellor, Sir John Ross.[139] The emotive language in a memorandum presented by the Irish Claims Compensation Association has been underlined in the copy now in the Hugh Kennedy Collection, University College, Dublin: a lack of tact may well have been more than matched by a political disinclination to respond.[140] On one matter pressure did prove successful. Among the refugees who arrived in England there were several cases of genuine hardship, and these the British Government assisted financially, first through the Irish Distress Committee and then through the Irish Grants Committee.[141]

Two other branches of law were appealed to by those whose property had been lost or destroyed: the law of the common carrier[142] and the law of insurance. Of the two, the latter, naturally, was the more pertinent. In a succession of cases where the facts lacked nothing in drama – the Rising itself,[143] armed robbery,[144] factory burning perhaps as part of the Belfast 'boycott',[145] commandeering of transport by the IRA[146] – the courts of Ireland and England were invited to interpret and apply exception clauses embracing incidents such as 'riot' and 'civil commotion'. Two of these cases, *Cooper's* and *Boggan's*, provide the only evidence within the *Irish Reports* of the strain which contemporary politics placed on the good temper of Irish judges towards one another.

The Free State Government set up a special Compensation Commission to deal with accumulated personal injuries claims under the malicious injuries code arising between 1919 and 1923.[147] In 1916 the same had been done for the benefit of the victims of the Rising[148] but, thereafter, until 1922, all claims were processed in the ordinary way. There was some relevant litigation on entitlement to workmen's compensation: a carter caught in the cross-fire on a Belfast street was held to have suffered an accident that arose out of and in the course of his employment, but not so a workman employed at horse-tram stables in Dublin who, defying instructions, met his death in similar circumstances.[149] But the main emphasis was again on the malicious

139 Ross, *Pilgrim scrip* (1927), 247ff. **140** Note, however, the terms of the Damage to Property (Compensation) (Amendment) Act 1926 (IFS). **141** *Correspondence between His Majesty's Government and the Provisional Government of Ireland relating to the liability for relief of Irish refugees* (Cmd. 1684; 1922); *Memorandum relating to compensation for injury to persons and property in the Irish Free State* (Cmd. 1844; 1923); *Second interim report of the Irish Grants Committee* (Cmd. 2032; 1924). Generally, see the *Report of a committee presided over by Lord Dunedin on compensation in the Irish Free State* (Cmd. 2748; 1926). **142** *Secretary of State for War* v. *Midland and Great Western Railway Co. of Ireland* [1923] 2 IR 102, 57 ILTR 110. **143** *Curtis* v. *Matthews* [1918] 2 KB 825, [1919] 1 KB 425; *Alexander* v. *British Dominion General Insurance Co.* (1916) 50 *ILTSJ* 195. **144** *London and Lancashire Fire Insurance Co.* v. *Bolands Ltd.* [1924] 2 IR 130, 58 ILTR 85; [1924] AC 836. **145** *Craig* v. *Eagle Star and British Dominions Insurance Co.* (1921) 56 ILTR 145. **146** *Cooper* v. *General Accident, Fire and Life Assurance Corporation* [1922] 2 IR 38, 43, 45 and 214; 55 ILTR 191; 56 ILTR 1 and 165; *Boggan* v. *Motor Union Insurance Co.* [1922] 2 IR 184 and 221, [1923] 2 IR 136; 56 ILTR 90 and 173, 57 ILTR 105; *Johnson & Perrott Ltd.* v. *Holmes* (1925) 21 Ll L Rep 330. See further, below, pp 296–314. **147** (1922) 57 *ILTSJ* 65 and 77. **148** (1916) 50 *ILTSJ* 276. **149** *Noble Ltd.* v. *Carragher* (1923) 57 ILTR 137; *Hogan* v. *Dublin United Tramways* (1916) 50 *ILTSJ* 264. Cf. the case briefly reported at 57 *ILTSJ* 93. For the case of an employment contract held to have been frustrated by the destruction of the premises in which the employment took place, see *Gilmore* v. *Bird & Co. (Belfast) Ltd.* (1922) 56 *ILTSJ* 242.

injuries code and here important legislative changes were to be made. Under the code, a policeman, to succeed in his claim, had to show that he had suffered injury while bringing a disturber of the public peace to justice.[150] The condition was strictly interpreted by the judges[151] and, as a result and in order to preserve police morale, the legislature substituted, in 1919, the condition that the policeman need only show that he had been engaged in the discharge of his duty.[152] Other remedial action by the legislature the same year followed similar dissatisfaction with the strict approach of the judges, in cases involving policemen killed or injured, to the method of fixing the level of compensation.[153] In further changes an amount of protection under the code was extended to private citizens: where they were victims of crimes arising out of a combination of a seditious character or of any unlawful association (in 1919)[154] or unlawful assembly (in 1920).[155] The legislative changes of 1919 and 1920 were carried over into the law of Northern Ireland,[156] but in the Free State in 1923 the two acts of 1919 and 1920 were expressly repealed and, once the Compensation Commission had finished its task, personal injury protection under the code there became limited in effect to members of the Garda Síochána and then only on a restricted basis.[157]

Wounded veterans of both the Anglo-Irish War and the Civil War, it might also be noted, were awarded pensions by the Oireachtas.[158] All veterans became entitled to pensions in any event,[159] as did the members of the special constabularies disbanded in the North in 1925.[160] In the case of anti-Treaty veterans of the Civil War, provision to this effect was made only after de Valera came to power in 1932.[161] Veterans on the Republican side in the Spanish Civil War were not to be so handsomely treated.[162]

As the political solution of the early 1920s to what was then thought to be the Irish problem began to be implemented, the courts, inevitably, were required to consider certain aspects of it. In the autumn of 1921 the courts in Dublin were asked to prevent the transfer to the new Northern Ireland Government of powers over national insurance; the proceedings were abortive.[163] In 1924 in London the Judicial Committee of the Privy Council determined that there were flaws in the plan, then current, to set up the Boundary Commission over the opposition of the Northern Ireland Government, but there was no flaw which legislative action in both Dublin and London could not cure.[164] The courts, then, did not seriously affect the march of events but, neverthe-

150 Grand Jury Act 1836, s. 106. **151** E.g., in *Lowe* v. *Cork C.C.* (1917) 51 ILTR 62. Cf. *Mills* v. *Dublin Corporation and Dublin C.C.* (1918) 53 ILTR 113. **152** Criminal Injuries (Ireland) Act 1919, s. 1(1)(a). The legislation was retrospective to 1 January 1917 (s. 1 (6)). Extra-statutory pensions had been awarded to members of the Irish police injured in the Rising or to relatives of those killed in it: (1921) 55 *ILTSJ* 212. **153** Criminal Injuries (Ireland) Act 1919, s. 1(3). **154** Ibid., s. 1(1)(b). **155** Criminal Injuries (Ireland) Act 1920, s. 7(a). For the relationship of the two acts of 1919 and 1920, see *Deehan* v. *Derry C.C.* and *Mangan* v. *Kerry C.C.* (1921) 55 ILTR 31. **156** For an early Northern Ireland case in which it was sought, unsuccessfully, to treat a group of policemen as an unlawful assembly, see *Grant* v. *Armagh C.C.* (1924) 58 *ILTSJ* 276. **157** *Summary of report of interdepartmental committee on malicious injuries* (Pr. 8142; 1965); Commission on the Garda Síochána, *Report on remuneration and conditions of service* (Prl. 933; 1970), pp 191-7. **158** Army Pensions Act 1923 (IFS). **159** Military Service Pensions Act 1924 (IFS). **160** *Northern Whig* newspaper, 16 December 1925. **161** Military Service Pensions Act 1934 (IFS). **162** Thomas, *The Spanish Civil War* (1961), p. 608. **163** *McCann* v. *A.-G. for Ireland and the Irish Insurance Commissioners* (1921) 55 *ILTSJ* 314. See, too, *Report of the departmental committee on the application of the Government of Ireland Act 1920 to National Health Insurance* (Cmd. 1575; 1922). **164** Calvert, *Constitutional law in Northern Ireland*, pp 46-8; introduc-

less, they did provide the answers to many important questions. This was particularly so in the South. There they helped resolve in favour of the pro-Treaty politicians any doubts as to the legitimate political authority within the State;[165] in this they were, doubtless, assisted by the decision to wind up the Dáil courts. Implications of independence were more slow to be grasped.[166] Before 1924 the judges leaned heavily on the provision in the Constitution of 1922 that, prior to the establishment of a new judicial system, they were to continue to exercise the same jurisdiction as was theirs before 1922.[167] On these grounds they refused to recognise jurisdictional bars in the enforcement of judgments obtained in English courts or in the extra-territorial operation of workmen's compensation.[168] After 1924 this began to be changed[169] but, despite the change in the source of authority of the new courts,[170] and with the exception of the controversy over the right of appeal to the Privy Council,[171] remarkably little else. Free State judges upheld the claim of the Government to take full advantage of a number of legal rules which implied a more central role for the Crown than it was ever permitted to hold in Irish politics after the débâcle of the Treaty.[172] Kennedy, the Chief Justice from 1924, had been prompted on the subject when Attorney General.[173] So it was that State debts enjoyed priority as had those of the Crown. Crown privilege became State privilege. The Crown could do no wrong was translated into a doctrine of State immunity in tort which a re-invigorated constitutionalist tradition was only able to dislodge in 1971.[174] It was within the alternative political tradition represented by de Valera that people began to question the legitimacy of these equations and it was the de Valera Constitution of 1937 which was to provide the legal stimulus for a fresh look to be taken.

Partition had an immediate impact. Neighbouring counties which, under the malicious injuries code, could be forced to share the cost of a successful claim had hence-

tion by Hand to *The report of the Irish Boundary Commission 1925* (1970). **165** *R. (Childers)* v. *Adjutant-General of the Forces of the Irish Provisional Government* [1923] 1 IR 5, 56 ILTR 183; *R. (Murphy)* v. *Military Governor of Mountjoy Prison* (1924) 58 ILTR 1; *Fogarty* v. *O'Donoghue* [1926] IR 531 and 551, (1924) 58 *ILTSJ* 185 and 191. **166** Speculation at the time turned on whether the Free State, as a Dominion, was a sovereign state. International law precedents embraced the unlikely trinity of Egypt, the Ionian Islands and the Cherokee nation. **167** Constitution of the Irish Free State 1922, art. 75. **168** *Gieves Ltd.* v. *O'Conor* [1924] 2 IR 182, 58 ILTR 135 (contra, in England, *Wakeley* v. *Triumph Cycle Co.* [1924] 1 KB 214); *R. (Armstrong)* v. *Wicklow County Court Judge* [1924] 2 IR 139, 58 ILTR 38 and 121. English maintenance decrees were also enforced: 57 *ILTSJ* 254. **169** *R. (Alexander)* v. *Circuit Judge for Cork* [1925] 2 IR 165 and 175; *Cahill* v. *A.-G.* [1925] IR 70, 59 ILTR 29. **170** See *Quinn & White* v. *Stokes & Quirke* [1931] IR 558, at 564, per Kennedy CJ. **171** *Hull* v. *McKenna, Freeman's Journal* v. *Fernstrom* [1926] IR 402, 57 ILTR 173; *Lynham* v. *Butler* [1925] 2 IR 231, 59 ILTR 58. **172** Kelly, *Fundamental rights in the Irish law and constitution* (2nd ed. 1967), pp 324-49. **173** In a memo. to Hugh Kennedy, then Attorney-General, in October 1923, seeking legal advice on the priority, as State debts, of accrued taxes, Ernest Blythe, Minister for Finance, wrote: 'the first step towards the solution of the problem appears to be to ascertain accurately the legal position of the King and if that is such as would suit the propaganda of the domestic opponents of the Free State, the second step is to ensure that it can so effectively be veiled, that the policy adopted will not interfere with or prevent the effective collection of revenue ... if any change is made taking away from taxes their description of Crown debts provision should be made that they will be entitled to the privileged treatment heretofore accorded to Crown debts': Hugh Kennedy Collection, University College, Dublin. (On the Kennedy Collection, see now A.C. Holland, 'The papers of Hugh Kennedy: a research legacy for the foundation of the State', (1989) 24 *IJ* (n.s.) 279.) **174** *Byrne* v. *Ireland* [1972] IR 241.

forth to be situated either in the North or in the South. Where cross-border activity had occurred, claimants, as a result, were well-advised to commence proceedings in both jurisdictions. Given the differences which grew up soon after partition in the malicious injuries codes North and South, many claimants were to find cause for complaint and not merely over the cost.[175] Jurisdiction in criminal matters was, of course, curtailed in the two parts of the country,[176] and at an early date informal North-South 'extradition' was also to be brought to a halt.[177]

Rulings were not always the prerogative of the courts. In 1926 the Treasury in London granted to the Northern Ireland Ministry for Finance the right to claim, on behalf of the crown, any treasure trove found in the Six Counties;[178] the Royal Irish Academy had previously been the sole designated agent in Ireland. In 1966 the Committee of Privileges of the House of Lords, sitting on the forlorn claim of Irish peers to be again admitted to the House of Lords in a representative capacity, examined afresh the sequence of legal and constitutional events in the early 1920s. Somewhat earlier, courts in Ireland, in disputes over the ownership of political funds, had returned to the period too.[179] The reasons given by the Committee of Privileges for refusing to admit the Irish peers were complex.[180] One proposition was unanswerable, as this survey, after its own fashion, has attempted to show: the Ireland of the Act of Union was indeed dead.

175 *Farrelly* v. *Fermanagh C.C.* (1921) 55 *ILTSJ* 261; *Plumb* v. *Fermanagh C.C.* [1923] 1 IR 54; *McCullagh* v. *Irish Free State* (1923) 57 ILTR 171. **176** The decision on the jurisdiction issue in *R.* v. *McQuillan* [1923] 2 IR 97, 59 ILTR 101 would presumably have been different had the theft occurred a few months afterwards. **177** *O'Boyle and Rodgers* v. *A.-G. and O'Duffy* [1929] IR 558, 63 ILTR 33. **178** *Report of the Ministry of Finance 1927-29* (Belfast, 1930), para. 30. This was an agency arrangement under s. 60 of the Government of Ireland Act 1920. **179** These inquiries had been conducted in rather different contexts: *Fogarty* v. *O'Donoghue* [1926] IR 531 and 551; and *Buckley* v. *A.G.* (1950) 84 ILTR 9. **180** Lysaght, 'The Irish Peers and the House of Lords', (1967) 18 *NILQ* 277.

Forcibly Commandeered Transport and Owners' Insurance: The Deciding of Two Test Cases in the 1920s

Transport played a not inconspicuous part in the Anglo-Irish war of 1919 to 1921. To launch its guerilla-type forays against the police and British military, the Irish Republican Army needed the use of motor vehicles, and, predictably, seized these by force when they could not be acquired by peaceful means. Later, during the period of the Civil War, also for strategic reasons, motor transport again risked being commandeered.

From the outset, the British authorities recognised the military importance to their adversary of motor vehicles and strove to deny him all access to them. Thus on 1 November 1919 it became obligatory on the private citizen to possess a permit for a motor car. A year later, on 12 November 1920, the Commander-in-Chief in Ireland, the competent military authority under the Restoration of Order in Ireland Act, initiated more drastic action. The fresh order he promulgated contained, first, the following recital:[1]

> And whereas it appears that motor-cycles and motor-cars have been largely used by evil-disposed persons in the commission of murders and other criminal offences; and it has become necessary further to restrict the having, keeping, or using of motor cycles and motor cars.

The order went on to restrict the authority of permits previously issued to the period between 6a.m. and 8p.m. and within a distance of twenty miles from the user's residence. This last provision was the inevitable response to a method of warfare involving the concentration, by means of motor transport, of large numbers of armed men on isolated barracks in the possession of the Royal Irish Constabulary. A considered judgment is that the order failed in its purpose of preventing 'rebel movement' by road.[2]

Practice, where motor cars were commandeered by the IRA, would appear to have varied. Commonly, a receipt was given. And sometimes, too, when vehicles were returned in a damaged condition, the local IRA agreed to bear the cost of repairs.[3] Vehicles were commandeered for any length of time, from a few hours to as many days or weeks, possibly even for an avowed indefinite period, as in the ballad about Dr Johnson's car, where its seizure was announced to be operative until Ireland gained her freedom.[4]

1 Conveniently set out in the judgment of Sir John Ross C. in *Cooper* v. *General Accident Assur. Corp.* [1922] 2 IR at 49. **2** Charles Townshend, *The British campaign in Ireland 1919-1921* (Oxford, 1975), p. 148. **3** As in the episode from Limerick related by a friend of Walter Long, details of which were passed on by him to the Irish Committee of the British Cabinet: Thomas Jones, *Whitehall diary, volume III: Ireland 1918-1925*, ed. Keith Middlemas (London, 1971), p. 24. The episode took place prior to 1 July 1920. **4** Johnson's car was

On the other hand, on occasion there was no receipt and sometimes, too, the appropriated vehicle was never seen again. Where this happened owners, understandably, became agitated. Their insurers were equally perturbed, for the question arose in such cases of whether the cost of the loss of a vehicle was carried on the owner's insurance or had to be borne by the owner himself. What was at stake was the scope of typical motor insurance cover in force in Ireland in the 1920s and, in particular, the scope of exceptions to the insurers' liability expressed to lie in respect of losses attributable to 'civil commotion' and 'riot'.

At bottom, these were legal issues and it was to the law and the established Irish court system that the protagonists – Irish motorists and their insurers – were to turn in order to seek the solution to them. This they did in two test cases which became famous in their day. *Cooper* v. *General Accident, Fire & Life Assurance Corporation*[5] and *Boggan* v. *Motor Union Insurance Co.*,[6] however, are of enduring interest to the lawyer. First, they remain important precedents in insurance law.[7] Secondly, and less obviously, the resolution of the two test cases provided the scenario for an extraordinary episode in the history of judicial decision-making, which is worth resurrecting on a number of counts.

In both *Cooper* and *Boggan* excitement attends the unfolding of the answers that the judges were finally to give. The drama is heightened both by the relationship of the two test cases one to the other as they progress through the various stages of appeal and by the exceptionally large number of such stages with which concurrent constitutional reform had chosen to confront the Irish litigant. In 1921-2 the previous year's Government of Ireland Act enjoined that the parties in the *Cooper* case should proceed from trial court to House of Lords by way of, first, the Irish King's Bench Division, second, the Court of Appeal for Southern Ireland and, third, the High Court of Appeal for Ireland. This elaborate court structure naturally prolonged the litigation and helped to foment bitter disagreement on how the legal arguments advanced in the two cases should be approached. The origins of this disagreement remain obscure, but I will be suggesting that they lay as much in the judges' collective problem of adjustment to rapid political change as in differences of individual temperament.

II

The basic facts in the two cases were uncontroverted. In the first, on the evening of 28 October 1920, a group of men called at the home of a Captain Cooper in Douglas, six miles from Cork, forcibly seized the Ford car in the garage and drove it off. In the second, a taxi, belonging to a Mr Boggan, was seized by a group of armed men on the evening of 7 November 1920 on the road between Wexford and Duncormick. Earlier

seized on the bridge separating Ballybofey and Stranorlar in Co. Donegal. Johnson had been lured out on a false call. The car, celebrated in the ballad for the 'din' it made, a criticism to which Johnson is supposed to have taken exception, was eventually recovered in Burtonport by troops landed from a Royal Navy ship. **5** [1922] 2 IR 38, 214. **6** [1922] 2 IR 184, 222, [1923] 2 IR 136. **7** E.R. Hardy Ivamy, *Fire and Motor Insurance* (2nd ed., 1973), pp 263-5. Professor Ivamy deals with two other litigated claims arising from damage to, or loss of, motor vehicles in Ireland at the same period: *Crozier* v. *Thompson* (1922) 12 Ll L Rep 291 and *Johnson and Perrott Ltd.* v. *Holmes* (1925) 21 Ll L Rep 330.

in the evening, a Sunday, the taxi had been engaged to take the hirer to a dance. The chauffeur, a Mr Meyler, and his passenger were forced out, and the chauffeur eventually made his own way back to Wexford. 'When we got to Katescross,' Meyler later testified,[8]

> going round the bend of a road, when I was travelling at a good speed, three or four men appeared across the road, each of them armed with a revolver. They used some word which I could not catch. One came over and asked me where I was going to. I told him I was bringing the man alongside me to Duncormick. He told us to get out of the car. He then brought us up the road about twenty or thirty yards. He told me he was taking the car from me. I was then blindfolded and brought across the land to an outhouse. I was told to sit down. I was kept there three and a half to four hours. They took my permit. I was blindfolded again. They brought me to a different road and let me go. Two men stayed with me the entire time.

Boggan was insured with Motor Union Insurance, Cooper with General Accident Assurance. Citing the terms of the relevant policies of insurance, the companies refused to honour the claims for compensation lodged in respect of the losses of their motor-vehicles by the two owners. By June 1923 something over three hundred claims identical with that lodged by Boggan awaited final processing,[9] and the caution which the two insurance companies had demonstrated was clearly vindicated. Well before then, however, dissatisfaction at the refusal of Motor Union and General Accident to pay any compensation had prompted both Boggan and Cooper to go to law.

Cooper's action against his insurer was heard first, on 6 May 1921, before Moore J, sitting without a jury. The insurance cover for Cooper's car was subject, inter alia, to the following exception:

> loss or damage occasioned through riot or civil commotion occurring within the land limits of Ireland.

General Accident relied on evidence presented by the local district inspector of the RIC. This revealed that in October 1920, the month Cooper's car had been taken, four other cars had been seized in the immediate vicinity, and two of them belonged to neighbours of Cooper. Evidence was also adduced that in the period between 1 October 1920 and 30 April 1921 (i.e. up to a week before the commencement of the court hearing) fourteen cars had been taken 'in whole South City of Cork and Rural District'. Moore J held in favour of Cooper. He could not find on the facts that there was either riot or civil commotion on Cooper's premises at the time the car was taken. The facts were consistent with simple armed robbery or burglary. There was no necessary inference that General Accident had discharged the burden of proof cast on them of bringing themselves within the exception.[10]

8 [1922] 2 IR at 185. **9** [1923] 2 IR at 142. The data was furnished by counsel for Motor Union. **10** [1922] 2 IR at 38–9.

On 16 June 1921 the King's Bench Division (Molony CJ, Pim and Gordon JJ) unanimously refused General Accident's application to set aside Moore J's judgment in favour of Cooper. Molony CJ chose to stress two principal matters. First, relying on *Gorman* v. *The Hand-in-Hand Insurance Co.*[11] and *Munro, Price & Co.* v. *War Risks Association,*[12] that the onus of proving that the loss was occasioned by riot or civil commotion, i.e. fell within the exception, rested firmly on the insurer. Second, that the insurer had to demonstrate a clear causal connection between the riot or civil commotion and the loss of which complaint was made. Molony CJ accepted Lord Mansfield's definition of 'civil commotion' –

> an insurrection of the people for general purposes, although it may not amount to a rebellion, where there is an usurped power ... an insurrection of the people for the purpose of general mischief, though not amounting to a rebellion –

and cited *Winicofsky* v. *Army and Navy General Assurance Co.*[13] (a case featuring an exception for a loss occasioned by hostilities) on the necessity for proof of a causal connection in regard to exception clauses generally. Molony CJ continued:[14]

> ... it is not established in this case that the theft was due to riot or civil commotion, although no doubt, the state of the city and county of Cork made things easier for thieves, because, as we all know, in the present disturbed state of affairs property cannot receive the same protection from the police as it would have if the police were confined to their ordinary police duties.

Gordon J, for his part, would have gone further than Moore J and held affirmatively that Cooper's loss of his car was not due to riot or civil commotion.[15] Pim J, on the other hand, followed the approach of Molony CJ, holding merely that there was insufficient evidence to suggest that the loss was so due:[16]

> It has even been submitted that the only possible explanation of the theft is that the car was taken by hostile forces. If we drew such an inference, it might be correct; but in my view, we are certainly not coerced to such a conclusion, nor even entitled to draw it. Thieves fish in troubled waters, and it is obvious that this car may have been taken by thieves with a view to theft and nothing more.

More was to be heard of this theory of Pim J on the background to the removal of Cooper's car. It was not completely implausible: evidence had been adduced that the RIC were satisfied that at the time of the car's disappearance a gang of motor thieves was operating in Macroom, 24 miles to the west of Cork.[17]

Four months later, on 2 November 1921, the Court of Appeal for Southern Ireland affirmed both Moore J and the King's Bench Division. Dodd J concurred with Ronan LJ, and the latter was content to uphold the judgment of Moore J primarily on the

11 (1877–8) IR 11 CL 224. **12** [1918] 2 KB 78. **13** (1918–19) 35 TLR 283. **14** [1922] 2 IR at 41. **15** [1922] 2 IR at 42–3. **16** [1922] 2 IR at 42. **17** See the reference in the judgment of Molony CJ: [1922] 2 IR at 40.

basis that he, as trial judge, had been best placed to weigh the relevant evidence. Ronan LJ also sought comfort in numbers:[18]

> Four Judges have already arrived at the same conclusion of fact – Mr Justice Moore and the three Judges of the appellate tribunal, who have concurred with his view. The House of Lords has repeatedly laid it down that when two separate Courts have agreed as to a question of fact, nothing but an overwhelming case would induce them to overrule that decision. In my opinion in this case the evidence shows only that the motor-car was stolen by two men who came there for that purpose; and it was perfectly open for the Judge on the evidence before him, according to the weight he attached to it, to arrive at the conclusion he did. Having regard to the fact that the King's Bench Division unanimously came to the same conclusion, this Court should not interfere with their decision.

The third member of the Court of Appeal, O'Connor LJ, delivered a judgment which marked the first breach in the ranks of the judiciary. O'Connor LJ did not press his views to a formal dissent, but his doubts over joining Ronan LJ and Dodd J in dismissing the appeal were nonetheless forcibly expressed and were to prove of critical importance. Moore J had not, in O'Connor LJ's view, given sufficient weight to several points which he, had he been the trial judge, would have regarded as most relevant:[19]

> First, there was the fact … of the existence of civil commotion in the district, and the desire of the insurrectionists to obtain motor-cars for the purposes of the insurrection. Second, there was the time of the happening. It was at seven or eight o'clock of an October evening, an appropriate enough time for an insurrectionary gang carrying out their objects by force, but not one that would be chosen by ordinary motor thieves. Third, there was the occurrence in the district at about the same time of five motor thefts, two of which were from neighbours of the plaintiff. Fifth, there was also the rarity of the crime of motor-stealing before these troubles arose.

O'Connor LJ's expansion of point five was plainly intended as a rejoinder to Pim J and his theory that thieves had been fishing in troubled waters. 'Speaking', added O'Connor LJ,[20]

> from my own experience in the Law Room of Dublin Castle during a period of four years, I never came across a single instance of this particular crime, though it may, no doubt, be said that once the forces of law and order are inoperative, thefts of every kind may occur more easily than before.

Doubtless encouraged by O'Connor LJ's virtual dissent, General Accident announced a further appeal. Meanwhile, Motor Union, Boggan's insurers, suffered an early reverse. On 25 November 1921 Molony CJ, as trial judge, held that Boggan's loss

18 [1922] 2 IR at 44. **19** [1922] 2 IR at 45. **20** Ibid.

fell outside the exception contained in his contract of insurance.[21] The exception was in different terms from that in Cooper's case:

> Loss or damage arising during (unless it be proved by the insured that the loss or damage was not occasioned thereby) or in consequence of earthquake, war, invasion, riot, civil commotion, military or usurped power.

The High Court of Appeal for Ireland handed down its decision on what was the third appeal in the Cooper litigation on 16 January 1922, i.e. a month after the court was first constituted[22] and nine days after a majority of Dáil Eireann had voted to accept the Anglo-Irish Treaty of the preceding December. The High Court of Appeal unanimously upheld (the first occasion any Irish court had done so) the arguments put forward by General Accident, and thus allowed the appeal.

Sir John Ross, the lord chancellor, gave the lead to the other members of the court, O'Connor MR and Andrews LJ. He did not mince his words in attacking the stances of judicial colleagues in the courts below. Criticised first by him was the 'onus of proof' argument on which members of the King's Bench Division had particularly relied. 'I cannot help thinking', Ross began,[23]

> with great respect to them all, that the attention of the learned Judges who have dealt with this case was too much occupied in considering the question of onus. A question of onus may be sometimes of immense importance, as, for instance, in an action for damages for malicious prosecution, where the plaintiff must produce evidence to satisfy the Judge that it is inconsistent with the existence of reasonable and probable cause before he can get to the jury at all. But in a case of this kind, where the facts are not in dispute, and where everything depends on the inferences to be drawn from the facts, there is little advantage in discussing the question of onus. The judicial mind derives a certain amount of comfort and satisfaction in arriving at a doubtful conclusion by throwing the onus argument into the scale. The truth is that the facts will support either of the two antagonistic conclusions. If to an equal degree, the question of onus is all-important, because if the facts are equally consistent with the two adverse conclusions, the party on whom the onus lies must fail.

The question, the lord chancellor continued, was one of a balance of probabilities, and the scale was to be turned by a correct conclusion founded on circumstantial evidence.

Ross examined next the critical question of the precise meaning of the exception, 'loss or damage occasioned through civil commotion occurring within the limits of Ireland', pausing, on the way, to aim another brickbat at Molony CJ:[24] 'We need not trouble to go back to Lord Mansfield's definition.' There then follows a passage where Ross barely concealed his impatience with colleagues who were either unwilling or unable to face political reality:[25]

21 [1922] 2 IR at 184–5. **22** 15 December 1921. **23** [1922] 2 IR at 47–8. **24** [1922] 2 IR at 48. **25** Ibid.

> Nobody can deny that at the time of this occurrence there existed civil commotion within the limits of Ireland. Some call this commotion war, others guerilla warfare, others rebellion or insurrection, others use more condemnatory descriptions. We have nothing to do with the ethics of the movement, whether it is criminal or excusable. We find that it existed, that it was highly organized and was systematically worked against the then established Government of the land. It operated all over the country, and it is proved in this case to have been operating in the City of Cork.

Lower court judges had equally, in Ross's opinion, adopted an unjustifiably stringent approach to proof of the causal connection between 'civil commotion' and 'loss'. Pim J was singled out for having spoken in terms of 'coercive evidence', and of the need to eliminate every explanation other than an act of a hostile force. 'This language', Ross declared,[26]

> is suitable to the degree of certainty required for the conviction of a criminal, and is wholly inapplicable to a case like this. If the takers had been recognized as connected with the civil commotion, even that could not have been made the basis of a necessary inference; they might, notwithstanding, have stolen the car for their private advantage. It has been contended here that even if one car had been found to have conveyed men who were attacking a military or police barrack, that would not have been sufficient.
>
> The words of the exception must receive a reasonable construction. A reasonable construction seems to me to be, that if the car was taken by some persons for the purpose of being used in the civil commotion, or of assisting those who were furthering the civil commotion, that is sufficient to establish the exception.

The lord chancellor found further fault with the reasoning of Pim J, echoing O'Connor LJ's incredulity at the thought that ordinary thieves had purloined Captain Cooper's Ford:[27]

> We know that expert motor thieves operate in London and in other large cities. But to dispose of a stolen car requires skill and careful planning. To anyone acquainted with the circumstances of Irish life, before the time of general disorder, the occurrence of such a crime would appear most improbable. The circumstances may have changed since the powers of the police have been diminished by the insurrectionary movement; but even in the present circumstances I find it hard to believe in the existence of gangs of ordinary motor thieves. Both sets of belligerents are known to be against ordinary robberies …
>
> I am not at all captivated by the suggestion that thieves fish in troubled waters. From what we know of the conditions of the present conflict, I should think it extremely unlikely that ordinary thieves would select these areas as a

26 [1922] 2 IR at 48–9. **27** [1922] 2 IR at 49.

> field for their operations; they would find it very difficult to either keep or dispose of the plunder.

Ross spoke even more plainly later. 'I cannot believe,' he remarked,[28] 'that there is anybody in the district – though this is hardly an argument – who would not have treated the theory of ordinary theft with derision.'

Other colleagues the lord chancellor also found wanting; O'Connor LJ was even mildly rebuked for his failure in the Court of Appeal to convert his doubts into a formal dissent.[29] Ross also pointed out, for the enlightenment of Ronan LJ, the distinction between a finding of fact and an inference from a fact, continuing that no House of Lords decision prevented an appellate court from disagreeing with inferences which, in its opinion, had been wrongly drawn by the lower court.[30]

Ross finally addressed himself to a further argument which was pressed, for the first time, before the High Court of Appeal.[31] Counsel contended that, as there was no evidence of 'civil commotion' actually on Cooper's premises when the car was taken, its loss could not be said to have been so occasioned. The contention Ross summarised thus:[32] 'The civil commotion may have been the cause that led to the theft of the car, but the Court, he insists, has no right to inquire into the causes of causes – the purpose is immaterial.' So narrow a notion of what 'civil commotion' meant would have severely limited the scope of any exception in respect of a loss expressed to be occasioned by it, and the lord chancellor rejected it:[33]

> The way in which the matter presents itself, to my mind, is this. Civil commotion may manifest itself in various ways – in homicide, in arson, in tumult, in kidnapping, in ambushes, in forcible capture of war material, and such like. Each of these things when it occurs is an incident or a constituent element in the civil commotion: it goes to constitute the civil commotion that is manifesting itself in this form for the time being. It is not clear thinking to hold that the civil commotion is an entity by itself, and that these manifestations of its operation are something distinct from it. For the time being the particular manifestation constitutes a form of civil commotion itself.

O'Connor MR briefly concurred with the lord chancellor's judgment. In a separate concurring judgment Andrews LJ covered some familiar ground: proof of civil commotion at the time and place of the occurrence was not requisite; in the circumstances, an appellate court was empowered to disagree with inferences of fact wrongly drawn by the lower court. Andrews LJ acknowledged that the onus of proving the facts to bring the case within the exception rested with the insurers, but, unlike the judges in the courts below, he held that General Accident had discharged that onus. Such a conclusion was not based upon 'mere conjecture' but 'upon legitimate and

28 [1922] 2 IR at 50. **29** [1922] 2 IR at 52. **30** Ibid. In fact, *Montgomerie* v. *Wallace James* [1904] AC 92 and *Dominion Trust Co.* v. *New York Life Insurance Co.* [1919] AC 257, as Ross pointed out, maintained the reverse. There was, of course, the Irish authority of *The S. S. Gairloch* [1899] 2 IR 1. **31** However, it would appear to have been urged before Moore J, the trial judge: [1922] 2 IR at 39. **32** [1922] 2 IR at 51. **33** Ibid.

natural inferences and deductions from facts proved'.[34] Earlier in his judgment, Andrews LJ added two facts to the list O'Connor LJ had drawn up in the Court of Appeal which pointed towards the inference that Cooper's car had been taken by insurrectionists. These were:[35]

> the fact that the plaintiff had his car in Cork City on the day of the occurrence, where it is quite possible that it may have been seen by some of those responsible for civil commotion in that area; and, further, that there is no evidence that any motor thieves, apart from the insurrectionists, were operating in this district.

Andrews LJ, in fact, had had little doubt what the true explanation for the theft of Captain Cooper's Ford was:[36]

> All the essential features of the occurrence point to the commission of the theft for the purpose of procuring the car to assist the members of the Irish Republican Army or those who were associated with them in their endeavour to overpower those to whom was lawfully entrusted responsibility for the preservation or restoration of peace and the maintenance of law and order in the country.

The unanimity of the High Court of Appeal did not deter Captain Cooper from initiating the final appeal to the House of Lords. To date, ten judges had pronounced on his claim and only three had held against him. Unfortunately for Cooper, however, under the rules of litigation, it was the judgment of the superior court which prevailed, and the three judges who had been hostile constituted the most senior court which had as yet expressed an opinion.

Boggan's case meanwhile had reached the Court of Appeal for Southern Ireland on 25 January 1922, nine days after the High Court of Appeal held against Cooper, and judgment was reserved, after a two-day hearing, on 30 January. The court's decision, however, was not made known until the following July. Ronan LJ, on behalf of the court, then explained that the case had stood over for so long because the court had been led to believe that the House of Lords would have heard the appeal in Cooper's case that month. When it was learnt that Cooper's appeal would not be heard in London before the start of the long vacation – it was not to be heard until November, in fact – the Court of Appeal acceded to the request of counsel appearing for Motor Union, and delivered judgment on 12 July.[37]

The court was divided, Ronan LJ and Dodd J voting to uphold Molony CJ's judgment in favour of Boggan. O'Connor LJ dissented. Fresh legal arguments were addressed to the Court of Appeal but of more importance was the surfacing of fundamental differences of judicial approach. Whether the show of these would have been avoided if the House of Lords had heard Cooper's appeal earlier than it did must remain conjectural. Both judges of the majority took pains to emphasise that, in their opinion, differences distinguished the two cases.

34 [1922] 2 IR at 56. **35** [1922] 2 IR at 54. **36** Ibid. **37** [1922] 2 IR at 186.

Though Ronan LJ and Dodd J agreed in dismissing the appeal, their reasons did not always coincide. The exception in Boggan's insurance policy embraced 'loss or damage' to the vehicle 'arising during ... or in consequence of ... riot, civil commotion ...' In Cooper's policy the words were loss or damage *caused* by riot or civil commotion. In Ronan LJ's opinion, this difference had the effect that it made inapplicable to Boggan's claim the definition of 'civil commotion' advanced in Cooper's case by the lord chancellor:[38]

> The language of the exception in the policy before us is very remarkable. It is not loss caused by riot or civil commotion. It is loss or damage arising 'during' or 'in consequence of' riot or civil commotion. To my mind these words point to the view that there is or has been a riot, as distinguished from the specific burglary, house-breaking, or theft, In the present case there was no such riot. The riot sought to be established consisted exclusively of the theft or robbery with violence.

In his judgment O'Connor LJ did not agree:[39]

> I am of opinion that the decision in [Cooper's] case would have been just the same if the words had been not 'caused by' but 'in consequence of' a riot; and I cannot follow Lord Justice Ronan when he says that because the word 'during' precedes 'in consequence of', the latter words are merely limited to a question of time, and have no reference to causation. I am of opinion that the true meaning and scope of this policy is that where the arm of the ordinary law is paralysed by commotion, disturbance, or riot, the insurers are not liable for theft by armed men.

On this issue, Dodd J agreed with Ronan LJ but, to make doubly sure, added his belief that the circumstances of the seizure of Boggan's motor-vehicle had not constituted a riot. Ronan LJ had assumed[40]

> that if an indictment for riot had been preferred against the perpetrators of this outrage it would have been the duty of the judge to tell the jury that the transaction amounted to riot.

Whether the hijacking at Katescross amounted to a riot was examined by Dodd J at considerable length. One conclusion he reached demonstrated his opposing view:[41]

> If depositions containing only the facts before us now had been submitted, a Judge would have had some strong observations upon Crown Counsel sending up a bill for riot, would have encouraged the Grand Jury to throw it out, and would not have prevented the jury from finding a verdict of not guilty.

Ronan LJ took issue with Ross over a second passage from the latter's judgment in the Cooper appeal, in which Ross had criticised Molony CJ in particular for dwelling

38 [1922] 2 IR at 188. **39** [1922] 2 IR at 192. **40** [1922] 2 IR at 187. **41** [1922] 2 IR at 195.

on the 'onus of proof' argument. Though Ronan LJ did not revise his judgment,[42] what is printed in the official report as his reaction to the lord chancellor's words is unusual, to put it no higher, and, certainly, should not be ignored. 'I cannot,' declared Ronan,[43]

> understand these observations. They must, I think, as Mr Justice Dodd has suggested to me, be regarded as dicta. Lord Campbell reminds us, in *Attorney-General* v. *Dean and Canons of Windsor*,[44] that dicta are to be treated with respect, but followed only so far as agreeable to sound sense and prior authorities.

Ronan continued his attack on Ross by answering the latter's further assertion in Cooper's case that no handicapping rule on onus of proof came into play since the inferences were, in the lord chancellor's opinion, so unmistakably clear. The attack this time reached a crescendo. 'On this branch of the case,' Ronan began,[45]

> I will only say, speaking for myself, that my own knowledge of the state of the country, my knowledge of Wexford, being absolutely nil, I am unable to say whether it is more probable that these men took the car in order to sell it than that they captured it as part of an insurrectionary system …
>
> … In judging a question of this kind in Ireland in the present day, probability depends largely upon the place where and the time when the incident happened. In a matter of this kind there is a loose way of talking. Everybody knowing anything about the country knows that different persons have different means of knowledge. The lord chancellor refers to the rarity of the crime of motor-stealing before the period of disorder. There is not one scrap of evidence of that in Cooper's case or in this case. In the course of his judgment in Cooper's case, O'Connor LJ says that while acting as law officer he never came across a single instance of motor-stealing; but on the other hand, Mr Justice Dodd told us that at Green Street he had tried several such cases. If one Judge happens to have had some special experience, and another Judge happens not to have had that experience, is it seriously contended that the judgment of the Judge at the trial is to be reversed because of some Judge's personal knowledge of facts which were not brought before either of the Courts below? I really know nothing myself about Wexford. I do not read the newspapers carefully, or remember what I read; I have nothing to guide me in this case except the evidence on which the Chief Justice acted; and on that evidence I am not satisfied that the car was taken as part of an insurrectionary system.

Dodd J was scarcely less circumspect in his judgment. Cooper's case, he was satisfied, established no new principles; it was a decision on the facts. The lord chancellor he exonerated of the charge of altering the law: the former's remarks on the onus and

42 See footnote 2 to the brief report of the outcome of the appeal in *Boggan* before the High Court of Appeal: [1922] 2 IR 222. **43** [1922] 2 IR at 190. **44** (1860) 8 HLC at 392. **45** [1922] 2 IR at 191.

standard of proof, properly understood, said nothing that was novel. 'It is,' Dodd J continued,[46]

> loyalty and not disloyalty to the High Court of Appeal to be careful to see that their judgment is not pushed beyond its legitimate limit. While this Court owes a special duty to the superior Court, it owes also a comity to the Court of first instance.

A call for the closing of the ranks followed:[47]

> It is essential, whatever view a Judge should entertain of his own, or may I say retain, that all our Courts should join together in the harmonious administration of the law.

The word 'harmonious' was presumably aimed principally at Ross; undoubtedly, it will have rankled.

Dodd J went on to recite his definition of 'riot' and then to reiterate Ronan LJ's emphasis on the need to interpret the word in the context of the insurance policy:[48]

> The word must find its meaning from the insurance standpoint of increased risk. It points to a condition of things in the body politic, some risk ejusdem generis with war, invasion, or civil commotion altering the normal risk – a tumultuous and violent disturbance of the peace in a local area – such as the Bristol riots, the Gordon riots, the Porteous riots, the Belfast riots, the Derry riots, the Bantry riots; such a state of things as would lead, if prolonged, to a reading of the Riot Act analogous to the general disturbance by invasion, or war, or civil commotion, military and usurped power, but not intended to apply to what was merely an incident in an ordinary theft. It points to something aliunde the theft itself.

In his judgment in *Cooper*, Ross had spelt out the implications for insurers of the courts' accepting a particular interpretation of the exception contained in the policy in that case. With equal frankness, Dodd J ended his judgment in *Boggan* by dwelling on the implications for insured persons of the particular interpretation that Mr Battersby, counsel for Motor Union, sought to place on the exception contained in Boggan's policy:[49]

> I desire to add that my decision is uninfluenced by any question as to onus of proof. I have been influenced by the consideration that if the insured owners of motor cars are not protected against risk such as this the premiums have been flung away. All Mr Battersby has to do is to say the loss occurred in Ireland and ask for judgment.

46 [1922] 2 IR at 195. **47** Ibid. **48** [1922] 2 IR at 197. **49** Ibid.

That was a prospect which his colleague, O'Connor LJ, was prepared to face, not necessarily with equanimity but because, in his reckoning, that was the only honest answer to the particular legal problem. Impatience, which he shared with Ross, with the ostrich-like attitudes of the other judges was demonstrated, in O'Connor's case, stylistically, by the inclusion in his judgment of exclamatory sentences:[50]

> Although I do not base my judgment on civil commotion, I wish to say one or two words on that question. There was a great deal of argument upon it, and some loose observations were made by witnesses to the effect that there was no civil commotion at the time. I wonder what those witnesses would designate civil commotion. No civil commotion at a time when the police had been forced from some of the outlying barracks! no civil commotion at a time when cars were being commandeered and receipts given for them! The ordinary burglar or thief does not give receipts for motor cars. Matters had not, indeed, come to a head – martial law had not been proclaimed; but the outbreak of civil commotion and the proclamation of martial law do not usually synchronize. Civil commotion did prevail in Wexford when armed men gagged the driver of the car in question here and took it away …

Cooper's appeal was heard by the House of Lords on 13 November 1922 before Viscount Cave LC, Viscount Finlay and Lords Dunedin, Atkinson and Sumner. Their lordships did not feel the need to call on counsel for the respondents and delivered unreserved judgments, unanimously dismissing the appeal and thus upholding the decision of the High Court of Appeal. In a disappointing final act, only Lord Sumner, perhaps, added anything new, in an appeal to the insurance company not to enforce its full claim to costs in respect of such arduous and prolonged litigation:[51]

> It was necessary for the insurance company to prosecute these appeals to such a stage as would result, if they could obtain it, in success, because it is obvious that to them this case is of very great and general importance. To the plaintiff, however, it is only a matter of his motor car, which these men have taken away from him. It is not, of course, the respondents' fault that your Lordships can only be reached from County Cork by so many and long stages but neither is it the plaintiff's. I cannot help thinking that if the insurance company could see its way to mitigate in some measure the heavy blow which falls upon the appellant in the matter of costs, it would neither be disregarding its own interest nor failing to obtain general approbation.

The legal battles were not yet over. Boggan's case was appealed by Motor Union to the High Court of Appeal for Ireland, and that court, on 27 November 1922, after hearing argument, affirmed the order of the Court of Appeal.[52] The court consisted of Sir John Ross, O'Connor MR and Henry CJ (the new chief justice of Northern Ireland). No judgments were delivered. This outcome was not, perhaps, expected. Though, on the occasion of the Boggan appeal, Henry CJ replaced Andrews LJ on the

50 [1922] 2 IR at 192. **51** [1922] 2 IR at 220. **52** [1922] 2 IR at 222.

court, its other two members, the lord chancellor and O'Connor MR, had participated in the previous hearing, and it seems improbable that Ross, for example, would have altered his general approach. A possible explanation was the need to secure a speedy termination of judicial business pending before the High Court of Appeal: its abolition took place a week later.[53]

Motor Union appealed to the House of Lords. On 14 June 1923 the earl of Birkenhead and Lords Atkinson, Wrenbury and Carson and, it would seem, also Shaw of Dunfermline[54] unanimously set aside the decision of the High Court of Appeal and entered judgment for Motor Union.[55] Boggan, like Cooper, was fated to lose as well. Motor Union greeted the news with the announcement that it would not ask for costs either in the House of Lords or in any of the inferior courts.[56]

As in Boggan's case, the judgments of the House were unreserved. The earl of Birkenhead and Lord Wrenbury, the only two members of the House to deliver judgments of any length, were satisfied that the seizure and subsequent loss of Boggan's vehicle were occasioned by both riot and civil commotion; this was the inexorable conclusion from the evidence. Cooper's case, in the opinion of both Lord Birkenhead and Lord Carson, constituted a binding precedent.[57]

A paragraph in the speech of Lord Wrenbury included a curious detail on the conduct of the case by counsel appearing for Boggan:[58]

> I have been, I confess, a good deal disturbed by the fact that although, as I understand from the respondent's counsel, there are six judgments of learned Judges in the Courts of Ireland given in his favour – judgments supported, I suppose, by reasoning – no one of those judgments has been read. Notwithstanding my invitation to the respondent's counsel to read them, or so much of them as is necessary to put me in possession of the reasoning of these learned Judges, he has elected not to read them. Lord Birkenhead has said that he has looked through these judgments, and that their reasoning has been put by counsel in the course of the argument. I should have been better satisfied myself if I had heard what these learned Judges had to say, in order to see whether the language which they used and the opinions which they expressed would modify in any way the opinion I have formed.

This departure from current practice was unusual enough to merit special mention from Lord Wrenbury. Boggan's counsel, E.A. Swayne KC and St. L.E. Devitt, were responsible for the decision. There was not a total suppression: the earl of Birkenhead had perused the salient judgments. But that they should have been deliberately kept back from the other law lords is extraordinary. The outcome, of course, was that the spectacle of unwontedly disputatious Irish judges was, at counsels' contrivance and with Birkenhead's apparent approval, not permitted to become, for the moment at least, a matter of common knowledge.

53 Irish Free State (Consequential Provisions) Act 1922, s. 2, sch. 21, para. 6. **54** Lord Shaw is said to have been present, but not even a brief concurring speech is recorded. **55** [1923] 2 IR 136. **56** [1923] 2 IR at 142. **57** [1923] 2 IR at 138 and 142. **58** [1923] 2 IR at 142.

III

Much was remarkable in this protracted litigation: the lengths to which the majority of Irish judges appeared prepared to go in order to forestall the denial to both Cooper and Boggan of the remedy that was felt their due; the acrimonious note in the exchanges between Irish judicial protagonists of the opposing legal points of view; the speed and unanimity of the law lords once it became their turn, in the calmer atmosphere of London, to settle the two disputes.

Many legal issues were raised by both cases. There was the problem of the precise legal interpretation to place upon the original events in counties Cork and Wexford. There was also the problem of defining the precise legal purpose for which that interpretation was required. This purpose was, basically, the application of words in a contract but, again, the rules for interpreting these words admitted of dispute. In addition to these two principal problems, many subsidiary difficulties were present: the aptness of introducing arguments based on the handicapping rules of dispute-solution (onus of proof, standard of proof); the scope of the *contra proferentem* rule in interpreting insurance contracts; the conventions applicable where an appeal court reviews decisions on facts reached by the trial court; the precedential value of earlier decisions. While all these problems and others besides were identified, it is important to realise that not all of them were equally obvious. The extent to which a number of judges chose to dwell on the less obvious justifies, I think, the verdict that they were not eager that Cooper and Boggan should fail.

Molony, the chief justice, was typical of those who found it impossible to reach any conclusion other than that the two men were entitled to compensation.[59] Molony himself reached an identical conclusion in a third reported case, *Craig* v. *The Eagle Star and British Dominions Insurance Co.*,[60] decided in July 1922, and in a fourth, *London and Lancashire Insurance Co. Ltd.* v. *Bolands Ltd.*,[61] decided contemporaneously, where Molony sat not only in the King's Bench Division, but also in the Court of Appeal. The Chief Justice had the merit at least of being consistent. Craig's claim arose out of the destruction of his premises in Dundalk in August 1920 as a result of arson, possibly in retaliation for the killing of Catholics in Belfast. In the case, Molony affirmed the arbitrator's finding that there was insufficient evidence that the destruction had been caused by riot or civil commotion and that the loss was therefore covered by the insurance policy. Counsel for Craig advanced an argument which may have impressed Molony and helped determine his attitude. It is identical with one explicitly acknowledged by Dodd in his judgment in Boggan:

> If the present fire is held to be an insurrectionary burning there could be no such thing as an accidental fire or a malicious non-insurrectionary burning in Ireland in recent times.[62]

59 For details of the curious lone battle waged by Molony in 1920 to retain the title of Lord Chief Justice of Ireland, and for insight into the workings of his mind, see 'The Title of the Last Lord Chief Justice of Ireland', below, p. 315. **60** (1922) 56 ILTR 145. Samuels J agreed. **61** [1924] 2 IR 130; [1924] AC 836. In the King's Bench Division Gordon J sat with Molony; in the Court of Appeal for Southern Ireland Ronan and O'Connor LJJ accompanied him. **62** 56 ILTR at 147.

It was Molony's reliance on the onus of proof argument which particularly affronted Ross. This, in Ross's view, was taking matters much too far. It provided him with the final proof that a majority of the judges were prepared to join a conspiracy in which logical gymnastics were to prevail over common sense. Conviction that the analysis was accurate provoked, in *Cooper*, a judgment that was bound to give offence. Read even today, it has the hallmark of a critical school report on junior colleagues. Ross's judgment cannot easily have been forgiven. Only a combination of fate and politics had determined that these colleagues should be junior to him in the hierarchy of courts. Equally distasteful was the effrontery of forthright language from him in a court which was not only a novelty but, worse, a superfluous novelty and, worse still, a novelty probably already under sentence of death. Ross by his conduct appeared to have done little to help ensure that he would survive its obsequies, however much for a while he had enjoyed the unique confidence of the British Government.[63]

It was Ross's descent into the arena in *Cooper* which marked the turning-point in the combined litigation. The squabble that ensued – it can scarcely be dignified by calling it anything else – centred, in part, on issues of principle: the place of handicapping rules in evolving the solution to the problems presented in the two cases; whether the personal experiences of a judge were matters that could properly be taken into account; the difference between 'facts' and 'inferences' from them. But even here the personal criticism is never far away. Never explicit, it is nonetheless very plain.

If the manoeuvring of Molony and others precipitated Ross's stern reproof, the terms of that reproof precipitated Ronan on to his collision course, a course, let it be said, upon which Ronan, for his part, was prepared to embark with some gusto. Dodd attempted to be more decorous, but his call for harmony on the bench and his stress on the need to honour the comity owing to a lower court could be seen as equally insulting. Dodd, a 'lower court' man himself, was already on record on comity: the comity owing to the dead. In February 1922 he had earlier, in *Leyburn* v. *Armagh County Council (No. 2)*,[64] as a member of the High Court of Appeal, reproved the Court of Appeal for inadequate examination of previous case law in the light of fresh doctrine.[65] In the excitement, however, any intended subtlety may have been misunderstood.

If Ross's forthright judgment in *Cooper* represented a turning-point, O'Connor LJ's in the Court of Appeal was equally significant, for it anticipated the answer that the legal system would eventually furnish. O'Connor's virtual dissent in *Cooper* and his actual dissent in *Boggan* could, I think, have been predicted. He had earlier dissented in *Tyler* v. *County Council of Cork*,[66] an important malicious injuries case, where a majority of the Court of Appeal had held that theft consequent on malicious damage was, in the special circumstances of the looting from the shoe shop in Fermoy,

63 Ross became lord chancellor in September 1921. He ceased to hold that office on its abolition, along with that of the High Court of Appeal, in December 1922. Hamar Greenwood viewed Ross as the only judge in Ireland he could trust: Thomas Jones, *Whitehall diary, volume III: Ireland 1918-1925*, p. 50. (The reference is to Cabinet discussions held on 14 February 1921.) **64** [1922] 2 IR 58 at 74. **65** The criticism was aimed at the Court of Appeal which decided *Tyler* v. *County Council of Cork* [1921] 2 IR 8. **66** [1921] 2 IR 8 at 28-33. The first paragraph of O'Connor's dissent should not be ignored by students of the prose style of the

compensatable under the malicious injuries code. He was to dissent again in *McKenna* v. *Stephens and Hull & Co.*[67] where a majority of Molony CJ and Ronan LJ strained the law in order to enable an accident victim to recover damages against a party, who was not the immediate tortfeasor, and indeed may not, properly, have been a tortfeasor at all. O'Connor's entire approach was clearly dominated by his refusal to stretch legal principles simply to enable a meritorious plaintiff or innocent claimant to recover.

Ross's approach in the insurance and malicious injuries cases that came before the High Court in 1922 was similar. Dodd argued in his Court of Appeal judgment in *Boggan*, delivered in July (as had counsel in *Craig's* case),[68] that he was concerned to avoid the result that insurance premiums paid in the Ireland of 1921–2 would have been shown to have been worthless.[69] In *McKnight's* case, an important malicious injuries decision the previous February, Ross had steered the High Court of Appeal away from the position that the Court of Appeal had embraced, of permitting sympathy for the claimant to dictate an extension in the scope of the malicious injuries code:[70]

> The change in judicial opinion came shortly before and during a most unfortunate time. What was the state of affairs? Armed bands in large numbers were contending all over the country; they were inflicting reprisals by destroying the property of persons supposed to be in sympathy with one side or other; they frequently came long distances in motor cars; the ordinary criminal courts had ceased to be operative; the inhabitants were powerless to suppress the crimes or to attempt to bring offenders to justice. The application of the original policy was quite out of touch with the circumstances then existing.
>
> ... Everyone will agree that innocent sufferers ought to be compensated from some source, but nothing can be more unjust and unreasonable than the imposition of these intolerable burdens at such a time and under such circumstances.

Earlier the same month, in *Leyburn's* case, another celebrated malicious injuries decision, Ross had presided over a five-man High Court of Appeal which overruled earlier Court of Appeal authority, prompted undoubtedly by similar considerations, bringing larceny *simpliciter* within the scope of the malicious injuries code.

With thefts increasingly unlikely to be found capable of compensation via the malicious injuries code, owners prudent enough to possess insurance cover against loss by theft of motor vehicles and the like may have started to cast themselves in the role of the wise virgins in the parable. Certainty of access to the funds of property insurers was their ultimate protection. As, in Ireland, the year 1922 wore on, the legal buttress for the pre-existing system of property ownership began to disintegrate, and the centrality of the issue of the scope of insurance protection, the meaning of the phrases 'riot' and 'civil commotion', became increasingly important. The freezing in January by the new Provisional Government of malicious injuries awards, the establishment in May

Irish judge. **67** [1923] 2 IR 112 at 132–5. On the case see further Osborough, 'The Demise of the State's Immunity in Tort', (1973) 8 *Ir. Jur.* (n.s.) 275 at 277–8. **68** (1922) 56 ILTR 145 at 147. **69** [1922] 2 IR at 197. **70** *McKnight* v. *Armagh Co. Council* [1922] 2 IR 137 at 148.

of the joint Provisional Government – British Government Commission (the Shaw Commission) to examine outstanding claims, the announcement later of the change in the method of satisfying claims:[71] none of this was an incentive to the owner of property in Ireland to remain, nor was it, perhaps, wholly intended to be.[72] The most plausible explanation for the disagreements of the Irish judges in *Cooper* and *Boggan* (and which were seen in the malicious injuries cases too) is that a majority sought to stem the collapse of the system of legal protection for property; the minority sympathised with the motive, but concluded it could not be done, at least not by the judicial organ of government.

There is no hint in Ross's judgment in *Cooper*, delivered in January 1922, that the signing of the Treaty the previous December and its recent ratification by a slender majority in the Dáil had prompted a more realistic judicial appraisal of recent events. In February, whilst again presiding in the High Court of Appeal, Ross faced problems of the court's jurisdiction and powers.[73] In resolving them and restating the intent behind the judiciary provisions in the Government of Ireland Act,[74] Ross did not choose to mention, as well he might have, the trend of political events which ensured by the end of the year his own involuntary retirement and the relegation of his court to that limbo reserved for British constitutional experiments which fail. Under the new dispensation, Ross must be seen, therefore, as a political innocent, and the explanation for his candour in dealing with Cooper's insurance claim cannot be that he agreed with the rising generation of ex-revolutionary politicians that the period 1919-21 demanded a fresh legal interpretation. The likeliest explanation for his role in the Cooper affair is much more prosaic: he did his job in the manner he thought any judge should. And if he did not know what the events of January 1922 betokened for himself personally, he at least sensed what was the reality behind the events at Douglas in October 1920: this had been the IRA at work.

Yet, Ross himself was not to be consistent. In December 1922 the High Court of Appeal rubber-stamped the Court of Appeal's decision in *Boggan*, and Ross let pass the opportunity to reply to the snide attacks of Ronan. And in a third test case, *London and Lancashire Insurance Co. Ltd.* v. *Bolands Ltd.*,[75] the High Court aligned itself both with the King's Bench Division and the Court of Appeal in upholding yet another claim by the insured against the insurer. The arbitrator had originally turned down Bolands's claim in respect of money taken during an armed raid on their premises: Ross and the rest of the court joined in a decision which the House of Lords, predictably, in view of their decision in *Boggan*, and in due course, were to reverse.

Had Ross himself had a change of heart? He himself was the victim of vehicle seizure. On two occasions his conspicuous Daimler was taken from his own home in Stillorgan, County Dublin,[76] but it is altogether too fanciful to suppose that this could have brought about any judicial volte-face. Besides, unlike Cooper or Boggan, Ross

71 See Provisional Government releases of 20 January, 11 February and 8 May 1922; Damage to Property (Compensation) Act 1923 (IFS). **72** See 'Law in Ireland 1916-1926', above, at 297-8. **73** *Leyburn* v. *Armagh Co. Council* [1922] 2 IR 15. **74** [1922] 2 IR at 18-19. **75** [1924] 2 IR 130; [1924] AC 836. **76** (1921) 55 *ILTSJ* 87; Sir John Ross, *The years of my pilgrimage* (London, 1924), pp 291-2. One 'borrowing' occurred on 26 March 1921.

was fortunate enough to have his car returned. Yet the thesis is not impossible. In *Pilgrim scrip*, his second book of memoirs, Ross reveals himself as the injured loyalist, sold down the river by Lloyd George and others, who had foolishly imagined that the British Government would be the ultimate guarantor of property in Ireland.[77] For Ross the beginning of wisdom can be traced to the period immediately after the signing of the Anglo-Irish Treaty and certainly no later than the spring of 1922.[78]

The unanimity of the House of Lords in dismissing the claims of Cooper and Boggan in the light of all that had occurred earlier in the Irish courts is as remarkable as the despatch with which that dismissal was ordered. As the months slipped by, from the time when the Irish judges had pronounced on the two claims, it naturally became easier for the law lords to adopt the simplest interpretation of what had happened in Cork and Wexford in October and November 1920. In addition, if, in the *Boggan* case, there were any waverers – and, conceivably, Lord Wrenbury may have been one – Lord Birkenhead, who enjoyed an intimate knowledge of the state of affairs in Ireland throughout, was on hand to bring them back into line.

Counsel's conduct in the third test case of *London and Lancashire Insurance Co. Ltd.* v. *Bolands Ltd.*[79] was somewhat different from what it had been in *Boggan*: Irish case law was opened before the law lords. In the result, it made no difference: Bolands lost their case as had Cooper and Boggan earlier. But whether out of sympathy with the predicament of the Irish property owner or out of respect for the views of the majority of Irish judges which on this occasion had been made available, one law lord, Lord Blanesburgh, was tempted to dissent:[80]

> I was personally very strongly predisposed in favour of the view taken of such a proviso as we find in this policy by Lord Justice Ronan in the passage from his judgment in *Boggan* v. *Motor Union Insurance Co.* ...

Judging it prudent not, in fact, to do so, Blanesburgh then retreated, though with little conviction:[81]

> I am personally constrained, however, albeit somewhat doubtfully, to come to the conclusion that the answer to that view of the proviso has just been stated by the noble and learned Lord who has just preceded me, and accordingly, although not without hesitation, I concur in the conclusion in this case which suggests itself as correct to the other members of the House.

Doubt over the correctness of what had been done had surfaced at last in England, but it was too late.

77 Sir John Ross, *Pilgrim scrip* (London, 1927), pp 247 ff. **78** Ross's failure to be consistent spoiled his track record. The contributor of the entry on Ross in the *DNB* claims that only twice, in a long judicial career, was Ross overruled by the House of Lords. **79** [1924] 2 IR 130; [1924] AC 836. **80** [1924] 2 IR at 137. **81** Ibid.

The Title of the Last Lord Chief Justice of Ireland

It is a matter of historical notoriety that the Government of Ireland Act 1920 failed in its objective of granting concurrent Home Rule to the two parts of Ireland which the Act set up. In the North, a parliament, government and judiciary duly came into existence, but in the South the summons of elected representatives to a parliament of Southern Ireland went largely unheeded, and the parliament itself thus died at birth. Months before the Act of 1920 was passed the Act had been shown unlikely to provide the framework for the evolution of government in the South; and so it turned out. By 1920–1 the politicians of the South had demands too large to be satisfied by a grant of mere Home Rule; they sought, instead, a republic. How many did and what precisely was involved are still matters of controversy – among Irish historians at least – but this much is clear: a certain proportion did and these were not all bewitched by idle rhetoric. The proof of that was to come later. When the Truce of July 1921 led to the Treaty of the following December, enshrining a Dominion settlement, a minority was not to rest content. The Civil War of 1922–3 was the result.

It needs to be remembered that in the South the Government of Ireland Act was not a complete dead letter. At the same time as the Supreme Court of Northern Ireland was established so, too, was that of Southern Ireland. This latter Supreme Court, indeed, remained the lynch-pin of the judicial system in the South until a new Courts of Justice Act was passed through the Free State legislature in 1924. The Court had a chequered history for the three years of its existence. From its creation until December 1922, it functioned alongside a High Court of Appeal for Ireland, which exercised appellate jurisdiction both North and South. Until the middle of 1922, its authority was challenged by that of the rival Republican courts created by Dáil Eireann in 1920. In June 1922 the Four Courts building in the heart of Dublin where the Court had its headquarters was destroyed in a military action which signalled the outbreak of the Civil War. Finally, it was an unconscionably long time under sentence of death. Article 75 of the Constitution of the Free State, adopted towards the end of 1922, clearly anticipated that the Court would soon be abolished, but political and other considerations forced the postponement of legislative action until 1924. In the meantime, however, erstwhile 'enemies of the Irish people' found themselves forced, among their other duties, to help consolidate the political authority of a government composed of former 'rebels against the Crown'.

In December 1922, on the abolition, contemporaneously with that of the High Court of Appeal, of the office of lord chancellor of Ireland, the effective leadership, as well as the titular headship, of the judiciary in the South devolved on the shoulders of the Lord Chief Justice. The then incumbent was Thomas Molony. Molony had had a distinguished legal career. Called to the Bar in 1887 and taking silk in 1899, he became Irish solicitor-general in 1912, moving on to attorney-general in 1913. Later in the same year he was made a judge of the then High Court and in 1915 was translated to the Irish Court of Appeal. He became Lord Chief Justice of Ireland in 1918 and was to be the last holder of that office.

Molony had previously served on a number of governmental inquiries. In 1919 he had been chairman of the Viceregal Commission on Intermediate Education in Ireland[1] and, somewhat earlier, a member of two royal commissions, one on the disturbances in Dublin in 1914 at the time of the Howth gun-running,[2] and the other on certain shootings, including that of Sheehy-Skeffington, which occurred during the suppression of the Easter Rising of 1916.[3] Molony had also displayed a considerable interest in matters of penal reform; this interest, indeed, he was to maintain throughout his life. In terms of Irish politics he was a Home Ruler of the old stamp, an assessment most clearly confirmed by his contribution 'The Judiciary, the Police and the Maintenance of Law and Order', to a collection of essays edited by J.H. Morgan and published in 1912 under the title *The New Irish Constitution*. In terms of the law, Molony was not, perhaps, an outstanding figure – sound rather than visionary. It might have been otherwise. Charles Monteith, in his appreciation of Molony in the *Dictionary of National Biography*, was to write: 'In times less poisoned by hatred and outrage he might have built up over the years a legal reputation equal to that of his greatest predecessors on the Irish bench.' As it was, in a series of martial law cases, Molony showed unequivocally that his first loyalty was to the rule of law. The stance cannot always have endeared him to the government in London who, from 1920, had reasons of their own for wishing the existence of a more pliable Irish judiciary.

Molony, along with most of the other senior judges of the old regime, retired on pension in the spring of 1924. He retired as Lord Chief Justice of Ireland, a title which a transitional provision in the Government of Ireland Act 1920 enabled him to continue to hold. Throughout 1920 Molony fought a hard battle to win the right to continue to hold that title. The draft Bill of 1920 had envisaged that he would become 'Lord Chief Justice of Southern Ireland'. Only in December 1920 was parliamentary support forthcoming for a device which took account of Molony's hostility to that proposal. On hearing, from Molony, that the House of Lords had accepted an amendment to this effect, Lord French,[4] the Irish viceroy, replied, on 13 December, that 'it was the least they could do'. It was an unambiguous, if modest, tribute to a man who, out of both opposition to Partition and concern to uphold the status and dignity of high judicial office, had undoubtedly made himself, in the eyes of members of the British Government, a thorough nuisance.

1 *Report of the vice-regal committee on the conditions of service and remuneration of teachers in intermediate schools, and on the distribution of grants from public funds for intermediate education in Ireland, 1919*, Cmd. 66, xxi. 645. **2** *Report of the royal commission on the circumstances connected with the landing of arms at Howth on 28th July 1914* (1914–16), Cd. 7631, xxiv. 805. **3** *Report of the royal commission on the arrest and subsequent treatment of Mr Francis Sheehy Skeffington, Mr Thomas Dickson and Mr Patrick James McIntyre* (1916), Cd. 8376, xi. 311. **4** Field-Marshal Sir John French (1852–1925); Lord-Lieutenant of Ireland 1918–21.

Molony's interest in the matter of his title dates from the early weeks of 1920 when he was first shown the draft sections on the judiciary for the Government of Ireland Bill. Macpherson,[5] the Irish Chief Secretary, invited Molony to travel to London to advise on the proposals so far as they related to the creation of a separate judiciary for 'Northern Ireland'. Molony declined the invitation and, in a letter of 9 February to Macpherson, left the latter and the British Government in no doubt as to his personal opposition to what was afoot. At the time the opposition of a majority of both the Irish Bar and the Irish solicitors was well known, but the views of the man who was the de facto head of the Irish judiciary, needless to say, were not widely broadcast, even though the shrewd observer might have guessed what they were. In his letter to Macpherson, Molony first referred to recent history:

> In 1914 when Mr Asquith brought in his amending Bill, which gave Ulster all it asked for, the integrity of the Irish Bench was maintained; and in 1916 when the Ulster Unionist Party put forward a proposal to give two Judges to Ulster, the authority of the Irish Court of Appeal was agreed to be maintained intact with the consent of all parties.

The proposal in the present Bill, Molony went on, was reactionary:

> It will impose an unnecessary expense on Irish revenue and Irish suitors. All the administrative offices of the Irish High Court will require to be duplicated, at immense cost. Every person in Northern Ireland who sues a person in Southern Ireland, or vice versa, will have to get leave to issue and serve his writ out of the jurisdiction, and, if he obtains judgment, will have to take proceedings analogous to those indicated under the Judgments Extension Act before he can proceed to execution.

Molony had reached

> the clear conclusion that the proposals are detrimental to the dignity and authority of the Bench, the prosperity and character of the Bar, the interests of suitors, and would tend to deepen and, perhaps, unfortunately, prolong the separation of the two parts of Ireland, which it is hoped ultimately to re-unite.

In the same letter Molony also expressed disquiet at the apparent proposal to lessen the dignity and prerogatives of his own office, a subject to which he returned in a further letter to Macpherson on 29 February. The effect of the Bill and the schedules to it, Molony then pointed out, was that he must either retire not less than one month before the appointed day, or else be automatically transferred to the Chief Justiceship of Southern Ireland and be deprived of the title of Lord Chief Justice of Ireland. The letter continued:

5 J.I. Macpherson, 1st Baron Strathcarron (1880-1937); Chief Secretary for Ireland 1919-20. Macpherson was a Scot with an interest in Gaelic studies.

> If this is what is intended, I would like to point out that it is a direct violation of the King's letter appointing me to the office of Lord Chief Justice of Ireland, and of my patent under the Great Seal.[6] I assume that this was not intended, or even thought of, and that there will be no difficulty in inserting in the Bill in committee a clause such as has already been inserted in the reference to the Master of the Rolls in section 43, that nothing in the Act shall affect the rank, title or precedence of the existing Lord Chief Justice of Ireland.

As Lord Chief Justice, Molony then pointed out, he held by act of parliament or royal charter many offices which he would cease to hold if the Bill passed unamended. The gauntlet had been well and truly thrown.

Macpherson replied on 3 March. He regretted that the exigencies of the Irish situation made it inevitable that a Home Rule Bill must do violence to 'many old traditions and associations'. 'It is essential to the Government scheme,' Macpherson continued,

> that there should be a Lord Chief Justice of Southern Ireland and a Lord Chief Justice of Northern Ireland at the head of each of the new Supreme Courts, and that the functions of the present Lord Chief Justice of Ireland must be transferred to them as regards their respective jurisdictions.

He then adverted to a point raised explicitly by Molony:

> The case of the Master of the Rolls is different, because his title connotes executive functions as custodian of the public records in Ireland, and although the custody of the records is transferred to the Lord Lieutenant, still the public services in connection with the public records are reserved as a common service as respects the whole of Ireland under clause 9(3) of the Bill, instead of being divided between Southern and Northern Ireland. There will be no Rolls or Master of the Rolls for Southern or Northern Ireland, and the all-Ireland title of the present holder of the office can thus be retained consistently with the establishment of the two new Supreme Courts.

In the same letter Macpherson nonetheless promised to ensure that the present incidents of Molony's office were continued during his tenure; he also foresaw no difficulty in providing for the retention of Molony's rank and precedence.

The reply did not satisfy Molony and, on receiving it in Monaghan where he was then on assize, he wrote yet again to Macpherson:

> I am not sure that you give sufficient weight to the depth of Irish sentiment, or you would feel more strongly than you do how serious it is to deprive the

6 In part the relevant Letters Patent provided: 'We do make constitute and appoint Our Right Trusty and Well Beloved Thomas Francis Molony ... to be Lord Chief Justice of Ireland ... To have hold and enjoy the same unto him the said Thomas Francis Molony for and during his good behaviour with all rights, privileges, pre-eminences, profits and emoluments to the said office belonging or appertaining.'

> occupant of a great office of the title which he holds with the most solemn assurances that the King and Parliament can give. I do not question any change of jurisdiction or duties. I am quite prepared to perform all the duties of the Chief Justice of Southern Ireland, but what I think I am entitled to is that during my tenure my Letters Patent under the Great Seal shall be respected.
>
> It may seem anomalous to have at one and the same time the Lord Chief Justice of Ireland and the Lord Chief Justice of Northern Ireland, but still we should prefer to have an anomaly than to do an injustice. Besides we have an Irish precedent which has lasted for about 500 years and has worked well. The Primacy of Ireland was claimed by the Archbishop of Armagh as successor of St Patrick, and by the Archbishop of Dublin as Prelate of the Metropolitan See. The dispute was carried to Rome, where a sagacious Pope decided that the Archbishop of Dublin should be Primate of Ireland, and the Archbishop of Armagh Primate of *all* Ireland, and so it has remained during all the succeeding centuries. Similarly you may make any number of Chief Justices of Northern Ireland you like, provided you leave me with the title I hold.
>
> If you have any doubt about my constitutional position, what would you say to referring the question to Lord Reading, or, if you prefer it, the Lord Justice General of Scotland? I would be quite satisfied with either.

On 12 March Macpherson briefly acknowledged this further letter; he undertook to make enquiries and see whether it was at all possible to secure for Molony the retention of his title. It was the last Macpherson was to hear directly of the affair, for on 3 April, disillusioned at the trend of affairs in Ireland, he resigned as Chief Secretary.[7] Molony wrote next to Macpherson's successor, Hamar Greenwood,[8] enclosing the previous correspondence with Macpherson. Greenwood replied on 27 April, promising that he would see what he could do.

It was at this stage that Molony sounded the opinions of others. He contacted Sir Frank Greer,[9] the parliamentary draftsman attached to the Irish Office. To Greer he made the suggestion that an amendment should be made in the schedule to the Bill which would have the effect of preserving the title of Lord Chief Justice during Molony's tenure. Molony was also in touch with the Irish Lord Chancellor, Sir James Campbell.[10] Here Molony appears to have been rather more successful, for Campbell actually raised the matter at a Cabinet Committee meeting held in London in mid-June.[11] At this meeting Campbell urged that the controversy be settled, but his report to Molony on what transpired can have given the latter little comfort. No final deci-

7 He became Minister of Pensions. **8** Sir Hamar Greenwood (1870–1948); Chief Secretary for Ireland (the last) 1920–2. **9** Sir Francis Greer (1869–1925); Parliamentary Draftsman in the Irish Office 1908–23. **10** Sir James Campbell, 1st Baron Glenavy (1851–1931); Lord Chancellor of Ireland 1917–21. **11** It was ironical that Molony should have had to turn to Campbell. Campbell's Unionist foibles had been implicitly assailed by Molony in his contribution to the collection of essays edited by J.H. Morgan and published in 1912. The final irony is that while Molony, after becoming Chief Justice, resigns in 1924 and goes to live in England, Campbell, the preceding Lord Chief Justice, retires from the lord chancellorship in 1921 but, as Lord Glenavy, is rehabilitated as the first chairman of the Senate of the Irish Free State.

sion had been taken, Campbell wrote, but the members in attendance had, in general, not been sympathetic to Molony's case.

Dissatisfied at the absence of any progress and concerned at the prospect that none now would be made, Molony wrote to Edward Shortt,[12] the Home Secretary, who had not been at the Cabinet Committee meeting attended by Campbell. In this letter of 25 June Molony enclosed once again the correspondence he had had with Macpherson. In the accompanying explanation he both restated an old argument and introduced a fresh one:

> I was appointed in June 1918. The Judicature Act enables the title to be conferred; the King, by his letter under the Royal Sign Manual, gives me the title, and Letters Patent under the Great Seal are issued to me in pursuance thereof. It is now proposed to treat the most sacred obligations which Parliament and the King can enter into with a subject as mere waste paper, and to deprive me of my title of Lord Chief Justice of Ireland. I am quite satisfied that this course, while within the powers of Parliament, is both unconstitutional and unjust, and I am sure that you, as a lawyer, considering the circumstances for a moment, will accept my view.

Molony then continued:

> It is no answer to me to say that under the Bill if I do not accept the proposed change I can retire on a pension. No matter what my personal feelings may be I am not going to retire at a time when it is most necessary that the Lord Chief Justice should do everything possible to maintain the King's Peace in this unhappy country where my retirement would certainly be regarded as a triumph for the forces of disorder. As you were not present at the Committee meeting when the Lord Chancellor voiced my views, I think it only right that I should let you know how strongly I feel on this subject and I will feel obliged if you convey my views to the Prime Minister and the Cabinet.

Molony sent Greenwood a copy of this letter to Shortt but the only response to these June letters came from Walter Long,[13] the First Lord of the Admiralty, to whom Shortt had forwarded the file. Long, in his letter of 6 July to Molony, was far from sympathetic. 'I have considered,' he wrote,

> your representations carefully, and quite appreciate your reasons for seeking to retain the title of Lord Chief Justice of Ireland. But I confess that, once the principle of dividing the judiciary is admitted, as it has been, both by the Government and by the House of Commons, it seems to be inevitable that the

12 Edward Shortt (1862-1935); Home Secretary 1919-22. Shortt had been Chief Secretary for Ireland 1918-19. **13** Walter Long (Viscount 1921) (1854-1924); First Lord of the Admiralty 1918-21. Long had been Chief Secretary for Ireland 1905-6.

> only possible course is to name the Heads of the two judicatures the Lord Chief Justice of Southern and of Northern Ireland. To have a Lord Chief Justice of Ireland along with, and parallel to, a Lord Chief Justice of Northern Ireland is an anomaly that I do not think we could defend.

Long did not see fit to allude to Molony's own reference to the actual anomaly of having a primate of Ireland alongside a primate of all Ireland, though it is possible that Shortt had not forwarded the entire correspondence and that he was not therefore familiar with it. Long ended his reply by stating that he would of course 'listen to any representation the Irish Government or the Lord Chancellor may have to make if, on grounds of policy, they consider desirable the alteration of nomenclature that you suggest'.

On 10 July Molony replied to Long's letter from Nenagh where he was on circuit. After the predictable expression of disappointment at its content, Molony went on to ask that, before the Cabinet finally resolved on 'an act of injustice', he might be given an opportunity of being personally heard before the Government of Ireland Bill left the Commons. He brought up a further point which echoed the substance of the very first letter to Macpherson where he declined to advise on the content of the Government of Ireland Bill: 'The concluding paragraph of your letter seems to be written under a misapprehension of my judicial position. As a Judge I cannot discuss matters of policy with the Irish Government, and must respectfully decline to make any representations to them on that subject.'

The general question was taken up again in the autumn. It drew from Dr Bernard,[14] the Provost of Trinity College, Dublin, the following observation, in a letter of 16 November: 'It seems to me a very extraordinary thing that the King's appointment by Letters Patent under the Great Seal can be set aside in the facile manner that the Government propose.' A month earlier Molony had sought more practical support from the Viceroy, Lord French, who was also a member of the British Cabinet. French in turn wrote to Walter Long in the middle of October, as did Molony himself, and it was eventually arranged that Molony would cross to London to meet the Cabinet Committee in mid-November.

This meeting was not a success. Long was ill and was not himself present. Indeed, the only member of the Committee who was there was Sir Laming Worthington-Evans.[15] Worthington-Evans was 'polite and patient' but, as Molony reported to French on 17 November, the discussion with him was 'of a somewhat unsatisfactory character, and ultimately matters were left very much as they were and nothing definite done'. Molony's report to Long on the same meeting ended bitterly:

> It is, I think, a striking example of the interest taken in Irish affairs by the Committee that no one else (other than Worthington-Evans) responded to your invitation to come and hear an Irishman unfold his grievance even

14 Dr J.H. Bernard (1860–1927); Provost of Trinity College Dublin 1919–27. Bernard had been Archbishop of Dublin 1915–19. **15** Sir Laming Worthington-Evans (1868–1931); Minister without Portfolio 1920–1.

when that Irishman happened to be the Chief Keeper of the King's Peace in Ireland.

The Government of Ireland Bill left the Commons towards the end of November. As it began its progress through the Lords, Molony canvassed the law lords for their support. Lord Phillimore[16] was written to on 27 November; he replied promptly on 1 December telling Molony that he intended to move two amendments in Committee to safeguard the latter's title. Molony also established contact with Lords Finlay,[17] Atkinson,[18] and Cave,[19] and with Birkenhead,[20] the lord chancellor. Birkenhead's reaction indicated that at long last a compromise was in sight. It came in a letter, dated like Phillimore's, 1 December, from Birkenhead's secretary, Sir Claud Schuster:[21]

> The Lord Chancellor wishes me to say with reference correspondence that has passed between you and him, that he has done his best to obtain a settlement which would meet your wishes. Unfortunately, after prolonged endeavour, he finds that the difficulty in the way of doing so fundamentally is insuperable. He thinks it best to state this frankly to you, and to express his regret that it should be so. At the same time, if you attach any importance to the matter on sentimental grounds – and the Lord Chancellor thinks that you may well do so – he wishes me to say that he is almost certain that he can retain for you personally the title of Lord Chief Justice of Ireland, and he would be glad to know whether you wish him to continue his efforts in that direction.

Molony replied at once on the 2nd:

> On sentimental and other grounds I have always attached great importance to the retention by me of the title of Lord Chief Justice of Ireland, and I shall be very glad if the Lord Chancellor will continue his efforts in the direction you state.
>
> I have received from Lord Phillimore this morning a copy of two amendments which he intends to propose in Committee, and which will enable me to retain for my time the title of Lord Chief Justice of Ireland, and if these amendments are accepted by the Government I will be quite satisfied. I do not think that anybody really wishes to deprive me of the non-judicial offices which have always appertained to my position, and which are really part and parcel of the history of Ireland for the last 250 years.

16 Sir W.G.F. Phillimore (Baron 1918) (1845–1929); Lord Justice of Appeal 1913–16; active in the judicial business of the House of Lords 1918–28. **17** R.B. Finlay (Viscount 1919) (1842–1929); lord chancellor 1916–19. **18** John Atkinson (Baron 1905) (1844–1932); Lord of Appeal 1905–28. **19** George Cave (Viscount 1918) (1856–1928); Lord of Appeal 1918; lord chancellor 1922–3, 24–8. **20** Earl of Birkenhead (F. E. Smith) (1872–1930); lord chancellor 1919–22. **21** Sir Claud Schuster (1869–1956); Clerk of the Crown and Chancery and Permanent Secretary to the Lord Chancellor's Office 1915–44.

On 6 December, in Committee in the House of Lords, Lord Phillimore, in fulfilment of the promise made Molony, moved his two amendments.[22] The first provided that the Lord Chief Justice of Ireland should have reserved to him the position he at present enjoyed with regard to a number of non-political, academic and other bodies. The second said that the existing Lord Chief Justice of Ireland should, if he consented, be the first Lord Chief Justice of Southern Ireland, but should retain his present title and rank and should continue to hold and exercise all non-judicial offices and duties annexed or appertaining to the office of Lord Chief Justice of Ireland.

Phillimore intended that his amendments should be embodied in the main text of the Government of Ireland Bill. Birkenhead, as we know from his letter to Molony of 1 December, was not totally unsympathetic to Molony's plight but he insisted, in his reply to Phillimore,[23] that the proper place for any changes to be made was in the detailed transitional arrangements relating to existing judges. Indeed, in schedule 4 of part III of the Bill the Lord Chief Justice of Ireland was already mentioned, for it was there provided that the Lord Chief Justice of Ireland should become the Lord Chief Justice of the Supreme Court of Southern Ireland unless he elected to retire or be transferred to the Supreme Court of Northern Ireland.

Birkenhead went on to assess the merits of the two amendments. The effect of the first, he reckoned, was merely to preserve the jurisdiction as academic visitor of the present incumbent and no objection could be taken to that. Nor could objection be taken to that portion of the second amendment dealing with the title and rank of the incumbent. 'So far as that goes,' Birkenhead observed,

> I see no objection to the proposal. It would be exposed, of course, to the superficial criticism that he is called the Lord Chief Justice of Ireland whereas, in fact, he would become Lord Chief Justice of Southern Ireland. But after all mankind is very much influenced by titles, especially when they have their roots in history. The title of the Lord Chief Justice of Ireland has been a distinguished title and, if the present holder of the office would feel some solace in the face of the changes by which he is confronted, I would certainly make a great effort to meet the views of the noble and learned Lord in that respect.

Birkenhead was less happy with the latter part of the second amendment. He thought it went too far;[24] conceivably, it could have the effect of depriving the Lord Chief Justice of the Northern Supreme Court of privileges and powers which would be incidental to and ought properly to be annexed to his office. In place of both the amendments, Birkenhead then proposed his own compromise amendment for inclusion in the Fourth Schedule:

> The existing Lord Chief Justice of Ireland, if he becomes Lord Chief Justice of Southern Ireland shall, so long as he holds that office be entitled to retain the

22 42 *H.L. Debs., 5th ser.*, col. 1083. **23** Id., col. 1084. **24** Col. 1085.

> rank and title of Lord Chief Justice of Ireland and to exercise any jurisdiction in respect of and on behalf of His Majesty as visitor to any college or other charitable foundation exercisable by him on the appointed day.

The concession to Molony of the major point about his title reflected credit on Birkenhead, for by now members of the Irish judiciary were looked on askance by elements within the British government.[25] The compromise Birkenhead suggested was formally accepted by Phillimore and then agreed in Committee without a division. The House of Commons accepted the amendment on 16 December, a matter which Birkenhead duly reported in the Lords on the following day.[26]

Two days earlier, on the 15th, Molony had written to Reading,[27] his English counterpart, to thank him for his support: 'I think Lord Phillimore's amendment goes a long way towards removing my personal grievance, and I am very glad that it commended itself to the House.' He added, percipiently: 'I am not very confident that the Bill will bring peace to Ireland.'

There is little more to tell. Molony's title as Lord Chief Justice of Ireland was assured under the terms of the Government of Ireland Act. But the political settlement which English politicians rather too optimistically fancied that measure might produce did not materialise. Instead, the guerilla warfare intensified and then first the Truce of July 1921 and later the protracted political manoeuvring of the ensuing autumn led to the Anglo-Irish Treaty of December. Many of the judges of the old regime, Molony included, saw the writing on the wall: their days on the bench were numbered and they knew it. Molony confessed as much to an English correspondent, John Simon,[28] in February 1922. Simon replied: 'No doubt the numbers of the Irish Bench will be cut down by the new Government and I can quite understand that you are not very anxious to hold your old position under the new dispensation.'[29]

Birkenhead in the House of Lords on 6 December 1920 spoke of his desire to offer Molony 'some solace' in the face of the changes by which he was then being confronted. In retrospect, this gesture can be seen to have been little enough. It was Molony's fate, on the implementation of further changes in the judicial system provoked by yet another political settlement, to be invested with the leadership of the judiciary in the 26 counties on the abolition of the office of lord chancellor of Ireland. It can have given him little satisfaction, for the change came in late 1922 when the Southern part of Ireland faced, arguably, an ever graver threat than it had done during the period of what is now termed the Anglo-Irish War. Early in 1922 John Simon had written Molony a depressing letter in which he expressed little hope that Ireland would settle down: 'It is one of the worst consequences of violent and unconstitutional acts that they are so infectious.'[30] As the year wore on, Simon's fears were only too obviously

25 T. Jones, *Whitehall diary*, ed. K. Middlemas, vol. 3 (London, 1971), p. 19. **26** 136 *H.C. Debs., 5th ser.*, col. 893; 43 *H.L. Debs., 5th ser.*, col. 395. The 'Molony' provision may be found in para. 1 (c) of part III of sch. 7 to the 1920 Act. **27** Earl of Reading (R. D. Isaacs) (Marquess 1926) (1860–1930); Lord Chief Justice 1913–21; Ambassador to the United States 1918–19. **28** John Simon (Viscount 1940) (1873–1954); lord chancellor 1940–5. **29** Simon to Molony, 15 Feb. 1922. **30** Ibid.

realised. In June the headquarters of the judiciary in the South, the Four Courts, were destroyed. Full-scale civil war broke out soon after.

Molony and his colleagues did not yet make their exit. The priority was quickly shown to be the need to consolidate what was left in the country of a tradition of law and order. For the judiciary, this meant, in simple terms, the adoption of a policy of 'business as usual'. It was not easy to pretend, behind barbed-wire defences, that things were normal but what is important was that, under Molony's leadership, the attempt was made. The burnt-out shell of the Four Courts had, of course, to be abandoned and the Courts moved, first to King's Inns, and then, in a move redolent of the Middle Ages, to Dublin Castle; accommodation at neither home was ideal. The interlude merely accentuated the difficulties of administering justice in Ireland at the time.

The Provisional Government had come to power early in 1922. All its members had, in constitutional terms, been rebels against the Crown. One of the many ironies of Irish history now took place. In the long political crisis which the Civil War of 1922-3 represented it fell to the loyalist judiciary of the former regime to help establish the legal authority of the new: such was the effect of a series of celebrated habeas corpus decisions.[31] In evaluating the role of the judiciary at this critical point in modern Irish history, Denis Gwynn prefers to lay stress on their contribution to a return to normality. And Gwynn singles out Molony as the man largely responsible.[32] Certainly, as the months passed, Molony's administrative burdens became no lighter. He it was who, in December 1922, administered the oath to the first governor-general, Tim Healy; but Molony had much more to do besides. For all the evidence of co-operation and mutual understanding, however, relations between the judiciary and the members of what was now the Government of the Free State were never free of strain; it was, perhaps, too much to expect that they could be.

In May 1924 most of the members of the judiciary went into involuntary retirement; among them was Molony. For him, as for the rest who had retired, there then re-commenced a different dispute with the British Government, this time over pension rights. Battle here had first been joined in 1922.[33] The dispute at that time must have seemed to Molony to represent one insult too many. It necessitated, yet again, the launching of a struggle which he could never have anticipated would be his lot when he first accepted judicial office. And to make a fuss was again to appear unseemly in a world which was almost beyond caring.

31 See above pp 284, 286. **32** 'A special tribute is due to Sir Thomas Moloney, who was Lord Chief Justice when the Free State came into existence. He held that position when the Four Courts were forcibly occupied by the Irregular forces under Rory O'Connor; and when the work of the Dublin Courts had to be transferred to the buildings of the King's Inns. Confidence was utterly shaken during those momentous days, and it looked as though anarchy was to gain control. But the firmness and dignity of the Lord Chief Justice, when he established his own court at the end of a large room and allotted their respective places to the other courts, did as much as anything else to restore a sense of security. And his personal example in arriving punctually at his work, regardless of all threats of assassination, did as much as that of any man to strengthen the morale of the country': D. Gwynn, *The Irish Free State 1922-1927* (London, 1928), pp 168-9.
33 *Memorandum on the position of the Southern Irish judges under the Treaty and the Irish Constitution* (copy in Molony papers). This memorandum was prepared some time in 1922 and forwarded to the British Government.

For three years and more Molony had continued to hold a title of which the British Government had earlier tried to deprive him. He had fought a personal campaign in support of his stand and, though, in the end, he did not gain everything he sought, the victory, in effect, was his. Whether his successors as Chief Justice in either part of Ireland have been either as jealous of the privileges of high judicial status or as determined to defend them it can be left to others, at some future date, to decide.

Molony himself, following his retirement, took up residence in England, living there until his death in 1949. Made a baronet in 1925, Molony chaired a British government inquiry into young offenders which reported in 1927.[34] He maintained his links with Ireland and, in particular, with his alma mater, Trinity College, where he served as vice-chancellor from 1931. It was to Trinity that Molony bequeathed his chain of office, a gold collar SS, that he had acquired from Campbell, his immediate predecessor as Lord Chief Justice. Molony attached a condition: the collar was to stay in the custody of the college only 'until such time as the office of Lord Chief Justice of Ireland shall be restored'.[35] Trinity retains custody, and, at a shrewd guess, it will continue to do so for some time to come.*

34 *Report of the departmental committee on the treatment of young offenders* (1927), Cmd. 2831. **35** V.T.H. Delany, 'The gold collar SS of Ireland' (1961) 77 *LQR* 169 at 171.

* This article is based in part on papers in the possession of the family of the late Sir Thomas Molony. I am grateful to Sir Joseph Molony, QC, for making these papers available to me for consultation and for permitting me to quote from them. I would also like to thank Sir Joseph and Professor R.F.V. Heuston for their valuable suggestions. Expressions of opinion, of course, remain my own.

Index